JOHN PHILIP KEMBLE

by Stuart

A
BIOGRAPHICAL
DICTIONARY

OF

ACTORS, ACTRESSES, MUSICIANS, DANCERS,
MANAGERS & OTHER STAGE PERSONNEL
IN LONDON, 1660–1800

Volume 8: Hough *to* Keyse

by

PHILIP H. HIGHFILL, JR., KALMAN A. BURNIM
and
EDWARD A. LANGHANS

SOUTHERN ILLINOIS UNIVERSITY PRESS
CARBONDALE AND EDWARDSVILLE

Publication of this work was made possible in part through a grant from the National Endowment for the Humanities.

Library of Congress Cataloging in Publication Data (Revised)

Highfill, Philip H

   A biographical dictionary of actors, actresses, musicians, dancers, managers & other stage personnel in London, 1660–1800.

   Includes bibliographical references.
   CONTENTS: v. 1. Abaco to Belfille.–v. 2. Belfort to Byzand.–[etc.]–v. 8. Hough to Keyse.
   1. Performing arts–London–Biography. I. Burnim, Kalman A., joint author. II. Langhans, Edward A., joint author. III. Title.
PN2597.H5   790.2′092′2 [B]   71–157068
ISBN 0–8093–0919–X (v. 8)

List of Illustrations

OPERAS, PROMPTBOOKS, AND PARTS

Volume 8

Hough *to* Keyse

Hough, Mr [*fl.* *1795–1800*], *boxkeeper.*
Mr Hough was one of the boxkeepers at
Drury Lane who was listed in annual benefit
bills from 5 June 1795 through 14 June 1800.

Hough, Peter *d. 1759, dancer, tumbler.*
The Mr Hough who danced a Servant in
Harlequin Restored at Drury Lane on 7 October
1735 was very likely Peter Hough, who was
active at Sadler's Wells the following decade.
During the remainder of the 1735–36 season
at Drury Lane Mr Hough was seen as the Constable in *The Harlot's Progress*, John Trot (probably the Servant) and Monsieur Roundall in
Harlequin Restored, Monsieur Roundall again
in *Taste à la Mode* (apparently a piece from
Harlequin Restored), and in an entr'acte turn
drawn from *Taste à la Mode*.

Hough continued dancing at Drury Lane
through the 1741–42 season, performing such
new characters as Fatty and the Clockmaker in
Poor Pierrot Married, Mother Midnight in *The
Harlot's Progress*, one of the Chinese Guards in
Harlequin Grand Volgi, the Egg Woman and a
Clown in *Harlequin Shipwrecked*, Slouch in
Robin Goodfellow, one of the crowd of citizens
in both *Oedipus* and *Julius Caesar*, and the King
of Antipodes in *Chrononhotonthologos*. He occasionally shared benefits in the spring with
other minor performers.

Hough's activity at Drury Lane ceased after
the spring of 1742, and it seems most probable
that he was the Mr Hough who had a benefit
at the New Wells, London Spa, on 23 February
1743 (the place seems to have been specially
opened for the occasion). On 7 February 1746
the Reverend John Lloyd leased Sadler's Wells
to Thomas Rosomon, who had previously
managed the New Wells, Spa Fields, and to
Peter Hough. The lease that Peter and Rosomon obtained was for 21 years at a yearly rental
of £100 plus the rates and taxes. The partners
opened Sadler's Wells in April 1746, and
Hough appeared there as a tumbler from time
to time. Dennis Arundell says that Peter
Hough died in 1759, apparently on stage at
Sadler's Wells. His epitaph, as reported by
Arundell, read, "Here lies the bones of Peter
Hough / Of Sadler's Wells, and that's enough."

Hough, Mrs [Peter?] [*fl.* *1741–1748*],
singer, dancer.
A Mrs Hough replaced Miss Minors as a
Gypsy in the pantomime *The Fortune Tellers* at
Drury Lane Theatre on 12 November 1741.
She was probably the Mrs Hough who danced
at Sadler's Wells in April 1746 and sang there
on 14 March 1748. The dates of her activity
coincide sufficiently with those of Peter Hough
that one may guess she may have been his wife.

Houghton. *See also* HAUGHTON.

Houghton, Mr [*fl.* *1784–1794*],
drummer.
Mr Houghton played kettledrums at the
Handel Memorial Concerts in Westminster
Abbey and at the Pantheon in May and June
1784. Doane's *Musical Directory* of 1794 listed
him as a member of the Academy of Ancient
Music and a participant in oratorio performances at Drury Lane and Westminster Abbey.
He also performed at Covent Garden, according to Doane, and may have been a permanent
member of the band there. Houghton lived in
Newport Street.

Houghton, [Robert?] [*fl.* *1776–
1793?*], *painter.*
A manuscript at the Folger Shakespeare Library lists a Mr Houghton as a painter at Covent Garden Theatre on 30 September 1793. It
is quite possible that he was Robert Houghton, whose name was recorded many times in
the accounts of the Theatre Royal in Liverpool.
The earliest mention of him there was in 1776,
when he was receiving 9s. weekly as a painter
during the winter season and was noted as
having worked a week cleaning scenes before
the 1776 summer season. Other entries, in
1776, 1777, and 1778, mention Houghton's
services in connection with scenery: grinding
colors, serving as a painter's man, assisting in
the preparation of *Harlequin's Invasion* (five and
a half days; 4s. paid him on 21 June 1777),
and working on "the stuff to make the New
Shapes of Robes" (£9 10s. 9d. paid him on 29
November 1786, probably for the materials—
and that night he received £2 3s. for his benefit
tickets).

A second Houghton, probably related to
Robert the painter, served in Liverpool as a
checker and general handyman at 4s. weekly.
He may have been the Houghton "Junr" who
was paid a shilling as an "Extra man" at Liverpool on 18 August 1777; he seems not to
have worked in London.

Houseman, Mr ₍fl. 1723₎, *dancer.*

A Mr Houseman danced the *Drunken Swiss* at the Haymarket Theatre on 26 and 27 December 1723, according to Latreille. *The London Stage* cites the dancer as "Noaseman" and lists him as dancing on 26 and 30 December. A clipping in the Burney Collection at the British Library cites him as "Nosemen" and as dancing on 30 December.

Houseman, William ₍fl. 1675–1676₎, *actor.*

The London Stage lists William Houseman as an actor in the King's Company at Drury Lane in 1675–76.

Howard. *See also* HAWARD.

Howard, Mr ₍fl. 1733–1745₎, *dancer.*

Mr Howard's benefit tickets were accepted at Covent Garden on 2 May 1733, and it is probable that he was the dancer who appeared there as an Ethiopian and as Euryale in performances of *Perseus and Andromeda* beginning on 13 February 1735. He was not otherwise noted in the bills, but he may have been in the dancing chorus throughout the season. The same person was probably the dancer Howard who was in the Goodman's Fields troupe in 1744–45 and was seen as the Farmer in *The Jealous Farmer* on 28 February 1745. The last mention of him in the bills was on 2 December 1745, when he shared a benefit with several others. A Mrs Howard was granted a benefit at Goodman's Fields on 6 February 1747; she is not known to have been in the troupe, though she may well have been.

Howard, Mr ₍fl. 1735–1736₎, *house servant.*

Latreille identified Mr Howard of the Covent Garden Theatre in 1735–36 as a pit office keeper at a salary of 2s. 6d. nightly. On 31 May 1736 Howard shared a benefit with two others, and at some point during the season he replaced Mrs Redfern as a boxkeeper.

Howard, Mr ₍fl. 1748–1758₎, *singer, actor.*

Mr Howard sang at the Smock Alley Theatre in Dublin in 1748–49 and 1749–50, and for the 1751–52 season in London he joined the Covent Garden company as a singer and actor. He made his first appearance there, so far as one can determine from the bills, on 30 September 1751, playing Cepheus in *Perseus and Andromeda*. Howard remained at Covent Garden until the early part of the 1758–59 season, playing such other parts as Merlin in *Merlin's Cave*, Charon in *The Necromancer*, Morpheus in *Apollo and Daphne*, the Lion in *Pyramus and Thisbe*, Pluto in *Harlequin Sorcerer*, Gubbins in *The Dragon of Wantley*, Valor in *The Triumphs of Hibernia*, Merlin in *Harlequin Skeleton*, Sir Trusty in *Rosamond*, the Magician in *Colombine Courtezan*, the Moon in *The Rehearsal*, Carefull in *The Press Gang*, an Attendant Spirit in *Comus*, and Gubbins in *Lady Moore*. Howard also swelled the choruses in performances of *Macbeth*, *Romeo and Juliet*, *The Prophetess*, and *Theodosius*.

Once, on 28 July 1753, Howard, advertised as from Covent Garden, played Hecate in *Macbeth* at Richmond. Howard began the 1758–59 season at Covent Garden, but on 30 November 1758 his name was dropped from the bill for *Romeo and Juliet*.

Howard, Mr ₍fl. 1773₎, *actor.*

Mr Howard was a member of Foote's troupe at the Haymarket Theatre from 17 May to 14 September 1773. He had unspecified roles in *The Nabob* and *The Rehearsal* and was seen as Governor Cape in *The Author*, Sir Richard in *The Minor*, Margin in *The Bankrupt*, Harwood in *The Register Office*, and Sir Jacob in *The Mayor of Garratt*.

Howard, Mr ₍fl. 1779₎, *actor.*

Mr Howard had an unnamed role in *The She Gallant* at the Haymarket Theatre on 13 October 1779.

Howard, Mr ₍fl. 1784₎, *singer.*

A Mr Howard (evidently not Samuel Howard, who was a tenor) sang bass in the Handel Memorial Concerts at Westminster Abbey and the Pantheon in May and June 1784.

Howard, Mr ₍fl. 1787–1800₎, *actor.*

Mr Howard performed at Kilkenny on 20 July 1787, and it was he, we believe, who was the Howard who acted Don Whiskers in *Harlequin's Frolick* and Squire Robert in *The Mock*

Doctor at Sayer's booth at Bartholomew Fair in London in 1788. The *Theatrical Journal* reported that Howard "was very pathetic in Col. Cohenberg" in *The Siege of Belgrade* in December 1793 at Woodbridge. The same Howard, probably, played Roderigo in *The Noble Pilgrim* and Jupiter in *Midas* at Worthing on 29 September 1796 and performed at the Crow Street Theatre in Dublin in 1799–1800.

Howard, Mrs ₁*fl. 1694–1699*₁, *actress.*
The London Stage lists Mrs Howard as a member of Betterton's troupe at Lincoln's Inn Fields in 1694–95, the season marked by the breakup of the old United Company. Mrs Howard is known to have played Kitty in *Love's a Jest* in June 1696, spoken the epilogue to *The City Lady* in December (advertised as "Miss" Howard), acted Peggy in *The Innocent Mistress* in late June 1697, and played Lebret in *The False Friend* in May 1699.

Howard, Mrs ₁*fl. 1747*₁, *performer?* See HOWARD, MR ₁*fl. 1733–1745*₁.

Howard, Henry *d. 1766, actor.*
Henry Howard made his first stage appearance as Falstaff in *The Merry Wives of Windsor* at Covent Garden on 22 April 1760. He acted only that one time, for Rooker's benefit, and though he should perhaps be classified an amateur and excluded from this dictionary, he evidently spent much of his time around the theatre and was typical of a number of semi-professionals the theatres had to put up with. The *Monthly Mirror* in January 1801 remembered him:

Mr. Henry Howard was a person extremely well known at the time . . . a choice spirit: a versifier, and a scribbler for the Papers. He wrote a Poem, a vile one called An Interview between Shakespeare and Garrick, and some Letters in the Gazeteer; he was one of those inconsiderate creatures who are continually hovering about a Playhouse, and pass the remainder of their lives in a Tavern, a Prison, or a Brothel. Though possessed of some humour in a Club Room [he had] none on stage. . . . [His] performance was so bad he never made another trial. He died in January 1766 from the effect of the bruises he received in a midnight broil, with some Irish Chairmen, about three weeks before. In G. A. Steevens Dramatic History of Master Edward and Miss Anne he is introduced into the plate

of the Choice Spirit's Club, and appears from it to have been a fat squab figure.

The article suggests that had Howard been successful, he would have continued in his stage career.

Howard, John ₁*fl. c. 1778–c. 1810*₁, *proprietor.*
Wroth in his *London Pleasure Gardens* tells us that about 1778 John Howard followed the bankrupt Holland as proprietor of Islington Spa. Howard opened the gardens during the mornings and afternoons, charging one guinea for a subscription or threepence or sixpence for individual tastes of the water. He added a bowling green and announced some "astronomical lectures in Lent, accompanied by an orrery." By 1784 a band played in the mornings, and tea drinkers were serenaded in the afternoons by horn players. The musicologist Sir John Hawkins died in 1789 a day after drinking Howard's mineral waters, but there was no proof that the waters were the actual cause of his death. After the beginning of the nineteenth century the Spa was less frequented, but Howard kept up the lovely gardens, and about 1810 he pulled down part of the old coffee house and changed the entrance from New River Head to Lloyd's Row. Howard lived in a house adjoining the new entrance.

Howard, Samuel *1710–1782, organist, singer, composer.*
Grove states that the musician Samuel Howard was born in 1710, served under Croft as a chorister in the Chapel Royal, and studied also under Pepusch. He became organist of St Clement Danes and St Bride, Fleet Street. Though better known as an organist and composer, Howard had a fine tenor voice and sang in the chorus in *Esther* when Gates presented a private performance of the oratorio at the Crown and Anchor Tavern on 23 February 1732. He was probably the Howard who sang at Covent Garden in *Alcina* in 1735 and was either Harbonah or an Israelite in *Esther* the same year, or so conjectures Dean in *Handel's Dramatic Oratorios and Masques*. By 1737 Howard's compositions were being heard at the theatres, and in 1738–39 some of his songs were used in the pantomime *Robin Goodfellow* at Drury Lane.

Samuel Howard was one of the original subscribers to the Royal Society of Musicians when it was formed on 28 August 1739. He composed music for the pantomime *The Amorous Goddess* for Drury Lane in February 1744, and about 1746 was published *A Collection of English Songs* written by Howard and Lampe. *Mortimer's London Directory* of 1763 cited Howard as an organist and noted that he lived in Norfolk Street in the Strand. From 1765 to 1777 he had lodgings in Bow Street, Covent Garden, according to the *Survey of London*. Howard received his doctorate in music from Cambridge in 1769.

Howard had returned to lodgings in Norfolk Street when he died on 13 July 1782, according to *Musgrave's Obituary*. Administration of his estate was granted to his daughter Anna Howard of the parish of Kingsburg, Middlesex. In that administration Samuel Howard was described as a widower. The *Catalogue of Printed Music in the British Museum* lists a sizable number of songs, overtures, act tunes, cantatas, and anthems by Howard. Most of his work was light in nature and designed for theatrical entertainments.

Howard, Thomas [fl. 1794], harpsichordist.

Doane's *Musical Directory* of 1794 listed Thomas Howard, of No 10, Church Street, Westminster, as a harpsichordist and a subscriber to the New Musical Fund.

Howard, William d. 1785, violinist, singer.

The William Howard who was elected a member of the Sublime Society of Beefsteaks on 28 December 1745 may have been the musician of that name who had replaced Valentine Snow in the King's Musick in 1749. The *New Universal Magazine* in November 1754 published a song, *Wine, wine is alone the brisk Fountain*, as sung by W. Howard. On 15 September 1757 Howard made Peter Clugh his attorney and described himself as one of His Majesty's Musicians in ordinary at £40 yearly, living in the parish of St Andrew, Holborn. On 23 May 1758, calling himself a member of the King's band and now living in the parish of St Dunstan in the West, Howard made Jacob Kirkman his attorney. Kirkman was a harpsichord maker of Broad Street.

By 6 February 1785 Howard was sufficiently incapacitated for his wife to petition the Royal Society of Musicians for relief for Howard, herself, and two daughters and a son, "they all being in want of every necessary for subsistence." They were granted eight guineas, to be paid at two guineas per month. On 3 April 1785, "Mrs Howard, widow of Mr William Howard sen: late member of this society attended and craved the usual allowance for the funeral of her said husband"; she was granted £5. A month later, on 1 May, Mrs Howard, whose Christian name Elizabeth was now given, was awarded a present of two guineas by the Society and an allowance of £1 10s. 4d. per month.

Their son William Howard (d. 1834) is noticed separately.

Howard, William d. 1834, violinist.

On 4 August 1776 William Howard "Junior" was admitted to the Royal Society of Musicians, at which time he was described as a single man. He was the son of William Howard (d. 1785), also a member of the Society, and his wife Elizabeth. The younger Howard was in the band at the King's Theatre in 1783 and 1791 (and probably other years), and in May and June of 1784 he played first violin in the Handel Memorial Concerts at Westminster Abbey and the Pantheon. From 1790 on, he played violin in the St Paul's concerts in May. The Drury Lane accounts list a Mr Howard as a member of the band at 5s. daily in May 1791, and in February 1792 he played in accompaniment to *L'Allegro ed il Penseroso* at Covent Garden.

Doane's *Musical Directory* of 1794 gave Howard's address as Stangate Street, Lambeth, and listed him as a member of the Royal Society of Musicians and a participant in the Professional Concerts, the opera at the King's Theatre, and the Handel concerts at Westminster Abbey. The Drury Lane accounts show that Howard (William, we assume) was paid £1 15s. weekly as a member of the band there in 1801. That salary had been raised to £1 16s. by the 1812–13 season. The accounts also indicate that Howard (William?) was a member of the band at the Haymarket Theatre in the summers from 1804 to 1810, though no salary was mentioned.

William Howard and his family figured in the minutes of the Royal Society of Musicians

Harvard Theatre Collection

William Broadhurst as Selim and MR HOWELL as the Grand Vizier

artist unknown

in the 1820s and 1830s, but in such a way as to imply that he was then no longer very active in the musical life of London. On 3 February 1822 Howard was granted the "usual" relief allowance for himself, his wife, and two children—Mary Ann, born on 22 January 1813, and William, born on 27 February 1815. The sometimes confusing accounts of the Society indicate that the Howards had at least two other children, born after 1815: a son, who died in 1831 before reaching the age of 14, and a daughter, Charlotte. Mrs Howard died in 1834; William Howard died shortly before 2 November 1834, when the Society paid £12 for his funeral expenses.

Howell, Mr [*fl.* 1798–1815], *dancer, actor, singer.*

Mr Howell was a chorus dancer and singer at Covent Garden Theatre from 1798–99 to 1802–3, appearing in modest roles such as a Sailor in *The Death of Captain Cook*, an unspecified character in *The Volcano; or, the Rival Har-*lequins, a Turkish Officer in *The Siege of Acre*, and a Country Lad in *The Deserter of Naples*. On 12 February 1800 he began to act the Count of Lindenberg in *Raymond and Agnes*, a piece in which he had previously performed as one of the domestics. His salary was £1 10s. per week in 1802–3.

Howell also performed at the Haymarket Theatre in the summers of 1800 and 1801, dancing in the chorus of *Obi* in the former year and in *The Corsair* in the latter. Probably he was the Howell who danced at the Royal Circus in June 1803, at Covent Garden again between 1811–12 and 1814–15 at £2 per week, at the Surrey Theatre in April 1814, and at the Royal Circus in August and November 1815.

Twopence-colored prints were published by Dyer of Mr Howell, actor at Covent Garden in 1811–12, as Robert de Fitzwalter in *Magna Charta*; and in 1812 W. West issued twopence-colored prints of Howell as the Grand Vizier and William Broadhurst as Selim in *Harlequin and Padmanaba*.

Howell, James *[fl. 1720–1733]*, proprietor.

In 1720, according to Warwick Wroth's *The London Pleasure Gardens*, Belsize House, once the residence of Lord Wotton, was converted by a Welshman named James Howell into a place of public amusement. He opened about April with an "uncommon solemnity of music and dancing" and, oddly, did not at first charge admission. The building and grounds were open from six in the morning to eight at night, and pleasure-seekers could be entertained by a variety of birds, "which compose a most melodious and delightful harmony," and have "breakfast on tea or coffee as cheap as at their own chambers." Twelve (later thirty) stout fellows, armed, were "always at hand to patrol timid females or other" along the road from London to Hampstead.

In July 1721 the Prince and Princess of Wales and an entourage dined at Belsize House and were diverted with hunting. In June 1722 a wild deer hunt was held, attracting 300 to 400 coaches full of the nobility and gentry from town. They were also entertained by athletic events and gambling. In 1722 a satire called *Belsize House* tried to expose "the Fops and Beaux who daily frequent that Academy" and the women who used it as a place to make assignations:

> *This house, which is a nuisance to the land*
> *Doth near a park and handsome garden stand*
> *Fronting the road, betwixt a range of trees*
> *Which is perfumed with a Hampstead breeze.*
> *The Welsh Ambassador [Howell] has many ways*
> *Fool's pence, while summer season holds, to raise.*

On 20 May 1723 Howell held a benefit concert for himself at Belsize House, and it is therefore probable that musical entertainments were a regular feature there. Certainly music was a daily feature by 1725, when races were also held. In the spring of 1733 a race was advertised for ponies twelve hands six inches high.

How long after 1733 Howell continued as proprietor is not known. He seems to have been an enterprising person, but he was once imprisoned in Newgate for some offense.

Howell, John *d. 1708, singer.*

At the coronation of James II on 23 April 1685, John Howell marched as one of the Children of the Choir of Westminster. He was sworn a Gentleman of the Chapel Royal (but without fee) on 30 August 1691, as a countertenor. He sang in the St Cecilia's Day celebration on 22 November 1692 and at the Queen's birthday on 30 April 1693 and 30 April 1694. He was admitted to the Chapel Royal in ordinary as Gospeller upon the death of John Sayer in January 1694, sworn Epistler on 1 October of that year, and made a salaried Gentleman of the Chapel Royal on 10 December 1695. On 23 March 1697 he replaced Alphonso Marsh in the King's private music. He and John Shore shared a benefit at York Buildings on 4 January 1699, when Daniel Purcell's music for the previous St Cecilia's Day festival was performed.

John Howell died on 15 July 1708. He had written his will on the eleventh, describing himself as from the parish of St Margaret, Westminster. The will provided bequests of £5 each to Howell's father John, his brother-in-law John Mathews, his sister Bridgett Mathews, his brother-in-law Marke Freake, his sister Elizabeth Freake, and his brother William. To his sister Sarah Howell, John left £5 for mourning plus an additional £5. Everything else, including his salary arrears, he left to his wife Katherine. She proved the will on 2 November 1708.

Howells, Miss *[fl. 1798–1800]*, singer.

Miss Howells, the daughter of a London watchmaker, sang with her sister Fanny Howells at Vauxhall Gardens between 1798 and 1800. Like her sister, she was probably a pupil of James Hook, many of whose songs listed in the *Catalogue of Printed Music in the British Museum* were published as sung by the Howells girls at Vauxhall. While they were engaged there, both sisters suffered "a very violent sort of fever" which ran through the Lambeth neighborhoods.

Although her sister Fanny enjoyed a theatrical career in the nineteenth century as wife of the Irish musician Thomas Simpson Cooke, this Miss Howells seems to have given up the profession after her Vauxhall appearances in 1800. We do not believe her to have been the Mary Ann Howell, of Bath, who became the second wife of the singer Charles Benjamin Incledon; that person was probably the daughter of the Bath musician Thomas Howell, the elder.

Howells, Fanny, later Mrs Thomas Simpson Cooke the first   *1785?–1824, singer, actress.*

Fanny Howells, the daughter of a London watchmaker, was born about 1785. Displaying musical precocity, at the age of four she was articled to the singer Michael Kelly. According to a press clipping in the Folger Library, Fanny sang at Vauxhall Gardens in 1786, but such a feat would have been impossible if she truly was only 15 years old, as claimed by the *Thespian Dictionary*, at the time of her debut at Covent Garden in 1800. With her sister, Fanny did sing at Vauxhall in 1798, and a collection of James Hook's songs as sung there by the two Misses Howells, Dignum,

Harvard Theatre Collection

FANNY HOWELLS

engraving by van Assen

Denman, Mrs Mountain, and Mrs Franklin were published that year. Other songs by James Hook were published in 1799 and 1800 as sung by the Howells sisters at Vauxhall.

Announced as a "Young Lady," Fanny made her "first appearance on any Stage" at Covent Garden Theatre on 29 September 1800 as Daphne in *Daphne and Amintor*. She was so nervous at her debut that when she came on she "fainted away" in the arms of Mrs Mountain, reported the press next morning. Revived after a few minutes, Fanny "was able to sing the Airs with much sweetness and taste amidst the warmest plaudits from every part of the House." Though very young—only 15 according to the report of one newspaper—and obviously inexperienced as an actress, she was possessed of a figure pleasing and genteel, though somewhat short, and a sweet and flexible voice guided by a good ear. After repeating Daphne on 3 and 10 October, she acted Clara in *The Duenna* on 22 October, when she was identified as Miss Howells. On 4 November she was applauded as Leonora in *The Padlock*.

Fanny remained engaged at Covent Garden for three seasons, earning £2 per week in the first two and £2 10*s.* in 1802–3. After her first appearance at the Haymarket Theatre on 25 June 1802 as Lucy in *The Review*, she continued to perform at that theatre each summer, except 1805, through 1806. On 26 June 1803 she was "rapturously received" at her first appearance at the Royal Circus, where she sang regularly through November of that year.

Early in 1804 Fanny was in Dublin. The name of Miss Howells is found in the Minute Books of the Irish Musical Fund for 5 March 1804, when she was appointed to assist at the annual concert of that organization. About December 1805 she married Thomas Simpson Cooke (1782–1848), an Irish singer, instrumentalist, and composer, the son of Bartlett Cooke, a well-known oboe player at Smock Alley Theatre. She remained mostly in Dublin, where her husband's career flourished. She was given a benefit at Crow Street Theatre on 4 May 1808. On 29 September 1808 the *Times* announced that "Mrs. Cooke, of the Dublin theatre, was delivered of a fine boy on Wednesday se'ennight [21 September]. The child has been christened by the name of Henry Angelo

Michael. Mr. Grattan and Madame Catalan stood sponsors." The Cookes were that year living at No 33, Lower Mount Street.

In July 1813 Mrs Cooke returned to London to sing with the English Opera at the Lyceum on the occasion of her husband's debut in the English capital. Both were announced as from the Dublin stage. When they played Lady Elinor and Lord William in *The Haunted Tower*, Fanny introduced the song "The Trumpet of Joy," which was not well received, though that was no fault of hers. The reporter in the *European Magazine* for that month found that she was not as pretty as he remembered her to have been. Another critic thought that though time had enlarged her dimensions, she was undiminished in grace. Her duet with her husband in the third act of *The Haunted Tower* was called for repeatedly, "amidst cheering acclaim." One paper on 27 July reported that she was an uncommonly sweet singer, with a clear, mellow, and original voice, and that she had been a pupil of Hook, whose songs she had introduced at Vauxhall when a child.

On 24 February 1816 Mrs Cooke made her first appearance at Drury Lane in her familiar role of Lady Elinor to her husband's Lord William. She remained there at £5 per week through 1818–19 and then retired. On the afternoon of 24 June 1824 she died of consumption at her home in the Edgeware Road.

Fanny's husband enjoyed a distinguished musical career in London, writing numerous songs and adaptations of operas and setting many plays to music, as well as conducting and singing in the leading concerts. His career is noticed in *Grove's Dictionary*. He died on 26 February 1848, leaving his estate to his second wife Angelina Cooke.

Henry Angelo Michael Cooke, the son of Fanny and Thomas S. Cooke, after being educated at the Royal Academy of Music, was for many years a principal oboist in London orchestras and bandmaster of the second regiment of Life Guards. He was usually called Grattan Cooke. He died at Harting, Sussex, on 12 September 1889.

According to a press cutting in the Folger Library, Fanny Howells had her portrait done when a child, sitting on a garden chair, with music in her hand. An engraved portrait of her by A. van Assen was published by Moore and Beauclere about 1800.

Howes. *See also* HAWES.

Howes, Burges *d. 1680, singer.*

Burges Howes, a bass singer from Windsor and very likely a relative of the musician William Howes, was sworn a Gentleman of the Chapel Royal on 11 September 1672, replacing Henry Cooke, who had died the previous July. The Lord Chamberlain's accounts did not mention Howes often, but he was doubtless the Howes "jr." who waited on Charles II at Windsor on 14 April 1674 and attended the King there again from 1 July to 11 September 1675. Howes died at Windsor on 10 January 1680 and was replaced in the Chapel Royal by John Abell.

Howes, William *fl. 1660?–1674?*, *musician. See* HOWES, WILLIAM *d. 1676*.

Howes, William *d. 1676, singer, instrumentalist, composer.*

William Howes (or Hawes) was born near Worcester and served as a wait in that town. He became a petty canon and sang at St George's Chapel, Windsor, until 1642 and then followed Charles I to Oxford, where he became a singer at Christ Church. He later returned to Windsor on a soldier's pay. On 25 November 1643 Howes was sworn a Gentleman of the Chapel Royal in ordinary, replacing the recently deceased Mr West. With other Commonwealth musicians in the employ of Cromwell, Howes signed a petition on 19 February 1657 asking the Protector to establish "a Corporacion or Colledge of Musitians" for the better regulation of musical activities in London.

By 20 June 1660 Howes was a member of the royal musical establishment under Charles II as was, we think, a second William Howes, probably our subject's son. Separating the two in the Lord Chamberlain's accounts and other early documents is almost impossible. Warrants called Howes a violinist replacing Robert Dowland in a list headed "(double places)," and he was also named as a member of the private music for lutes, voices, theorboes, and virginals, replacing John Mercure. Those two posts would seem to refer to one William Howes, but we cannot be certain, for on 9 November 1660 a warrant listed Howes as a replacement for John Hickson at 1*s*. 8*d*. daily plus £16 2s. 6d. annually for livery, and it also cited Howes again as Robert Dowland's replacement at a salary of £40 12s. 8d. yearly. A document in the *State Papers Domestic* dated autumn 1663 cited Howes twice, again suggesting two musicians of the same name.

Howes was one of the teachers of Susannah Perwich, and on occasion he also augmented his income by serving the King at Windsor for a fee of from 5s. to 8s. daily. On 10 July 1665 Howes was appointed to John Banister's elite band of violinists at court. By 1668 his salary as a violinist was up to £42 12s. 8d. annually, and a warrant dated 9 January 1669 listed him as receiving £46 10s. 10d. for service as both a violinist and a wind instrumentalist. A warrant dated 14 April 1674 cited two different singers named Howes: the younger was called a bass and the elder a tenor. To confuse matters further, there was a singer in the Chapel Royal at that time (he joined in 1672) named Burges Howes; he may have been the bass singer referred to.

On 28 March 1676 William Howes (the elder, we would assume, to whom most of the references above probably point) may have been close to death, for a warrant was issued granting Richard Tomlinson the place of either Howes or John Jenkins, whichever should be vacated first by "death or avoydance." Howes died in Windsor on 21 April 1676; on 3 May Tomlinson replaced him in the band of violins, and Edmund Flower took his post in the wind instruments. The *Old Cheque Book of the Chapel Royal* contains a record of Howes's death and lists Alphonso Marsh the younger as his replacement. Howes was buried in the yard of St George's Chapel, Windsor. William Howes was also a composer, one of his songs being in Hilton's *Catch that Catch Can*.

The second and younger William Howes (if, in fact, there was one) would seem to have been a minor member of the Chapel Royal, active from perhaps 1660 to 1674.

Howey, Mrs ₁*fl. 1723–1724*₁, *actress.*
Mrs Howey made her first stage appearance as Clarinda in *The Female Fops* in a performance at the Haymarket Theatre given by a group of amateurs on 12 December 1723. She apparently turned professional, however, and was seen at the same house on 5 February 1724 as Violante in *Sir Courtly Nice*, with William Milward as Belguard.

Howis, Mr ₁*fl. 1796*₁, *puppeteer.*
The Pie Powder Court Book at the Guildhall lists Mr Howis as exhibiting his puppets at Bartholomew Fair in 1796.

Howles, John *c. 1761–1812, violinist, violist, clarinetist.*
When John Howles was recommended for membership in the Royal Society of Musicians on 1 February 1784, he was said by Charles Linton to be 23 years old, married but with no children, a member of the guards, a performer at the Royal Circus, and a musician proficient on the violin and clarinet. The John "Howlds" who was one of the second violinists at the Handel Memorial Concerts at Westminster Abbey and the Pantheon in May and June of 1784 was surely John Howles. On 10 and 12 May 1784 John played tenor (viola) at the St Paul's concert, but in 1790, 1792, 1794, 1795, and 1797 he was listed as playing the violin. Doane's *Musical Directory* of 1794 stated that John played also at the Professional Concerts, in the oratorios at Drury Lane, and at Westminister Abbey. He lived at St James's Palace.

The Drury Lane accounts show that as of 1801 Howles was earning £2 weekly as a member of the band, a fee he was still getting in 1807. He played at the Haymarket Theatre at least some summers; the accounts mention him from 1804 through 1810. John was also active in the Royal Society of Musicians, serving on the Court of Assistants in 1807, 1808, 1811, and perhaps other years as well.

John Howles wrote his will on 8 February 1806, leaving everything to his wife Deborah. He died in 1812, and his widow proved the will on 11 April of that year. On the following 3 January 1813, the Royal Society of Musicians received from her a petition for a widow's allowance (amount unspecified), which was granted. On 4 April the Secretary of the Society was ordered to investigate the amount of the annuity Mrs "Howlds" was receiving from St James's and to adjust her pension from the Society accordingly.

Howton. *See* HOOTEN.

Hoy, Robert *[fl. 1791–1807]*, actor, manager.

The "Gentleman" making his first appearance on any stage who played Henriquez in *The Double Falsehood* at Covent Garden on 6 June 1791 was identified in Reed's "Notitia Dramatica" as Mr Hoy. Hoy did not pursue a London career further but spent the rest of his time in the provinces. In late December 1798 he and a troupe he organized began performing in Wolverhampton, according to the *Monthly Mirror* of February 1799. The periodical chided Hoy for making exaggerated claims for his company, but the players were complimented for their work. In Hoy's group were Campbell, Eastmure, Fox, and Mmes Edwards, Belfille, and Harlowe.

The same periodical placed Hoy's company in Worcester in 1801. There Hoy featured Fox, Shuter, Chambers, Field, Holmes, and Mmes Field, Belfille, Edwards, and Chambers. By 1803 Hoy was operating at least two theatres on the Worcester circuit, for James Winston's notes for *The Theatric Tourist* (at Harvard) state that Hoy offered in August 1803 a free benefit from each of his theatres to the patriotic fund. From the 1803 will of the actor William Fox of Worcester and from the *Gentleman's Magazine* of April 1807 we learn that Hoy's Christian name was Robert. The latter source reported that Hoy had that month married a Miss Burne.

Hubb, John *[fl. 1739]*, musician.

John Hubb was one of the original subscribers to the Royal Society of Musicians when it was founded on 28 August 1739.

Hubbard, Mr *d. 1786, bassoonist.*

Mr Hubbard played bassoon in the Handel Memorial Concerts at Westminster Abbey and the Pantheon in May and June 1784. According to *Musgrave's Obituary*, Hubbard's lodgings were in Goodge Street, and the bassoonist died on 10 October 1786.

Hubbert. *See* HOBART.

Hubert, Mr *[fl. 1777]*, actor.

At the China Hall playhouse in Rotherhithe on 20 June 1777, a Mr Hubert was part of the Mob in *The Mayor of Garratt*.

Hubert, Robert *[fl. 1664–1665]*, exhibitor, impresario?

Robert Hubert, alias Forges, was in 1664 the master of the Mitre tavern in London House Yard, near the west end of St Paul's Cathedral. The Mitre was used for musical concerts, but it is not certain that Hubert himself organized the presentations. He did, however, exhibit "natural rarities" which he had collected "with great industrie, cost, and thirty years' travel into foreign countries," a catalogue of which he published in 1664. He spoke of himself in the catalogue as a "sworn servant to his Majesty" and said that his collection was "daily to be seen at the place called the Musick-house, *at the Mitre*."

Hubert's catalogue listed

a mummy; a giant's thigh-bone, more than four feet in length, found in Syria; a haget, that sleeps for six months; it is a creature of the island of Mayonto in the lake Yondarro; the hornes of a dog of a land near China; the ribb of a Triton or Mereman, taken by Captain Finney on the shoutts of Brazil, 500 leagues from the Maine; the vein of the tongue of that whale, that was taken up at Greenwich a little before Cromwel's death; a manucodiata or bird of Paradise with feet, for it hath great feet, to shew that it perches on trees in a land as yet unknown, for they are never seen alive, but are always found dead in the Malacoo's Islands, by reason of a continual wind that bloweth six months one way and six months the other way, and because of their sharp head, little body, and great feathered tayle, they are blown up so high that they fall dead in another climate or country. . . .

—and so on. The collection was sold in 1665 and later bought by Dr Hans Sloane; it formed one of the bases for the British Museum.

Hubert, Samuel Morton *[fl. 1794]*, singer.

Samuel Morton Hubert, according to Doane's *Musical Directory* of 1794, sang bass for the Choral Fund and the Surrey Chapel Society in London. He lived at Mr Mitchener's in Arundel, Sussex.

Huddart, Thomas *d. 1831, actor, dancer.*

The "Young Gentleman" who made his Covent Garden debut on 15 October 1798 as Othello was making his fourth appearance on any stage. He was Thomas Huddart, said the *Monthly Mirror*, and hailed from the Crow

Street Theatre in Dublin. He "displayed considerable sensibility in several scenes of this difficult character; his figure is elegant, and his voice possesses some fine commanding tones; he has undoubtedly much to learn and unlearn before he can become eminent in the profession; but, upon the whole, we have a right to expect every thing from a debut so promising." The *Morning Herald* was impressed with Huddart's tender and gentle scenes but found him too boisterous in the impassioned moments: "from his too eager exertion, he exhausted himself, in a great measure, before the conclusion of the piece."

The *Authentic Memoirs of the Green Room* noted that Huddart had performed in Dublin "for a few nights; and was obliged, not from ambition, but necessity, to make the stage his profession." He came from a respectable but not affluent family. The author of the *Memoirs* found his voice sweet but not powerful enough for Othello. "In an humbler line Mr. Huddart may be found a useful character. At present he has no permanent situation." Despite the critical attention, Huddart left London.

He acted at Norwich and at Crow Street in 1799 and also appeared at Limerick and Cork. During the 1799–1800 season at Crow Street he married Miss Ann Gough, the sister of Mrs Galindo; Mrs Huddart had a modest acting career in Dublin and elsewhere in the early years of the nineteenth century, but she did not appear in London. The Huddarts had a daughter, Mary Amelia, in 1804; she became an actress and the wife of Robert W. Warner and lived until 1854.

Thomas Huddart performed in Dublin in 1800–1801 and, according to a playgoer's journal in the National Library of Ireland, was in *The Votary of Wealth* on 26 May 1801: "about the middle of the piece Huddart as the rejected lover, carrying off in his arms a mistress [played by Miss Brown] fainting at the prospect of rape, exposed her legs, & made use of some freedom which she resented, and a battle royal ensued behind the scenes. . . ." He did not return the following season.

The *Monthly Mirror* reported that Huddart made his Manchester debut as Frederick in *Lovers Vows*, drawing

the loudest applause we remember ever to have heard in this theatre. He possesses very considerable

requisites for the stage, and has great advantages of voice, figure, and expression of countenance. We could only wish to recommend to him a little more firmness and majesty of deportment, though in that respect he is at present far from inelegant.

Huddart performed at Manchester through the 1804–5 season, appearing in such roles as Faulkland in *The Rivals*, Moneses in *Tamerlane*, Rolla in *Pizarro*, Jaffeir in *Venice Preserv'd*, Octavian in *The Mountaineers*, Young Norval in *Douglas*, Henry V, Macduff in *Macbeth*, Osmond in *The Castle Spectre*, Oakly in *The Jealous Wife*, Posthumus in *Cymbeline*, Hotspur in 1 *Henry IV*, and Hamlet. He also appeared as a dancer.

The *Townsman* and the *Theatrical Inquisitor* gave Huddart considerable attention during his years in Manchester. The *Townsman* was much impressed with Huddart's Rolla:

. . . I cannot hesitate to say, that this performer appears to be the principal support of the company. In the exertions of the evening, he gave proofs of much judgment and considerable powers; but his powers are limited, tho' they might, with study, be greatly improved. Yet how can the efforts of great study be hoped for, from one, however great his talents, who is called up to play, generally a long part every night. Indeed Mr. Huddart would fill the second line of serious characters with great success, and with satisfaction to the town; but it is indispensible that the company should have a principal tragedian of the *first rate* abilities.

He was liked as Henry V, though he misread (purposely or not, the critic could not tell) a line and cried, "God for Harry, England, and King George!" There was too much rant in his Osmond, and he was too youthful as Oakly, but the *Townsman* critic was usually able to give Huddart praise.

The *Theatrical Inquisitor* criticized Huddart severely for caricaturing Cooke when he played Hotspur. The critic ridiculed "H[uddar]t's entering; here he is—see with what contempt he looks upon his brother actors, and how his sparkling eyes turn to boxes, pit, and gallery-gods, waiting, or expecting, nay, even as it were, commanding, their plaudits, before we must expect one word of the author." During his Manchester years Huddart is known to have performed also at Buxton and Chester, and he may well have appeared in other towns.

Huddart performed again at the Crow Street Theatre in Dublin in 1808, and on 16 May

1811 he made his second London appearance, at the Haymarket as Muley (in *Don Sebastian?*). On 29 September 1813 at Drury Lane, Huddart was seen as Shylock in *The Merchant of Venice*. The *Theatrical Inquisitor* said "The attempt was more bold than successful. His face is destitute of varied expression, his manner hard, his voice unsusceptable of varied modulation." Huddart tried London once again on 11 November 1819, when he played Macbeth at Covent Garden.

Sometime after that Thomas Huddart retired from the stage. He died in 1831. *Tallis's Dramatic Magazine* in January 1851 said that Huddart had served as a common councilman in Dublin and had been a member of the firm of Jenkins, Huddart, and Company, wholesale chemists.

Huddy, Master   [*fl. 1732*],   *actor.*

Master Huddy played the Duke of York in *Richard III* on 20 March 1732 at the Goodman's Fields Theatre and was seen there again on the following 1 December as Lucius in *Julius Caesar*. Philip Huddy acted Tressel in the first production and the title role in the second; it is very likely that Master Huddy was his son.

Huddy, Philip   *d. c. 1745?, actor, singer.*

Perhaps the actor-singer Philip Huddy was related to Hugh Huddy, a writer of song lyrics who was active in London about 1720. Philip Huddy's earliest notice was on 10 May 1723, when he shared a benefit with Davies at Lincoln's Inn Fields and played Alcander in *Oedipus*. The two players divided £107 7s. 6d., probably before house charges were subtracted. The benefit would suggest that Huddy had been active at the theatre throughout the 1722–23 season, though we have no record of other parts for him. On 22 August 1723 he played the King in *The Blind Beggar of Bednal Green* at the Pinkethman-Norris booth at Bartholomew Fair. It is likely that he repeated the role at Richmond on 2 September, and on 5 September he was at Pinkethman's Southwark Fair booth acting the King in another droll, *Jane Shore*.

In 1723–24 Huddy was again unnoticed in the Lincoln's Inn Fields playbills until late in the season, when, on 13 May 1724, he shared a benefit with Lanyon and played Duncan in *Macbeth*. The receipts came to £124 5s. In the summer Huddy acted Menander in *Sophonisba*, Pizarro in *The Indian Emperor*, and Pedro in *Massaniello*, and he had a role in *The Roman Maid*. He returned to Bartholomew Fair on 22 August to act, again, the King in *The Blind Beggar* at Pinkethman's booth; on 5 September at the same manager's Southwark Fair enterprise, Huddy was the King in *Valentine and Orson*.

The Lincoln's Inn Fields accounts show that Huddy was earning 8s. daily as of 25 September 1724, but the bills did not cite him until benefit time. On 1 May 1725 he portrayed Ratcliff in *Richard III* and shared £125 7s. with Hulett. Huddy acted King Ninus in *Semiramis* for Pinkethman on 23 August at Bartholomew Fair.

The Life of Lavinia Beswick, Alias Fenton tells us that Huddy was turned out of John Rich's company at Lincoln's Inn Fields the following season. On 24 February 1726 he held a benefit for himself at the Haymarket Theatre, playing Acasto in *The Orphan*. Over a year later, on 19 May 1727, he was back with Rich, acting Claudius Caesar in *Caradoc the Great*; but he may not have been a regular member of the troupe, for that is the only record of his acting between his Haymarket benefit and his activity in York in the summer of 1727.

Huddy purported to be organizing a provincial company and, on 16 June 1727, assured the people of York that he had contracted with Boheme, Wilks, Spiller, Wilcocks, Ray, Mrs Egleton, and other London players to perform in York during the races. The following 20 July Anthony Boheme advised the public through *Mist's Weekly Journal* that his name was listed by Huddy "without my consent or Knowledge," and that he had no intention of appearing in York. Perhaps Huddy's "company" did not perform at all.

Not until 8 December 1729 does Philip Huddy's name appear again in surviving London playbills. On that date he made his first appearance on the Goodman's Fields stage as Horatio in *The Fair Penitent*, after which he was seen in many major roles until his retirement at the end of the 1734–35 season. Among his characters at Goodman's Fields were Vainlove and Bluff in *The Old Bachelor*, Horatio in *Hamlet*, Myrtle in *The Conscious Lovers*, Sir George in *The Drummer*, Manly and Sir

Francis in *The Provok'd Husband*, Page and the Host in *The Merry Wives of Windsor*, Belvil in *The Rover*, Leon in *Rule a Wife and Have a Wife*, the Elder Worthy in *Love's Last Shift*, Careless in *The Busy Body*, King Lear (though later he played Kent), Vandunck in *The Royal Merchant*, Omar in *Tamerlane*, Pounce in *The Tender Husband*, Sempronius in *Cato*, the title role and Raymond in *The Spanish Fryar*, Priuli in *Venice Preserv'd*, the Mad Taylor in *The Pilgrim*, Clincher Senior in *The Constant Couple*, Phoenix in *The Distrest Mother*, Hothead in *Sir Courtly Nice*, the Governor in *Love Makes a Man*, the Uncle in *The London Merchant*, Bonniface in *The Stratagem*, the King in *1 Henry IV*, Kite in *The Recruiting Officer*, Dalton in *The Lover's Opera*, Blunt in *The Committee*, Tressel in *Richard III* on 20 March 1732 (Master Huddy, probably Philip's son, played the Duke of York), Lockit in *The Beggar's Opera*, the title role in *Julius Caesar* on 1 December 1732 (Master Huddy acted Lucius), Brumpton in *The Funeral*, and Driver in *Oroonoko*. Huddy's last recorded performance was on 3 May 1735, when he played one of the Grenadiers in *Britannia*. During the 1730s Huddy made occasional appearances at Tottenham Court and at the late summer fairs.

Huddy was a Mason, and when *The Provok'd Husband* was presented at Goodman's Fields on 29 November 1732, the bill announced that "The Brethren are desir'd to meet at two a-Clock at Brother Huddy's at the Theatre Tavern, there to Dine, and proceed afterwards in order to the Play." By that date Huddy had become proprietor of that tavern. After his retirement from the stage the actor apparently spent the rest of his life running his establishment. From time to time the newspapers mentioned him. The *Daily Advertiser* of 6 September 1736 reported, for example, that Huddy had suffered a robbery. The same paper on 26 September 1738 mentioned Huddy and supplied us with his first name. He was still operating his tavern in the spring of 1739.

On 20 January 1746 a Mrs Huddy, described as a widow in distress, was given a benefit at the Goodman's Fields playhouse; tickets were available from her at the Fleece Tavern on the corner of Ayliffe Street, Goodman's Fields. She was surely Philip Huddy's widow, and we may guess that he had recently died—perhaps late in 1745.

Hudgson. *See* HODGSON.

Hudson. *See also* HODGSON and HODSON.

Hudson, Mr [*fl.* 1771–1789], *actor, singer, dancer, manager.*

A Mr Hudson acted Young Dudley in a performance of *The West Indian* at the Haymarket Theatre on 15 April 1771. In the same cast, playing Miss Dudley, was his wife. No doubt they were the Hudsons who had long and active provincial careers in the 1770s and 1780s.

Mr Hudson, usually accompanied by his wife, acted occasional supporting roles at Bristol in 1772 and 1778–89 and was with Tate Wilkinson's company on the York circuit between 1775–76 and 1780–81. In 1783–84 he acted at Derby, and in the spring of 1786 he was at Brighton. At the opening performance of the Royalty Theatre, London, on 20 June 1787, Hudson acted Duke Frederick in *As You Like It*. At the Royalty through at least September 1788, he also sang and danced in such pieces as *The Patriotic Barber*, *The Deserter at Naples*, and *Don Juan*. Announced as from the Royalty, he played at Gloucester in 1789, where he co-managed with Grist.

Hudson, Mr [*fl.* 1782?–1798], *dancer, musical-glass player, tumbler.*

A Mr Hudson danced the role of Abbot in *Alfred the Great*, a historical ballet performed at Sadler's Wells during 1797. The following summer there he and Wilkinson played on "a Double Set of HARMONIC GLASSES" on 9 April and 30 July 1798.

Possibly this person was the Master Hudson who in "Exhibitions of Sadler's Wells" presented by Andrews's company at Coopers' Hall, Bristol, in March 1782, performed feats of "Ground and Lofty Tumbling" with Miss Richards. Several years later Master Hudson was a member of Hilliard's acrobatic entertainment from Sadler's Wells performing at Brighton in the summer of 1785.

Hudson, Mrs [*fl.* 1705], *boxkeeper.*

On 24 January 1705 Luttrell noted in his diary: "captain Walsh quarelling with Mrs. Hudson, who keeps the boxes in the play house, she pulled out his sword and killed him." Nothing more is known of the incident, nor can we tell which playhouse Mrs Hudson worked for.

Hudson, Mrs [*fl.* 1769–1780?], *singer.*

A Mrs Hudson sang frequently at Vauxhall Gardens during the 1770s, and she was probably the Mrs Hudson who performed in the oratorios at York in 1769 and 1770. Songs published as sung by her at Vauxhall included: *A Collection of Favorite Songs sung at Vauxhall Gardens by Mrs Weichsell, Mrs Hudson, & Mr Vernon,* 1773; Hook's *Beneath a green shade,* 1774; *While others sing in cheerful lay* (1775?); *When first the east begins to dawn* (1775?); *Jockey's left me for a while,* 1778; and *A Third Collection of Favourite Songs sung at Vauxhall by Mr. Vernon and Mrs Sherbourne, Mrs Hudson & Mrs Weichsell* (1780?). Possibly she was the Mrs Hudson referred to in a letter by Kitty Clive on 23 November 1773: "Mrs Hudson is an agreeable woman, but I am always afraid she will Break in two, I never saw anything human so thin."

Hudson, Mrs [*fl.* 1771–1789], *actress, singer?*

A Mrs. Hudson acted Miss Dudley in a performance of *The West Indian* at the Haymarket Theatre on 15 April 1771. In the same cast, playing Young Dudley, was her husband. They were no doubt the Mr and Mrs Hudson who had long and active careers in the provinces in the 1770s and 1780s.

At Bristol in 1772 and 1773 Mrs Hudson acted supporting roles. In 1775 she was engaged for the York Theatre by Wilkinson, who described her as "a lady of fame in the west, from Exeter. . . . Her person was not very good, but her face was remarkably handsome." In May of that year she made her debut at York as Jane Shore but, according to Wilkinson, "was not much approved of, but being very perfect, with perseverance and assiduity, she by degrees grew into good favour" on the circuit and especially at Doncaster was held "in first-rate esteem." At Hull that season she and Mrs Montague caused "frequent commotions" in Wilkinson's company because of their rivalry for public favor. The ill will persisted through several years, and on 3 January 1777, for Mrs Hudson's benefit night at Hull, Mrs Montague balked at playing the Queen to Mrs Hudson's Rosamond in *Henry II,* though she

did agree to read the role, a circumstance which caused the audience to drive her from the stage.

At the end of the York season of 1777, Mrs Hudson quarreled with Wilkinson and left him. They were reconciled by 1779, when she and her husband were re-engaged. She had meanwhile acted at Bristol in 1778–79. She was also at Derby early in 1782.

Mrs Hudson returned to London for a single night on 31 January 1785 to play the Duke of York in *King Charles I* and a character in *A Comic Sketch of the Times* at the Haymarket Theatre. In 1786 she was at Cheltenham and Brighton. Probably she was the Mrs Hudson who sang at the Royalty Theatre with Mrs Gibbs in a musical piece called *The Muses in Motion* during November 1787, when her husband was a member of that company. In 1789 she played at Gloucester, Swansea, and Brecon, taking her benefit at Brecon on 4 December 1789.

Hudson, Master. *See* HUDSON, MR [*fl.* 1782?–1798].

Hudson, George *d.* 1672, *violinist, lutenist, singer, composer, dancing master.*

Anthony à Wood wrote that George Hudson began his professional life as a dancing master. On 3 December 1641 Hudson was sworn a musician for lutes and voices extraordinary (that is, without fee) in the King's Musick. He was probably given a salaried post not long afterward, but evidence is lacking. Hudson busied himself during the Commonwealth by teaching and composing; Playford's *Musical Banquet* in 1651 listed Hudson as a London teacher of "Voyce or Viol." In 1656 he and Dr Charles Coleman composed the instrumental music for Sir William Davenant's historic production of *The Siege of Rhodes* at Rutland House.

In 1660 Hudson and Davis Mell were given a joint appointment as masters of the King's violins, at a shared salary of £110 annually. The records would indicate that Hudson replaced Stephen Nau, whose salary had been £42 12*s*. 10*d*. yearly, and he also took over Estien Nau's post as composer for the violins at £200 annually. In addition, Hudson received (rarely on schedule) £16 2*s*. 6*d*. each year as a livery fee. Mell and Hudson were

Faculty of Music, Oxford

GEORGE HUDSON

artist unknown

advised by the Lord Chamberlain on 31 May 1661 that they had better exercise stricter discipline over their band of violinists, for negligence in practice and performance had been reported. Hudson, along with four other top men in the royal musical establishment, received a total of £50 on 4 July 1661 to cover the rental of two rooms they used for musical instrument storage and for practice during the previous year. The payment continued the following year and in 1663.

In addition, like so many court musicians, Hudson attended the King on trips out of London, as in the summer of 1662, when Charles II was at Hampton Court, and each musician in attendance was paid 5*s*. daily above his usual salary. Hudson was with the King at Windsor in the summer of 1663. On 10 July 1665 Hudson became one of the members of the King's band of violins under the direction of John Banister the elder. By 1668 Hudson was receiving £42 10*s*. 10*d*. yearly as one of the King's composers.

A warrant in the Lord Chamberlain's accounts dated 26 April 1669 suggests that the widow of Richard Hudson, a violinist and probably a relative of George, was to receive £32 5*s*. "by vertue of an assignment from George Hudson" of his livery payments for 1665 and 1666. Richard must have loaned George some money, taking as collateral the arrears in liveries. By 21 January 1670 George had become a warden in the Corporation of Music, though that position probably brought him no income.

A warrant dated 10 January 1672 indicates that by that date George Hudson must have been ill and perhaps close to death. Thomas Purcell and Pelham Humphrey were appointed composers in ordinary for the violins without fee, to assist Hudson and to receive salaries at Hudson's death or "other avoydance"—a device frequently used to assure continuity in a post when a court musician was near death. Hudson was still alive on 24 June 1672, however, for he was cited on that date as an active member of the Corporation of Music. On St Andrew (30 November) he was listed on a livery warrant, but on 10 December the accounts cited a nuncupative will of George Hudson of the parish of St Martin-in-the-Fields, made at the house of John Warrells, East Greenwich, Kent. He left £100 each to Humphrey and Elizabeth Warrells. When Purcell and Pelham Humphrey took over Hudson's post as composer for the violins, they received (together, apparently) £42 15s. 10d. plus £200 annually, which was presumably what Hudson had been earning at his death. For several years after his death George Hudson was cited in the Lord Chamberlain's accounts, for arrears in livery payments were due his executors for some years afterward. On 29 January 1675, for example, his executors were to receive £64 10s. due for the years 1665, 1666, 1667, and 1670.

George Hudson composed a few dance pieces during his life, some of which were published in 1669 in *Musick's Recreation* and in 1655 in *Court Ayres*. Some of his music exists in manuscript at the British Library and some at Christ Church Library, Oxford.

A portrait of George Hudson by an unknown artist is at the Music School, Oxford. For many years it was misidentified as a portrait of Robert Hudson, the eighteenth-century singer.

Hudson, John [fl. 1724–c. 1749], violinist.

A Mr Hudson "of the Musick" at Lincoln's Inn Fields Theatre was cited several times in the company accounts from 6 November 1724 through the 1728–29 season. His salary was 5s. weekly, though he put in extra time at the same rate and increased his income. He was mentioned occasionally on the free list, one citation, on 22 February 1729, indicating that he had a brother (Samuel?). In 1725–26, during which season Mr Hudson's name disappeared from the theatre accounts, John Hudson the violinist played for the Duke of Chandos at Cannons for £17 1s. It seems very probable that the theatre musician was John.

The Lord Chamberlain's accounts show that John Hudson was in the royal musical establishment on 29 December 1730, and the accounts continued citing him into the 1740s.

On 28 August 1739 Hudson, described as of the parish of St Martin-in-the-Fields, became one of the founding governors of the Royal Society of Musicians. Sometime around 1749 Edward Gibbs replaced Hudson in the King's Musick.

Hudson, Mary *d. 1801, organist, composer, singer.*

Mary Hudson was taught music by her father, Robert Hudson (d. 1815), a singer and organist. She was among the sopranos in the Handel Memorial Concerts at Westminster Abbey and the Pantheon in May and June 1784 and from 1794, perhaps earlier, until her death was the organist of St Olave, Hart Street, and St Gregory, Old Fish Street. Her address in 1794 was No 1, St Peter's Hill.

Her compositions included several hymns and *Applaud so great a guest*, the latter being an English version, set for five voices, of the Latin epitaph on Purcell's gravestone.

She died at St Peter's Hill, London, on 28 March 1801. Administration of her estate, valued at under £1000 was granted to her father on 17 April 1801.

Hudson, Richard *d. 1668, violinist, wind instrumentalist?, instrument keeper.*

Richard Hudson was one of the small group of London musicians who, on 19 February 1657, petitioned Cromwell to form a "Corporacion or Colledge of Musitians" to control the practice of music in London. Hudson was one of Cromwell's court musicians and followed the Protector's body to the grave in 1658. At the Restoration Richard became part of the musical establishment of Charles II, being appointed on 16 June 1660 to replace "Mr. Noe"—that is, Simon Nau, the violinist. Hudson was to receive Nau's salary of £46 12s. 8d. annually, plus livery. By 20 June 1662 he was given the additional position of "keeper of his Ma^{ts} Lutes and Vyolls" at a fee of 12d. daily, replacing Richard Moller, who had died.

The Lord Chamberlain's accounts contain frequent citations of Hudson, sometimes in connection with money he spent for violin strings, sometimes for trips he made with the King to Portsmouth, Oxford, Windsor, and other towns or with the Queen to Tunbridge, sometimes (as on 20 December 1664) in connection with performances at the King's Theatre in Bridges Street under Thomas Killigrew, and sometimes for storing and repairing musical instruments used at court.

One warrant, dated 15 April 1663, directed Hudson to collect the court musicians' viols, violins, and lutes and "cause his Majesty's Armes to be cut in mother of pearl and inlayed in the finger boards of the several instruments"; the warrant also commanded Hudson to see to it that the instruments stayed "in his Majesty's house" so as to keep them from being changed or broken. Hudson was one of the elite group of 12 violinists in the King's private music under John Banister the elder and from 14 March 1667 onward under Louis Grabu.

Richard Hudson died in 1668, probably shortly before 18 February, on which date Thomas Fitz was named to replace him in the band of violins. Two days later Henry Brockwell was granted Hudson's post as keeper of the lutes and viols. Frequent warrants were issued in subsequent months repeating those appointments, and Hudson's name did not disappear from accounts until late in 1683. The reason seems to have been financial. On 26 April 1669 the sum of £32 5s. was to be paid to Richard Hudson's widow and executrix, "by vertue of an assignment from George Hudson"—also a court musician and doubtless a relative—for livery payments due Richard Hudson for 1665 and 1666. Richard seems to have loaned George some money, taking George's unpaid livery fees as security. By the time of Richard's death in 1668 the debt had not been paid, nor had the livery payments from the King.

On 12 January 1671 the accounts show again how far behind were payments to court musicians. Thomas Fitz was the replacement for Hudson among the violinists, and "There being some money in arrears due for the service of Hudson which ought to be paid unto his widow, half of the first year's salary due to Fitz shall be given to Elizabeth, relict of Richard Hudson, who is very poor and much in necessity. Thomas Fitz to receive the like sum out of the arrears of Hudson's salary."

Though it appears that Richard Hudson was in a position at some point in his career to loan money to George Hudson, at another time he had to borrow. A warrant of 27 February 1672 stated that

Whereas Richard Hudson, late keeper of his Majesty's lutes and violls, did assign unto Alphonso Maley [Alphers Maley?] all his wages and salary due for the said place during his life and at his death, amounting to the sum of £71 4s, £18 5s to be paid annually, Henry Brockwell since coming into the said place, these are to pray you, to make stop of half the said wages payable to the said Henry Brockwell, and pay the same to Mr. Maley until the said sum be fully paid.

Elizabeth Hudson apparently found the problem of untangling her late husband's financial affairs too much for her, for on 8 July 1675 she appointed Lewis Peare of Westminster her lawful attorney.

When Nicholas Staggins took over Grabu's post as Master of the King's Musick, a warrant dated 3 November 1675 mentioned that Staggins was also made "musician in ordinary to his Majesty for the wind instruments in the place of Richard Hudson, deceased." Hudson is not otherwise known to have been a wind instrumentalist, and perhaps the post was merely an administrative one to provide him with extra pay. Staggins, however, was cited regularly in the accounts as a replacement for Hudson through the rest of the 1670s and until as late as St Andrew's Day, 1683—after which Hudson's name disappeared from the accounts.

Hudson, Robert *1732–1815, singer, organist, composer, choirmaster.*

Robert Hudson was born in London on 25 February 1732. He became assistant organist of St Mildred, Bread Street, in 1755 and was appointed vicar choral of St Paul's Cathedral in 1756. In 1758 he was made a Gentleman of the Chapel Royal and in 1773 almoner and master of the children of St Paul's, a post he held until he resigned in 1793. In his *Reminiscences*, Thomas J. Dibdin, who was one of the choir children, called him a very kind instructor. He was also the music master of Christ's Hospital, for which he composed numerous hymns.

On 18 January 1760 Hudson was one of the vocalists in a performance of *Judas Maccabaeus* at the Great Music Room, Dean Street, Soho.

On 12 February 1762 he sang Acis in *Acis and Galatea* at Hickford's Room, and on 1 April 1762 in a concert at Drapers' Hall he sang the song *While joyful here we meet*, published in that year. In the summer of 1762 he appeared at Ranelagh Gardens, and he continued to perform there and at Marylebone Gardens during the 1760s. From about 1760 to 1775 Hudson also served as organist at Finch's Grotto Gardens. In 1763 *Mortimer's London Directory* listed his address as St Peter's Hill.

Hudson was one of the tenor vocalists in the Handel Memorial Concerts at Westminster Abbey and the Pantheon in May and June 1784. In 1794, according to Doane's *Musical Directory*, he was still living at No 1, St Peter's Hill. In 1798 he sang at Sadler's Wells.

He died at Eton on 19 December 1815 and was buried in St Paul's Cathedral. His daughter, Mary Hudson, also an accomplished musician, had left him her estate upon her death in 1801.

Among his numerous compositions was *The Myrtle* (a collection of songs in three books, published in 1767), chants and hymn tunes, and a setting for five voices of the inscription on Child's monument at Windsor which begins, "Go, happy soul." A list of over 130 of his songs is given in the *Catalogue of Printed Music in the British Museum*. A portrait by an unknown artist at the Music School, Oxford, has often been mistaken for Robert Hudson, but it is actually of George Hudson, the Restoration musician.

Hudson, Samuel [*fl. 1739*], *musician*.

Samuel Hudson was one of the original members of the Royal Society of Musicians when it was organized on 28 August 1739. Perhaps he was the brother of the violinist John Hudson.

Hudson, William *d. 1815, violinist*.

When William Hudson was recommended for membership in the Royal Society of Musicians on 7 July 1776, he was described as a person who had practiced music professionally upwards of seven years and was a married man with no children. Little is known of his musical activities in London except that he was admitted to the Society on 1 September 1776 and played the violin in the Society's May concerts at St Paul's in 1792 and 1797.

About 1800 Hudson moved to York. On 2 February 1802 the Royal Society of Musicians granted him four guineas for immediate assistance. A similar grant was made on 2 November 1806. On 6 May 1811 his yearly allowance of £68 8*s.* from the Society was reduced to £14 12*s.* Hudson died on 21 April 1815, and the Governors of the Society determined on 7 May 1815 that his widow's circumstances were such that no allowance from the Society was needed.

Hues or Huges. *See* HUGHES.

Huette, Mme [*fl. 1751–1757*], *dancer*.

Mme (sometimes Mlle) Huette made her first appearance on the English stage at Covent Garden Theatre on 12 April 1751 dancing for the benefit of Mr Cooke. After dancing for the second time, on 17 April, she appeared on 26 April in three pieces, *The Characters of Dancing*, *La Paisane*, and a *Louvre and Minuet*, the last with Villeneuve. She danced again in *La Paisane* on 29 April, performed a *Scotch Dance* and the *Louvre and Minuet* with Froment on 4 May, and shared benefit tickets on 14 May.

In 1752 Mme Huette was with the company at Jacob's Wells Theatre, Bristol, where on 28 March she danced the *Louvre and Minuet* with Pitt; on 18 July she danced with Grandchamps· in several numbers for her own benefit. By the second half of 1753–54 she was back at Covent Garden, performing with Settree on 27 April 1754 and sharing in benefit tickets with Jervais and Mrs Gwinn on 4 May. In 1756–57 she danced at the Smock Alley Theatre in Dublin.

Huggins, John [*fl. 1661–1662*], *violinist*.

John Huggins was listed as one of the violinists in the King's Musick receiving wages of 1*s.* daily plus £16 2*s.* 6*d.* annual livery in 1661–62.

Hughes. *See also* HEWS.

Hughes, Mr [*fl. 1731–1733*], *boxkeeper*.

Mr Hughes the boxkeeper shared benefits at Lincoln's Inn Fields on 2 June 1731 and 16 May 1732 and at Covent Garden on 17 May 1733.

Hughes, Mr [*fl.* 1750–1759?], *tailor.*

A Mr Hughes was a tailor at Covent Garden Theatre in the 1750s. On 31 January 1750 the theatre paid him £55 for clothes. In 1759, in a letter to Charles Macklin, Spranger Barry referred to Mr Hughes as a tailor to the theatre.

Hughes, Mr [*fl.* 1755], *actor.*

A Mr Hughes played the title role in *The Happy Gallant* on 6 September 1755 at Bence's Room, the Swan Tavern, in West Smithfield, at the time of Bartholomew Fair.

Hughes, Mr [*fl.* 1757–*c.* 1775], *proprietor.*

In 1757, a Mr Hughes, "a man curious in gardening," then the tenant of Bagnigge House, in the West Side of King's Cross Road, discovered that his plants did not thrive on the water drawn from his garden well. An analysis of the water by Dr John Bevis showed the water to be a valuable chalybeate; another well, newly sunk, was then discovered to have cathartic properties. Capitalizing on the commercial potential, by April 1757 Hughes opened the house and gardens to the public, on a daily schedule, including Sundays. In 1760 Bevis published a pamphlet on the waters there.

The Bagnigge Wells became a popular resort for taking water, tea, and breakfasts and for walking. Charley Griffith entertained at the organ in what was called the Long Room; a picture of him, captioned "THE BAGNIGGE ORGANFIST" (*sic*) was published about 1792, long after Hughes's proprietorship. Hughes sold out to John Davis about 1775.

Hughes, Mr *d. 1791, porter, call man.*

A Mr Hughes served as a porter or messenger at Drury Lane Theatre beginning at least by February 1781. On the seventeenth of that month he was paid £1 11s. for two bills "for calling performers." On 29 September 1781 he received £1 6s. for the same services. By 1784–85 his salary was 18s. per week, at which level it continued until 30 April 1791, when the account books noted "Hughes dead," and the weekly paylist was lowered by that amount.

Hughes, Mrs [*fl.* 1807]. *See* PARISOT, MLLE.

Hughes, Mrs [*fl.* 1737]. *See* HUGHES, MISS M. [*fl.* 1732–1737].

Hughes, Charles 1747–1797, *proprietor, manager, equestrian.*

Born in 1747, Charles Hughes was, by the age of 23, in 1771, a featured equestrian at Philip Astley's "Riding School" on Westminster Bridge Road, where he performed with as many as four horses at a time. Also about that time he gave equestrian performances in the open air at Cromwell's Gardens. Described by Decastro as "a man whom nature had not been niggardly to in her favours," Hughes had neither breeding nor education, but he did possess social felicity, extraordinary talent on the horse, and strength enough, it was said, to carry an ox upon his shoulders. Above all, he was ambitious.

Soon Hughes deserted Astley, with whom his subsequent relations were to be bitter, and on 23 April 1772 opened Hughes's Riding School in Blackfriars Road, due south of Blackfriars Bridge. Later that year he changed the name to the British Horse Academy. In reality it was little more than an open-air fenced ride. There he introduced the celebrated Sobieska Clementina, Miss Huntly, an "astonishing Young Gentleman (son of a Person of Quality)" who could leap over a horse 40 times without pause, and his own wife, who entertained by riding full tilt while standing on pint pots.

Perhaps to stimulate business at both the school and the exhibitions, Hughes published in 1772 *The Compleat Horseman; or, the Art of Riding Made Easy. Illustrated by Rules drawn from Nature . . . Adorned with various Engravings, finely executed.* The entire venture was short-lived, however. In July 1773 both his and Astley's establishments were closed by the Surrey magistrates. Astley took his troupe to Dublin for a year, while Hughes took his to the Continent for eight years.

Between 1773 and 1781 Hughes established a reputation for himself performing before the majesties of France, Sardinia, Naples, Spain, and Portugal, the Emperor of Germany, and the Sultan of Morocco. At Valencia his company entertained in the Plaza de San Domingo on 27 and 29 September and on 2 October 1778. He left there the following document, dated 22 September 1778: "I,

Charles Hughes, declare that for each day that I shall give performances with my company in the equestrian show which I am to produce in the Ring of the Plaza de Santo Domingo, I shall give to the Santo Hospital twenty-four pounds in this currency, and that I have obtained the corresponding permits for the purpose."

Hughes returned to England at either the end of 1781 or the beginning of 1782 in time to become involved in Charles Dibdin's scheme to establish an equestrian theatre, the idea being, as Dibdin described it, "to have a stage on which might be represented spectacles, each to terminate with a just [*sic*] or tilting-match, or some other grand object, so managed as to form a novel, and striking *coup-de-theatre* . . . that the business of the stage and ring might be united." Having arranged financial backing which required no investment on the part of either Dibdin or Hughes, they built a new amphitheatre in St George's Fields on land leased to them by Colonel West, the son of Vice Admiral Temple West. In return for providing the lease, which had to be reverted from another party, Colonel West had to be admitted to the partnership.

The equestrian theatre project suffered considerable opposition from the authorities and especially from the Reverend Rowland Hill, to whom any theatre was "a temple of sin" and who was in the process of erecting a new chapel close to the site chosen by Dibdin and Hughes. Their application to the Surrey magistrates for a license failed, causing the press to comment that "It is most extraordinary that any man or men should erect such a building without a certainty of lawful leave to carry on the purposes intended therein to be performed." But Hughes and Dibdin persisted and on 4 November 1782 opened the Royal Circus and Philharmonic Academy without a license. The fashionable opening-day audience saw a varied bill, with Hughes's troupe, Dibdin's ballet *Admetus and Alceste*, and Dibdin's pantomime *Mandarina; or, the Refusal of Harlequin*.

According to the plan, Dibdin was the chief manager of the Royal Circus, and Hughes commanded the horse department. Hughes had a house next to the theatre, on the south side, which eventually became the Circus Coffee House and now stands as the Flowers of the Forest Inn. His brother-in-law, Charles Tom-linson, rented the Equestrian Coffee House which stood on the north side of the theatre.

From the outset, the Royal Circus was plagued by internal squabbles, especially when Giuseppe Grimaldi was appointed to supervise dancing instruction for the juvenile performers in the academy. Each party made repeated charges of conspiracy by his partners. Hughes left no memoir, but Dibdin made clear in his that from his point of view Hughes was a cunning man, a "weak, unstable, absurd creature"—"While the leech Hughes, was sucking the blood of the proprietors, and fastening on the concern, the serpent of Grimaldi, was coiled up till a proper opportunity should arrive to seize the management."

After only nine nights of playing, a complaint was lodged against the Royal Circus; Hughes was arrested but, upon an appeal, was discharged by a split decision of the magistrates. In all, however, the Royal Circus performed only 14 nights in its first year and suffered as well the competition and animosity of Philip Astley. In 1785 Dibdin extricated himself from the proprietorship, but only after three years of frustrating conflict and litigation, the details of which may be found in George Tuttle's dissertation, "The History of the Royal Circus, Equestrian, and Philharmonic Academy, 1782–1816" (Tufts University, 1972), in memoirs by the Dibdins and Decastro, and in such pamphlets as Dibdin's *Royal Circus Epitomized* (1784). For Charles Dibdin's professional contributions to the Royal Circus, the reader should also consult his entry in this dictionary.

Emerging as manager in 1785, Hughes operated the Royal Circus until 1791. Hughes's effort to procure a local audience transformed the house in 1787 into what his stage manager Thomas Read called a bear garden. He obtained a liquor license and the Circus became "A scene of nocturnal orgies, riot, disipation [*sic*], and confusion." Though the proprietors continued to lose money on the venture, Hughes developed a reputation as a premier equestrian performer and promoter. An advertisement for an evening in 1785, typical of most, describes the fare he offered:

ROYAL CIRCUS
For the Benefit of Hughes
This Day, the 21st of October [1785]

HUGHES takes the liberty to acquaint the Nobility, Gentry, and Public, that he will continue the NEW PERFORMANCES, at this place, until the 30th instant, assisted by his TROOP from DUBLIN, in Addition to his wonderful Horse CHILIBY, which Horse will dress and undress a Lady's Head, jump on and off the Stage, take off the Lady's Cap, &c.

Also will be exhibited,

The Whole of his SAGACIOUS HORSES,

And a NEW JOCKEY RACE,

With a Representation of the Beacon Course at Newmarket.

The TROOP from DUBLIN against HUGHES's MARPLOT, rode by Jack Jeffries, in Red. WILDMAN, by Jack Holland, in Mixture. OLD LATH, by Tom Camel, jun. in Yellow. HIGH-FLYER'S COLT, by Tom Robinson, in Red. CHILIBY, by Giles Sutton, in Yellow. CROP, by Manuel Periera, in Blue.

Also TILTS and TOURNAMENTS by both Troops.

To the above were added a new dance called *The Sailor's Return*, a burletta called *The Milk-Maid's Disaster*, and specialty equestrian demonstrations by the Little Devil and Master Robinson. In April 1787 Hughes advertised the arrival from the Continent of "The Royal Troop," some 80 in number, who would perform "alternately every evening during the summer season." That troop, joined to his own, boasted Hughes, made his establishment the most brilliant and preeminent place of public entertainment.

But Hughes's fiery character continued to create problems for his associates, particularly Thomas Read, who felt obliged to air his grievances in *The History of the Royal Circus, introductory to the Case of Mr. Read, late Stage Manager of that Theatre; in a Letter to a Friend* (1791). The proprietors accused Hughes of taking three Circus horses to the Stourbridge Fair, Cambridge, in 1788 "for his own private emolument." Hughes, however owned the horses and employed the riders. On 2 August 1790 he found it necessary to sue the proprietors in the court of the King's Bench "to recover a large sum of money for the keep and training of the horses for the year 1788 to the year 1789." Judgment in his favor was reported by the press in January 1791. By 1789, in order to curb Hughes, the proprietors had placed the theatre under the direction of John Palmer, who was responsible for producing

that August one of the Royal Circus's great successes, *The Triumph of Liberty; or, the Destruction of the Bastille*. Hughes was again relegated to the management of the equestrian events only, and the bills began to read, "Horse Department under the Direction of Mr. HUGHES."

Soon the circumstances at the Royal Circus became extremely complicated. In order to extricate himself from financial chaos, Hughes contrived to be declared bankrupt on 10 March 1791. One of his creditors, Charles Carpenter, a lawyer who had served Hughes for some years, finding himself in jeopardy of losing £510 in legal fees, petitioned to have the bankruptcy rescinded. While it may have been bogus, Hughes's bankruptcy proved to be legal nevertheless, so Carpenter's petition was dismissed by Lord Thurlow, the Lord Chancellor, on 23 June 1791.

Hughes still held the license to the Royal Circus, which first had been issued in his name alone on 7 October 1783 and which had been regularly renewed to him. So he opened the interior of the Circus as a coffee house. Soon, however, he left for Russia at the invitation of the Russian Count Orlov, to whom he had been introduced by an influential friend, Sir John Dick. Hughes had been commissioned by Orlov to buy horses for Empress Catherine, a mission which he fulfilled so expertly that Orlov invited him to accompany the animals to St Petersburg. The Empress also provided Hughes and some of his company with equestrian amphitheatres in St Petersburg and Moscow. In 1792 Hughes also taught horsemanship to the Russian aristocrats.

Precisely when Hughes left for Russia, however, is not known to us. On 31 December 1791 three of his horses were rented by Drury Lane Theatre for use in a spectacular revival of *Cymon*. On 28 January 1792 that theatre paid £10 17s. 6d. to "Mr Hughs for the Use of Horses." Similar payments "for his Horses and attendants," totaling about £115, continued until December 1792. During his absence he had let the Circus out to a number of independent equestrian troupes.

In the fall of 1793 Hughes was forced to return to London because Jane West was suing him for the ground rent, which was in arrears. Evidently he made peace with Miss West and for a short time in 1793 turned the Circus into a menagerie, caring there for a number of various kinds of animals brought back from Algiers by Sir John Dick. That winter he supplied Covent Garden Theatre with foxes, hounds, and horses for a fox-hunting scene.

In the latter half of 1794 Jane West finally repossessed her property and leased it to James Jones and George Jones (not relatives), thereby bringing Hughes's role there to an end. The license was granted to him as usual in October 1796, but in October 1797 it was transferred to James Jones.

Charles Hughes died on 7 December 1797, at the age of 50, and was buried in the churchyard of St George's, Southwark. Nothing is known to us about his wife except her equestrian performances in 1772. In a legal document relating to Hughes's arrest in 1782, he mentioned his only child at that time, Wilhelmina Frederica Maria Sophia Hughes, whose age was about 21 months in December of that year.

Hughes is shown in three illustrations on a crude engraving published in London in 1789, which depicts scenes from *The Destruction of the Bastille*. The engraving is reproduced and discussed by A. H. Saxon in *Theatre Notebook*, 28 (1974).

Hughes, Mrs Charles [*fl.* 1772–1782], *equestrienne*.

Little is known about the wife of Charles Hughes, the proprietor of the Royal Circus, beyond her performances at Hughes's Riding School in Blackfriars Road in 1772. She entertained by riding full tilt while standing on pint pots, a feat which the advertisements claimed instilled "terror" in the spectators. Her daughter, Wilhelmina Frederica Maria Sophia Hughes, was born in 1781. Mrs Hughes was alive when her husband made a statement concerning his arrest in December 1782.

Hughes, Francis *c.* 1667–1744, *singer, impresario?*

Francis Hughes was born about 1667 and was probably the impresario who advertised in the London Gazette of 2–6 January 1690 as follows:

These are to give notice, That the Consort of Musick (at Mr Hughs's, in Freemans Court in Cornhill near the Royal-Exchange) will be perform'd on Wednesday next, being the 8th instant, and so to continue every Wednesday for the future, beginning between 7 and 8 of the Clock in the Evening.

By 1700 Hughes's name began appearing as a singer in published songs. Raphael Courteville's *To touch your heart*, which was printed about that year, cited Hughes as the singer at Drury Lane. Hughes is known to have sung in *The Grove* there on 19 February 1700. Daniel Purcell's *Ofelia's Aire, her Meen, her Face* was sung by Hughes in *Love Makes a Man* at Drury Lane, presumably when it opened on 9 January 1701, according to a separately published copy of the song.

During the first decade of the eighteenth century, Hughes was busy singing at Drury Lane and at occasional concerts elsewhere; for instance, he was paid £2 3s. for singing in *The Judgment of Paris* when it was performed with Weldon's music sometime during 1702 at Lincoln's Inn Fields Theatre, at a special performance for the Duke of Bedford. During the same year he sang Daniel Purcell's "Since Celia 'tis not in our Power" in *The Inconstant*, probably when it opened in February 1702 at Drury Lane, and he sang between the acts at that theatre on 9 June that year. In the summer of 1702 he also appeared as a singer at Hampstead and at Pawlet's Dancing School. In subsequent years, in addition to his regular appearances at Drury Lane, he sang at Mr Barker's Great Dancing Room in Mincing Lane, Fenchurch Street, at York Buildings, at Nottingham (during the races, about 1 August 1707), at court (for the Queen's birthday on 6 February 1713), and at Stationers' Hall.

Among the Coke papers at Harvard is a paylist for opera singers which shows Hughes receiving £60 yearly. Most of his career was spent singing occasional songs within plays—between the acts, or at recitals—but on 16 January 1705 at Drury Lane he sang the part of Ormondo in Clayton's *Arsinoe*, an English opera after the Italian manner. He sang Turnus in *Camilla* when it was first presented at the same playhouse on 30 March 1706. On 1 April 1707 when *Thomyris* was performed, Hughes seems to have played the role of Orontes alternately with Valentini. He made only occasional appearances during the ensuing ten years.

Burney wrote of Hughes later in his *General History of Music*:

Mr. HUGHS had been a favourite singer at concerts, and between the acts of plays, for several years before he was assigned the part of first man, in the first opera that ever was performed on our stage in the Italian manner. His voice was a *counter tenor*, as we are told in the dramatis personae of *Thomyris*; and, indeed, as the compass of his songs discovers. He continued to perform the first part till the arrival of Valentini [in 1706–7], after which he either quitted the stage or the world, for no further mention is made of him either in opera or concert annals.

Burney evidently did not know that on 14 September 1708, nine months after his last known appearance as a singer at Drury Lane, Francis Hughes was sworn a Gentleman of the Chapel Royal. On 6 February 1713 he was among the court singers who offered Handel's *Ode for the Birthday of Queen Anne*; Dudley Ryder heard him singing a chief part in an anthem at St Paul's on 14 June 1715; Hughes participated in concerts at Stationers' Hall on 13 and 27 March and 23 December 1717 and at York Buildings on 5 December 1718; but he was infrequently mentioned in musical circles after he gave up his post at Drury Lane.

Francis Hughes died on 16 March 1744 at the age of 77 and was buried in the West Cloister of Westminster Abbey on 21 March. His will, dated 5 June 1740, was proved on 24 March 1744. The residuary legatees were Theophilus Hughes and Susan, Jane, and Mary Vaughan, daughters of Margaret Vaughan, Hughes's sister. The only other relative mentioned by Hughes in his will was a nephew, William. The singer Hughes should not be confused with John Hughes the poet, dramatist, and amateur violinist, who was active in London during the first decades of the eighteenth century.

Hughes, Miss H. [*fl.* 1734], *actress.*

Miss H. Hughes played Lappet in *The Miser* at the theatre in James Street on 31 May 1734. The performance was a benefit for Norris which was intended for Lincoln's Inn Fields but which, because of an opera production at that house, was moved to James Street. In the cast as Wheedle was Miss M. Hughes, probably our subject's sister.

Hughes, Miss J. [*fl.* 1733], *actress.*

Miss J. Hughes played Myrtilla in *The Provok'd Husband* at the Haymarket Theatre on 28 May 1733. In the cast as Jenny was Miss M. Hughes, probably a sister.

Hughes, Miss M. [*fl.* 1732–1737], *actress, singer?, dancer?*

On 10 April 1732 Miss Hughes, hailed as from Dublin, made her first appearance at the Goodman's Fields Theatre playing Flora in *She Wou'd and She Wou'd Not* and speaking a humorous epilogue with Miss Norris. Nothing is known of Miss Hughes's activity before her arrival in London, though she probably gained stage experience as a young girl in Ireland. Miss M. Hughes, very likely our subject, acted Jenny in *The Provok'd Husband* at the Haymarket Theatre on 28 May 1733 (Miss J. Hughes— her sister?—played Myrtilla); the players were advertised as being from the Goodman's Fields playhouse, and it is possible that after her debut at the Haymarket Miss Hughes remained in the troupe playing parts too small to be cited in the playbills.

On 17 October 1733 she appeared as Prince Edward in *Richard III* at Drury Lane (Miss Norris acted the Duke of York), but she seems not to have been a regular member of the company. In late May 1734 she was at the James Street playhouse and at the Haymarket. At the former she acted Marcia in *Cato* on 23 May and then Lucy in *George Barnwell*, Lady Loverule in *The Devil to Pay*, and Wheedle in *The Miser*. Also appearing in *The Miser* was Miss H. Hughes—probably a sister. We are guessing that the career set forth here belonged to Miss M. and not to one of the other Hughes girls. Miss M. Hughes was clearly a young girl still, for the James Street performance of *Cato* was advertised as "At the Lilliputians Theatre," and the casts there were made up largely of youngsters. At the Haymarket Theatre on 27 May 1734 (in the middle of Miss Hughes's run at James Street) she played Kissinda in *The Covent Garden Tragedy*.

In 1734–35 Miss Hughes was with the Goodman's Fields troupe under Henry Giffard, and she remained with his company in 1735– 36 at the same house and in 1736–37 at Lincoln's Inn Fields. For Giffard she played such parts as Clarinda in *The Double Gallant*, Cordelia in *The Fond Husband*, an Attendant and a Nymph in *Jupiter and Io*, Clarinda in *Woman Is a Riddle*, a Haymaker in *The Necromancer*, Clarissa in *The Temple Beau*, Dorinda in *The*

Stratagem, Lucinda in *The Conscious Lovers*, Fainlove in *The Tender Husband*, Teraminta in *The Wife's Relief*, Trusty in *The Provok'd Husband*, Lady Betty Manly in *A Tutor for the Beaux*, an Attendant on Britannia in *Britannia*, and Hillaria in *Love's Last Shift*. Her pantomime roles would suggest that Miss Hughes was either a singer or a dancer or both. The "Mrs" Hughes listed in *The London Stage* as acting Charlotte in *The Independent Patriot* on 12 February 1737 at Lincoln's Inn Fields was probably Miss M. Hughes. Her last known appearance was as Teraminta in *The Wife's Relief* at Lincoln's Inn Fields on 17 May 1737.

Hughes, Margaret   *d. 1719, actress.*

The prompter John Downes, writing in 1708, remembered Margaret Hughes as one of the first actresses in the King's Company in the 1660s, and on the basis of that statement some historians assumed that she joined the troupe perhaps as early as 1660 and surely by 1663, when the company began acting at the Bridges Street Theatre. John Harold Wilson argued in the October 1956 *Notes and Queries* that there was no certain evidence that Mrs Hughes appeared on stage before 1668 and felt that she was the newly arrived actress named "Pegg" who was kissed by Pepys on 7 May of that year.

We should probably not accept as authentic the following poem quoted in John Payne Collier's "History of the British Stage" at Harvard, but it suggests that Mrs Hughes was the rival of Anne Marshall, who acted in the same troupe from the Restoration to 1666 (after which she appeared as Mrs Quin):

Who must not be partial
To pretty Nan Marshall?
Though I think, be it known,
She too much does de-moan,
But that in the Moor
May be right, to be sure,
Since her part & her name
Do tell her the same
But none can refuse
To say Mistress Hughes
Her rival out-does

. . . .

Yet—I swear—honest Coz.,
With a critical oath
That Ned [Kynaston] beats [i. e. betters] them
*   both.*

Collier claimed to have found the doggerel poem at Bridgewater House, but who can say that he did not write it himself? (But Downes said that Mrs Hughes did, indeed, play Desdemona.) A more reliable source, a manuscript cast dating about 1661–62 in a Folger Shakespeare Library copy of the 1637 edition of *The Royall King*, lists a "Hews," along with (Mrs) Eastland, as a cast member; the evidence is ambiguous, for "Hews" may not refer to an actress—though the only known male Hughes, William, seems not to have acted until much later. Wilson is very likely correct in dating Mrs Hughes's first appearance in 1668, but there is still the possibility that she acted earlier.

When Pepys went backstage at the Bridges Street playhouse and kissed a young actress named Pegg, a performance of *The Virgin Martyr* had just been completed, and perhaps Margaret Hughes appeared in it—if she was, in fact, the Pegg referred to. Pepys called her a recent mistress of Sir Charles Sedley, "a mighty pretty woman, and seems, but is not, modest." Pinto, in his edition of Sedley's works, suggests that Mrs Hughes may have acted in *The Mulberry Garden* on 18 May 1668 when it opened, but there is nothing to support that conjecture beyond Pepys's statement that she was Sedley's mistress. During the 1668–69 season, probably between January and August 1669, Margaret Hughes played Angellina in a revival of *The Sisters*, according to prompt notes in a Folger Library copy of the 1653 edition of the play.

On 2 October 1669 "Mrs. Hues" was listed in a Lord Chamberlain's warrant as a member of the King's Company due livery for the period 1668–1670, which listing certainly suggests that she acted regularly during that period despite scanty references to her. On 20 June 1670 Lady Chaworth wrote her brother Lord Roos at Belvoir Castle that "one of the K[ing's] servants hath killed Mr. Hues, Peg Hues' brother, servant to P[rince] Robert [Rupert] upon a dispute whether Mis Nelly [Gwyn] or she was the handsomer now att Windsor." By that time Margaret Hughes had probably become the mistress of Prince Rupert, and a visitor at Windsor. Peg's brother seems not to have been the actor William Hughes.

The Memoirs of Grammont tell us that Mrs

The Tate Gallery

MARGARET HUGHES

by Lely

Hughes "made out of this poor prince such an odd character, that the figure he cut seemed positively too extravagant for real life—an adventure which delighted the King and produced great rejoicing at Tunbridge" where the King and Queen had taken the court and the players. In 1673 Margaret bore the Prince a daughter, Ruperta. She may earlier have had a son, Arthur, who in 1681 signed his name to a manuscript of the play *The Frolicks*.

Mrs Hughes returned to the stage in 1676 to act for the Duke's Company at the Dorset Garden Theatre. She played Mirva in Settle's *Ibrahim* in March 1676 and then Octavia in *The Wrangling Lovers*, Mrs Monylove in *Tom Essence*, Gerana in *Pastor Fido*, Charmion in *Antony and Cleopatra* (Sedley's version), Valeria in *The Rover*, Cordelia in *The Fond Husband*, and Leonora in *The French Conjurer*. After the 1676–77 season Mrs Hughes retired from the stage again and was set up by Prince Rupert in a house near Hammersmith, which was later called Brandenburg House. (Prince Rupert is said by *The Dictionary of National Biography* to have bought Margaret the Hammersmith house in 1683, but he died in 1682.) About 1678 a lampoon, preserved at Harvard and probably written by Captain Alexander Radcliff, came out:

> Had I been hang'd I could not chuse
> But Laugh att Whores that drop't from slewes
> Seeing that Mᵣ Margaret Hewghs
> soe fine is.

In his will, dated 1 December 1682, Prince Rupert specified that his estate should be put in the hands of the Earl of Craven in trust for "Margaret Hewes and . . . Ruperta, my naturall daughter begotten on the bodie of the said Margaret Hewes, in equal moyeties." He asked Ruperta to be obedient to her mother and not marry without her consent and the advice of the Earl of Craven. (Ruperta eventually married Emanuel Scrope Howe.) The house near Hammersmith was said to have been worth £25,000. Rupert had squandered so much of his fortune on Mrs Hughes while he was alive, that most of the £200,000 (Doran said £20,000) worth of jewels he left had to be sold to pay his debts, according to Sybil Rosenfeld in her edition of Etherege's letters. Mrs Hughes gambled away what she had left and had to sell some of her jewelry to

Harvard Theatre Collection

MARGARET HUGHES
engraving by Cooper, after Lely

Nell Gwyn and the Duchess of Marlborough. Tom Brown, in his *Letters from the Dead to the Living* (1703), had Peg Hughes write to Nell admitting that she had not been able to keep the money Rupert had left her.

Margaret Hughes died on 1 October 1719 and was buried at Lee, Kent, on the fifteenth. On the following 2 November administration of the estate of Margaret Hewes, late of Eltham, Kent, was granted her sister and next of kin, Judith Hawley.

Lely painted a portrait of Margaret Hughes, which is in Lord Jersey's collection at Middleton Park, Oxfordshire; in 1706 the portrait was in the collection of Sir Francis Child of Osterley. There are at least four other versions by Lely: an oil on canvas in the collection of Lord Dartmouth; a studio version at Rockingham Castle; an oil on canvas, once owned by Countess Craven, bequeathed to the Tate Gallery in 1965; and an oil on canvas, of another composition, with a more rural setting and showing Margaret with a straw hat, in the collection of Margaret Yeatman-Biggs. The portrait was engraved by Bocquet, Schneker (published by E. and S. Harding in 1792), E. Scriven (as a plate to Grammont's *Memoirs* in 1811), and Cooper (as a plate to *La Belle Assemblée*, published by John Bell in 1819).

Hughes, Richard *d. 1810, treasurer.*

In a letter dated 21 February 1800 to Thomas Harris, the Covent Garden manager, Richard Hughes wrote that he had been with that theatre for 16 years, or from about 1784. For about ten of those years he was a subtreasurer, becoming in September 1793 the treasurer upon the dismissal of Edward Barlow. It was Hughes who signed the letter of 26 July 1799, posted for the performers, to the effect that charges for benefit nights would be raised £20 and that only three weeks' notice would be available for the assignment of a night. The letter began the altercation between the performers and managers which resulted in the publication in 1800 of *A Statement of Differences Subsisting Between the Proprietors and Performers of the Theatre Royal, Covent Garden*. Hughes seems to have continued as the treasurer until his death on 26 September 1810 at Millbank, Westminster.

His will, signed on 31 October 1809. reveals that Hughes had lived in comfortable circumstances. In it he described himself as of the Great Houses in the Parish of St George, Hanover Square, and of Covent Garden and expressed his wish to be interred in the burial ground of the South Audley Chapel in St George, Hanover Square, "in a private manner." Specific bequests were made to relatives: £100 to his niece Maria, the wife of William Roberts; £50 each to his niece Louisa Hay and his nephews Francis and Richard Hay; and £100 to one of his executors, Robert Lewis. His executors were directed to sell at his death, the stock and crop of his business as a gardener, along with all his horses and carts, and to collect the money and stock due to him from Richard Harris at Covent Garden. These proceeds, combined with the conversion of the remainder of the estate into cash, were to be laid out in three-percent bank annuities or funds in trust for his wife, whom he did not name, for the rest of her life. Upon her death Richard Edwards, another executor, was to receive £500, Richard Hay £100, and any per-

sons whom his wife might designate up to £100; the residue would then pass to his niece Maria Roberts. In a codicil of 15 November 1809, Hughes took precautions that his wife's legacy should not pass to a subsequent husband by directing that if his nieces and nephews died before his wife, then upon her death the estate should pass to Richard Edwards. The will was proved by the executors on 8 October 1810.

Hughes, Richard *d. 1814, manager, proprietor, actor, scene painter.*

Although the varied theatrical career of Richard Hughes endured for at least 48 years, there is relatively sparse documentation of it. According to the *Thespian Dictionary* (1805) and Gilliland's *Dramatic Mirror* (1808), Hughes was a native of Birmingham, and of Welsh extraction. Originally apprenticed to a button painter at Birmingham, Hughes began his stage career in a spouting club and then joined Roger Kemble's touring company as a scene painter and general utility actor. Even after Hughes became the impresario of several provincial theatres, it is said, he continued to assist in scene painting.

Hughes probably played numerous supporting roles in Kemble's company as it traveled throughout England. He acted Colonel Tomlinson in *King Charles I* at Worcester on 12 February 1767, the night on which the manager's 12-year-old daughter Sarah, later Mrs Siddons, made her first known appearance, as the young Princess Elizabeth, and her brother John Philip Kemble, age 10, acted the Duke of York. About 1770 Hughes engaged with the theatre at Plymouth Dock and soon married Lucy Williams, the manager's daughter. In November 1772 they acted as Mr and Mrs Hughes at Derby. Soon after, Hughes took over the management of the theatre at Plymouth and then began to expand his interests. By 1781 he was managing the theatre at Exeter, where he is known to have acted Sir Peter Teazle in *The School for Scandal* in December of that year and Dominick in *The Spanish Fryar* in May 1783. At Exeter on 23 April 1784, one of his sons, Master Hughes (probably Richard), had a benefit; in the company at that time were also a Mr and Mrs B. Hughes, who perhaps were related.

In 1787 Richard Hughes bought the Exeter

Theatre from the provincial manager Samuel Freeman Foote and continued to manage it, sometimes assisted by his son Richard, for many years. Eventually he gained control of the theatres at Weymouth, Guernsey, Truro, Penzance, Dartmouth, and Lyme. A letter dated 4 September 1791 in James Lackington's *Memoirs* described Hughes at Weymouth as

. . . industrious to an extreme, as he is scarce a moment idle. For besides managing his company, performing himself six, sometimes eight characters in a week, he paints all his own scenes, and attends to many other subjects; and although he has had a large expensive family (nine children), the theatre there and also at Exeter is his own. Weymouth theatre he rebuilt about four years since, every thing is very neat; his scenes are fine, and his company a very good one. . . .

When Richard Wroughton was searching for ways to save the failing Sadler's Wells Theatre in 1791 (it was rumored that it might be turned into a Methodist Chapel), Hughes took advantage of the opportunity to venture into London management. A new partnership was formed at the Wells in which Hughes secured one fourth of the shares, probably at a cost of about £120. The other shareholders were Wroughton and the younger Samuel Arnold, who retained one eighth and one fourth respectively, John Coates, a Bermondsey tanner, with one eighth, and William Siddons, Sarah's husband, with one fourth. Hughes, no doubt the most experienced member of the partnership, exercised an important influence over the affairs of the Wells for the next 25 years. In 1798 he signed a document, now in the British Library, as "Manager and Director of the theatre called Sadlers Wells."

Although Hughes seems not to have performed on the Sadler's Wells stage during his management, he did make two appearances at the patent houses, the first at Covent Garden on 8 April 1795 as Jobson in *The Devil to Pay*, for the benefit of John Quick, and the second in the same role at Drury Lane on 2 May 1796, for the benefit of Mrs Siddons. Both times he was described as the manager of the Theatre Royal, Weymouth, but oddly no mention was made of his position at Sadler's Wells. In the latter instance one critic reported his talents to be "not of the first rate," but another claimed he was "an excellent substitute for Moody in Jobson."

The first several years of the new partnership at Sadler's Wells were profitable, but by the end of the century the enterprise had become a losing proposition. In March 1802 the Reverend Lloyd Baker granted a renewed 21-year lease at £210 per year to a reconstituted proprietorship in which Hughes with 10 shares was the principal. The other shareholders, each with five shares, were the younger Charles Dibdin, Thomas Dibdin, William Yarnold, Thomas Barfoot, the composer William Reeve, and the scene painter Robert Andrews. At a cost of between £1200 and £1700 the auditorium of the Wells was remodeled from square to semicircular shape by the architect and machinist Rudolphe Cabanel, according to a model by Hughes. In 1812—a season in which the profits were only £132—Yarnold and Andrews sold their shares, so that Hughes then owned 14, Thomas Dibdin five, and Charles Dibdin, Barfoot, and Reeve each seven. Since 1803 Hughes had also enjoyed, in lieu of salary, the large house attached to the theatre, free of rent and with the perquisites of coals, candles, and a servant. He was also a quarter-partner in "The Temple of the Muses," a celebrated bookstore in Finsbury Square which had originated with the eccentric James Lackington.

Richard Hughes died on 20 December 1814 and was buried in his family vault at St James, Clerkenwell, on the twenty-sixth. His son-in-law Joe Grimaldi wrote in his *Memoirs* of being compelled to rehearse the current pantomime on the day of the funeral and "to run to the funeral, to get back from the churchyard to the theatre to finish the rehearsal, and to exert all his comic powers at night to set the audience in a roar." Hughes's widow continued as principal shareholder in the Wells for a number of years, often interfering in the affairs of management, much to the dismay of the Dibdins. Although she had performed in her husband's provincial theatres, there is no evidence of her having played in London in the eighteenth century. She died at Exeter on 18 December 1839, at the age of 90.

Hughes's son Richard, who was an assistant to his father in provincial management, became a co-proprietor of Sadler's Wells after his father's death and then proprietor of Vauxhall Gardens in the 1830s. In 1837 he was bequeathed Joe Grimaldi's five shares in the

Wells and became the executor of the will of his famous brother-in-law and the possessor of his manuscript memoirs. In the spring of 1842 the younger Hughes became bankrupt and his 10 shares in the lease of Sadler's Wells were put up for auction.

According to the *Thespian Dictionary*, by 1805 the elder Richard Hughes had buried three of his daughters, one of whom was Maria, a dancer who had become the first wife of the great Sadler's Wells clown Joseph Grimaldi on 11 May 1799 but had died in childbirth on 18 October 1800 at the age of 25. Another daughter, Julia, became Mrs Bennet and was still alive when Joe Grimaldi made his will in 1836.

By some accounts Richard Hughes was tight-fisted, chilly, and a difficult man to please. The younger Charles Dibdin, recognizing his partner's reserved character, spoke well of him:

This Gentleman . . . acquired a large fortune, thro' Industry, economy, perseverance, and judicious speculation. He was a singular Man, and had an appearance of repelling reserve in his manner, that occasioned many to augur ill of his social disposition, but it was merely what I may call a constitutional manner; I always found him a very pleasant, intelligent companion, and full of information and anecdote. As a Man of Business I never found any more ready, judicious and effective. He possessed also many benevolent traits of character, of the exercise of which I have seen repeated instances; and have been informed of some which placed him in no common grade upon the scale of humanity.

The *Thespian Dictionary* reported that Hughes's success as a manager, especially in the provinces, was accountable to his strict insistence upon the punctuality, propriety, and attentiveness of his performers.

Hughes, Thomas *d. 1668, singer.*

On 16 February 1661 Thomas Hughes was installed one of the singing men in the Chapel Royal. Hughes is known to have sung at Princess Mary's funeral, for which he received on 30 March 1661 7*s.* 4*d.*, and Dr Busby mentioned Hughes in 1664 as being one of the members of the choir at Westminster Abbey. Thomas Hughes was buried at the Abbey on 10 November 1668.

Hughes, William [*fl. 1661?–1670?*], *actor.*

The Mr "Hughs" who was said by the prompter John Downes in 1708 to have been "Bred up from [a boy], under the Master Actors" in the King's Company in the early 1660s was certainly William Hughes, but we cannot be certain just when he began working for the troupe. One "Hews" is noted in a manuscript cast dating 1661–62 in a Folger copy of the 1637 edition of *The Royall King*, but the reference could be to the actress Margaret Hughes. William Hughes, who may not have been related to Margaret, is not otherwise known to have been in the King's troupe until 1667.

On 15 April 1667 when *The Change of Crownes* was performed by the King's troupe at Bridges Street, William Hughes, according to the manuscript promptbook that has survived, played a Messenger. The following 23 July he was listed on a Lord Chamberlain's warrant as a member of the company; on 2 October 1669 he was granted livery for the period 1668–1670; and on 13 January 1670 Mary Hunt sued him for a debt of £80. On 20 June 1670 Lady Chaworth wrote that "One of the K[ing's] servants hath killed Mr. Hues, Peg Hues' brother, servant to P[rince] Robert upon a dispute whether M[is] Nelly or she was the handsomer now att Windsor." Was Margaret Hughes's brother, William the actor? There is no evidence to confirm it.

Hulett, Mr [*fl. 1765–1778*], *numberer, housekeeper.*

On a Drury Lane paylist dated 9 February 1765 a Mr Hulett was down for 2*s.* 6*d.* daily, or 15*s.* weekly, as a numberer at the theatre. His total pay for the 1766–67 season was £25, and when that was noted in the accounts on 4 June 1767 Hulett was described as the assistant housekeeper. The last mention of him in the playbills was on 19 May 1778, when his benefit tickets were accepted.

Hulett, Charles *1700?–1735, actor, singer.*

Charles Hulett (sometimes Hulet) was born in either 1700 or 1701; reports vary, but there appears to be some agreement that he was 35 when he died, and Reed in his "Theatrical Obituary" at the Boston Public Library gives his death date very specifically as 8 October 1735. Charles was the son of John Hulett, a yeoman of the Guard, Warden of the Tower, and Steward of the Earl of Northampton, according to O. Smith's notes at the British Library. He was born in Russell Street, Bloomsbury, received a tolerable education, and was apprenticed as a boy to the bookseller Edmund Curll, one of Pope's butts in the *Dunciad*.

After two years of apprenticeship under Curll, the story goes, Hulett was permitted by his master to try for a theatrical career. *The Dictionary of National Biography* has it that Hulett acted for a season in Dublin, but there is no evidence of that. His first mention in London advertisements seems to have been on 21 May 1720, when he received a benefit performance of *Othello* at Lincoln's Inn Fields. There was nothing in the bill to indicate Hulett's participation that evening. A year later (perhaps after laboring in bit parts) Hulett, on 9 May 1721, shared with two others a benefit which grossed £75 7s. His first named role was Lenox in *Macbeth* on 26 October 1721 at Lincoln's Inn Fields.

Hulett is said to have been patronized by the actor James Quin, who performed at John Rich's Lincoln's Inn Fields, and perhaps he was schooled by Quin in the bombastic style. Hulett's roles at Lincoln's Inn Fields during the 1720s and early 1730s, before Covent Garden opened, included a number of parts that might have lent themselves to Hulett's corpulent figure and strong voice. Among them were Haly in *Abra Mule*, Bajazet and later Omar in *Tamerlane*, the First Tribune in *Domitian*, Lucius in *Titus Andronicus*, Casca in *Julius Caesar*, Achilles in *Troilus and Cressida*, Hotman in *Oroonoko*, Aegeon in *Oedipus*, Kent and later Gloucester in *King Lear*, Hannibal in *Sophonisba*, Odmar in *The Indian Emperor*, Seyton in *Macbeth*, Alvarez in *Don Sebastian*, Renault in *Venice Preserv'd*, Philip in *Philip of Macedon*, the Master of the Madhouse in *The Pilgrim*, the Ghost in *Hamlet*, Salisbury in *Sir Walter Raleigh*, Worcester in *1 Henry IV*, Diphilis in *The Maid's Tragedy*, Polyperchon in *The Rival Queens*, Gratiano and Montano in *Othello*, Sir Walter in *The Unhappy Favorite*, Hogstye in *Aesop*, Humphrey in *The Conscious Lovers*, Sir Thomas in *The Gamester*, the Provost in *Measure for Measure*, Bonniface in *The Stratagem*, Raymond in *The Spanish Fryar*, the Governor in *Love Makes*

a Man, Cacafogo in *Rule a Wife and Have a Wife*, one of the Avocatori in *Volpone*, Cassander in *The Rival Queens*, Mopsus in *Damon and Phillida*, and Thorowgood in *The London Merchant*. His engagement with John Rich's troupe ran out just before Covent Garden opened, and he was lured by better terms to Henry Giffard's company at the Goodman's Fields Theatre in the fall of 1732.

During those years at Lincoln's Inn Fields, Hulett made frequent appearances elsewhere. On 2 September 1721 (called "Hewlet") he had a role in *King Saul*, a droll, at the Hall-Leigh booth at Southwark Fair. He was at Bartholomew Fair in August 1722 in *Darius*, and on 14 March 1723 he appeared at the Haymarket Theatre to play Aimwell in *The Stratagem*. On 24 August 1724 he acted the title role in *The Prodigal Son* at Bartholomew Fair, raising the ire of local authorities because of the lewdness of the piece (according to a manuscript at Cambridge). He was at the Fair again in August 1727 playing Lord Lovewell in *The Unnatural Parents*. Hulett was not mentioned in London bills in 1727–28 nor in the fall of 1728; Joseph Knight in *The Dictionary of National Biography* suggests that Hulett was in Dublin during that year and a half. Surviving Dublin bills contain no mention of him, however.

From February through August 1729 Hulett acted at the Haymarket, playing some parts he had not attempted before, among them the title role in *Oroonoko*, Macheath in *The Beggar's Opera* (he was favorably compared to Walker, the original Macheath), the title part in *Hurlothrumbo*, Vulcan in *The Smugglers*, and Friendly in *Flora*. (*The London Stage* has him playing Mopsus in *Damon and Phillida* on 16 August 1729 at Drury Lane, but that must be an error for the Haymarket.) Hulett wound up that summer at Bartholomew and Southwark fairs. He appeared at both fairs again in 1730, and in 1731 he added Tottenham Court Fair.

Hulett's finances during the 1720s are only partly known. He shared a benefit with Orfeur in May 1722 that brought in almost £75; the benefit he shared with Chapman in May 1724 came to about the same figure. When he shared with Huddy in 1725, the income jumped to over £125, and with Morgan in 1726 he split a gross of £102 9s. 6d. It is likely that he usually did well at benefit time. The Lincoln's Inn Fields accounts show Hulett to have been earning a daily salary of 10*s.* as of 25 September 1724.

We do not know whether or not Hulett was married in the 1720s, but the following parish register entries could concern the actor: at St Paul, Covent Garden, on 8 March 1726 James, the son of Charles "Hulit," was buried; at St Clement Danes on 8 March 1727 Henrietta-Maria "Hewlet," the daughter of Charles and Mary, was baptized.

On 2 October 1732 Charles Hulett made his first appearance at Goodman's Fields, playing Falstaff in *1 Henry IV.* A number of new and sometimes serious roles were open to him at his new home. *The Comedian,* which came out in the fall of 1732, called Goodman's Fields "The Theatre next in Reputation to that of *Drury-Lane*" but cautioned Hulett that he had "Talents for Tragedy which want Improvement." The new roles Hulett tried at Goodman's Fields during the 1732–33 season were Kite in *The Recruiting Officer,* Falstaff in *The Merry Wives of Windsor,* Brabantio in *Othello,* the King in *The Mourning Bride,* Claudius in *Hamlet,* Chamont in *The Orphan,* Cassius in *Julius Caesar,* Henry VIII in *Vertue Betray'd,* Mrs Haverly in *The Decoy,* Gloucester in *Jane Shore,* Banquo in *Macbeth,* Timophanes in *Timoleon,* Ely in *The Mad Captain,* Jobson in *The Devil to Pay,* Hali-Vizem in *Scanderbeg,* Sir Tunbelly in *The Relapse,* Hob in *Flora,* Sempronius in *Cato,* and Sealand in *The Conscious Lovers.* The author of the *Life of Mr Wilks* called him "[T]hat improving Young Fellow *Charles Hulett*" in 1733.

During the summer of 1733 Hulett bounced around a bit: he played Manly in *The Provok'd Husband* at the Haymarket on 28 May and then appeared at Covent Garden in June and July as Momus in *Momus Turn'd Fabulist,* Hannibal in *Sophonisba,* and Jobson in *The Devil to Pay.* He concluded the summer at Bartholomew Fair acting Jeptha in *Jeptha's Rash Vow* and Apollo in *The Fall of Phaeton.* Except for appearances at the two late-summer fairs in 1734, the rest of Hulett's career was spent at Goodman's Fields.

From the fall of 1733 to his death two years later, he acted such new parts at Goodman's Fields as Trusty in *The Funeral,* Scandal in *Love for Love,* Clytus in *The Rival Queens,* Alvarez in

The Mistake, Sancho Panza in *Don Quixote,* Marcian in *Theodosius,* Montezuma in *The Indian Emperor,* the Serjeant, Lord Rake, and the Master of the Elephant in *Britannia,* Horatio in *The Fair Penitent,* Richard III, Chaunter in *Phebe,* a Spirit in *The Necromancer,* Freehold in *The Country Lasses,* Creon and the Ghost of Laius in *Oedipus,* Pierre in *Venice Preserv'd,* and Clause in *The Royal Merchant.*

On 15 May 1735 Hulett sent a note to the papers concerning his benefit on that date:

We hear, it has been industriously and maliciously spread about Town, that Mr. Hulett designs to leave the Company in Goodman's Fields, by which he was much hurt in his former benefit [on 17 March 1735], and believes the said Report is continued to detriment him in the present [benefit]; this is to assure the Town, it is entirely groundless, he being engaged by Article for two succeeding Years in the said Theatre.

How his second benefit fared is not known.

True to his word, however, Hulett was at Goodman's Fields again in the fall of 1735. The bills showed that his last appearance was as Pierre in *Venice Preserv'd* on 3 October. Stories of the cause of Hulett's death vary somewhat, but the London *Daily Post and General Advertiser* on 9 October reported the event: "Yesterday, between One and Two o'Clock, died of a Haemorrage . . . Mr. Charles Hulett, belonging to Goodman's Fields, whose natural Qualifications to the Stage, had he the Application of many of less Merit, would have render'd him one of the most considerable Performers now alive [*sic*]." Hulett was buried at St Mary, Whitechapel. His widow and child (William Charles?) were given a benefit at Goodman's Fields the following 19 November.

Chetwood in his *General History* in 1749 said that Hulett "took too much Pride in the Firmness of his Voice; for he had an odd Custom of stealing unperceiv'd upon a Person, and, with a Hem! in his Ear, deafen him for some time . . . the last Hem! he gave broke a Blood-Vessel, which was the cause of his Death in Twenty-four Hours After." O. Smith followed Chetwood's story in all essential details. In his *Dramatic Miscellanies* Davies added that two eminent physicians were unable to help Hulett after his blood vessel broke. *The Dictionary of National Biography* said the accident happened at the theatre during a rehearsal.

All the sources are in agreement on Hulett's strong, clear, melodious, and powerful voice and the fact that he was, as Chetwood said, a "Mountain of Flesh" and "a great Benefactor of the Malt-Tax." But, Davies said, along with his obesity and his careless habits of dress, Hulett was lively in conversation, good natured, and an excellent mimic.

Hulett has often been identified as one of the Nightwatch in Zoffany's famous painting of Garrick in *The Provok'd Wife*, but Hulett was dead before Garrick came to the stage. The actor in the painting was Hull.

Hulett, Mrs Charles ₁*fl. 1731–1736*₁, *actress.*

Mrs Charles Hulett played the Queen of the Beggars in *Phebe* at Tottenham Court on 12 August 1731 and Lucy in *The Devil to Pay* at the Lee and Harper booth at Southwark Fair on 8 September of the same year. That appears to have been the extent of her theatrical career. She was the wife of the actor Charles Hulett, who died in 1735; his theatre, Goodman's Fields, gave a benefit performance on 19 November 1735 for Hulett's "widow and child."

Hulett, William Charles ₁*fl. 1753–1754*₁, *dancer, violinist, singer, impresario.*

Dunlap in his *History* states that William Charles Hulett (or Hewlet) had been an apprentice to William Hallam at the Goodman's Fields Theatre in London before he went to New York in 1753 to join the elder Lewis Hallam's Old American Company. Since the actor Charles Hulett had been a member of the Goodman's Fields troupe in the early 1730s and is known to have left a wife and child when he died in 1735, perhaps William Charles was his son.

In any case, on 24 September 1753 in New York, Hulett provided a *Scotch Dance* and a hornpipe as entertainments at a performance of *Tunbridge Walks*. He was also a singer, and led the band in the Hallam company. At the end of the 1753–54 season Hulett left the troupe, settled in New York, and opened a dancing school, where he also taught fencing and music. He and Alexander Dienval, according to Julian Mates in *The American Musical Stage before 1800*, established the first subscription series of concerts in New York. Dunlap said that for some time Hulett was the only

dancing master in town and a "worthy man." Odell in his *Annals* states that Hulett had a son, William Charles, who performed with Clinton's Thespians at the John Street Theatre in New York during the Revolution.

Hull, Mr ₁*fl. 1714?*₁, *wardrobe keeper?*

An "Inventory of Playhouse Cloaths of Chr[istopher] Rich . . . by Mr Hull & Mr Hunt" was discovered in the British Library by Sybil Rosenfeld, who conjectures it was made after Rich's death in 1714.

Hull, Mr ₁*fl. 1732*₁, *singer.*

At the concert at Hickford's Room on 24 April 1732, in a series sponsored by Geminiani, Hull sang with one of the Young sisters. Signor Pasquale, "appearing in public for the first time," played the violoncello. The "rest of the instruments" were played "by the performers of Geminiani's Concert." The evening was for Hull's benefit. He is otherwise unknown.

Hull, Thomas *1728–1808, actor, singer, manager, playwright, novelist.*

Thomas Hull was born in 1728 in a house in the Strand, "where his father was in considerable practice as an apothecary," according to the brief sketch in the 1812 *Biographia Dramatica*. He received some education at Charterhouse. Only two other pieces of information about Hull's family are known. In his edition of *Select Letters* (1778), Hull, in footnoting a reference to *Essay on Delicacy*, identified it as the work of "Dr. Nathaniel Lancaster, many years Rector of Stanford Rivers, near Ongar, in Essex, Uncle to the Editor of these Letters," and continued with high praise for Lancaster's talents. In his will, Hull mentioned a niece, Jane Elizabeth Awsiter. Hull's sister, Anna Maria, had married John Awsiter.

James Winston remembered that Thomas was later sometimes facetiously called "Dr Hull," but the *Biographia Dramatica* account says that he failed at his father's profession of apothecary after refusing to continue his education for the church and then "took to the stage, and appeared first at the theatre in Smock Alley, Dublin, and then at that of Bath. . . ." Certainly he was in Sheridan's company at Smock Alley in 1753–54, but his only known roles there were Longbottom in *The Country Lasses*, Fabian in *The Fatal Mar-*

National Portrait Gallery

THOMAS HULL

by G. Dance

riage, Perez in *The Mourning Bride*, Diocles in *Oedipus*, Scale in *The Recruiting Officer*, and Smith in *The Rehearsal*. He was not re-hired at Smock Alley. He acted at Bath from 1754–55 through 1757–58. He seems also to have engaged in literary controversy and to have revived or continued his profession as apothecary.

In 1759 he published a pamphlet (*Mr. Hull's Case, Address'd to the* Public, " . . . given *Gratis* at Mr. HULL's, in *Bradley's* Buildings, Horse-street, and no where else") which attacked the Bath theatre's proprietor, John Palmer, for crowding him out of the managership, depriving him of his accustomed characters, reducing his salary, and finally, driving him from the theatre without a benefit. During the course of his verbose account, which includes a long exchange of letters, Hull states the terms of his articles, which are of considerable interest:

. . . I was engaged (in *September* 1757,) as *Actor* on, and *Manager* of, the Theatre in Orchard-street, for the Sum of Seven Pounds: This Engagement was attended with a *Solemn Promise* that it should continue in Force for *three Years*, that I should have an additional Reward of ten, twenty, or thirty Pounds, according to the Success of each Year. . . .

The pamphlet concludes, significantly, with the following:

Advertisement.
At Mr. HULL's House, in *Bradley's Buildings*, may be had Genuine Eau de Luce, Best Hungary, Lavendar, and Honey Waters, Ladies Black Sticking Plaister, Palsey Drops, Universal Balsam (being the most immediate Remedy for all Green Wounds, Scalds, Burns, &c.) Tooth-Powder, Lip-Salve, Heartburn Lozenges, &c.&c. at the *lowest Prices*.

Hull made his London debut at Covent Garden on 5 October 1759, playing the Elder Woud'be in *The Twin Rivals*. He was to perform at Covent Garden during the winter seasons for the next 48 years, the very epitome of the slowly-developing, responsible, dependable journeyman actor. He earned £2 per week his first few seasons, ascended to £6 per week for acting plus £150 additional per season when, from 1775–76 through 1781–82, he took over as acting manager from Colman at Covent Garden. In 1789–90 he dropped to £5 per week. He was, despite heavy inflation, earning only £4 per week at Covent Garden in the waning days of his career in 1806–7. But his benefits were well attended and he conducted managerial ventures outside London. He managed with Younger at Birmingham in 1762. He acted leads at Bristol in the summers from 1769 through 1773. From 1790 to 1792 he managed at Margate in the summers. In the summer of 1795 he was acting at Brighton.

Thomas Hull's roles, arranged in sequence, will illustrate his development and his solid importance to Covent Garden Theatre, where he acted indefatigably from each season's be-

ginning to its end. He often played on three or four successive nights in different parts. It was his boast that he had missed the prompter's call but once in 54 years—and then he was in bed with a violent fever.

Hull's Covent Garden roles were: (1759– 60) Charles in *The Non-Juror*, the First Spirit in *Comus*, Le Noble in *The Country House*, and Manly in *The Provok'd Husband*; (1760–61) Pembroke in *King John*, Renault in *Venice Preserv'd*, Friar Lawrence in *Romeo and Juliet*, the King in *Florizel and Perdita*, Don Juan in *Rule a Wife and Have a Wife*, Worcester in 1 *Henry IV*, Morelove in *The Careless Husband*, Lenox in *Macbeth*, Francisco in *Wit Without Money*, Springlove in *The Jovial Crew*, Horatio in *Hamlet*, Aimwell in *The Stratagem*, Exeter in *Henry V*, Worthy in *The Recruiting Officer*, Blandford in *Oroonoko*, Heartwell in *The Country Lasses*, and Clerimont in *The Miser*; (1761–62) Page in *The Merry Wives of Windsor*, Heli in *The Mourning Bride*, Burgundy in *Henry V*, Buckingham in *Richard III*, Westmoreland in 2 *Henry IV*, Lysimachus in *The Rival Queens*, Young Meriton in *The Counterfeit Heiress*, Sharper in *The Old Bachelor*, the Frenchman in *Lethe*, the Elder Brother in *Comus*, Colonel Ravelin in *Marplot in Lisbon*, Richard Wealthy in *The Minor*, and Myrtle in *The Conscious Lovers*; (1762–63) the Player in *The Beggar's Opera*, Cassio in *Othello*, Vizard in *The Constant Couple*, and Carlos in *Love Makes a Man*; (1763–64) Truman in *The Squire of Alsatia*, Lenox in *Macbeth*, and Loveless in *Love's Last Shift*; (1764– 65) Charles in *The Busy Body*, Galesus in *Coriolanus*, and Edgar in *King Lear*; (1765–66) Scandal in *Love for Love*, Fantome in *The Drummer*, Elder Freeman in *The Double Mistake*, Octavius in *Julius Caesar*, Paulet in *Cleone*, Granger in *The Refusal*, Sempronius in *Cato*, Rovewell in *The Fair Quaker of Deal*, the Dauphin in *King John*, and Davison in *The Albion Queens*.

In 1766–67 Hull played often but added only four roles to his repertoire: Wellbred in *Every Man in His Humour*, Don Juan in *The Double Perplexities*, Roderick in *The Double Falsehood*, and Antony in *Julius Caesar*. In the years following he added: (1767–68) Chatillion in *King John*, Dervise in *Tamerlane*, Pharon in *Mahomet*, Pisanio in *Cymbeline*, Antonio in *The Merchant of Venice*, Albany in *King Lear*, Classic in *The Englishman in Paris*, Pyrrhus in

Harvard Theatre Collection

THOMAS HULL as King Charles
engraving by Reading, after Roberts

The Distrest Mother, Pinchwife in *The Country Wife*, and Freeman in *A Bold Stroke for a Wife*; (1768–69) the Uncle in *George Barnwell*, Harpagus in *Cyrus*, Gloster in *Jane Shore*, and Young Knowell in *Every Man in His Humour*; (1769–70) Jenkins in *Man and Wife*, Sir William Douglas in *The English Merchant*, Old Goodwin in *The Brothers*, and Oakly in *The Jealous Wife*; (1770–71) Chaplain in *The Orphan*, Sadi in *Barbarossa*, Priuli in *Venice Preserv'd*, Belmour in *Jane Shore*, Escalus in *Measure for Measure*, Aeson in *Medea*, King of France in *Henry V*, Camillo in *The Winter's Tale*, and Burleigh in *The Earl of Essex*; (1771–72) Young Cape in *The Author*, Goodwin in *The Brothers*, Axalla in *Tamerlane*, Fairfield in *The Maid of the Mill*, Voltore in *The Fox*, Ballance in *The Recruiting Officer*, Seyfel in *Zobeide*, Don

Ferdinand in *Ximina*, Eumenes in *The Siege of Damascus*, Orsino in *Twelfth Night*, and Syphax in *Cato*.

Hull added (1772–73) Cromwell in *Henry VIII*, Edwin in *Elfrida*, the King in *All's Well that Ends Well*, Old Knowell in *Every Man in His Humour*, Clifford in *Henry II*, Cassius in *Julius Caesar*, Scandal in *Love for Love*, and Northumberland in *Lady Jane Gray*; (1773–74) Captain Dudley in *The West Indian*, the High Priest in *Herod and Mariamne*, Vernon in *1 Henry IV*, Raymond in *The Spanish Fryar*, Don Alvarez in *Don Sebastian, King of Portugal*, and Trusty in *The Funeral*; (1774–75) Cranmer in *Henry VIII*, Sealand in *The Conscious Lovers*, Dion in *Philaster*, Melanthon in *The Grecian Daughter*, Leonato in *Much Ado about Nothing*, Brabantio in *Othello*, Teramenes and then Artabasus in *Cleonice* in successive performances, Leontine in *Theodosius*, and Strictland in *The Suspicious Husband*; (1775–76) Hubert in *King John*, Kathul in *The Fatal Discovery*, Locrine in *Eldred*, Duke Senior in *As You Like It*, and Horatio in *The Fair Penitent*; (1776–77) Boccalini in *News from Parnassus*, Seofrid in *Ethelinda; or, The Royal Convert*, Megistus in *Zenobia*, Duncan in *Macbeth*, Mador in *Caractacus*, Gonzales in *The Mourning Bride*, Prospero in *The Tempest*, Angelo in *Measure for Measure*, Poliphontes in *Merope*, the Earl of Northampton in *Sir Thomas Overbury*, Sir John Flowerdale in *Lionel and Clarissa*, and Antonio in *The Merchant of Venice*; (1777–78) Morat in *The Orphan of China*, the Chief Bard in *Caractacus*, Sir Hubert in *Percy*, Mr Johnson in *The Rehearsal*, Adam in *As You Like It*, Sir Friendly Moral in *The Lady's Last Stake*, Ethelwin in *The British Heroine*, the Archbishop of Canterbury in *Henry V*, and Lord Audley in *Edward the Black Prince*; (1778–79) Aegeon in *The Comedy of Errors*, Greenwood in *A New Prelude and Prologue*, Suffolk in *The Earl of Warwick*, the Governor in *The Chelsea Pensioner*, and Cecil in *The Albion Queens*; (1779–80) the Cardinal in *The Duke of Milan* and Eumenes in *The Siege of Damascus*.

Hull continued to build repertoire: (1780–81) Jarvis in *The Gamester* and Bishop Juxon in *King Charles I*; (1781–82) Grey in *The Chapter of Accidents* and Drelincourt in *The Walloons*; (1782–83) Dolabella in *Philadamus*, Valetta in *The Knight of Malta*, and Mr Shandy in *Tristram Shandy*; (1783–84) Baptista in *The Magic Pic-*

ture, Charinus in *The Prophetess*, Everard in *The Heroine of the Cave*, and the Duke in *The Two Gentlemen of Verona*; (1784–85) Villers in *The Belle's Stratagem*, Sir John Lambert in *The Hypocrite*, and the Chief Justice in *2 Henry IV*; (1785–86) Count Baldwin in *Isabella*, Melville in *The Man of the World*, the Duke of Mantua in *The Bird in a Cage*, and Flavius in *Timon of Athens*.

Hull was active in 1786–87 and 1787–88 but his rate of playing diminished and in those seasons, apparently, he learned no new parts. Thereafter, through the season of 1799–1800, he added the following: (1788–89) Sir William Honeywood in *The Good-Natured Man* and Haswell in *Such Things Are*; (1789–90) Colonel Dormant in *The Farmer*, Sir John Bevil in *The Conscious Lovers*, Antigonus in *The Sheep*

Harvard Theatre Collection

THOMAS HULL as Jarvis

engraving by Leney, after De Wilde

Shearing, Count Kolberg in *The German Hotel*, Serapion in *All for Love*, and the King in *Hamlet*; (1790–91) Banks in *Wild Oats*; (1791–92) Nouri in *Zelma* and Seville in *The Child of Nature*; (1792–93) Stanley in *Richard III*; (1793–94) Willows in *The World in a Village*, the Count in *Nina*, Peter in *Fontainville Forest*, Sedgly in *British Fortitude and Hibernian Friendship*, Courtney in *The Fatal Extravagance*, and Mithranes in *Cyrus*; (1794–95) Perkins in *The Town Before You*, the Father in *The Bank Note*, and the Principal Judge in *The Secret Tribunal*; (1795–96) Sir Stephen Bertram in *The Jew*; (1796–97) Heartley in *A Cure for the Heart Ache* and Octavio in *The Italian Villagers*; (1797–98) Acasto in *The Orphan* and the Bishop of Winchester in *England Preserv'd*; (1798–99) Chevalier Cuno von Hallwyl in *The Count of Burgundy*; (1799–1800) Old Maythorn in *The Turnpike Gate*.

After the turn of the century Hull's advancing age and the growing ascendancy of younger "character" actors like Munden and Emery (and even Waddy) left Hull in possession of few of his roles. He kept his Friar Lawrence and still appeared as Duncan in *Macbeth*. He even added a few new parts: Pandulph in *King John* in 1802–3, old Sir Thomas Erpingham in *Henry V* in 1803–4, the Friar in *Hamlet* and Campeius in *Henry VIII* in 1805–6. As John Genest remarked, "he stayed on the stage until he was quite worn out."

He acted for the last time on 28 December 1807, bringing to a close a career of at least 54 years in which he had learned the lines for upwards of 225 characters. It was said that he acted in all but three of the 29 of Shakespeare's plays which were performed in the eighteenth century. (A wide interpretation, however, must be given "Shakespeare's plays." The phrase would include some drastic alterations, including Hull's own.)

The opinions of Francis Gentleman in *The Dramatic Censor* (1770), delivered after Hull's first decade on Covent Garden's stage, seem not materially different from those of other critics throughout his career: "a respectable performer" of "tender sensibility," fitted for "graver parts of comedy," and "better calculated for exhibiting amiable and tender feelings, than any which border on gloomy and sanguinary designs."

Mr. Hull, very capable of supporting paternal characters with propriety and feeling . . . always convinces a sensible auditor, that he thoroughly understands his author; had nature given him executive requisites equal to his judgment and assiduity, he would have been a capital pillar of the stage; what he is possessed of he exerts with judgment and modesty.

Less friendly critics saw Hull another way, as dull, imitative, and uninspired. In 1792 the vitriolic satirist "Anthony Pasquin" (John Williams) condemned his acting and his attempts to write tragedy and suggested that he had been on the boards too long:

> Lo! Chearfulness flies from the haunts of poor
>   HULL,
> Who's adust, melancholic, somnific and dull;
> The flame of his mind lacks additional fuel,
> His passions are cold, and his words—water-
>   gruel.
>
> .   .   .   .
>
> He's a sort of stage Patriarch, whose heart should
>   wed ease,
> As he's lauded in life by all ranks and degrees.
> To lacerate acting like his with my pen,
> Were charging a cannon to tear—a poor wren.

So also observed Francis Godolphin Waldron in *Candid and Impartial Strictures* (1795): Hull "has long enjoyed a respectable rank in the theatrical world in personating old trusty *Stewards*, and parts that require an apparent honest sincerity of expression. . . . Time has long whitened his locks, and would fain advise him to quit the bustle of the mimic world, but the veteran appears to be still determined to hold his place."

Charles Dibdin remarked in his second *Tour* (1798) that Hull was "the apologist-general at Covent-Garden Theatre for about five and twenty years," which probably reflects appreciation not only of the many prologues which Hull spoke but also the numbers which he wrote.

Hull's placid amiability made him popular with his audiences and his fellow actors. A quick "study" and always "perfect," never in need of the prompter's whisper, he often stepped in on short notice when sickness threatened a performance. His compassionate concern for the misfortunes of the aging actress Esther Hamilton impelled him finally to put

in motion a scheme he had long deliberated, and in 1765 he founded the Covent Garden actors' fund to assist ill or indigent and aged actors.

James Winston in one of his jottings (at the Huntington Library) called Hull "a good scholar," though there is no record of any formal schooling after he left the Charterhouse. In his day he was known nearly as well for his writing as for his acting. He wrote 20 or more theatrical offerings, a novel, and some tales and supervised several editions. He altered Shakespeare's *Comedy of Errors* as *The Twins* (Covent Garden, 24 April 1762, published 1793). His farce *The Absent Man* (Covent Garden, 28 April 1764) was not published. *Pharnaces*, an opera altered from Lucchini's *Farnace* (1731) and set by William Bates, was performed at Drury Lane 15 February 1765. *The Spanish Lady, a Musical Entertainment* (Covent Garden, 2 May 1765) was published in 1765.

The farce *All in the Right*, a translation and alteration from Detouches, was brought out as an afterpiece, partly to introduce Hull's niece Sophia Potts as Emily ("with songs in Character") at his Covent Garden benefit 26 April 1766 and was not published. His comedy *The Perplexities* (Covent Garden, 31 January 1767), founded on Sir Samuel Tuke's *Adventures of Five Hours*, was published in 1767. It shared the bill with *The Fairy Favour*, a masque concocted by Hull for some of J. C. Bach's music. Also in 1767, on 14 December, Hull brought forth a comic opera *The Royal Merchant*, based on Beaumont and Fletcher's *The Beggar's Bush*, with Thomas Linley's music. (The Neville manuscript diary noted: "At the beginning of the 2nd act some fellows in the 2s. Gallery began a disturbance, but were turn'd out and carried before [the Bow Street magistrate] Sir John Fielding, where they confessed that they were hired to disturb this performance by a publican, but refused to say whom. . . .") The opera was published in London and Dublin in 1768. Hull's oratorio *The Prodigal Son*, never heard, was published in 1773 and reissued in 1777.

On 1 May 1773, Hull's benefit night, he staged his popular tragedy *Henry II; or, The Fall of Rosamond*, based on the 1749 play by William Hawkins. It was published in 1774. The work, in a preliminary state, had been

Harvard Theatre Collection

THOMAS HULL

engraving by Leney, after Graham

produced by Hull at Birmingham on 28 August 1761—"A hasty and imperfect Compilation of some scenes, on the subject," Hull later called it. On the following day his friend the poet William Shenstone had written with suggestions for changes, which were incorporated in the Covent Garden version. On 18 March 1775, for Mrs Barry's benefit, Hull donated a revision of another old play—this time of James Thomson's *Edward and Eleonora*, which had been refused a license in 1739 for what Walpole's licenser had thought were seditious reflections. Hull tamed the piece into "what the Ladies call 'a very pretty tragedy,'" said the reviewer for the *Westminster Magazine*.

True Blue, or The Press Gang, altered from Henry Carey's *Nancy*, sometimes acted as *The Spaniards Dismayed; or, True Blue Forever*, began its considerable career as an afterpiece on 23 December 1776. It was not published. Arthur Murphy's 10-year-old comedy *The School for Guardians* was the next grist to come to Hull's alteration mill. He married it to music by Thomas Augustine Arne, J. A. Fisher, and Antonio Sacchini to produce *Love Finds the Way* (Covent Garden, 18 November 1777, published that year). Fisher also contributed incidental music to the staging of *Iphigenia; or, The Victim*, a tragedy, a considerable alteration of Abel Boyer's *Achilles; or, Iphigenia in Aulis* (which was a translation of Racine). It was devised only to oblige Mrs Barry, as a novelty for her benefit. It played only once, on 23 March 1778, and was not published. F. W. Bateson has suggested that Hull may have collaborated with R. W. Sheridan on the latter's popular musical interlude *The Camp*, which played at Drury Lane first on 15 October 1778. Hull staged his second revision of *The Comedy of Errors* on 22 January 1779, hewing closer to Shakespeare's text than he had in *The Twins*. The tragedy *The Fatal Interview*, first played on 16 November 1782 is sometimes ascribed to Hull and sometimes to Samuel Jackson Pratt, who wrote the epilogue. It ran only three nights and was not published.

Hull's third alteration of a play by Shakespeare, *Timon of Athens*, was based on Thomas Shadwell's alteration of 1678. It was played for Hull's benefit on 13 May 1786 and speedily forgotten. Nicoll lists also for 1786 a work apparently neither performed nor published, *The True British Tar, or, A Friend at a Pinch*. Another quick alteration, for his benefit on 30 May 1798, was the last of Hull's works to reach the stage. It was *Disinterested Love*, a comedy taken from Philip Massinger's *The Bashful Lover*. The single performance was marred by the illness of the actor Alexander Pope, causing the lead part of Hortensio to be read by H. E. Johnstone. It was not published. Hull's oratorio *Elisha; or, The Woman of Shunem* was published in 1801 but evidently never given a performance.

Hull's nondramatic works include: *Mr. Hull's Case, Addressed to the Consideration of the Public*, Bath, 1759; a novel, *The History of Sir William Harrington*, 4 vols., 1771, 1772, 1797 (translated into German, Leipzig, 1771; into French, Lausanne, 1773); *Genuine Letters from a Gentlewoman to a Young Lady, her Pupil*, edited and revised by Hull, 2 vols. 1772; *Richard Plantagenet, a Legendary Tale*, 1774 (at least six editions); *Select Letters between the Late Duchess of Somerset, Lady Luxborough, and Others, including a Sketch of the Manners, etc. of the Republic*

Harvard Theatre Collection

THOMAS HULL as Voltore

engraving by Pollard, after Roberts

of Venice, edited by Hull, 2 vols., 1778; *A Collection of Poems and Translations in English and Latin*, Bath, 1780?, Reading, n.d.; *Moral Tales in Verse*, 2 vols., 1797; *The Advantages of Repentance. A Moral Tale Attempted in Blank Verse*, n.d.

Hull married the actress Anna Maria Morrison, evidently at some time between 1762, when she acted at Birmingham under her maiden name, and 6 April 1766, when Hull addressed a birthday poem to his wife (now in the Garrick Club: "Length of Life & Happiness / Ever my Maria bless!"). The Master Hull who acted briefly at Bristol in 1769 was doubtless their child. Mrs Hull died on 23 October 1805.

Thomas Hull died at his house in Dean Yard, Westminster, on 22 April 1808 and was buried in the churchyard of St Margaret, Westminster, on the north side of the Abbey green, near the entrance to the north porch of the Abbey. Wewitzer's *Dramatic Chronology* (1817) purports to give an epitaph inscribed on the gravestone (which has been destroyed):

> Hull, long respected in the scenic Art,
> In Life's great stage sustain'd a virtuous part
> And some memorial of his zeal to shew
> For his lov'd Art, and shelter age from woe,
> He form'd that noble fund which guards his name,
> Embalm'd by Gratitude, enliven'd by Fame.

But the transcription published by W. G. Wright in *Notes and Queries* in 1931 does not include poetry:

Sacred to the Memory of Mrs. Anna Maria Hull. Died 23 Oct., 1803 [*recte* 1805] in the 77th Year of her Age. Also to the Memory of Thomas HULL, Esqr. late of the Theatre Royal, Covent Garden. Founder of the Theatrical Fund. Died 22 April 1808, in the 79th Year of his Age. Also to the memory of Mrs. Jane Elizabeth . . . Sister of the above Mrs. HULL. Died 6 February 1838, in the 75th Year of her Age.

In a will signed on 24 February 1806 and proved on 28 September 1808, Hull left to the actor George Holman the portrait of Hull's friend William Shenstone. He also left to Holman a portrait of himself but wished him eventually to

deliver it to the committee . . . of the Theatrical ffund instituted at the Theatre Royal Covent Garden . . . to be by them transmitted to the next committee and in like manner to be continued thro' all future Committees, and to be by them kept in the room wheresoever . . . they may hold meetings in humble hope that the said portrait may be considered as brotherly testimony of my ardent wish that the said Institution may long continue to answer the salutary purposes for which it was intended.

To Jane Holman, George's wife, he left "my two small medallions carved indubitably on pieces of Shakespeare's Mulberry tree with the Heads of Shakespeare and Garrick." To "George Archdale, son of Richard Archdale, Esq" he left "my bust of the late Earl of Halifax" and "To John Richards Esquire Secretary of the Royal Academy Somerset Place my snuff Box form'd unquestionably out of the wood of Shakespeare's mulberry tree with the arms and crest of that incomparable poet engraved thereon." Hull left the residue of his property, including much plate and many books and pictures, to his niece, Jane Elizabeth Awsiter, who was joint executrix of the will with Elizabeth, wife of John Richards. (The marriage register of St George's Chapel, Mayfair, for 30 June 1752 records the wedding of "John Awsiter & Anna Maria Hull of S: Margaret's, Westm^r.") The content and tenor of a letter written by Thomas Hull, now in the possession of Charles Beecher Hogan, suggests that the actress Elizabeth Edmead may have been Hull's natural daughter.

On 23 and 24 May 1808 "the excellent & valuable library of books, the property of Mr. Tho. Hull, late of Covent Garden Theatre. . . . Also a quantity of music" was, according to the catalogue, sold by the auctioneer Fisher "by order of the executrix."

Portraits of Thomas Hull include:

1. By George Dance, 1799. Pencil and wash drawing at the National Portrait Gallery. Engraving by W. Daniell.

2. By John Downman. In 1777 Downman did studies of six performers who appeared in the premiere of Mason's *Caractacus* at Covent Garden on 6 December 1776, including Hull, who played Mador. In his sketchbooks Downman recorded sketching the studies, but stated that he did not have the time to make the picture intended.

3. By J. Graham. Canvas at the Garrick Club; seated left, head to right, book in left hand, silver-rimmed spectacles in right. In the Garrick Club catalogue (No 121) as artist unknown, but the engraving by W. Leney, published by G. Cawthorn in 1797, is marked "Graham fecit."

4. As Edwin, with Mrs Hartley as Elfrida and Mrs Mattocks as one of the Chorus, in Elfrida. By unknown engraver. In the Harvard Theatre Collection but not listed in the catalogue.

5. As Gloster in *Edward and Eleanora*. Engraving by W. Leney, after J. Roberts. Published as a plate to *Bell's British Theatre*, 1791, and Cawthorn's *British Library*, 1795.

6. As Jarvis in *The Gamester*. Canvas by Samuel De Wilde. At the Garrick Club. An engraving by W. Leney was published as a plate to *Bell's British Theatre*, 1791; a copy by an unknown engraver was published in *British Drama*, 1817.

7. As Jarvis, with Mrs Wells as Charlotte,

Alexander Pope as Beverley, and Mrs Pope as Mrs Beverley. Canvas (79 × 100½) by Mather Brown. At the Garrick Club.

8. As King Charles in *King Charles I*. Engraving by B. Reading, after J. Roberts. Published as a plate to *Bell's British Theatre*, 1777.

9. As Pisanio in *Cymbeline*. India ink and watercolor by Thomas Parkinson. At the British Museum. Engraving by C. Grignion. Published as a plate to Bell's *Shakespeare*, 1775.

10. As Voltore in *Volpone*. Engraving by R. Pollard, after J. Roberts. Published as a plate to *Bell's British Theatre*, 1777.

11. As one of the Watch, with Garrick as Sir John Brute, in *The Provok'd Wife*. Canvas by Zoffany, exhibited at the Royal Academy in 1765. Engraving by Finlayson, published 1768. For details of the provenance and the two versions of this painting, see the notice of David Garrick in this dictionary, iconography list, No 232.

12. In the "Immortality of Garrick." Large canvas by George Carter depicting 17 actors bidding farewell to Garrick as he is borne to Parnassus. In the Art Gallery of the Royal Shakespeare Theatre, Stratford-upon-Avon. Engraving by J. Caldwall and S. Smith, published by the artist with a key plate, 1783. The supplement to the *British Museum Catalogue of Engraved British Portraits* mistakenly identifies Hull as Hall.

13. By unknown artist. Seated with bust of Shenstone. In the National Portrait Gallery (No 4625).

Hull, Mrs Thomas, Anna Maria, née Morrison *1727–1805, actress, dancer.*

Anna Maria Morrison was the daughter of the minor actress Mrs Morrison (née Anne Saunders?). Anna Maria was first noticed (but only as "Miss Morrison") with 10 other children, in the bill for 19 November 1737 at Drury Lane, when she danced in the pantomime *The Burgomaster Trick'd* and the ballet *The Shepherd's Mount*. She was next in the bills for 19 May, dancing a saraband with young Miss Wright. On 25 May she and Miss Wright danced a minuet and *The Bretagne* and they danced unnamed figures also on 26 May and repeated the saraband on 31 May. On 23 August, during Bartholomew Fair, the "Lilliputian company" appeared at Hallam's booth in

George Inn yard where Miss Morrison played Punch in the *Grand Ballet*.

Miss Morrison's name did not appear in the bills again until the following spring, when she danced on four evenings in April and May: a *Peirates* with Master Ferg, a solo Serious Dance, *Pierrots* with Master Ferg, and a saraband and tambourine, both solo. The pattern was repeated the next season, when she danced only in April and May, except that then she appeared twice at Drury Lane and three times at Covent Garden. Her partner on 24 April 1740 at Drury Lane was "Master Gillier, a Boy of Six and Scholar of Muilment," and the youngsters repeated their minuet for Mrs Stevens and Mrs Vincent's benefit at Covent Garden the following evening. Anna Maria danced alone at Covent Garden on 7 May and with Master Ferg in a *Miller's Dance* the next evening at Drury Lane. Her brief season terminated on 23 May at Covent Garden when she danced her saraband. Folger manuscript accounts show Miss Morrison to have been entered on the Covent Garden paylist on 17 November 1740 at the rate of a shilling a day. The playbills do not mention her dancing, but few dancers were cited that season.

Anna Maria continued to dance at Covent Garden throughout her adolescence and young womanhood. She was there in the regular company, but obscurely functioning in the dance corps, from 1740–41 through 1753–54, except for 1743–44. She also began acting minor parts in comedy at the summer theatres in Richmond and Twickenham in 1746 and 1747—Dicky in *The Constant Couple*, Lucia in *The Squire of Alsatia*, Lady Humkin in *Diversions of the Morning*.

Perhaps discouraged by her lack of success, Anna Maria left London after the 1753–54 season and took to the provinces. Her wanderings cannot be fully traced, but there was a Miss Morrison at the Orchard Street Theatre, Bath, each season from 1753–54 through 1758–59. Tate Wilkinson said that she was at Maidstone in 1757 and she came to the Portsmouth theatre from service at Bath in 1759. She rejoined the Covent Garden company in September 1760—at 5*s*. per night, according to the Covent Garden account book in the British Library. Her duties were still menial. She opened as Dolly Trull in *The Beggar's Opera*

on 24 September. It ran for only a few nights, being overwhelmed by a competing *Beggar's Opera* at Drury Lane. She acted Serina in *The Orphan* on 23 October and 16 December, and then Miss Morrison's name dropped out of sight again until her appearance at Birmingham in the summer of 1762. At Covent Garden on 28 April 1764, for that night only and for Thomas Hull's shared benefit, she played the Lady in *Comus*.

Anna Maria Morrison had apparently married the Covent Garden actor Hull by the time he wrote the birthday poem dated 6 April 1766 (now in the Garrick Club): "Length of Life & Happiness / Ever my Maria bless!" She acted, but only occasionally, at Bristol in 1769 and 1770. She returned to Covent Garden on 26 April 1770, now under the sponsorship of her husband, the stage manager, to play Mrs Oakly opposite his Oakly in *The Jealous Wife* and for his benefit.

Hull invited his wife to play Paulina in *The Winter's Tale* (revived after 29 years and in Hull's own revision) for his benefit on 24 April 1771. She played four times in 1771–72, including, once again, Paulina in *The Winter's Tale* for her husband's benefit and, for Miss Macklin's benefit, Lady Wrangle in *The Refusal*. That part she learned by sitting up two nights in a row when Ann Pitt, who was cast for it, fell ill. She also played the Queen in *The Earl of Essex* twice. For Hull's benefit on 1 May 1773 she was Queen Eleanor in *Henry II*.

Mrs Hull's fullest season at Covent Garden was her last. In 1774–75 she acted the following roles: the Countess in *All's Well that Ends Well*, Sisigambis in *Alexander the Great*, Lady Capulet in *Romeo and Juliet*, Mrs Fulmer in *The West Indian*, Isabella in *The Conscious Lovers*, the Duchess of York in *Richard III*, the Duchess of Suffolk in *Lady Jane Gray*, the Queen in *Hamlet*, and the Queen in *Cymbeline*. But most of her appearances were in the fall. After 24 May 1775, when she played Mrs Fulmer, she never again acted in London. The only bill available for the Birmingham theatre in 1791, that for 28 July, names a Mrs Hull, and perhaps that was she.

Anna Maria Morrison Hull died on 23 October 1805 and was buried in the churchyard of St Margaret, Westminster. Her husband, by his direction, was buried beside her in 1808.

Mrs Hull was the niece of the actress Margaret Saunders who appointed Anna Maria's mother, Ann Morrison, executrix of her will of 1743 and left unspecified property to her, with Anna Maria as residuary legatee.

Hullet. *See* HULETT.

Hüllmandel, Nicholas Joseph 1751–1823, *pianist, harpsichordist, composer.*

Nicholas Joseph Hüllmandel was born in Strasbourg in 1751, studied under C. P. E. Bach, and came to London to teach and perform in 1771. He played the harpsichord at the Haymarket Theatre at Duport's benefit on 27 April 1772 and doubtless performed on other occasions. He traveled to the Continent, visiting Italy, and lived for some time in Paris, where he may have met Mozart. Mozart had a good opinion of Hüllmandel's sonatas, and Nicholas Joseph's uncle, Rodolphe, was the one who recommended Mozart for the position of organist at Versailles. In 1787 Hüllmandel married the aristocratic Mlle Cazan.

In 1789 he sent his wife to London, and he followed her there in 1790. They spent the rest of their lives in England. Haydn in his *First London Notebook* in 1792 listed Hüllmandel as a pianist and composer of note. Most of Hüllmandel's compositions—concertos, violin duets, piano sonatas, trios, and other works—were published between 1785 and 1800. The Hüllmandels had a daughter, Evalina, who married the painter Bartholomew, and a son Charles Joseph (1789–1850), who was a lithographer with a shop at No 51, Great Marlborough Street about 1820. The elder Hüllmandel died on 19 December 1823 at the age of 72.

He was pictured in a group portrait consisting of medallion miniatures of 26 musicians and singers, engraved by Landseer, after a design by De Loutherbourg, from miniature cameos by H. de Janvry, published in London in 1801 by de Janvry and sold by Colnaghi & Co.

Hulme, Mr ₍fl. 1779₎, *actor.*

A single performance of *Falstaff's Wedding* was presented at the Haymarket Theatre on 27 December 1779; a Mr Hulme played an Officer.

Hulstone, Mr ₍fl. 1735₎, *actor.*

Mr Hulstone acted Loveless in *The Relapse* at York Buildings on 17 July 1735 and Appletree in *The Recruiting Officer* at the Haymarket Theatre on the following 13 December.

"Hum, Mr" ₍fl. 1759₎, *actor?*

Galligantus was presented at the Haymarket on 17 September 1759 and on subsequent dates. The bill called it "A new English Burletta. Taken from the Memoirs of Jeffrey Ap Arthur of Monmouth, interspersed with Critical Remarks by Mess Snarler and Hum for Mr Bombast the Author." From that description it is not clear whether Mr "Hum" had a hand in the writing of the piece or, with "Snarler," performed in it. In any case, the whole thing sounds like an antic of Christopher Smart, who used such pseudonyms for his cohorts.

Humer, Mr ₍fl. 1791–1792₎, *dancer.*

Smith in *The Italian Opera* lists a Mr Humer as one of the dancers in the opera company at the Pantheon and the Haymarket Theatre during the 1791–92 season.

Humerston. *See* HOMERSTON.

Humfrey. *See* HUMPHREY.

"Humm, Sir Henry." *See* STEVENS, GEORGE ALEXANDER.

Hummel, J. Louis ₍fl. 1792–1794₎, *singer. See* HUMMEL, JOHAN NEPOMUKA.

Hummel, Johan Nepomuka 1778–1837, *pianist, composer, singer, teacher.*

Johan Nepomuka Hummel was born at Pozsony, Hungary, on 14 November 1778, the son of Joseph Hummel, director of the Imperial School of Military Music and leader of the theatre band at Pozsony.

Johan was given lessons on the violin at a very early age but rejected that instrument in favor of the pianoforte, on which he at once revealed an astonishing talent. When the boy was about seven years old, his father went to conduct at Schikaneder's Theatre in Vienna. Mozart heard the boy play and took him under his tutelage and into his house in the Grosse Schülerstrasse.

Harvard Theatre Collection

JOHAN N. HUMMEL
engraving by Esslinger, after Müller

Hummel's first public appearance was in 1787 at a concert in Vienna supervised by Mozart. The elder Hummel, impressed by his son's success, took him in 1788 on a concert tour of Bohemia, Germany, and Denmark and then to Edinburgh, where the father taught pianoforte for some time. Father and son then played their way south through Newcastle-on-Tyne, Durham, and Cambridge. On 27 October 1788 Johan, not yet 10 years old, heard his own quartet played and performed a sonata for harpsichord at the Oxford Music Room.

In London, Johan received instruction from Muzio Clementi and is known to have played concerts at a number of locations. He appeared in a recital with J. B. Cramer at the Crown and Anchor Tavern in January 1791. Anthony Le Texier presented *A New Kind of Concert* at the King's Theatre on 19 May 1791, in which a brilliant collection of dancers, singers, and instrumentalists performed. The great young violinist Master Franz Clement played a concerto. The singer Giacomo Davide sang a new song by Haydn, who accompanied him at the harpsichord. Vestris and Mlle Hilligsberg

danced a pas de russe, and Master Hummel played "on the Piano Forte some favourite *Airs with Variations*" (no doubt revealing to Londoners the beginning of that marvelous ability at improvisation which was said in time to rival Beethoven's). On 20 April 1792, under Johann Peter Salomon, Hummel introduced a Haydn sonata at the Hanover Square Rooms and there on 5 May played a concerto by Mozart. In the summer of 1792 Hummel went on to perform at Bath and Bristol.

On 15 February 1793 "Master Hummell" appeared for the first time on the oratorio bill at the King's Theatre, singing with Master Welsh "O lovely peace" from *Judas Maccabaeus* and with Miss Leak "My faith and truth" from *Samson*. In February also he sang and accompanied himself on the pianoforte at Spring Gardens during the showing of scenes from Philip James de Loutherbourg's *Eidophusikon*. *Grove's Dictionary* asserts that, after leaving Bath and Bristol Hummel "made a short stay in Holland and by way of that country returned to Vienna in 1793." But he may have returned to Britain after a brief time on the Continent, for on 7 March 1794, in another pastiche of Handel's sacred music, a "Master Hummel" sang at Covent Garden under the direction of the Ashleys. Either Johan had returned or there was another young singer named Hummel in London at the same period. (C. B. Hogan, in the index to one of his volumes of *The London Stage*, identifies the singer of 1794 as "J. Louis Hummel.") Doane, in his *Musical Directory* (1794), writes of a Master Hummel who played "the Pia[no] Forte, [at] Salomon's Concert" and who sang in "Oratorios [at] Colman's [i.e. Covent Garden] Theatre" and adds that he also sang in one of the Handelian celebrations in Westminster Abbey.

At any rate, during the nineties Hummel was studying in Vienna with the aging but competent contrapuntist Johann Georg Albrechtsberger and occasionally receiving lessons from Haydn. Beethoven was also the pupil of both teachers, and, though he was eight years older than Hummel, the two may nevertheless have become acquainted.

Accounts of Hummel's life, like that in Grove, are vague about the period following study and before Hummel's satisfying concert tour to Russia in 1803. But the fact is that by February 1801, and perhaps by 1800, both

Johan and his father were again in England. A manuscript diary (now in the Folger Shakespeare Library) kept by Jane Porter—then only 24 and not yet a famous novelist—describes the pair on 19 February 1801. Jane was then the guest of Mrs Claude Champion Crespigny at Champion Lodge, Camberwell:

About noon the two Mr Hummells, father and son, called on Mrs Crespigny. She sent for me down. Their profession is music, and as it is one of my ruling passions, I had a most delicious banquet of sweet sounds. They dined with us. It rained in the evening, which compelled them to stay all night. Young Hummell has great execution and taste, both on the Grand Piano Forté, and the Harp. His voice is rich and full of feeling. He sang with dissolving pathos, the beautiful lines of Moore, beginning "sweet are the dreams &c." As we conversed after tea, I found him well-read, even philosophical, and possessing a kind of brilliant naiveté, that I never saw in any one before. He is young and handsome. He never drinks wine for this reason. When a boy, he observed its degrading effects upon men, and he supposed it must have a bewitching quality upon those who had once tasted it, to make them taste it again— He resolved never to run the risk. The abhorrence grew with him to manhood; and though he has tasted it, and does not dislike it, yet aware of the use of his resolution, in no company whatever, and at no time does he break through what he has made a principal, never to drink a glass of wine. At first his acquaintance laughed at him and quarrelled with him; but he was firm, and is now free.— What an example is this, set by a young lively man of one-and-twenty!!

In 1803 Hummel was engaged by the Court Theatre in Vienna. In 1804 he went to Eisenstadt to Haydn's old post as *Kapellmeister* to Prince Esterházy; he was there until 1811 but was dismissed for inattention to his duties. In 1813 he married the opera singer Elizabeth Röckl (1793–1883). From 1812 through 1816 he supported himself by performing and teaching at Vienna. In 1816 he became *Kapellmeister* at Stuttgart. From 1819 until the end of his life he was *Kapellmeister* at Weimar, a service interrupted by professional tours—to St Petersburg and Paris in 1822 and to Paris and London in 1829. In 1833–34 he came back to London for one season as conductor of the German opera company at the King's Theatre. He died at Weimar on 17 October 1837.

A discussion of Hummel's contribution to instruction and of his compositions, along with a competent catalogue of his works, by Duncan Hume, may be found in *Grove's Dictionary*.

An engraved portrait of Hummel was published in *The Harmonicon* in June 1824 and was reproduced in *Musical Quarterly*, 56. It is a copy of an engraving by C. Mayer, after F. H. Müller, published in Hamburg, n.d. Another engraving, by M. Esslinger, after Müller, was published by Schumann, n.d. A third engraving, by Fleischmann, after Müller, appeared in 1822. There is also an engraved portrait of Hummel by Scröber, after Grinler.

Humpage, Mr [*fl.* 1788–1790], *constable.*

Mr Humpage was added to the paylist at Drury Lane on 11 October 1788 at 2s. daily as a constable. He was still working at the theatre in 1789–90.

Humphrey, Pelham *1647–1674, singer, composer, lutenist, violinist.*

According to Anthony à Wood, Pelham Humphrey (or Humfrey) was the nephew of Colonel John Humphrey, an amateur musician. Pelham was born in 1647, and in 1660 he became one of the Children of the Chapel Royal under Captain Henry Cooke. Pepys, on 22 November 1663, was at the chapel at Whitehall and wrote later that "the Anthem was good after sermon, being the 51 psalme—made for five voices by one of Captain Cookes boys, a pretty boy—." Humphrey was the pretty boy, and Pepys noted that the other lads could do as well. They were, indeed, a remarkably talented lot: Michael Wise, John Blow, Thomas Tudway, William Turner, and the elder Henry Purcell were among Humphrey's fellow choristers. Pelham's anthem was later published in Boyce's *Cathedral Music*, and five anthems which Humphrey set to music were included in Clifford's *Divine Services and Anthems* in 1664.

The precocious boy was sent abroad by Charles II in 1664 to further his musical training; funds from the Secret Service to the amount of £450 over the following two years were granted to support Humphrey's trip to France (where he studied with Lully) and Italy. In addition to monies paid Pelham for his travel and maintenance on the Continent, there were payments to him, as a former

Chapel boy, through Henry Cooke, amounting to perhaps £40 annually (Cooke was paid that sum, at any rate, on 17 May 1665, for Humphrey's maintenance.)

The Lord Chamberlain's accounts show that on 10 March 1666 Humphrey, described as a lutenist, was appointed to replace Nicholas Lanier, in the King's Musick at £40 yearly plus livery. Probably, as Grove suggests, Humphrey was given the appointment *in absentia*, for Pepys's comments on him in late 1667 imply that he did not return from the Continent until then. On 23 January 1667 Pelham, apparently still on the Continent, was given Thomas Hazard's place in the Chapel Royal, and on the following 26 October he was sworn a Gentleman of the Chapel Royal—the implication being that he had only then returned.

Back in London, Humphrey, only 20 years old, was quite taken with himself. Pepys provides us with reports of Pelham's skill and vanity. On 1 November 1667 the diarist was at Whitehall, and at the chapel he heard "a fine anthem, made by Pelham (who is come over) in France, of which there was great expectation, and indeed is a very good piece of musique, but still I cannot call the Anthem anything but instrumentall musique with the voice, for nothing is made of the words at all." On 15 November Pepys found Humphrey at his mercer's with "Caesar" (that is, William Smegergill, the composer and lutenist) and judged Humphrey

an absolute Monsieur, as full of form, and confidence, and vanity, and disparages everything, and everybody's skill but his own. The truth is, everybody says he is very able, but to hear how he laughs at all the King's musick here, as Blagrave and others, that they cannot keep time nor tune, nor understand anything; and that Grebus [Grabu], the Frenchman, the King's master of the musick, how he understands nothing, nor can play on any instrument, and so cannot compose; and that he will give him a lift out of his place; and that he and the King are mighty great! and that he hath already spoke to the King of Grebus would make a man piss.

Despite that opinion, Pepys fed the two musicians, and then they made music, Pepys on his viol, Caesar on the French lute, and Humphrey on the theorbo.

On 16 November 1667 Pepys wrote that he went

to White Hall; and there got into the theater-room, and there heard both the vocall and instrumentall musick, where the little fellow [Humphrey] stood keeping time; but for my part, I see no great matter, but quite the contrary in both sorts of musique. The composition I believe is very good, but no more of delightfulness to the eare or understanding but what is very ordinary.

Nevertheless, a 1668 warrant in the Lord Chamberlain's accounts indicates that Humphrey and Thomas Purcell were named composers in the King's Musick, replacing George Hudson and Matthew Locke. (Oddly, a warrant dated 10 January 1672, shortly before Hudson's death, specified that Humphrey and Purcell should assist Hudson and succeed to his post.) Another 1668 order directed that Humphrey should replace the lutenist Nicholas Lanier in the King's private music at £56 2s. 6d. annually plus livery; the date of the appointment was 27 January, but the fees were retroactive to 25 March 1666, shortly after Lanier's death. Humphrey was also to receive £48 7s. 6d. in livery fees due Lanier for 1666, 1667, and 1668.

On 21 January 1670 Humphrey was made one of the assistants of the Corporation of Music. Busy though he was, he also made occasional trips to attend the royal family outside London, as in the summer of 1671, when he was in attendance at Windsor for an extra 8s. daily fee. By the summer of 1672 Humphrey had become a warden in the Corporation of Music, and when Henry Cooke died on 13 July Pelham succeeded to Cooke's positions as Master of the Children of the Chapel Royal and composer for voices to the King. Zimmerman, Purcell's biographer, states that Humphrey was Cooke's son-in-law. One of Humphrey's students was the younger Henry Purcell.

A map of Covent Garden made by a John Lacy in 1673 shows a 65′ × 30′ plot of ground in Russell Street, touching the Theatre Royal property, assigned to a Mr Humphreys. He owned another parcel measuring about 100′ × 20′ in Bedford Street. Possibly the man was Pelham Humphrey.

The Lord Chamberlain's accounts contain many warrants directing payments to Humphrey to cover his expenses in teaching the boys in the Chapel Royal (he had at least 12 under him) and maintaining them after their voices broke. One warrant, dated 24 July 1673, stated that Humphrey was paid £24 yearly for every boy he kept. To that fee was added £40 annually which he was paid as a member of the private music, and £20 for lute strings each year. From other warrants we know that, as one of the composers for the violins, Humphrey annually shared £42 15*s*. 10*d*. plus £200 with Thomas Purcell. And he received, though seldom on time, £12 2*s*. 6*d*. annually for livery.

On 29 September 1673 Humphrey let John Lilly take over the instruction of four of the children of the Chapel for £30 yearly, though, as the accounts in 1672, 1673, and 1674 show, Humphrey still spent much of his time working with the boys. On 14 July 1674 Pelham Humphrey died at Windsor at the age of 27. He was buried on 17 July in the cloisters of Westminster Abbey. Within a few days his posts as Master of the Children and composer of the private music for voices were taken over by John Blow. Robert Smyth replaced him as musician in ordinary in the King's Musick. As late as 1677 Humphrey was still being named in the accounts for arrears in livery payments; they presumably were due his widow.

Humphrey had written his will on 23 April 1674, which, considering his age, suggests that he was probably very ill. It contained no signatures of witnesses. On 30 July, when the will went through probate, John Blow testified that he was present when Humphrey wrote the will. It was proved by Pelham's widow and executrix, Catherine. Humphrey left everything to his wife but asked that 20*s*. each for mourning rings should be given to John Blow, Besse Gill, and Pelham's cousin Betty Jelfe. Catherine and Pelham Humphrey had at least one child, a daughter Mary, who was buried in the cloisters of Westminster Abbey on 23 February 1674. That Humphrey died in debt is indicated by a warrant in the Lord Chamberlain's accounts dated 19 November 1675. A debenture for 1672 and 1673 amounting to 12*s*. 6*d*. was received from Mrs Humphrey for her late husband.

Catherine (or Katherine) Cooke Humphrey had brought her husband a fair amount of money when they married, sometime after Henry Cooke's death in July 1672. Cooke left his daughter £300 due him from the Exchequer plus 120 broad pieces of gold. Rimbault

in his notes to the *Old Cheque Book of the Chapel Royal* says that Humphrey's wife was praised for her beauty in Richard Veel's *An Hymeneal to his dear friend Mr. P H* (1672).

Pelham Humphrey was typical of the court musicians of his day, many of whom had a variety of talents. According to Pulver, Humphrey sang tenor, taught singing as well as several musical instruments, educated and maintained the Chapel boys, was the disciplinarian of the court musicians, and composed a great many anthems and songs, including a number of works for theatrical productions. One of his songs, *The Phoenix*, published about 1705, had lyrics by King Charles himself, and in some instances Humphrey wrote his own words. He, John Banister the elder, and James Hart wrote music for *The Tempest*—probably the Dryden-Davenant version which was performed at Lincoln's Inn Fields on 7 November 1667, for about 1670 was published *The Ariel's Songs (sic)* from the play. (The Shadwell version of *The Tempest* came out in April 1674, near the time of Humphrey's death and some years after he did most of his composing.)

In addition to music for *The Tempest*, Humphrey is known to have written songs for *Charles VIII* (1671), *Love in a Wood* (1671), *The Conquest of Granada* (1672), and *The Indian Emperor* (1675, posthumous). Music by Humphrey appeared in such collections as Playford's *Choice Songs* (1673), *Choice Ayres, Songs and Dialogues* (1676–1684), and *Harmonia Sacra* (1688). His music for *The Tempest* exists in a manuscript at the Paris Conservatoire, and much of his music can be studied in manuscript form at the British Library, Cambridge, Ely, Windsor, Oxford, and the Royal College of Music. His music displays a lightness of touch and yet a dramatic style that was followed by later English composers. He was the first to introduce the continental flavor to English musical composition, and his influence can be found in the work of his talented student, Henry Purcell.

Humphreys, Mr [*fl.* 1791–1806], *house servant.*

Mr Humphreys (or Humphries) was cited in the Drury Lane Theatre accounts as an employee in 1791–92. With the troupe at the King's Theatre on 15 June 1792, he was listed among personnel whose benefit tickets were admitted. He was similarly noticed in the bills in subsequent years, and the accounts cited him as late as 1806. His weekly salary seems to have been £2. He was variously named a doorkeeper, a first gallery cheque taker, and a ticket taker. It seems probable that he was a son of the doorkeeper Walter Humphreys.

Humphreys, Mr [*fl. 1793–c. 1814?*], *manager, clown, actor, singer.*
A Mr Humphreys was co-manager with Jones of a circus from Edinburgh which played at York in August 1793. Humphreys served as clown to the horsemanship at the Royal Circus in London in April and May 1795. Perhaps he was the Humphreys who performed at Wheatley's Riding School in Greenwich, playing an Officer in *Douglas* and Robin in *The Waterman* on 8 June 1798 and Diggory in *She Stoops to Conquer* and Lingo in *The Agreeable Surprise* on 17 May 1799. On the first occasion Master Seabrook also performed (as will be seen, a Mr "Humphries" and a Mr Seabrook were associated some years later). On the latter occasion Humphreys joined his wife and Mr Twaits in a comic song.
At the Royal Circus on 25 April 1803, Humphreys was one of Bireno's Officers in *Louisa of Lombardy*; in November he played an Officer in *The Black Forest*; and on 18 June 1804 he played Crispin Bristle in *Haste to the Wedding*. A Mr "Humphries" was co-manager with Seabrook at Greenwich about 1814 and may have been our subject.

Humphreys, Mrs [*fl. 1798–1812?*], *actress, singer.*
At Wheatley's Riding School in Greenwich, Mrs Humphreys played Anna in *Douglas* and Wilhelmina in *The Waterman* on 8 June 1798 and Cowslip in *The Agreeable Surprise* on 17 May 1799. On the latter date she also sang a comic song with her husband and Mr Twaits. She may have been the Mrs "Humphries" who acted at Drury Lane from 1800–1801 through 1802–3 for £2 weekly and at Covent Garden from 1803–4 through 1811–12 for £4 weekly. That woman or another of the same name played at Weymouth in 1802.
Mrs Humphreys of Covent Garden was pictured in an engraving by T. Cheesman, after A. Buck, published by W. Holland in 1808;

Harvard Theatre Collection

MRS HUMPHREYS
engraving by Cheesman, after Buck

a half-length copy was published as a plate to *La Belle Assemblée* in 1813.

Humphreys, Miss [*fl. 1769*], *actress.*
Miss Humphreys, possibly the daughter of the doorkeeper Walter Humphreys, made her first appearance on 19 May 1769 at Drury Lane Theatre as Bell in *The Deuce is in Him*. That seems also to have been the only time she was mentioned in the bills.

Humphreys, John [*fl. 1663*], *trumpeter.*
John Humphreys was appointed a trumpeter extraordinary (without fee) in the King's Musick on 23 May 1663. A salaried position must not have become available, for Humphreys was not mentioned again in the Lord Chamberlain's accounts.

Humphreys, Richard d. c. 1799, *pugilist, actor.*
Henning in *Fights for the Championship* (about 1890) said that the pugilist Richard Humphreys may have been born at Clapham, the son of a general dealer, or he may have been the son of a former army officer who had

Harvard Theatre Collection

RICHARD HUMPHREYS

engraving by Young, after Hoppner

a post in the Pipe Office and died, leaving his son destitute. In any case, "the Gentleman Boxer," as he was called, fought "on a Stage at Newmarket" in 1786, according to Pierce Egan in *Boxiana* (1812). The *Public Advertiser* reported that Humphreys performed at Covent Garden Theatre on 26 December 1788 in the new pantomime *Aladdin*. After his appearance in *A Sparring Match* on 30 December, the *Town and Country Magazine* said, "This degradation of a theatre royal was properly reprobated by the audience in general." That may have been so, but though Humphreys was dropped from the bill on 5 January 1789, the sparring match entertainment continued with the equally famous pugilist Mendoza, who was paid £21 for his pains.

In September 1790 at Doncaster, Mendoza defeated Humphreys in a bout, after which "Gentleman" Humphreys retired from the ring and set himself up as a coal merchant in the Adelphi. G. O. Rickwood in the March 1951 *Notes and Queries* said that Humphreys died in affluent circumstances in 1827, but the *Monthly Mirror* of January 1799 had reported the recent death of "The once-celebrated pugilist, Humphries, for some time a coal-merchant." The *Gentleman's Magazine* in 1799 had also reported Humphreys's death and had given his address as Tudor Street, Blackfriars.

John Hoppner's painting of Humphreys in a fighting attitude was in the possession of Wilson Braddyll in 1788, the year in which an engraving by J. Young was published by the artist. Its present location is unknown to us. Another engraving by Young, after W. Whitby, was also published in 1788. The match between Humphreys and Daniel Mendoza at Odiham in Hampshire on 9 January 1788 was engraved by J. Grozer after Einsle. An anonymous engraving of Humphreys fighting Mendoza in 1790 was printed as a plate to Egan's *Boxiana* in 1812.

Humphreys, Walter [*fl.* 1757–1776], doorkeeper.

The Drury Lane doorkeeper Walter Humphreys (or Humphrys, Humphries) was named in benefit bills from as early as 20 May 1757 to as late as 17 May 1776. A paylist dated 9 February 1765 shows his salary to have been 1s. 6d. daily, or 9s. weekly. He was involved in the squabble between Colman and Harris at Covent Garden Theatre in 1768. Humphreys testified that he was a friend of Harris and that on 11 August 1768, at one in the afternoon, he accompanied Harris into the housekeeper's room at Covent Garden Theatre. They were prevented from going farther into the building by guards placed by the company housekeeper and the sheriff. Humphreys said that he believed he had prevented Harris's being struck by one or more of the defenders. It is likely that the Miss Humphreys who performed at Drury Lane in 1769 was the doorkeeper's daughter.

Humphries, Mr [*fl.* 1769–1770], actor.

Mr Humphries performed at Richmond on 1 July 1769 and appeared as Eustace in *Love in a Village* at the Haymarket Theatre on 20 September 1770.

Humphries, Mr [*fl.* 1794–1799?], actor, puppeteer?

A Mr Humphries acted Harlequin in *The Life and Death of Harlequin* at Mrs Sturmer's booth at Bartholomew Fair in 1794. Perhaps he was the Humphreys who is placed by Speaight in *The History of the English Puppet Theatre* at Bartholomew Fair from 1796 to 1799 as a puppeteer.

Humphries, Eliza [*fl.* 1797–1802], actress.

The "Young Lady" who made her first appearance at Drury Lane Theatre on 14 October 1797 as Lady Emily in *The Heiress* was identified by a manuscript note on a Kemble playbill as Miss (Eliza) Humphries, who had acted previously at the Private Theatre in Tottenham Court Road. The *Thespian Dictionary* later said that Eliza "was announced as a second Miss Farren, and . . . fell a sacrifice to the Art of Puffing." Similarly, the *Authentic Memoirs of the Green Room* felt it was extravagant to have compared Miss Humphries with Miss Farren, especially in view of the fact that Miss Humphries had a "fine figure and expressive countenance, but no taste, no voice, and her expressions [were] frequently vulgar." Nevertheless, Drury Lane kept her on at £4 weekly, and she was seen as Miss Titup in *Bon Ton* on 20 November and Angelica in *Love for Love* on 28 November.

Miss Humphries performed at Richmond in 1799, and she may have continued regularly at Drury Lane during the winters without being noticed in the bills. On 18 June 1800 she was the Marchioness Merida in *The Child of Nature*, and the Drury Lane accounts show her to have been on the paylist at £2 weekly that season. Dutton's *Dramatic Censor* of 1800 noted that she was "a lady whose name we seldom meet with in the bills. . . ." She was described as from Drury Lane when she appeared at the Lewis Theatre in the summer of 1802.

"Hungarian Twins, The" *c. 1700–c. 1722, freaks.*

Caulfield in his *Remarkable Persons* cited the *Philosophical Transactions* as his source for the following description of Hungarian twin sisters who were shown in London about 1708, when they were about eight years old:

They were united behind, from the small of the back to the parting of the legs, so that when one went forward, the other went backward; and when one stooped she lifted the other from the ground. They were very active, and one of them talked a good deal; they had not the sense of feeling in common, any where but in the parts that joined. They could read, write, and sing, very prettily; they could also speak three languages, Hungarian, High and Low Dutch, and French: and while they were here, they learned English. Their faces were very beautiful, and they were well-shaped; they loved each other with great tenderness, and one of them dying in her twenty-second year, the other did not long survive.

Hunn, Mrs Richard. *See* CANNING, MRS GEORGE.

Hunt, Mr [*fl.* 1714?], *wardrobe keeper.*

An "Inventory of Playhouse Cloaths of Chr[istopher] Rich . . . by Mr Hull & Mr Hunt" was discovered in the British Library by Sybil Rosenfeld, who conjectures it was made after Rich's death in 1714.

Hunt, Mr [*fl.* 1782], *actor.*

Mr Hunt performed an unspecified minor role in *The Taylors* at the Haymarket Theatre on 25 November 1782.

Hunt, Mrs [*fl. c.* 1673–1675], *actress.*

The Lord Chamberlain's accounts listed Mrs Hunt (sometimes, apparently incorrectly, Blunt) as a member of the King's Company from about 1673 to 1675. No roles are known for her in the public theatre, though she acted the African Woman in the court masque *Calisto* on 15 February 1675.

Hunt, Mrs [*fl.* 1704–1719], *actress.*

The actress Mrs Hunt (not to be confused with the celebrated amateur singer and lutenist Arabella Hunt, who died in 1705) was first mentioned in a play cast in 1704, when her name was listed for the role of Dolly in *The Stage Coach* in the first edition of that play. The work was performed at Lincoln's Inn Fields on 2 February that year. Similarly, the 1705 edition of *The Gamester* shows her to have acted Favourite; the work was presented at Lincoln's Inn Fields on 22 February 1705. Mrs Hunt played Prudence in a revival of *The Amorous Widow*, according to the 1706 edition of the play, and since casts for revivals about 1705 or 1706 were not always listed in the playbills, it is difficult to guess what performances she may have acted in. The work was given at the Queen's Theatre on 12 and 20 November 1705 and again the following 3 and 20 April 1706. *The London Stage* under 18 December 1699 cites the cast and suggests rightly that Mrs Hunt was probably not acting in the work that early.

Mrs Hunt's name disappeared from printed casts until 1710, when, on 25 March, she acted Jiltup in *The Fair Quaker of Deal* at Drury Lane. On 23 May she was Mrs Security in *The Gamester*, and on 6 June she played the Nurse in *Love for Love*. Again she was not listed in casts for several years. She joined John Rich's company at the new Lincoln's Inn Fields playhouse to act a schedule of fair-sized roles in the spring and summer of 1715: Lucy in *The Old Bachelor* (on 4 January) and then Jiltup in *The Fair Quaker of Deal*, Amlet in *The Confederacy*, Ruth in *The Squire of Alsatia*, Ben in *Love for Love* (for her benefit on 10 May, when she received £65 7*s*. 6*d*. in receipts, probably before house charges were subtracted), Rachel in *The City Ramble*, Jenny in *Love in a Sack*, Prate in *The Doating Lovers*, and Jacinta in *The False Count*. The following season she added such

roles as Teresa in *2 Don Quixote*, Mrs Mixum in
A Woman's Revenge, Widow Blackacre in *The
Plain Dealer*, the Aunt in *The London Cuckolds*,
Mopsa in *Presumptuous Love*, and Lady Greasy
in *The Northern Heiress*. Her benefit on 14 April
1716 brought her a poor £44 8s. 6d. before
charges.

Mrs Hunt moved to Drury Lane Theatre in
1716–17 in hopes of better luck, but the rec-
ords suggest that she did little better. On 29
October 1716 she acted Lady Faddle in *The
Country Wit*, and between then and the 1719–
20 season she added only a few new parts that
were listed in the bills: Lady Cockwood in *She
Wou'd if She Cou'd*, Sarsnet in *Three Hours after
Marriage*, Dol Troop in *The Old Troop*, Lady
Maggot in *The Scowrers*, Crowstitch in *Love for
Money*, the Nurse in *Love for Love*, Chat in *The
Committee*, Mrs Joyner in *Love in a Wood*, Cor-
sica (*recte* Corisca) in *The Bondman*, the Hostess
in *1 Henry IV*, the Landlady in *The Chances*,
and Abigail in *The Scornful Lady* (on 14 November 1719—her last recorded appearance).

A letter printed with the Dublin edition of
Gay's *Three Hours after Marriage* (reported by
Hughes in *A Century of English Farce*) relates an
anecdote concerning the fourth performance of
the work on 19 January 1717 at Drury Lane.
Colley Cibber, playing Plotwell, dressed himself in one scene as an Egyptian mummy. He
was onstage with Mrs Hunt, who played the
maid Sarsnet, when William Pinkethman, as
Plotwell's rival Underplot, made his entrance.
Trying to outdo Cibber's outdoing, as Cibber
would say, Pinkethman dressed himself as a
crocodile. The audience loved it, and in his
parade around the stage to show off his long
tail, Pinkethman inadvertantly knocked Mrs
Hunt head over heels, so that "she disclosed
more linnen than other habiliments, and more
skin and flesh than linnen: this began the first
uproar in the audience." At the following performance the audience wanted a reprise of the
comic turn, but Mrs Hunt ran off the stage in
a fright, provoking more laughter.

The Drury Lane accounts show a note from
the managers to the treasurer: "let Mrs Hunt
be reduc'd to forty Shilts per week only, from
ye . . . Nov:r 28th 1719." Mrs Willis took
over Mrs Hunt's roles in January 1720; Mrs
Hunt seems to have left the company in mid-
season, and she was not mentioned in London
casts again.

Hunt, Master   [*fl.* 1795–1809?], *actor,
dancer*.

Master Hunt performed a Cupid in the pantomime *Harlequin Invincible* at Astley's Amphitheatre, Westminster Bridge, on 22 August 1795 and probably on other dates that
year. Perhaps he was the Mr Hunt who danced
the character of Old Mause in *Highland Laddie*
at the Royal Circus, St George's Fields, on 1
and 8 June 1807 and played Lover in *Fashion's
Fools* at Sadler's Wells in 1809.

Hunt, Durant   *d. 1671*, *singer*.

Durant (or Durantius, Dubartus) Hunt was
double-cast with Gregory Thorndell as Ville-
rious in Davenant's *The Siege of Rhodes* at Rutland House in 1656. He was a member of the
Chapel Royal by the time of the coronation of
Charles II on 23 April 1661 and was mentioned, but seldom, in the Lord Chamberlain's
accounts through 10 December 1663. He died
on 23 April 1671 and was buried in the nave
of Salisbury Cathedral. His will was written
the day before he died and proved on 15 May
1671.

The will described Hunt as one of the "vic-
cars Chorall of the Cathedral Church of Sarum
in the County of Wilts . . . sicke and weake
in body." His estate was mostly bonds and bills
to the value of about £500 "in good debts
(besides suspected debts)." Hunt left bequests
to a number of people: his nephew Richard
Worme, his niece Mary Worme (Mrs William
Covey), his niece Anne Worme (Mrs Richard
Robinson)—the children of his late sister Mary
Worme; his niece Dulcebella Whitewell,
daughter of William Whitewell; his niece
Mary Hutchins and her four children—Giles,
James, John, and Mary; his godson John
Clarke, son of his nephew John Clarke; his
godson William Pope, son of Silvester Pope;
Frances Whitewell, the wife of Dr Whitewell,
and her sister Margaret Swanton; his friends
William Swanton, Lawrence Swanton, Fran-
cis Swanton, Thomas Swanton, Dr William
Whitewell, Mrs Prudence Plott, Mrs Barbara
Pinsbury, Jane Swanton (Mrs Francis Swan-
ton), and Edward Marke; Elizabeth Smedmore
(Mrs John Smedmore); Anne Vinfurbish,
widow of William Vinfurbish, of Lincoln; and
Alice Hall, wife of Edward Hall.

Hunt also left money to the poor of both
Salisbury and Chichester and to the vicars and

choirmen of Salisbury Cathedral. His residuary legatees were the children of his sister Mary Worme: Richard Worme, Mary Covey, and Ann Robinson.

Hunt, Joseph ₁ *fl. 1796–1812*₁, *pyrotechnist.*

Joseph Hunt was paid occasional sums for providing fireworks at Drury Lane Theatre between 1796 and 1809. His first payment of £2 3*s.* was on 24 December 1796. He received a total of £3 19*s.* in 1797–98, £4 11*s.* 8*d.* in 1799–1800 (in connection with *Lodoiska*), and £2 9*s.* 2*d.* in 1800–1801. Similar small amounts were paid to him in the first decade of the following century, the last of £4 16*s.* coming on 7 January 1809. In 1811–12 Hunt received small amounts for fireworks at the Lyceum. The Mrs (Ann?) Hunt who was paid £1 12*s.* on 24 December 1796 by Drury Lane for sewing canvas may have been his wife.

Hunt, Mrs ₁ **Joseph?, Ann?**₁ ₁ *fl. 1796*₁, *house servant. See* HUNT, JOSEPH.

Hunt, Mrs William, Henrietta, née Dunstall ₁ *fl. 1769–1779*₁, *actress, singer.*

Henrietta Dunstall, the daughter of the performers John Dunstall and his wife, Mary, did not, as we have mistakenly stated in her parents' notices, play Lucy in *The Beggar's Opera* at Drury Lane on 13 February 1744. Her father, who acted Lockit in that performance, was only 26 years old at the time, so even if Henrietta had been born by that date, she would have been too young for Lucy. Therefore, the listing in *The London Stage* bill of *Miss* Dunstall for that date is, we believe, an error for her mother, *Mrs* Dunstall. Indeed, Henrietta was announced—as Miss Dunstall—as making her first appearance on any stage at Covent Garden on 14 April 1769 in the singing role of Sally in *Thomas and Sally*, for her father's benefit. At the end of that year, on 6 December 1769, she married William Hunt at St Paul, Covent Garden; in the marriage register her husband was described as a bachelor of that parish and she as a spinster of the parish of St Martin-in-the-Fields.

Perhaps she then played in the provinces for several years until, announced as "A young

Gentlewoman," she returned to the London stage on 1 October 1771 to perform Leonora in *The Padlock* at Drury Lane. The prompter Hopkins recorded in his diary that night that "Mrs Hunt Daughter of Mr Dunstall made her first appearance in Leonora a tolerable Voice figure & face, So, So,—pretty well receiv'd." The critics seemed pleased enough: "making proper allowance for timidity, having never trod the stage but once for her father's benefit," thought the reviewer in *Town and Country Magazine* of that month; she "was characteristically innocent. Her person is agreeable, and her voice harmonious." The critic in the *Theatrical Review* found her voice clear and her figure "well suited to the character" and predicted that "when time has rendered her familiar to the Stage, she will amply recompence the Public for the favourable reception, and the general applause she experienced on this occasion."

Her second role was Rosetta in *Love in a Village* on 8 October 1771, when she was still advertised as "A young Gentlewoman" and Hopkins noted that she was "pretty well receiv'd." On 22 October her name finally appeared in the bills for Patty in *The Maid of the Mill*. Hopkins thought her "very Indiff[erent]," but the critic in the *Theatrical Review* judged her "very pleasing" and again predicted success after more experience. On 13 November she repeated Leonora, and on 14 December she played the title role in *Amelia*, an unsuccessful alteration by Cumberland of his *Summer's Tale*. She was seen again as Leonora on 27 May and 1 June 1772.

After a summer of playing soubrettes at Bristol, Mrs Hunt returned to Drury Lane for her second season, in which she performed in the choruses of *Romeo and Juliet*, *The Witches*, *The Elopement*, and *Macbeth* and also played Jenny in *The School for Fathers* for her benefit on 3 May 1773. That summer at the Haymarket she appeared as Patty in *The Maid of the Mill* on 20 September and then settled in at Drury Lane for a third season in 1773–74. Her early promise sensed by the *Theatrical Review* critic seems not to have blossomed, for she spent most of her on-stage time in the choruses of *Alfred*, *The Genii*, *A Christmas Tale*, *As You Like It*, and *The Heroine of the Cave*, though she performed Meriel in *The Ladies Frolick* on 15

April and 23 May and Rhodope in *A Peep Behind the Curtain* on 14 May 1774. In the summer of 1774 she played at Birmingham.

Mrs Hunt's name was not to be found in the Drury Lane bills in 1774–75, but she acted Rosetta in *Love in a Village* at Covent Garden on 28 April 1775 for her father's benefit. She returned to play with Younger's company at the King Street Theatre in Birmingham in the summer and fall of 1775, when the critic of *The Campaign* in that city wrote harshly of her, stating that Mrs Hunt was "a very, very poor capital actress. Exclusive of her voice, she has not one single grain of merit, which is a plain proof, that the best of educations and instructions are fruitless in this profession, unless when they center in a person who is ordain'd and stamp'd an actor or actress by the sovereign hand of nature." Also in the Birmingham company that summer was a Mr Hunt, who perhaps was her husband.

After playing at Bristol in the summer of 1777, Mrs Hunt made two more appearances in London, at Covent Garden: Nell in *The Devil to Pay* on 22 April 1777 and Jenny in *Lionel and Clarissa* on 28 April 1778, both times for her father's benefit. In her father's will, drawn on 29 June 1774, Henrietta had been bequeathed the proceeds from the sale of his property at Huntington, which presumably she received after his death on 31 December 1778. Her mother Mary Dunstall had died in 1758.

On 5 February 1779 the *Morning Chronicle* announced the death of Mrs Hunt, but on the next day the report was denied as "premature."

Hunter, Mr [*fl.* 1755], *house servant?*
A Mr Hunter, probably a house servant, shared in benefit tickets at Drury Lane on 15 May 1755.

Hunter, Mr [*fl.* 1774?–1805?], *actor.*
A Mr Hunter acted several times at the Haymarket Theatre in the winter season of 1783–84, when his roles were Henry in *Richard III* and Whittle in *The Irish Widow* on 15 December 1783, a principal character in *The Patriot* on 23 February 1784, Owen in *The English Merchant* on 22 March, and Pedro in *The Spanish Fryar* on 30 April. Perhaps he was the same Mr Hunter who acted Patie in *The Gentle Shep-*

herd on 12 December 1791 and Gratiano in *Othello* and Captain Loveit in *Miss in Her Teens* on 6 February 1792, also at the Haymarket.

An actor named Hunter played at Edinburgh in March 1774, at Crow Street in Dublin in 1788–89, and at Edinburgh from 1801 to 1805.

"Hunter, The English." *See* "ENGLISH HUNTER, THE."

Hunter, Mrs Maria [Susanna?, née Cooper?] [*fl.* 1774–1799], *actress.*
It is indicated by William S. Clark in *The Irish Stage in the County Towns* (1965), without documentation, that the Maria Hunter who acted in London and the provinces during the last quarter of the eighteenth century was born Maria Susanna Cooper. If so, then the actress was the authoress of *The History of Fanny Meadows. In a Series of Letters*, published in 1775 in imitation of *Pamela*.

Mrs Hunter was acting at the Theatre Royal in Shakespeare Square, Edinburgh, between January and March 1774, when she performed such substantial roles as Belvidera in *Venice Preserv'd*, Calista in *The Fair Penitent*, the title roles in *The Grecian Daughter* and *The Irish Widow*, Lady Macbeth, and Lady Randolph in *Douglas*. Also in the Edinburgh company at that time was a Mr Hunter who perhaps was her husband.

On 21 October 1774 Mrs Hunter, announced as "A Lady" making her first appearance on the English stage, acted Mrs Oakly in *The Jealous Wife* at Covent Garden Theatre. She was identified as Mrs Hunter by Hopkins in his prompter's diary. The critic in the *Westminster Magazine* for that month gave her a mixed notice:

when she has unlearned certain habits contracted on the other Stages, she is likely to become a very pleasing Actress, and to hold a respectable station. Her voice, face, and person, are much in her favour; but her mode of utterance, as well as some of her actions, is often reprehensible. Her execution in the first two Acts was not only animated, but appeared to proceed from a very just conception of the situation in which she was engaged, which was not entirely the case in the three last. The cool, sneering, and sarcastic turn she gave to her part in the third Act, is evidently opposite to the business of

Harvard Theatre Collection

MARIA HUNTER as Mrs Belville
engraving after De Wilde

the scene, and she was not fully possessed of the variety of passions in the fifth Act, though a perfect mistress of hysterics. On the whole, however, her performance gave great satisfaction, and deserved the applause it received.

Of Rosamond in *King Henry II*, her next character, on 24 October 1774, the same critic reported she had played "with approbation." At the Haymarket sometime in December 1774 she acted Belvidera in *Venice Preserv'd* and Widow Brady in *The Irish Widow* for her own benefit, concerning which she advertised her

gratitude for the "indulgence She received from the Public on her first appearance in the character of Mrs. Oakly" and begged humbly "for their protection this evening, being the last time of her performing in England this Season, She having an engagement at Dublin." (*The London Stage* does not list such a performance at the Haymarket that month.)

After performing at Smock Alley, Dublin, and Cork in 1775, Mrs Hunter returned to Covent Garden on 13 October 1775 to play Mrs Oakly once more. She was "very well received," reported one newspaper, playing the part "throughout better than it has been performed for some time at either house." Her other roles at Covent Garden that season were Roxana in *Alexander the Great*, Valeria in *The Roman Father*, the Queen in *Hamlet*, the Queen in *Richard III*, Lady Winterly in *The Man of Reason*, Goneril in *King Lear*, and Calista in *The Fair Penitent* (for her benefit on 8 May 1776).

In the summer of 1776 Mrs Hunter acted at the Theatre Royal, Liverpool, between 15 July and 16 September at a salary of £2 10*s*. per week. Because she "refused to play" the week of 20 July, her salary was withheld for that period. Though not at a London winter house in 1776–77, she was engaged by Colman for the 1777 summer season at the Haymarket. Her appearance there was delayed, however, because she went to Norwich to act between March and early May. On 3 March 1777 the committee of the Norwich Theatre voted "That on account of Mrs Cornelys's Indisposition, Mrs Hunter be engaged at one Guinea & a half p Week & a proper Allowance for her Charges in coming to perform at Norwich as long as Mr Colman can admit of her absence from the Theatre Royal in the Haymarket, with a Benefit in Course of Salaries, on her paying the usual Charges paid by the other performers." On 25 April 1777 it was ordered that she should be paid five guineas "for her Charges in coming from London to perform at this Theatre."

Mrs Hunter returned to London by 15 May 1777, when she acted Lady Alton in *The English Merchant* at the Haymarket, where also that summer she played a role in *The Nabob*, Nerissa in *The Merchant of Venice*, the Queen in *Hamlet*, Margarita in *Rule a Wife and Have a*

Wife, Lady Anne in *Richard III*, the First Constantia in *The Chances*, and Lady Brute in *The Provok'd Wife*.

By 1777 Mrs. Hunter had become the mistress of General John Hayes St Leger (1756–1800). Under the auspices of St Leger, she was introduced to Tate Wilkinson, manager of the York circuit, who brought her on as Mrs Oakly at Doncaster on 26 September 1777. In his *Wandering Patentee*, Wilkinson stated that

Mrs. Hunter had the talents of pleasing in a peculiar degree, on and *off* stage; but *on* the stage, by her time being more pleasantly occupied when off, pleasure had led her to be inattentive to a memory not of itself to be depended upon, and was a great bar to her stage success. At a table Mrs. Hunter was a woman of great good-breeding, sense, and conviviality, and knew how to *dissect* with a grace and point.

In order to oblige his "best friend" General St Leger, Wilkinson once again engaged Mrs Hunter at York for a few nights in 1779, but she did not enjoy much success. By then "she had rapidly fallen off in figure, stage-manners, voice, &c. to what she had been." She also was

Harvard Theatre Collection

MARIA HUNTER as Lady Anne
artist unknown

with Wilkinson's company at Birmingham in the summer of 1779.

The *Public Advertiser* of 28 July 1781 reported that Mrs Hunter had accompanied General St Leger to the West Indies, where he had been posted as commandant. Perhaps she did some acting there. Having returned to London in the spring of 1782, she made her first appearance in five years at Covent Garden on 17 April, as Queen Elizabeth in *The Earl of Essex*. On 30 April she acted her standby role of Mrs Oakly at Drury Lane for the benefit of Mrs Wells. The following season, 1782–83, engaged at Covent Garden for £5 per week, she played three queens—in *Hamlet*, *Richard III*, and *King Henry II*—and Paulina in *The Winter's Tale* and Lady Medway in *The Discovery*. For her benefit on 20 May 1783, when she acted Mrs Oakly, she received £170 17s. 6d., less house charges of £105. Her performance of the Queen in *Hamlet* that season was castigated by the *Public Advertiser*'s critic: "Mrs. Hunter's Queen is . . . among the very worst. Residing . . . in so polite a Place as Cleveland-Row, it is astonishing that her Manners and Deportment can be so much asunder from every thing that is so polite."

Having no permanent engagement for some years, Mrs Hunter made occasional appearances at the Haymarket, playing Clarinda in *The Suspicious Husband* on 26 April 1785 and Mrs Oakly on 9 and 29 April 1788. She played at Crow Street, Dublin, in November 1788 and at Brighton in the summer of 1789. She returned to the Haymarket to act Lady Brute in *The Humours of Sir John Brute* on 26 December 1791 and the Queen in *Richard III* on 16 April 1792. Probably she was the Mrs Hunter who was with the company at Richmond, Surrey, in the summer of 1792 playing Amelia in *Wild Oats*, Mrs Racket in *The Belle's Stratagem*, and Mrs Warren in *The Road to Ruin*.

Her activities during most of the 1790s are obscure. On 12 June 1799 she reappeared at Covent Garden Theatre to act an unspecified principal role in *Lovers' Vows* for the benefit of the General Lying-In Hospital, Bayswater, and later that summer was a member of Winston's company at Richmond. On a manuscript list of the Richmond company, now in the Richmond Reference Library, Maria Hunter's address is given as No 12, Leicester Street,

Leicester Square. The same address was advertised on the bills of a benefit she took at the Haymarket Theatre on 21 October 1799, when she was described as "late of Covent-Garden Theatre." That night she spoke the original epilogue to *Every One Has His Fault*; probably she acted in the piece, but the cast for that performance is not known.

Portraits of Mrs Hunter include:

1. By J. Roberts. Pencil drawing. In the Harvard Theatre Collection. Acquired in 1976 from Thomas Agnew, London.

2. As Mrs Belville in *The School for Wives*, a role she is not known to have acted in London. Engraving by Thornthwaite, after DeWilde. Published as a plate to *Bell's British Theatre*, 1792.

3. As Mrs Belville. By an unknown engraver, after DeWilde. Printed by C. Cook, 1808.

4. As Boadicea in *Boadicea*, a role she is not known to have acted in London. Engraving by Thornthwaite, after J. Roberts. Published as a plate to *Bell's British Theatre*, 1778.

5. As Lady Anne in *Richard III*. Watercolor by unknown artist. In the Harvard Theatre Collection.

6. As Lady Anne. By an unknown engraver. Published as a plate to Bell's *Shakespeare*, 1785.

7. As Penelope in *Ulysses*, a role she is not known to have acted in London. Engraving by Thornthwaite, after J. Roberts. Published as a plate to *Bell's British Theatre*, 1778.

Huntley, Mr ₁*fl.* 1775–1788₁, *acrobat, dancer.*

Mr Huntley was a tumbler at Sadler's Wells as early as 1 May 1775 and as late as the summer of 1788. He appeared in an unnamed pantomime at Birmingham on 27 and 30 December 1776 and served as a harlequin at Derby in early February 1777. At Derby he was advertised as coming from Sadler's Wells and Astley's riding school at the south end of Westminster Bridge. His wife appeared at Sadler's Wells as a dancer as early as 23 September 1774 and continued performing there until as late as 14 September 1787, when she figured in a dance called *Swan Hopping*.

Huntley, Mrs ₁*fl.* 1774–1787₁, *dancer.* *See* HUNTLEY, MR.

Huntley, Miss ₁*fl. c.* 1773–1795₁, *equestrienne.*

Miss Huntley was an equestrienne with Philip Astley from about 1773. A bill for Astley's Amphitheatre for 24 September 1777, her benefit night, stated that she was "the Young Lady that performs divers Feats of Activity on Horseback." At some point she performed at the Royal Circus; an undated bill in the Minet Public Library said Miss Huntley rode one or two horses, doing astonishing (but undescribed) feats at full speed. At the end of her demonstration she would "throw a Somerset from the off-side Horse to the Ground, with Elegance and Ease." She was with Hughes's circus at Stourbridge Fair in Cambridge in 1788 and rode at the Lyceum in 1795.

Huntley, Miss ₁*fl.* 1790–1791₁, *singer, actress.*

Miss Huntley made her stage debut as a singer in the new pantomime *The Picture of Paris* at Covent Garden Theatre on 20 December 1790. On 26 February 1791 she played Polly in *The Woodman*. Her salary was £2 weekly.

Huntley, John ₁*fl.* 1794₁, *singer.*

Doane's *Musical Directory* of 1794 listed John Huntley, Junior, of No 2p10, Narrow Well, Lambeth, as a bass who sang for the Choral Fund. Nothing is known of the senior John Huntley.

Hurd. *See* HEARD.

Huri, Signor ₁*fl.* 1777₁, *acrobat.*

On 23 September 1777 Signor Huri joined some fellow acrobats in an "Exhibition of Egyptian Pyramids" at Astley's Amphitheatre.

Hurrell, Thomas ₁*fl.* 1734–1768?₁, *actor, manager.*

Cecil Price in *The English Theatre in Wales* records that Thomas Hurrell and his wife Elizabeth managed a company of strolling players at Booth Hall, Gloucester, in September 1734. In 1741 the couple were members of Jones's troupe at Cardigan, but Thomas, Elizabeth, and four other players bolted on 8 May of that year and formed a new troupe, headed by Morison. They performed at Cardigan, Carmarthen, Llandilo, Llandovery, Hay, Crickowell, Abergavenny, and Caerleon, sometimes to pitifully small houses. The Hurrells left the troupe after 12 June.

It seems most likely that the Mr "Hurrel" who acted the Fryar in *The Rival Queens* "Intermixed with a Comic called A Wife Well Manag'd" at Tottenham Court on 4 August 1741 was Thomas. A. S. Brown's manuscript list of players at Norwich places Thomas Hurrell there in 1742–43. Hurrell seems to have been a member of Whitley's company in the 1760s, and when John Cunningham's *Poems* were published in 1766 Thomas Hurrell "comedian" was one of the subscribers.

On 14 April 1768 a "Gentleman" acted Campley in *The Funeral* at Drury Lane; Latreille identified the player as a Mr Hurrell, and it is certainly possible that he was Thomas. But Latreille transcribed the bill as saying the gentleman was making his first appearance on any stage (*The London Stage* records it as "1st appearance on the stage"), so unless the playbill lied, the actor may have been a different Hurrell.

Hursfall. *See also* HORSFALL.

Hursfall, Mr ₁*fl. 1761*₁, *barber.*

Mr Hursfall was cited in the Covent Garden accounts on 25 April 1761 as the company barber; he was paid £2 1s. 6d. for work done for Mr Sodi's new dance.

Hurst, Mr ₁*fl. 1794*₁, *serpent player.*

A Mr Hurst, living in Petty France, Westminster, was listed in Doane's *Musical Directory* of 1794 as a member of the first regiment of guards and a player on the serpent in the Oxford Meeting of 1793 and the Handelian performances in Westminster Abbey.

Hurst, Miss ₁*fl. 1778?–1781*₁, *actress.*

A Miss Hurst, announced as making her first appearance on that stage, acted Leanthe in a revival of *Love and a Bottle* at the Haymarket Theatre on 26 March 1781. She appeared again at the Haymarket on 16 October 1781, as Louisa in *The Artifice.*

Perhaps she was the Miss Hurst who was a member of Joseph Austin's provincial company in 1778 and performed at Chester in September 1779. It is unlikely that she was the Miss Hurst who acted many leading roles at Edinburgh in 1780–81; the latter actress was performing in Edinburgh during the period that our subject was in London in March 1781. Both Misses Hurst may have been related to the actors Mr and Mrs Richard Hurst and the dancer T. Hurst.

Hurst, Richard *d. 1805, actor, manager, dancer?*

Richard Hurst, whose career in London and the provinces lasted some 48 years, made his first appearance on the stage, announced as a young gentleman who had never appeared before, at Covent Garden Theatre on 26 October 1754 as Tressel in *Richard III.* Next he acted Paris in *Romeo and Juliet* on 20 November; during the remainder of that season he appeared in only two roles: an Aedile in *Coriolanus* on 10 December and Young Rakish in *The Schoolboy* on 9 May 1755, when he shared benefit tickets with several other minor performers.

Perhaps it was Thomas Sheridan, the Irish actor-manager and player of the leading roles in the first three plays in which Hurst had appeared at Covent Garden, who recommended young Hurst's engagement to Victor and Sowden at Smock Alley, Dublin, for the 1755–56 season. Hurst seems to have arrived in Dublin in mid-December 1755, so it is possible that he was the Mr "Hust" whose name had appeared in the bills as one of the performers in Noverre's grand ballet, *The Chinese Festival*, which had had a tumultuous opening at Drury Lane on 8 November 1755. After several attempts to perform *The Chinese Festival* in the face of rioting anti-French audiences, Garrick gave up the piece on 18 November. Also named as a dancer in the bills for that ballet was a Master "Hust"; he was perhaps the Master T. Hurst who was at Drury Lane in subsequent years. While it is likely that Richard Hurst was related to T. Hurst, we doubt that Richard would have been old enough in 1755 to have been the young dancer's father. They may have been brothers. When Richard Hurst went to Dublin in December 1755, where he was engaged for at least five seasons, Master T. Hurst remained in London.

In any event, Richard Hurst was acting at

Smock Alley by 19 December 1755. Little is known of his performances that season, but in 1756–57 at Smock Alley, then again under Thomas Sheridan's management, Hurst acted the Constable in *The Recruiting Officer*, Simon in *The Suspicious Husband*, Dr Bolus in *The Double Gallant*, Tybalt in *Romeo and Juliet*, Steward in *The Twin Rivals*, Don Felix in *The Wonder*, Corrigidor in *She Wou'd and She Wou'd Not*, Othman in *Barbarossa*, Stanmore in *Oroonoko*, Fenton in *The Merry Wives of Windsor*, The Duke in *Rule a Wife and Have a Wife*, Montano in *Othello*, and Fabian in *The Fatal Marriage*.

In his third season at Smock Alley, 1757–58, Hurst acted some 30 roles, the most important of which were Orlando in *As You Like It*, Sealand in *The Conscious Lovers*, Horatio in *The Fair Penitent*, Claudius in *Hamlet*, Don Felix in *The Wonder*, Duncan in *Macbeth*, Antonio in *The Merchant of Venice*, and Angelo in *Measure for Measure*. From the calendar of that theatre presented in Esther Sheldon's *Thomas Sheridan of Smock Alley*, it is evident that Hurst was resident and busy throughout the season. According to Dorothy Eshelman's introduction to her edition of *The Committee Books of the Theatre Royal Norwich*, when the new theatre in Chapel Field opened on 31 January 1758 with *The Way of the World*, Richard Hurst was serving as acting manager for the Norwich builder and proprietor Thomas Ivory. On that night, however, Hurst was acting Phoenix in *The Distrest Mother* at Smock Alley and, according to Sheldon's calendar, continued to perform there in February and March. Another Hurst, perhaps related, was the manager at Norwich from 1758 to May 1763. Richard Hurst, meanwhile, played at Cork in the summer of 1758 and was back at Smock Alley in 1758–59 and then was a member of the Crow Street Theatre company in 1759–60.

In 1765–66, Richard Hurst joined the Drury Lane company, appearing there on 22 October 1765 as Cornwall in *King Lear*. That season at Drury Lane he also acted the Doctor in *Macbeth*, Heli in *The Mourning Bride*, Sir Charles in *The Foundling*, Page in *The Merry Wives of Windsor*, Vizard in *The Constant Couple*, Pisanio in *Cymbeline*, and Lysimachus in *The Rival Queens*. On 3 May 1766, when he played Colonel Blunt in *The Committee*, he shared a benefit with Moody and Mrs Dorman. That

summer Hurst acted for Foote at the Haymarket: Gargle in *The Apprentice*, Sullen in *The Beaux' Stratagem*, and unspecified roles in *The Orators*, *The Commissary*, and *A Woman Is a Riddle*. In the second half of the summer season of 1766 he joined Barry's competing company at the King's Theatre, where he played Lodovico in *Othello*, Renault in *Venice Preserv'd*, Friar Lawrence in *Romeo and Juliet*, Cornwall in *King Lear*, Manly in *The Provok'd Husband*, Acasto in *The Orphan*, Sealand in *The Conscious Lovers*, Adam in *As You Like It*, Sciolto in *The Fair Penitent*, and Leontine in *Theodosius*.

Hurst returned to Drury Lane in 1766–67 at a salary of 6s. 8d. per day, or £2 per week. Among the roles he added to his repertoire were Orasmin in *Zara*, Antonio in *Much Ado about Nothing*, Herbis in *The Siege of Damascus*, Traverse in *The Clandestine Marriage*, Hotman in *Oroonoko*, Gratiano in *Othello*, a Citizen in *King John*, and Norfolk in *Richard III*. On 13 May 1767, when he played Macduff in *Macbeth*, Hurst shared a benefit deficit of £4 6s. 6d. with Tassoni and Mrs Dorman. About that time, in his *Thespis*, Kelly wrote that Hurst had talent for portraying the physical infirmities of old age, but he spoiled all by bellowing so.

In the spring of 1767, Hurst engaged in an obscure contention with Sir Edward Littleton that disturbed Garrick greatly. On 7 April 1767 Garrick wrote to his brother George that Littleton had received some scandalous letters which he thought could be traced to "our Hurst." Having promised Littleton his assistance, Garrick asked his brother to call on Sir Edward but to say nothing to Hurst—"I believe Hurst is a Tartar." By 28 April, Garrick had found out more, and he wrote to George that "Sir Edward Lyttleton's affair shocks me: I long to know the event. Hurst must be discharged—what a villain! Pray let me know the whole in your next." George's reply has not survived, but on 4 May, David, who then knew more, warned his brother, "For Heaven's sake! say not one word about Hurst's affair."

Though Garrick had been shocked by Hurst's mysterious and scandalous behavior, the actor was not, as the manager had declared he must be, discharged. On the contrary, Hurst remained engaged at Drury Lane throughout the rest of Garrick's management, which ended after 1775–76, and also into the first four years of Sheridan's, through 1779–80. He labored nightly as an actor of little consequence in dozens of modest tertiary roles but occasionally was brought on in a more substantial part. He acted Cymbeline on 10 October 1767 and then played that role in subsequent revivals over the years. He was also often seen as Thorowgood in *The London Merchant*, Antonio in *The Tempest*, Pedro in *The Spanish Fryar*, and Ascanio in *The Law of Lombardy*. On 5 May 1769 he played in *The Tempest* for a benefit "By Desire of the most noble Grand of the Honorable Order of Select Albions, for their Brother Hurst."

For a benefit he shared with Rooker on 3 May 1771, Hurst played Jarvis in *The Gamester* and Sturgeon in *The Mayor of Garratt*, both for the first time. When he shared £155 5s. in net benefit receipts with Rooker on 16 May 1772, he acted O'Flaherty in *The West Indian* for the first time, and Hopkins noted in his prompter's diary, "not enough upon the Brogue." Other roles he played for the first time at Drury Lane included Major Oakly in *The Jealous Wife* on 30 March 1773, Sciolto in *The Fair Penitent* on 4 May 1773, Sterling in *The Clandestine Marriage* on 21 December 1773, Ventidius in *All for Love* on 28 April 1774, Aubrey in *The Fashionable Lover* on 6 May 1775, and Claudius in *Hamlet* on 30 October 1779. Hurst's salary in 1776–77 was still £2 per week. He lived in a house at No 374, the Strand, in May 1778; at No 368, the Strand (opposite Norfolk Street), in May 1779; and at More's, the pastry cook, the east end of the New Church, the Strand, in April 1780.

In "Poetical Essays" in the *Gentleman's Magazine* for January 1772, where the performers of Drury Lane were briefly sketched in an alphabetical catalogue, Hurst was referred to as an actor long respected by the town. But the same year, Francis Gentleman in *The Theatres* described him as "a laborious, imitative drudge," whose acting was "Discordant, stiff, nay everything that's bad, / An heap of Mossop's errors, quite run mad." In a list of the "Alphabetical Characters" of performers found in a British Library press clipping dated 16 April 1777, Hurst was condemned for his bawling, ranting, and staring. Another press clipping, from 13 November 1777, alluded to his lack of spirit in acting and the fact that he had compensated by "lately" becoming a wine

merchant, an occupation he must have followed on the side while he kept up his full schedule at Drury Lane. Hurst suffered an accident on 18 April 1776 while representing Posthumous in *The Jubilee*; engaged in the fighting scene with Palmer, who played Jachimo, Hurst received a severe wound in the temple, narrowly escaping the loss of his eye.

During the summer of 1771 Hurst had become joint manager of the Canterbury Theatre with Dimond. In 1773 Hurst enlarged the theatre, which was located over the butter market, but the season was such a financial disaster that, according to a letter Charles Mate wrote to James Winston some years later, in 1803 (letter now in the Birmingham Public Library), "poor Hurst was oblig'd to fly by night." However, according to a clipping in the British Library dated 13 November 1777, Hurst was still (or again) managing at Canterbury in the summer of 1777.

After the 1779–80 season, Hurst either left his engagement at Drury Lane or it was terminated by the managers. In 1780 he neglected his payment to the retirement fund of that theatre, to which he had subscribed £1 1s., beginning in 1766. He had, in fact, been one of the committee of Drury Lane actors established, on 18 May 1774, to make rules and orders for the fund's operation, and he had signed the citation given to Garrick by the members of the fund.

Hurst passed the rest of the century as a provincial performer. He played at Cork and Kilkenny in the summers of 1780 and 1781. Between 1781–82 and 1783–84 he was at the Crow Street Theatre and in 1784–85 at Smock Alley. In April 1786 Hurst was imitated as Cymbeline by G. A. Stevens at Leeds. Hurst acted at Manchester in 1787 and 1788, in various Irish towns from 1784 through 1795, and again at Crow Street in 1791–92 and in the summer of 1794.

By the autumn of 1801 Hurst was acting with the Liverpool company, when he received £104 at his benefit. In December 1802 his Liverpool benefit brought him £173, at which time the *Monthly Mirror* described him as an "old man, in bad state of health." He died at his lodgings in Castle Street, Liverpool, on 21 January 1805. In his brief obituary, the *Gentleman's Magazine* of that month remembered him as one "who, for upwards of 40 years, performed as an actor on the London and Liverpool theatres." That year the *Thespian Dictionary* claimed that while acting in Ireland in his later years, Hurst's "abilities were even below mediocrity."

Hurst's wife did not perform in London, but she was acting with him at Crow Street in 1781–82, 1782–83, and 1791–92 and in various Irish towns in the early 1790s. She was probably the Mrs Hurst who had acted at Coopers' Hall, Bristol, from November 1772 to April 1773 and with Austin's company at Chester in June 1770 and September 1775. The dancer T. Hurst, who performed in London between 1755 and 1782, and the actress Miss Hurst, who played at the Haymarket in 1781, may have been their children or were otherwise related. Richard Hurst may also have been related to Benjamin Hurst Newton, who performed in London in the 1770s and 1780s and was, according to Everard, the uncle of the famous dancer Nancy Dawson.

Hurst, ₁Robert?₁ ₁*fl.* 1724₁, *performer?*

A Mr Hurst received a benefit at Lincoln's Inn Fields Theatre on 25 April 1724. Receipts came only to £35 5s., apparently before house charges. Perhaps Hurst was a performer, or he may have been Robert Hurst, whose play *The Roman Maid* was performed at Lincoln's Inn Fields on 11 August 1724.

Hurst, T. ₁*fl.* 1755?–1782₁, *dancer, actor.*

The first appearance in London of the dancer T. Hurst was marked by two misfortunes. First, his name was incorrectly spelled in the bills as Master "Hust," and, second, his debut occurred at Drury Lane on 8 November 1755 in Noverre's ballet *The Chinese Festival*, an entertainment which provoked the anti-French London public to riot. After several attempts to perform it before tempestuous audiences who tore up his theatre, Garrick was obliged to withdraw the piece on 18 November. Also named in the bills for *The Chinese Festival* was a Mr "Hust," who was perhaps Richard Hurst and may have been the brother of the younger dancer, since Richard himself was, we believe, too young to have been the father. When Richard Hurst went to Dublin in December 1755,

where he played for at least five seasons, Master Hurst remained in London.

Over the next several seasons, Master Hurst seems to have performed infrequently. He was one of the children in the cast of Garrick's new farce called *Lilliput*, which opened at Drury Lane on 3 December 1756 and had several other performances that season. On 31 October 1757 Master Hurst's name was advertised in the bills for one of the pantomime characters in *The Farmer Trick'd*, performed by children at the Haymarket Theatre. He was Puff in performances of *Miss in Her Teens* given by children at Drury Lane on 5 and 20 April 1759.

By 1764–65, still called Master Hurst, he was a regular member of the Drury Lane dancing chorus, earning in that season 2s. 6d. per day, or 15s. per week. On 4 February 1765 he played an unspecified role in James Townley's farce, *The Tutor*, which was, according to Benjamin Victor, ill-received the first night and damned the next. Master Hurst's name appeared on the Drury Lane paylist in 1766–67 for 3s. 4d. per day, or £1 per week, but no roles for him are known.

On 26 December 1768, then called Mr Hurst, he appeared as the Milk Woman in the first performance of *The Elopement*, a pantomime in which he performed many times that season and the next. On 10 October 1768, the character of the Milk Woman was specified for "T. Hurst."

Though his name appeared on no more bills, Hurst, it seems, was dancing in the choruses at Drury Lane through 1774–75 and perhaps in 1775–76. In 1775 he subscribed 10s. 6d. to the Drury Lane Fund but neglected his payment in 1776. The Hurst who appeared frequently as one of the Spirits in *A Christmas Tale* at Drury Lane in 1776–77 was probably not the dancer, but Richard Hurst.

At Covent Garden on 4 May 1779, Master Davies, described as a scholar to Hurst, made his first appearance in public dancing a hornpipe at the end of Act IV of *The Comedy of Errors*. On 25 November 1782 Hurst danced in the pantomime-burlesque *The Taylors* at the Haymarket Theatre and then was not heard of again.

Miss Hurst, who performed at the Haymarket in 1781, and another Miss Hurst, who

acted at Edinburgh in 1781, may have been
related to him.

Hurt. *See* HART.

Hus, Mons [*fl. 1779–1787*], *dancer,
ballet master.*

Monsieur "Huss" is included among the
dancers at the King's Theatre in 1779–80 in
a manuscript list found in the Burney papers
at the British Library. He is described as one
of the first dancers, *demi-caractères*. Probably he
was the same Hus who was ballet master at the
King's Theatre in 1786–87. New ballets created by him then were an untitled allegorical
ballet on 20 January 1787, *La Fête provençale*
and *La Bergère capricieuse* on 8 March, *Sylvie* on
22 March, and *Le Cossac jaloux* for his benefit
on 17 May 1787, when tickets could be had of
him at No 80, Haymarket.

Almost certainly he was one of many dancers
named Hus from Belgium or France who were
active throughout the eighteenth century, but
there is no way of telling which one might be
the dancer who came to London. Fuchs lists
many of them in his *Lexique*, and Marian Hannah Winter gives details of some of their careers in *The Pre-Romantic Ballet* (1974).

Two other performers named Hus danced at
the King's Theatre in the 1786–87 season.
"Hus Sen[ior]" danced the role of the Father of
Zemira in *Zemira and Azor* on 13 February
1787; in that ballet a Mlle Hus danced a Slave
to Sander.

Hus, Mons [*fl. 1787*], *dancer. See* HUS,
MONS [*fl. 1779–1787*].

Hus, Mlle [*fl. 1787*], *dancer. See* HUS,
MONS [*fl. 1779–1787*].

Husband, Benjamin 1672–1756, *actor.*
Chetwood in his *General History* said that
Benjamin Husband was born in January 1672
in Pembrokeshire. "He fell in Love with the
Tragic Muse very young, but dangled after the
Drama full two Years, sighing, at great Ex-
pence, before he was suffered to declare his
Passion publicly." Sometime before December
1694, if Chetwood was correct,

he gained Permission to personate Sir *Walter Ralegh*
in the *Earl of Essex* [*The Unhappy Favorite*]; but he
came off so well, that, the following Pay Day, he
received a Week's Salary, the usual Stipend of young
Actors (Ten Shillings a Week); but, unluckily, the
Death of good Queen Mary put a Stop to their
Acting for near Six Months. However, when Per-
mission was given to open the Theatres again, Mr.
Husband soon gained better Parts, and a larger
Salary.

The London Stage contains no record of *The
Unhappy Favorite* being performed in 1694,
nor, indeed, have we any other record of Husband's activity that year.

The Lord Chamberlain's accounts reveal that
Husband was a member of the United Company as of 22 February 1695 and that during
the summer of 1696 he was twice sued for debt
by two different glovers. In the fall of that year
he was with Betterton's troupe at the Lincoln's
Inn Fields playhouse. There he acted Alonso
in *Rule a Wife and Have a Wife* in October. On
the twenty-eighth of that month he was discharged for some reason, but the order was
canceled. Before the end of 1696, however,
Husband left London.

Thomas Doggett was responsible for rec-
ommending Benjamin to the Dublin theatre
manager Joseph Ashbury, and, with Theophilus Keene and (according to Chetwood) Joseph
Trefusis, Husband moved to Ireland. Of his
work in Dublin between 1696 and 1700 we
know little. John Dunton mentioned Husband
in *A Tour in Ireland* in the spring of 1698 as
being among the Smock Alley players who
were "no way inferior to those in London," but
we know of no roles he played.

He was back with Betterton's troupe at Lincoln's Inn Fields in London for the 1700–1701
season. He acted the small role of Tygranes in
The Double Distress in March 1701, Count
Baldwin (Kynaston's old role) in *The Fatal
Marriage* on 24 April, and Edmund in *King
Lear* on 19 May (the last two roles are mentioned in manuscript notes in British Library
copies of the plays). Husband may also have
performed in *King Lear* on 27 January 1701—
the copy has both dates. He acted Zama in
Tamerlane about December 1701, but a year
later he moved to Drury Lane, and in November and December 1702 he acted there Don
Alphonso in *All for the Better*, Don Philip in

the first performance of *She Wou'd and She Wou'd Not*, Lorenzo in *The Patriot*, and Richmore in *The Twin Rivals*. The scanty records of the time show no other parts for him in 1702–3, but we may guess that he acted regularly in roles of some importance. Similarly, in 1703–4 he doubtless acted frequently, though we know only of his playing Albovade in *The Faithful Bride*.

Christopher Rich, the Drury Lane manager, complained in December 1704 that Husband was being wooed by the rival Queen's Theatre management. He was certainly at the Queen's in 1705–6 and is known to have played Antinous in *Ulysses* on 23 November 1705. After that he was seen as Don Lorenzo in *The Mistake*, the Viceroy of Sweden in *The Revolution of Sweden*, Florestan in *The British Enchanters*, probably a role in *Oedipus* at his benefit on 11 April 1706, and Bellmour in *Adventures in Madrid*. Husband continued at the Queen's Theatre in 1706–7, adding such new parts as Glendower in *1 Henry IV*, Decius Brutus in *Julius Caesar*, Hemskirk in *The Royal Merchant*, Cromwell in *Henry VIII*, Vizard in *The Constant Couple*, and Winwife in *Bartholomew Fair*.

At the Queen's in the first half of the 1707–8 season he added, among other parts, Orbellan in *The Indian Emperor*, Sir Charles Freeman in *The Stratagem*, and Seward in *Macbeth* and, at Drury Lane during the last half of the season, Dervise in *Tamerlane* and Scandal in *Love for Love*. In 1708–9 at Drury Lane, Husband tried such new parts as Horatio in *Hamlet*, Burleigh in *The Unhappy Favorite*, Cassio in *Othello*, Dowglass in *1 Henry IV*, and Diomedes in *Troilus and Cressida*. On 10 May 1709 he signed a five-year contract that provided him with an annual salary of £65, a benefit each April with house charges of £50, and vacations from 10 June to 10 September each year—but the agreement may have been canceled when the actors went back to the Queen's in the fall of 1709.

Husband continued in many of his old parts in 1709–10 at the Queen's Theatre and added such roles as the Elder Worthy in *Love's Last Shift* and Claudius in *Hamlet*. In the summer of 1710 he appeared at Pinkethman's theatre in Greenwich in such new characters as Pierre in *Venice Preserv'd*, Antonio in *The Tempest*, Banquo in *Macbeth*, and Brazen in *The Recruiting Officer*. Husband and his fellow players began

the 1710–11 season at the Queen's, but by the end of November the actors had returned to Drury Lane, and the prosperous years of group management and company stability began. Husband remained at Drury Lane through 1713–14, playing, for the most part, roles he had offered before. Very few appearances were recorded for him his last two seasons, and in 1713–14 we know only that he acted Catesby at the first performance of *Jane Shore* on 2 February 1714 and, for his shared benefit with Boman on 17 May, Apemantus in *Timon of Athens*.

On 3 January 1715 Husband appeared as Castalio in *The Orphan* at the new Lincoln's Inn Fields playhouse, and there he continued acting through 1717–18. He was seen in several of his old parts plus Vainlove in *The Old Bachelor*, Constant in *The Provok'd Wife*, Biron in *The Fatal Marriage*, Vasquez in *The Indian Emperor*, Blandford in *Oroonoko*, and Horatio in *The Wife's Relief*. During his summers he may have made excursions to Ireland, for Chetwood claimed that Husband settled there in 1713— an error, we would guess, for 1718, but possibly indicative of Husband's continuing interest in the Dublin theatre.

Company lists and surviving playbills gathered by the late William Smith Clark show that Husband acted at the Smock Alley Theatre from 1720–21 through 1732–33, at the Ransford Street Theatre from 1733–34 through 1735–36, at Smock Alley again from 1736–37 through 1742–43 with the exception of 1739–40, at the Aungier Street playhouse in 1743–44 and 1745–46—and for the United Company in the two seasons between. Clark's lists show him as at Smock Alley again from 1746–47 through 1754–55 with the exceptions of 1751–52 and 1752–53. But he may have played seldom or not at all in those final years and perhaps was only given annual benefits. The last record we have of his acting was his performance of Sir John in *The Conscious Lovers* at Aungier Street on 12 March 1744. A few roles in Dublin are known for him: Constant in *The Provok'd Wife*, Scandal in *Love for Love*, Belvil in *The Rover*, Guiscardo in *The Rival Generals*, Ben and Sir John in *The Conscious Lovers*, Don Philip in *She Wou'd and She Wou'd Not*, Dion in *Philaster*, Cassander in *The Rival Queens*, Valentine in *Love for Love*, Hearty in *The Contrivances*, Hemskirk in *The Royal*

Merchant, the Attorney in *The Squire of Alsatia*, the King in *1 Henry IV*, and Heartwell in *The Old Bachelor*.

On 9 November 1741 a Mr "Husbands" acted Blunt in *The London Merchant* at the James Street Theatre in London. Possibly that actor was Benjamin, though he was in the Smock Alley Company during the 1741–42 season. Who was the Master Husband—Benjamin's son?—who had played Tom Thumb in *The Tragedy of Tragedies* at Smock Alley on 4 February 1737?

Benjamin Husband's Smock Alley benefit on 19 March 1746 was a special one: he was advertised as "the oldest actor now living . . . and as such the Father of the Stage," and David Garrick performed for him. Two days later Husband printed a note of gratitude:

I do hereby return my most humble thanks to the numerous and polite audience who favoured my Benefit Play the 19th Instant. And I must ever acknowledge Mr. Garrick's free and generous offer to play Sir Harry Wildair for me; to whose eminent talents as an actor I am so much indebted for the success of it.

Despite his age Husband must have been remarkably spry: on 8 January 1747 he was set upon by footpads in Marlborough Street but made such stout resistance that he got clear of them. His last benefit was years later, on 21 May 1755 at Smock Alley, when Spranger Barry performed for him. *Faulkner's Dublin Journal* reported that Benjamin Husband died on 20 September 1756.

Husband, John   [*fl.* 1794],   *singer.*
John Husband of Philadelphia was listed in Doane's *Musical Directory* of 1794 as an alto singer who had participated in the oratorios at Covent Garden and Westminster Abbey and had been a member of the Cecilian Society.

Husband, William   [*fl.* 1794],   *singer.*
William Husband of Philadelphia was listed in Doane's *Musical Directory* of 1794 as a tenor who had sung for the Cecilian Society and in the Handel performances at Westminster Abbey.

Husbands, Charles   *d. 1678, singer.*
Charles Husbands, a countertenor, was sworn a Gentleman of the Chapel Royal on 14 March 1664. Husbands was described as from Windsor and a "probacōner, &c." He attended the King at Windsor in May, June, and July 1671 for 8*s*. daily, but his musical activity is otherwise unknown. Husbands died at Windsor on 26 March 1678. The Charles Husbands who was a Chapel boy in the 1680s may have been his son.

Husbands, Charles   [*fl.* 1685–1687], *singer.*
At the coronation of James II on 23 April 1685 Charles Husbands marched among the Children of the Chapel Royal. By 23 November 1687 his voice had broken, and he was awarded a suit of clothes and an allowance of £20 for one year as a former Chapel boy. He may have been the son of the singer of the same name who died in 1678.

Huss. *See* HUS.

Hussey, Mr   [*fl.* 1732–1739],   *singer.*
A Mr Hussey sang the role of Gozanes in *Teraminta* at Lincoln's Inn Fields Theatre on 20, 23, and 30 November 1732 and the Priest of Baal in Handel's oratorio *Deborah* at Covent Garden Theatre on 28 March 1735. The following season at Lincoln's Inn Fields he appeared as Charles in Henry Ward's new ballad opera *The Happy Lovers* on 31 March 1736. At the same theatre he sang in the choruses of *King Arthur* on 28 September 1736 and *Harlequin Shipwrecked* on 21 October 1736. On 16 January 1739, Hussey sang the role of the Apparition of Samuel in Handel's *Saul* at the King's Theatre.

Hussey, Mr   p6[*fl.* 1743–1746],   *house servant?*
A Mr Hussey, probably a house servant, shared in benefit tickets at Lincoln's Inn Fields Theatre on 3 June 1743 and at Drury Lane Theatre on 21 May 1744 and 22 April 1746.

Hussey, Mr   [*fl.* 1794],   *violinist, dancing master.*
A Mr Hussey, of Clapton, was listed in Doane's *Musical Directory* (1794) as a violinist and dancing master.

Hussey, Abraham [fl. 1745–1780], actor, dancer, booth proprietor.

Most of the career of Abraham Hussey was spent as the proprietor of theatrical booths at the London and provincial fairs. At Hussey's Booth at May Fair in 1745, he presented *Jane Shore*, *The Adventures of Harlequin*, and *The Merry Cobler of Preston*, but no casts were listed in the advertisements. Using the familiar concert formula, he and Phillips gathered a company to play *The Prodigal Son* and *The Harlot's Progress* at Goodman's Fields Theatre on 1 May 1746 and at least nine other times that month. At the New Wells, Shepherd's Market, near Piccadilly, on 28 July 1746 Hussey acted Scrub in *The Stratagem* and Hob in *Flora*. The event was a benefit for his wife, but her function as a performer, if any, is not known. In August of the same summer Hussey operated a booth in the George Inn Yard, Smithfield, at which was performed "An Historical Piece" by Shakespeare and *The Schemes of Harlequin*. The following month at Southwark Fair he and Phillips operated at the "New Theatre" on the Bowling Green.

Hussey subsequently opened booths in the George Inn Yard, Smithfield, in August 1747, at Bartholomew Fair in August 1748 and 1749, and at Southwark Fair in September 1753. He took a benefit at Goodman's Fields Theatre on 3 March 1747 but his role is unknown. At Stourbridge Fair, near Cambridge, in 1748 and 1749, Hussey exhibited "Drollery and Fireworks." He performed again in London, on 3 September 1755 as the Clown in *The Drunken Peasant*, a dance performed at the Haymarket Theatre.

On 26 December 1757, Hussey danced Mlle Ragonsby in *Le Carnevale de Venice* at the Haymarket. Playing the Clown in the same production was his son, John Hussey, who as Master Hussey had begun his career at the Haymarket in the summer of 1757. Abraham Hussey seems not to have appeared again in London until 2 September 1780, when he was the Clown in *The Genius of Nonsense* at the Haymarket, announced as making his first appearance on any stage in 20 years. Although his first name was not given on the bills, that Mr Hussey could not have been John, for the latter had continued to perform in London during the 1770s.

Abraham Hussey was probably the Mr Hussey who advertised in the *General Advertiser* on 4 May 1752 the renting-out of masquerade costumes at the Two Green Lamps, near Exeter Exchange in the Strand.

Hussey, Mrs Abraham [fl. 1746], performer?

The wife of the actor and booth proprietor Abraham Hussey was given a benefit at the New Wells, Shepherd's Market, on 28 July 1746, at which time her husband performed Scrub in *The Stratagem* and Hob in *Flora*. No roles for Mrs Hussey are known, but presumably she performed in or assisted with her husband's enterprises.

Hussey, John [fl. 1757–1778], dancer, ballet master, actor.

Although he may have performed with his father's troupe in the provinces, John Hussey, the son of Abraham Hussey, was first noticed in London bills on 17 June 1757 at the Haymarket Theatre, when, called Master Hussey, he danced in the comic ballet *The Marine Boys Marching to Portsmouth* and performed the Clown in a Lilliputian production of *Harlequin's Frolics*. As Master Hussey he appeared in the same pieces on 5 July and played Pierrot in *Harlequin's Maggot* on 22 August 1757.

Several months later, on 31 October 1757, he played in *The Farmer Trick'd* at the Haymarket. At the same theatre on 26 December 1757, now in his majority, he was called, incorrectly, T. Hussey in the role of Harlequin in the ballet *Le Carnevale de Venice*, in which his father performed Mlle Ragonsby. On 6 January 1758 his name was corrected to J. Hussey. He next danced at the Haymarket on 2 June 1760.

In 1760–61 Hussey was engaged as a chorus dancer at Covent Garden at a salary of £35 for the season. He made his first appearance there on 11 December 1760 in *Comus* and then danced as a Hussar in *The Hungarian Gambols* on 9 March 1761 and in *The Painter in Love with his Picture* on 8 May 1761.

Hussey continued as a utility dancer at Covent Garden through 1774–75 and also served for some time as a ballet master. His salary in 1767–68 was 5s. per night, or £1 10s. per week. He signed his full name to a letter from the Covent Garden performers to George Colman which was printed in the *Theatrical Monitor* on 5 November 1768. On 19 May 1768 he had married a Miss Griffith at St Martin-in-the-Fields.

After the season 1774–75, Hussey's appointment at Covent Garden was not renewed. His next and last notice was on 8 September 1778, when he shared in benefit tickets at the conclusion of the summer season at the Haymarket.

Hussey, Matthew ₁*fl.* *1739–1763*₁, *organist.*

Matthew Hussey was one of the original subscribers to the Royal Society of Musicians when it was established on 28 August 1739. In 1763 a Matthew Hussey, an organist of Newington Butts, was listed in *Mortimer's London Directory*.

Hussey, T. *See* HUSSEY, JOHN.

Hust. *See* HURST.

Hutchinson, Mr *c.1606–1682. See* BEESTON, WILLIAM.

Hutchinson, Mr ₁*fl.* *1783–1785*₁, *dresser. See* HUTCHINSON, F.

Hutchinson, Mr ₁*fl.* *1795*₁, *boxkeeper.*
A bill for Handy's circus at the Lyceum, dated 10 February 1795, instructed patrons to apply for box tickets from Mr Hutchinson.

Hutchinson, F. ₁*fl.* *1783–1785*₁, *dresser.*
The opera accounts for 1783, 1784, and 1785 show a Mr Hutchinson and a Mr F. Hutchinson to have been men's dressers at the King's Theatre.

Hutley. *See* HUTTLEY.

Hutson, Miss ₁*fl.* *1782*₁, *equestrienne.*
A bill for Astley's Amphitheatre from the summer of 1782 stated that one of the entertainments would be horsemanship on three horses, the riders being Griffin, Jones, Miss Hutson, and the clown: "they ride in a variety of different attitudes. Also form a pyramid on 3 horses."

Huttley, Mr *d. 1796, singer, actor, oboist, flutist.*

A number of references in the late 1780s and early 1790s in Bath, Bristol, Dublin, and London to a Mr Huttley (or Hutley) all seem to point to the same person. The earliest mention of Huttley appears to have been in 1784; he played the flute in the Handel concerts at Westminster Abbey and the Pantheon in May and June of that year. "Hutley" accompanied Mrs Warrell on the oboe at the Royalty Theatre in Wellclose Square at one of "Brush" Collins's performances on 26 July 1788.

Huttley made his Bristol debut on 6 October 1790 and performed in a concert at the Assembly Rooms on 21 October. On the latter date he and other musicians advertised a forthcoming series of concerts. On 23 October Huttley made his debut at Bath, stating that his appearance was his third on any stage (but whether he meant as an actor, singer, or instrumentalist—for he was all three—is uncertain). Huttley played small parts, sang, and played the oboe at Bristol and Bath from 1790–91 through 1794, two of his known roles at Bristol being Crop in *No Song, No Supper* on 19 October 1791 and Careless in *The School for Scandal* on 31 March 1792.

The *Diary, or Woodfall's Register* on 26 March 1793 said that Huttley had recently married Harriet Peach—probably at Bath. On the following 6 August, for that night only, he played Crop again for his first appearance at the Haymarket Theatre in London. He was advertised as from the Theatre Royal, Bath (the Bath and Bristol companies were almost identical). He was similarly hailed as from the Bath company when he made his Irish debut at the Capel Street Theatre on 17 November 1795. The *European Magazine* in April 1796 reported that Mr Huttley, formerly of Bath, had died in London.

Hutton, Mr ₁*fl.* *1773–1779?*₁, *actor, imitator.*
Mr Hutton was a member of Samuel Foote's summer company at the Haymarket Theatre in 1773, his first notice in the bills there being on 26 May (as "a Young Gentleman") when he played Shift in *The Minor* and gave some imitations. During the remainder of the summer Hutton played the Watchman in *The Apprentice*, Dr Catgut in *The Commissary*, and a Waiter

in *A Trip to Portsmouth*. The bills occasionally noted that he entertained the audience with imitations. Not listed in *The London Stage* is a benefit at the Haymarket on 12 April 1774 which Hutton shared with Stewart and Jefferson; Hogan cites it in *Shakespeare in the Theatre*. Hutton reappeared at the Haymarket on 7 September 1775 and, with Bannister, did some imitations. He was there again the following 30 October and on 27 August 1776. At his last recorded London appearance, on 17 September 1777 at the Haymarket, Hutton gave "Vocal and Rhetorical" imitations.

The performer we have been following was probably the Mr Hutton who played at Belfast in 1776 and appeared at Newry in 1778 and 1779. He may have been related to Catharine Hutton, who married Michael Atkins.

Hutton, Mrs [*fl. 1730–1749?*], *actress.*
The London Stage lists a Mrs Hutton as an actress at the Haymarket Theatre in 1730–31. The same Mrs Hutton, perhaps, acted Emilia in *Othello* at the Haymarket on 17 October 1749.

Hutton, Mrs [*fl. c. 1770*], *singer.*
About 1770 was published the song *Take me Jenny*, as sung by a Mrs Hutton at "the new Garden" and at Ranelagh. She is otherwise unknown, so we should suggest the possibility that she was the singer Mrs Hudson (fl. 1769–1780?).

Hutton, Miss [*fl. 1720–1722*], *dancer, actress.*
A female dancer named Hutton, sometimes listed in the Lincoln's Inn Fields playbills as Miss and occasionally as Mrs, was first cited on 6 December 1720, when she provided entr'acte dances with *The Amorous Widow*. She was in the bills through the end of the 1720–21 season and returned to dance and act in 1721–22. She was named for only one part, Betty in *The Old Bachelor*, which opened on 13 January 1722. On 7 May Miss Hutton shared with two others a benefit that brought in £103 2s.

Hutton, William *d. 1680, singer.*
William Hutton was one of the Gentlemen of the Chapel Royal by 16 February 1661 and sang, for 7s. 4d., at Princess Mary's funeral on the following 30 March. Dr Busby listed Hutton as a member of the Westminster School choir in 1664. Hutton died in May 1680 and was buried in the cloisters of Westminster Abbey on the twelfth of that month, described as "a Quire Man."

Huxtable, Anthony *d. 1818, violinist.*
Anthony Huxtable, according to the account his son Christopher sent to Sainsbury for his dictionary, was one of the first violins at the King's Theatre; he played in the principal concerts in London, and performed in the Handel concerts at Westminster Abbey and the Pantheon in May and June 1784. Doane's *Musical Directory* of 1794 added that Huxtable was a member of the New Musical Fund (he was still one of the subscribers in 1815), but by 1794 the musician had moved to Castle Hill, near South Molton, Devonshire. There he taught violin and pianoforte and led public concerts. Anthony Huxtable died in 1818, leaving two sons, Christopher and William, both musicians.

Hyam. *See also* HAYM *and* HIEM.

Hyam, Mrs [*fl. 1781–1783*], *actress.*
Mrs Hyam was seen in two performances at the Haymarket Theatre; on 12 November 1781 she was in *The Spendthrift*, and on 17 September 1783 she was in *Cheapside*.

Hyat, Miss [*fl. 1763–1764*], *singer.*
Wroth in his *London Pleasure Gardens* states that a Miss Hyat sang under Thomas Lowe's management at Marylebone Gardens in 1763 and 1764.

Hyde, Mr [*fl. 1733–1739*], *actor.*
Mr Hyde had a very odd career: he appeared few times during the course of his six years in the theatre, but he almost always acted leading roles, usually for his benefit, and he rarely repeated himself. Had he not appeared at the patent houses, one might suppose he was an amateur. His first appearance was on 17 April 1733 at the Goodman's Fields playhouse, where he took the title part in *The Spanish Fryar* for his benefit. He was seen in the title

role in *The Old Bachelor* at the same house the following 17 September. On 19 October he played the Fryar agai, this time at Drury Lane, for his first appearance on that stage. He acted Falstaff in *1 Henry IV* for his benefit at that house on 2 May 1734. The following season his benefit came on 5 February, and he was seen as King Henry in *Richard III*.

Hyde's next appearance was at Covent Garden, where, on 24 February 1736, he acted King Lear for his benefit. He was back at Drury Lane on 4 March 1737 for his next benefit, at which he essayed Carlos in *Love Makes a Man* and Timothy in *The What D'Ye Call It* "(after the manner of the late facetious Mr Penkethman)." At the same theatre on 11 May 1738 for his benefit he acted Othello; then on 25 September 1739 he tried Mirabel in *The Way of the World* at Covent Garden. He concluded his odd career on 6 December 1739 at the same playhouse, playing Falstaff in *2 Henry IV*. In every case he played one-night stands; the Fryar was evidently the only part he acted twice.

Hyde, Mr [*fl.* 1760], *actor.*

Mr Hyde played R. Wealthy in *The Minor* at the Haymarket Theatre on 28 June 1760.

Hyde, Mr [*fl.* 1768], *carpenter.*

Mr Hyde was cited as a master carpenter at the Covent Garden Theatre in the 1768 deposition of Walter Humphreys in the lengthy lawsuit involving George Colman.

Hyde, Mrs [*fl.* 1734], *actress.*

Mrs Hyde (or Hide) played Jezebel in *Don Quixote in England* at the Haymarket Theatre on 5 April 1734.

Hyde, John [*fl.* 1789–1817], *trumpeter, violinist, proprietor.*

The Mr Hyde who was paid 9*s.* weekly at Drury Lane in 1789–90 was very likely John Hyde the trumpeter. Hyde was in the band at the King's Theatre on 24 February 1792 at the Handel Memorial Concert, as he was on 14 March 1794 at Drury Lane for a similar tribute. The theatre accounts show Hyde as a member of the Drury Lane band in 1792, 1793, and 1799 and a member of the band during the summers at the Haymarket Theatre from 1804 to 1810. At Drury Lane he was once cited as an extra trumpet, and payments to him appear to have been only for the spring or summer months.

Doane's *Musical Directory* of 1794 noted that Hyde also played the violin, that he had performed at the Oxford Meeting in 1793, and that in addition to the oratorio performances at Drury Lane he had also participated in those at Westminster Abbey. Hyde's address was No 6, Diana Place, Portland Road. Adam Carse in *The Orchestra in the XVIIIth Century* calls Hyde the sponsor of the English slide trumpet.

Hyde played in a performance of the *Messiah* at the Haymarket Theatre on 15 January 1798. In 1800 he purchased the Tottenham Street Rooms, which for many years after were called Hyde's Rooms. There he provided concerts, sometimes performing as well as serving as the proprietor. A curious note in the Drury Lane accounts in 1803–4 shows a payment of £30 7*s.* 6*d.* to "Hyde's Boys Bugles." We may guess that Hyde had trained a group of buglers for some production. Hyde was in the band at the King's Theatre, playing for the operas, in 1817 and had been playing there before that date.

Hyll. *See* Hill.

= I =

"Iago." *See* RYAN, LACY.

"Ianthe." *See* BETTERTON, MRS THOMAS.

Ibbings. *See* EVANS.

Ibbott, Sarah [*fl. c. 1750–1825*], *actress, proprietress.*

Miss (later Mrs) Sarah Ibbott may have been performing at Bath about 1750, according to Penley's *Bath Stage.* She was certainly in Simpson's troupe there in 1751. Francis Gentleman in his preface to *The Modish Wife* called Simpson's company a "very imperfect odd jumbled crew" but gave Miss Ibbott credit for the success of Gentleman's alteration of *Richard II.* She was, he said, "the best declamatory actress I ever heard. . . ."

In the summer of 1752 she was at Richmond and Twickenham, and a number of bills have survived to indicate the importance of her position in the troupe. At Richmond she played Indiana in *The Conscious Lovers* on 13 June and then was seen as Ann Lovely in *A Bold Stroke for a Wife*, Kitty Pry in *The Lying Valet*, Hortensia in *Aesop*, Sylvia in *The Recruiting Officer*, Lucy in *The Beggar's Opera*, Miranda in *The Busy Body*, Alicia in *Jane Shore*, Mrs Sullen in *The Beaux' Stratagem*, Mrs Kitely in *Every Man in His Humour*, Mrs Marwood in *The Way of the World*, Lady Townly in *The Provok'd Husband*, the title role in *The Silent Woman*, Lady Allworth in *A New Way to Pay Old Debts*, Angelica in *The Gamester*, Zara in *The Mourning Bride*, Cordelia in *King Lear* (with Cooke as Lear, for her benefit on 29 August), and Lady Brute in *The Provok'd Wife.* The troupe played only rarely at Twickenham; Miss Ibbott, for her benefit there on 12 August, chose *The Silent Woman.*

Sarah was at the Orchard Street Theatre in Bath in 1752–53, one of her known roles there being Mrs Beverly in *The Gamester* on 29 Feb-

ruary 1753. *The Bath Comedians* (1753), a lampoon, had kind words for her:

> I'll censure some, and some I'll rally
> And first begin with charming S—lly,
> I–b–tt, I–b–tt, that's her Name,
> And faith she is a lovely Dame;
> They say her Voice can charm like Magick
> In Comick Scenes as well as Tragick;
> She acts well, and speaks well too,
> What more can any Woman do?
> So, Madam, that's enough for you.

The eccentric Charlotte Charke prompted for Simpson's company in Bath and said Miss Ibbott gave her precious little work, for Sarah was always perfect in her part. Charlotte praised her as Isabella in *The Fatal Marriage*, saying she "blended Nature and Art so exquisitely." Charlotte's remarks probably refer to the 1753–54 season at Bath, when Sarah returned to Simpson's theatre. She was there again in 1754–55, one of the few performers who attracted audiences to Simpson's venture, according to Mrs Charke. With Simpson's troupe on 31 March 1755, she played in *The Gamester* at the Jacob's Wells Theatre in Bristol. In 1755–56 she was at Simpson's theatre in Bath under Thomas King. A note in the Sarah Ward–West Digges correspondence states that she contemplated playing Hamlet at Bath at one point but decided not to.

Sarah Ward wrote from Liverpool to West Digges on 17 July 1758 that Miss Ibbott would be a good actress for him to hire. Mrs Ward's knowledge of Miss Ibbott's work would suggest that between 1756 and 1760 Miss Ibbott may have made the rounds of the provincial theatres as well as playing regularly at Bath. On 14 January 1760 Sarah Ibbott made her first appearance in Ireland playing Millwood in *George Barnwell* at the Crow Street Theatre in Dublin.

Finally she tried London. On 22 October 1760 she played the Queen in *The Earl of Essex* at Covent Garden. But either she did not make much of an impression on London audiences or she preferred theatrical activity in the smaller provincial theatres, for she did not appear in London again. She spent the 1761–62 season back in Dublin at the Smock Alley Theatre and was in Birmingham in June 1762. There is another blank in her record until 1766–67, when she played at Norwich, her home for the rest of her career.

Pinn's *Roscius* (1767) found Mrs Ibbott (now no longer "Miss") a fine Lady Macbeth, good at "raging Anguish, or a deep despair."

> *Extensive merit, variously great,*
> *From Lady Randolph, down to Muslin's Prate!*

The following year, on 17 December 1768, Neville recorded in his *Diary* a visit to the Norwich theatre: "At 6 went into the Pit at the Norwich Theatre, which is a minature [*sic*] Drury-Lane, but too much ornamented with carving, gilding etc. Saw the 'Way of the World' with 'High Life below Stairs.' Mrs Ibbott, who did Lady Wishfort, is a pretty good actress." From that one might suppose that there was a Miss Ibbott active in the 1750s and a Mrs Ibbott at Norwich from 1767 onward, but it would appear that only one actress was involved. Indeed, if in the early 1750s Miss Ibbott was in her early twenties, by the late 1760s she might well have been playing Lady Wishfort.

Tate Wilkinson at Newcastle in the summer of 1769 engaged Sarah from the Norwich company to replace Mrs Baker.

> She possessed great merit [Tate wrote in *The Wandering Patentee*], good voice, education, and understanding—not equal in expression to Mrs. Baker, her manner far from accomplished: however, if size was necessary, though Mrs. Baker was not a skeleton, yet Ibbot made more than treble amends as to the quantity. She acted Queen Elizabeth, take it all together, better than any person I have seen (Mrs. Pope excepted).

Mrs Ibbott left Wilkinson at Hull in the winter of 1769 and returned to Norwich, though she played at York in August 1769 and joined the troupe there as a regular, evidently, in the spring of 1770. As elsewhere, her Queen in *The Earl of Essex* was one of her chief vehicles.

From 14 January 1774 until 22 April 1825 Sarah Ibbott's name appeared fairly regularly as a proprietress in the books of the Norwich theatre. At first she was acting and receiving a salary, for on 11 May 1775 the Committee Books there record Mrs Ibbott's salary as being reduced to one guinea weekly. On 15 June of that year she is known to have played Mrs Willoughby in *A Word to the Wise*. Hannah More wrote to Garrick from Bungay on 16 June 1777 that she had seen Mrs Ibbott with the Norwich troupe there; Sarah had done "more than tolerably" as Mrs Heidelberg in *The Clandestine Marriage*. Perhaps because of her continued work as an actress, Mrs Ibbott, though a proprietress of the Norwich troupe, was increased to one and a half guineas weekly on 13 August 1777. Burley in *Players and Playhouses of East Anglia*, without providing any evidence, states that the Mr Ibbott in the Norwich troupe in the 1770s was Sarah's husband; but we have found no evidence of her having married. Ibbott could have been her brother or cousin. Burley also claims that Sarah acted Falstaff for her benefit at some point.

On 11 April 1783 Mrs Ibbott was requested by the Committee to superintend the ladies' wardrobe at the theatre; when she and Mr Pye did so, the Committee gave them power to displace any personnel in the wardrobe they deemed unfit and to appoint others. Though involved in managerial tasks, Mrs Ibbott was still acting, for a bill of 12 February 1783 records her playing Miss Dreadnought in *The Fair American*. The Committee books indicate her presence at the meetings very frequently in 1784, but they mention her less and less after that. Tate Wilkinson said that a wealthy relative of Mrs Ibbott died in April 1787 and left her most of his fortune. She retired, Tate said, and in 1795 was living well, but, he noted, she was "ever of a penurious turn." The Norwich Committee books show her to have attended no meetings in 1785 (though that may simply reflect omissions in the records), one in 1786, none in 1787, three in 1788, one in 1790, one in 1799, and one in 1801. At Norwich as a proprietor from 1811 to 1814 was H. Ibbott, who did not appear in London but was surely a relative of Sarah Ibbott. The last mention of her in the accounts is of her attendance at a Committee meeting years later, on 22 April 1825.

Sarah Ibbott was, according to William "Gentleman" Smith in a letter to Lord Chedworth (now at the Folger Shakespeare Library), "a very unwieldly, large & ugly [woman] but declaimed admirably, & with personal requisites wou'd have stood respectably in London."

Iggs. *See* ₍ B₎IGGS.

Igl. *See* ECCLES.

"Il Bolonese." *See* GABRIELLA, TOMASO.

Iliff, Edward Henry ₍*fl.* 1785–1805₎, *actor, playwright, novelist.*

Edward Henry Iliff was declared by the author of *The Thespian Dictionary* (1805) to be "the son of a clergyman." Iliff "in his early days went to sea as a midshipman." (A less-complete account in *The Secret History of the Green Room* in 1792, had called the father a curate of St Mary le Strand.) The later account continued: "On his return home [from a voyage], he procured, through the interest of his father, a comfortable situation in the India House, but an attachment to the stage seduced him from his employment, and he made his first appearance at Brighton, under the assumed name of *Williams.*"

At Brighton (or Richmond, according to *The Secret History of the Green Room*), Iliff (or Williams) ran into debt, quarreled with his manager, and received "pecuniary assistance" from Miss Maria Palmer, a singer. They were married at Sheffield in 1786, according to the manuscript "Dramatic Register" in the Harvard Theatre Collection. But the wedding probably took place late in 1785, for an extant bill of the Derby players names a Mrs Iliff on 15 December 1785 and Mrs Norma Armstrong has found that Mrs Iliff with her husband Edward Henry were in Edinburgh as early as 16 January 1786.

Iliff's roles at the Theatre Royal, Shakespeare Square, in 1786 were: Bassanio in *The Merchant of Venice*, Beaumont in *The Humourist*, Benedict in *The Pageant*, Captain Savage in *The School for Wives*, Carlos in *Isabella*, the Dauphin in *King John*, Don Octavio in *She Wou'd and She Wou'd Not*, the title role in *Douglas*, Edmund in *King Lear*, Edward Knowell in *Every Man in His Humour*, Ferdinand in *The Tempest*, Hamlet, Horace in *Set a Beggar on Horseback*, Lackland in *Fontainebleau*, Lord Gayville in *The*

Heiress, Lord Raymond in *The Countess of Salisbury*, and the title role in *Theodosius*. It was a various list, mostly in comedy and usually in secondary or tertiary parts. His only capital role was for his introductory night, Hamlet on 19 January 1786.

The new Mrs Iliff's mother had been for many years housekeeper for the excellent actress Ann Street, who was, successively, Mrs William Dancer, Mrs Spranger Barry, and Mrs Thomas Crawford. Long ago, in 1767, Ann Barry had instructed little Miss Palmer and had put her on at Drury Lane in some juvenile parts. Though past her prime, Ann Crawford was still influential and she now prepared to help the new husband of her protégée. Tate Wilkinson recounted in *The Wandering Patentee* how Mrs Crawford, always popular at York, came for a two-night engagement in May 1786:

Mrs. Crawford introduced Mr. and Mrs. Iliff. The latter was to supply Miss Wilkinson's singing cast. Mr. Iliff acted Douglas to Mrs. Crawford's Lady Randolph, in which part his figure, youth, and sense of his author, with the aid of his able instructress, made him appear to very great advantage.

The Iliffs were both well-practiced when they returned to Edinburgh in January 1787 to stay through July. Edward Henry's roles the second season there were (in addition to his old ones): Banquo in *Macbeth*, Beauford in *The Fool*, Blushingly in *The Natural Son*, Captain Ambush in *The Young Quaker*, Captain Clement in *Hunt the Slipper*, Dangle in *The Critic*, Fenton in *The Merry Wives of Windsor*, Lawson in *The Gamester*, Lord Flint in *Such Things Are*, Mandeville in *He Wou'd Be a Soldier*, Marquis in *The Widow's Vow*, the title role in *Percy*, Prince Volscius in *The Rehearsal*, Roderigo in *Othello*, Sir George Airy in *The Busy Body*, Sir George Euston in *I'll Tell You What*, Sir Richard Vernon in *1 Henry IV*, Sparkish in *The Country Girl*, Squire Richard in *The Provok'd Husband*, Squire Thistleton in *The Virtuous Chambermaid*, Woodville in *The Chapter of Accidents*, Young Fashion in *A Trip to Scarborough*, and Young Whimsey in *The First Floor*.

Maria Iliff went to London to fulfill a singing engagement at Vauxhall in the summer of 1787, and her husband accompanied her (they were living at No 20, Charles Street, Westminster in 1788) but apparently found no theatrical employment for several months. He was introduced to the elder George Colman, who hired both him and his wife at the theatre in the Haymarket in the summer of 1788, where he added the following roles to his repertoire during the four years following, in order: (1788) Young Meanwell in *Tit for Tat* ("Ilett"), the title role in *The Minor*, Trip in *The School for Scandal*, and Campley in *Inkle and Yarico*; (1789) Lord Simper in *A Quarter of an Hour before Dinner*, Lord Falbridge in *The English Merchant*, Captain Berry in *Half an Hour after Supper*, Easy in *The Manager in Distress*, Laertes in *Hamlet*, Lord Megrim in *As It Should Be*, Melvil in *Vimonda*, the original Count de Wurzendal in the anonymous comedy *The Swop*, Lieutenant Dormer in *The Sword of Peace*, the original Jack Spriggins in the younger George Colman's new farce *The Family Party*, Count Almaviva in *The Spanish Barber*, a Nobleman in *The Battle of Hexham*, and Ensign Frederick in Thimble's *Flight from the Shopboard* (1790); Egbert in *The Battle of Hexham*, Captain Nightshade in *Seeing is Believing*, Solarino in *The Merchant of Venice*, Heartwell in *The Farm House*, and Mr Hammond in *Modern Breakfast*; (1791) Sir Walter Blunt in *1 Henry IV*, an Officer in *The Surrender of Calais*, and Sprightly in *The Author*.

The two Iliffs joined Tate Wilkinson for race week at Doncaster late in September 1788. A Hull playbill of 10 December 1788 described Iliff as "from Dublin." Both Iliffs were at York in 1788–89. The register of St Martin's, York, shows that a daughter, Clara, of "Mr. Iliff, comedian," was baptized there on 4 March 1789. She was probably the Miss Iliff who performed at Covent Garden in 1800–1801. There was also a Master Iliff at that theatre that year.

In July 1790, when Joseph Fox opened the Duke Street Theatre, Brighton, the Iliffs were in the company ("Iliffe"). Speaight listed an Edward Iliff, puppeteer, in Savile Row in 1791–92. The *Thespian Magazine* located Iliff in the Manchester company from December 1793 to March 1794. In that year Doane's *Musical Directory* gave Mrs Iliff's address as No 5, Gilbert Row, St George's Fields.

Like his wife, who wrote poetry, Edward Henry Iliff was literary. In 1796 he followed the Gothic-sentimental fashion, publishing *Angelo, A Novel Founded on Melancholy Facts*.

His burlesque *The Ugly Club* was given one performance, at Drury Lane for Robert Palmer's benefit on 6 June 1798; it was published that year as "By Edmund Spenser, the Younger." The *Thespian Dictionary* said in 1805 that the Iliffs were separated by a difference in politics.

Iliff, Mrs Edward Henry, Maria, née Palmer ⌊*fl.* 1767–1815⌋, *actress, singer, poet.*

Maria Palmer was the daughter of a long-time and devoted housekeeper for the notable actress Ann Street, who was, successively, Mrs William Dancer, Mrs Spranger Barry, and Mrs Thomas Crawford. The author of *The Thespian Dictionary* (1805), agreeing with all other early accounts, wrote:

To this lady, (who in every respect treated her as her own child) [Maria] was indebted for her education; she brought her forward in Prince Arthur, and other little characters, at Drury Lane, but as she encreased in years, took her from the stage, and provided her with proper masters, intending her for some less dangerous situation in life. Her mind, however, being bent on the drama, she eloped from her patroness, and commenced actress in a country company in the west of England.

It is not impossible that *The Thespian Dictionary* invented the intention of Mrs Dancer to obviate that "dangerous situation," which all theatrical annalists of that period professed to feel the theatre to be. Certainly Mrs Dancer did bring Maria Palmer onto the boards as a child and did encourage both her and her husband later. The phraseology of the Haymarket bill of 21 August 1767—"Miss Palmer, first appearance in this kingdom"—probably assures us that she had made a debut in Ireland, the only other kingdom where theatre really flourished at that date. Mrs Dancer was well connected in Dublin. The Haymarket role was Lord William (a juvenile) in *The Countess of Salisbury*. Foote's company then contained Spranger Barry, Thomas Barry, and Mrs Dancer. The offering was repeated eight times during the summer at the Haymarket and revived at Drury Lane in January and May 1768 and April 1769 with Miss Palmer and the two Barrys still in the cast. Also in January, and again in April and May 1768, Miss Palmer was a Page in *The Orphan*, a role she was still young enough to assume on 22 December

1772. After that she ceased for a number of years to appear on the London stage. But the evidence persuades that she was still being trained for the stage by Mrs Dancer and perhaps also by Spranger Barry, who had been living with Mrs Dancer and who late in 1767 or early in 1768 married her.

In the summer of 1775 a Miss Palmer, probably Maria, was in the company at Crow Street, Dublin. She was said by *Farley's Dublin Journal* to be playing for the first time on 20 June, advertised as "A Young Lady." She acted again on 20 July.

Maria Palmer met Edward Henry Iliff when both were playing at Brighton in the summer of 1785. *The Thespian Dictionary* claimed that she helped him financially. They were married at Sheffield, "Mr. Pero, the Manager, giving the Lady away," declared *The Secret History of the Green Room*. That was probably sometime before 15 December 1785, on which date a Derby bill carried "Mrs Iliff" (though she may have been only acting under that name: the "Dramatic Register" in the Harvard Theatre Collection gives the year of their marriage as 1786.)

In the winter-spring season of 1786 the Iliffs were in the company at the Theatre Royal, Shakespeare Square, Edinburgh. Maria's roles were various, though predominantly comic, sentimental, or melodic (or all three). She may have been rather small—she played Prince Arthur in *King John*, usually a child's role—and she was probably shapely, for she sang Captain Macheath in *The Beggar's Opera*, a "breeches part." Her other roles, in alphabetical order, from mid-January through late May 1786, were Angelica in *The Fair American*, Beatrice in *The Pageant*, Diana in *Lionel and Clarissa*, Emma in *Peeping Tom of Coventry*, Jenny in *The Deserter*, Jessica in *The Merchant of Venice*, Lauretta in *St Patrick's Day*, Nysa in *Midas*, Ophelia in *Hamlet*, Page in *The Follies of a Day*, Queen Dollalolla in *Tom Thumb the Great*, Rosa Seymour in *Fontainebleau*, Rosetta in *Love in a Village*, Signora Lorenzo in *The Castle of Andalusia*, a Singing Witch in *Macbeth*, and Wilhelmina in *The Waterman*.

In May 1786, says Tate Wilkinson in his *Wandering Patentee*, Mrs Crawford (Mrs Barry until July 1778) came to York for a two-night engagement. "Mrs. Crawford introduced Mr.

and Mrs. Iliff. The latter was to supply Miss Wilkinson's singing cast." Wilkinson also noted that Mrs Crawford assisted Iliff in his career.

In the winter-spring season of 1787 the Iliffs returned to Edinburgh. Maria added the following to her growing repertoire: Betsy Blossom in *The Deaf Lover*, Clorinda in *Robin Hood*, Diana in *The Maid of the Oaks*, Donna Clara in *The Duenna*, Fanny in *The Maid of the Mill*, Gillian in *The Quaker*, Ismene in *The Sultan*, an Italian in *The Critic*, Jenny in *Hunt the Slipper*, Jenny Cullender in *The Dramatic Phrensy*, Kathleen in *The Poor Soldier*, Laura in *The Agreeable Surprise*, Leonora in *The Padlock*, a Maid in *The Ephesian Matron*, Norah in *Patrick in Prussia*, Signora Figurante in *Gretna Green*, both Sylvia and Urganda in *Cymon*, Usaminta in *The Young Quaker*, and Viola in *The Strangers at Home*.

In the summer of 1787 Maria Iliff obtained an engagement to sing at Vauxhall and left for London accompanied by her husband. She sang at the pleasure garden, but he seems to have been unemployed until the following summer, when he was admitted to the Haymarket summer company. Mrs Iliff did not appear in the bills at that theatre that summer, but she may have sung in choruses, for Tate Wilkinson remembered that the Iliffs joined him at Doncaster in race week, toward the end of September, coming "I believe that season from the Haymarket Theatre."

Mrs Iliff, alone so far as is known, was in Pero's traveling company at Derby, Hull, and other towns in 1788–89. Both Iliffs also played at York that season. She joined her husband at the Haymarket in the summer of 1789 and part of 1790, singing in the chorus and also featured a few times in "breeches" parts (Macheath, Young Meadows in *Love in a Village*, and Young Quaver in *Ut Pictura Poesis*) and at least once in a pantomime, as Columbine in *The Portrait*. She was also the original Julia in the comic opera *New Spain; or, Love in Mexico* by John Scawen. But on 13 July 1790, when Joseph Fox opened his Duke Street Theatre in Brighton, the Iliffs were among a substantial company which included John Henderson, Mrs Crouch, and Michael Kelly.

Mrs Iliff is recorded acting at Drury Lane during the winter of 1794–95 and at Covent

Garden in 1797–98 and every season thereafter through 1815–16. But her salary was never higher than £1 5s. per five-day week. She was employed principally as a chorus singer, adding to her repertoire of named characters only Wowski in *Inkle and Yarico* in 1790, Araminta in the *Young Quaker* in 1791, Mrs Vixen in *The Beggar's Opera* in 1795, a Lapland Witch in *Harlequin's Return*, Norah in *The Poor Soldier*, Narcissa in *Inkle and Yarico*, a Scotch Lassie in *Oscar and Malvina*, and Penelope in *The Romp in* 1798, and Kitty in *Marian* and Orsanana in *Ramah Droog* in 1800.

Meanwhile, she was finding engagements in the provinces (she was at Brighton on 17 July 1798 and at Birmingham on 13 June 1799) and at the pleasure gardens (songs were published "as sung by" her at Vauxhall, Apollo Gardens, and Bermondsey Spa Gardens). In the season of 1810 she was again in the company at the Haymarket as a chorus singer.

The Secret History of the Green Room described her as she was in 1792: "Her person is thick and short; her countenance and demeanor vulgar; and to vocal refinement or delicacy she is an utter stranger;—she has, however, a clear, strong voice, and an useful degree of confidence on the stage."

The miniscule account in *The Thespian Dictionary* related that "She is now [1802] separated from her husband, a difference of political sentiments having . . . obliterated the love which gratitude had inspired." It is not clear when the separation occurred. In 1791–92 Iliff was operating a puppet show in Savile Row. In 1793–94 he was in Manchester, but in 1794 Doane's *Musical Directory* gave Mrs Iliff's address as No 5, Gilbert Row, St George's Fields, London.

Mrs Iliff is credited by William Upcott, in the *Biographical Dictionary of Living Authors* (1814), with the authorship of *Poems on Various Subjects* (1808).

The Iliffs had at least two children. The parish register of St Martins', York, records a daughter, Clara of "Mr Iliff, comedian," baptized there on 4 March 1789. Very likely she was the Miss Iliff who performed at Covent Garden in 1800–1801. There was also a Master Iliff at the theatre that year.

Illingham, Miss. *See* ILLINGSWORTH, MRS.

Illingsworth, Mrs [*fl.* 1793–1799], *singer.*

Though the evidence is vague and confusing, it would seem that references in bills of the 1790s to Miss Illingsworth, Miss Illingham, and Mrs Hillingsworth are all to the same person—a minor singer who seems most of the time to have been cited as Mrs Illingsworth. She was so designated on 4 October 1793 when she was at Sadler's Wells and on 31 August 1795 at the same theatre, when she was a Lass in *England's Glory. The London Stage* indexes her as Miss Illingham, a minor singer at Drury Lane in 1797–98 and 1798–99; but in the playbill for 8 November 1797 she was cited as Mrs Hillingsworth (she was in the chorus of Peasants in *Richard Coeur de Lion*), as she was when she was a Peasant in *Blue-Beard* on 16 January 1798. But she was called Miss Illingham when she was a Minstrel in *Feudal Times* on 19 January 1799. The company accounts reveal that she was paid 25s. weekly for her chorus chores.

Illingsworth, Miss. *See* ILLINGSWORTH, MRS.

Imanuel. *See* EMMANUEL.

Imer, Marianna [*fl.* 1746], *singer.*

Marianna Imer, the older sister of Teresa Imer Cornelys, the notorious singer and entrepreneur, sang at the King's Theatre in *La caduta de giganti* on 7 January 1746 and subsequent dates and was Berenice in the *pasticcio Antigone* on 13 May.

Imer, Teresa. *See* CORNELYS, TERESA.

Immyns, John *d.* 1764, *singer, instrumentalist.*

John Immyns was a lawyer, but an indiscretion of some sort kept him from practicing, and he had to settle for being a clerk to a city attorney. His interest in music led to a position as amanuensis to Pepusch and copyist for the Academy of Ancient Music. Immyns was a countertenor and played the flute, violin, viola de gamba, harpsichord, and lute (he taught himself the last instrument with the help of Mace's *Musick's Monument*). He succeeded to

John Shore's post as lutenist in the Chapel Royal when Shore died in 1752.

Immyns sang the countertenor role of Mordecai for Handel in *Esther*, according to Dean's *Handel's Dramatic Oratorios and Masques*; *The London Stage* lists a performance of the oratorio on 26 March 1740 at the Lincoln's Inn Fields playhouse. The following year Immyns founded the Madrigal Society. The original members were, according to Hawkins's *General History*, "mostly mechanics" who had been used to the "practice of psalmody." The group included "some weavers from Spitalfields, others of various trades and occupations," and they gathered at The Twelve Bells in Bride Lane, Fleet Street, to sing for their own entertainment. From time to time Immyns served as president of the Society.

John Immyns died of asthma in Coldbath Fields on 15 April 1764. He had written his will on 3 October 1763, describing himself as of the parish of St James, Clerkenwell, and gentleman lutenist to the Chapel Royal. He left his entire estate to his wife Sarah, who proved the will on 16 April 1764. William Immyns, of St Michael Loudon, printer, had testified on 23 October 1763 to John Immyns's signature on the will. He may have been John's brother.

Immyns, John *b. 1764, singer, instrumentalist.*

The younger John Immyns was the son of William and Catharine Immyns. According to the registers of the Congregation of the United Brethren in London, John was born on 26 October 1764 and baptized two days later. Grove seems to be in error in citing John as the son of the lawyer and musician John Immyns (d. 1764) and in saying that the younger John died in 1794.

Our subject sang tenor at the Handel Memorial Concerts in Westminster Abbey and the Pantheon in May and June 1784. He was paid £2 10*s.* for the 1787–88 season playing "tenor violin" for the Academy of Ancient Music. On 2 August 1789 he was recommended for membership in the Royal Society of Musicians, and for that organization the information given above concerning his birth and baptism was assembled. When John was proposed for membership he was described as married and the father of one child, Elvia, 15 months

old. He was proficient on the harpsichord, violin, tenor (viola), and violoncello and was in 1789 serving as organist of St John Bedford and Jury Chapel, Aldgate. He was elected to membership and signed the Society's book on 6 December 1789.

For the Society he played viola at the annual concerts at St Paul's in 1790 and all succeeding years (except for 1795) through 1800. Doane's *Musical Directory* of 1794 described Immyns as an organist and 'cellist and stated that he was a member of the Royal Society of Musicians and organist at the Surrey Chapel. His address was No 68, Red Lion Street, Clerkenwell. The last mention of Immyns was in January 1803 when he visited the Royal Society of Musicians meeting.

Imry. *See* EMERY.

Ince, Mr [*fl. 1797–1799*], *house servant?*

Mr Ince was one of several people allowed benefit tickets at Covent Garden Theatre on 6 June 1797, 19 May 1798, and 29 May 1799. He was probably a house servant.

Inchbald, George *d. 1800, actor, singer.*

George Inchbald was a son of Joseph Inchbald the actor. Nothing is known of George's mother. She may have been Joseph's first wife. In James Boaden's *Memoirs of Elizabeth Inchbald*, George is a shadowy figure who seems to have been a grown man when he arrived at Edinburgh on 10 January 1774, bringing letters from London to Joseph and Elizabeth Inchbald. He is liable to confusion with the (apparently) somewhat younger Robert Inchbald, his brother or half brother.

He seems to have been a good actor. Tate Wilkinson said that

Young Mr. INCHBALD was engaged [for the York circuit] (at the request of his lovely mother-in-law, Mrs. Inchbald) in July 1779, and did not leave me till May 1786. He was a young man of great service in a theatre, though not so attentive always as he should be, but of good behaviour: when he left me, he cost me two performers at least to supply his loss.

In the summers of 1780 and 1781 he was at the Theatre Royal, Shakespeare Square, in Edinburgh, playing Strickland in *The Suspi-*

cious Husband, Roby in *Percy*, Villars in *The Belle's Stratagem*, Sir John Graham in *Sir William Wallace*, and Young Cape in *The Author* in 1780 and Merlin in *Tom Thumb the Great*, Posthumus in *Love and Ambition*, and Sir John Trotly in *Bon Ton* in 1781.

In the fall of 1786 Inchbald went to London. His career there was short. On 25 September he stepped on at short notice as Stukely in *The Gamester* at Covent Garden in place of Francis Aickin, whose wife had died. On 4 October he appeared in the Covent Garden bill for the first time as Don Diego in the afterpiece *The Padlock*. On 16 October he was entrusted with the title role in the premiere of Leonard Macnally's *Richard Coeur de Lion*. The *Morning Chronicle* the next day related the evening's interesting conclusion:

Inchbald we thought [was] rather hardly dealt with. His voice happened to fail him in a particular turn of the tune he was singing, and some of the audience were ungenerous enough to disconcert him so far that he made a modest bow and retired. . . . [Thus] a duet that was to have been sung by the King from the battlements of the castle, and Blondel without the walls, on which the turn of the fable hinged, was omitted; a circumstance that could not but materially affect the interest, as it destroyed the connexion of the fable.

He withdrew from his engagement the same night and went back to the provinces.

From 1787 through 1789 Inchbald was acting at Norwich. On 27 August 1792, at Spalding, Lincolnshire, he married the widow Sarah Reily, daughter of the "York Roscius," Bridge Frodsham, and herself an accomplished actress. On 25 November 1793, as "from Edinburgh," an Inchbald who was probably George made his Irish debut at Smock Alley Theatre, Dublin. He played there for a few nights only. A surviving playbill of the Theatre in Worthing, Sussex, shows a Mr Inchbald playing two leads, Pedro in *The Noble Pilgrim* and Sileno in *Midas* on 29 September 1796.

A Mrs Inchbald, who could not have been Elizabeth the actress-playwright but who may have been George's wife, was reported by the *Monthly Mirror* acting with a small but good company under Butler's management at Kendal, Westmoreland, in March 1797 and before. And the same journal in April, speaking of Masterman's company at Cardiff, remarked:

"Mr. Inchbald, the son-in-law [*recte*, stepson] of the celebrated dramatic writer, has succeeded Fotterall in the heroic walk—he is an actor of considerable promise."

Elizabeth Inchbald's notebooks record several benefactions to George Inchbald and his wife during his final illness in the fall of 1800. He died on 28 October 1800.

Inchbald, Mrs George. *See* Frodsham, Sarah.

Inchbald, Joseph *1735–1779, actor, scene painter, singer.*

Joseph Inchbald was born in 1735, according to obituaries which stated his age to be 44 at the time of his death in 1779. Details of his youth and education and the employments of his early manhood are unknown. He was first noticed as a member of "Mr. Goodhall's Band" of players at Stourbridge Fair, near Cambridge, from early September to early October 1767, playing Shift, Smirk, and Mother Cole in *The Minor*. He acted at Norwich from 1768 to 1770. He had by 1769 acquired a son, for the Norwich Committee Books of 22 May that year included "Mr Inchbald & Son" in a list of people whom the Committee agreed "to retain as performers for the ensuing year . . . at the same Salary & . . . Terms as last year." The boy was either George or Robert Inchbald, both of whom were sons by some early liaison and both of whom performed.

In 1770–71 Inchbald was engaged at Drury Lane, making his debut there on 8 October 1770 as Osmyn in *The Mourning Bride*, billed, with a deceit not uncommon, as a young gentleman making his first appearance. He was identified by Hopkins in his prompter's diary: "Mr Inchbald from the Norwich Compy. made his first appearance in Osmyn very bad Figure, Indifferent voice and a very bad Actor. a Small hiss at End of Play."

Inchbald's roles during the rest of the 1770–71 season were Aldamon in *Almida*, Oswald in *King Arthur*, Rhadamistus in *Zenobia*, and an undesignated part in *The Capricious Lady*. He was re-engaged the following season, 1771–72, adding the Chief Druid in *The Institution of the Garter*, Capulet in *Romeo and Juliet*, a part unspecified in *Timon of Athens*, Calippus in *The Grecian Daughter*, Eschylus in *Timoleon*, Petruchio in *The Chances*, Gloster in *Jane Shore*, the title part in *Tamerlane*, and Old Wilful in *The Double Gallant*.

In the spring of 1771 he had met the beautiful, talented, and eccentric Elizabeth Simpson, who was on a visit to relatives in London. On 9 June 1772 they were married at the house of Elizabeth's sister Mrs Slender, in London, by a Father Rice, a Roman Catholic priest. The following day there was a Protestant ceremony at St Andrew, Holborn. John Palmer ("Plausible Jack"), the handsome Drury Lane comedian of the time, was asked to give the bride away. It was probably his voice behind the anonymous account in the *Thespian Magazine and Literary Repository* (1793) which describes Inchbald, shabbily-dressed and 18 years older than his 18-year-old bride. The priest mistook Palmer for the bridegroom. The account charges that Inchbald "paid no attention whatever to his appearance, and . . . presented himself with beard unshaven, and face unwashed," certainly consonant with his reputation for personal slovenliness.

On 11 June 1772 the newly-weds set off for Bristol, where Inchbald had an engagement and took lodgings with the Winstone family near College Green. There Inchbald, a talented amateur painter, acted and practiced his hobby of painting portraits. There also he coached his wife for her first appearance, as Cordelia to his Lear, on 4 September. On the eighteenth they left for London.

Despite the variety of his offerings of the previous season at Drury Lane, he had not been critically successful. In addition to Hopkins's stricture, Francis Gentleman in *The Theatres* had also blasted his Osmyn:

> Inchbald, who long on Norfolk dumplins fed,
> Those solid emblems of his solid head;
> Imported to the capital, was shewn
> As one well-form'd to mount the tragic throne;
> A first appearance smooth'd the thorny way,
> Yet, candid judgment damn'd his wild essay

and no comparable critic had come to his assistance. So he was not engaged for a third season at Drury Lane.

He and Elizabeth had managed, however, to attract the notice of West Digges, struggling to put together a company for Edinburgh and Glasgow. On 10 October 1772 they took ship for Scotland, arriving at Leith on 17 October after a stormy passage. They left in a chaise for Glasgow on the nineteenth, and on 26 October they presented there their Lear and Cordelia. On 6 November Elizabeth was Anne Bullen and he Cranmer in *Henry VIII*. After that, the record is unclear. She had a few small parts; his son Robert, living in the same house with them, acted juvenile roles such as Fleance in *Macbeth*.

In any account of the Inchbalds, the focus shifts very early to the distaff side. The lovely and strong-willed Elizabeth, born with a speech impediment which she had already largely conquered, made use of her husband's experience, obliging him to walk hours on the Edinburgh hills and Firth beaches listening to her declamation and coaching her dramatic lines. Many of her roles after the company moved on to Edinburgh in November 1772 are known, but we know none of Joseph's until 8 April 1773, when he played Othello.

The Inchbalds were together on the Edinburgh roster every winter from 1772–73 through 1775–76. Joseph Inchbald's recorded roles at Edinburgh, in approximate sequence, are: Othello, the title role in *Tamerlane*, Jaffeir in *Venice Preserv'd*, Albany in *King Lear*, Smith in *The Rehearsal*, Ghost in *Hamlet*, Colonel Tamper in *The Deuce Is in Him*, Thomas in *Thomas and Sally*, Colonel Bully in *The Provok'd Wife*, the title role in *Julius Caesar*, Pembroke in *Lady Jane Gray*, Sullen in *The Beaux' Stratagem*, Foresight in *Love for Love*, Horatio in *The Fair Penitent*, the King in *The Mourning Bride*, King Henry in *1 Henry IV*, Linco in *Cymon*, Ford in *The Merry Wives of Windsor*, Myrtle in *The Conscious Lovers*; Raymond in *The Spanish Fryar*; Simon in *The Invasion of Harlequin*, Stephano in *The Tempest*, Aubrey in *The Fashionable Lover*, Banquo in *Macbeth*, Devil in *The Devil upon Two Sticks*; Don Diego in *The Padlock*, Woodcock in *Love in a Village*, Major Sturgeon in *The Mayor of Garratt*, Old Philpot in *The Citizen*, Scrub in *The Beaux' Stratagem*, Russet in *The Deserter*, Martin in *Wit's Last Stake*, the title role in *King John*, Tullus Hostilius in *The Roman Father*; Ben Black in *The Reprisal*, Colonel Oldboy in *Lionel and Clarissa*, an unspecified role in *The Commissary*; Gaffer Gubbin in *The Dragon of Wantley*, General Savage in *The School for Wives*, Lord Ogleby in *The Clandestine Marriage*, Gregory in *The Mock Doctor*, Hawthorn in *Love in a Village*, Patrick

O'Carrol in *The Register Office*, the President in *The Devil upon Two Sticks*, Sealand in *The Conscious Lovers*, Sergeant Puzzle in *The Lecturer*, Sir Benjamin Dove in *The Brothers*, Sir Francis Wronghead in *The Provok'd Husband*, and Sir John Trotly in *Bon Ton*.

In the autumn of 1775 Inchbald was among those celebrated in *The Edinburgh Rosciad*, a wretchedly rhymed critical sheet:

Inchbald, the all-work player of the house,
Comes next to get his ditty from the muse;
Tonight he's Jaffier, Henry, *or* Othello,
To-morrow Quixotte, *or a* Punchinello.

In addition to acting a wide range of roles at Edinburgh and also on the excursions to Scottish provincial towns by members of the Theatre Royal, Shakespeare Square, it appears, from the elliptical language of James Boaden in the *Memoir of Mrs Inchbald*, that he was also from time to time engaged in painting stage scenery.

But an ambition to be a portraitist had simmered in Inchbald from his earliest youth. On 2 July 1776 he and his wife left Edinburgh and, going to Shields, took ship for St Valleri. He had determined to devote a year to the study of painting at Paris, with the visionary purpose of subsisting by the art. His wife accompanied him because she wanted to study the French language and acting technique. Their money ran out, they were miserable, and at the end of 11 weeks they went home.

Inchbald's next professional stop was Liverpool, where he and his wife had been engaged by Joseph Younger to play from 10 October 1776. At Liverpool they made the acquaintance of Mrs Siddons, who was to be a staunch friend to Mrs Inchbald for many years. On 17 December they left Liverpool for Manchester, surviving without much hurt the overturning of their coach. On 18 January 1777, sipping tea with Mrs Siddons, they first met her 20-year-old younger brother John Philip Kemble.

During the spring of 1777 a group of performers, including the Inchbalds, the Siddonses, and Kemble, lived together in country lodgings on Russell Moor, and Inchbald busied himself painting likenesses of his wife and Kemble. In May they returned to Manchester, where a quarrel between Inchbald and Younger over costumes sent the couple to Birmingham. There again they lived with the Siddons-Kem-

ble group until their theatrical performances were stopped by the magistrates. Early in 1778 Inchbald and his wife were at Canterbury for two months. They then joined Tate Wilkinson's company on the York circuit for the last and happiest period of Inchbald's theatrical career.

At York, Inchbald acted and was also pressed into service again as a scene painter, providing the picture scene for *The School for Scandal* in April 1778 and scenes for *Tony Lumpkin in Town* on 2 February 1779 and a perspective view for *The Camp* on 20 February 1779.

On 4 June 1779 the Inchbalds made an excursion to Halifax, as much for pleasure as performance, though they both acted. Joseph, in good spirits, accompanied the ladies' coach on horseback. On 5 June the party went to Leeds. Next day Inchbald suddenly died—in his wife's arms, according to Wilkinson's rather fevered account. He was buried at Leeds. John Philip Kemble furnished an elaborate Latin epitaph for his tomb.

Joseph Inchbald by most accounts was a good actor, a pleasant man, and an indulgent, faithful, and almost uxorious husband to his beautiful young wife. She vexed him repeatedly with her innocent coquetries and capricious behavior, and there were many small quarrels, soon made up. She was deeply grieved by his death and did not remarry, though she outlived him by half a century. Inchbald's dear friend Tate Wilkinson left a testimonial:

Mr. Inchbald was my friend, my worthy man, my esteemed actor, in all my long 'Pilgrim's Progress.' For the time he was engaged with me, I never experienced more ingenuousness, honour, and integrity, nor did I ever know an actor of such universal worth, who confessed at least weekly, (if not daily) the comforts he felt in his Yorkshire situation, and ardently expressed an anxiety for the success and life of me, his manager, whose interest he, by every means, endeavoured to support. He soon grew into great favour, particularly by his performing Justice Credulous, Sir Anthony Absolute, and many comic old gentlemenlike characters; his painting (to which he had I believe been bred) also aided his popularity: His picture-scene, now in full sight, whenever the School for Scandal is represented, proves his talents, execution, and design: In short, it was a continuance, during his engagement with me, of the utmost satisfaction; and he adored his lovely Mrs. Inchbald to a degree of enthusiasm. . . .

Inchbald, Mrs Joseph, Elizabeth, née Simpson *1753–1821, actress, singer, playwright, novelist, poet.*

Elizabeth Simpson was born on 15 October 1753 at Standingfield, near Bury St Edmunds in Suffolk, one of the numerous children of John and Mary Simpson. Her parents were substantial farmers and Roman Catholics, part of a considerable society of yeomen and gentry of that faith in the locality. She had a grave defect in her speech, and she resented the fact that her brothers were sent to school and the girls in the family were not. But from her earliest years she repaired her deficiencies by earnest reading.

Elizabeth's family were fond of plays and attended often at the theatre in Bury. Despite her stutter the child early determined that she would one day become an actress, and when her brother George left home to go on the stage her resolve increased. After several times fruitlessly applying to Griffith, the Norwich manager, on 11 April 1772 Elizabeth left a note for her mother and departed in the Norwich fly for London. Two (?) of her sisters and other relatives lived in London, but from motives of pride she avoided them until a series of adventures, occurring as she wandered the town alone, frightened her into their care.

Elizabeth called several times on Thomas King and Samuel Reddish, who offered wary encouragement but no theatrical engagement, and on James Dodd, who offered only indecent proposals. She was, as he said, "terrified and vexed beyond measure at his behavior" and, according to James Boaden, her biographer, found it necessary to dampen his ardour by throwing a basin of hot water in his face. It was only the first of many times that her extraordinary beauty would tempt men to excessive behavior. Among several actors whom she had seen with her brother George on the stage in Norfolk was Joseph Inchbald who was then performing in London. Though twice her age, he began a courtship which culminated with their marriage by a Catholic priest, one Father Rice, in her sister's house on 9 June 1772. Inchbald was said by James Boaden to be a Catholic also, but some doubt is raised by the fact that a Protestant ceremony was performed for the couple at St Andrew, Holborn the following day.

On 11 June 1772 the couple set off for Bristol, where Inchbald had an engagement and where he arranged a trial for his wife. Her debut was on 4 September 1772 as Cordelia to his Lear. Evidently only her beautiful face and slender figure rendered her performance tolerable. Though she had resolutely practiced elocution, her efforts had only produced a stage delivery which was forced and artificial. Her devoted husband set about coaching her until "at length she hit upon a better tone of declamation than she had set out with," though apparently she was never able to achieve an entirely satisfactory diction in performance.

In September 1772 Inchbald completed his Bristol engagement, and the pair, along with Robert, Inchbald's son by a former connection, returned to London, embarked for Scotland, arrived at Leith on 17 October after a stormy

Harvard Theatre Collection

ELIZABETH INCHBALD

engraving after Drummond

passage, and set out to join West Digges's company, then at Glasgow. Elizabeth was allowed Anne Bullen in *Henry VIII* on 6 November, with her husband playing Cranmer. After that she apparently got no other important parts at Glasgow but performed a Witch in *Macbeth* and "walked" in the pantomimes.

When the company went to Edinburgh, Elizabeth accelerated her attempts to cast off her impediment and master an acting style, and she and Joseph walked on the hills and by the seashore for many hours "spouting" verse. Digges cast her in *Jane Shore*, Cordelia in *King Lear* and Calista in *The Fair Penitent* and she played Anne Bullen again; she was Calpurnia to her husband's Julius Caesar and Aspasia to his Tamerlane, Lady Anne in *Richard III*, Lady Percy in *1 Henry IV*, Lady Elizabeth Gray in *The Earl of Warwick*, Fanny in *The Clandestine Marriage*, Mrs. Strickland in *The Suspicious Husband*, and the Tragic Muse in *The Jubilee*. She also sang in the chorus of the *Beggar's Opera* and served as a Bacchante in *Comus*.

On 26 April 1773 the company returned to Glasgow and there she performed several times a week, adding to her repertoire Clarissa in *All in the Wrong*, Lucia in *Cato*, Mary Queen of Scots in *The Albion Queens*, Zulina in *The Princess of Tunis*, the title role in *Lady Jane Gray*, Miranda in *The Tempest*, and Louisa Dudley in *The West Indian*. On 17 June the playhouse at Greenock opened for a month and Elizabeth added Miss Aubrey in *The Fashionable Lovers*, Angelica in *The Constant Couple*, and Violante in *The Wonder*.

On 2 August the players embarked at Leith for Aberdeen but were caught by a storm so violent that the ship was unable to make headway. They were set ashore, forced to walk in the rain, and begged rides in carts. Both Inchbalds suffered bad attacks of ague and fever. Her constitution may have been undermined permanently, for she was in fragile health often thereafter throughout her life. Though very ill for a fortnight, she recovered sufficiently to play 33 characters on 31 nights from 12 August through 8 November, adding Mary Queen of Scots in *The Albion Queens*, Imogen in *Cymbeline*, Miss Neville in *She Stoops to Conquer*, the Queen in *The Spanish Fryar*, Belvidera in *Venice Preserv'd*, Desdemona in *Othello*, Monimia in *The Orphan*, Palmira in *Mahomet*, Silvia in *The Recruiting Officer*, Indiana in *The*

Conscious Lovers, and Sigismunda in *Tancred and Sigismunda*. In their return toward Edinburgh on 9 November 1773, the theatrical party again had to walk much of the way in the rain and don wet clothes after sleeping in a draughty inn. Their illness returned, and Inchbald had to be carried in a chair when he was required at the theatre.

In January 1774 Mrs Inchbald began a serious study of French. In April she and her husband returned to Glasgow to act and during the stay visited Glamis Castle and took excursions to perform at Haddington and Kelso. Early in 1775 her brother George Simpson and his wife joined the Edinburgh company, Elizabeth playing Juliet in his first performance and George Benvolio. By 20 April the Simpsons had quarreled with Digges, had been discharged, and had been reinstated by the mediation of the Inchbalds. In May Joseph and Elizabeth performed at Aberdeen. In July a recurrence of the ague caused her to faint onstage in Edinburgh. Her health continued poor through the summer, but she plunged on with her reading and her French study. The Inchbalds continued to act with success at Edinburgh and its dependent theatres through 1775–76. On 12 June 1776 Joseph gave some undescribed offense to the spectators and engaged in a dispute with them which they avenged by rioting on 15 June when Elizabeth played Jane Shore. On 2 July, they left Edinburgh.

The years in Edinburgh had brought unhappiness as well as artistic success and some prosperity. In the first winter the desire for adoration which was one of the strongest strains in Elizabeth Inchbald's nature had drawn the quiet but pointed attentions of the actor Sterling, which in turn excited the jealousy of Joseph. Joseph indulged in excursions and carousings, led astray by their libertine friend, the actor Dick Wilson, and incurred the suspicion of infidelity. There were later violent quarrels over the assiduous attentions to Elizabeth of a Mr Webb and over her capricious acts—like suddenly cutting off her hair. The quarrels were always made up; Inchbald was always brought to heel by his uxorious nature. She was kept faithful by her religious principles and her rather cool view of men.

The Inchbalds now determined to spend a year in France, he with the naïve notion of perfecting his technique as an amateur painter to the point where he could subsist upon it professionally, she with the more practical purpose of studying the French language and acting techniques. Also (though this was far back in her mind) she was storing up impressions for the writing she was to do. (Already, as early as 1769, or earlier, she had begun to keep a careful journal.) They sailed from Shields for St Valleri on 2 July 1776 and, by way of Abbeville and Amiens, made their way to Paris. But money ran out, and at the end of eleven weeks they took the packet for Brighton.

Coming to London, where Dick Wilson was a favorite at Covent Garden as Don Jerome in *The Duenna*, they sought his aid and that of Digges to gain a foothold in the capital. They stayed until 4 October in fruitless supplication to the managers. Joseph Younger at Liverpool took them on, and there Elizabeth added to her growing string of parts Leonora in *The Mourning Bride* and Cleopatra in *All for Love*.

ELIZABETH INCHBALD

engraving by Wooding, after Russell

At Liverpool also was begun the important friendship with Mrs Siddons, which was to last for Elizabeth for 45 years. On the journey to play at Manchester on 17 December 1776, the Inchbalds' coach overturned, but they were only shaken up. Sipping tea and supping with Mrs Siddons on 18 January 1777, they for the first time met her 20-year-old brother John Philip Kemble.

Early in 1778 Mrs Inchbald proclaimed herself "remarkably unsettled" and domestic bickering broke out again. But on 24 March the couple went to country lodgings on Russell Moor, living in serene communal harmony with fellow performers Mr and Mrs Siddons, John Philip Kemble, Thomas Jefferson, and William Lane. While her husband painted portraits, Mrs Inchbald read long hours with Kemble. There were conversations, long walks, cardplaying, and childish games like blindman's buff on the moors.

That year Mrs Inchbald's strange and restive nature was newly perplexed in doubts about religion, though she had continued an irregular communicant of the Church. She corresponded with Father Jerningham in Paris and he replied with consoling equivocation.

In May 1778 the party returned to Manchester. On 26 May, after a quarrel over costumes between Inchbald and Younger, the Kembles, Siddonses, and Inchbalds left for Birmingham to act under Mattocks's management, but the performances there were stopped by the magistrates. The Inchbalds next went for two months to Dimond's company at Canterbury, where they met Thomas Holcroft, the radical actor and writer, who was to figure largely in Elizabeth's future. She played opposite him in 19 performances and added to her repertoire Rosamund in *Henry II*, Julia in *The Rivals*, Emma in *Henry and Emma*, Elizabeth in *King Charles I* (her benefit with Jones), Leonora in *The Revenge*, Portia in *The Merchant of Venice*, Angelina in *Love Makes a Man*, Isabella in *Sir Thomas Overbury*, the title part in *Semiramis*, Clarissa in *The Hotel*, Eleonora in *Edward and Eleanora*, and Perdita in *Florizel and Perdita*.

On 20 September 1777 the Inchbalds left Canterbury and made their way to Hull to join Tate Wilkinson's Yorkshire circuit. The whimsical Wilkinson recalled in his *Wandering Patentee* "my well-beloved, my beautiful Mrs.

INCHBALD" playing the lead Horatia in *The Roman Father* for her debut at Hull on 28 October. The Inchbalds followed the circuit—York to Leeds to Wakefield to Doncaster to Hull—she adding the new parts Lady Sneerwell in *The School for Scandal* and Selima in *Tamerlane*. There were frequent quarrels because of Inchbald's jealousy of the minor player Davis, who dressed Mrs Inchbald's hair, and also over the division of their salaries. Kemble turned up and chose Mrs Inchbald to take the leading part and speak the epilogue in his new tragedy *Belisarius* on 28 December 1778. Mrs Inchbald, inspired, went hard to work on her novel *A Simple Story*.

On 4 June 1779 the Inchbalds made a carefree excursion with a party to perform at Halifax. Joseph gallantly accompanied the ladies' coach on horseback. They returned to Leeds the following day. On the next, 6 June, Joseph suddenly died.

The company gave Elizabeth a benefit on 14 June. She welcomed George Inchbald to the company on 26 June and then spent a few weeks resting at Pontefract. In September she resumed acting, at Wakefield and Doncaster. She finished a rough draft of her novel *A Simple Story* and sent it off to the publisher John Stockdale in London by way of her friend Dr Brodie. Stockdale politely refused it. Tate Wilkinson's rough kindness helped her sustain the twin shocks of her widowhood and the publisher's refusal. He not only promised her the top salary of a guinea and a half per week if she would sign his articles for the following year but raised George Inchbald's weekly wage several shillings. On 8 April 1780 Elizabeth went into breeches to act Hamlet for the benefit of her stepson, who that night played Horatio.

Six months after her husband died Elizabeth had to reject diplomatically a proposal of matrimony from the comedian Dicky Suett; and a year and a half after Joseph's death his old friend the rake Richard Wilson also suggested marriage and was found wanting. Elizabeth and everyone else seems to have expected overtures from Kemble, and he seems to have been tempted. (Years later he asked her if she would have had him, and she is supposed to have replied: "I'd have *jumped* at you.")

For all his admiration of her person and intellect, Wilkinson found Mrs Inchbald captious. She disliked Lady Sneerwell; she resented playing in pantomimes. She tried unsuccessfully to transfer her services to Palmer at Bath. There were reasons for her difficult behavior. For many weeks she was ill; she was oppressed by the poverty of members of her family, to whom she had continually to send money. Her old friend Dr Brodie sought to become her lover and was so importunate that she had to refuse to see him again.

In July 1780 Elizabeth returned to Edinburgh to play a selection of lead and secondary roles: Edwina in *Percy*, Clarinda in *The Suspicious Husband*, Mrs Sullen in *The Beaux' Stratagem*, Widow Racket in *The Belle's Stratagem*, and Lady Dainty in *The Double Gallant*.

On 3 October 1780 Elizabeth made her first appearance at Covent Garden Theatre playing Bellario in *Philaster*. Her salary was £2 per week that season. It was the beginning of a nine-year acting career there. To the list of characters she is known to have played she added Mariana in *Measure for Measure*, Angelina in *Love Makes a Man*, Lavinia in *The Fair Penitent*, Lady Touchwood in *The Belle's Stratagem*, Lady Elizabeth Grey in *The Earl of Warwick*, Charlotte in *The Gamester*, the Lady in *Comus*, the Abbess in *The Comedy of Errors*, the Queen in *King Charles I*, Lady Allworth in *A New Way to Pay Old Debts*, Violante in *Sir Courtly Nice*, and First Constantia in *The Chances*. In 1781–82 she added Melissa in *Duplicity*, Wat Dreary in an all-female production of *The Beggar's Opera*, the Marchioness di Quintano in *The Banditti*, Nottingham in *The Earl of Essex*, and Miss Mortimer in *The Chapter of Accidents*. In the summer of 1782 she engaged with George Colman at the Haymarket, but he gave her only 30s. a week. Her new roles that summer (besides Ben Budge in a transvestite *Beggar's Opera*, in which her dissolute friend Becky Wells was Macheath) were Miss English in *The Separate Maintenance*, the original Emma Cecil in Frances Burney's new comedy *The East Indian*, and Belinda in *Tunbridge Walks*.

On 6 October 1782 Elizabeth went to Shrewsbury and acted a month thereafter with Miller for a guinea a week and a benefit which cleared £10. She refused to return to York and closed an agreement for £5 per week with the unscrupulous Richard Daly at Smock Alley Theatre, Dublin, arriving there on 9 Novem-

ELIZABETH INCHBALD as the Lady Abbess

engraving by Scriven, after Ramberg

ber. Kemble was in Dublin, and they resumed the practice of reading to each other. She continued to read on her own and to concoct comedies which went to Harris and Colman for quick rejection. At Dublin she added to her repertoire Adelaide in *The Count of Narbonne*, Julia in *Which is the Man?*, Octavia in *All for Love*, Statira in *The Rival Queens*, Erixene in *The Brothers*, and Jacintha in *The Suspicious Husband*. Daly made (of course unsuccessfully) the squalid demands with which he usually oppressed actresses under his management. Elizabeth boarded the packet for Liverpool on 25 May 1783.

Elizabeth returned in June 1783 to her disappointingly thin round of parts at the Haymarket, adding Caelia in *The Fox*, Emma Howard in *A Friend in Need is a Friend Indeed*, Emily in *The Lawyer*, and Olivia in the *Good-Natured Man*. She continued to act some parts she had learned outside London.

Other additions to her London repertoire,

by year and theatre, were as follows: Covent Garden, 1783–84, Sukey Tawdry in *The Beggar's Opera*, Florimel in *The Positive Man*, Hermione in *The Winter's Tale*, Lady Blanch in *King John*, and Aurelia in *The Prophetess*; Haymarket, 1784, a "Principal Character" (so in the playbill, but doubtless Irene, which she is listed for in 1786) in her own successful interlude *A Mogul Tale*, which came out on 6 July 1784; Covent Garden, 1784–85, Nerissa in *The Merchant of Venice*, Mrs Fainall in *The Way of the World*, Mrs Page in *Merry Wives of Windsor*, Bertha in *Matilda*, and the Duchess in *Women Pleas'd*; Haymarket, 1785, Lady Margaret Russel in *Lord Russel*, Lady Frances in *The Two Connoisseurs*, Laura in *Tancred and Sigismunda*, Bell in *The Deuce is in Him*, and the Countess in *All's Well that Ends Well*; Covent Garden, 1785–86, Imoinda in *Oroonoko*, Lady Charlotte in *The Funeral*, Regan in *King Lear*, Lucinda in *The Conscious Lovers*, Eliza in *The Plain Dealer*, Zelmira in *Zenobia*, Melissa in *Timon of Athens*, Lady Eusten in *I'll Tell You What*, and Laura in *A Bold Stroke for a Husband*; Covent Garden, 1786–87, Lady Lambert in *The Hypocrite*, Dorinda in *The Beaux' Stratagem*, Harriet in *The Miser*, and Britannia in *Omar*; and Covent Garden, 1788–89, Julia in *The Midnight Hour* and Constance in *Animal Magnetism*. At the end of the Covent Garden season of 1788–89, with her articles expiring and hopes of eminence as a first-line actress dimming, Elizabeth turned resolutely from the stage to her writing.

Whether it was her impatient nature or her early experience as a provincial stroller which made her peripatetic, Mrs Inchbald never settled down to a permanent abode in London. In 1782–83 she lodged with a Mrs Smith at No 2, Leicester Court, Castle Street, Leicester Fields. Before 1786 she lodged with the Morells in Hart Street but that year moved to the residence of a Mrs Hall in Great Russell Street, Covent Garden, which had in Addison's time been the famous Button's Coffee House. From 1789 she was to be found in a room in Frith Street, Soho, and in 1792 went (with great expectations) to live at a Mr Shakespear's in Leicester Fields. (He did not turn out to be literary.) Before 1803 she was somewhere on Leicester Square but on 11 June that year went to live at Annandale House, Turnham Green, a community of Roman Catholic women. She found the superintendent offensive and stayed only until December, when she moved to a small room on the top floor of No 163, the Strand. In June 1810 she moved to a house, No 5, in St George's Row "looking over Hyde Park, upon the Surrey Hills" but lived unquietly because of a squabble between her landlord and the owner. In May 1811 she moved down to No 1, St George's Row, in 1817 to No 4, Earl's Terrace, Kensington, and in mid-April 1819 to Kensington House.

There she died on 1 August 1821, after a short respiratory illness, an ailment which had been recurrent for years. She was buried on 4 August in Kensington churchyard.

Elizabeth died debt-free and with an estimated £6,000 in investments, which she dispersed in her will to a variety of friends and relations. The principal beneficiaries were her nephew George Huggins and niece Ann Jarrett. But she left sums to her laundress (a former theatrical hairdresser) and even £20 per year "to the person calling himself Robert Inchbald, the illegitimate son of my late husband." Other beneficiaries included the old actress Isabella Mattocks, who received £50, and the Theatrical Fund of Covent Garden, £50.

Her exceptional beauty and strong character carried her further as an actress than her histrionic talents warranted and further than she herself expected, considering her handicap in speech. It was perhaps unfortunate that she persevered so long—until her thirty-seventh year—before turning to writing full time.

That point was made in one of the very few contemporary allusions—the only really cruel one—to both her acting and writing, in the lines by the savage "Anthony Pasquin" (John Williams) in *The Children of Thespis* (1788):

A truant to Modesty, wild without rule,
She roams after Folly, and raves in her school;
Guts novels for sentiment, plot, pun, and diction,
And looks to the cieling for objects of fiction.

. . . .

As an Actress her claims but dishonour her station,
And debase the attempts of my investigation;
For her scribbling rage has extinguish'd the player,
And impell'd her to slight both her practice and
*   prayer*

. . . .

But INCHBALD, *decreed more absurd than her*
*   neighbours,*
With God and the Devil besprinkles her labours;
Sure the traits of her mind must be oddly directed,

Harvard Theatre Collection

ELIZABETH INCHBALD as Lady Jane
engraving by Audinet, after De Wilde

When her bawdry destroys what her morals ef-
*   fected.*

It was sheer slander. Her morals were safe enough, protected both by her piety and her wary view of the world. Her chaste charms were often a vexation to others of her sex. William Godwin's daughter Mary, Mrs Shelley, wrote that she had heard a "rival beauty complain" that when Mrs Inchbald came into a room every man in it would be attracted to her immediately. A description written by an admirer, which she preserved among her papers, endorsed "Description of Me," portrayed her as fair but freckled, and "with a tinge of sand, which is the colour of her eyelashes; no bosom; hair of a sandy auburn; . . . face beautiful in effect and beautiful in every feature; . . . countenance full of spirit and sweetness, excessively interesting, and, without indelicacy, voluptuous; . . . dress always becoming and very seldom worth so much as eight-pence."

A letter of 6 December 1773 in the Burney collection in the British Library remarks that "from an absolute stuttering she can hardly make herself intelligible" in private conversation but that on the stage she was highly articulate. She retained a slight stammer to the end of her life. She was vain of her beauty, and of her intelligence, and used both in her recurrent warfare with managers and editors. A letter of 3 April 1780 addressed by her to Wilkinson, in which she is insistent about parts and salary for a summer engagement ends: ". . . consider how Peaceable I am—how *Good-natured*—how *tall*—and how *Pretty*." John Nichols preserves in his *Illustrations* an appraisal by George Hardinge:

I doat upon her. Her manners are gentle, easy, and elegant, . . . She is of the middle height, and by nature fair; but she has rather too settled a colour in her face. Her figure is excellent, her features pretty, and her mouth [possesses] as fine teeth as ever you saw. She is very short-sighted, and cannot see three inches from her nose without a little round glass, which is a most graceful implement in her hand. She is perfectly modest; but arch, clever, and so interesting, that if she had no genius you would long to be acquainted with her. What [people] seem to enjoy in her most is her *naiveté*, and she gave us two or three capital traits of it. She lives alone—her character has no *tache* upon it—and Mrs. Siddons said she was as cold as ice: but I cannot believe it, for at least I see a little of the coquette in her, but well disciplined, and well bred.

Elizabeth Inchbald's literary output was enormous, especially considering her tardy start. She completed a four-volume autobiography but on the advice of her spiritual adviser, Dr Poynter, burned it shortly before her death. (Fortunately for our knowledge of at least the external events of her life, she also kept for over half a century a minute record of her daily activities, expenditures, and receipts, from which James Boaden was able to extract the two volumes of his *Memoirs of Mrs. Inchbald*. Many of the original notebooks have disappeared, though some survive at the British Library and others at the Folger Library.)

In the cramped, uncomfortable surroundings of lodgings Mrs Inchbald had doggedly hammered out her plays, novels, and critical essays, had done her editing, and had kept up her diary day by day until it eventually numbered 52 annual volumes. Her writings for the stage were very profitable. She received as much as £600 for a single comedy, an enormous sum for her day. She was also determinedly frugal, doing her own housework and carrying scuttles of coals up flights of stairs. But her benefactions, to family and friends, were large. At the same time she lived a brilliant social life, with a wide and respectful acquaintance among the nobility and the literati alike. She said herself that she had sometimes finished scrubbing her floor while a nobleman's coach waited at her door.

In addition to several wooers inclined to marriage, she was until very late in life surrounded by would-be lovers, some of whom she could not quite bring herself to accept and others of whom (like John Kemble) could not bring themselves to propose—among them Francis Twiss, a close friend and adviser, who eventually married Frances Kemble; her physician Dr. Gisborne; and the eccentric divine, medical man, and satirical poet John Wolcot ("Peter Pindar"). She remained good friends with the several generations of Kembles and with Elizabeth Farren and her mother, and she stubbornly befriended the unfortunate actress Mary ("Becky") Wells, whose indiscretions shocked Mrs Inchbald's proper acquaintances, providing her an allowance until Becky's death in 1812.

Her dramatic productions were *A Mogul Tale; or The Descent of the Balloon*, an interlude, Haymarket 1785 (published 1824); *I'll Tell You What*, comedy, Haymarket, 1785 (1786); *Appearance is Against Them*, Covent Garden, 1785 (1785); *The Widow's Vow*, Haymarket, farce, 1786 (1786); *Such Things Are*, melodrama, Covent Garden, 1787 (1788); *The Midnight Hour, or War of Wits*, translated from the French, Covent Garden, 1787 (1787); *All on a Summer's Day*, comedy, Covent Garden, 1787; *Animal Magnetism*, farce, Covent Garden, 1789; *The Child of Nature*, from the French of Madame the Marchioness Sillery, formerly Countess of Genlis, Covent Garden, 1788 (1788); *The Married Man* from *Le Philosophe Marie* of Néricault Destouches, Haymarket, 1789 (1789); *The Hue and Cry*, farce,

Drury Lane, 1791; *Next Door Neighbours* from the French dramas *L'Indigent* and *Le Dissipateur*, Haymarket, 1791; *Young Men and Old Women*, farce, Haymarket, 1792; and "The Massacre," 1792, tragedy, neither produced nor published in Mrs Inchbald's time. (Boaden appends it to vol I of *Memoirs*, where he explains that, though it was printed, it was suppressed "in deference to political opinions, which we do not absolutely condemn.")

Every One Has His Fault, comedy, Covent Garden, 1793, (1792); *The Wedding Day*, farce, 1794, (1794); *Wives As They Were and Maids As They Are*, comedy, 1797, (1797); *Lovers' Vows*, drama from the German of August Friedrich von Kotzebue, Covent Garden, 1798, (1798); *The Wise Man of the East*, drama, from the German of Kotzebue, Covent Garden, 1799, (1799); *A Case of Conscience*, melodrama, 1800, neither acted nor published (Boaden appends it to vol II of *Memoirs*, with her note explaining her withdrawing it from Covent Garden); and *To Marry, or Not to Marry*, Covent Garden, 1805, (1805). Other dramas which have sometimes been attributed to Elizabeth Inchbald are *Cross Purposes* "By a Lady," comedy, Haymarket, 1792, (1792); and *The Spoiled Child*, a farce, Drury Lane, 1790.

Mrs Inchbald also edited several anthologies of plays: *The British Theatre*, 25 volumes, 1806–1809; *The Modern Theatre*, 10 volumes, 1809: and *A Collection of Farces and Other Afterpieces*, seven volumes, 1809.

Her most lasting influence was exerted through her four-volume romantic novel *A Simple Story*, published in 1791. It went through many editions and was translated early into French and German. The novel concerns the contrast between a mother who has had a conventional upbringing and a daughter who has received in her education an infusion of "modern" ideas. *Nature and Art*, Mrs Inchbald's second novel, employs Rousseau's theme of the natural man. Henry, who was brought up on a wild island, is a child of nature, simple and kind. William, who has had an English education, is rakish and insensitive. The novels were widely influential, especially among bluestocking ladies who aspired to write romantic fiction.

Mrs Inchbald contributed critical articles to the *Edinburgh Review* and other publications.

John Murray tried to interest her in writing for the new *Quarterly Review* in 1808 but failed, and John Bell offered her the editorship of *La Belle Assemblée* in 1809, but she declined.

Elizabeth Inchbald was a favorite subject for portraiture. Following is a list of likenesses:

1. By Richard Cosway. Watercolor. Location unknown.

2. By George Dance. Pencil drawing in the National Portrait Gallery. Engraving by W. Daniell.

3. By Mrs Douce. In his *Memoirs of Mrs. Inchbald* (1, 343), Boaden wrote that "in the month of March, 1794, Mrs. Inchbald sat for her portrait to Mrs. Douce, of Upper Gower Street." Location unknown.

4. By S. Drummond. Location unknown. Engraving by W. Ridley. Published as a plate to the *Monthly Mirror*, 1797. Another engraving, by unknown engraver, after Drummond, with some variations, was published as a plate to *La Belle Assemblée*, 1821.

5. By G. H. Harlow. Pencil drawing in the Garrick Club (catalogue No 402).

6. By G. H. Harlow. Canvas in the Players Club (catalogue No 5).

7. By William Hoare. Location unknown.

8. By John Hoppner. Canvas. Property of Madame E. André in 1914. Location unknown.

9. By Thomas Lawrence, 1796, unfinished. Owned by H. M. Adams, Cambridge, England. Engraving by S. Freeman. Published as a plate to the *Monthly Mirror*, 1797.

10. By Thomas Lawrence. Similar to No 8, perhaps a repetition. Sold by Lady Blessington at Christie's on 20 June 1846; in the Dutton family, Birch Hall, Windlesham, 1913. Sold at Sotheby's, 23 March 1807 (lot 85). Reproduced in *Burlington Magazine*, March 1977.

11. By Thomas Lawrence. Perhaps identical with No 9, but not certainly Mrs Inchbald. Owned by Mr and Mrs Morrie A. Moss, Memphis, Tennessee.

12. By John Opie. In the collection of Lord Leconfield.

13. By John Opie. At Petworth House, Sussex. Probably the painting that sold for five and a half guineas at Opie's sale on 6 June 1807.

14. By Sir Henry Raeburn. Location unknown.

15. By George Romney. In the Tennant Collection, 1904. Reproduced in Gower's *Romney*, 1904. The portrait was purchased by Sir Charles Tennant from Miss Romney, late of Whitestock Hall, Ulverston. Engraving by Heath, published by Longman & Co, 1806.

16. Engraved portrait by J. Hopwood, Jr, after R. E. Drummond. Published as a plate to *Ladies' Monthly Museum*, 1819.

17. Engraved portrait by W. Ridley. Published by Vernor & Hood, 1798.

18. Engraved portrait by T. S. Seed. Published as a plate to *Thespian Magazine*, 1794.

19. Engraved portrait by Walker, after Cook. Published by Bellamy, 1787. Also in reverse by unknown engraver, after Cook, published as a plate to *Hibernian Magazine*, October 1787. Other engravings, copied after Walker's, by J. Chapman, and by Holl; the latter was published on 1 May 1800 on a plate with portraits of John O'Keeffe, Thomas Dibdin, and R. B. Sheridan.

20. Engraved portrait by Wooding, after J. Russell. Published as a plate to *European Magazine*, 1788. Also engraved in reverse by Page, with another copy by an unknown engraver.

21. As the Lady Abbess in *The Comedy of Errors*. Engraving by C. Sherwin, after H. Ramberg. Published by J. Bell, 1806; a copy by E. Scriven, also after Ramberg, was printed for J. Cawthorn, 1806.

22. As the Lady Abbess. Engraving by Wooding. Published as a plate to *New Lady's Magazine*, 1786.

23. As Lady Jane Gray in *Lady Jane Gray*. By Samuel De Wilde. In the Garrick Club. Engraving by P. Audinet. Published as a plate to *Bell's British Theatre*, 1791.

Inchbald, Robert *[fl. 1769?–1815]*, *actor, instrumentalist.*

Robert Inchbald was the son ("illegitimate," he admitted) of Joseph Inchbald the actor. The actor George Inchbald was either his brother or half brother. Robert was probably at Norwich acting juvenile parts in 1769 when "Mr Inchbald & Son" were named in the Committee Books of Norwich Theatre as persons to be rehired that season, though that may have been his brother George. The first sure notice we have of him is in the autumn of 1772 when he, his father, and his (reluctant) stepmother Elizabeth Simpson Inchbald were at Glasgow,

residing in the same house while they acted at the theatre. He was given such roles as Fleance in *Macbeth*. He seems to have annoyed his stepmother, both then and afterward, and when they returned to Edinburgh she required him to lodge separately from her and his father, her new husband. His age at the time was perhaps somewhere between 9 and 12 years old.

According to Norma Armstrong's calendar of performances at Edinburgh he played Lucius in *Julius Caesar* on 15 December 1773, Tom Thimble in *The Rehearsal* on 23 December, William in *The Jealous Wife* on 5 January 1774, Robin in *The Merry Wives of Windsor* on 9 April.

There is no further record of Robert's having acted. But we believe he was probably the Robert Inchbald who was listed by Charles Burney as among the second violins at the Handel Memorial Concerts at Westminster Abbey and the Pantheon in May and June 1784. He was also a violoncellist, succeeding Monroe as first violoncellist of the band of the Musical Society of Oxford, which played concerts at the Oxford Music Room in 1791. He was succeeded there by Reinagle in 1795. He belonged to the New Musical Fund and was on its lists as a resident of Oxford in 1794 and of Winchester in 1805. In 1815 he was living in Southampton.

Mrs Joseph Inchbald was tart in her will: "To the person calling himself Robert Inchbald, the illegitimate Son of my late husband, I leave twenty pounds a year."

Ineledon, Charles Benjamin *1763–1826, singer, actor.*

Charles Benjamin Incledon was christened at St Keverne, Cornwall, on 5 February 1763 with the name of Benjamin; later he took the name of Charles. He was the son of Bartholomew Incledon, a surgeon and apothecary of St Keverne, and his wife Loveday. His father was probably related to the Incledons of Gratton in Devonshire, who intermarried with the Glinnes of Cornwall; he may also have been a relative of Benjamin Incledon (1730–1796), the Devonshire genealogist, who is noticed in *The Dictionary of National Biography*.

Placed in the Exeter cathedral choir at the age of eight, Incledon received his early tuition from Richard Langdon and then from William Jackson. Quickly he became a little idol at the concerts and musical parties of Exeter. It is

Royal College of Music

CHARLES INCLEDON

attributed to Shee

reported that when at a divine service Judge Nares heard him sing the solo "Let the Soul live," the magistrate was reduced to tears and gave the lad five guineas. Incledon abandoned his studies in 1779 to serve in the man-of-war *Formidable*, under Captain Cleland, bound for the West Indies. Afterwards he transferred to the *Raisonnable*, on board which he experienced several naval engagements in 1782. His vocal talents were much appreciated by his officers, who, it is said, dubbed him "Singer to the British Fleet." After his discharge in 1783 Admiral Pigot, Lord Mulgrave, and Lord Hervey furnished him with letters of introduction to Colman and Sheridan, the London managers. Nothing came of his auditions, if indeed they ever occurred.

According to Gilliland, it was Royle, a member of the band at the Southampton theatre, who was instrumental in obtaining an engagement for Incledon there under Collins's management at 10s. 6d. per week in 1784. Incledon's first appearance at Southampton was as Alphonso in *The Castle of Andalusia* on a date unrecorded. He joined the Bath theatre in 1785, making his first appearance as Belville in *Rosina*. Among his other roles there was Edwin in *Robin Hood*, but most of the time he served as a chorus singer, at a salary reported to have been 30s. per week. At Bath he was tutored by Rauzzini, who introduced him to the concerts in Bath and Bristol. Among the first in which Incledon seems to have sung was the concert given on 25 August 1785 under the younger Brooks's direction for the benefit of Leoni at the Assembly Rooms in Bristol. Rauzzini's patronage helped Incledon to obtain an engagement in the summer of 1786 at Vauxhall Gardens, where, announced as from the Theatre Royal, Bath, he made his debut on 29 May.

Incledon sang every summer at Vauxhall through at least 1791, and many songs, especially those by James Hook, were published as sung there by him. These included *The Triumph of Beauty* (1786), *The Musical Courtship* (1787?), *I'll think on thee* (1788?), *Sweet Robinette* (1788?), *The Volunteer* (1789?), *Je pense à vous* (1790), *Lash'd to the Helm* (1790?), and *Adieu ma Liberté* (1790?). In December 1786 at the Free Masons' Hall he sang *Ma Chère Amie*, a popular ballad by Hook, which he had introduced at Vauxhall the pre-

vious summer and which was published about that time. In 1789 at Vauxhall he sang Sir Samuel Egerton Leigh's *The Genius of England's Invocation to Britain*, a song on the restoration to health of George III, typical of the many patriotic tunes with which Incledon would rouse audiences throughout his career.

During his Vauxhall years, Incledon continued to be seen in the second walk of roles on the stage at Bath and Bristol. He also became a great favorite in concerts and was flattered by the society of such persons as Dr Henry Harrington, physician to the Bath hospital and a talented musician and writer. Incledon also participated in the annual subscription concerts presented at the Bristol Assembly Rooms between 1786 and 1792. For his own benefit he organized a concert at Coopers' Hall in Bristol on 23 October 1787, which he announced in the press "will be got up in a Stile that will ensure the Approbation of all Lovers of Music and Vocal Harmony," adding:

Mr Incledon's Engagement at Vauxhall, London, obliging him to quit this City each Season before the Benefits, it is presumed is a sufficient Apology for advertising this Concert; when he hopes for the Approbation and Encouragement of his Friends and a generous Public.

In the spring of 1790, the Covent Garden manager Harris visited Bath and articled Incledon for the next three seasons at £6, £7, and £8 per week. Soon after, according to "The Manager's Note-Book," Linley proposed to engage him at Drury Lane at £12 per week, but Incledon declined the offer because he felt obliged to honor his oral promise to Harris. He always regretted that Linley's offer had come late, believing that under him he would have become "a much better singer."

On 17 September 1790, Incledon made his Covent Garden debut as Dermot in *The Poor Soldier*. The death of the Duke of Cumberland then closed the theatres for a week, so Incledon's second appearance, again as Dermot, did not occur until 29 September. He played the title role in *Cymon* on 1 October, followed by Sandy in *The Highland Reel* on 5 October, a chorus role in *Macbeth* the next night, Carlos in *The Duenna* on 12 October, Lord Winlove in *Fontainebleau* on 15 October, and Aluph in *The Crusade* on 19 October. On 23 November he appeared as Squire Thicket in the premiere of J. C. Cross's *A Divertisement*, a very popular musical interlude that ran 22 nights and in which Incledon sang the songs "To Batchelor's Hall," "Come, Painter, with thy happiest flight," and "Of all Sensations Pity brings."

That first season at Covent Garden, Incledon also sang in *A Picture of Paris, Taken in the Year 1790* and played Edwin in *Robin*, Wilford in the premiere of Henry Bates's comic opera *The Woodman*, which opened on 26 February 1791 and ran for 28 performances, Lubin in *The Chapter of Accidents*, Alphonso in *The Castle of Andalusia*, and Wakely in the premiere of the musical entertainment *The Cottage Maid* (on 3 June). In *The Soldier's Festival*, first played on 3 May 1791, he sang General Wolfe's favorite song "How stands the Glass around" and several patriotic songs with Bannister, Johnstone, and others. In *The Union* on 18 May he sang "A Sailor's life's the life for me" and a "Scotch Song" and with others offered "Sigh no more Ladies," "Goody Groaner," and "Beviano tutti tre;" at the end of Act II of *The School for Wives* he sang "Black-Ey'd Susan." For his benefit on 20 May 1791 he played Young Meadows in *Love in a Village* (a role he acted at Bath on 28 October 1789). Gross receipts that night were £278 0s. 6d., and tickets had been available from Incledon at No 19, Martlet Court, Bow Street.

Incledon also appeared at the Covent Garden oratorios conducted in the spring of 1791 by Bartleman and Harrison, in which he sang such sacred airs as Handel's "Justly, these evils" and "Why does the God of Israel sleep?" from *Samson*, "Blooming virgins" from *Athalia*, and "The flocks shall leave" from *Acis and Galatea*, among others.

Some contemporary reports indicate that, during his first season at Covent Garden, Incledon suffered the prejudice of having been a Vauxhall singer. It was suggested that his coarse style of singing cultivated in that somewhat vulgar environment prevented him from obtaining the better roles at the patent house. More likely the reason he could not yet compete with the likes of Johnstone and Bannister was the fact that he was an actor of very humble stamp. His fine tenor, correct ear, and finished shake, according to Parke, won him some warm popularity, but his unskillful acting, caused in part by a vulgar accent and bad memory, was a liability. Whenever he had dif-

ficult music to prepare, it was said that Incledon used to lock himself up in a room with his old Exeter friend Davy, who was in the Covent Garden orchestra, and two bottles of wine; thus he would practise until he perfected the piece.

After playing at Crow Street, Dublin, and at Cork in the summer of 1791, Incledon returned in the autumn for his second season at Covent Garden, to be seen as Captain Macheath in *The Beggar's Opera* for the first time, on 20 September 1791. His other new roles were Saib in *Love and War*, Arbaces in *Artaxerxes*, Selim in *A Day in Turkey*, Hilliard in *The Jovial Crew*, Somerville in *The Magician No Conjurer*, Sir Henry Freeman in *Marian*, Orpheus in *Orpheus and Eurydice*, Hazem in *Zelma*, Leander in *The Padlock*, Captain Melville in *Just in Time*, and Mercury in *The Golden Pippin*. When the visiting Haydn saw him perform in *The Woodman* on 10 December 1791, he judged that "he has a good voice and quite a good style, but he uses the falsetto to excess. He sang a trill on high C and ran up to G." (Haydn had previously heard him sing at a meeting of the Anacreontic Society on 12 January 1791.) For his benefit on 9 May 1792, when he received £399 6s. (less house charges of £105) and lived now at No 5, Bow Street, Incledon played the Captain in *Love in a Camp* for the first time and introduced a new song set by his former teacher Rauzzini. He also sang in the oratorios directed by Linley at the King's Theatre that spring and appeared in private theatricals at Wargrave.

The summer of 1792 found Incledon again at Crow Street. In London on 15 October 1792 he sang for Sim's benefit at the Haymarket Theatre, the only time, it seems, that he performed on that stage in the eighteenth century. In his third winter season at Covent Garden he played Captain Fieldair in the first production of *Hartford Bridge* on 3 November 1792; that popular musical farce by William Pearce enjoyed 36 performances before the end of the season. He also sang in 19 performances of *The Relief of Williamstadt*, a musical interlude which was premiered on 23 March 1793. His other assignments included a vocal part in *Harlequin's Museum*, Earl Fitzallan in *The Armourer*, a Lieutenant in *True Blue*, and Don Florio in *Money at a Pinch*. He also sang in the Covent Garden oratorios.

For his benefit on 10 May 1793, when he was living at No 12, Bow Street, Incledon played Macheath and sang in *The Sailor's Festival*. His receipts that night, the substantial amount of £469 15*s*. (less house charges), indicate that by that time he had earned a popular following. The Bristol *Journal* of 8 September 1794 claimed that he had acquired his reputation not by any help of the managers— "they did not bring him so forward as his talents deserved"—but by "the irresistible force of his own merit." He had by then, argued the Bristol journalist, performed various characters "in so masterly a manner" as to warrant the leads in all operas. (Moreover, that paper reported, in his previous summers in Ireland he had received more tributes than any previous singer, even Mrs Billington.) A week after his Covent Garden benefit, on 16 May 1793 Incledon gave up his usual role of Dermot in *The Poor Soldier* to Mrs Clendining (whose benefit night it was) and took the role of Fitzroy; the experiment proved successful

Harvard Theatre Collection

CHARLES INCLEDON as Macheath

engraving by Thomson, after Singleton

and Incledon's Fitzroy, according to a diary cited in *The London Stage*, "gave a rich feast to the musical amateur."

Hoping to capitalize on his growing reputation, Incledon set off for a busy summer's touring. In June and July 1793 he played ten nights at Liverpool, earning £177 at his free benefit. His travels took him to Southampton, Winchester, Portsmouth, and Plymouth. At Brighton he made his first appearance, playing Young Meadows and Dermot to great applause from the largest audience of the season, including almost every person of fashion in town. Packed houses approved his Macheath and Sandy on 6 August and Alphonso and Belville on 8 August. On the latter night, in the presence of the Prince of Wales, he introduced the songs "Sally in our Alley" and "Streamlet that flowed round her cot." For his benefit on 9 August the small theatre yielded £90, the largest house ever known in Brighton.

Incledon returned to Covent Garden in 1793–94 with new articles for five years at a salary of £12 per week; his terms were the third highest in the company, equal to Holman's and exceeded only by those of Lewis and Quick. He earned his worth by almost nightly appearances in many of his familiar roles, as well as in the new ones of Julian in *The Midnight Wanderers*, Sinclair in *Sprigs of Laurel*, Sir Bertram in *The Ward of the Castle*, Lubin in *The Quaker*, Germueil in *Nina*, Cable in *The Positive Man*, Dalton in *The Travellers in Switzerland*, Captain Oakland in *Netley Abbey*, Edward in *British Fortitude and Hibernian Friendship*, Signor Arionelli in *The Son-in-Law*, Woodford in *The Packet Boat*, Colin in *The Speechless Wife*, Patie in *The Gentle Shepherd*, a principal character (with the song "Hark! the drum beats to Arms") in *The Fall of Martinico*, Valentine in *The Farmer*, and Tom Tug in *The Waterman*.

At the premiere of the anonymous musical piece *Love and Honor; or, Britannia in Full Glory at Spithead* on 9 May 1794, for the benefit of Mrs Martyr, Incledon played William and sang "Rule Britannia," "The Wandering Tar" (a new song by Shield to Sheridan's epilogue to *The Rivals*), "Sally in our Alley," and "Water parted from the Sea," the last in the manner of "a celebrated Italian Opera Singer." That night he also introduced George Alexander Stevens's celebrated description of a storm in a "A Sea Storm," a song he delivered in the character of a sailor and without accompaniment. That number, especially when backed by a scenic exhibition, became one of Incledon's greatest hits and always could be relied upon to draw people to his benefits in later years. For his own benefit that season, on 2 May 1794, Incledon played Edwin in *Robin Hood* and Ensign Platoon in the first performance of J. C. Cross's *Naples Bay*. Receipts were £396 12s. 6d. (less house charges) and tickets had been available from him at No 15, Charlotte Street, Bloomsbury, his address for the remainder of the century. Earlier that spring he had gone to Bristol to sing in a concert of sacred music in St Michael's Church on 14 April 1794.

Venturing north for the summer of 1794, Incledon acted at Manchester in June and then went for a few nights to Edinburgh, where he first appeared on 5 July as Young Meadows in *Love in a Village*; he acted Leander in *The Padlock* on 7 July, followed by Signior Arionelli in *The Son-in-Law* and Captain Campley in *Inkle and Yarico* on the eighth and Edwin in *Robin Hood* and Lubin in *The Quaker* on the twelfth. Later in July he began a fortnight at Liverpool, receiving £138 at his benefit on the thirtieth. During assize week at York, beginning on 11 August, Incledon made £114 12s. playing his principal characters for Wilkinson. Then he acted at Leeds, Wakefield, Scarborough, and Harrowgate. Later in August he returned to York for race week. In his *Wandering Patentee*, Wilkinson stressed especially Incledon's industry and application to his business while at York, contradicting other reports that the singer was a lazy and troublesome character:

. . . surely to no performer was I ever more indebted, for not only his success, but for his unremitted and I may add his very laborious endeavours to please. . . . He should be termed the HERCULES of a theatre, for his toils and labours are far beyond description: Instead of not doing enough, he did more; yet, to my astonishment, was the next day ready for duty. To enumerate his merits as a singer, they are so universally known, allowed, and admired, as to render it needless: But I think he will die like the swan, tuning delightful music. . . .

In 1795 Francis Waldron, in his *Candid and Impartial Strictures on the Performers*, asserted that Incledon had the finest voice of any male English singer on the stage:

Clear, mellow, and extensive in its tones, it is capable of executing almost any piece of vocal music.

His forte is evidently in the plain English ballads; and the sea songs, which have always been peculiarly grateful to a British ear, were never better sung than by this gentleman. The less we say of his acting powers the less cause he will have to blame our freedom of observation.

At Covent Garden for the next 20 years, Incledon remained one of London's brightest stars. Among the roles he "created" in the last six years of the eighteenth century were Magnet in *Arrived at Portsmouth* on 30 October 1794, Montauban in *The Mysteries of the Castle* on 31 January 1795, Sir Ralph Neville in the spectacular *Windsor Castle* on 6 April 1795, Cheerly in *Lock and Key* on 2 February 1796, Harcourt in *Abroad and at Home* on 19 November 1796, Michael (an Egyptian Peasant) in *The Mouth of the Nile* on 25 October 1798, Henrico in *Albert and Adelaide* on 11 December 1798, Henry Blunt in *The Turnpike Gate* on 14 November 1799, and Darbony in *Joanna* on 16 January 1800. In the summer of 1795 he was again at Liverpool, Dublin, and Cork. On 20 September of that year he also played at Richmond. He sang at the Oxford Music Room in 1793 and in June 1796; during the latter year he also acted again at York and Edinburgh. He played for short periods at Birmingham in the summers of 1796, 1797, 1798, and 1800. On 18 March 1799 he sang in the *Messiah* at the British Assembly Rooms at Birmingham and later that year returned to Edinburgh and Dublin.

On 6 June 1797 Incledon made a single appearance at Drury Lane Theatre, when for the benefit of Sedgwick he played Edwin in *Robin Hood* and sang his famous "Storm" song. He also sang at Ranelagh Gardens with Madame Mara in the summer of 1798.

Despite Wilkinson's testimonial to his good nature, Incledon sometimes displayed a restive and troublesome personality. Parke, with whom he had sometimes shared lodging, believed him to be "a singular compound of contrarieties, among which frugality and extravagance were conspicuous." Leigh Hunt remembered his "lax and sailor-like twist of mind," while H. Crabb Robinson commented on his vulgarity, relating how he met Incledon on 15 October 1811 in a coach flaunting "seven rings on his fingers, five seals on his watch-ribbon, and a gold snuffbox." In February 1798 he quarreled with the Covent Gar-

Harvard Theatre Collection

CHARLES INCLEDON as William

engraving by Alais, after Foster

den management, refusing to appear as a British Officer in the third performance of the pantomime *Joan of Arc* on the fourteenth after having played in the first two performances on 12 and 13 February. Objecting to "holding up the fag end of a pantomime," he demanded his articles from Harris on 16 February and was promptly obliged. Except for command performances on 22 February in *Lock and Key* and on 15 March as Balthazar in *Much Ado about Nothing* (for Townsend who was ill), Incledon did not renew his engagement until 14 April. The incident did not damage his benefit on 21 April 1798 at which the receipts totaled £528 10s. 6d. (less house charges), a handsome sum to add to his total salary that year of £413 6s. 8d.

The year 1800 closed the century with double tragedy for Incledon. His first wife, Jane Lowther, the daughter of a mason of Bath, whom he had married at Walcot Church in that city on 17 August 1787, lost an infant in childbirth in January 1800. Mrs Incledon sur-

vived the trauma for only a few days, dying on the twenty-sixth. Her dangerous condition had prevented Incledon's playing Darbony in *Joanna* the night before, and the part was assigned to Hill. For a few days the bereaved singer "laboured under a derangement of intellect," reported the *Monthly Mirror* of January 1800, but soon he proved that "his *voice* had suffered no *derangement*" on his return to the boards as Captain Sidney in *Ramah Droog* on 4 February 1800. He played a full schedule the balance of the season. On 27 March 1800 he sang Shield's "Battle Song" from *The Italian Villagers* in Mr Franklin's concert at Willis's Rooms. The following night, 28 March 1800, at Covent Garden he sang in the first performance of *The Creation*. On 12 June he sang "The Storm" for the blind dramatist O'Keeffe's Covent Garden benefit, "an obliging condescension," reported the *Monthly Mirror*, "which he had refused to every other applicant, reserving this Song solely and exclusively for his own Benefit." (But Incledon had sung that number for Sedgwick's benefit on 6 June 1797.)

In 1800 Incledon was one of the "glorious eight" principal actors (the others being Knight, Fawcett, Holman, Johnstone, H. Johnstone, Pope, and Munden) who signed the manifesto on the *Differences subsisting between the Proprietors and Performers of Covent Garden*, the actors' protest against what they considered to be the tyranny of the management in increasing benefit charges by £20, restricting the number of free "orders," and other infringements. Defending the proprietors in his *Dramatic Censor*, Dutton claimed that the total income earned by Incledon in 1799–1800, including salary and benefit receipts after charges, was £888 14s. 2d. The figure seems appropriate, for the account books indicate that Incledon's salary that season was £13 per week; for his benefit on 15 April 1800 the gross receipts were £579 13s. Though plainly impatient with Incledon for the part he played in the rebellion against the management, Dutton praised him as a singer, reporting the many demands by audiences for encores; yet, as did most observers, Dutton damned his acting.

While playing in Dublin during the summer of 1800, Incledon and Holman tried to buy the Crow Street Theatre from Jones for a sum of £31,500, but they broke off the negotiations, according to "The Manager's Note-Book," when they discovered that a mortgage of £2000 had been granted by Barry.

Making his peace with the Covent Garden managers, Incledon returned to London in 1800–1801 at a salary increased to £14 per week for three years. On 8 February 1801 at St Paul, Covent Garden, he married Mary Ann Howell, a spinster of Bath, who was perhaps related to the Bath musician Thomas Howell. The second Mrs Incledon evidently was not a performer.

Incledon continued to perform at Covent Garden through 1814–15, except in 1811–12, a year in which the management would not meet his salary demands. His wages in 1803–4 and 1804–5 were £16 per week, reported as two pounds higher than those of any other Covent Garden performer. In 1805–6 they were raised to £18, and then to £20 in 1806–7, the level at which his salary remained through 1810–11. His benefits continued to bring excellent sums.

He supplemented his already handsome income by summer excursions, enjoying full houses at his benefits in Dublin and Southampton in 1801. At the Arthur Street Theatre in Belfast he played nine nights, beginning in late July 1801, and with Mrs Addison sang Handelian oratorio selections at St Anne's Church for the benefit of the local poor house. In 1802 he toured the provinces with an entertainment called *Variety, or Something New*, a program of songs and recitations, including "The Thorn," "Black-Eyed Susan," and "The Storm," accompanied on the piano by Davy. In the summer of 1803 Incledon took out a new but similar entertainment called *The Wandering Melodist; or, the Rose, Shamrock, and Thistle*, now accompanied by Major. On the passage from Holyhead to Dublin he was shipwrecked and nearly lost his life. The packet boat struck on the Dublin Bar with the loss of several lives. In the dark and confusion Incledon showed great courage, assisting his wife and Major to mount above the level of the sea, where they clung to the round-top for several hours until saved by fishermen. "In the midst of these horrors," Major related to Angelo, "Incledon uttered a strange mixture of oaths, prayers, and confessions." Appropriately, upon reaching Dublin, he announced "The Storm," which attracted large audiences. As he said, the song

"paid him well for doing the duty of the top." That year he also sang in the Three Choirs meeting at Worcester.

In 1804 Incledon was with the Duke of Cumberland's sharpshooters. In addition to holding fine regimental dinners at the Bedford, they practiced military strategy over the fields of Hampstead and Highgate, but by that time Incledon had become so large and bulky that he was often "much blown." (On 9 May of that year a thief stole all the silver spoons from the singer's residence at Brompton Crescent—but, as the story goes, "he was quickly observed, quickly taken, quickly tried [on the 15th], quickly found guilty, and *Quickly* was his name.")

Incledon played at the new Bath Theatre Royal in Beaufort Square in 1806. He made appearances at Bristol in April and December 1805, March 1805, July 1810, April and November 1811, and May 1812. He was at Norwich in April 1807, whence he wrote to Elliston on the tenth, "I perform here every night this week. & Damn'd deal of *applause* but little *money*." Between 24 August and 14 September 1807 Incledon performed four nights a week at the Lyceum in the Strand in a new entertainment, *A Voyage to India*, which he styled an "Operatic Romance." It consisted of "interesting oral matter" delivered by Bartley and "fifteen new songs" sung by Incledon, accompanied by the younger Kellner. The license granted to Incledon for the entertainment, as recorded in the Public Record Office, was for "Recitation Music & Dancing."

The following summer he toured with *Hospitality; or, the Harvest Home*, another program consisting of recitations by Bartley and songs by Incledon, accompanied this time by Horn. Earlier that summer, in June 1808, he had had another narrow escape when a coach in which he and Beverley were returning from the Woolwich theatre overturned, pinning one passenger under the wheels. Though the vehicle was shattered to pieces, Incledon "exerted his vocal powers" to call for help, and he was extricated from the wreck having suffered only minor bruises. With Mathews, he toured an entertainment of the familiar format of recitations and songs in the summer of 1811. At Hull they were obliged to perform at the Circus, because Wilkinson—despite his claim of indebtedness to Incledon expressed in the *Wan-*

dering Patentee—refused to let them have the theatre.

Incledon's second wife died at Bath in May 1811. Two years later in November 1813 he married his third wife, a widow named Mrs Martha Hunt, who outlived him. His request to Elliston for an engagement at Drury Lane having come to naught, after a year's absence Incledon returned to Covent Garden in 1812–13 at a salary of £17 per week, a figure he was also paid during the next two seasons there. He reappeared on that stage in September 1812 as Macheath, a performance which dispelled the rumors that he had lost his voice.

With Sinclair, in the summer of 1814, he took out on the circuit a "theatrical bouquet" entitled *Mirth and Minstrelsy; or, Two to One against Care*. After his final season at Covent Garden, Incledon toured in the summer of 1815 with Broadhurst in an entertainment titled simply *Minstrelsy*. That year he also played Macheath to Mrs Mountain's Polly at the Surrey Theatre; it was a performance which revealed that both talents were fading, for, according to Oxberry, though Mrs Mountain was a shadow of her former self, her effort was superior to the "elephantic effort of Incledon." He toured throughout England and Ireland with his *Minstrelsy* early in 1816 and then performed a few nights at the Lyceum in August and at the Surrey in September. The bills for his benefit at the Surrey on 14 September announced "that a report. most industriously circulated to his disadvantage, stating that he had been offered terms from Drury Lane Theatre, was utterly without foundation; on the contrary, an application made to that house, on behalf of Mr. Incledon, but without his knowledge, was most decidedly rejected." It was a face-saving statement, for a British Library manuscript reveals that Incledon had written to Robbins that "if he could get an eligible situation at Drury Lane he should prefer it to anything." After the brief engagements at the Lyceum and the Surrey, Incledon played for a while at the East London Theatre, another minor house, in Wellclose Square, where he had a benefit on 17 October 1816.

Incledon had planned to sail from Bristol to America in September 1816, but sentiment, it was said, prevented his doing so. More likely he needed more money, for he returned to London to announce a farewell benefit at the King's Theatre, "by permission of the sub-committee of Drury Lane Theatre, and the proprietors of Covent Garden Theatre," for 31 March 1817. The performances of *Love in a Village* and *Three Weeks after Marriage* were supported by talent from both patent houses. A tremendous crush, including the nobility, attended, to yield over £1000. "Many were hurt, and the screams of the females were appalling," according to "The Manager's Note-Book." Three persons were carried out in a senseless state. Dowton spoke the following lines in tribute:

The tuneful fav'rite of your youthful days,
Raised by your smiles and nurtured by your praise,
Whom you proclaim'd from competition free,
Unrivall'd in his native melody,
Now forced, alas! in foreign climes to roam,
To seek beyond th'Atlantic waste—a home,
Ere yet to England's shore he bids adieu,
Pours forth one parting, grateful strain—to you.
Oh! let the men, who with him trod the stage,
Who mark'd the promise of his earlier age—
Who saw, with joy, his talents ripen'd bloom—
Who hail'd his progress, and now mourn his
     doom—
Shed, for such talents lost, the pitying tear,
While yet they may behold their brother here.—
Here—where the friends who nerved his youthful
     power
Now meet to consecrate his farewell hour:
Here, where the plaudits he has felt so long
Now, for the last time, cheer your child of song.
To you his claim for kindness he preferr'd—
Your presence shows that his appeal was heard.
No actors here, as actors, now attend;
But friends assembled to support a friend:
Those friends would waft above one fervent pray'r,
One anxious wish for him who owns their care;
May he, in lands where British accents sound,
Experience what he felt on British ground;
While to his ear your language they impart,
Oh! may they speak your language to his heart—
May all the social joys which here exist
There wait upon the wand'ring melodist!

Incledon received warm letters from Shield, whose many songs he had made popular, and from Mrs Mountain, who wished he would be "prosperous in other climes!" Thomas Welsh wrote to Miss Merry at Bath:

I never heard such a thing as Incledon's singing 'The Lads of the Village' and 'The Storm' last night. Nature was in a generous fit when she gave him

CHARLES INCLEDON singing "The Storm"
by De Wilde

that divine voice: as to his feeling, I really think he has more genuine and natural taste then all the singers put together of the whole country. He is, I believe, determined to visit America, and it is a disgrace to this kingdom to suffer it. I am sorry you did not hear him—'twas an invaluable lesson.

On 21 August 1817 Incledon sailed from Liverpool on the *John and Edward*, sending back with the harbor pilot a most sentimental and affecting letter of farewell to his friends, in which he wrote of his children and grandchildren clinging "forcibly round my heart" and thanked his theatrical and musical breth-

ren. He ended by expressing the hope that this new speculation would "enable me finally to deposit my bones near the graves of my ancestors; and that, on the moment of my dissolution, I may have the satisfaction of seeing my progeny surround me."

Incledon made his American debut at the Park Theatre in New York on 17 October 1817 as Hawthorn in *Love in a Village*. According to "The Manager's Note-Book," his first night was a great success, exceeding Cooke's by $12; and his first six nights produced $7730, netting him £619 sterling. New York may have fêted him at a public dinner, as "The Manager's Note-Book" claimed, but the *Records of the New York Stage* indicate that Incledon, careless in dress, gross in figure, poor as an actor, and with a voice past its prime, did not create a favorable impression. It may have been more than anti-English sentiment which caused an incident on the night he played in *The Beggar's Opera*; one New York paper reported that "much to the credit of the audience, not even the popularity of Incledon, nor his excellent songs, were found sufficient to stifle the marks of disapprobation which were loudly heard from all parts of the theatre at the dropping of the curtain." Early in 1818 an erroneous report circulated in London that Incledon had died in New York, but it was contradicted by a letter in March.

Incledon performed in Baltimore in November 1817, in Philadelphia in December, and in Washington in February 1818. He also toured north to Albany, Montreal, Quebec, and Halifax with his performance of *The Wandering Melodist*, a nickname by which he had become known. In Providence he appeared with Bianchi Taylor in the summer of 1818, singing his favorite songs, "Washington's Star," "Black Ey'd Susan," "Sailor's Last Whistle," and "The Storm," among others.

He sailed from New York in August 1818, with a reported profit of nearly £5000 for his American venture, arriving in Liverpool in September. Mrs Incledon's "alarming illness" had brought him home earlier than he had intended. Soon after his arrival in London he published in the papers a charitable and laudatory letter about his American experience:

Unwilling as I always have been to intrude myself on the public, I cannot avoid noticing, with feelings of regret, the misrepresentations which I have observed in the newspapers, since my return from America, upon the state of music in that country; and I avail myself of the first moment of my return to the metropolis to correct this error. I am proud, at the same time, publicly to express my very high sense of the liberal and enlightened hospitality with which I have been treated everywhere in the United States. With regard to musical science in America, I must say that I was agreeably surprised at finding it, in every province, in such high cultivation. At St. Paul's church, New York, I sang in an oratorio, which was, throughout, performed in a style which would have done credit to London. If any additional proof were wanting of their real fondness for music, it is to be found in the facility I everywhere experienced, during my tour, where I was offered the use of halls for my performance, free of expense. I could enumerate more instances of generosity than your leisure would permit you to read, besides which it might be thought irrelevant to the subject; I must, therefore sum up the expression of my feelings in this declaration, that I have never yet been more agreeably surprised than by my rapid glance at America; and I shall always hold in affectionate remembrance the country which welcomed me as a stranger, and patronised me with as much ardour as she could have shown had I been her own son. . . .

In April 1819 Incledon reappeared at the Surrey Theatre. That month he wrote to William Farren at Dublin asking "for the last time to put my feet on the Boards of Crow St. Theatre." Indeed, he went to Ireland that summer, beginning his tour with a fortnight at Sligo. From Dublin on 27 August 1819 he wrote to Elliston, who had just taken over the management of Drury Lane, that he was about to go to Belfast for four or five nights and then planned to visit his daughter in Sunderland for about a month before returning to London. He advised Elliston that, once back in the capital, "I shall be happy to treat with you for an engagement at Drury for one or two years (*not more*)." Engaged by Elliston at £15 per week, Incledon appeared at Drury Lane on 29 February 1820 as Steady in *The Quaker*. But he had lost his brilliant tone. When asked to perform in May he declined because his new set of teeth was not finished.

Incledon took his leave of the London stage in a farewell performance at the English Opera House on 19 April 1822 as Steady in *The Quaker* and Henry Blunt in *The Turnpike Gate*. Before his farewell address, as might have been

expected, he sang "Black Ey'd Susan" and "The Storm." He went immediately to Brighton and on the twenty-sixth of that month was reported to be seriously ill at his lodgings in Prospect Place. But he survived to live in retirement at Brighton for another four years.

Evidently in need of money, he made another and final appearance on the stage in October 1824 at Southampton, the theatre where he had started his career some 40 years before. He did not act but offered a program of his favorite songs: "Black-Eyed Susan," "The Death of Admiral Benbow," "Scots wha hae wi' Wallace bled," "All's Well," and "Then farewell my trim-built wherry." The critic in the *Hampshire Telegraph* was respectful: "To criticise the singing of a man upwards of sixty would be ridiculous, who had undergone the hardships he has—that was not the thing looked for; suffice it to say, his singing showed what he once could do." After his last song, Incledon addressed the audience (according to "The Manager's Note-Book") nearly as follows:

Ladies and gentlemen,—It is with sincerest feelings of gratitude I am capable of that I stand before you this evening to return you my most heartfelt thanks for the distinguished patronage you have ever conferred on me. In this town, and on these boards, I first appeared as a singer; and the encouragement I then received from you has proved, I may say, my passport to fame. Ladies and gentlemen, since that period I have passed through many vicissitudes; I have served his Majesty in many engagements—there is not a ship in the navy, nor are there many towns in the country, that I have not sung in; but still your early liberality has never been effaced from my memory: it is now six years ago since I left the stage, but it has always been my wish to appear once more before you. Ladies and gentlemen, age, sickness, and infirmities have altered me much from what I once was, but I have always done my best to please my kind patrons; and I repeat it, ladies and gentlemen, while I live I shall never forget the support and encouragement I have received from the inhabitants of Southampton.

In January 1826 Incledon suffered a paralytic stroke. He recovered sufficiently to attend the Glee Club meeting at the Rein Deer in Worcester in February but declined to sing for the company. Low in spirits, he went back into the kitchen, gathered the servants round him, sang "Then farewell my trim-built wherry," and left. He died a few days later, on 11 Feb-

Harvard Theatre Collection

CHARLES INCLEDON as Steady

engraving by Woolnoth, after Wageman

ruary 1826, at Worcester, of a stroke according to *The Dictionary of National Biography*. But Grove states that he died at London on 18 February. He was buried with his first two wives and five of his children in the family vault in the burial ground of the Hampstead Parish Church on 20 February. The burial register indicates that his abode at the time of his death (the date of which is not recorded) was All Saints, Worcester.

Incledon had at least eight children by his three wives. Five were named in his will drawn on 2 August 1817, some nine years before his death: Jane Catherine, Charles Venanzio, William Shield, Mary Ann, and Frederick Francis. Three others had died earlier. One of them was the infant in 1800; another may have been the William Incledon, late of Braunton in Devonshire, a seaman on the merchant ship *London Mary Planter*, whose estate of less than £20 was granted to his widow Elizabeth on 21

April 1802. Of the five children mentioned in the will, all save William Shield Incledon survived their father. Charles Venanzio Incledon (1791–1865), the eldest son, left his farm in Bury St Edmunds to appear at Drury Lane as Meadows in *Love in a Village* on 3 October 1829 but left the theatre after a season; he then taught English in Vienna for many years before his death at Bad Tüffer in 1865. The second son, Frederick Francis Incledon, took up trade in London. One daughter, Jane Catherine, married Walker Featherstonehaugh of Sunderland. The other, Mary Ann, was married to William Pace by the time she was granted the second administration of her father's will on 20 June 1864. Possibly related to the family was Richard Incledon, late of Gosport parish in Alverstroke, Southampton, a commander in the Royal Navy, whose estate of £300 was granted to his widow Ann on 23 December 1831.

Charles Incledon's estate, reported to have been worth about £8000, was divided equally among his surviving children. He provided a modest annuity of £50 to his third wife and widow Martha Hart Incledon. The date of her death is unknown to us. Incledon's will was proved at London on 22 March 1826.

Anecdotes told about Charles Incledon suggest that he could be a vain and somewhat overbearing man. He called himself "the English Ballad-Singer," claimed Mrs Mathews, who knew him well, "a distinction he would not have exchanged for the highest in the realm of talent." In his early years he displayed eccentricity and sometimes wit. When he visited the island of Dalkey, near Dublin, in 1795, he was knighted "Sir Charles Melody" by a party of friends who established a mock kingdom and court. In the *Thespian Olio* (1796), G. S. Carey gave Incledon's five reasons for drinking as

Good wine, a friend, or being dry,
Or lest we should be by and by,
Or any other reason why.

Incledon was pretentious about his reading: it was reported that once, having bought a handsome bookcase, Incledon measured it, then entered a bookshop to buy "two feet of books," specifying only handsome bindings. Another tale, designed to show his "conceit and ignorance," claimed that when once asked in company his opinion of Aristotle, he replied, "My opinion is that many who talk so much of Aristotle, have never been near the place." Some manuscript verses in the National Library of Scotland, attributed to Incledon, evidently from the early part of his career, complain of being neglected in England and having to seek fame in "Popish" and "Lutheran" lands.

As a theatrical singer few persons could rival him. His voice was described as powerful, brilliant, melodious, sweet, liquid, and rich. His ear, it was said, was so perfect he could not sing out of tune. Shield wrote of him in tribute:

I have written as much for Charles Incledon as any man living, perhaps more, and, if I were to content myself with saying that he never disappointed my expectations in the performance of any song that I composed for him, I should do him injustice: he did more; often has he imparted to my melodies a grace, a beauty, a charm, which I did not previously suppose them to have possessed. Of the popularity they enjoy I am willing to ascribe a large share to his unrivalled excellence in their execution.

Some details of his style and voice were provided by another contemporary in the *Dictionary of Music* (1827):

He had a voice of uncommon power, both in the natural and falsette. The former was from A to g', a compass of about fourteen notes; the latter he could use from d' to e" or f" or about ten notes. His natural voice was full and open, neither partaking of the reed nor the string, and sent forth without the smallest artifice; and such was its ductility that when he sang pianissimo it retained its original quality. His falsette was rich, sweet and brilliant, but totally unlike the other. He took it without preparation, according to circumstances either about d', e' or f', or ascending an octave, which was his most frequent custom; he could use it with facility, and execute ornaments of a certain class with volubility and sweetness. His shake was good, and his intonation much more correct than is common to singers so imperfectly educated. . . . He had a bold and manly manner of singing, mixed, however, with considerable feeling, which went to the hearts of his countrymen. He sang like a true Englishman. . . . His forte was ballad.

Many of the songs composed by Hook, Shield, Reeve, and others that were sung by Incledon are listed in the *Catalogue of Printed Music in the British Museum*. In addition to

some cited above, included is *The Thorn* by William Shield, as sung by Incledon at Covent Garden and in his entertainment called *Variety*, published about 1802 on music sheets with the statement that the words were written by Robert Burns. The lyrics were lines from several epigrams which Burns had sent to the Edinburgh bookseller William Creech on 30 May 1789. After Burns died they were published in the *Edinburgh Advertiser* of 8 August 1800.

Portraits of Incledon include:

1. By William Beechey. Present location unknown to us.

2. By M. Brown. Present location unknown to us. Engraving by Ridley published as a plate to the *Monthly Mirror*, September 1801.

3. By George Dance. Pencil drawing, 1798. In the National Portrait Gallery (No 1145). Acquired from sale of the property of the Rev George Dance, deceased, grandson of the artist, at Christie's on 1 July 1898.

4. By Samuel De Wilde. Watercolor drawing. In the Huntington Library.

5. By Thomas Lawrence. Painting in the possession of Herr Brausewetter at Wagram in 1867. Present location unknown to us.

6. Attributed to M. A. Shee. Painting in the Royal College of Music.

7. By unknown artist. Silhouette on paper. In the Garrick Club.

8. By unknown artist. Oil on compo-board. Bust portrait 14 high × 11½ wide. Sold for $7.50 in the Evert Jansen Wendell sale at the American Art Association, New York, 15–20 October 1918.

9. Engraving by Godby, after G. Engleheart.

10. Engraving by K. Mackenzie, after R. Dighton. Published as a plate to *Thespian Dictionary*. Also a plate to *The Myrtle and the Vine* (1800), vol 1.

11. Engraving by W. Ridley, after Edridge. Published as a plate to Parson's *Minor Theatre*, 1794.

12. As Captain Macheath in *The Beggar's Opera*. Engraving by H. R. Cook, after Clater. Published as a plate to Oxberry's *New English Drama*, 1818. A copy by an unknown engraver, after Clater, was published as a plate to Oxberry's *Dramatic Biography*.

13. As Captain Macheath. Watercolor by Samuel De Wilde. In the Garrick Club. An-

other portrait by De Wilde of Incledon as Macheath was originally listed in the *Mathews Collection Catalogue* (No 130) but evidently is not in the Garrick Club.

14. As Captain Macheath. Engraving by J. Thomson, after Singleton. Published as a plate to the *Theatrical Inquisitor*, 1816.

15. As Captain Macheath. By unknown engraver, undated. In the Harvard Theatre Collection.

16. As Captain Macheath, with Eliza Bolton as Polly. By unknown engraver. In the Harvard Theatre Collection, but not listed in Hall catalogue.

17. As a Sailor singing "The Storm." Engraving by J. Ayton. Published by W. Kenneth, 1826.

18. As a Sailor singing "The Storm." By J. T. Barber-Beaumont. Miniature in the Garrick Club. Engravings were made by: H. Meyer, published as a plate to *The Drama*, 1824; Page, published as a plate to Oxberry's *Dramatic Biography*; Reading, published by T. Williams; J. Vendramini, published by J. P. Thompson, 1804, and James Sumford, 1812.

19. As a Sailor singing "The Storm." Watercolor by De Wilde. In the Harvard Theatre Collection.

20. As a Sailor singing "The Storm." Engraving by Roberts, after J. Emery. Published by Roberts; another impression published by Laurie & Whittle, 1806.

21. As a Sailor singing "Poor Jack." By unknown engraver. Published 10 August 1790.

22. As Squire Thicket in *A Divertisement*. Engraving by Springsguth.

23. As Steady in *The Quaker*. Pencil sketch by T. Wageman, offered for sale at Christie's on 15 March 1977 (lot 83). This sketch is the original for the engraving by Woolnoth which was published as a plate to Oxberry's *New English Drama*, 1820.

24. As William in *St David's Day*. Engraving by Alais, after Foster, Jr. Published by J. Roach.

25. Caricature, with John Braham. By T. Rowlandson.

26. Satirical print by G. Cruikshank, entitled "Theatrical Faux Pas." Published in the *Satirist*, 1 March 1814. Depicts Mrs H. E. Johnston's abandoning of her paramour, Harris, the Covent Garden Manager, to run off with Drummond. One of the onlookers, Incle-

don, stands in profile as a handsome young sailor. His figure is closely copied from Roberts's engraving, after Emery, of Incledon as a Sailor singing "The Storm," above, No 19.

"Incombustible Man, The." *See* RICHARDSON, MR [fl. 1672–c. 1677].

"Inconnu." *See* "L'INCONNUE."

"Indian Chiefs, The" [fl. 1795], *dancers, singers*.

Arundell, in his *Story of Sadler's Wells*, cites a 1795 bill for that theatre advertising two American Indian Chiefs from the Catawba Nation, the first to appear (on stage) in Europe. The Indians demonstrated their dexterity with the tomahawk and the bow and arrow and gave exhibitions of war dances and songs. "Those who wish for a nearer communication with the Indian Chiefs than the Stage exhibition will admit of," the advertisement said, "may be gratified, by applying at the Middleton's Head Coffee-House, near Sadler's Wells."

"Indian Princes, The" [fl. 1720], *dancers*.

At York Buildings on 1 April 1720 was presented a *"War Dance* by the Indian Princes" for their shared benefit with Raphael Courteville (d. 1772).

"Indian, The Spotted." *See* "PRIMROSE THE PIEBALD BOY."

"Infant Hercules, The" *b. c.* 1778, *acrobat*.

On 23 June 1788 at Sadler's Wells "The Infant Hercules" exhibited feats of strength. Another bill for that summer described him as 10 years old and stated that he turned a somersault on the rope.

"Infant Musician, The" *See* CROTCH, WILLIAM.

"Infant Pierrot, The" [fl. 1798], *tumbler*.

The Royal Circus playbill for 23 April 1798 announced that there would be tumbling "By a Capital Group, in which the *Infant Pierrot* and *Modern Hercules* will make their first Appearance."

"Infant Rossignol, The" [*fl.* 1795], *bird imitator.*

"The Infant Rossignol" was to imitate "the Notes of various Birds, and also accompany the band on a Dumb Violin" at Astley's Amphitheatre on 27 July 1795. He may have been the son of the bird imitator, tumbler, and equestrian Mr Adams (fl. 1782–1800) who was active in the 1780s and 1790s.

Ingall, Mr [*fl.* 1784–1805?], *actor.*

Mr Ingall played Mat o' the Mint in *The Beggar's Opera* for one night only, on 13 December 1784 at the Haymarket Theatre. On 15 October 1792 he was again at the Haymarket, for a single performance of *The Country Girl*, in which he acted Sandford. According to the *Hiberian Journal* of 7 November 1792, Ingall made his debut at the Crow Street Theatre in Dublin on that date, advertised as having come, not from London, but from the York theatre. He seems to have remained at Crow Street for the 1792–93 season. Perhaps he was the Mr "Ingle" who was at Sadler's Wells in London on 2 April 1804 and who, according to the *Memoirs* of the younger Charles Dibdin, acted there also in 1804–5.

Ingall, Mrs [*fl.* 1748], *actress.*

Mrs Ingall played Lady Wealthy in *The Unnatural Parents* on 24 August 1748 at the Lee and Yeates booth at Bartholomew Fair. She acted the role again on 7 September at Southwark Fair, but the title was changed to *The Fair Maid of the West*. She appeared in it again on 1 October at Blackheath Fair.

"Ingenious Artist, The" [*fl.* 1783], *pyrotechnist.*

"The Ingenious Artist" provided fireworks displays at Astley's Amphitheatre to conclude the performances on 29 January and 3 February 1783.

Ingham, Mr [*fl.* 1793–1794], *acrobat.*

The Bristol newspapers on 20 April 1793 advertised that the circus performers at the amphitheatre in Limekiln Lane included a Mr Ingham. When Ingham appeared at the Royal Circus in London in 1793 and 1794, throwing "an innumerable Row of Flipflaps," he was hailed as from Dublin.

Ingle, Mlle. *See* HEINEL, ANNE FRÉDÉRIQUE.

Inglefield, Thomas *b. 1769, oddity.*

Thomas Inglefield was born at Hook in Hampshire on 18 December 1769 with truncated arms and legs, without hands and feet. He was exhibited at No 8, Chapel Street, Tottenham Court Road, in 1787. An engraving by F. Grose of Inglefield sitting at a desk, drawing, was published that year. Another portrait of him sitting at a desk, drawn by Riley and etched and sold by Inglefield himself, was also issued in 1787 with an inscription which provided his birth date and place and related that his affliction was "occasioned as his Mother supposes by a Fright she suffered when pregnant with him." Inglefield learned

By permission of the British Library Board

THOMAS INGLEFIELD

engraving by Inglefield, after Riley

to write and draw "holding his Pencil between the stump of his Left Arm and his Cheek & guiding it with the Muscles of his Mouth."

"Inglesina." *See* Davies, Cecilia.

Innes, Albert ₁*fl. 1787–1788*₁, *violinist.*
During the 1787–88 season the Academy of Ancient Music paid Albert Innes, a violinist, £4 4s. He was apparently a replacement for a Mr Woodcock. Innes was possibly related to the bookseller and music publisher William Innys, who worked in London from 1711 to 1756, sometimes in partnership with John Innys.

Invill, Kiza, née Garman   ₁*fl. 1757–1787*₁, *dancer, actress.*
Miss Garman made her first stage appearance as a child in a "Grand Dance by Lilliputians" at the Smock Alley Theatre in Dublin on 20 January 1757. On 10 May 1759 she and other children performed *Cleone* and *Lethe* at the Haymarket Theatre in London; her part in the latter work was not named in the bill, but she played Paulet in *Cleone*. After that, Kiza Garman either left the stage for several years or performed in the provinces. She was certainly related to the Mr and Mrs (Peter?) Garman who were in Dublin in 1756–57 when Kiza made her first appearance; she may well have been their daughter.
On 6 May 1769 Miss Garman attempted Rose in *The Recruiting Officer* at Covent Garden. She was advertised as making her first appearance on (that) stage as an actress; the phrasing of the bill suggests that Kiza had been performing as a dancer that season, and, indeed, she had signed with other players a letter to Colman on 5 November 1768. She shared a benefit when she played Rose, but the house was evidently not good, and her share came to only £5 13s. The following season, 1769–70, Miss Garman danced in *The Rape of Proserpine* and acted Juliet in *Measure for Measure*.
Once more Kiza's name dropped from London bills. She had become Mrs Invill sometime before returning to Covent Garden for the 1771–72 season. All that she did that season, unless she was once again dancing, unheralded, in the chorus, was to perform in *The Recruits* on 1 May 1772. The following season, again, she was rarely cited in the bills; she

danced minuets and cotillions on 26 May 1773, and she did the same in May 1774. Though she was in the company in 1774–75, her name seems not to have appeared in any bills; then, once again, she dropped from sight. On 27 April 1782 at Covent Garden she was in some quadrilles and cotillions, and we know that she was on the paylist that season for £1 5s. weekly. She danced in a turn called *Hibernian Dotage* in the fall of 1786 and in a dance entitled *Mirth by Marriage* in the fall of 1787. Mrs Invill remained in obscurity at Covent Garden through at least the early part of the 1787–88 season.

Ion, Mr ₁*fl. 1720*₁, *performer?*
Mr Ion and Mr Brown shared a benefit at Lincoln's Inn Fields Theatre on 23 May 1720. Ion's function in the troupe was not specified in the bill.

Irearte, Mr ₁*fl. c. 1785*₁, *performer?*
Among the Lord Chamberlain's papers in the Public Record Office is a document relating to accounts at the King's Theatre; one Irearte (if that is the correct spelling) was paid £11 12s. 8d. about 1785 for services unspecified.

Irebeck. *See* Trebeck.

Iredale, Mr ₁*fl. 1789–1795*₁, *dresser.*
Mr Iredale's benefit tickets were accepted at Covent Garden Theatre on 17 June 1789 and so, too, in 1790, 1791, and 1792. The theatre accounts for the 1794–95 season cited Iredale as a dresser at 11s. weekly.

Ireland, Mr ₁*fl. 1741–1746*₁, *actor.*
Mr Ireland, "who never performed before," acted Jobson in *The Devil to Pay* at Goodman's Fields Theatre on 22 April 1741. Ireland shared a benefit with Bucknall on 18 March 1746.

Ireland, Mr ₁*fl. 1799–1805*₁, *acrobat.*
Decastro in his *Memoirs* said that "*Ireland,* the celebrated 'Yorkshire Flying Phenomenon,' first performed his extraordinary feats of agility during [John Cartwright Cross's] period of unrivalled success" at the Royal Circus at the end of the eighteenth century. The *Monthly Mirror*

in June 1799 reported that "Notwithstanding the attraction of Pizarro, at Drury Lane, the Circus continues to be crowded, night after night . . . Ireland's astonishing leaps" being partly responsible. Ireland apparently hurt himself in one of his leaps in 1801, for a bill from that year noted that he was "now perfectly recovered" and would perform as before.

A bill in 1804 indicated that Ireland had been on a tour of the provinces:

[T]he above Professor of excentric Ability, having, during his Tour through the United Kingdom acquired a variety of astonishing Improvements in his nouvello Performances, will make his reappearance for a short Period only at the above Theatre [i.e. the Royal Circus] To-morrow Evening, in the course of which among others too numerous to enumerate, he will leap over a Horse lengthways with a Man on his Back [the horse's, presumably] supporting a Hoop only three feet in Diameter, through which his leap will be taken.

On 21 May 1804 it was advertised that Ireland would jump over "a long coach lengthways."

The bill of 11 October 1804 listed six of Ireland's "Leaps and Kicks": "Over a Pole 10 Feet high," over a horse and through a hoop, "Hop and Kick a Baloon 18 Feet high," "Leap through a Hogshead of Fire, heels foremost," "Over a large six-wheel Stage-coach," and "Over a Row of Chandeliers." Ireland performed his acrobatics in Edinburgh in 1805, after which year we find no further mention of him.

Ireland, Master [*fl.* 1759], *actor. See* IRELAND, THOMAS.

Ireland, John [*fl.* 1754], *musician.*
On 29 January 1754 William Felton was bound apprentice to John Ireland of the Worshipfull Company of Musicians. Ireland may have been related to the John Ireland of Leicester who in 1754 published a book of music called *The Sacred Melody*. On 9 May 1769 a John Ireland, musician, became a freeman in the Worshipfull Company of Musicians; he was, one would guess, our subject's son. His address was given as the Old Change.

Ireland, John [*fl.* 1769], *musician. See* IRELAND, JOHN [*fl.* 1754].

Ireland, Thomas [*fl. c.* 1750?–1759], *proprietor.*
About 1750 the proprietorship of Lambeth Wells came into the hands of a Mr Ireland. He instituted monthly concerts given by a musical society under the direction of Starling Goodwin, organist of St Saviour, Southwark, according to Wroth's *London Pleasure Gardens*. Erasmus King, once a coachman to Dr Desaguliers, read lectures and exhibited experiments in natural philosophy for a sixpence. Lambeth Wells was condemned as a nuisance about 1755 and was given over to Methodist services.

Perhaps that Mr Ireland was Thomas, who on 5 May 1759 was granted a license to perform *Cleone* at the Haymarket Theatre for one night only. The performance, according to *The London Stage*, had taken place on 18 April and was given by children "not above thirteen years of age." Playing Sifroy was Master Ireland, doubtless Thomas Ireland's son.

Iremells. *See* TREMELLS.

Irish, Mr [*fl.* 1682], *mountebank?*
Charles Killigrew, Master of the Revels, was directed in 1682 "to suppress one Mr. Irish, Mr. Thomas Varley, and Mr. Thomas Yates, Mountebank, who have no Licence" to perform at Bartholomew Fair.

Irish, Mr [*fl.* 1791–1820], *boxkeeper.*
Mr Irish, a boxkeeper at Drury Lane, was first mentioned in the theatre's account books in the 1791–92 season, and on 15 June 1792 at the King's Theatre (where the Drury Lane company had been performing) Irish's benefit tickets were accepted. He was similarly listed in the bills in other years. The accounts show him to have been earning 15s. weekly in 1801, though in 1803–4 and in many later seasons he was listed as being paid 12s. weekly. A note dated 1813–14 described Irish as a "private" boxkeeper. He was still working at Drury Lane in 1819–20. A Mrs Irish, presumably his wife, was cited in the accounts in June 1802; her function in the company is not known, and she seems not to have worked for the theatre in the eighteenth century.

"Irish Dwarf, The" [*fl.* 1791], *strong man.*

A newsclipping at the Huntington Library, pen-dated "3 June?" 1791 is an advertisement for the exhibitor Pidcock, who was presenting a variety of entertainments at the Lyceum in the Strand:

The Double-jointed IRISH DWARF, whose strength is beyond conception. He will engage to carry two of the largest men now existing; as he, a few days back, carried Mr. O'Brian, the Irish Giant, and Mr. Samuel M'Donald, the Prince of Wales's porter, both at the same time.

"Irish Giant, The" *See* BYRNE, CHARLES, and O'BRIEN, PATRICK.

"Irish Johnstone." *See* JOHNSTONE, JOHN HENRY.

"Irish Nightingale, The" *See* KELLY, MICHAEL.

"Irish Roscius, The." *See* BARRY, SPRANGER.

"Irish Tartar, The." *See* JOHNSON, THOMAS.

"Iron Legs." *See* GRIMALDI, JOHN BAPTIST [*fl.* 1740–1742].

Irwin. *See also* ERWIN.

Irwin, Mr [*fl.* 1790], *actor.*

A Mr Irwin played Hastings in *She Stoops to Conquer* at the Haymarket Theatre on 29 September 1790.

Isaac, Mr [*fl.* 1631?–1716], *dancer, dancing master, choreographer.*

Mr (or, when he first appeared, Monsieur) Isaac danced in the court masque *Calisto* on 15 February 1675. Jennifer Martin informs us that Isaac may have been born in France, but he was in London by 1631 (unless that was an earlier Isaac) when, according to Aubrey's *Brief Lives*, he and John Lacy were apprentices to John Ogilby. Isaac may have studied under Thomas Caverley. He was to become one of the most important dancers of the Restoration and early eighteenth century, yet remarkably little

Harvard Theatre Collection

MR ISAAC, dancing master
engraving by White, after Goupy

is known about him. Indeed, there is much doubt as to his identity and the spelling of his name. It appeared variously as Isaac and Isaack but also as Le Sac and L'Sac. Mentioned in the Lord Chamberlain's accounts between August 1671 and April 1677 are two children of the Chapel Royal, Peter and Bartholomew Isaac, who may have been our subject's relatives.

John Evelyn recorded in his *Diary* on 7 February 1682 that his "Daughter *Mary* now first began to learne Musick of Signor *Bartholomeo*, & Dauncing of Monsieur *Issac*, both reputed the best Masters &c." Jennifer Martin discovered that an English dancing master named Isaac visited France in October 1684 and taught the court ladies there English country dances. André Lorin, a dancing master at the court of Louis XIV, visited London in the late 1680s and referred to our subject as Isaac d'Orléans, a title Isaac may have used while in France. In 1686 was published *The New Droll*, a song which contained mention of Isaac:

And to keep good wits together
Better far than cards or dice
Isaac's balls are quaint device
Made up with fan and feather

Isaac also performed at the theatre. We take the "L'Sac" at the Lincoln's Inn Fields Theatre on 5 July 1700 to have been Isaac, and since the playbills in the early years of the eighteenth century are both scarce and often uninformative when found, perhaps Isaac danced far more at the theatre than we know. He shared a benefit with Smith at York Buildings on 4 January 1705. There are also references to appearances by his scholars at public performances, as on 2 May and 29 December 1702 at Drury Lane.

But most of Isaac's energy was directed toward the court and the composition of dances. For example, about 1703 was published *The Marlborough, a New Dance Compos'd by Mr. Isaac, Perform'd at Court on Her Majestie's Birth dat. Feb^r ye 6th 17* (sic). From 1703 to the death of Queen Anne (when Isaac gave up his post as court dancing master) the composer James Paisible wrote the tunes for most of Isaac's dance compositions. The *Catalogue of Printed Music in the British Museum* contains more than half a dozen items under Isaac's name, a great many more under Paisible's, and a number of others scattered throughout the volumes. On 1706 John Weaver dedicated his *Orchesography* to Isaac and included some of his dances. Each year Isaac composed a dance for the Queen's birthday. Isaac occasionally composed dances for public theatre performances as well, as he did for the Queen's Theatre on 22 March 1712 for Mrs Santlow and young Mr Camille.

Most of Isaac's dances had rather undescriptive titles: *The Royall Ann, The Union, The Rigadoon Royal, The Northumberland, The Gloucester, The Royall, The Favourite, The Pastorall, The Saltarella, The Spanheim,* and so on. After he gave up his court post in 1714 Isaac evidently went into retirement, for though we hear occasionally of his teaching private pupils or, as on 10 January 1716 at Lincoln's Inn Fields playhouse, of his composing a dance, most references to him cease.

Hardly any commentary has been found on Isaac and his work. E. Pemberton included a chaconne by Isaac in *An Essay for the Further Improvement of Dancing* in 1711 and spoke cryptically of the dancer as "So Great a Master that as he wants no Encomium, [he] is likewise above the Malice of petty Upstarts. . . ." John Essex in *The Dancing Master* (1731) said that the late Mr Isaac

had the Honour to teach and instruct our late most Gracious Queen [Anne] when a young Princess, first gained character and afterwards supported that Reputation of being the Prime Master in England for 40 years together; He taught the first quality with Success and Applause, and was justly stiled the Court Dancing Master.

Matthew Dubourg the violinist was born in London in 1703, the reported natural son of the dancer Isaac. *Musgrave's Obituary* lists the dancing master's death as 1740, though the statement by Essex suggests that Isaac died before 1731.

A portrait of a Mr Isaac, by Louis Goupy, was engraved by George White; it was published by S. Sympson without a date.

Isaac, Bartholomew   [*fl.* 1674–1677], singer.

Bartholomew Isaac (or Isaack, Isack) was one of the Children of the Chapel Royal in the early 1670s. He received his training from John Blow, and with Blow from 18 May to 3 September 1674 he attended Charles II at Windsor. By 23 April 1677 his voice had broken, and he left the Chapel Royal. It was customary, however, to maintain the former Chapel boys for a period, and the Lord Chamberlain's accounts contain several references in 1677 to money spent on clothing for Bartholomew and some of his fellow students. On 19 June, for example, he was to be given hose, two suits, and, with three other boys, "coloured Suites with all small furniture." Bartholomew was probably related to Peter Isaac, another Chapel boy.

Isaac, Matthew.   *See* DUBOURG, MATTHEW.

Isaac, Peter   [*fl.* 1670–1672], singer.

Peter Isaac (or Isaack) had been one of the Children of the Chapel Royal under Henry Cooke, but by Christmas 1670 his voice had changed. A note in the Lord Chamberlain's accounts dated 8 August 1671 stated that Cooke was to receive £30 annually, retroactive to Christmas 1670, for maintaining young Peter, "whose voice has changed." In March and April 1672 other notes in the accounts referred to Isaac. He was to be given livery as a former Chapel boy, and, apparently, after giving up his post among the Chapel boys he served as a Chapel page, a position he left on 4 April 1672. Peter was probably related to the boy singer Bartholomew Isaac.

Isaacson, Mr ₍fl. 1791₎, *singer, actor.*
Mr Isaacson performed in the musical play *Ceyx and Alcyone* at Sadler's Wells on 25 April 1791.

Isabella. *See* AUBERT, ISABELLA, and GIRARDEAU, ISABELLA.

"Isabella, Lady." *See* "LADY ISABELLA."

Isack. *See* ISAAC.

Isham, John *c. 1680–1726, organist, composer.*
Grove states that John Isham (originally Isum) was born about 1680. He was educated at Merton College, Oxford, after which he served as deputy organist to William Croft at St Anne, Westminster, where Croft was appointed in 1700. On 27 January 1707, at York Buildings, a concert was presented for the benefit of Sweet and Isum; we take that to be a reference to Isham and an indication that he performed outside the church. On 22 January 1711 Isham was appointed to the post of organist at St Anne's, upon Croft's resignation. Two years later, on 17 July 1713, Isham received his Bachelor of Music degree at Oxford.

On 3 April 1718 he took the position of organist at St Andrew, Holborn, at £50 annually and gave up his post at St Anne's. Soon after, he was made organist of St Margaret, Westminster, a post he held until his death. Isham was unsuccessful in his application for the position of music master of Christ's Hospital on 28 January 1720.

Isham wrote a number of anthems, but most of his compositions were light songs, some of which were published in *Wit and Mirth* in 1719—an indication of their popularity. About 1710 he and William Morley published *A Collection of New Songs*. John Isham was buried at

St Margaret, Westminster, on 12 June 1726, and on 8 July his post as organist there was granted to Edward Purcell at £30 annually.

Isle. *See* DE LISLE.

"Islington Strong Man, The." *See* "STRONG MAN FROM ISLINGTON, THE."

Isnell, Mr ₍fl. 1794₎, *singer?*
Doane's *Musical Directory* of 1794 listed a Mr Isnell, of Craysford, Kent, as a bass (singer, apparently) who participated in the Handel performances at Westminster Abbey.

Issack. *See* ISAAC.

Isum. *See* ISHAM.

"Italian Female Samson, The" ₍fl. 1752–1753₎, *strong woman.*
An unidentified clipping at the Huntington Library dated 30 August 1753 reads:

THIS NOTICE is given, without any Design to deceive, or impose, That the True and Original Italian Female Samson, or Strong Woman, having had the Honour to perform, with Applause, and great Satisfaction, before the chief Nobility of England, in London, as well as in many other Cities of this Kingdom; does therefore think it necessary, on Account of the Encouragement she has been so fortunate to meet with in this Nation, to advise the Publick, that immediately after this next Bartholomew Fair, she is determined to go to Germany: Whoever therefore has a Curiosity to see her perform these amazing Feats of Strength, with many other new and surprising Things, which she will exhibit during the Time of this next Bartholomew Fair, may see her at the Sign of the King's Head in Smithfield, at the Price of One Shilling each Person, for the best Places; and Six-pence each Person for the other Places.

At the same time desiring every one will take Notice, That she is the same Person that perform'd at the Fair the last Year; and that there are many Counterfeits, who have Persons to give out Bills, and impose on the Publick, under the Pretence of their being the true Strong Woman.

N.B. That at Charing-Cross, 'till this Time, she has perform'd at Half a Crown for each Person. And to make it appear that she is really the same Person, she will lay a Wager, of 500 Guineas, that no one can do the Things that she is able to perform.

"Italian Grimacier, The." *See* "CELEBRATED GRIMACIER, THE."

Ives, Mr [fl. 1750], actor.

Mr Ives played La Merluche in *L'Avare* at the Haymarket Theatre on 26 February 1750 in the "Anti-Gallic" troupe that tried to counteract the visiting French players under the managership of Monnet. On 13 March Ives was seen as Alain in *Arlequin fourbe Anglois*.

Ives, Mr [fl. 1778–1795], actor, manager.

Mr Ives had a booth at Bartholomew Fair in 1778, according to Morley's *Memoirs of Bartholomew Fair*. The same Ives, probably, was listed in the Pie Powder Court Book as a comedian at the Fair in 1795.

Ives, Mr [fl. 1798], actor.

Mr Ives acted Lord Randolph in *Douglas* and Bundle in *The Waterman* at Wheatley's Riding School in Greenwich on 8 June 1798. The troupe performed one night only, advertising that they had an engagement in another town. The names of the performers in this troupe do not match the personnel at the Norwich Theatre; otherwise one might be tempted to identify Ives as a member of the Ives family of theatre folk at Norwich.

Ives, Miss [fl. 1795–1796], singer, actress.

Miss Ives was a minor singer and actress at Covent Garden Theatre during the 1795–96 season. She sang in *Macbeth* on 14 September 1795—the first notice of her—and then was a member of the chorus in *Romeo and Juliet*, played Belinda in *The Ghost* and Sukey Tawdry in *The Beggar's Opera*, was a supernumerary in *The Lad of the Hills*, and sang in *Zorinski*. Her last notice came on 26 April 1796.

Ives, Simon 1600–1662, organist, singer, instrumentalist, composer.

Simon Ives (or Ive) was baptized on 20 July 1600 at Ware, Hertfordshire. Nothing is known of his early years. By 1633 he must have gained a fair reputation, for he was involved in the elaborate masque *The Triumph of Peace* by James Shirley, which was performed at Whitehall on 3 February 1634 under the joint auspices of the four Inns of Court. Bulstrode Whitelocke, according to his *Memoirs*, was in charge of the music for the masque:

I made choice of Mr. Simon Ives, an honest and able musician, of excellent skill in the art, and of Mr. Lewes, to compose all the airs, lessons, and songs for the Masque, to be the masters of all the musicke under me. . . . I was so conversant with the musitians, and so willing to gaine their favour, especially at this time, that I composed an aier myselfe, with the assistance of Mr. Ives, and called it *Whitelocke's Coranto*. . . .

Greg in his *Bibliography of English Printed Drama* transcribes the title page of the 1633 edition of the masque and quotes the praise Ives received: his "Art gaue an Harmonious soule to the otherwise languishing Numbers." Ives received £100 for his labors.

When Anthony à Wood jotted down his brief biographies of musicians in his "Lives of Musicians" (at the Bodleian), he called Simon Ives

a singing man in ye Cath. Ch. of S. Paul in London and a teacher of musick before the Rebellion broke out, after it did break out lost his singing mans place, and stuck to his instruction in musick wch. kept him in a comfortable condition. He was excellent at the Lyra-Viol [viola da gamba] and improved it by excellent inventions.

Ives served as a vicar choral at St Paul's Cathedral and was organist of Christ Church, Newgate. One of Ives's students was the remarkable Susannah Perwich. In *The Virgin's Pattern* (1661) it is recorded that "one of her Masters (Mr. Ives by name) was wont to say he could play no *new* Lesson *before* her, but she would have it *presently*."

In 1661 Ives was made a minor prebendary at St Paul's. He died in London on 1 July 1662. He had made his will on 4 February 1662, describing himself as of the parish of Christ Church. To his son-in-law Joseph Body, citizen and joiner, and his wife Mary, Simon's daughter, he left a parcel of freehold land in Southwark, near the Corn Market, which he had lately purchased from Thomas Thicknesse of Long Sutton, Lincolnshire. Ives also left to Mary and Joseph Body a lease of four or five houses near the windmill in Moorfields, at the west end of Grogg Lane, plus other leases held for Ives by Thomas Fuller. Mary Body was designated residuary legatee.

To the poor of Ware, Ives's birthplace, he left 40s.; he also asked that a similar amount be given to the poor of the parish where he died. To his sister (-in-law, presumably) Rose Kendall he left £5, and to Rose's daughter Anne, £10 when she should marry or reach 21. To his sister-in-law Mary Ives, his brother Edward's wife, he bequeathed £5, and to her daughter he left a similar amount. To John Keyes of Cambridge, who accommodated Simon Ives's son at the University when he studied there in January 1645, Ives left 40s. To his kindred at Colchester, his brother John and brother William's children, he left mourning rings.

Ives left his youngest son, Andres, £100 on demand, the money to be paid by Ives's executors in portions spread out over 18 months. To the petty canons of St Paul's Cathedral, Ives left a chest of viols made by Thomas Alred; the chest contained three tenors (violas), one bass, and five trebles. Ives also left another bass viol made by one Muskett, Thomas Alred's man. The will was proved on 7 July 1662 by Mrs Ives. The spelling of Ives's name which we have used here is that found in most sources, though the scribe who wrote the will consistently used Ive.

The elder Ives composed a number of catches and rounds which appeared in popular collections in the 1650s, 1660s, and 1670s. Much of his music is in manuscript at the British Library. Simon Ives's son Simon was also a musician.

Ivory, Abraham   *d. 1680?, actor.*

The Key (1704) to the Duke of Buckingham's *The Rehearsal* stated that "*Abraham Ivory* had formerly been a considerable Actor of Womens Parts; but afterwards stupify'd himself so far, with drinking strong Waters, that, before the first Acting of this Farce [in 1671], he was fit for nothing, but to go of Errands; for which, and meer Charity, the Company allow'd him a Weekly Sallary." The company in question was the King's, at the Bridges Street playhouse, and *The Rehearsal* was presented there on 7 December 1671 with Ivory playing him-

self. At the end of Act I a player tells Bayes, "Sir, Mr. *Ivory* is not come yet; but hee'l be here presently, he's but two doors off." Abraham appeared in the battle scene in Act V, for after the scene Bayes says, "Mr. *Ivory*, a word."

Ivory was probably the "Abram" cited in the Bodleian promptbook of *Brennoralt* as playing one of the Guards and in the Harvard promptbook of *The Maides Revenge* as a Servant; the plays were acted about 1673–1675.

Montague Summers in his edition of *The Rehearsal* suggested that Ivory may have begun acting about 1638–39, but there is no proof of that. The earliest pre-Restoration notice of him was probably the report of a raid on the actors at the Cockpit Theatre, provided by the *Kingdom's Weekly Intelligencer* of 2–9 January 1649:

. . . Abraham had a black Satten gown on, and before he came into the durt, he was very neat in his white laced pumps. The people not expecting such a pageant looked and laughed at all the rest, and not knowing who he was, they asked, what had that Lady done?

Ivory's name is unusual enough that it seems most probable that the following entries in the parish registers of St James, Clerkenwell, concern Abraham Ivory the actor, and since the registers reveal that Ivory lived near the Red Bull playhouse in Clerkenwell, it is probable that he acted at that theatre at some point. William, the son of Abraham Ivory, was christened on 1 May 1652. Elizabeth, the daughter of Abraham and Susan Ivory, was born and christened on 28 May 1654 and buried on 31 July 1656. Their daughter Margarett was born on 5 April 1656, christened on the twentieth, and buried on 3 November 1657. Their son Felix was born on 11 April and christened on 22 April 1657. Their son Frauncis was christened on 6 November 1659 and buried on 11 July 1661. On 15 February 1680, Abraham "Ivery" and his wife, from Dagger Lane, were buried.

Ixon, Mrs.   *See* BEAUMONT, MRS [*fl. 1800–1802*].

= J =

"Jacio, General." *See* "JACKOO, GENERAL."

"Jack." *See* HAINES, JOSEPH.

"Jack, Blind." *See* KEILING, JOHN.

Jack Pudding. *See* PUDDING, JACK.

"Jackoo, General" ₁*fl.* 1785–1786₁, *performing monkey.*

A bill for Astley's Amphitheatre, hand-dated 28 May 1785, at the Huntingon Library stated that "GENERAL JACKOO, the celebrated Monkey from Paris, will, for the first time this season, change the whole of his dress in a surprising manner, and perform his war manoeuvres, dance on the Tight Rope with fetters on his feet, &c." In "The Manager's Note-Book" is a letter from Philip Astley in Paris to Mr and Mrs Pownall, dated 4 December 1786. He said, "Genl Jacio did not arrive before the 18th and we opend the 19th . . ." That entry would appear to be a reference to the performing monkey.

Jacks, Mr ₁*fl.* 1774–1799₁, *actor, house servant.*

Mr Jacks was listed in the Drury Lane accounts in 1774–75 as a supernumerary. He seems also to have been one of the house servants, for an entry dated 1 October 1799 named Jacks and others as advancing £600 for old renters—whatever that may have meant.

Jackson, Mr ₁*fl.* 1742–1750₁, *actor, dancer, singer.*

A Mr Jackson acted Orasmin in a performance of *Zara* given at the James Street Theatre on 7 April 1742 for the benefit of "a tradesman in distress." That night he also sang a dialogue with Miss Sharp. He was perhaps the Jackson who acted the Constable in a production of *The*

Recruiting Officer given by Theophilus Cibber's company at the Haymarket Theatre on 27 September 1744. A Mr Jackson, perhaps the same person, danced a Demon in at least seven performances of *The Tempest* at Goodman's Fields Theatre in February 1745 and on 1 May 1745 shared in benefit tickets. In 1745–46 he again danced there in *The Tempest.*

In 1748 a Jackson performed the Prince of Wurtemburgh in *Northern Heroes* in Bridges, Cross, Burton, and Vaughan's booth in the George Inn Yard on 24 August during Bartholomew Fair and in September in their booth on the Bowling Green, Southwark, during Southwark Fair. He, or another Jackson, was with a company that performed in French at the Haymarket Theatre in February and March 1750; Jackson acted Plumet in *L'Officier en recrue* (a translation of *The Recruiting Officer*) on 9 and 12 February, Laronneau in *L'Opéra du Gueux* (a translation of *The Beggar's Opera*) on 16 and 21 February and 8 March, and Cléante in *L'Avare* on 28 February and 1, 7, and 13 March. On the last night he also performed Clerimont in the pantomime *Arlequin fourbe Anglois.*

An actor named Jackson was a member of the company at Norwich in 1743–44.

Jackson, Mr ₁*fl.* 1758–1759₁, *actor.*

The "young Gentleman" who acted the title role in *Theodosius* at Covent Garden Theatre on 18 December 1758 is identified as Mr Jackson by Joseph Reed in a manuscript in the British Library. He played the role again on 20 December. A year later, Mr Jackson, announced as making his third appearance on any stage, acted Osman in *Zara* at Covent Garden on 12 December 1759, at his own benefit for which the receipts were £163, 15*s.* 6*d.*, less house charges of £84. No other appearances for Jackson are known to us.

Jackson, Mr [fl. 1766], *office keeper.*

A Mr Jackson was an office keeper at Covent Garden Theatre in 1766, according to a manuscript in the British Library (Egerton 2272).

Jackson, Mr [fl. 1768], *actor.*

Announced as from the Theatre Royal, Dublin, a Mr Jackson acted Manly in *The Provok'd Husband* at Covent Garden on 30 May 1768. On the same evening another actor named Jackson played an unspecified role in *The Devil upon Two Sticks* at the Haymarket.

Jackson, Mr [fl. 1768–1770], *actor, singer.*

On 30 May 1768 a Mr Jackson's name appeared in the Haymarket bills for an unspecified role in *The Devil upon Two Sticks*. Presumably he was not the Jackson announced as from the Theatre Royal, Dublin, who acted Manly in *The Provok'd Husband* at Covent Garden on the same night. The Haymarket Jackson also played Puff in *Miss in Her Teens* on 8 June 1768, Bonniface in *The Stratagem* on 23 June (when a Miss Jackson acted Gipsey in the same piece and a Mrs Jackson appeared as Mrs Bruin in *The Mayor of Garratt*), Lockit in *The Beggar's Opera* on 27 July, Sir Thomas Testy in *Hob in the Well* on 8 August, Corydon in *Damon and Phillida* on 19 August, and a role in *The Orators* on 24 August. Perhaps he was the Jackson who acted Wingate in *The Apprentice* at the Haymarket on 19 December 1768 and Mungo in *The Padlock* at the same theatre on 29 October 1770.

Jackson, Mr [fl. 1776–1800], *dancer.*

A dancer named Jackson performed in the choruses at Covent Garden and shared in annual benefits almost every season from 1776–77 through 1799–1800. Among his earliest appearances was one in a naval ballet *All in the Downs* on 25 April 1777, on a night when Master Jackson, probably his son, also danced. Jackson's salary in 1776–77 was £1 10s. per week, a figure which remained constant at least through 1795–96.

His dancing roles included the Doctor in *Harlequin's Chaplet* in 1789–90, a principal character in *The Provocation* in 1790–91, a Demon of Revenge in *Blue-Beard* in 1791–92, a Creolian in *The Governor* in 1792–93, one of

the Bridemen in *Harlequin and Faustus* and a Midshipman in *The Shipwreck* in 1793–94. He also danced at Richmond on 1 September 1797.

Jackson, Mr [fl. 1778–1788], *actor.*

An actor named Jackson, who seems not to have been either John or Thomas Jackson, appeared occasionally in London in the 1770s and 1780s. He acted Lovegold in *The Miser* with a company playing at China Hall, Rotherhithe, on 24 June 1778, the same night that Thomas Jackson was busy at the Haymarket. A Mr Jackson played Goosequill in *The Rival Milliners* and Pleadwell in *Falstaff's Wedding* at the Haymarket Theatre on 27 December 1779. At the same theatre Mr Jackson performed unspecified roles in *Love at a Venture* on 21 March 1782 and *The Taylors* on 25 November 1782. His other characters in specially-licensed performances at the Haymarket over the next several seasons included Lord Stanley in *Richard III* on 17 September 1784, a principal role in *The Fair Refugee* and Cadwallader in *The Author* on 10 February 1785, Fulmer in *The West Indian* and Sprightly in *The Author* on 12 March 1787, and the Prince of Tanais in *Tamerlane* on 22 December 1788.

Perhaps he was the same Jackson who, announced as from Norwich, acted at Newbury from November 1785 to January 1788 and played at Blackburn with a Mrs Jackson in April 1787.

Jackson, Mr [fl. 1784], *violist.*

A Mr Jackson was listed by Dr Burney as one of the tenor players (violists) in the Handel Memorial Concerts at Westminster Abbey and the Pantheon in May and June 1784. He was not William Jackson (fl. 1784–1807?), who was also listed, as a violinist.

Jackson, Mrs [fl. 1729?–1749], *singer, actress.*

A Mrs Jackson acted Jenny in *The Beggar's Opera* at Drury Lane Theatre on 17 October 1740 and several other times that month. Perhaps she was the same Mrs Jackson who played Mme Cajoleuse and Diane in performances of *L'Opéra du Gueux*, a French translation of *The Beggar's Opera*, presented at the Haymarket Theatre by English actors on 29 April 1749 and some seven times in May. A Mrs Jackson was a member of the company at Norwich between 1729 and 1741.

Jackson, Mrs ₁*fl. 1768*₁, *actress.*

At the Haymarket Theatre in the summer of 1768 a Mrs Jackson acted Mrs Bruin in *The Mayor of Garratt* on 23 June, the Lady in *Rule a Wife and Have a Wife* on 8 July, and Molly in *The Beggar's Opera* on 27 July, 1 and 10 August, and 7 September. She was probably the wife of Mr Jackson (fl. 1768–1770) and the mother of Miss Jackson (fl. 1768), who also performed at the same theatre that summer.

Jackson, Mrs ₁*fl. 1782–1787?*₁, *actress.*

A Mrs Jackson acted the Queen in *Richard III* at the Haymarket Theatre on 4 March 1782, at a time when Mrs John Jackson is known to have been in Edinburgh. Perhaps she was the Mrs Jackson who acted at Blackburn with a Mr Jackson in 1787.

Jackson, Master *b. c. 1730, musician.*

At the Castle Tavern or 13 March 1741 the violinist William Jackson (d. 1782?) received a benefit. That evening a concerto and solo were played by "Jackson's Brother, a lad of eleven years of age," whose Christian name and instrument were not identified.

Jackson, Master ₁*fl. 1775–1779*₁, *dancer.*

Master Jackson, who was probably the son of the Covent Garden dancer Mr Jackson (fl. 1776–1800), made his first appearance on that stage dancing with his tutor Aldridge in a dance called *The Indiaman Returned* on 29 April 1775. On 12 December 1775 he performed in a new pantomime dance *The Irish Wedding*, with Aldridge, Miss Besford, and others. They appeared on 2 January 1776 in another new dance called *Mirth and Morality*. He danced a comic dance with Miss Parish and a new dance, *The Coopers*, with Languish and Miss Nicols on 25 April 1777, the night Mr Jackson appeared in a naval dance, *All in the Downs*.

After dancing at Bristol in the summer of 1777, Master Jackson returned to Covent Garden, where his name appeared in the bills through 1778–79 for various specialty numbers such as *The Humours of Leixlip* with Al-

dredge and Miss Besford. Some of the dancing performances we have listed for Mr Jackson during the last two decades of the century may have been given by this lad after he matured.

Jackson, Miss ₁*fl. 1740–1745*₁, *dancer.*

Earning 15s. per week, a Miss Jackson danced at Drury Lane Theatre in 1740–41, in such chorus roles as a Gypsy Woman in *The Fortune Tellers*. The next season at Drury Lane she was in the chorus of *The Harlot's Progress* and *Harlequin Shipwrecked*. She transferred to Covent Garden in 1742–43, where she danced as a country lass in many performances of *The Rape of Proserpine*, and was sometimes billed as Mrs Jackson. At the New Wells, Clerkenwell, on 27 December 1742 she danced for the benefit of Mrs Starkey. In 1744–45, still a member of the Covent Garden company, Miss Jackson shared a benefit with Anderson, Stede, and Mrs Le Brun on 7 May 1745.

Jackson, Miss ₁*fl. 1768*₁, *actress.*

A Miss Jackson acted Gipsey in *The Stratagem* at the Haymarket Theatre on 23 June 1768. Probably she was the daughter of Mr Jackson (fl. 1768–1770) and Mrs Jackson (fl. 1768), who also performed at the theatre that summer.

Jackson, Miss ₁*fl. 1795–1799*₁, *singer.*

Miss Jackson was employed as a chorus singer at Drury Lane from 1795–96 through 1799–1800. She performed vocal parts in *The Surrender of Calais*, *Alexander the Great*, and *The Iron Chest* in 1795–96; a Villager in *The Honey Moon*, and a Captive in *Lodoiska* in 1796–97; a Peasant in *Richard Coeur de Lion* in 1797–98; a Peasant in *The Captive of Spilburg* and a Villager in *Feudal Times* in 1798–99; and a Peasant in numerous productions of *Blue-Beard* in 1797–98 and 1798–99.

Jackson, Miss *d. 1806?, actress, singer, dancer.*

A Miss Jackson acted a principal character in the premiere of the anonymous comedy *A School for the Ladies* and Damaris in the afterpiece *No Wit Like A Woman's* at the Haymarket Theatre on 5 April 1780. In other specially-licensed performances at the same theatre she played Mrs Tripe in *The Detection* on 13 November 1780 and Trudge in *Love and a Bottle* on 26 March 1781.

Possibly she was the Miss Jackson who was at the Orchard Street Theatre, Bath, from 1782–83 through 1787–88, at Brighton in Fox's company in 1790, at Chesterfield in January 1800, at York and Hull between 1800 and 1802, and at Nottingham and Chester in 1802. A Miss Jackson was a regular member of the Manchester company from 1803 to 1805, mainly as a singer. Though she would fill the second cast of vocal characters "with very great propriety," the Manchester *Townsman* of 4 January 1804 judged that she was "not what such a town as Manchester has the right to expect as a first performer in that line." The *Gentleman's Magazine* of November 1806 reported that Miss Jackson, "late of the Manchester theatre," had died at Doncaster that month.

Jackson, Elizabeth. *See* LACY, MRS WILLOUGHBY THE SECOND.

Jackson, "Gentleman." *See* JACKSON, JOHN *1769–1845, pugilist.*

Jackson, Jane. *See* BIANCHI, MRS FRANCESCO.

Jackson, John *1730–1806, actor, manager, playwright.*

According to *The Dictionary of National Biography*, John Jackson was born in 1742, the son of a clergyman who had livings at Keighley and at Beenham in Berkshire. But Jackson's obituary in the *Scots Magazine* of December 1806 claimed he was 76 at the time of his death, an age indeed confirmed in the manuscript "Recorder's Book of the Calton Burying Ground" at Edinburgh, which sets the year of his birth at 1730. In his *History of the Scottish Stage* (1793), Jackson claimed to have been educated for the clergy.

In his own narrative, Jackson placed his stage debut at Edinburgh on 9 January 1762 as Oroonoko. Subsequently that winter at Edinburgh he acted Romeo, Osmyn in *The Mourning Bride*, Prospero in *The Tempest*, and Hamlet. He almost lost the role of Douglas when the manager Love intended to give it to Digges, just returned from Ireland, but Jack-

JOHN JACKSON as Albertus
artist unknown

son threatened to resign, won his point, and was well applauded despite Digges's conspicuous presence "in the centre of the third row of the pit from the orchestra." The play's author Home also saw the performance to his expressed satisfaction. Soon after, Digges tested Jackson with another contention, by insisting on top billing when he played Old Norval to the newcomer's Douglas; they finally compromised by sharing the first line on the bills. Jackson then acted Jaffeir to Digges's Pierre in *Venice Preserv'd* and Juba to his Cato. In the middle of May Jackson played Romeo to Mrs Bellamy's Juliet and Castalio to her Monimia in *The Orphan*.

Despite receiving "a very pressing invitation" to remain in Edinburgh for another season at salary to be increased by £1 per week, Jackson determined to leave, believing that as Digges and Mrs Bellamy were to remain, his own situation "would not be rendered very pleasing." He went down to London, where he made his debut at Drury Lane on 7 October 1762 as Oroonoko, advertised as a "Young Gentleman" but identified by the prompter Cross in his diary as Jackson. Garrick used him sparingly that season, for Jackson's only other performances were Lord Guilford Dudley in *Lady Jane Gray* on 15 and 22 October and 23 November, Moneses in *Tamerlane* on 4 November, Southampton in *The Earl of Essex* on 20 April 1763 (for his benefit), and Cornwall in *King Lear* on 12 May.

In the 1763 edition of *The Rosciad* Churchill treated Jackson with typical virulence. An anonymous writer to the *Theatrical Review* in June 1763 sent the editor an interlude which had been proposed for performance at Jackson's benefit in retaliation (Garrick having expunged the exceptionable lines), but both Lowe and Vernon made excuses about playing in it, so the piece was not given. The *Theatrical Review* critic that season had been kinder to Jackson:

This young gentleman appeared Oct. 7—His figure, as to height and proportion, is excellent: but he was a little deficient in that graceful ease, which, possessed, would render his person the most elegant on the theatre. This necessary qualification however, he may, no doubt, attain by a due attention to the polite accomplishments. His first character was Oroonoko, and it is but justice to say, that we scarce observed a single sentiment that he did not impress with all the sense of the author. On the other hand, his voice was so exceedingly weak, that unless, like Demosthenes, he can hit on a method to improve it, we fear it will not a little impede his progress to eminence on the stage. Besides—notwithstanding his tones, in general, were perfectly harmonious, yet now and then his pronunciation was tinctured with something of the provincial; which, though not strong enough to absolutely mark the place that gave birth to it, was nevertheless, conspicuously harsh and disagreeable. With respect to his deficiency in power, an attendance on Mr. Angier of Bishopsgate-street, (if any credit is to be given to assertions in the public papers) would soon remove it; and as to the latter, nothing more is needful than a frequent rehearsing before a real and judicious friend. These difficulties (as they at present seem) surmounted, we will venture to pronounce a success to Mr. Jackson equal to his warmest wishes and most sanguine expectations.

In 1763–64 Jackson enjoyed a slightly better opportunity at Drury Lane under Colman, who was minding the theatre while Garrick was on his grand tour. His roles included Paris in *Romeo and Juliet*, Sir Richard Vernon in *1 Henry IV*, a Wounded Captain and Malcolm in *Macbeth*, Guiderius in *Cymbeline*, Fenton in *The Merry Wives of Windsor*, Poins in *2 Henry IV*, Bellamy in *The Suspicious Husband*, Lysimachus in *The Rival Queens*, and Hamet in *The Orphan of China*. On 14 February 1764 he acted Polydore in *The Orphan*, a performance which the prompter Hopkins found "very bad." His lot failed to improve in his third Drury Lane season, in which he earned £3 per week. For his benefit on 4 May 1765, when he acted Polydore, tickets could be had of him in Palsgrave's Head Court, Temple Bar.

In the summer of 1765 Jackson was a member of the first company at the newly-built theatre in Richmond, Surrey, under the management of James Love. The critic in the *Universal Museum* of August 1765 complained that Jackson and Packer, who played such capital roles as Hamlet, Richard III, Lord Townly, and others, were "extremely inadequate to the load," so that scarcely a piece was offered "but what becomes languid and uninteresting." After his benefit at Richmond on 5 August 1765, Jackson left London to play at Smock Alley, Dublin, for several seasons. He may have been the Jackson who, announced as from the Theatre Royal, Dublin, acted Manly in *The Provok'd Husband* at Covent Garden toward the end of the season on 30 May 1768; but such a role seems not to have been in his line, so that actor was perhaps Thomas Jackson (1741–1798), with whom John is often confused, or yet another Jackson. John performed at the Millgate Theatre in Belfast with James Parker's company in August 1768 and at Cork in the summer of 1769. Between Belfast and Cork he had played at the New Concert Hall, Edinburgh, in the spring of 1769, acting Hamlet on 15 March. He returned late in 1769 to Edinburgh, where he is known to have played Iago on 18 November and Pierre in *Venice Preserv'd* on 31 January 1770. For the rest of that season Jackson was at the Capel Street Theatre, Dublin. In 1771–72 he acted at Smock Alley with Mrs Jackson, the former Hester Brown, whom he had married sometime in the summer of 1769, probably in Ireland. Though a daughter of the Irish actor John Sowdon, she had used the professional name Brown before her marriage to Jackson.

During the early 1770s the Jacksons played regularly at Edinburgh and Dublin. Jackson's tragedy *Eldred: or, The British Freeholder* was performed at Edinburgh on 19 March 1774 and probably had been played earlier at Capel Street. Husband and wife played at York in May 1774, she having a benefit on the twentieth, the last night of their engagement there. From that city on 18 June 1774 G. C. Swan wrote to David Garrick: "Pray have you seen the Jacksons? and have I done justice to them, and to their performances? I am somewhat surprised that I have not yet heard from him . . . as he left his wardrobe at my house." The Jacksons acted in Younger's company at Liverpool in December 1774.

With his wife, Jackson was engaged by Foote at the Haymarket Theatre for the summer of 1775. He made his first appearance on that stage in his own *Eldred* on 7 July, when he also spoke the prologue and his wife the epilogue. His tragedy was repeated with some success on 10 and 14 July, though according to a critic's notation in a manuscript at the Folger Library "it will not bear the test of criticism in scarce any one point." That summer Jackson was also seen as Sir Jealous's Servant in *The Busy Body* on 19 September. On 20 November 1775 he acted Sir William in a specially-licensed performance of *The Gentle Shepherd* given at the Haymarket by "Desire of the Masons." Mrs Jackson, without her husband, was engaged at Covent Garden for 1775–76; however, for her benefit on 1 May 1776 he did appear at that theatre in the title role of his own play *Eldred*, in which Mrs Jackson played Edwena.

Although his wife's career flourished in London during the late 1770s, Jackson himself was obliged to lead the life of a stroller. In the summers of 1775 and 1776 he played at Birmingham, where he was criticized by an observer writing in *The Campaign*:

[Jackson] seems possest of almost every requisite for the Stage; and yet we hardly know any one who affords less satisfaction to his auditors: He always seems to understand his [text] perfectly, but his method of conveying it to others is so laboured, that it rather offends than pleases; would he endeavor to acquire a little more ease he would be much better received.

Occasionally he acted at Bristol in the summers of 1776 and 1777, when he and his wife were advertised as from Covent Garden. In 1776–77 he was at Edinburgh and Dublin but returned to Covent Garden once more to act Zanga in *The Revenge* for his wife's benefit on 7 May 1777. He performed similar service for her benefit on 5 May 1778, this time playing Hareb in the first London performance of his second tragedy *The British Heroine* (which had been first acted at Crow Street on 13 January 1777 as *Gerilda*). Never published, the play survives as No 448 in the Larpent manuscripts at the Huntington Library. That night Quick delivered a monologue called *Tony Lumpkin's Ramble Through London*, which Jackson claimed as his composition when he produced it at Edinburgh on 26 July 1780 with the revised title of *Tony Lumpkin's Rambles Through Edinburgh*. *The Dictionary of National Biography* assigns John Jackson the role of Tony Lumpkin in *She Stoops to Conquer* at the Haymarket on 9 June 1777, but that player was probably Thomas Jackson, a regular Haymarket actor at that time.

Early in 1780 Jackson began to acquire interests in northern theatres which he tenanted in the summer months. With the provincial actor John Bland (1721–1808) and a Mr Mills he intended to take over the management of the Alston Street Theatre in Glasgow in May 1780. While waiting for the proposed opening date, Jackson took a company to play in theatres he had established at Dundee, Aberdeen, and Dumfries. He returned to Glasgow on 5 May to discover the theatre "a smoky ruin," it having burned to the ground that morning with all his wardrobe and properties. The building may have been sabotaged by a fanatical element opposed to players and playhouses. It had been insured for £1000, but the proprietors had neglected the premium; the Sun Fire company made a generous present of £300 against the loss. The proprietors advised Jackson that they had no intention to rebuild the theatre, but that he was at liberty to erect a house at his own risk, and that if he should choose to build on the same spot they would present him with the ground and the remaining walls. Jackson, however, determined on a site less removed from the city, in St Enoch's Croft, later known as Dunlop Street, a pleasant seat on the Clyde.

Purchasing the ground from Robert Barclay, a Glasgow writer, Jackson began to build. As Jackson told the story, just as he with trowel in hand was about to lay the foundation stone on 17 February 1781, a paper was handed him from Dr Gillies and Mr Porteus advising of their intention "to join with other proprietors in Dunlop Street to apply to the magistrates to prevent the building of a Playhouse or Concert Hall for acting plays in this street, as being an injury to their property, and inconsistent with the conditions granted by Mr. Dunlop to the feuars." In a long letter of reply Jackson avowed that as "the son of a clergyman, and brought up for holy orders, he will ever pay honour to the sacred characters of that order"; he then effectively persuaded their tolerance, concluding "let us show to each individual of [our] world, that brotherly love and charity are the characteristics of good Christians." Completed at a cost of more than £3000, the Dunlop Street playhouse, which held about £90 to £100, was opened by Jackson in January 1782.

While the negotiations and construction had been proceeding in Glasgow, Jackson continued to perform in Edinburgh. His third tragedy, *Sir William Wallace, of Ellerslie; or, The Siege of Dumbarton Castle*, was performed there on 26 July 1780 without success. On 10 November 1781 Jackson purchased the patent and the Theatre Royal, Shakespeare Square, Edinburgh, from David Ross. At the cost of some £7000 he re-roofed and refurbished the building, provided new scenery, costumes, and ornaments, and, with his wife now joining him from London opened it under his management on 1 December 1781 with *The Suspicious Husband*. The next month he opened the Glasgow house. Afterwards, wrote Jackson, "the seasons of performing were so settled, that one set of performers supplied both houses. The actors, wardrobe, and exhibitions were the same; its theatrical arrangements being upon a conjunct plan with that of the metropolis [London]."

In his *Random Records*, the younger George Colman hinted that Jackson and his wife "made a system of suppressing talent superior than their own," for it was his opinion that the members of the regular Edinburgh company seldom "rose much above mediocrity, and most of them fell under it." The record shows, however, that Jackson's stages were regularly graced by the finest players up from London, including Henderson, Holman, King, Mrs Baddeley, Miss Farren, Mrs Jordan, Mrs Pope, Mrs Siddons, and Mrs Yates. John Williams warmly praised Jackson in *The Pin Basket to The Children of Thespis* for his enterprise, claiming that to him "that part of the Scotch people who are fond of theatrical entertainments are highly indebted, for his spirit and skill in giving their theatres importance."

Considering the treacherousness of theatrical management and the vagaries of the personalities involved, it is remarkable that Jackson's management succeeded during the 1780s. There was a curious quarrel with the public in July 1788 over the casting of James Fennell in preference to Woods as Jaffeir in *Venice Preserv'd*. In 1789 he had to embarrass Mrs Jordan publicly for her unprofessional conduct. She had signed with him for 17 nights, but played only 15 and then tried to pressure him for more money; when he refused to raise her pay, she defected to London and circulated injurious lies about him.

By 1790, however, Jackson began to experience—as he put it—"derangements" of his finances, brought on, it would seem, by overextending his resources and energies in his attempt to coordinate his theatres at Edinburgh, Glasgow, Aberdeen, and Dundee. He was obliged to make over his properties to a trustee, who disposed of the Aberdeen theatre to pay debts. From 21 July to 21 August 1790 Jackson left King to run the Edinburgh house, having found it necessary to seek his "personal safety with only nine shillings" in his pocket.

The lease of the Edinburgh and Glasgow theatres was put up for auction on 2 November 1791. What subsequently occurred makes a confusing and contradictory story. As told by Jackson in his *History* and by Charles Lee Lewes in his *Memoirs* the facts are essentially the same but the points of view differ. Essentially, it seems that Jackson had persuaded Stephen Kemble, then the Newcastle manager, to take the lease at a rent of some £1350 for one year, assuming that by then Jackson could settle with his creditors, whereupon, as he had promised, he would keep Kemble as partner in the concern. Jackson claimed he would have preferred to have made the lease over to Harriet Esten, a competitor for it, but delays on her side complicated that possibility. Lewes, on the other hand, claimed that Jackson had supplicated Kemble to take it in order to prevent Mrs Esten from obtaining it, for fear it would never revert to Jackson again. Kemble got the lease. But when Jackson presented his security for one-half the rent, Kemble objected that that was insufficient, and refused to allow him to return to the management. Jackson accused Kemble of sharp practice, and Kemble refused Jackson admission to his own building at Edinburgh. The dispute was put before Henry Erskine, Dean of the Faculty of Advocates, for arbitration. Erskine ruled on 9 August 1792 that Kemble was to pay Jackson half the profits from the theatre so long as he leased it from his creditors, but, whereas Kemble was obliged to be half proprietor, he was to be sole manager at a salary to be determined by the Dean.

The decision was a long while in coming. During the previous season, 1791–92, while Kemble had operated the theatre, Jackson had busied himself applying pressure and subterfuge. In July 1792 he persuaded his trustee Robert Playfair to lease the Edinburgh theatre to Mrs Esten for the ensuing season at a rent of £1000, a substantially lower figure than Kemble had paid. Immediately a scramble for the right to the patent began, with solicitations of all sides to the Duke of Hamilton and Henry Dundas, to whom it had originally been issued. Dundas asked the Lord Advocate, the Dean of the Faculty, and the Lord Provost to decide, and they nominated Kemble. Hamilton, however, had already authorized Mrs Esten to use the patent, and she had the right to the lease. She opened the Theatre Royal and Kemble managed to obtain permission from Jones to fit up the Circus as a theatre, which he opened on 12 January 1793. But Kemble's establishment was shut down on 6 February because it was unauthorized. The mess was resolved by the following January 1794, when Mrs Esten gave up the lease to the Theatre Royal to Kemble, who for its use agreed to pay Jackson's creditors £1000 and Mrs Esten £200 each year.

It was that struggle and the conviction that he had been duped by Kemble which impelled Jackson to publish *A Statment of Facts, Explanatory of the Dispute Between John Jackson and Stephen Kemble, relative to the Theatre Royal of Edinburgh* in 1792 (reprinted with slight variations in his *History of the Scottish Stage, from its first establishment to the present time; with A Distinct Narrative of Some Recent Theatrical Transactions*, in 1793). Jackson performed at Dublin in 1795–96, at Bury and Stockport in 1796, and at Nottingham in 1799.

When the Edinburgh and Glasgow theatres were advertised for sale in 1800, Jackson, "on assurance of support from his friends" purchased them for a reputed £8020, and immediately sold a half-interest to Francis Aickin, the manager at Liverpool. Together they opened the theatres in 1801–2 and the new managers fared well for several seasons. One "Candidus" in a pamphlet of 1802 voiced disappointment in the physical condition of the Edinburgh theatre and the assignment of characters. When Jackson and Aickin faced the competition of a new theatre in Queen Street, Glasgow, they agreed to close their smaller theatre in Dunlop Street and take over the management of the new house, renting it till 1808 for five percent of the cost, which amounted to about £800 per year. When Master Henry West Betty appeared in his theatres in 1804, Jackson published his *Strictures upon the Merits of Young Roscius* (Glasgow, 1804).

In the spring of 1806 Aickin sold his interests in Edinburgh and Glasgow to Anthony Rock. That season had been disappointing, causing the *Monthly Mirror* of May 1806 to state that "The experience of this and the two or three previous last seasons ought to convince Mr John Jackson that the tide of popularity, though never in his favour, has irretrievably turned against him. It would be 'kicking against the pricks' to attempt a new management."

Jackson was then 76 years of age. His wife had died in January 1806 of "a Decline of Nature" at the age of 55, in the phrase of the manuscript "Recorder's Book of the Calton Burying Ground," now in the General Registry Office for Scotland. At the end of that year, Jackson died also of "a Decline of Nature" at his house in Shakespeare Square on 4 December 1806. The *Gentleman's Magazine* that month reported that as a tribute of respect the

Edinburgh theatre was closed for a few days. He was buried "in his own ground" on 6 December, according to the "Recorder's Book."

One of Jackson's children, Anna Moriah Jackson, had died of "Water in the Head" at the age of five years and five months, and was buried in his ground in Edinburgh on 8 September 1790. Jackson was survived by a son, John, and two daughters, Jessy and Elizabeth. A letter in the National Library of Scotland signed by the three siblings and dated 1809 petitions Viscount Melville to renew his patent (due to expire that year), under which their father had operated the Theatre Royal in Shakespeare Square. The building was by then encumbered with debt and its affairs were in the hands of trustees, but the three Jacksons assured Melville of the headway they were making in lifting the debts. The petition had been initiated by them in order to save their rightful inheritance and only means of livelihood. Obviously they feared further injury from Henry Siddons who was preparing a new theatre in the Circus in Leith Walk but who would be unable to operate without the patent's sanction. The patent, however, went to Siddons, through the influence of Walter Scott, who opposed the renewal to Jackson's heirs, and on 14 November 1809 Siddons opened the new Theatre Royal, Leith Walk.

An anonymous engraving of John Jackson as Albertus in *The Siege of Harlech* was published in the *Hibernian Magazine* in February 1777.

Jackson, Mrs John, Hester, née Sowdon, stage name Miss Brown   *1751–1806, actress, singer, dancer.*

The actress and singer Hester Jackson, the wife of the Scottish manager John Jackson (1730–1806), was the daughter of John Sowdon (d. 1789), a London actor and sometime manager of Smock Alley Theatre in Dublin during the 1750s. Her father adopted the professional name of Sowdon, probably to save his parents embarrassment, for according to the *Dublin Journal* of 5–9 June 1753, he came of a good family, being brother to "Thomas Otway of Castle Otway, Esq." When Hester went upon the stage she adopted the professional name of Brown. According to the register of her burial in January 1806, Hester died at the age of 55; thus she was born in 1751.

HESTER JACKSON as Britannia

by Bonnor

(Her obituary in the *Scot's Magazine* for January 1806 also stated that she died at 55, but claimed she was the daughter of an actor named Brown.)

Some uncertainty surrounds Hester's early career. We do not believe that she was the Miss Brown who acted Isabella in a performance of *Cleone* given by children at the Haymarket Theatre on 10 May 1759, or the Miss Brown who was a popular singer at Sadler's Wells between 1762 and 1767. More likely, Hester made her debut not in London, but in Dublin, where she appeared first as Polly in *The Beggar's Opera* at the Smock Alley Theatre in January 1767. Several years later she made her first appearance in Edinburgh under Ross's management at the New Concert Hall as Thamyris in *The Royal Shepherd* on 26 January 1769 and repeated that role on 30 January and 21 March. At Edinburgh that winter season she also played Harriet in *The Jealous Wife* on 13 March, Ophelia to her future husband's Hamlet on 15 March, Angelica in *The Constant*

Couple on 23 March, and Harriet in *The Guardian* (with Jackson in the title role) and Polly in *The Beggar's Opera* on 25 March. In his *History of the Scottish Stage*, John Jackson claimed to have acted Romeo to his future wife's Juliet about that time.

Sometime shortly before 31 July 1769 Hester married John Jackson in Ireland, for on that date she played Polly at Cork, announced as Mrs Jackson from Edinburgh. Back at Edinburgh on 18 November 1769, the opening night of the new Theatre Royal in Shakespeare Square, advertised as Mrs Jackson, she acted Desdemona to her husband's Iago. During that 1769–70 season she was also seen as Belvidera in *Venice Preserv'd*, Charlot in *The Lame Lover*, Charlotta in *The Apprentice*, Miss Lucy in *The Virgin Unmask'd*, Sally in *Thomas and Sally*, and Ophelia in *Hamlet*.

In May 1771 the Jacksons returned to Dublin to act at the Crow Street Theatre. During the early 1770s they played regularly in Dublin and Edinburgh. Among her numerous known roles in Edinburgh were Andromache in *The Distrest Mother*, Belinda in *The Old Bachelor*, and Lady Charlotte in *The Funeral*. They played at York in May 1774, she having a benefit there on the twentieth, the last night of their engagement. In December of 1774 they were with Younger's company at Liverpool.

With her husband Mrs Jackson was engaged by Foote in 1775 for his summer company at the Haymarket in London. There she made her first appearance on 7 July, as Edwena (and spoke the epilogue) in Jackson's tragedy *Eldred*. She had performed the role in Edinburgh on 19 March 1774 and perhaps previously in Dublin. Performances of *Eldred* on 10 and 14 July were her only others that summer. She was taken on for the following season at Covent Garden, where, on 25 September 1775, she first appeared as Juliet to Lewis's Romeo and danced a minuet in a masquerade scene with D'Egville in Act I. The *Westminster Magazine* for that month, identifying her as the lady who had performed in her husband's tragedy at the Haymarket, found her extremely stiff in her delivery and action, but believed that if she could "divest herself of stage formalities, there would be few better *Juliets* at either house, and she would prove a very decent second-rate Actress."

Harvard Theatre Collection

HESTER JACKSON as Juliet

artist unknown

After performances of Juliet on 2 and 9 October 1775, Mrs Jackson continued in her Covent Garden debut season with appearances as Rosetta in *Love in a Village*, Selima in *Tamerlane*, Queen Catherine in *Henry VIII*, Daphne in *Midas*, Lucia in *Cato*, Indiana in *The Conscious Lovers*, Cynthia in *The Double Dealer*, and Polly in *The Beggar's Opera*. For her benefit on 1 May 1776 she acted Edwena, and her husband (who was not a regular member of the Covent Garden company) acted the title role in his *Eldred*. She went to Bristol with him in the summer of 1776 (and in 1777); she returned to work at Covent Garden for another four seasons without her husband, who was resigned to the provinces. Among her more important roles during that period were the Queen in *Richard III*, Zelmira in *Zenobia*, the Lady in *Comus*, Isabella in *Measure for Measure*, the Queen in *Hamlet*, the title role in *Merope*, the Countess of Somerset in *Sir Thomas Overbury*, Mrs Bromley in *Know Your Own Mind*, Birtha in *Percy*, Cordelia in *King Lear*, Millwood in *George Barnwell*, and Mrs Strickland in *The Suspicious Husband*. On 28 December

1778 she acted Lady Macbeth. Among the few press comments on her was one in the *Morning Chronicle* in February 1777 which noted her beauty, abilities, and spotless private virtues. For her benefit on 7 May 1777, when her address was in the Great Piazza, Covent Garden, she played Leonora in *The Revenge* and received net proceeds of some £125. That night her husband returned to London to play Zanga for her. A year later on 5 May 1778 he played Hareb and she Gerilda in his tragedy *The British Heroine* (first offered at Crow Street by the title of *Gerilda* on 13 January 1777) for her benefit when net receipts were a more modest £83. She acted Lady Randolph in *Douglas* for the first time for her benefit on 30 April 1779, when her address was still in the Great Piazza. She also delivered the prologue, in the character of Britannia, to the London premiere of Dodd's farce *Gallic Gratitude* that night. Several weeks later on 10 May 1779 Mrs Jackson accommodated Fosbrook, the boxkeeper at Drury Lane, by playing Mrs Strickland in *The Suspicious Husband* for his benefit, her only performance of record at that theatre.

When John Jackson began to develop his northern theatrical empire in 1780, Mrs Jackson joined him at Edinburgh, where she acted regularly in the 1780s and early 1790s, at least through May 1794. She was also at Manchester in the summers of 1789 and 1790, and at York in 1791. Perhaps she was the Mrs Jackson who played Queen Eleanor in *King Henry II* at the Haymarket on 26 December 1791, and acted at Cork in May and September 1796, and at Richmond in the summer of 1799.

Genest wrote that Mrs Jackson "was a disagreeable actress." But in his edition of *Gallic Gratitude* published in 1779, James Solas Dodd appended "Critical remarks on Mrs Jackson's performance of Lady Randolph in the tragedy of *Douglas* . . . April 30, 1779," in which he wrote: "She possessed many requisites for the Stage; a pleasing person, an expressive countenance, a voice, at once exceedingly powerful and melodious, a great variety of tones, an action, void of stiffness or extravagance, and a just conception of the sense of her Author."

Hester Jackson died at Edinburgh on 7 January 1806. The "Recorder's Book of the Calton Burying Ground" in the General Registry Office for Scotland notes her burial on 13 January: "Esther Jackson Spouse of John Jackson Esq. ♀ of the Theatre Royal Edinburgh from his house Shakespeare Square died of a decline of Nature buried in his own ground Aged 55." Her husband followed her to a grave in the same ground within a year, dying on 4 December 1806, at the age of 76. Information on their children will be found in his notice.

An engraving by T. Bonner of Mrs Jackson in the character of Britannia in *Gallic Gratitude* was published in 1779. A drawing in India ink by an unknown artist of her as Juliet is in the British Museum; an engraving by an unknown engraver was published by F. Wenman in 1778.

Jackson, John *1769–1845, pugilist.*

The pugilist John Jackson, known as "Gentleman" Jackson, was born at London on 28 September 1769, the son of a builder. Three bouts in the prize ring are recorded for him. In a contest of one hour and seven min-

Harvard Theatre Collection

JOHN JACKSON, pugilist
engraving by Busby, after Marshall

National Trust for Scotland

JOHN JACKSON–DANIEL MENDOZA bout at Hornchurch
artist unknown

utes, before the Prince of Wales, he defeated Fewterel of Birmingham at Smitham Bottom, near Croyden, on 9 June 1788. While fighting George Ingleston, the Brewer, at Ingatestone, Essex, on 12 March 1789, he fell, dislocating his ankle and breaking a small bone in his leg, and thus was defeated. Jackson volunteered to continue the bout chained in one spot, but Ingleston refused. In ten and a half minutes he defeated Mendoza at Hornchurch, Essex, on 15 April 1795.

In the summer of 1790 Jackson gave exhibitions at the Royal Circus in St George's Fields. An advertisement for 24 July 1790 announced: "For the last time, the Art of BOXING will be displayed, by Mr. MENDOZA, Mr. WARD, Mr. JACKSON, and Mr. RYAN."

Jackson reigned as Champion of England from 1795 to 1803, when he retired, and was succeeded by Jem Belcher. At a school he established at No 13, Bond Street, he taught the nobility the art of self-defense. With 18 other fighters, dressed as pages, he formed a guard to the entrance of Westminster Abbey at the coronation of George IV. He also at some time was the publican of the Sun and Punchbowl in Holborn and of the Cock in Sutton.

Possessing a superb body, five feet 11 inches in height and 196 pounds in weight (14 stone), Jackson was also an accomplished jumper, weight-lifter, and short-distance runner. He posed for the vast, nude figure of Satan in Lawrence's extraordinary "Satan Summoning up his Legions," which was exhibited at the Royal Academy in 1797; the face of Satan, however, is that of J. P. Kemble. Byron, one of Jackson's pupils who thought his manners were "infinitely superior to those of the fellows of the college whom I meet at the high table," alluded to him several times in his poems, writing in his "Hints from Horace," "And men unpracticed in exchanging knocks / Must go to Jackson ere they dare to box."

Jackson died at No 4, Lower Grosvenor Street, West London, on 7 October 1845 at the age of 76. His grave at the West London and Westminster Cemetery in Brompton was marked by a large monument erected by subscription, which bore the inscription:

'Stay, Traveller,' the Roman record said,
To mark the classic dust beneath it laid;
'Stay, Traveller,' this brief memorial cries,
And read the moral with attentive eyes:
Hast thou a lion's heart, a giant's strength,
Exult not, for these gifts must yeld at length:
Do health and symmetry adorn thy frame,
The mouldering bones below possessed the same.
Does love, does friendship, every step attend,
This man ne'er made a foe, nor lost a friend;
But death full soon dissolves all human ties,
And, his last combat o'er, here Jackson lies.

Additional information on Jackson may be found in Pierce Egan's *Boxiana* (1812).

Portraits of the pugilist include:

1. By B. Marshall. An engraving by C. Turner was published by the engraver, 1810; another engraving by T. L. Busby was published by G. Smeeton, 1813.

2. By Sharples. At Rossie Priory.

3. By unknown artist. "Jackson-Mendoza Fight." Painting at Brodick Castle.

4. By unknown artist. Painting owned by Sir Henry Smythe in 1880, in which year it was reproduced in Miles's *Pugilistica*.

5. By unknown artist. Watercolor, standing, stick in right hand. In an extra-illustrated set of Genest, Widener Library, Harvard University.

6. Engraved portrait by Perry Roberts. At the Huntington Art Gallery and Library.

7. Engraved portrait by C. Turner. Published by the engraver, 1821.

8. By unknown engraver. Of Jackson sparring. Published by W. Cole.

9. By Thomas Lawrence. A study of Jackson's arm. In the sale of the property of Matthew Hutchinson at Christie's, 22 February 1861 (lot 67). Probably drawn in connection with Lawrence's preparation for painting "Satan Summoning up his Legions."

10. By Thomas Lawrence. The nude figure of Satan in "Satan Summoning up his Legions." The face, however, is that of John Philip Kemble. This vast painting is at the Royal Academy of Arts.

Jackson, Mrs John, Mary. *See* THURMOND, MARY.

Jackson, Paul *1742–1828, violinist, flutist, horn player.*

Paul Jackson was born in 1742, probably at Oxford, and very likely the son of Joseph Jackson, leader of the Oxford Music Room Concerts from 1748 until his death in the autumn of 1759. The London violinist William Jackson (fl. 1741–1763), who frequently went to assist Joseph with the Oxford concerts, may have been his kin.

Most of Paul Jackson's career was spent as a flutist and violinist in the band of the Oxford Music Room, where, on 6 April 1775, Jackson enjoyed a benefit, in an unusual departure from the rule which provided benefits only for the leading violinist and cellist. Jackson participated in the Handelian concerts at Westminster Abbey, according to Doane's *Musical Directory* of 1794. In *The Oldest Music Room in Europe* Mee calls him an "excellent performer on the horn and flute."

A notation in the Minute Books of the Royal Society of Musicians on 7 July 1799 indicates that Jackson was then a member. On 4 April 1824, then aged 83, he was granted five guineas for relief by the Governors of the Society. He died in June or early July 1828, at the age of 86. On 6 July 1828 his widow was granted 30 guineas per year by the Society and on the following 3 August £12 was granted for the expenses of her husband's funeral. At the latter meeting the Governors decided to give her widow's allowance to her friend Mr Marshall in trust to appropriate for Mrs Jackson's sole use and comfort, "she being so old." She died on 24 November of the same year, aged 88; on 7 December the sum of £8 was granted for her funeral expenses. Their son, Charles Jackson, was also a flutist and music seller in Oxford; he died on 22 April 1832, aged 55.

Jackson, Thomas *1741–1798, actor, dancer, singer.*

Thomas Jackson was born on 21 December 1741. According to *The Dramatist; or, Memoirs of the Stage* (1809), written in a somewhat confusing chronology by his daughter Ann Catherine Holbrook, Jackson was encouraged to a stage career by George Alexander Stevens, the lecturer, and Samuel Foote, the Haymarket Theatre manager. Impressed when he heard Jackson rehearse the part of Scrub in *The Beaux' Stratagem* in a London spouting club, Stevens took him on tour to Cambridge and Lynn. Probably Thomas was the Mr Jackson who as a member of Foote's company acted an unspecified role in the premiere of the manager's comedy *The Mayor of Garratt* at the Haymarket on 20 June 1763 and in a number of subsequent performances of the piece that summer. Jackson also played a role in *The Diversions of the Morning* several times, a King of Brentford in *The Rehearsal* on 1 and 11 August 1763, Tallyhoe in *The Englishman Return'd from Paris* on 5 and 22 August, and Charino in *Love Makes a Man* on 7 September.

The ensuing five years Jackson probably passed as an obscure stroller. (It seems unlikely that he was the Jackson who was in Foote's company in the summer of 1768; also in Foote's company that summer was a Mrs Jackson and a Miss Jackson. According to the testimony of Thomas Jackson's daughter, her mother was not an actress, and Ann Catherine herself was not born until 1780. It is possible, of course, that Thomas had two wives, the first an actress and mother of his first daughter, and a second, the mother of Ann Catherine.

At Edinburgh in 1769 and 1770, Thomas Jackson became "a favourite with all the first people," according to his daughter. In the same company at the Theatre Royal in Shakespeare Square was John Jackson (1730–1806), later the Edinburgh manager, with whom Thomas has often been confused. Their careers during the 1770s and 1780s are sometimes difficult to distinguish, inasmuch as both went to play subsequently at Bath and Dublin, sometimes in the same years. Thomas's line, however, was comedy and farce, while John's essentially was more serious. After Edinburgh, Thomas went to Bath and then to Dublin, where he played at Smock Alley from 1772 to 1776. (A Master Jackson performed at Smock Alley in the summer of 1774 and at Crow Street in the summer of 1775, but we find no evidence to relate him to Thomas.) In 1775 he played at Cork several times. About that time he married Ann Cumming (b. 1753), a native of Cork. She has sometimes been confused with Hester Jackson, the wife of John Jackson.

Thomas Jackson returned to the Haymarket in the summer of 1776 to play Transfer in *The Minor*, Tim in *The Knights*, Mungo in *The Padlock*, Caleb in *Taste*, Jackides in *The Taylors*, Dametas and Pan in *Midas*, Crispin in *The Mayor of Garratt*, Foigard in *The Stratagem*, and roles in *The Nabob* and *The Cozeners*. So pleased with his performances was Foote, according to Mrs Holbrook's memoir, that the manager decided to write characters especially for Jackson, as he had done for Weston. But Foote sold his theatre to Colman, and in the summer of 1776 Jackson acted for the new manager such roles as Tony Lumpkin in *She Stoops to Conquer*, Francisco in *The Chances*, Argus in *The Spanish Barber* and Justice Woodcock in *Love in a Village*. He remained at the Haymarket for two more summers. One of his best roles was Orator Mum in O'Keeffe's *The Son-in-Law*, which was first performed at the Haymarket on 14 August 1779.

Dissatisfied with what he considered Colman's neglect, Jackson left the Haymarket in September 1779 to join the Bath Theatre under the management of Palmer, who needed a replacement for Edwin, now engaged at Covent Garden. Jackson's defection, claimed his daughter, enraged Colman, who vowed "never to forgive him." He remained at Bath for about eight years, and also appeared regularly at Bristol. In the summer of 1788, when his Bath colleague John Brunton took the management of the Theatre Royal at Norwich, one of the most important provincial theatres in England, Jackson went with him. At Norwich and the playhouses of the surrounding circuit in East Anglia—Colchester, Ipswich, King's Lynn, Cambridge, Yarmouth, Barnwell, Beccles, Bury—Jackson played for ten years, until his death in 1798.

The *Norwich Mercury* of his era contains notices of his variety as a performer. On 9 May 1789 he danced with Mrs Chesnut (wife of the company hairdresser). On 16 May 1791 he and his daughter delivered a "Dialogue." Jackson recited "Scrub's Description of Norwich" on 12 May 1792 and probably regularly thereafter. On 8 May 1793 he sang "Tippy Bob." He and Blanchard delivered a comic dialogue on 22 April 1795, and on 27 May 1797 Jackson was in a "Garland Dance."

Various sources have reported the place and date of his death and his place of burial incorrectly. The *Mirror of the Stage* (1823), for example, gave his date of death as 17 March 1798 and quoted an epitaph supposedly on his tombstone at Gillingham, Norfolk. Jackson's daughter recalled "the handful of dust thrown on his coffin" but failed to mention where; she claimed he had been born in 1742 and had died on 22 March 1798. She also quoted the epitaph, "lately written on my father, that fell into my hands by accident," but said nothing about its having been put on his tombstone. The confusion is clarified by an entry in the burial register of St Peter Mancroft in Norwich for 1798: "28th March, Thomas Jackson, widower, died 24th March, aged 57." An "epitaph" given in the *Era Almanack* of 1870, with an incorrect date of death, would seem too long for even a tombstone of the larger variety:

Sacred to the memory of Thomas Jackson, Comedian, who was *engaged* December 21, 1741, *to play a comic cast of characters* in this *great Theatre*, the World, for many of which he was *prompted* by nature to excel. The *season* being ended, his *benefit* over, the *charges* all paid, and his *account* closed, he made his *exit* in the *Tragedy* of 'Death,' on the 17th of March, 1798, in full assurance of being *called* once more to *rehearsal*; when he hopes to find his *forfeits* all cleared, his *cast of parts* bettered, and his *situation* made agreeable by Him who paid the great *stock-debt* for the love he bore to *performers* in general.

In his obituary in the *Norwich Mercury* of 31 March 1798 it was stated of Jackson: "In private life his manners were truly inoffensive; in his public character he possessed extensive professional merit. By his death the Norwich stage has lost an able actor, and his daughter an indulgent parent."

Thomas Jackson's wife Ann had died at Norwich on 22 March 1794 at the age of 41 and had been buried at St Peter Mancroft on 26 March, according to the burial register there. At his benefit on 14 May 1794, Jackson

pleaded for the public's generous support, as he had had great expenses resulting from his wife's long illness and funeral. Their daughter Ann Catherine, born in 1780, appeared as a young child on the Bristol stage as early as June 1783, when she was billed as "only 4 years old." She performed at Bristol occasionally from that date until 1788. Also performing children's roles at Bristol in 1783–84 was a Master Jackson, no doubt Thomas's son, although in her memoirs Ann Catherine never mentioned a brother. Also, in 1784 a Mrs Jackson acted occasional breeches parts at Bristol, but she was not Thomas's wife, if there was truth in Ann Catherine's assertion that her mother was not a performer. Ann Catherine married the Norwich actor William Holbrook at the Battle Parish Church on 26 November 1798. She claimed to have acted Juliet, Roxana, and Alicia at Norwich before she was 18. After her father's death she acted for a while at Lewes in Sussex. With her husband she performed at Taunton, Lancaster, Daventry, Cheltenham, and Manchester. She died in London in January 1837. Mrs Holbrook's writings included the aforementioned *The Dramatist; or, Memoirs of the Stage* published at Birmingham, 1809; *Memoirs of an Actress*, Manchester, 1807; *Tales Serious and Instructive*, Uttoxeter, 1821; *Constantine Castroit, an Historical Tale*, Rugeley, 1829; and *Realities and Reflections. A Series of Original Tales*, 1834.

Jackson, Thomas *c. 1700–1781, organist, composer.*

On 17 February 1721 Thomas Jackson was sworn a musician in ordinary in the Chapel Royal (in place of Thomas Roberts, deceased), so he would have been born about 1700 and not about 1715 as stated in *British Musical Biography* and *Grove's Dictionary*. Jackson's annual stipend in royal service between 1735 and 1759 was £40. He was one of the original subscribers to the Royal Society of Musicians upon its establishment in 1739.

On 26 May 1764 Thomas Jackson, "now of Uckfield in the County of Sussex, Gent; and one of His Majesty's Musicians in Ordinary," appointed Henry Ann Monchet of the Custom House his "true friend & lawful attorney." Compositions by Jackson include the songs *The Happy Man* (1750?), *On Greenwich Park*

Royal College of Music

THOMAS JACKSON

artist unknown

(1740?), *A Favorite Lesson for the Harpsichord* (1778?), and *Twelve Psalm Tunes and Eighteen Double and Single Chants with a new Species of Chant to the Benedicte . . . for four Voices* (1780?). One of his psalm-tunes was called "Jackson's."

He was organist of St Mary Magdalen and master of the song school at Newark-on-Trent, where he died on 11 November 1781. A portrait of Thomas Jackson painted by an unknown artist is at the Royal College of Music.

Jackson, William *d. 1664, singer.*

William Jackson entered Christ Church, Oxford, on 1 April 1656 as a servitor, received his B.A. on 1 November 1659 and his M.A. on 15 July 1662. He was sworn a Gentleman of the Chapel Royal on 14 November 1662, taking the following oath:

I, William Jackson, Master of Arts, being to be admitted into a Priest's place in his Maties Chappell Royall, doe faithfully promise by the grace of God to doe my best endeavour to make my selfe fitt by all meanes for skill with pious, discreet, and sober demeanour for the sayd place as shall be approved of by the Deane and Subdeane of the sayd Chappell. And in case I shall not so approve myself in this yeare of probation, I shall at the end of it yield up and resigne my sayd place into the hands of the Deane or Subdeane. . . .

Jackson was referred to only a few times in the Lord Chamberlain's accounts. He died on 27 February 1664 and was buried two days later in the West Cloister of Westminster Abbey.

Jackson, William ₁*fl.* 1726–1739₁, *musician, composer, music master.*

The music master William Jackson was the author of *A Preliminary Discourse to a Scheme, demonstrating and shewing the Perfection and Harmony of Sounds* which was published in octavo and folio editions in 1726. We believe he was the William Jackson senior who was a charter member of the Royal Society of Musicians upon its establishment in 1739 and the father perhaps of William Jackson, the Vauxhall musician (d. 1782?).

Jackson, William *d. 1782?, violinist, organist.*

A musician named William Jackson "junior" was a charter member of the Royal Society of Musicians when it was established in 1739. He was probably the son of William Jackson "senior" (fl. 1726–1739), who also was listed as a charter member.

It was probably the younger William Jackson who played first violin in a concert given for his benefit at the Castle Tavern on 13 March 1741. That evening a concerto and solo were played by "Jackson's Brother, a lad eleven years of age."

Our subject was probably the William Jackson who played for performances of the *Messiah* at the Foundling Hospital in May 1754 and April 1758, when he was paid 10s. in each instance. He played for Charles Barbandt's new oratorio *David and Jonathan* at the Haymarket Theatre on 28 January 1761 (repeated 19 and 26 February). According to Mee's *Oldest Music Room in Europe*, Jackson often assisted Joseph Jackson (d. 1759), possibly a relative, with the Oxford Music Room concerts from 1748 to 1759. In 1763 William Jackson, violinist, was listed in *Mortimer's London Directory* as living in Windmill Street.

A press clipping in the Minet Public Library—hand-dated "1782"—announced the sale of "The genuine household furniture, linen, china, a numerous collection of music, and many valuable instruments of Mr. WILLIAM JACKSON, Musician, deceased who, for 40 years past, was the principal performer at Vauxhall and 50 . . . years, organist to the Parish of St. Allhallows."

Jackson, William ₁*fl.* 1784–1815₁, *violinist, horn player.*

The Mr Jackson who was one of the second violins in the Handel Memorial Concerts at Westminster Abbey and the Pantheon in May and June 1784 was probably the William Jackson, musician, of Vine Street, Lambeth Marsh, who was granted a patent (No 1449) on 20 August 1784 for a new musical instrument to be called "The British Lyre." In 1794 William Jackson, violinist and horn player of No 61, Poland Street was listed in Doane's *Musical Directory* as a member of the New Musical Fund, a player at the Royal Circus and with the band of the second regiment of guards.

No doubt he was the violinist named Jackson who played in the Covent Garden band for the oratorios between 1797 and 1800. He also played at the Haymarket Theatre on 15 January 1798 in a performance of the *Messiah* presented for the benefit of the Choral Fund. A Mr Jackson was a member of the Drury Lane band in 1807–8 at a salary of £2 per week. In 1815 William Jackson served on the Committee of the New Musical Fund, to which he had subscribed as early as 1794.

Jacob, Signor ₁*fl.* 1777₁, *acrobat.*

The bill for Astley's Amphitheatre on 23 September 1777 included an exhibition of

"Egyptian Pyramids" by a group including a Signor Jacob.

Jacob, Benjamin *1778–1829, instrumentalist, singer, conductor.*

In an autobiographical letter replying to Sainsbury's inquiries for his musical dictionary, Benjamin Jacob stated that he was born on 15 March 1778, and the parish registers of St Giles in the Fields show that he was christened there on 26 April. Grove, therefore, is in error in giving Jacob's birthdate as 15 May. Benjamin's parents were Benjamin and Mary Jacob. His father was an amateur musician and taught his son to play the violin. At the age of seven our subject began receiving singing lessons from Robert Willoughby and became a chorister at Portland Chapel. He learned the harpsichord and studied under the organists William Shrubsole and Matthew Cooke at Spa Fields Chapel and St George, Bloomsbury, respectively. When he was only 10 years old, Benjamin was appointed organist of Salem Chapel, Soho, and at 11 he became organist of Carlisle Chapel, Kennington Lane. From 1790 to 1794 he was organist at Bentinck Chapel, Lisson Green, after which he became organist at Surrey Chapel, where he played until 1824.

Jacob sang as a "Treble" boy at the Handel concerts at Westminster Abbey in 1790 and 1791. When Doane's *Musical Directory* was published in 1794, it listed Benjamin "Jacobs" as also a participant in the oratorio performances at Drury Lane and a resident at No 13, Queen Street, Seven Dials. Jacob began studying harmony under Arnold in 1796. On 24 January 1799 he played the organ at a performance of the *Messiah* at the Haymarket Theatre—"A New Organ, built by Lincoln, will be opened on this occasion," the bill stated. Arnold proposed Jacob for membership in the Royal Society of Musicians on 4 August 1799. At that time Jacob was living at No 24, Great James Street, Bedford Row, and was described as a single man with many students. He was unanimously elected on 3 November.

In the spring of 1800 Jacob conducted a series of oratorios under the direction of Barthélemon (not Bartleman, as stated in Grove), in Cross Street, Hatton Garden. That year he married, he said, Miss Tay of King's Norton, Warwickshire, by whom he had one son and four daughters. For several years Jacob played the organ at the Choral Fund's annual concert, with Arnold conducting at the piano and Barthélemon leading the band. In 1803 he gave an organ concert at Surrey Chapel, and the following year he and Samuel Wesley "united in an Organ Performance playing alternately the Fugues of Sebastian Bach, and Handel, with many Overtures, Airs, and Choruses. About 3000 persons of the highest respectability," Jacob wrote, " . . . continued to sit with the greatest attention, through a four hour's performance, on the Organ only." In 1811, 1812, and 1814 those performances were repeated with Dr William Crotch and Jacob sharing the organ.

Jacob was called upon to "open" a number of new organs. In addition to the instrument at the Haymarket in 1799 he opened the organs at St Swithin's in 1809; Camden Chapel, Camberwell, in 1810; and Christ Church, Birmingham, in 1815. He also served numerous times as an "umpire" in the selection of organists for churches in and around London.

In 1818 at the Lenten oratorios at Covent Garden Theatre Jacob conducted at the organ and pianoforte and, he said, performed a concerto on the organ nearly every night of the oratorio season. He was elected an Associate of the Philharmonic Society in October 1818 and a member of the Court of Assistants of the Royal Society of Musicians in December 1823. He regularly presented concerts at Surrey Chapel for the benefit of the Alms Houses. Jacob's involvement in performances prevented him from composing much music, but he wrote a few glees and psalm tunes and a collection called *National Psalmody*, which was published in 1817. When he wrote to Sainsbury in 1824 Jacob was living at Urn House, Westminster Road, near the Asylum. At that time he reported that of his five children one, his son, had died in 1817 at the age of 16. The boy had shown promise as a musician. In 1824 Jacob left his post at Surrey Chapel to take a similar position at the new church of St John, Waterloo Road.

Grove reports that Benjamin Jacob died of consumption in London on 24 August 1829 and was buried in Bunhill Fields. We have found his will, which was written on 18 July 1829. Jacob left his entire estate to his wife Mary (presumably the former Miss Tay). Witnessing his will were two of Jacob's daughters,

Royal College of Music

BENJAMIN JACOB

artist unknown

Mary Lucretia and Sarah Jane, of "Malboro" Cottage, Brompton. No mention was made of Jacob's two other daughters. The will was proved on 3 November 1829.

In 1875 Eliza Wesley published the *Letters of Samuel Wesley to Mrs. Jacobs relating to the* *works of John Sebastian Bach* (the spelling Jacobs is not incorrect; Benjamin seems to have added the s in the nineteenth century). In *The Musical Times* in April 1966 Walter Emery discussed the letters, showing that the printed texts are corrupt.

A portrait of Benjamin Jacob by an unknown artist, dating about 1820, is at the Royal College of Music in London.

Jacoba, Mrs [fl. 1725], dancer, actress.

Mrs Jacoba (or Jacobs), "The new Colombine" in the French troupe at the Haymarket Theatre in the spring of 1725, was advertised as "An actress lately arrived from France [who] will perform the Part of Colombine in the Woman Captive, and in the Amoureuses Follies the Part of Agate" on 19 April. The plays referred to were Montfleury's La Fille Capitaine and Regnard's Les Folies Amoreuses. At her benefit on 7 May, when Les Deux Arlequins and The Doctor Against His Will were performed, Mrs Jacoba danced with Roger.

Jacobs. See also JACOB.

Jacobs, Mr [fl. 1768–1783], actor, singer.

Mr Jacobs was a member of Samuel Foote's company at the Haymarket Theatre in the summer of 1768, his first mention in the bills being on 23 June, when he played Roger in The Mayor of Garratt. During the remainder of the summer he was seen as Tally in The Minor, Nimming Ned in The Beggar's Opera, a Servant in Hob in the Well, and an unnamed character in The Orators. Jacobs also appeared at the Haymarket during the 1768–69 season: on 7 October 1768 as a Drawer in The Busy Body and on 15 May 1769 in The Devil upon Two Sticks. He joined Foote once more in the summer of 1769 to add such parts as Dick in The Minor, Bernardo and Francisco in Hamlet, the Printer's Devil in The Author, and Ratcliff in Richard III.

He became a member of the Drury Lane company in 1769–70 and acted with them in the winters through 1773–74; during the summers, through 1775 except for 1771, he acted at the Haymarket. His first advertised role at Drury Lane seems to have been Supple in The Double Gallant on 16 January 1770. After that he appeared in such characters as Abram and a Welshman in Harlequin's Invasion, the Bookseller in The Committee, Simple in The Merry Wives of Windsor, List in The Miser, Philotus in Timon of Athens, the Old Miser in The Witches, Justice Statute in The What D'Ye Call It, the Shopkeeper in The Chances, Dapper in The Citizen, a Sailor in The Fair Quaker of Deal, Sideboard in The Way to Keep Him, Harry in The Male Coquette, and Tom Epping in The Note of Hand. He also filled numerous unnamed parts in afterpieces and pantomimes.

In some years (usually toward the end of the winter season) Jacobs played both at Drury Lane and at the Haymarket, occasionally at both houses on the same evening. At the Haymarket over the years he added such parts as Lucianus in Hamlet, John and Robin in The Patron, Barnaby in The Old Bachelor, the Painter's Boy in Taste, Simon in The Apprentice, Davy in The Mock Doctor, the Cook in The Lying Valet, Ninny in Cupid's Revenge, Twig in The Cooper, Sneer in A Trip to Portsmouth, Frisseau in The Pantheonites, Launcelot in The Merchant of Venice, the Coachman and Dr Catgut in The Commissary, and Transfer in The Minor. His last appearance in London before departing, perhaps for the provinces, was on 30 October 1775, when he played Abel Drugger in The Tobacconist at a special performance for his benefit ("for Brother JACOBS, by particular desire of the Masons").

During those years in London Jacobs occasionally had his benefit tickets accepted, and on 24 May 1773 at Drury Lane he shared a benefit with two others; the three divided £168 19s. 6d. in profits. In 1774 he was granted a license for plays and entertainments at the Haymarket for 21 September, according to the Lord Chamberlain's accounts (he played Simone in The Apprentice on that date, at the end of Foote's summer season).

On 17 September 1783, at the Haymarket, Cheapside was performed by actors, some of whom were from the provinces. In the cast was Jacobs, from the Theatre Royal, Edinburgh. Of his provincial career we know nothing further.

Jacobs, Mr d. 1793, carpenter.

The Drury Lane accounts show a payment of £25 in December 1793 to a Mrs Jacobs, the sum being the arrears of her deceased husband's salary. He was identified as a carpenter. A similar entry, dated 2 October 1794, concerned a payment of £10 and indicated that Mr Jacobs had died in December 1793. It seems likely that the man in question was a son of the Drury Lane carpenter Richard Jacobs, who was active through 1802. (The 1794 reference to a payment to the deceased carpenter's widow, in a Folger manuscript, cites the woman as Mrs Jacobson, but that spelling would seem to have been an error for Jacobs.)

Jacobs, Mrs [*fl.* 1790], *actress.*

At Bartholomew Fair in 1790 a Mrs Jacobs played Donna Whiskerendoes in *The Spaniard Well Drub'd* at the old Yates and Shuter booth.

Jacobs, Miss [*fl.* 1781?–1792], *dancer, actress?*

The Miss Jacobs who danced in London in the early 1790s may have been the Miss Jacobs who took children's parts at Bristol in 1781–82. In the Rowbotham bills at the Folger Shakespeare Library is one dated 14 May 1782 which indicates that a Miss Jacobs performed at the manager Keasberry's benefit with the Bath-Bristol troupe. From February to July 1791 Miss Jacobs was a "danseuse et coryphée" with the opera company at the Pantheon in London. On 17 February she was the Muse de l'Astronomie in the pantomime ballet *Amphion et Thalie*, and on 22 March she danced a Nymph in *Telemachus in the Island of Calypso*.

During the 1791–92 season Miss Jacobs danced with the Drury Lane troupe at the King's Theatre, appearing in *Don Juan* and the afterpiece *The American Heroine*, and as a Grace in *Neptune's Prophecy* (a dance which concluded *Dido Queen of Carthage*). For her chores that season the company paid her £5 weekly. In June and July of 1792 at the Haymarket she danced in an allemande and in the afterpiece *The Enchanted Wood*.

Jacobs, C. [*fl.* 1798], *house servant?*

On 1 December 1798 the Drury Lane accounts show that C. Jacobs was added to the paylist at 3*s.* 4*d.* per day. That lowly salary suggests that Jacobs was probably a house servant.

Jacobs, Miss E. [*fl.* 1798–1804?], *singer, actress.*

At a salary of £1 10*s.* weekly Miss E. Jacobs sang in the chorus at Drury Lane in 1798–99 and 1799–1800. She was a Peasant in *The Captive of Spilburg* on 14 November 1798, after which she sang in *The Surrender of Calais, Aurelio and Miranda, Pizarro, Blue-Beard, Feudal*

Times, Lodoiska, and *De Montfort.* On 6 June 1800 the Page in *The Siege of Belgrade* was performed by "A Young Lady" making her first appearance on any stage in a speaking role; the manuscript list in the Kemble playbills identified the Lady as Miss E. Jacobs, previously a chorus singer.

It is probable that Miss Jacobs continued swelling the choruses at Drury Lane during 1800–1801; near the end of the season she was again given a chance to act. On 6 May 1801 she played the Page again, advertised as making her first appearance of the season (as an actress) and her second appearance on any stage (again, as an actress). Then during the rest of May and early June she tried Sally Shamrock in *The Shipwreck*, Marietta in *The Pirates*, and Nina in *The Prisoner*. The last work was presented on 3 June, and the bill noted that Miss Jacobs was a pupil of Mrs Crouch. Miss E. Jacobs was very likely the Miss Jacobs who sang in the operas at the King's Theatre in 1802, 1803, and 1804. One would suppose that she was the daughter of the Drury Lane carpenter Richard Jacobs.

Jacobs, Miss R. [*fl.* 1799–1801?], *singer?*

Miss R. Jacobs sang in the chorus of *Feudal Times* at Drury Lane from 19 January to 5 March 1799. Also in the chorus was Miss E. Jacobs, who was probably her sister; they were, we would guess, daughters of the Drury Lane carpenter Richard Jacobs. On 4 March 1800 a Miss Jacobs was cited in the Drury Lane accounts as receiving 13*s.* 4*d.* weekly; a second list has her down for 16*s.* 8*d.* Neither salary matches that of Miss E. Jacobs, so perhaps these references are to Miss R. Jacobs. In September 1800 this woman was called Kelly's pupil, which fact suggests that she was a singer. The last mention of her in the accounts is a note saying that "Miss Jacobs engagement [for the 1801–2 season, presumably] took place on the 28th of November, 1801."

Jacobs, Richard [*fl.* 1787–1802], *carpenter, machinist.*

Richard Jacobs served Drury Lane as master carpenter from as early as the 1787–88 season through at least 1801–2. He was occasionally cited in the playbills as having collaborated with Cabanel, Johnston, and others on the machinery and decorations for such spectacles as *Harlequin Captive*, *Alexander the Great*, *Jack of Newbury*, and *Robinson Crusoe*. His duties were evidently those of the modern technical director. He was responsible for the construction of the scenery and machinery (sometimes he was listed as a machinist), the fabrication or procurement of such stage properties as pistols, the payment of the salaries of the scenemen whom he probably supervised, and the care of horses used in entertainments.

The account books mentioned Jacobs frequently through the years from 23 June 1787 ("Mr. Jacobs to compleat his Sal^ry 12/–/–") through 1801–2, when his weekly salary was noted as £3. The accounts show that his weekly income was constant at £3, though at the ends of some seasons—in May 1792, for instance—he was dropped from the paylist, which might mean that during some summers he worked elsewhere. In April 1799 Mr and Mrs Jacobs were taken off the paylist; she was a member of the Drury Lane singing chorus, and the couple appear to have had a son, who served Drury Lane as a carpenter, and two daughters, both of whom sang and one of whom also acted. It is probable that the Jacobs who worked at Drury Lane for 12*s*. weekly as a sweeper in 1812–13 and as a porter the following season was also related to Richard Jacobs.

Jacobs, Mrs Richard ₍*fl.* 1798–1799₎, *singer*

Mrs Richard Jacobs, the wife of the Drury Lane master carpenter, sang in the chorus at that theatre, according to the accounts, in 1798–99 at a salary of 5*s*. daily. She was not named in any of the bills, though the Misses E. and R. Jacobs, probably her daughters, were.

Jacobs, T. ₍*fl.* 1800–1811₎, *bassoonist*.

T. Jacobs was a bassoonist who played for the Royal Society of Musicians in the May concerts at St Paul's in 1800, 1802 through 1804, 1806, and 1811.

Jacobson. *See* JACOBS.

Jacolet, Mons ₍*fl.* 1788₎, *dancer*.

Monsieur Jacolet danced in Noverre's ballet *L'Amour et Psiché* at the King's Theatre on 29 January 1788 and in the same choreographer's new tragic ballet *Euthyme et Eucharis* beginning on 13 March.

Jacondus, Signor ₍*fl.* 1777₎, *acrobat*.

At Astley's Amphitheatre on 23 September 1777 an exhibition of "Egyptian Pyramids" was performed by a group of acrobats that included Signor Jacondus.

Jacques, Mr ₍*fl.* 1799₎, *singer, actor*.

Mr Jacques performed an unspecified role in *The Oracle at Delphi*, a musical piece composed by Lonsdale, at Sadler's Wells on 17 April 1799.

Jaeder, Mr ₍*fl.* 1786₎, *performer?*

On 7 October 1786 Mr Jaeder's name was added to the Drury Lane paylist at 10*s*. daily, a salary that suggests he may have been a performer.

Jagger, Mr ₍*fl.* 1761–1762₎, *trumpeter*.

The Covent Garden accounts show that for performances of *The Coronation*, which began on 13 November 1761 and continued to the last day of the season, 24 May 1762, a Mr Jagger was paid 5*s*. daily as one of the six trumpeters. He was not named in the bills, nor do the accounts indicate whether or not he performed the following season when the spectacle was revived.

Jagger, William ₍*fl.* 1760–1782₎, *singer*.

William Jagger was a popular singer at Vauxhall Gardens from as early as 1760, when his name began to appear in printed versions of songs sung there. Every song in the British Library's collection that has Jagger's name cited as the performer is a work by Thomas Augustine Arne. Among the Arne pieces Jagger sang at Vauxhall were *Long time I serv'd young Rosalind*, *Why Caelia this constant upbraiding?*, and *In infancy our hopes and fears* from *Artaxerxes*.

Jagger sang at the Smock Alley playhouse in Dublin in 1764–65 and was at the Crow Street Theatre there in 1778–79. The *Kentish Gazette* on 25 August 1781 announced Jagger's

Canterbury debut for the twenty-seventh and noted that he was from Dublin. In the same periodical on 7 September 1782 was an announcement of Jagger's benefit, with his full name given.

James, Mr ₁*fl. 1667–1672?*₁, *actor.*

A Mr James is mentioned in two related promptbooks from the Restoration period, *The Wise Woman of Hogsdon*, in which he is down for the role of Sir Boniface, and *The Comedy of Errors*, in which he is listed as Aegeon. The promptbooks may relate to performances at the Nursery in London about 1672. Indeed, James may well have been active in both places, and he may have been related to the King's Company's actress Elizabeth James and the boxkeeper James of 1677.

James, Mr ₁*fl. 1677*₁, *boxkeeper.*

According to *The Theatrical Inquisitor and Monthly Mirror* of July 1816 (a source so late that it should be approached with caution), one James was a boxkeeper at the Bridges Street Theatre in December 1677. The periodical published a document showing receipts for *All for Love* on Wednesday 12 December and *The Rival Queens* on Wednesday 26 December. On the former date "James's boxes" brought in £2; on the latter he made £2 4*s*. There is a possibility that James was not the boxkeeper's surname but his Christian name.

James, Mr ₁*fl. 1723–1724*₁, *dancer.*

Mr James danced at his shared benefit with two other dancers at the Haymarket Theatre on 13 February 1723. He continued appearing at the Haymarket through 30 December 1723, but the bills were often uninformative, and his citations were few. At his last appearance he danced a *French Peasant*. Lincoln's Inn Fields hired James in the summer of 1724. The accounts show that he appeared 18 times between 23 June and 20 August, though the bills seldom mentioned him. He danced at the Bullock-Booth-Spiller booth at Southwark Fair on 24 September, but after that date his name disappeared from London bills.

James, Mr ₁*fl. 1741*₁, *harpsichordist.*

A Mr James played a concerto on the harpsichord at a Masons' night benefit for brothers Montgomery and Excell on 29 April 1741 at Goodman's Fields playhouse. During the course of the evening Excell sang "Advice to the Sons of Bacchus," for which he had written the lyrics and James had composed the music.

James, Mr ₁*fl. 1781–1791*₁, *actor.*

Mr James played a principal role (not specified) in *The Sharper's Last Shift* at the Haymarket Theatre on 22 January 1781, Cripple in *Love and a Bottle* on 26 March, a Servant in *The Beaux' Duel* on 21 January 1782, and an unnamed character in *The Taylors* on the following 25 November. He was probably the Mr James who was at the Theatre Royal, Edinburgh, from January through May 1783 acting Antonio in *Much Ado about Nothing*, Buillard in *The Camp*, Canton in *The Clandestine Marriage*, Degagee in *The Dead Alive*, Dr Caius in *The Merry Wives of Windsor*, the French Lover in *Robinson Crusoe*, Fulmer in *The West Indian*, La Varole in *A Trip to Scarborough*, Monsieur in *Love Makes a Man*, Monsieur le Médicin in *The Anatomist*, the Old Woman in *Rule a Wife and Have a Wife*, and Sir Peter Pride in *Barnaby Brittle*. A Mr James was in Pero's troupe at Derby in 1788–89 and 1789–90. Hare in *The Georgian Theatre in Wessex* states that James was hailed as from Exeter when he performed at Salisbury in 1790–91.

James, Mrs ₁*fl. 1733*₁, *actress.*

A Mrs James made her first appearance "on any stage" as the Dumb Lady in *The Mock Doctor* at the Haymarket Theatre on 14 February 1733.

James, Miss ₁*fl. 1740–1741*₁, *performer?*

Miss James was on the Covent Garden paylist at 5*s*. per day in 1740–41. She may have been a performer.

James, Elizabeth ₁*fl. 1669–1703?*₁, *actress, singer.*

Though Elizabeth James may have been a member of the King's Company at the Bridges Street Theatre in the early or mid-1660s, her first known role was Damilcar, a singing part in *Tyrannick Love*, on 24 June 1669. The scanty records of the Restoration period show her other roles to have been Isabella in both parts of *The Conquest of Granada*, Isabel in *Love in a Wood*, and Alleria in *Generous Enemies* in 1670–71; Amalthea in *Marriage à la Mode* in 1671–72; Sophronia in *The Assignation* and Julia in *Amboyna* in 1672–73; Arabella in *The Amorous Old Woman* in 1673–74; Alithea in *The Country Wife*, Bianca in *Othello*, and Aurania in *Love in the Dark* in 1674–75; and Julia in *Gloriana* 1675–76. It is perhaps significant that in the early part of her career she appeared in a number of Dryden's works.

Elizabeth was occasionally mentioned in the Lord Chamberlain's accounts, as on 7 August 1671 when a Mrs Corney was given leave to sue her, perhaps for a debt.

Very little is known of Elizabeth James's personal life. Ward in his *Life of Dryden* states, without providing his source, that Mrs James probably gave birth to a child about May 1670. It has been guessed that the actor James whose name appeared in the promptbooks for *The Wise Woman of Hogsdon* and *The Comedy of Errors* may have been related to Elizabeth, as, indeed, he may have been, but in what way we cannot tell. J. H. Wilson in *All the King's Ladies* helpfully suggests that some character descriptions in plays might reveal something of the personality and person of Mrs James; Alleria in *Generous Enemies*, for example, is called "Young, Fair, witty, modest, tall, slender, and a thousand other things."

Elizabeth was the subject of several satirists, as were so many players. Among the manuscript poems of Rochester at Harvard is a *Lampoon* of about 1678 which says

> Pride that ill natur'd distemper of the mind
> Keeps Rich women honest, but makes poore ones
>   kind
> Like a damn'd daub'd Picture upon the Ale house
>   Wall
> So James is ill painted, and Expos'd to all
>   A Virgin as shee'l vow and sweare
>   Poore Girl she forgetts the Couch at the Beare.

(Wilson notes that at the Bear at Charing Cross there was indeed, as Shadwell has Hazard remark in *The Miser*, "a very convenient Couch.") Though Mrs James is not known to have performed after the 1675–76 season, the satirists would hardly have continued mentioning her had she not been in the public eye in some way. In 1685 in the first version of *The Playhouse* Robert Could points to "Mistress James"

as a mercenary jilt, and Tom Brown in his *Letters from the Dead to the Living* in 1703 implied that "Madam Ja—es" was little better than a whore.

James, Harris *d. 1751, actor, dancer.*

Harris James was first mentioned in London playbills on 14 October 1732 when he played Pert in *The Inconstant* at Goodman's Fields Theatre. Considering the number of billings he had during the remainder of the 1732–33 season, and the fact that he was evidently a fairly accomplished actor and dancer, it is probable that he had had some experience in the provinces before appearing in London. Before the end of the season he was seen as Blunt in *The London Merchant*, the Soothsayer in *Julius Ceasar*, Monsieur in *Love Makes a Man*, an Attendant in *The Amorous Sportsman*, the second Drawer in *The Tavern Bilkers*, Trapland in *Love for Love*, Jack in *Oroonoko*, Sir Thomas Pairnails in *The Decoy*, James in *The Mock Doctor*, the Bookseller in *The Committee*, Simon in *A Bold Stroke for a Wife*, Blunt in *Richard III*, Davy in *The Mock Mason*, and, for his benefit, shared with Jenkins on 8 May 1733, Jeremy in *Love for Love*.

The day after his benefit at Goodman's Fields he played his role of James the Welshman in *The Mock Doctor* at Drury Lane, hailed as making his first appearance at that playhouse. Such alternation was to be typical of James's career, for unless there were two men of the same name and similar lines in London during the years that followed, Harris James managed at times to flit back and forth between theatres, sometimes appearing at two houses on the same night. Those appear to have been special occasions—when he filled in for indisposed friends at another playhouse perhaps (we cannot tell for certain what the reasons may have been)—for during his career James was usually a regular member of one of the companies: Goodman's Fields from 1732–33 through most of 1733–34, then Covent Garden for the remainder of that season; the Haymarket during the summer of 1734; Covent Garden from 1734–35 through 1747–48; and Drury Lane from 1748–49 through 1750–51. After following that rather stable career we will note the occasional appearances James made which broke that pattern.

Before leaving Goodman's Fields in February 1734 to finish out the 1733–34 season at Covent Garden, James added to his repertoire Petit in *The Inconstant*, Arcas in *Damon and Phillida*, and Lopez in *The Wonder*. At Covent Garden in April and May of 1734 he acted Dicky in *The Constant Couple*, Jeremy in *The Strollers*, and Gomez in *The Spanish Fryar*. In the summer of 1734 James was seen at the Haymarket Theatre as Shallow in *The Humours of Sir John Falstaff*, Mrs Slammekin in *The Beggar's Opera Tragedized*, Basset in *The Provok'd Husband*, Daniel in *Oroonoko*, Jack in *The Lottery*, Scrub in *The Stratagem*, Charles in *The Non-Juror*, Gregg in *The Beggar's Wedding*, Robin in *The Contrivances*, and Robin in *The Humorous Election*.

In the fall of 1734 James began his long, full-time association with John Rich at the Covent Garden Theatre. During the ensuing 13 years he played such parts as Sancho and Don Lewis in *Love Makes a Man*, Richard in *The Provok'd Husband*, Davy and the title role in *The Mock Doctor*, Roger in *The London Cuckolds*, Finder in *The Double Gallant*, Jeffery in *The Amorous Widow*, Gardner in *The Drummer*, a Valet de Chambre in *Perseus and Andromeda*, Galloon and Hector in *The Gamester*, Belfond Senior and Scrapeall in *The Squire of Alsatia*, Snap in *Love's Last Shift*, the Beggar in *The Beggar's Opera*, Waitwell in *The Way of the World*, a Witch in *Macbeth*, Rag, Mrs Fardingale, and Tom in *The Funeral*, Corydon in *Damon and Phillida*, Daniel in *The Conscious Lovers*, Obadiah and Abel in *The Committee*, Ralph in *Wit Without Money*, Dick in *Flora*, Syringe and Lory in *The Relapse*, Whisper in *The Busy Body*, Jachimo in *Cymbeline*, a Carrier in *1 Henry IV*, Slender, Pistol, and Caius in *The Merry Wives of Windsor*, Verges in *Much Ado about Nothing*, Nicodemus in *The Stage Coach*, Pistol and Feeble in *2 Henry IV*, Alphonso and the Mad Welshman in *The Pilgrim*, Numps in *The Tender Husband*, Vulture in *The Country Lasses*, Ben and Trapland in *Love for Love*, Appletree, Pearmain, and a Recruit in *The Recruiting Officer*, Setter in *The Old Bachelor*, Harlequin in *The Emperor of the Moon*, Thomas and Filbert in *The What D'Ye Call it*, Razor in *The Provok'd Wife*, Teague in *The Twin Rivals*, Lucianus in *Hamlet*, a Tumbler in *The Necromancer*, Corin in *As You Like It*, Charino in *Love Makes a Man*, Rakehell in *She Wou'd If She*

Cou'd, Quaint in *Aesop*, Sir Politic in *Volpone*, Shylock in *The Merchant of Venice*, Cutbeard in *The Silent Woman*, the Shoemaker in *The Man of Mode*, Perriwinkle in *A Bold Stroke for a Wife*, Charles in *The Busy Body*, Jasper in *Miss in Her Teens*, Simon in *The Suspicious Husband*, Higgen in *The Royal Merchant*, and Petulant in *The Way of the World*.

On 10 September 1748 James began his three-year engagement at Drury Lane with Whisper in *The Busy Body*. After that he played some roles he had acted at Covent Garden in previous seasons, but many of his parts were additions to his repertoire, such as Macmorris in *Henry V*, Foigard in *The Stratagem*, Sampson in *Romeo and Juliet*, Saygrace in *The Double Dealer*, Lolpoop in *The Squire of Alsatia*, Old Gerald in *The Anatomist*, Puff in *Miss in Her Teens*, Polonius (but only once) in *Hamlet*, the Town Clerk and Dogberry in *Much Ado about Nothing*, Tribulation in *The Alchemist*, Mustachio in *The Tempest*, and Doodle in *The London Cuckolds*. His last Drury Lane appearance was as Blunt in *The London Merchant* on 14 May 1751, after which Harris James left the stage; he had only a few more months to live.

During that long career James made fleeting appearances elsewhere, as noted before. The earliest example was in September and October 1734: on 20 September he acted Sancho in *Love Makes a Man* at Covent Garden; on 26 September he was seen at Richmond as Butler in *The Drummer*; he was back at Covent Garden on 9 October in an unnamed role in *See If You Like It*; three days later he acted the Constable in *The Recruiting Officer* at Lincoln's Inn Fields; and on 14 October he again played in *See If You Like It* at Covent Garden.

The next occasion called for some speedy traveling. On 7 April 1735 James was seen as Kite in *The Recruiting Officer* at Southwark in the early evening and as the Valet de Chambre in the afterpiece *Perseus and Andromeda* at Covent Garden. There is no reason why he could not have made both engagements. Another interesting sequence came in the fall of 1737. On 26 October James acted Ralph in *Wit Without Money* at Covent Garden, his home base; the following day he appeared at Drury Lane as Punch in *The Harlot's Progress*; on the twenty-eighth he played Finder in *The Double Gallant* at Covent Garden and crossed over to

Drury Lane, where he played Punch again. That pattern continued until 9 November, when his stint as Punch concluded. Again, it would have been possible for him to play the mainpiece at his home theatre and the afterpiece at the rival house, and evidently the managers were not averse to his doing so. He was probably the Mr James who danced a hornpipe at the James Street playhouse on 7 April 1742. But that ended James's split engagement until 26 December 1748, when he contrived to play Perriwinkle in *A Bold Stroke for a Wife* at Drury Lane and Obadiah in the same play at the New Wells, Clerkenwell.

James also made a few appearances away from his home theatre that did not call for special haste. He may have been the Mr James who acted at the Aungier Street Theatre sometime during the 1740–41 season, but only if that actor appeared there during the summer of 1741, when James's schedule in London was free. On 22 August 1741, he was back in London, playing Crack in *The Modern Pimp* at Bartholomew Fair. He danced a hornpipe at the James Street Theatre on 7 April 1742 and was Harlequin in *Harlequin Hussar* at Tottenham Court on 4 August 1743 at a theatrical booth, the management of which he shared with Daniel and Malone. On 26 September 1747 he acted Tom in *The Conscious Lovers* and Jasper in *Miss in Her Teens* at Richmond; he then made his first appearance of the season at Covent Garden on 31 October.

Beyond the many roles he played and his juggling of his schedule, little is known about Harris James. He was married, and his wife made her first stage appearance on 10 May 1736 at Covent Garden at his benefit, which lost him £41 4s. During that 1735–36 season the Covent Garden accounts noted that James acted 172 days at 5s. daily for a season salary of £43. He was still earning 5s. daily in 1740–41 at Covent Garden, for though he was obviously a busy player, he acted mostly secondary and tertiary roles. By 1746–47 he was down to £1 weekly, presumably for a six-day week.

The Drury Lane prompter Cross noted in his diary that Harris James died at eight o'clock on the morning of 12 October 1751. Latreille picked up from some newspaper account the fact that James had been ill for some time.

Like so many hard-working employees of the patent houses, he died unsung. No critical comments on his work have been found.

James, Mrs Harris [fl. 1736–1754], actress, singer.

Mrs Harris James, the wife of the Covent Garden actor-dancer, made her first appearance on any stage on 10 May 1736 at her husband's benefit, playing Amanda's maid in *Love's Last Shift*. That was a very modest beginning for a woman who quickly moved into roles of considerable importance. During her first full season at Covent Garden, 1736–37, Mrs James played an Amazon in *Perseus and Andromeda*, Lucy in *The Beggar's Opera*, Mrs Mixem in *A Woman's Revenge*, Theaspe in *Achilles*, Queen Elizabeth in *King John*, the Chambermaid in *The Intriguing Chambermaid*, and Mrs Quickly in *The Merry Wives of Windsor*. She also sang in the chorus in *Macbeth*. On 2 June she went over to Lincoln's Inn Fields for one performance of *The Beggar's Opera*.

With her husband Mrs James remained at Covent Garden through 1747–48, making only rare appearances elsewhere. At Covent Garden she built up a very respectable repertoire that included, in addition to the roles already mentioned, Queen Elinor in *King John*, Moretta in *The Rover*, Widow Lackit in *Oroonoko*, Mrs Sealand in *The Conscious Lovers*, Lady Laycock in *The Amorous Widow*, the Duchess of Gloucester in *Richard II*, the Hostess in *2 Henry IV*, Queen Isabel in *Henry V*, the Countess of Auvergne in *1 Henry VI*, the Bawd in *The Chances*, Jiltup in *The Fair Quaker of Deal*, Sysigambis in *The Rival Queens*, Lady Wishfort in *The Way of the World*, the Aunt in *The Tender Husband*, Lady Darling in *The Constant Couple*, Lady Bountiful in *The Stratagem*, Mopsophil in *The Emperor of the Moon*, Lady Pliant in *The Double Dealer*, Lady Wronghead and Mrs Motherly in *The Provok'd Husband*, Lady Woodvill in *The Man of Mode*, Mrs Clearaccount in *The Twin Rivals*, Mrs Topknot in *The Gamester*, Araminta in *The Old Bachelor*, Roger in *The London Cuckolds*, Emilia in *Othello*, Sophronia in *The Assignation*, the Duchess of York in *Richard III*, Gertrude in *Hamlet*, Goneril in *King Lear*, Calpurnia in *Julius Caesar*, (those last six roles all came in the winter of 1743–44), Isabella in *The Re-*

venge, Nottingham in *The Unhappy Favorite*, Alicia in *Jane Shore*, Mrs Otter in *The Silent Woman*, the Player Queen in *Hamlet*, Audrey in *As You Like It*, Mrs Foresight in *Love for Love*, the Queen in *Cymbeline*, and Mrs Prim in *A Bold Stroke for a Wife*.

During her career Mrs James put in an appearance at Goodman's Fields on 5 December 1740 as Mrs Goodfellow in *Tunbridge Walks* and at Bartholomew Fair on 22 August 1741 as Betty in *The Modern Pimp*.

Mrs James moved with her husband to Drury Lane in the fall of 1748, her first part there being Mrs Amlet in *The Confederacy* on 15 September. Between that date and her retirement in the winter of 1754 she was given such new parts as the Nurse in *Romeo and Juliet*, Doll Common in *The Alchemist*, Isabella in *The Conscious Lovers*, Tag in *Miss in Her Teens*, Melissa in *The Comical Lovers*, and Tib in *Every Man in His Humour*. Most of her roles at Drury Lane were those she had acted earlier at Covent Garden.

As of the 1746–47 season Mrs Harris was earning only £1 weekly at Covent Garden—a rather low salary considering the importance of some of her roles, but probably the managers were unwilling to pay her more than her husband. Harris James died after a long illness on 12 October 1751. Mrs James continued acting until 23 October 1754; she played Lady Wishfort on that date. Then a month later, on 22 November, Drury Lane granted her a benefit, and the prompter Cross noted in his diary that she was "going to leave the stage, and retire . . . to a Nunnery."

The address of the Jameses in April 1751 was at Mr Duke's, a watchmaker in Little Wild Street. Her lodgings were at Mr Saunders, a carpenter in Little Wild Street, in April 1752. She was still living in Little Wild Street in 1753 and 1754.

James, James   [*fl.*   1730–1740?],
trumpeter.

On 27 December 1730, according to the Lord Chamberlain's accounts, James James replaced Thomas Lund among the trumpeters in the King's Musick. He continued in the royal service for ten years and was replaced, apparently on 7 May 1740, by Justice Willis. James had become one of the original members of the Royal Society of Musicians on 28 August 1739.

James, John   *d. 1745, organist, composer, trumpeter?*

The John James who was listed in the Lord Chamberlain's accounts in 1736 as a trumpeter in the King's Musick was perhaps the John James who served as deputy organist and then organist at St Olave, Southwark, and was noted for his skill at extemporaneous performing. In 1738 he resigned his Southwark post and became organist of St George in the East. James died in 1745. He composed a few organ works and some songs.

Jameson, Mr   [*fl.* 1782], *actor.*

At the Haymarket Theatre on 21 March 1782 a Mr Jameson played an unnamed role in *Love at a Venture* and Subtle in *The Tobacconist*.

Jameson, Miss   [*fl.* 1782], *actress.*

A Miss Jameson, apparently not the singer Mary Jameson, had an unnamed role in *The Taylors* at the Haymarket Theatre on 25 November 1782.

Jameson, Mary, later Mrs Stewart Amos Arnold   [*fl. c. 1770–1786*], *singer, actress.*

Mary Jameson was singing at Vauxhall Gardens from about 1770, when printed songs began citing her as the soloist. Among those dating about 1770 were *The Fields now are looking so gay*, *Now Winter is Flown*, *Attend all ye Nymphs*, *As now my Bloom*, and *Tho' still so Young and scarce Fifteen* (was she, perhaps, that young?). In 1771 was published a collection of songs that had been favorites at Vauxhall that year. The singers were Mrs Weichsell, Vernon, and Miss Jameson. Mary was certainly in first-rate company. Songs with her name attached kept coming off the presses: *I do as I will with my Swain* in 1773; *My Patie is a Lover gay* in 1774; *To fly like a Bird from Grove to Grove*, *Among the Swains upon the Green*, and *Corn Riggs are bonny* about 1775; and *Miss in her Teens* about 1780. She was clearly one of the most popular of the pleasure garden singers.

On 29 September 1773 she made her first appearance on any stage as Rosetta in *Love in a Village* at Covent Garden. She was cited only as a young lady, a pupil of Dr Arne, but she was later identified in the bills as Miss Jameson. She was on the weekly payroll at 16s. 6d. The *Westminster Magazine* was disappointed, feeling that her musical powers were not extraordinary and her acting powers still worse. The *Covent Garden Magazine* found her awkward but felt that she had done her master credit. She repeated the role, and the fourth performance was at the command of the King. The *Morning Chronicle* of 14 October reported that his Majesty seemed to be in raptures throughout, and when the favorite song "In love should you meet a fond pair" was completed, the Queen said to the Duchess of Ancaster that Miss Jameson had "An amazing voice, and an exquisite judgment." During the rest of the 1773–74 season Mary played Patty in *The Maid of the Mill*, Mandane in Arne's *Artaxerxes*, Margery in *The Dragon of Wantley*, and, replacing Miss Catley, Thetis in *Achilles in Petticoats*.

Miss Jameson appeared at the Haymarket Theatre as an entr'acte singer on 16 February 1775 offering "Diana's Chace" and on 1 May singing a "Trumpet Song." Then she went to Dublin where she appeared at the Smock Alley Theatre in 1775–76, at the Crow Street Theatre from May 1776 through 1776–77, and at Fishamble Street in 1777. She is known to have played Diana in *Lionel and Clarissa* at Crow Street on 7 June 1777. In the *Hibernian Magazine* in July 1776 was published "Love resigns this Season," a song sung by Miss Jameson in the Rotunda. She appeared at Cork and Kilkenny in 1779 and at Cork again in 1780. During the 1780–81 season she was back at Smock Alley, and in 1781–82 she sang at the Crow Street Theatre.

It seems unlikely that Mary was the Miss Jameson who had an unnamed role in *The Taylors* on 25 November 1782 at the Haymarket Theatre in London, though she may have been. W. J. Lawrence's notes on the Dublin theatre, examined by the late W. S. Clark, indicate that she was in Dublin during the 1782–83 season, appearing at both Smock Alley and Capel Street. During that season she appeared in Belfast, and when she was advertised on 24 January 1783 as newly engaged there by the manager Atkins, he boasted that she was "the best public singer in Ireland." But, according to Clark's *The Irish Stage in the County Towns*, if

she went to Belfast it could not have been for a long engagement, for she was back at Smock Alley on 25 February. In the fall of 1783 she performed at Cork.

The Irish records show Miss Jameson at Smock Alley in 1783–84, and since she seems not to have been in Ireland in 1784–85, it seems reasonable to conjecture that perhaps she was the Miss Jameson who took a principal part (unnamed) in an untitled burletta at the Royal Circus in London in 1785. Also participating were Matthews, Johannet, and Mr and Mrs Hanley. The Irish records Clark investigated show that Mary was back at Smock Alley in 1785–86 and in July and August 1786 playing at Waterford, Limerick, and Cork. At Cork on 24 October 1786 she was advertised as Mrs Arnold, according to Clark. But the marriage license at the Dublin Public Records Office of Stewart Amos Arnold and Mary Jameson is dated 1788, and the *Hibernian Magazine* in May 1788 spoke of Mrs Arnold as "late Miss Jameson" when she sang on 12 April in the *Messiah*.

Janiewicz, Felix   *1762–1848, violinist, composer.*

Felix Janiewicz (sometimes Yaniewicz) was born in Wilno (Vilnius), Russia, in 1762. In his younger years he was attached to the court of Stanislaus, King of Poland, where he received considerable musical encouragement and a pension to allow him to travel and study. In 1784 he went to Vienna, where he heard Haydn and Mozart conduct their own works and where Michael Kelly often heard Janiewicz perform. Kelly said Janiewicz "touched the instrument [the violin] with thrilling effect, and was an excellent leader of an orchestra. His concertos always finished with some pretty Polonaise air; his variations also were truly beautiful."

From Vienna Janiewicz traveled to Italy, where he spent three years. Fétis asserts that the violinist gave a concert in Milan in 1786 and then came to England, but it seems clear that his journey to England did not come before 1790, after Janiewicz had spent some time in Paris. In Paris Janiewicz performed at the Concert Spirituel in 1787 and at the Olympiens. For a while he had a pension from the Duc d'Orléans, but the French Revolution drove him from Paris. Pohl claimed that Janiewicz lost all of his possessions when the Revolution broke out. Grove suggests that the violinist may have returned to Poland, but conditions both there and in France evidently persuaded Janiewicz to give up the Continent and make for the British Isles, where he spent the rest of his life.

Beginning in March 1790, concerts, organized mostly by Salomon, were given at the Hanover Square Rooms. Janiewicz was listed among the violinists who performed there, his first appearance being in February 1792, according to Grove. In that year Haydn recorded in his *First London Notebook* that "Yaniewicz" was among the musical folk in London; he listed him as a violinist and as a composer, for Felix had already published some works in France. On 15 February 1793 at the King's Theatre he played a concerto on the violin, his appearance being advertised as his first public performance in England. Thereafter he appeared at the theatres on occasion, especially during the oratorio seasons in the spring, to offer concertos on the violin. He also performed, according to Doane's *Musical Directory* of 1794, at the Professional Concerts. His address was No 40, Brewer Street, Soho. Hester Thrale's *Diary* on 17 March 1795 indicated that Janiewicz was turned out of Rauzzini's Bath concerts because he was a public performer. Hogan's *Anglo-Irish Music* states that the violinist performed in Dublin between 1796 and 1821 and visited Cork and Limerick in 1796. Dr Burney heard him in London in May 1799.

One of Janiewicz's students in England was Joseph Bottomley, who wrote to Sainsbury for his dictionary in 1824 that about 1798–1800 Janiewicz was engaged to perform at Manchester. In his travels around the British Isles he mixed business with pleasure, as the *Monthly Mirror* in March 1800 noted: he "combines the *utile* with the *dolce*. He is *married* at Liverpool; leads the *concerts*; and is (a la Liverpool) a *man of business*." And indeed he was. Humphries and Smith in *Music Publishing in the British Isles* list Janiewicz as a violinist, composer, music seller, and publisher. He ran his business at No 25, Lord Street, Liverpool, from about 1801 to 1805 and at No 29 from about 1805 to 1810. For two years after that he was in partnership with a Mr Green at No 29, Lord Street, then from about 1812 to 1817 he was

alone at No 60. His business became Janiewicz and W. G. Weiss at the same address from about 1817 to 1827; then for the following two years they had a shop at No 2, Church Street. In 1829 Janiewicz left the Liverpool partnership and Weiss carried on alone.

Janiewicz also had a shop in London at No 22, Devonshire Street, Bloomsbury, about 1810 and at his pianoforte rooms at No 49, Leicester Square, about 1811–12.

Janiewicz married a Miss Breeze of Liverpool in 1800. They lived in Upper Birket Street, St Anne's, for a while, but when the violinist began his music selling and publishing shop they moved to Lime Street. Sainsbury's dictionary states that the couple had one son and two daughters. Both daughters, Felicia and Pauline, became musicians.

In 1810 Janiewicz was granted a license for six concerts at his London house in Leicester Square, from 25 April to 31 May. He was one of the original founders in 1813 of the Philharmonic Society and one of the leaders of the orchestra during its initial season. He moved to Edinburgh in 1815 without giving up his Liverpool interests. In Edinburgh he led the orchestra in the 1815, 1819, nd 1824 festivals. He made his last appearance in 1829. Felix Janiewicz died in Edinburgh on 21 May 1848.

Luigi Scotti pictured Janiewicz in a large group of musicians in an engraving published in Florence about 1805.

Janiot. *See* GARRAT.

Janno, Mons [*fl.* 1733–1747], *dancer, acrobat.*

The earliest notice we have found of Mr Janno (or Jano, Janny) was that of 23 August 1733, when he danced one of the Rival Swains in *The Gardens of Venus* at the Mills-Miller-Oates booth at Bartholomew Fair. On 4 September at the Cibber-Griffin-Bullock-Hallam booth at the same fair he was Punch in *Riddoto al' Fresco*. Janno was with Theophilus Cibber's company of Drury Lane seceders playing at the Haymarket in the fall of 1733. He danced between the acts on 26 September, and then he was one of the College Youths in *The Festival* in November and December and Scaramouch and a Peasant in *The Burgomaster Trick'd* in January and February 1734. He also played the King of the Antipodes in *Chrononhotontho-logos* before the troupe went back to Drury Lane.

At Bartholomew Fair in August 1734 Janno danced and tumbled. From 1734–35 through 1736–37 at Drury Lane Janno offered entr'acte dances and appeared in such pantomime parts as a Masquerader in *Colombine Courtezan*, a Waterman in *The Tempest*, a Drawer in *Harlequin Restored*, Punch in *The Harlot's Progress*, and Slouch in *Poor Pierrot Married*. He appeared as a dancer at Bartholomew Fair in August 1736 and the following year was in *All Alive and Merry* at both Bartholomew and Southwark fairs.

Janno was not mentioned again in a London bill until 23 August 1740, when he again appeared as a dancer at Bartholomew Fair. In February and March 1741 he was earning £1 1s. (weekly, evidently) for playing Pluto in *The Royal Chace* at Covent Garden Theatre. In April 1746 Janno tumbled and rope-danced at Sadler's Wells. On 16 January 1747 he danced in *The Tempest* at the Goodman's Fields playhouse. He was probably the "Mr Jonno" in Dominique's company at the theatre in Stoke's Croft, Bristol, on 20 February 1746. Dominique, to quell criticism of his troupe's being Gallic, stated in the papers that "Jonno" was from Milan, Italy. The Master Janno who appeared at Drury Lane briefly in 1749 was probably our subject's son.

Janno, Master [*fl.* 1749], *dancer*.
The Master Janno (or Jonno) who was one of the Children Savoyards in a dance called *The Savoyard Travelers* at Drury Lane on 9 November 1749 was probably the son of the dancer Monsieur Janno of the 1730s and 1740s. *The London Stage* notes that on 10 November Master Janno was replaced by the "Little Swiss" and that possibly there had been no replacement but merely a change in name. But the Little Swiss had been dancing before November 1749, and it would have been odd for only one bill to carry him under a different designation. It is more likely that Janno and the Little Swiss were two different boys.

Janny. *See* JANNO.

Jansolet. *See* JANSOLIN.

Jansolin, Mme [*fl.* 1756–1762], *dancer*.
Madame Jansolin (or Jansolet) was a minor dancer at Covent Garden, usually found in the corps de ballet. Though she may have been dancing at the theatre for some years before a bill mentioned her name, the first reference to her was on 19 May 1756, when her benefit tickets were accepted. Beginning 1 February 1758 she danced in *The Prophetess*, and she was in that work again when it was revived the following season. On 14 October 1758 she was in a comic dance called *The Threshers*; then during the rest of the season she was a Bacchante in the pantomime ballet *The Feast of Bacchus*.

Madame Jansolin continued at Covent Garden through the 1761–62 season, appearing in *The Fair*, *Comus*, *The Rape of Proserpine*, *Apollo and Daphne*, *The Hungarian Gambols*, and doubtless other works. As of 22 September 1760 she was being paid 6s. 8d. daily. Her annual salary in her last season was £53. She seems not to have made much of a success at dancing, nor did Mlle Jansolin—her daughter, most likely—who appeared in 1757–58.

Jansolin, Mlle [*fl.* 1757–1758], *dancer*.
On 30 April 1757 Mlle Jansolin's benefit tickets were accepted at Covent Garden Theatre. She was a minor dancer, rarely cited in the bills, but she is known to have participated in a comic ballet on 28 April 1758. She was perhaps a daughter of Mme Jansolin.

Janson, [F.?] [*fl.* 1787–1794?], *singer*.
Mr Janson sang at Covent Garden for £1 10s. weekly in 1787–88 and 1789. He was in the *Macbeth* chorus on 16 November 1787; later that season he sang in *The Roman Father*, *Alexander the Great*, *Romeo and Juliet*, and *A King and No King*. On 15 December 1788 he was one of the group which sang "God Save the King" after the first of George III's mental breakdowns. It is possible that our subject was the F. Janson who was an honorary subscriber to the New Musical Fund in 1794. A Francis Janson married a Mary Smith on 9 May 1804 at St George, Hanover Square, but there is no way of knowing whether or not he was the singer.

Janson, Jean Baptiste Aimé Joseph [1742–1803], *violoncellist, composer.*

At Drury Lane on 6 March 1772 a Mr Janson performed a solo on the violoncello; the *Theatrical Review* on that date reported that Janson was "lately arrived from Paris, said to have been a pupil of Mr. Duport's, but though his taste and execution is very astonishing, we cannot give him the preference of his master." Since, according to Grove, Jean Baptiste Aimé Joseph Janson, the Netherlands violoncellist and composer, took to touring extensively in 1771, it is probable that the Janson who played in England in March and April 1772 was Jean Baptiste. He was born in Valenciennes in 1742 and studied in Paris under Berteau before Berteau's death in 1756. Janson's debut was at the Concert Spirituel in 1766, after which he went to Italy until 1771. He then returned to Paris before embarking on tours that took him to Germany, Poland, Denmark, Sweden, and, we believe, England. During the oratorio season in March and April of 1772 a Janson regularly offered a 'cello solo.

Jean Baptiste Janson became a professor at the newly-founded Paris Conservatoire in 1795 but lost his position when the Conservatoire was reorganized in 1802. He died in poverty in Paris on 2 September 1803. In addition to playing the 'cello, Janson composed a number of sonatas, trios, and concertos for his instrument, and three symphonies.

Jaquet-Droz, Henri Louis. *See* DROZ, HENRI.

Jardin. *See* DE JARDIN.

Jarnowick or **Jarowez.** *See* GIORNOVICHI.

Jarper. *See* HARPER.

Jarrall, Mrs [fl. 1774], *house servant?*
In the Winston manuscripts is a note that 5s. was a "night's pay" for a Mrs Jarrall in 1774. Perhaps she was one of the house servants.

Jarratt. *See also* GARRAT.

Jarratt, Miss [fl. 1759?–1786], *actress, singer, dancer?*

Possibly the Miss Jarratt who acted in London between 1772 and 1777 was the daughter of the singer Samuel Garrat (sometimes Janiot or Jarratt). If so, she danced at Covent Garden in 1759–60 when still a child, for the accounts of that theatre show a payment to Garrat of £21 on 30 May 1760 for his daughter's dancing that season.

Announced as "A Young Gentlewoman" making her first appearance, Miss Jarratt acted Miss Biddy in *Miss in Her Teens* at Drury Lane on 3 November 1772. In his diary the prompter Hopkins identified her: "Miss Jarratt (an apprentice to Mr Jefferson) a pretty little figure & met with Applause. Not much of an Actress." The critic in the *Town and Country Magazine* that month, however, thought she promised to become "an agreeable actress" in such parts as Biddy. Announced as the "young Gentlewoman who played the part of Biddy," on 6 November she played Theodosia in *The Maid of the Mill*. She was named as Miss Jarratt in the bill of 8 December for the role of Miss Melville in *The Duel*, an ill-fated comedy by William O'Brien that was hissed from the second act and was not suffered to be played again. Her other roles that season included Jessica (with a song) in *The Merchant of Venice* on 4 and 5 January 1773, Harriet in *The Jealous Wife* on 30 March, when according to Hopkins she was hissed, and Miss Rivers in *False Delicacy*, for her mentor Jefferson's benefit on 16 April.

Miss Jarratt remained at Drury Lane through 1776–77 but caused no great stir as an actress. In 1773–74 she added to her repertoire Celia in *As You Like It*, Miss Leeson in *The School for Wives*, Harriet in *The Guardian*, Blanche of Spain in *King John*, a role in *The Conjuror*, and Arabella in *The Committee*. In 1774–75 her new roles included one of the Country Girls in *The Elopement*, unspecified characters in *A Christmas Tale* and *The Genii*, Rose in *The Recruiting Officer*, Meriel in *The Ladies' Frolick*, Lucinda in *Love in a Village*, and the Milliner in *The Suspicious Husband*. Among his remarks on "the inferior performers," William Hawkins described her in *Miscellanies in Prose and Verse* in 1775 as "very agreeable in all she undertakes" and still "promising."

After playing the summer of 1775 at Richmond, Miss Jarratt returned to Drury Lane as Celia on 26 September. On 20 October she appeared for the first time as Cherry in *The Stratagem*, and Hopkins thought she did "pretty well." When she played the role again on 1 December she suffered an embarrassing accident which suggests the possibility she was pregnant or, even more likely, drunk. She stumbled and fell upon the stage, and Garrick, playing Archer, "could not very easily raise her," wrote Hopkins, because of Miss Jarratt "being in certain condition."

That season she also performed Miss Griskin in *A Trip to Scotland*, a Country Lass in *May Day*, and sang in the funeral procession of *Romeo and Juliet*. After another summer at Richmond, she returned in 1776–77 for what proved to be her last season at Drury Lane, during which she toiled busily almost every night to earn her £2 10s. per week in such roles as Wilhelmina in *The Waterman*, a Spirit and Camilla in *A Christmas Tale*, Flavia in *The Hotel*, Fairy in *Selima and Azor*, and one of the chorus of Spirits in *The Tempest*.

Possibly Miss Jarratt played again at Richmond in the summer of 1777. She came once more to London on 6 October 1777 to perform Polly in *The Beggar's Opera* for a special benefit for Digges at the Haymarket Theatre, and then she proceeded to the Theatre Royal in Edinburgh where she appeared on 8 December 1777 as Miss Hardcastle in *She Stoops to Conquer* and Louisa in *The Deserter*. She acted Silvia in *Cymon* and Violante in *The Wonder* on 10 December, Polly Peachum on 15 December, and Ophelia on 22 December. Then through April she appeared in a number of comedy and musical parts, including Beatrice in *Much Ado about Nothing*, Fanny in *The Clandestine Marriage*, Leonora in *The Padlock*, Prue in *Love for Love*, Rosalind in *As You Like It*, and Rosetta in *Love in a Village*.

In July 1778 she joined Wilkinson's company on the York circuit, playing Rosetta, Leonora, and other roles at Leeds, Halifax, York during race-week, Scarborough, Wakefield, and Doncaster. Acting with her was Jefferson, her former teacher. Wilkinson had a very high opinion of her, stating in his *Wandering Patentee* that she was "a beautiful girl, with a good voice . . . deservedly much ad-mired, not more so in any of her performances than when singing the song of the 'Jockey and the Rose'."

Later in 1778 Miss Jarratt went to sing leads at Bristol. In 1780 she was at Plymouth with Jefferson and his wife; on 19 July she was named in the bills for the male role of Don Carlos in *The Duenna*, a circumstance which suggests that she was still quite young. A garbled report in the *Morning Chronicle* of 19 October 1780 had her dying while performing at Plymouth on 17 October, but the press had confused her with the unfortunate actress Mary Bradshaw, who became so distressed when her daughter was hissed that she fell into a fit and died shortly thereafter.

Miss Jarratt then played at the Crow Street Theatre, Dublin, in 1780–81 and 1781–83 and then at Smock Alley in 1782–83 and 1784–85. She was at Cork in September 1784. Audiences at Richmond saw her again in the summer of 1785.

According to Winston's notation in the Drury Lane Fund Book at the Folger Library, Miss Jarratt, who had subscribed to the fund in 1775, neglected her payment in 1786.

Jarriot or **Jarrut.** *See* GARRATT.

Jarvis. *See also* JERVIS.

Jarvis, Mr [*fl. 1734–1762*], *housekeeper, office keeper.*

Mr Jarvis, the Covent Garden housekeeper, shared a benefit with Gwinn on 15 May 1734, the earliest notice of him. The benefit bills and theatre accounts from then until 8 May 1762 cited Jarvis fairly regularly, often identifying him as the housekeeper, but Latreille found one note, dated 1735–36, that called Jarvis the pit office keeper and gave his salary as 2s. 6d. nightly. He may well have held both positions. By the 1740–41 season he was earning £1 weekly, but the accounts on 4 October 1746 put him at 2s. daily (that might have been the fee for one of his two posts). References to Jarvis are rare in the 1740s and 1750s, though he apparently continued working at Covent Garden until the last mention of him in May 1762. He was sometimes call "Jervais."

Jarvis, Mr ₁*fl. 1744*₁,   *actor.*

Mr Jarvis (or Jervis) played Guildenstern in *Hamlet* on 29 June and 3 and 6 July 1744 at the Haymarket. He was probably related to the Miss Jarvis who acted at the same house earlier that year.

Jarvis, Mrs ₁*fl. 1758*₁,   *house servant?*

A Mrs Jarvis was listed in the 8 May 1758 benefit bill at Covent Garden as one of four people whose benefit tickets would be accepted. Since this is the only reference we have found to Mrs Jarvis, we may guess that perhaps she was a minor house servant, but there is the possibility of a misprint: the citation could be for Mr Jarvis, the Covent Garden housekeeper, who was noted in a benefit bill in May 1756 but not in 1758.

Jarvis, Miss ₁*fl. 1744*₁,   *actress.*

Miss Jarvis played Charlotte in *The Mock Doctor* and Wheedle in *The Miser* at the Haymarket Theatre on 10 May 1744. She repeated the role of Charlotte on 16 May.

Jarvis, Robert *d. 1755, bassoonist.*

The *Public Advertiser* reported on 30 July 1755 that Robert Jarvis, bassoon player for 40 years at Lincoln's Inn Fields and Covent Garden theatres, had died on 24 July. The only other references to him that have been found concern his membership in the Royal Society of Musicians. He was an original subscriber to that organization when it was founded on 28 August 1739, and in May 1754 he played bassoon for 8*s.* when the *Messiah* was performed at the Foundling Hospital.

Jarvis, Tom ₁*fl. 1754*₁,   *acrobat, equestrian?*

The bill for Covent Garden on 6 April 1754 promised as entertainment a "Dialogue-Epilogue between Tom Jarvis (an itinerant Turner) and his Horse." A "turner" was an acrobat.

Jatter, Mr ₁*fl. c. 1661–1662*₁,   *actor.*

In a manuscript cast in the Folger Shakespeare Library's copy of Heywood's *The Royal King*, "Jatter" is given the small part of Lansprisado Match. The King's Company probably presented the play about 1661–62 at the Vere Street Theatre.

Though there is a possibility that Jatter was actually one of Shatterells, there is not sufficient evidence either to prove or disprove such an identity.

Jay, Mr ₁*fl. 1748*₁,   *performer?*

On 18 July 1748 at the "Great Til'd Booth on the Bowling Green" in Southwark *The Unhappy Favourite* and *The Mock Doctor* were presented for the benefit of a Mr Jay, otherwise unknown. He may have been a performer.

Jealous, Mr ₁*fl. 1789–1794*₁,   *house servant?*

The benefit tickets of a Mr Jealous were accepted at Covent Garden Theatre on 13 June 1789 and then almost yearly through 17 June 1794. He may have been one of the house servants.

Jeames. *See* JAMES.

Jeani, Mr ₁*fl. 1790*₁,   *dancer.*

Mr Jeani performed with the Ferreres and Bourkes in the dance *Double Infidelity* at the Royalty Theatre on 5 April 1790.

Jee. *See also* LEE.

Jee, John *b. 1746, violist, organist, singer?, violinist?*

John Jee was proposed for membership in the Royal Society of Musicians on 6 March 1785. At that time he was 39 years old, a violist, and a widower with a son 17 then apprenticed to a stationer. He was admitted to the Society on 1 May and listed both as a violist and as an organist. Jee played viola in the St Paul's concerts on 12 and 14 May 1789, but when he asked to be excused from that duty in 1790 he was refused on the grounds that he was a new member of the Society. He played in May 1790 (listed in the minutes as what looks like "Lee"), and on 3 June 1792 he was proposed as a Governor of the Society. The minutes in 1793 indicate that he was elected.

It seems very probable that the John "Lee" listed in Doane's *Musical Directory* of 1794 was our subject. Doane noted that he was proficient on the viola and violin and sang tenor and alto. He participated in performances by the Handelian Society and Cecilian Society and in the oratorios at Drury Lane and Westminster Abbey. His address was given as No 2, Black Horse Court, Aldersgate Street.

Jefferies, Mr [*fl.* 1764–1771?], *actor.*
See JEFFERIES, MRS, later MRS JOHN LEE.

Jefferies, Mrs, later Mrs John Lee [*fl.* 1764–1778], *actress, singer.*

The date and place of Mrs? Jefferies's birth are not known, but *Theatrical Biography* (1772) asserted that she had married at a very early age the son of a reputable linen draper in London, whose father had set him up in the braziery business with good capital and connections. The young couple soon gave up the shop for the stage, however, and the pretty and gay Mrs Jefferies for her debut played Miss Grantham (or Grantam, Grantom) in *The Lyar* "about the year 1762 [recte 1764]." Reed in his "Notitia Dramatica" transcribed a bill for the Haymarket Theatre dated 30 June 1764 which listed Mrs Jefferies (or Jeffreys, Jeffries) as Miss Grantham in *The Lyar. The London Stage* omits that performance, though it does have her down for Lightning in *The Rehearsal* on 20 August and Dame Kitely in *Every Man in His Humour* on 1 September. After her summer engagement under Samuel Foote at the Haymarket, according to *Theatrical Biography*, Mrs Jefferies was without a contract, so with her husband she performed in the provinces and then enlisted in Mossop's troupe in Dublin.

Faulkner's Dublin Journal on 27 November 1764 announced that "A Young Gentlewoman" would play Belinda in *All in the Wrong* on the twenty-ninth at Smock Alley Theatre; when that actress made her eighth appearance on any stage on 5 January 1765 at Smock Alley in the same role she was revealed to be Mrs Jefferies. She and her husband performed at Smock Alley in 1764–65 and 1765–66.

According to *Theatrical Biography*:

The decline of Mr. Mossop's affairs, which was brought on by the powerful opposition of Barry and Woodward, made the generality of the performers under him revolt. Their weekly salaries became first to be curtailed, which brought on large arrears, and afterwards an almost total bankruptcy, so that his corps hourly went over to the enemy. . . .

Mrs Jefferies, who had been befriended by Mossop, felt that she could not desert him for the rival camp, so she and her husband returned to England.

On 8 June 1767 Mrs Jefferies was again at the Haymarket Theatre in London, playing once more Miss Grantham in *The Lyar.* On 2 July she was one of the Taylors' Ladies in *The Taylors*, and on 6 July she attempted Alicia in *Jane Shore. Momus* admonished her for trying a role so far out of her range:

> With bold presumption, in despite of shame,
> J—ff—s attempts to join the rank of same,
> And void of judgment, attitude and speech,
> She aims at characters above her reach;
> When poor Alicia with distraction raves,
> And calls for racks, for thunderbolts, and graves;
> Did Cinderella ever scold so well,
> When in her airs she bid you go to h–ll?
>
> . . . .
>
> In third-rate parts, where nature don't require
> Such skill in action, or such force of fire,
>
> . . . .
>
> There spite of censure shalt thou justly raise,
> The smile of pleasure and the voice of praise.

Other roles played that summer by Mrs Jefferies were Jenny in *The Provok'd Husband*, Parisatis in *Alexander*, Diana Trapes and Mrs Peachum in *The Beggar's Opera*, Juliet in *The Parson*, Desdemona in *Othello*, and Miranda in *The Busy Body*. Sylas Neville told his diary that "Mrs Jeffries could scarce do her part [in *The Taylors*] for laughing at Foote" on 25 August and that she played "Doll Trapes better than she does Mrs P[eachum]."

Only one part is known for Mr Jefferies, though he may have been seen in small roles all summer; on 6 July 1767 he was Mercury in *Lethe.* He returned alone to Dublin in 1767–68 to act at Smock Alley. In the provinces he "has ever since continued," said *Theatrical Biography*, "'dead to the world, and by the world forgot.'" He may have died by the fall of 1771, when Mrs Jefferies had become Mrs John Lee.

Mrs Jefferies performed at Drury Lane Theatre in 1767–68, making her first appearance on 25 September 1767 as Belinda in *The Provok'd Wife.* She was "not perfect" in her lines, the prompter Hopkins noted, but she "was pretty well received.—is a little smart figure." That season Mrs Jefferies came on also as Jacintha in *The Suspicious Husband*, Lucy in *The Lon-*

don Merchant, the Chambermaid and Miss Sterling in *The Clandestine Marriage*, Bridget in *Every Man in His Humour*, Fidelia in *The Plain Dealer*, Miss Grantham in *The Lyar*, Mlle Florival in *The Deuce is in Him*, Miss Rivers in *False Delicacy*, Miss Frolick in *The Absent Man*, Nerissa in *The Merchant of Venice*, Myra in *Wit's Last Stake*, and Clarissa in *All in the Wrong*.

In 1768–69, except for a single appearance at the Haymarket as Miranda in *The Busy Body* on 7 October 1768, Mrs Jefferies performed again at Drury Lane, adding to her repertoire such new roles as a Shepherdess in *Cymon*, Alithea in *The Country Girl*, Catherine in *Catherine and Petruchio*, Mrs Lovemore in *The Way to Keep Him*, and Sift in *The Widow'd Wife*. She returned to the Haymarket in the summer of 1769 to act Mrs Sullen in *The Beaux' Stratagem*, Mrs Ailwou'd in *The Doctor Last in His Chariot*, Mrs Vixen in *The Beggar's Opera*, Lucy in *The Minor*, Arabella in *The Author*, the Queen in *Richard III*, Miss Grantham in *The Lyar*, Sylvia in *The Old Bachelor*, and Emilia in *Othello*.

Mrs Jefferies continued at Drury Lane in 1769–70 and 1770–71, playing at the Haymarket between seasons. Among her new characters at Drury Lane were Lady Lambert in *The Hypocrite*, Mrs Frail in *Love for Love*, Mrs Willoughby in *A Word to the Wise*, Fainlove in *The Tender Husband*, Violante in *The Double Falsehood*, Phaedra in *Amphitryon*, Marcella in *'Tis Well It's No Worse*, Foible in *The Way of the World*, Lady Fuz in *A Peep Behind the Curtain*, and Mistress Page in *The Merry Wives of Windsor*. At the Haymarket in the summer of 1770 she acted two new roles: Cordelia in *King Lear* and Leonora in *The Wrangling Lovers*.

The reporter for *Theatrical Biography* said that after she abandoned her husband Mrs Jefferies went from lover to lover, one a prominent lawyer and another a "son of Mars"—an army officer. When she appeared once more in Dublin, she had become Mrs John Lee. She acted at the Crow Street Theatre, beginning on 11 November 1771. W. S. Clark in *The Irish Stage in the County Towns* mistakenly identified Mrs Lee's husband as Samuel Lee the Dublin musician, but his Christian name, according to Charles Beecher Hogan, was John. Clark also erred in stating that our subject's maiden name was Grantham; that, of course, was the role she played frequently throughout her career. Clark traced Mrs Lee to Limerick in

1771 (just before her appearance in Dublin) and to Cork in 1774 and 1775; she acted in Derby in 1775–76 and in Edinburgh from 1776 to 1778.

Several of Mrs Jefferies's Edinburgh roles were recovered by Norma Armstrong: Alicia in *Jane Shore*, Andromache in *The Distrest Mother*, Belinda in *All in the Wrong*, Charlotte Rusport in *The West Indian*, Clarinda and Jacintha in *The Suspicious Husband*, Dolly Ship in *The Invasion of Harlequin*, the First Ariel Spirit in *The Institution of the Order of the Garter*, Juliet in *The Patron*, Juliet in *Romeo and Juliet*, the Lady in *Comus*, Lady Brute in *The Provok'd Wife*, Lady Harriot in *The Funeral*, Lady Macbeth, Sophia in *The Brothers*, Lady Townly in *The Provok'd Husband*, Lavinia in *The Fair Penitent*, Lydia Languish in *The Rivals*, Maria in *The Citizen*, Miss Bridgemore in *The Fashionable Lover*, Miss Griskin in *The Trip to Scotland*, Miss Sterling in *The Clandestine Marriage*, Miss Walsingham in *The School for Wives*, Mrs Brittle in *Modern Union*, Mrs Oakly in *The Jealous Wife*, Mrs Sullen in *The Stratagem*, Olivia in *Twelfth Night*, the Queen in *King Charles the First of England*, and Sylvia in *The Recruiting Officer*.

Our subject was the Mrs Lee who appeared at the Haymarket Theatre again on 23 March 1778 as Mrs Oakly in *The Jealous Wife*. She played Mrs Prim in *A Bold Stroke for a Wife* on 31 March. At some point after that Mrs Lee retired from the stage and set up as mistress of a school in Aberdeen. She died before April 1784, when the *Scots Magazine* reported that John Lee her husband had been hanged for forgery at Newgate on 4 April.

Jefferson, Mr [fl. 1776–1788], *actor, prompter.*

The Mr Jefferson, "prompter," who shared in a benefit at the Birmingham Theatre on 21 August 1776 may have been the Jefferson who was at the Liverpool theatre on a salary of a guinea a week from 12 October to 20 December 1776. A Mr Jefferson, perhaps the same, acted once at the little China Hall Theatre in Rotherhithe, on 20 June 1777, as one of the mob in *The Mayor of Garratt*. Mr Jefferson was seen at Liverpool in the third week of July 1778 and evidently played through October at a guinea a week. A Mr Jefferson acted Zama in *Tamerlane the Great* on the occasion of a special benefit for a Mrs Farrer licensed by the Lord Chamberlain at the Haymarket on 22 December 1788.

Jefferson, Mr [*fl. 1799*], *musician.*

According to a manuscript company list in the Richmond (Surrey) Reference Library, a Mr Jefferson was leader of the band in that theatre in 1799.

Jefferson, Thomas *1732–1807, actor, manager.*

Thomas Jefferson, born 31 January 1732, was "the son of a respectable farmer of Carthorp, in the North Riding of Yorkshire," according to the biographical sketch in the *Monthly Mirror* for July 1804. His mother died when he was young and he was placed under the care of her brother, Mr Burton of Beadle Woodhouse "who, finding his nephew's ideas above those of a ploughboy, articled him, when fourteen years old, to a neighboring attorney." For six months he prospered at law, but told by his master to prepare for a journey to London and then disappointed in that expectation by the attorney's decision to go instead, Jefferson threw up his apprenticeship and decamped. "A remarkably fine charger having been purchased in the neighborhood for General Fawkes, Young Jefferson offered to ride it to London," where he arrived in January 1747. His adventure then took a serious turn:

One of his relations was the person who kept the Tilt Yard Coffee House, and while on a visit to him, on Tuesday the 7th of April, 1747, he had the misfortune to be blown up there, with the powder allotted to the Soldiers who were to guard Lord Lovat to his execution the Thursday following. His life was miraculously preserved by the intervention of a falling beam, which halted immediately over his head.

Attending the theatre, he was captivated by Peg Woffington as Ruth in *The Committee*. His uncle, moved by the narrow escape from the coffee-house explosion, helped release him from his articles with the attorney, and Thomas set about learning roles.

The well-known Charlotte Skinner, formerly engaged in [Samuel] Foote's Tea [satirical performances camouflaged lightly from the eye of the licenser as "tea-parties"], advertised a play at the Little Theatre [in the Haymarket] to be performed by amateurs—to her he immediately went, offered his services, and was desired, in return, to get ready in the part of Horatio, in the Fair Penitent.

The High Constable prohibited the performance, but Jefferson applied to Foote and Delaval, who suggested advertising "a play gratis" and themselves offered to collect "an optional contribution from every person" present. The scheme worked, and on the strength of his acting that night, Jefferson waited on Garrick, who, "as usual, advised a country excursion, with the promise of a future engagement." (From this stage onward the *Monthly Mirror* account must be heavily supplemented from several other narrative sources and by playbills and documentary evidence.)

Jefferson's friend Ellis Ackman procured him an engagement with a Kentish company, and he performed under the name of Burton. Acting at Rye, he met Elizabeth May, the daughter of a sea officer, who, before he would consent to a marriage, obliged Jefferson to enter into a bond of £500 that Elizabeth would never perform. Her father later was persuaded to cancel the bond, and Mrs. Jefferson acted

Harvard Theatre Collection

THOMAS JEFFERSON

engraving by Ridley, after Vanderburg

publicly for the first time as Lady Charlotte in *The Funeral* while she and Thomas were with Williams's company at Lewes.

While Thomas and Elizabeth Jefferson were performing in "Harlequin" with Phillips's company at Weybridge, Lacy the Drury Lane co-manager saw them and engaged them. On 24 October 1753 Jefferson first stepped onto the Drury Lane stage, as Vainlove in *The Old Bachelor*. From then until the end of the 1757–58 season the Jeffersons remained at Drury Lane. Thomas added to his repertoire Rossano in *The Fair Penitent*, Burgundy in *King Lear*, Handy in *The Man of Mode*, Trinobanitans in *Boadicea*, the Lieutenant of the Tower in *Richard III*, Essex in *King John*, an Aedile in *Coriolanus*, Silvius in *As You Like It*, Worthy in *The Recruiting Officer*, Indent in *The Fair Quaker of Deal*, Stanmore in *Oroonoko*, both Ratcliffe and Catesby in *Jane Shore*, Cash in *Every Man in His Humour*, an Irishman in *The Apprentice*, an Officer in *Tancred and Sigismunda*, the Music Master in *Catherine and Petruchio*, Cleomenes in *The Winter's Tale*, Dunelm in *Athelstan*, the Captain of the Guards in *Chrononhotonthologos*, Daniel in *The Conscious Lovers*, Brandon in *Henry VIII*, Guildenstern in *Hamlet*, Paris in *Romeo and Juliet*, Leander in *The Mock Doctor*, Burgundy in *King Lear*, Tranio in *Amphitrion*, a Mutineer in *Cato*, Lyon in *The Reprisal*, Robin in *The Author*, Gayless in *The Lying Valet*, Heli in *Tamerlane*, Bellford in *The Fatal Marriage*, Littlestock in *The Gamesters*, Pedro in *The Spanish Fryar*, Rhesus in *Agis*, Trueman in *The Squire of Alsatia*, and Clerimont in *The Miser*. James Winston in *The Theatric Tourist* (1805), claimed that Jefferson was also at Maidstone in 1757 with Wignall's sharing company.

The Drury Lane prompter Cross wrote in his diary on 16 September 1758: "Mr. [Henry] Woodward has enter'd into partnership with Mr. [Spranger] Barry in a new Theatre [Crow Street] in Ireland & has taken from us . . . Mr. Jefferson & Wife" and others. The decision to join the Dublin enterprise was fateful and nearly disastrous for the Jeffersons. They reserved passage across St George's Channel in a small vessel called the *Dublin Trader* which sailed from Parkgate on 27 October 1758 with 60 passengers and a crew of three. The ship struck a sandbar near the harbor. Sensing im-

pending disaster because of the dangerous overloading, the Jeffersons, John Arthur, Mrs Chambers, and others took a small boat and abandoned ship. That same evening the *Dublin Trader*, caught in a sudden autumn storm, sank with all on board, including Theophilus Cibber, Maddox the wire dancer, and other performers.

It is not known how the Jeffersons proceeded to Dublin, but the bills show that they acted successfully at Smock Alley Theatre in 1758–59 and then at the theatre in Crow Street in 1759–60, 1760–61, and 1761–62. Jefferson took professional excursions to Cork in August and October 1760 and in July and September 1761. Jefferson, and possibly Mrs Jefferson, may have performed elsewhere in the Irish provinces or in small towns in England before the record picks them up again, now in Exeter, where (Winston said) Jefferson joined the widow of "Harlequin" (probably George) Pitt in managing the Exeter Theatre in 1764. In 1765 Jefferson and Josiah Foote, a butcher of Exeter, purchased Mrs Pitt's property in the theatre and renewed the lease. Jefferson seems to have retained his interest at Exeter until about 1767.

Jefferson had frequently visited the theatre at Plymouth as a performer, and at the behest of the owner of the house, Anthony Kirby, he agreed to manage there. He was to receive, besides his salary as a performer, one third of the profits. On this understanding he sent crews of workmen from Dublin about 1764 to refurbish the interior. At that point Kirby died and the unsupervised carpenters ran up a debt of £261 in Jefferson's name. Finding himself so far involved, Jefferson purchased the scenery and wardrobe, secured a long lease, and remained sole proprietor at Plymouth until 1770 (or 1773, according to the *Monthly Mirror* article), when he sold one third to Joseph Foote and another third to a Mr Wolfe. The partnership continued according to Thomas Gilliland's *Dramatic Mirror* (1808) not very harmoniously until 1784, when Foote died, leaving half his share to Thomas Jefferson and Jefferson's son (George?) and the other half to Wolfe in trust. The bequest left Jefferson again the major shareholder in the Plymouth Theatre.

But the Plymouth managership, like the

earlier Exeter and later Richmond enterprises, was secondary, it seems, to Jefferson's ambitions as an actor. He returned to perform at Drury Lane in the fall of 1767. His wife Elizabeth had died at a rehearsal at Plymouth in July 1766 and he had married Rebecca Bainbridge in Exeter Cathedral on 27 December 1766.

On 17 September 1767 at Drury Lane Jefferson played Buckingham in *Richard III* "for the first Time, as a tryal, and is engaged for the next season.—Pretty well" wrote the prompter Hopkins in his stage diary. Jefferson continued "pretty well" in important supporting characters, with an occasional lead, for the next 11 seasons, until the end of the 1776–77 season.

In those seasons Jefferson repeated many of his old roles and added the following to his repertoire: Modely in *The School for Lovers*, Clytus in *The Rival Queens*, Colonel Briton in *The Wonder*, the King in *The King and the Miller of Mansfield*, Carlos in *The Revenge*, Lord Randolph in *Douglas*, Colonel Lambert in *The Hypocrite*, Megistus in *Zenobia*, Cubla in *Zingis*, Blanford in *Oroonoko*, Gratiano in *The Merchant of Venice*, Cloten in *Cymbeline*, Lord Trinket in *The Jealous Wife*, the Archbishop of York in *1 Henry IV*, Manly in *The Provok'd Husband*, Lord Morelove in *The Careless Husband*, Palamede in *The Frenchified Lady Never in Paris*, Renault in *Venice Preserv'd*, Trinculo in *The Tempest*, Careless in *The Committee*, Fairfield in *The Maid of the Mill*, Oswald in *King Arthur*, Mirabel in *The Way of the World*, Beau Clincher in *The Constant Couple*, Jarvis in *The Gamester*, Truman in *The Twin Rivals*, Johnson in *The Rehearsal*, Claudius in *Hamlet*, the Poet in *Timon of Athens*, Orsino in *Twelfth Night*, Aubrey in *The Fashionable Lover*, Charles in *Marplot in Lisbon*, Flip in *The Fair Quaker of Deal*, Wellbred in *Every Man in His Humour*, Iachimo in *Cymbeline*, Velasco in *Alonzo*, Colonel Rivers in *False Delicacy*, Don Frederick in *The Chances*, the Earl of Devon in *Alfred*, Strickland in *The Suspicious Husband*, Gloucester in *Jane Shore*, Captain Worthy in *The Fair Quaker*, Sunderland and Elder Rivers in *The Note of Hand*, the Emperor of Germany in *The Heroine of the Cave*, Goodwin in *The Brothers*, Jacques in *As You Like It*, Heartfree in *The Provok'd Wife*, Count Baldwin in *Isabella*, Methusius in *Timanthes*,

Justice Ballance in *The Recruiting Officer*, Leonato in *Much Ado about Nothing*, Tullus Hostilius in *The Roman Father*, and Major O'Flaherty in *The West Indian*.

In 1774, in conjunction with the dancer Simon Slingsby, Jefferson began to direct the affairs of the theatre at Richmond, Surrey, in summers, after the cessation of his duties at Drury Lane. But "at the close of the third season [1776], at the request of the proprietors, (who wished to dispose of their property)," they relinquished their lease, according to James Winston in *The Theatric Tourist*. (*The Monthly Mirror* says their tenure extended through 1777.) According to a letter dated 27 February 1804, from William Smith to James Winston, now in the Birmingham Public Library, both the theatre and the assembly rooms at Richmond were taken by Jefferson and Slingsby, for an annual rental of £250. "The assembly succeeded well—Theatre [a] loss—They held it 4 years, when they resigned it." Certainly Jefferson performed at Richmond through the summer of 1773, for Tate Wilkinson remembered having seen him there that summer.

Jefferson's well-wishers at Richmond had been sent for benefit tickets each summer to "his house, near the river," the only description on the playbills. Wilkinson and his wife spent a day there with Jefferson who "liked the good things of this world." The Wilkinsons found "excellent cheer and welcome."

With the retirement of his benefactor and friend Garrick and the cessation of his business at Richmond, Jefferson was not tied to London either in winter or summer. He went to Edinburgh's Theatre Royal in Shakespeare Square for the season from December through March, 1777–78, playing a round of 18 roles, several of which he had not tried in London: Benedick in *Much Ado about Nothing*, Don John in *The Chances*, Don Juan in *Braganza*, the title roles in *Hamlet* and *Othello*, Horatio in *The Fair Penitent*, Lord Ogleby in *The Clandestine Marriage*, Shylock in *The Merchant of Venice*, and Sir Charles Racket in *Marriage à la Mode*. From November 1778 until 8 March 1779 he and Josiah Foote rented the Bristol house for £300, but barely made expenses.

In 1780 he returned again at last to his own theatre in Frankfort Place, Plymouth. There he lived next door to the playhouse and did more managing than acting. But he still appeared fairly regularly there and at the circuit's satellite towns, like Exeter (where, in the winter of 1784–85 surviving notices show him, his wife, and Master and two Misses named Jefferson, and where he first essayed King Lear, on 17 December 1784). Playbills for Plymouth are scarce, but surviving ones throw up a few more of his late-learned roles: Sir Oliver Surface in *The School for Scandal*, Foigard in *The Beaux' Stratagem*, the High Priest in *The Death of Captain Cook*, Dick in *The Belle's Stratagem*.

In 1788 John Bernard acquired a share in the Plymouth partnership. Complicated squabbles and negotiations occurred, especially after Jefferson's gout began to curb his activity and after the entry into the concern of one Freeman (who later called himself Foote—no relation to Josiah or to Samuel). In or about 1796 Jefferson gave up all rights in the theatre and his properties there to Freeman for a clear annual benefit, which he continued to receive until near the end of his life.

Said the *Monthly Mirror* in 1804:

From severe and repeated fits of the gout for these last twelve years, he has been incapable of walking, but he appears every season before his friends, who always greet him heartily in such parts as he may with propriety be *seated*; in the sick King in the Second Part of Henry IV.—Lusignan, in *Zara*, and Lord Chalkstone, in *Lethe*. He also delivers occasional addresses, Shakespeare's Seven Ages, &c. &c. Independent of the gout, he enjoys a good state of health, is an excellent companion, and still retains a great portrait of his theatric ability. . . .

Winston in *The Theatric Tourist* confirmed that testimony, adding that the Earl of Mount Edgecombe generally was the patron of his benefit night—"always well, and fashionably attended, and we are happy to add [in 1805], the last two years have been particularly lucrative."

Yet nearly twenty years along in Jefferson's career Francis Gentleman in *The Dramatic Censor* (1770) had found him "faint indeed" in such young men as Myrtle in *The Conscious Lovers* and other impudent, dashing (or even sentimental) heroes. The clever Colonel Lambert in *The Hypocrite* should be "in the hands of some person possessing more vivacity than Mr. JEFFERSON." The daring Ranger in *The Suspicious Husband* was a "part above his cut." He was approved by Gentleman only as old men. Jefferson may have preferred himself in secondary young lovers, and Garrick may have preferred to shine in Archer against Jefferson's duller Aimwell, and Hopkins the prompter noted on 27 October 1775 that his Mirabel in *The Way of the World* was "hiss'd." Yet he earned Garrick's approbation and, apparently, good money. What purports to be a Drury Lane paylist of 13 February 1773 (reported by Lt Col Alex Fergusson in *Notes and Queries* in 1881) shows him making £8 per week. But that may have represented compensation for his wife as well. His salary evidently fluctuated, perhaps because in some seasons he may have had extra duties. James Winston, in his notes at the Folger Library, gives him £5 per week in 1773–74. The Drury Lane accounts at the Folger show him to have been earning £8 per week in February 1775 but only £4 in 1776–77. In some seasons he took a cash payment in lieu of a benefit night. In 1776–77 it was £80.

In 1805 the *Thespian Dictionary* gave him a patronizing valedictory:

many years an able assistant to the Drury Lane boards under Garrick; he possessed a pleasing countenance, strong expression, and compass of voice; was excellent in declamatory parts, and is a cheerful and entertaining companion: though latterly much debilitated with gout still his spirits are good; he is now obliged to be removed from his bed to his chair; is on the fund [i.e. drawing a pension] of Drury Lane, and has an annual benefit at Plymouth, where he has resided many years.

Inspection of the list of Jefferson's roles shows the breadth of his endeavors and also the growth, then decline (except in one line) of his capabilities. He was Garrick's foil in comedy after comedy for years. Michael Kelly thought him "very like" Garrick. "His eye was very expressive, and he was excessively proud to be considered like the great actor, of whom he spoke with enthusiasm." As Charles Dibdin remarked in his first *Tour*:

He was constantly, as everybody knows, the Colonel Briton to [Garrick's] Don Felix—the Claudio to his Benedick—the Aimwell to his Archer—the Frederick to his Don John—and I could name many other similar instances—nay when [Garrick] left off walking as Benedick in the Jubilee, he chose

Jefferson as the only person who could represent him. Jefferson is like Garrick in the face, and he gives you a strong idea of him altogether, only larger.

Thomas Jefferson had at least six children by his two wives. His first wife, Elizabeth May Jefferson, bore him two sons, Frank, who became an officer in the British Navy, and Joseph (d. 1832) the actor. (The date usually given for the birth of Joseph—1774—is obviously wrong. The well-documented death of his mother was in 1766. The name "John" which was furnished by S. W. Ryley in *The Itinerant* for one of these boys, is an error for Frank or Joseph.)

Nothing further is known of Frank. Joseph married the actress Euphemia Fortune, sister of the Esther Fortune who married the Bath actor William Warren. Joseph and Euphemia had seven children, all actors: Thomas, John, Joseph II, Hester, Euphemia, Elizabeth, and Mary Anne. The second Joseph Jefferson, by his wife the actress Cornelia Thomas (widow of Thomas Burke the actor), had two children, both actors, Joseph III and Cornelia. The third Joseph Jefferson (famed as Rip Van Winkle) by his first wife, Margaret Clements Lockyer, had five children, Charles, Thomas, Margaret Jane, Joseph Warren, and William Winter Jefferson. Margaret Jane Jefferson married B. L. Farjean, the novelist, and they, in turn, produced another line of artists, playwrights, poets, and composers close to the theatre in the first half of the twentieth century.

By his second wife, Rebecca Bainbridge Jefferson, the first Thomas Jefferson had at least five children. George, Elizabeth, and Frances Maria Jefferson were all actors, Frances Maria was the second wife of Samuel Butler, actor and manager. A "Harriet Mary Daugr of Thomas Jefferson by Rebecca his Wife" was baptized at St Paul, Covent Garden, on 2 March 1771, and a "Thomas Son of Thomas Jefferson" was buried there on 26 January 1776, according to the parish register.

The first Thomas Jefferson was seen, when immobilized by gout at Ripon in 1806, by the nineteenth-century comedian Drinkwater Meadows. Meadows was the source of a number of improbable anecdotes of Jefferson's early life, tales which he lived to tell to the third Joe Jefferson, and which some nineteenth-century biographers of that actor (including William Winter) have embraced. Some stories may have been inspired by Thomas Jefferson himself, for Michael Kelly remembered him as "a most entertaining man, and replete with anecdotes, which he told with peculiar humour," but Meadows has expanded and embroidered some. S. W. Riley's *Itinerant* and John Bernard's *Retrospections of the Stage* (1830) also contain anecdotes showing Jefferson's kindliness, independence of spirit, love of practical jokes, drollery, and ability as a trencherman.

A portrait of Jefferson, engraved by W. Ridley, after Vanderburg, was published as a plate to the *Monthly Mirror*, 1804. A copy by an unknown engraver, with the erroneous title, "Mr. Thomas Jefferson. Late President of the United States of America," was published as a plate to the *Hibernian Magazine*; another copy, also by an unknown engraver, was issued without a date.

Jefferson, Mrs Thomas the first, Elizabeth née May   *d. 1766, actress.*

Elizabeth May, daughter of an officer in the merchant marine, according to several accounts met the actor Thomas Jefferson at Rye, probably about 1751. Her father forbade the marriage until Jefferson submitted to a bond of £500 restraining him from putting his wife on the stage. Mr May was later persuaded to cancel the bond, and Mrs Jefferson appeared in a public performance for the first time at Lewes, as Lady Charlotte in *The Funeral*, according to James Winston in *The Theatric Tourist* (1805). The date is not known.

The young couple barnstormed for a while. They were seen by James Lacy, Garrick's associate at Drury Lane, when they acted at Weybridge. He brought them to London where, on 6 October 1753, Mrs Jefferson performed Anne Bullen in *Henry VIII*. She was slightly employed during the season, adding only Hippolita in *The Fairies*, the title role in *Britannia*, Sylvia in *The Recruiting Officer*, and some role unknown in *Fortunatas*. Repeating some of those parts during the five seasons following, Mrs Jefferson added only Lucinda in *The Conscious Lovers*, Isabella in *The Revenge*, Melissa in *The Lying Valet*, and Lady Macduff in *Macbeth*—not a very strenuous schedule if those were her only new roles.

At the end of the 1757–58 season Mr and

Mrs Thomas Jefferson were drawn away to Ireland by Henry Woodward, who had entered into a partnership with Spranger Barry at the Crow Street Theatre, Dublin. The Jeffersons had booked passage on the coastal vessel *Dublin Trader* which sailed from Parkgate on 27 October 1758 and foundered that same evening with the loss of all hands. The Jeffersons and some others, sensing the danger, had disembarked from the vessel before she cleared the harbor. The Jeffersons were performing in Dublin from 1758–59 through the 1761–62 season. Both acted at Cork in 1760 and 1761. They were at Exeter in 1764 and Plymouth the same year. In both places he was concerned in management as well as performance, and she acted in both theatres. It was at Plymouth, on 18 July 1766, that she suffered her ironic and poignant death. Thomas Davies in his *Memoirs of the Life of David Garrick* (1780) recounts how she was seized by a sudden pain in the midst of a hearty laugh, as she watched the rehearsal of a comedy. The comedian Moody caught her as she fell, and she expired at once. She was buried at St Andrew's, Plymouth, on 20 July 1766.

Davies also gives the most extended description of Mrs Jefferson's person and character:

the most complete figure in beauty of countenance and symmetry of form I ever beheld. This good woman (for she was as virtuous as she was fair) was so unaffected and simple in her behavior that she knew not her power of charming. Her beautiful figure, and majestic step, in the character of Anne Bullen, drew the admiration of all who saw her. She was very tall; and, had she been happy in abilities to act characters of consequence, she would have been an excellent partner in tragedy for Mr. Barry.

Tate Wilkinson concurred in the judgment: "She had one of the best dispositions that ever harboured in a human breast; and, more extraordinary, joined to that weakness, she was one of the most elegant women ever beheld."

Elizabeth May Jefferson bore her husband at least two children—Frank, who became a naval officer, and Joseph, who became a notable actor. The date (1774) usually given for the birth of Joseph Jefferson is obviously incorrect, for the fact that he was Elizabeth's child seems clear, both from family tradition and from the fact that he complained about poor treatment

from a stepmother, for Thomas Jefferson seems to have married only twice.

(The John Jefferson said by Samuel William Ryley in *The Itinerant*, 1808, to have been one of two sons of Thomas and Elizabeth Jefferson is really either Frank or Joseph or is entirely fictitious. He "was very tall, very slim, very sallow, and a very poor actor," and very religious and thus called "The Parson.")

Jefferson, Mrs Thomas the second, Rebecca, née Bainbridge [*fl.* 1776–1807], *actress.*

Rebecca Bainbridge (perhaps related to the theatrical family Bainbridge or Bambridge) was married to the actor-manager Thomas Jefferson at Exeter Cathedral on 27 December 1766, a little over five months after the death of his first wife.

If the second Mrs Jefferson had a provincial career as an actress before coming to London—and very likely she did—we have no record of it. Her metropolitan debut was at Drury Lane on 6 October 1773 as Miss Grantham in the afterpiece called *The Lyar.* The prompter Hopkins noted in his diary: ". . . a Small figure Not Handsome no Spirit & not at all like the Character. Some applause." Her husband was already at the theatre and a good friend of the manager, David Garrick, so perhaps influence had brought her there.

She remained only two seasons at Drury Lane, 1773–74 and 1774–75, presenting the following characters: Flavia in *Albumazar*, Clara in *Rule a Wife and Have a Wife*, Isabella in *The Wonder*, Mrs Strickland in *The Suspicious Husband*, Regan in *King Lear*, Mrs Fainall in *The Way of the World*, and Arabella in *The Committee*.

Thomas Jefferson remained one more season, 1775–76, at Drury Lane. Perhaps his wife was the Mrs Jefferson seen at the Birmingham theatre in the summer of 1776. She was probably in her husband's company at Plymouth from then on, with occasional time off for the births of her children. A surviving bill of 19 July 1780 shows her playing both Donna Clara in *The Duenna* and Lady Racket in *Three Weeks after Marriage.* Mrs Jefferson in 1788 was Dorcas in *Rosina*, Lady Harwin in *The Cottagers*, and Mrs Candour in *The School for Scandal.* After that her name does not occur in extant records again until the winter season of 1784–

85 at Exeter, where Jefferson was manager. Mr and Mrs Jefferson, a Master, and two Misses Jefferson were on the roster.

Thomas Jefferson died in January 1807. On 15 February the secretary of the Drury Lane Actors' Fund noted in its ledger: "Committee sent Mrs. Jefferson ten pounds," but with the apology that "the fund cou'd allow no more."

Rebecca Jefferson was the mother of George Jefferson, an actor, who assisted his father in managing the theatre at Plymouth; Frances, who married the actor-manager Samuel Butler; and Elizabeth, an actress. Two other children of the union probably died in infancy: the parish register of St Paul, Covent Garden, shows the baptism on 2 March 1771 of "Harriet Mary Daug! of Thomas Jefferson by Rebecca his Wife"; and on 26 January 1776, according to the burial register, "Thomas son of Thomas Jefferson" was buried.

Jeffries, Mrs ₁*fl. 1793*₁, *actress.*
Mrs Jeffries had an unspecified role in *The Generous Turk* at Astley's Amphitheatre on 3 April 1793.

Jeffries, Master ₁*fl. 1740*₁, *actor.*
Master Jeffries played a Dwarf in *Orpheus and the Death of Eurydice* at Bartholomew Fair on 23 August 1740.

Jeffries, ₁Tom?₁ ₁*fl. 1787?–1822*₁, *dancer, equestrian, clown.*
The Mr Jeffries who danced at the Royal Circus in April 1787, the "Young Jeffries" who was an equestrian in 1788, and the clown Jeffries who performed for Astley in the early 1790s were all, perhaps, Tom Jeffries, a clown mentioned in John Richardson's notice in *The Dictionary of National Biography.* An undated bill in the Minet Public Library for Hughes's Royal Circus, probably belonging to 1788 or thereabouts, said "Young" Jeffries "will ride full speed, one Foot on the saddle, the other in his Mouth." He was again referred to as Young Jeffries when Hughes and his troupe performed at Stourbridge Fair at Cambridge in 1788, after which no age indication was mentioned in the bills.

At Astley's Amphitheatre on 29 May 1792 Jeffries was the Clown in *Harlequin's Vagaries*; on 5 August he appeared as a Doctor in *Bagshot-Heath Camp*; on 31 January 1793 he was

in *La Forêt noire*; and on 22 August 1795 he played a Haymaker in *Harlequin Invincible.* The Royal Circus bill of 20 July 1797 listed Jeffries as an equestrian, and a bill of 1798 said that he and others in a show of horsemanship would perform still-vaulting and trampoline—presumably jumps onto or off their horses. The Circus bills for the summers of 1800 and 1801 again cited Jeffries as an equestrian.

The entry on the manager John Richardson in *The Dictionary of National Biography* states that Richardson appeared at Edmonton, just north of London, with Tom Jeffries, a clown of high repute from Astley's. In the same troupe were Edmund and Henry Kean, and though the exact date was not mentioned, it is likely the Edmonton engagement was around the turn of the century. Jefferies, along with his wife, performed in *The Jubilee of 1802* at the Royal Circus on 20 September 1802. Beginning in 1804–5 Jeffries was on the Covent Garden paylist at £1 10s. weekly, but by 1809–10 he was up to £3, and by 1814–15 he was earning £4. James Winston noted in his diary on 13 August 1820 that Jeffries had been hired to perform at Drury Lane for £4 weekly. In 1821–22 he was on the pay list at £3 weekly.

During the summers of 1807, 1808, and 1809 a Jeffries appeared at the Royal Circus, but if the bills were correct he was not our subject, for on 5 July 1807, when he served as clown to the horsemanship, he was advertised as making his first appearance in London. He was probably related to our subject. At some other point in 1807 the same or a different Jeffries was advertised at the Circus as an "eminent equilibrist" who would perform "on the moving ladder" and present *Horsemanship Burlesqued.* The Circus bill of 18 April 1808 cited a Jeffries as clown to the horsemanship and as the servant character Lounge in the pantomime *The Farmer's Boy.* He was advertised as making his first appearance on that stage. In July he was the clown in *Harlequin Robin and Robin Harlequin*, and a year later, on 10 July 1809, he served as "Clown to the Rope."

Jelkins, Mr ₁*fl. 1794–1795*₁, *dresser.*
The Covent Garden accounts for 1794–95 list a Mr Jelkins as a men's dresser at 9s. 6d. weekly.

Jell, Mrs ₁*fl. 1728*₁, *actress.*

Elvira in *The Spanish Fryar* was played by a Mrs Jell, otherwise unknown, in a performance at the Haymarket Theatre on 9 August 1728.

Jellico, Mr ₁*fl. 1782*₁, *actor.*

Mr Jellico acted Vincent in *An Adventure in St James's Park* and Toper in *The Beaux' Duel* at the Haymarket Theatre on 21 January 1782.

Jenings, Mr ₁*fl. 1782*₁, *tumbler.*

A Mr Jenings entertained with tumbling feats, along with Garman and Lonsdale, at Astley's Amphitheatre on 4 November 1782.

Jenings, Thomas *c. 1660–1734, singer.*

Thomas Jenings (or Jennings) was born about 1660, and by 23 April 1685, when James II was crowned, Jenings was a member of the Choir of Westminster. On 8 November 1697 he was sworn a Gospeller of the Chapel Royal, replacing Morgan Harris, and on 2 March 1700 he became a Gentleman of the Chapel. He died on 26 March 1734 at the age of 74 and was buried in the south cloister of Westminster Abbey three days later. Jenings had made his will on 11 February 1726 leaving his son John £5, his daughter Elinor (baptized Hellen) Shrider £5, and his second wife Elizabeth the remainder of his estate, including his house in Dean Yard. His children were to inherit the house after his wife's death. The will was proved on 27 March 1734.

Jenings had been married twice, both times to women named Elizabeth. His first wife was Elizabeth Loton of St Margaret, Westminster; their marriage allegation was dated 21 February 1688, when Elizabeth was about 25. She and Jenings had a daughter Hellen (also called Elinor), who was baptized on 1 May 1689; the notes to the published Abbey registers state that Hellen married the organ builder Christopher Shrider; she died on 21 March 1752. The discrepancy between the name in the will and the one in the parish register is obvious, but we take the Mrs Shrider in each document to have been the same woman.

The Jenings' son John was baptized at Westminster Abbey on 12 February 1691 and was buried there on 11 January 1737. Their son Thomas was baptized on 13 May 1693 and buried the following 24 November; Thomas

"Jenins" was buried at the Abbey on 29 July 1701; he may have been a son who was born sometimes after the first Thomas died in 1693.

Thomas Jenings's first wife died on 12 July 1720 and was buried on the sixteenth. The musician's will seems to indicate that he married again and that his second wife was also named Elizabeth. The will also suggests that Jenings and his second wife did not have any children.

Jenkes, Jonathan ₁*fl. 1671*₁, *musician.*

The Corporation of Music issued the following order on 4 August 1671:

Whereas John Beardnell, junior, Thomas Stone, Robert Perrey, Jonathan Jenkes, Rutland [*sic*], Francis Pendleton, Francis Cooper, Thomas Mathewes, Kingston [*sic*], doe take upon them to teach, practice and exercise musick in companyes or otherwise, to play at publique meetings without the approbation or lycence of the Marshall and Corporation of musick and in contempt of his Majesty's authority and the power granted to the said Marshall and Corporation under the Greate Seale of England. These are therefore to require you to apprehend and take into your custody the bodyes of the said John Beardnell and others abovenamed, and bring them before me to answer unto such things as shall be objected against them, and all mayors, sheriffs, justices of the peace, bayliffs, constables, headboroughs, and all other his Majesty's officers, civil and military, are required to bee ayding and assisting in the execution of this warrant.

Jenkins, Mr ₁*fl. 1731–1749*₁, *actor, singer.*

With comedians from the London patent theatres Mr Jenkins played Hunter in *Phebe* on 12 August 1731 and subsequent dates at the new theatre in Tottenham Court. On 8 September he appeared at Southwark Far as Trueman in *The London Merchant* and Gardener in *Merlin*. On 28 September at the same fair he acted Sir Philip in *A Bold Stroke for a Wife* at Fielding's booth.

Jenkins was with the Goodman's Fields troupe in 1731–32 and remained there through 1734–35. His first appearance was as Tradelove in *A Bold Stroke for a Wife*, after which he was seen in such parts as the Prince in *Tamerlane*, Edgar in *The Lover's Opera*, Indent in *The Fair Quaker of Deal*, Filch in *The Beggar's Opera*, Sir John in *The Devil to Pay*, the Captain in *Lady Jane Grey*, Dominico and a Witch in

Father Girard, Harry in *The Footman*, Ratcliff in *Richard III*, Basil in *The Stage Coach Opera*, Blandford in *Oroonoko* (for his benefit on 9 May 1732), a Yeoman in *Harlequin's Contrivance*, a Bravo in *The Inconstant*, Alonzo in *The Mourning Bride*, Ligarius in *Julius Caesar*, an Attendant in *The Amorous Sportsman*, Sanchio in *Rule a Wife and Have a Wife*, Squire Spendthrift in *The Decoy*, Clerimont in *The Mock Mason*, Tattle in *Love for Love* (for his shared benefit on 8 May 1733), Philip in *The Rival Queens*, Bernardo in *Hamlet*, Damon in *Damon and Phillida*, Monsieur in *Love Makes a Man*, a Witch and Donalbain in *Macbeth*, a Waterman in *Britannia*, Stanmore in *Oroonoko*, a Witch in *Jupiter and Io*, and Sir John in *The Relapse*. At the Haymarket on 28 May 1733 Jenkins was Leander in *The Provok'd Husband* and he was at Bartholomew Fair in August 1733 to play Octavian in *A Cure for Covetousness*.

His name disappeared from London bills after the end of the 1734–35 season, which leads us to believe that the Jenkins who performed in Dublin in 1736–37 and 1743–44 may have been our man. He is known to have played Macheath in *The Beggar's Opera* on 8 November 1737 at the Aungier Street Theatre, then Wildair in *The Constant Couple* on 11 November, and Comic in *The Rival Theatres* on 10 January 1737. The only other Dublin record we have of him is a shared benefit with three others at the Smock Alley Theatre on 2 February 1744.

The same performer, probably, acted Merry in *The Adventures of Sir Lubberly Lackbrains and His Man Blunderbuss* at Cushing's Bartholomew Fair booth on 23 August 1749.

Jenkins, Mr ₁*fl. 1782–1795*₁, *acrobat, equestrian, dancer.*
Master Jenkins was listed in the bills for Astley's Amphitheatre as an equestrian on 24 October and 2 November 1782 and as a tumbler on 27 September 1785. Thereafter "Master" became simply Jenkins in the bills, and it is likely that Jenkins was near his majority in 1785–86. Jenkins was once listed as "Clown to the Horsemanship" during the years that followed, and he was occasionally cast in dancing roles in pantomimes. Most of the bills were vague about his work, but some provided details. On 8 June 1789, for example, Jenkins was in an entertainment described as horse-

manship burlesqued and served as the clown; on 31 January 1793 he was an unnamed character in the pantomime *La Forêt noire*; and on 22 August 1795 he was cast as a Haymaker in *Harlequin Invincible*. The same Jenkins, most likely, had performed on a trampoline with a group of other acrobats at the Royal Circus in April 1787.

Jenkins, George ₁*fl. 1798*₁, *drummer.*
George Jenkins was listed as a double drummer in a performance of the *Messiah* at the Haymarket Theatre on 15 January 1798.

Jenkins, John *c. 1592?–1678, lutenist, bass viol player, composer.*
Andrew Ashbee in *Music and Letters* in 1965 provided much new information concerning the musician John Jenkins. Though Jenkins's birth is usually given as about 1592 in Maidstone, Kent, there is a good possibility, in view of statements made in her will by John's mother, that John was born after 1595. John's parents were "Henrie Gynken and Anne Jordaine," who were married on 28 June 1591 at All Saints Church in Maidstone. The registers there show the christening on 8 February 1594 of their daughter Mary and on 4 May 1595 of their son Henry. Anne Jenkins's will spoke of Henry as her eldest son, which fact suggests that either he was baptized long after his birth, or that his younger brother John was not born about 1592 but rather after 1595.

John is said to have become a musician early in life, and the wills of his father and mother would certainly suggest that though his father was a carpenter, John grew up in a musical household. Henry Jenkins's will (nuncupative) was dated 20 December 1617: "First he gave to his son Henry A Trebble Viall, to his son John A Pandore and to his son William A Trebble Viall. . . ." The probate date was 20 March 1618. John's mother's will, also nuncupative, was dated July 1621. She left her eldest son Henry a treble violin (viola) and 10*s*; to John, who by then was perhaps self-supporting or already under the protection of some noble family, she left 5*s*. To her son William she left another treble violin.

John Jenkins was patronized by one Dering or Deering and by Sir Hamon L'Estrange of Norfolk; the musician spent much of his life as one of Sir Hamon's family and became Roger

L'Estrange's teacher. About 1660 Jenkins replaced John "Coggeshall" among the theorbo
(lute) players in the King's Musick; on 16 June
1660 a warrant in the Lord Chamberlain's accounts lists Jenkins as replacing John "Cock-
shall, lute." Jenkins received annually the
usual livery fee of £16 2*s*. 6*d*., but Charles II
became increasingly slow in his payments as
the years went on. John's annual salary, in
addition to his livery fee, was £40.

An odd note in the accounts on 16 July
1661 has Jenkins receiving £20 for strings for
the 1660–61 period, but he is described not
as a string player but as a flutist, possibly an
error for lutenist. But the early records are
incomplete and Jenkins may have held two
appointments—one in the strings and one
among the "windy" instruments. By the 1670s
Jenkins was well along in years, and though
his fees continued he spent little time at court.
On 28 March 1676 an arrangement was made
for Richard Tomlinson to take the place of
either John Jenkins or William Howes—
whichever post should become vacant first. As
it turned out, on 19 April 1678 John Moss
was admitted to Jenkins's place in the private
music.

Much of Jenkins's time was given to musical
composition, and both Grove and Pulver discuss his music in some detail. His student
Roger North said that Jenkins became famous
before the Restoration, and his compositions
were much sought after. He was a lutenist,
North wrote, was very good upon the "consort" viol, and "used the lyra way upon the
[bass] violl." Though the court records are
mute, North said that Jenkins played the viol
da gamba for Charles I and "did wonders upon
an inconsiderable instrument." His compositions, North felt, showed his sense of humor,
and Jenkins "got the better of the dullness of
the old Fancys." Yet his music lacked the fire
and fury of the Italians and had repetitious
runs rather than Italian leaps; Jenkins did not
"dash upon harsh notes, as the Italians doe,
which makes their consorts more saporite [i.e.,
tasty]."

Jenkins was always a welcome visitor, according to North. In "most of his friends'
houses there was a chamber called by his
name," and he was regularly "courted to stay."
He was "a person of much easier temper than
any of his faculty, he was neither conceited nor

morose, but much a gentleman and had a very
good sort of wit, which served him in his
address and conversation, wherein he did not
please less than in his compositions." Indeed,
as he grew older and appeared less and less at
court despite his obligations there, "the Court
musitians had so much value for him that advantage was not taken, but he received his
salary, as they were payd."

Despite the fact that in his prime, which
was before the Restoration, he was an innova-
tor, introducing a "more aiery sort of composition," Jenkins's works lost favor. "For nothing is more fashion than musick," said Roger
North, "and the grand custome of all is to
effect novelty, and to goe from one thing to
another and despise the former." Jenkins simply fell out of fashion. During his later years
most of his time was spent with the family of
Sir Philip Wodehouse, Bart., at Kimberley,
Norfolk, where he died on 27 October 1678.
He was buried in Kimberly Church on 29
October. The inscription on his tombstone
seemed to set his birth in 1592, though perhaps the statement of his age at his death was
incorrect:

> *Vunder this stone Rare Jenkyns lie*
> *The Master of the Music Art*
> *Whom from y*ᵉ *Earth the God on High*
> *Call*ᵈ *unto Him to bear his part*
> *Aged eight six October twenty sev'n*
> *In Anno sev'nty eight he went to Heaven.*

Of Jenkins, the antiquarian Anthony Wood
said, "tho' a littel man, yet he had a greate
soule."

Jenkins, Thomas ₍*fl.* 1739₎, *musician.*

Thomas Jenkins was one of the original
members of the Royal Society of Musicians
when it was founded on 28 August 1739.

Jenkins, William ₍*fl.* 1749?–1789₎, *trumpeter.*

William Jenkins replaced William Douglass
as a trumpeter in the King's Musick perhaps
as early as 1749 or in 1754 (the Lord Chamberlain's accounts are not clear concerning the
date). He was mentioned as a member of the
royal musical establishment as late as 1759.
He was probably the trumpeter Jenkins cited
in the Drury Lane Theatre accounts as early as
13 November 1761, when he was paid 5*s*. for

playing in *The Coronation*, and we take him to have been the William Jenkins who performed at Drury Lane at least through 1775–76.

Mortimer's London Directory in 1763 gave his address as Duke's Court, Bow Street, Covent Garden. In 1769 Jenkins also played at Sadler's Wells. In 1784 he was one of the trumpeters in the Handel Memorial Concerts at Westminster Abbey and the Pantheon in May and June, and the following year he played in the St Paul's Concert in May. His last discovered notice was in May 1789, when he again performed in the St Paul's Concert.

Jenkins, William Kinnaird *b. c. 1778, dancing master, musician.*

On 6 April 1792 William Kinnaird Jenkins, the son of the dancing master George Jenkins of High Holborn, was apprenticed to the dancing master Colin Macrae for seven years. One may guess, therefore, that young Jenkins was then about 14 and had been born about 1778. William Kinnaird Jenkins was admitted a freeman in the Worshipfull Company of Musicians on 9 July 1799 and admitted to livery on 6 April 1803. In 1799 his address was No 15, Carlisle Street, Soho. Jenkins was a subscriber to the New Musical Fund in 1815 (and perhaps earlier and later), and he was still accepting apprentices—presumably as a dancing master—in 1844.

Jenkinson, Mr [*fl. 1796*], *actor, dancer?*

A Mr Jenkinson performed the role of Rabbit Man in *The Magician of the Rocks* at Astley's Amphitheatre, Westminster Bridge, on 16 May 1796. Playing the Postman in the same production was Joseph Jenkinson, probably a relative.

Jenkinson, Joseph *1770–1797, equestrian, actor, dancer, tumbler.*

By the time he was 15 in 1785, Joseph Jenkinson was performing at Astley's Amphitheatre, Westminster Bridge, advertised as "Master" Jenkinson. In 1788 he was still styled Master in the bills, but by 1791 he was called Mr Jenkinson. In the summer that year he danced at Astley's in *The Irish Fair* and played Harlequin in *The Emperor of the Moon*. In 1792 he performed the Old Man in *Harlequin's Vagaries*, and in 1793 he offered feats of horsemanship. In August 1795 he played Pantaloon

in *Harlequin Invincible*, a production in which a Mrs Jenkinson, probably his wife, danced as one of the Haymakers. He performed the Postman in *The Magician of the Rocks* on 16 May 1796, in which he or another Mr Jenkinson was Rabbit Man.

In 1795 Jenkinson also served as ring clown at the amphitheatre opened by Benjamin Handy at the Lyceum in the Strand. He also was a member of the Royal Circus company by that year. While performing on the trampoline at the Royal Circus for Mrs Parker's benefit in October 1797, he "overthrew himself"—reported De Castro in his *Memoirs*—and broke his breastbone and spinal cord. A few days later, on 16 October, he died, at the age of 27, leaving a widow and three children. He was buried at Christ Church, Lambeth, where a stone was erected to his memory. The Master and Miss Jenkinson who danced at the Haymarket Theatre in 1801 and at the Royal Circus in 1803 and 1804 were probably his children. A child named Jenkinson was on the Covent Garden company list in 1800–1801.

Jenkinson, Mrs Joseph [*fl. 1795–1797*], *dancer. See* JENKINSON, JOSEPH.

Jenkinson, William *1765–c. 1829, bassoonist, drummer.*

William Jenkinson was baptized at Hough on 13 September 1765, the son of John Jenkinson by his wife Frances. Perhaps his father was the musical-instrument maker, J. Jenkinson, who about 1797 had a shop at No 39, Fashion Street, Spitalfields, and printed J. A. Parrin's song *Come Slumbers steal me soft away*.

At the age of 18 William Jenkinson played the bassoon in the Handel Memorial Concerts at Westminster Abbey and the Pantheon in May and June 1784. He was paid £4 4s. as a bassoonist in the concerts presented by the Academy of Ancient Music in 1787–88. When recommended by Robert Munro for membership in the Royal Society of Musicians in August 1790, Jenkinson was described as a single man, "aged twenty four years last August," very sober and industrious, a performer on the bassoon, who belonged to the third regiment of guards and had engagements at Ranelagh Gardens and the Royal Circus. On 7 November 1790 he was unanimously elected to the Society. He was appointed to play the bassoon at the May concerts at St Paul's given by the Society every year from 1791 through 1800, except in 1797 and 1800, when he played the kettledrum. In the latter year he also served as a Governor of the Society.

In 1793 Jenkinson played bassoon at the Oxford Meeting. In Doane's *Musical Directory* of 1794 his address was given as No 2, Charlotte Street, Pimlico, and he was described as a bassoonist and drummer with engagements at the places mentioned above, as well as in the Covent Garden oratorios, in which he continued to perform as a drummer every spring through 1800. Jenkinson played at the Worcester concerts in 1803. He was on the orchestra list as a drummer at the King's Theatre in 1817 and perhaps had been engaged there in earlier years.

On 2 December 1827, Jenkinson applied for aid from the Royal Society of Musicians, stating in his petition that he was a widower, over 62 years old, "and totally incapable of further exertion for support, his sight, hearing, and limbs failing." That day the Society granted him £40 3*s*. per year. The Society's minute books record a grant to him of £4 on 4 January 1829, the last mention of Jenkinson, who presumably died soon after.

Jenning[s?], Mr [*fl.* 1673–1674], *actor.*
The promptbook for Shirley's *The Maides Revenge* at Harvard contains a cropped note indicating that a Mr Jenning or Jennings played a Servant. The work was probably presented by the King's Company at Lincoln's Inn Fields Theatre in 1673–74, before the troupe moved to their new Drury Lane playhouse. Perhaps the actor was related to the Mrs Jennings who played for the Duke's Company in the 1660s.

Jennings, Mr [*fl.* 1778–1779], *actor.*
Announced as from Dublin, a provincial actor named Jennings made his debut at the Theatre Royal, Edinburgh, on 14 November 1778 as Touchstone in *As You Like It*. At Edinburgh that winter, he acted among other roles Acres in *The Rivals*, Filch in *The Beggar's Opera*, Gage in *The Camp*, Hodge in *Love in a Village*, Ralph in *The Maid of the Mill*, and Young Philpot in *The Citizen*. On 28 November 1778 he played Oliver Surface in Scotland's first pro-

duction of *The School for Scandal*. He remained at Edinburgh through August 1779.

Jennings made his first appearance in London at Drury Lane Theatre on 12 October 1779 as Mungo in *The Padlock* (a role he had acted at Edinburgh on 28 November 1778). The *Morning Chronicle* next day reported that "The new Mungo, like all country bred actors, did too much for the part, and was infinitely too redundant in his action." That proved to be his only London performance, after which, presumably, he returned to anonymity in the provinces.

Jennings, Mr [*fl.* 1782–1783], *house servant?*
A Mr Jennings shared benefit tickets with minor house servants at Covent Garden Theatre on 29 May 1782 and 4 June 1783.

Jennings, Mrs [*fl.* 1661–1671], *actress.*
Mrs Jennings was one of Sir William Davenant's original group of eight actresses, and one supposes she was performing as early as 1661 even if no records of her acting that year have been found. She played Rosabella in *Ignoramus* on 1 November 1662 at court with the Duke's Company. The next mention of her was on 6 February 1668, when she acted Ariana in *She Wou'd If She Cou'd* at the Lincoln's Inn Fields playhouse. She was Mrs Philadelphia in *Mr Anthony* in December 1669, Galatea in *The Forc'd Marriage* in September 1670, and Phedima in *Cambyses* on 10 January 1671 and subsequent dates. She may have played that last part at Oxford the following 12 July. The prompter Downes said that after that Mrs Jennings was "by force of Love . . . Erept the Stage."

"Jenny, Dear." *See* FOURMANTEL, CATHERINE.

Jenny, Miss. *See* JONES, JANE.

Jenu, Mr [*fl.* 1794–1795], *carpenter.*
A note in the Drury Lane accounts on 2 September 1794 indicates a payment of £10 10*s*. to the master carpenter Richard Jacobs for Jenu and Beeton, evidently his helpers, for five weeks of work. On 15 October 1795 Jenu, cited as a carpenter in the accounts, was given a gift, paid £1 1*s*., and discharged.

Jermaine, Mr [*fl. 1681*], *actor.*

Mr Jermaine played Sir Walter Wiseacre in *Sir Barnaby Whigg* with the King's Company at Drury Lane in the summer of 1681. (*The London Stage* dating—of late October 1681— is, according to Robert Hume, too late.)

Jerman, Roger [*fl. 1657?–1670*], *carpenter.*

When *London's Triumphs* by John Tatham was published about 1657, the edition contained a note stating that "The several Fabricks and Structures of the whole daies Tryumph, were performed by the Industry of Mr German." "German" was almost certainly a variant spelling of Jarman or Jerman, and we know that there were at least three people of that name active in London in connection with theatres and Lord Mayor's shows. Anthony Jarman was a London carpenter and held one share of the lease on the Fortune Theatre as of 20 May 1622. Edward Jarman was the City Surveyor and helped produce the Lord Mayor's show in 1650. Roger Jerman, who may well be the man referred to in connection with *London's Triumphs* above, was cited in John Ogilby's *Relation of His Majesties Entertainment* in 1661 as one of the carpenters who helped prepare the entertainment for the coronation of Charles II.

Roger Jerman held a long-term lease on the property at the south end of Dorset Garden, which on 11 August 1670 he leased to Henry Harris and John Roffey of the Duke's Company. The Dorset Garden Theatre was built on the site. In the documents concerning the property, as examined by Leslie Hotson in *The Commonwealth and Restoration Stage*, Jerman is described as a carpenter.

Jermoli, Guglielmo [*fl. 1777–1779*], *singer.*

The tenor Guglielmo Jermoli made his first appearance at the King's Theatre on 4 November 1777 singing the Cavaliere della Piuma in *Le due contesse*, a burletta by Paisiello. His manner of singing, according to Dr Burney, "more resembled that of a German, than an Italian; but neither in voice, taste, nor action, did his performance ever surpass mediocrity." Signora Jermoli, no doubt his wife, sang Livietta in the same production.

Jermoli's other roles at the King's in 1777–

78 included Il Cavaliere in *Vittorina*, Conte Enrico in *La vera costanza*, Giannino in *L'amore artigiano*, a principal character in *Il marchese villano* (for his benefit on 26 March 1778, when tickets could be had at his lodgings, No 29, Cockspur Street, Charing Cross), a principal character in *La buona figliuola*, and Faustino in *L'amore soldato*.

In 1778–79, his second and last season at the King's, Jermoli appeared as Gervasio in *L'Avaro deluso*, principal characters in *La Frascatana* and *La buona figliuola*, and Antonio d'Ercilla in *La governante*. Burney found him "still more feeble [than Trebbi], and less in favour with the public."

Jermoli, Signora Guglielmo [*fl. 1777–1779*], *singer, dancer.*

Signora Jermoli made her first appearance at the King's Theatre on 4 November 1777, singing Livietta in *Le due contesse*. Also performing in that burletta was Guglielmo Jermoli, presumably her husband. Her other roles that season included principal characters in *Il marchese villano* and *La buona figliuola*, Lisandrina in *L'amore soldato*, and Angiolina in *L'amore artigiano*. On 10 March 1778, Signora Jermoli, in her character of Angiolina, also danced a minuet with Simonet in place of Mlle Baccelli, who was ill.

In 1778–79 at the King's she sang Modesta in *L'Avaro deluso*, principal characters in *La Frascatana* and *La buona figliuola*, and Fatima in *Zemira e Azore*.

Jerrold, Miss *b. 1777, actress.*

Announced as a child of three, Miss Jerrold spoke the prologue to *The Suspicious Husband* on 19 April 1780 at the Crown Inn, Islington, where her parents were playing a brief engagement. Her father was the provincial actor and manager Samuel Jerrold and her mother was his first wife, an actress born Simpson. Miss Jerrold was sister to Robert Jerrold, who performed at the Crown Inn that winter at the age of seven and later acted in the provinces under the name of Fitzgerald. Another brother, Charles, became a naval officer. She was also half-sister to Douglas William Jerrold, the author of *Black-Eyed Susan* and other theatrical pieces, who was one of the children of Samuel Jerrold by his second wife Mary, née Reid.

Jerrold, Robert, stage name Fitzgerald
1773–1818, actor, manager.

Robert Jerrold, born in 1773, was the elder and evidently illegitimate son of the provincial actor and manager Samuel Jerrold by his first wife (née Simpson) also a provincial performer. Their other son, Charles Jerrold, became an officer in the Royal Navy. When about seven years old, Master Robert spoke the prologue to *The West Indian* on 29 Feburary 1780 at the Crown Inn, Islington, where his mother and father were playing for a while with a strolling company. On 6 March he performed the young Duke of York in *Richard III* and then was seen as Peter in *Romeo and Juliet*. At the Jerrolds' benefit on 19 April 1780, Robert's name did not appear in the bill, but his sister, a child of three, spoke the prologue to *The Suspicious Husband.*

So far as can be determined, Robert Jerrold did not again appear on the London stage either under his given name or as Fitzgerald, the stage name he later assumed. He was, according to Thomas Dibdin, a young man working in 1789 in the Dover company under the management of Richland, who was his uncle and therefore probably the husband of Samuel Jerrold's sister. Jerrold acted in his father's Kent company and at Hull beginning 27 December 1797. In the nineteenth century he spent his career on the Norwich and York circuit. He joined the Norwich company by 1801. There, according to Joe Cowell (*Thirty Years Passed among the Players of England and America*, 1824), "ashamed of his father and his name," Jerrold adopted the stage name of Fitzgerald.

As Fitzgerald he managed for a while at York and acted at Norwich until his death. In June 1813 he bought the Sheerness theatre from his father.

Robert Jerrold died while performing at Wakefield on 31 May 1818, at the age of 45, and was buried there in St John's church. (According to William Blanchard Jerrold's biography of Douglas William Jerrold, Robert died on his way from Sheffield to Leeds.)

A Mrs Fitzgerald, no doubt Robert's wife, was an actress at Norwich from 1802 to 1828. Robert was also half brother to the nineteenth-century dramatist and man of letters, Douglas William Jerrold, author of *Black Eyed Susan*,

who was the eldest child of Samuel Jerrold by his second wife Mary, née Reid.

Jerrold, Samuel   *1749–1820, actor, manager.*

Samuel Jerrold, who passed most of his career as a provincial manager, was born in 1749, the son of a horse dealer in Hackney and reputedly descendant of landed gentry. He was supposed to have remarked bitterly one time about playing in a barn on an estate his ancestors had once owned.

With his first wife (née Simpson) and young family, Jerrold acted in a company which played at the Crown Inn, Islington, between February and April 1780. Among his roles there were Belcour in *The West Indian* and Sir John Trotley in *Bon Ton* on 29 February, Richard III on 6 March, Mercutio in *Romeo and Juliet* on 13 March, Marplot in *The Busy Body* and Colonel Tamper in *The Deuce is in Him* on 17 March, Gauge in *The Camp* on 27 March, and Ranger in *The Suspicious Husband*, to his wife's Clarinda, for their benefit on 19 April, when their daughter spoke the prologue. Their son Robert Jerrold also appeared in children's roles during that engagement.

By 1789 the Jerrolds were with the Dover company under the management of Richland, who evidently was the husband of Samuel's sister. Jerrold soon became manager of a company at Eastbourne and toured Kent. In December 1792 he acted at Gainsborough and in July 1795 at South Shields. In May 1798 he brought his company to play at the Wheatley Riding School in Greenwich. Jerrold was said to appear on the stage in every role wearing shoes which once belonged to Garrick. Also in the 1790s he operated a barn theatre at Cranbrook, and lived in the nearby village of Willsley.

In January 1807 Jerrold took over the lease of the theatre at Sheerness, which he operated until he sold it to his son Robert in 1813. The family moved to London in 1816, where the second Mrs Jerrold and two daughters acted for a while, though Jerrold seems to have retired. He died in London in January 1820, at the age of 70, and was buried at St Paul, Covent Garden, on 6 February.

By his first wife, who died about 1792, Jerrold had at least three children: Robert Jerrold (1773–1818), who acted under the name of Fitzgerald because he was ashamed of his reputed illegitimacy; Charles Jerrold, who became a naval officer and died about 1846; and a daughter, born 1777, who at the age of three spoke the prologue at the Crown Inn in April 1780.

Jerrold married his second wife, the young actress Mary Reid, who was half his age, at Wirksworth, Derbyshire, on 20 April 1794. She died at Liverpool in 1851. By her, Jerrold became the patriarch of a large and far-reaching theatrical family. Their son Douglass William Jerrold (1803–1857) was a successful author, best known perhaps for his *Black Eyed Susan*; he married the actress Mary Swann (1804–1859) and their children included Jane Matilda Jerrold, who married the author Henry Mayhew (1812–1887); William Blanchard Jerrold (1826–1884), author, who married Lily Blanchard (daughter of Samuel Laman Blanchard); and the author Thomas Serle Jerrold (1833–1919), who married the author Jane Matilda Copeland (1835–1919).

Samuel and Mary Jerrold's other children, all of whom became performers, included Henry Jerrold; Jane Matilda Jerrold, who married the actor W. J. Hammond; and Elizabeth Sarah Jerrold, who married the actor William Robert Copeland. Information about the nineteenth- and twentieth-century Jerrolds can be found in William Blanchard Jerrold's *The Life of Douglas Jerrold* (1859), Walter Jerrold's *Douglas Jerrold, Dramatist and Wit* (1914), and Richard M. Kelly's *Douglas Jerrold* (1972). Douglas William Jerrold and his son William Blanchard Jerrold are also noticed in *The Dictionary of National Biography*.

Jerrold, Mrs Samuel the first, Elizabeth, née Simpson *d. c. 1792, actress.*

A provincial actress named Elizabeth Simpson was the first wife of the Kent actor-manager Samuel Jerrold. Their son Robert Jerrold, born in 1773, presumably was illegitimate and later changed his name to Fitzgerald when he joined the York and Norwich circuit about 1801. A second son, Charles Jerrold, became a naval officer and died about 1846. A daughter, Miss Jerrold, in 1780 spoke a prologue at the age of three at the Crown Inn, Islington,

and no doubt made later provincial appearances with her parents.

Mrs Jerrold acted with her husband at the Crown Inn, Islington, between 29 February and 19 April 1780. Her roles there included Lady Minikin in *Bon Ton*, Charlotte Rusport in *The West Indian*, Tagg in *Miss in Her Teens*, the Queen in *Richard III*, Lady Capulet in *Romeo and Juliet*, Patch in *The Busy Body*, Emily in *The Deuce is in Him*, Nelly in *The Camp*, Millwood in *The London Merchant*, Mrs Sullen in *The Beaux' Stratagem*, and, for her benefit with her husband on 19 April 1780, Clarinda in *The Suspicious Husband*, when Samuel acted Ranger and their daughter spoke the prologue.

No doubt she acted in her husband's company around Eastbourne, Kent, and at Cranbrook, where he had converted a barn into a theatre. They lived in the small nearby village of Willsley. Mrs Jerrold died about 1792; and her husband married the young actress Mary Reid in 1794.

The first Mrs Jerrold possibly was one of the five daughters of the Drury Lane actress Mrs Elizabeth Simson (*recte* Simpson) and her actor-husband, who died in 1758, but we have no real evidence to that effect. If she was the Simpsons's daughter, however, she was also sister to the actor John Simson (named Simpson in his will); he died at Madras, India, about 1770. One of her sisters would have been the actress Mary Simson (c. 1752–1807), who later became Mrs Charles Fleetwood, the younger, and then Mrs White.

Jerrold, Mrs Samuel the second, Mary, née Reid *1772–1851, actress, singer.*

The provincial actress Mary Reid, at the age of 22, became on 20 April 1794 at Wirksworth, Derbyshire, the second wife of Samuel Jerrold, an actor-manager more than twice her age. He managed a company in the Eastbourne area of Kent and had a small barn theatre at Cranbrook; they lived, when not on tour, in the village of Willsley. No doubt Mrs Jerrold performed regularly in the company. At South Shields on 15 July 1795 her name was in the bills for Dame Dunkley in *The Wheel of Fortune* and Nelly in *No Song No Supper*.

At the Wheatley Riding School in Greenwich, where Jerrold brought his company for a few nights in May 1798, she is known to have played Miss Newcastle in *She Stoops to Conquer* and Fringe in *The Agreeable Surprise* on the seventeenth.

During a brief visit to London by the Jerrolds in 1803, their son Douglas William Jerrold was born on 3 January; eventually he became a successful dramatist and man of letters. In 1807 the Jerrolds moved to the seaport of Blue Town, near Sheerness, where they operated a theatre for six years. Mrs Reid, Mary Jerrold's mother, assisted in the box office and cared for her daughter's children. When they settled in London after 1813, Mrs Jerrold and two daughters, Jane Matilda and Elizabeth Sarah, became employed as performers for several years; Mrs Jerrold's name was on the Lyceum company lists in the summer of 1817 and 1818.

Mary Jerrold died at Liverpool on 31 December 1851 at the age of 79, according to her great-grandson Walter Jerrold's biography of his grandfather, *Douglas Jerrold, Dramatist and Wit* (1914). The *Dramatic Register* (1852) states that she died on 1 January 1852, nearly 76. Her husband had died at London 31 years earlier, in 1820. In his notice will be found information on their children and grandchildren, who formed a large theatrical and literary network in the nineteenth and twentieth centuries.

"Jerry Sneak." *See* RUSSELL, SAMUEL THOMAS.

Jervais. *See* JARVIS.

Jervis. *See* JARVIS.

Jevon, Mr [*fl.* 1733], *actor.*
Mr Jevon played the Son in *Love Runs All Dangers* at the Haymarket Theatre from 20 to 26 March 1733.

Jevon, Mrs [*fl.* 1720], *actress.*
Mrs Jevon played Clarinna in *Cymbeline* at Lincoln's Inn Fields Theatre on 14 March 1720, replacing Mrs Gulick. When the play was presented again on 9 June, Mrs Jevon's role was omitted.

Jevon, Thomas *1652–1688, actor, dancer, singer, playwright.*

Thomas Jevon was born in 1652, became a dancing master, and may have become a member of the Duke's Company at the Dorset Garden Theatre by the 1673–74 season. His first recorded appearance was in *The Conquest of China*, which was performed on 28 May 1675. The prompter Downes recorded an anecdote concerning Jevon's performance in Settle's play:

Mr Jevon Acting a Chinese Prince and Commander in it, and being in the Battle, [was] Vanquisht by the Tartars; he was by his Part to fall upon the point of his Sword and Kill himself, rather than be a Prisoner by the Tartars: Mr Jevon instead of falling on the point of his Sword, laid it in the Scabbard at length upon the Ground and fell upon't, saying, now I am Dead; which put the Author into such a Fret, it made him speak Treble instead of Double. Jevons answer was; did not you bid me fall upon my Sword.

Thereafter Jevon, a low comedian by nature, was cast in serious roles at a playwright's peril.

Before the union of the Duke's and King's companies in 1682 Jevon is known to have acted Osric in *Hamlet*, Young Bellair in *The Man of Mode*, Hazard in *The Virtuoso*, Harry in *Madame Fickle*, Agrippa in *Antony and Cleopatra*, Don Antonio in *The Rover*, Sneak in *The Fond Husband*, Avarito in *The French Conjurer*, Melibeus in *The Constant Nymph*, Eumenes in *The Siege of Babylon*, the Poet in *Timon of Athens*, Caper in *Friendship in Fashion*, Sir Frolick Whimsey in *The Virtuous Wife*, Cinna in *Caius Marius*, Escalus in *The Loyal General*, Fourbin in *The Soldier's Fortune*, Trickwell in *The Revenge*, Fabritius in *Lucius Junius Brutus*, the Gentleman Usher in *King Lear*, Furnish in *Mr Turbulent*, Sir Paul Eitherside in *The Royalist*, and Fopington in *The City Heiress*. In March 1682, not long before the companies joined, Jevon spoke the epilogue to *Like Father, Like Son*. He soon became a popular speaker of prologues and epilogues and is said to have introduced into them snatches of songs and dances.

With the United Company, usually at Drury Lane but occasionally at Dorset Garden, Jevon played a Swordsman in *A King and No King*, Mayenne in *The Duke of Guise*, probably Fourbin in *The Atheist*, Gillet in *Dame Dobson*, Cinna the Poet in *Julius Caesar*, Master Clack in *The Jovial Crew*, Widgine in *The Northern Lass*, Quick-Silver in *The Cuckold's Haven*, Franvil in *The Commonwealth of Women*, Scaramouch in Mountfort's *Dr Faustus*, Frisco in *The Banditti*, Jobson in his own play *The Devil of a Wife* (which opened at Dorset Garden on 4 March 1686), Bearjest in *The Luckey Chance*, Woodly in *Epsom Wells*, Harlequin in *The Emperor of the Moon*, a Soldier in *The Injured Lovers*, Toby in *A Fool's Preferment*, and Belfond Senior in *The Squire of Alsatia*.

In his early version of his *Satyr on the Players* about 1684 Gould said

Jeverns chief Bus'ness is to swear and eat
He'l turn procurer for a Dish of meat
Else the poor hungry Ruffian must I fear
Live on Gray Pease and Salt for half a year

The revised version some years later was more vicious:

A Third, a punning, drolling, bant'ring Ass,
Cocks up, and fain wou'd for an Author pass,
His Face for Farce Nature at first design'd,
And match it, too, with as Burlesque a Mind:
Made him, as vilely born, so careless bred,
And gave Him Heels of Cork, but Brains of Lead.

In *The Restoration Theatre* Montague Summers claimed that Jevon, Thomas Shadwell's brother-in-law, was a Catholic and in 1680 was living in the parish of St Dunstan in the West. In *Notes and Queries* in June 1890 W. R. Tate cited information on Jevon's tombstone to the effect that Jevon died on 20 December 1688 at the age of 36. Lysons recorded in his *Environs of London* that Jevon was buried on 24 December in Hampstead churchyard. His tombstone was removed by the late eighteenth century. In the Hampstead registers Lysons found the record of the burial of an infant, Thomas Jevon, possibly the comedian's son, on 13 September 1684. But the name Jevon (with its many variants, such as Jevan, Gevon, Jevorn, etc.) was quite common in the seventeenth century.

After his death Jevon was remembered in a number of books. Gildon said in his *Lives and Characters* in 1699 that Jevon, "A Dancing-Master and Player, was a Man of uncommon Activity." In his *Letters from the Dead* in 1701 Tom Brown, writing to the deceased Joe Haines, said, "your friend Mr. *Jevon* wou'd hang himself to see how much the famous Mr.

Harvey exceeds him in the Ladder-dance." The biography of Joe Haines (1701), possibly written by the actor Tobias Thomas, contains a lengthy but questionable anecdote concerning Haines and Jevon. The pair pretended to be a squabbling Frenchman (Haines) and an English country gentleman, newly come to town (Jevon). They acted out a growing antagonism, attracting a crowd which followed them to Tottenham Court and then to a Saw Pit in Hampstead, into which the two combatants jumped to fight, out of sight of the mob. When the crowd discovered that the pair were friends perpetrating an April Fool's joke, they beat Haines and Jevon all the way home. Another anecdote about Jevon, probably no more authentic, was told in *The Egotist* in 1743. Jevon walked into an elegant "Club of his Acquaintance with dirty Shoes, contentedly took a clean Napkin from the table to wipe them; when the Waiter desiring him to stay till he could fetch him a coarse Cloth, *Jevon* gently replied, No! no! thank you, my good Lad; this will serve me well enough."

Jevon's greatest contribution to the theatre was probably not his low-comedy acting but his play, *The Devil of a Wife*, which, as the *Biographia Dramatica* (1812) said, had "since undergone almost as many transformations as the Brahmins of the East Indies fable their deity Vishnou to have passed through." The most popular eighteenth-century adaptation of Jevon's play was *The Devil to Pay*, by Charles Coffey.

"Jew." *See* BARRETT, JOHN *d. 1795,* and DAVIS, "JEW."

Jewell, William   *c. 1729–1828, treasurer, general manager.*
Although William Jewell served as treasurer for several London theatres over a period of 47 years, little is known of his personal life save his appointments, his numerous benefits, his devotion to Samuel Foote, and his marriage. By the summer of 1765 Jewell was the treasurer of Foote's Haymarket Theatre, taking a benefit in that capacity on 8 August. He continued in that position for many years after Foote's death in 1777, under the management of the Colmans through the summer of 1804, until he was replaced by D. Morris in 1805.

In 1781–82 Jewell also became treasurer for

the opera at the King's Theatre in the Haymarket, a position he retained until about 1813, including the season 1791–92, when the opera played at the Pantheon. Sometimes at the King's Theatre he was referred to as the general manager or director. In July 1797 the *Monthly Mirror* suggested that the troublesome problems at the opera would be rectified greatly if Jewell were made the sole manager, since he had "the confidence of the nobility, and the love of every person employed." A dispute with William Taylor, the opera manager, in 1807 brought about Jewell's discharge but he was reinstated as the result of arbitration between Taylor and Edmund Waters; the decision by the arbitrators William Ogilvie and the Marquis of Headfort was published on 9 January 1808. In 1795–96 his salary at the King's Theatre was £500 per year. His earnings at the Haymarket are unknown to us, but he must have profited well at his regular late-summer benefits because of his influential position.

Jewell was Foote's faithful attendant during the latter's confinement after the tragic fall from a horse in February 1766 which resulted in the loss of his leg. In December 1773 Jewell saved Foote's life by dragging him from a burning bed in his Dublin lodgings. "The bed was burnt and poor Jewel's hands most miserably scorched," Foote wrote to Garrick on the thirty-first of that month. It was in large measure Jewell's testimony in the Court of the King's Bench on 9 December 1776, when he affirmed that Foote had not been in London at the time of the manager's alleged homosexual attack on John Sangster, which was responsible for Foote's acquittal. It was Jewell who brought Foote's body back to London after his death at Dover on 21 October 1777, arranged for his burial in Westminster Abbey, and raised a tablet to his memory in St Mary's Church, Dover. Jewell has been suggested as the author of *Aristophanes*, a collection of witticisms and jests attributed to Foote and others which was published anonymously in 1778.

In his will, dated 13 August 1768 and proved on 22 October 1779, Foote was generous to Jewell, charging "my Theatre Royal in the Haymarket and all my buildings thereto belonging with the payment of ten shillings and six pence every night that any theatrical or other performances shall be publickly exhib-

ited to be paid nightly to my Treasurer Wm. Jewell which I give him for his own use during my term." But that directive, written 13 years before Foote's death, may not have profited Jewell and perhaps became void when Foote leased away many of his theatrical prerogatives to Colman in 1776–77. Foote also gave Jewell the right to a rent-free benefit every year, a provision which the executors were charged to write into any manager's contract. Also, Jewell was extended the right to sell wine, tea, and fruit at the theatre without paying fees. Foote directed that if both his "Natural Children" Francis and George Foote should die before Jewell did his treasurer should receive £1000 from his bequests to them.

According to William Cooke, one of Foote's early biographers, Jewell took as a ward one of Foote's illegitimate sons. If so, a possible irony is raised, for in January 1769 at St Martin-in-the-Fields, Jewell had married the young Haymarket actress Ann Edwards, whom Boswell had called "Foote's favorite." The marriage incurred Foote's displeasure, causing the discharge of both, but they were quickly rehired. Mrs Jewell retired from the London stage in 1780. She died suddenly of apoplexy in London on 8 September 1798.

From 1779, and perhaps earlier, until about 1815, Jewell lived in a house at No 26, Suffolk Street, near the Haymarket Theatre, and Foote's house. When he retired, "having acquired a competency by the honest discharge of his responsible duties" (according to the *Gentleman's Magazine* of April 1828), he took a house at No 8, Bridge Row, Battersea, near Putney, where he died in early April 1828, almost at the age of 100. "From the peculiar cast and character of his features and person," informed his obituary in the *Gentleman's Magazine*, "no one unacquainted with the fact would have suspected him to have arrived at sixty."

In his will signed on 18 May 1815 while he was still living in Suffolk Street, Jewell requested that he be buried in the same vault with his wife at St Martin-in-the-Fields. He left his estate in trust to his executors George Fournier of Ironmonger Lane, Cheapside, Francis Glossop of Compton Street, Soho, and Robert Farthing of Bury Street, St. James's, who were directed to pay £200 to his daughter Ann for herself and her daughter Julia La Prade and to purchase £2000 of three-percent annuities from available money for the support of his granddaughter Julia. The residue of his stocks and annuities was given to his daughter Ann, except for his clothes, boots, and bedroom furniture and furnishings, which he left to Agnes Cadwallader, commonly called Agnes Jones, who had been his housekeeper for many years.

In a codicil dated 8 February 1823 he left a silver watch to his friend Thomas Barber of the Haymarket and a mourning ring to Thomas's wife, Anne Barber. He revoked the bequest of £2000 in annuities to his granddaughter Julia, substituting £2000 sterling in trust and £150 to be paid immediately after his death; he also gave her many household effects, books, silver spoons, and candlesticks, as well as the furniture previously bequeathed to Agnes Cadwallader, who had since died. He also gave some silver to his daughter Ann, who was by then married to Robert Orby Sloper of West Woodhaye House in Berkshire, and books and other effects to Ann's daughters Julia, Ann Orby Sloper, and John Sloper the younger. A second codicil dated also 8 February 1823 added gifts of silver to Miss Louisa Orby Sloper, evidently another of his granddaughters. On 17 April 1828 Philip Edwards and Philip Edwards the younger, probably relatives of Jewell's late wife, swore acquaintance with the deceased, late of Battersea, and identified his writing in the codicils. The will was proved by Jewell's executors on 22 April 1828.

According to the younger George Colman's *Random Records*, William Jewell had been "remarkable for that figure of speech which is denominated *slip-slop*." His colorful expressions served as a model for the humorous lines given by Colman to Daniel Dowlas in his comedy *The Heir at Law.*

Jewell, Mrs William, Ann, née Edwards
d. 1798, actress, singer.

According to the anonymous author of *Theatrical Biography: or memoirs of the principal performers of the Theatres Royal*, published in 1772, Ann Edwards had been for "many years" a serving girl in Samuel Foote's household. Admiring her singing about the house, Foote proposed her for the stage. He engaged a dancing and music master for her, and within a few months it was found that Ann could "slide upon the stage with a tolerable grace." An-

nounced as a "Young Gentlewoman," she made her debut at the Haymarket on 30 May 1768 as Harriet in the premiere of the manager's comedy *The Devil upon Two Sticks*, a role she then played many times that summer. For the fourth performance, on 6 June, her name appeared in the bills. It also was found in the cast list for the edition of the play printed that year.

In her debut summer Miss Edwards was also brought on as Sally in *Thomas and Sally*, Amelia in *The Statesman Foil'd*, Polly in *The Beggar's Opera*, Phillida in *Damon and Phillida*, and Venus in *The Judgment of Paris*. In specially-licensed performances at the Haymarket in the winter season she acted Phillida (with a new song) on 19 September 1768 and sang in *An Attic Evening's Entertainment* on 2 February 1769. On the latter date her name was given as Mrs Jewell, she having married William Jewell, the Haymarket treasurer, at St Martin-in-the-Fields in January. One of the auditors at the concert of 2 February was Sylas Neville, who wrote in his diary that "Miss Edwards (now Mrs. Jewel) has the sweetest voice I ever heard." William Jewell's marriage to Ann, whom Boswell called Foote's favorite, angered the manager to the point that it is said he discharged the couple but soon relented and rehired them.

After appearing several more times in the *Attic Evening's Entertainment* and singing in *Samson* at the Haymarket on 22 February 1769, Mrs Jewell returned to that theatre as a member of Foote's company that summer to play Zorayda in *The Captive*, Polly in *The Beggar's Opera*, Ophelia in *Hamlet*, and Leonora in *The Padlock*. There the following summer she added to her repertoire Charlot in the premiere of Foote's *The Lame Lover* on 25 June 1770, Nysa in *Midas*, and Maria in *The Citizen*.

With her husband she was with the company taken by Foote to play at the Theatre Royal, Edinburgh, in the winter season 1770–71, where she made her first appearance on 14 February 1771 as Polly Peachum. Though in ill health at the time, she played with great spirit, reported the Edinburgh *Courant* of 16 February: "She seems already to be a great favourite, & will, it is hoped, when her health is perfectly recovered, display musical talents hitherto unknown in this country." She also played Sally in *Thomas and Sally* and Patty in

The Maid of the Mill and participated as well in the concerts of the Edinburgh Musical Society. Reports of her reception at Edinburgh conflict. Boswell wrote to Garrick from that city on 30 March 1771 that Foote had "made a Very good Campaign of it here" and that Woodward "has been exceedingly admired & has a great support to the house" but that Mrs Jewell had failed—"her poorness of figure & awkward inanimate action digust us much." Garrick replied on 18 April that the account from Foote differed, for Mrs Jewell "was much approv'd of." Mrs Jewell also performed at Edinburgh in 1773, 1774, and 1775 (being paid on 21 October of that year £5 10s. for 4 days) and at Smock Alley Theatre, Dublin, in 1773–74.

As a member of the Haymarket summer company each year through 1781, Mrs Jewell appeared in a number of comedy and musical roles, a selection of which includes Miss Linnet in *The Maid of Bath* and Venus in *Dido* in 1771; Fanny in *The Cooper* and Tulippa in *Cupid's Revenge* in 1772; Lucy in *The Minor*, and a role in *The Bankrupt* in 1773; a role in *A Trip to Portsmouth* and Wilhelmina in *The Waterman* in 1774; Lady Anne in *Richard III* in 1775; Jenny Minnikin in *The Capuchin* in 1776; Polly Pattens in *Piety in Pattens* in 1777; Charlotte in *Man and Wife* in 1778; and an Actress in *The Manager in Distress* in 1780.

On 30 September 1775 she made her first appearance on the Drury Lane stage as Lucinda in *Love in a Village* and was "well receiv'd with great applause," according to the prompter Hopkins. She repeated the role there on 24 November 1775, then sang in *The Maid of the Oaks* on 28 November. Despite only two more notices of her name in the bills for *The Maid of the Oaks* on 26 March and 9 April 1776, she seems to have been a regular member of the company that season, for she was allowed to subscribe to the Drury Lane Fund.

In 1772 the *Theatrical Biography* judged her to be a good singer but an actress lacking in the understanding that there are better requisites for sentimental comedy than a "*bawling monotony*, and *sawing of the air.*" A poem highly laudatory of her power and charm in singing in *The Devil upon Two Sticks* and *The Maid of Bath* appeared in the press on 29 June 1773. About 1775 was published the song *The Birks of Endermay* as sung by Mrs Jewell in *The Maid of Bath*. She was taken to task by a writer in the *Morning Post* of 17 September 1777 for not powdering her "intolerable and offensive black wig." The critic also suggested that "A little less affectation & conceit would not be amiss," and "Some of her swells & trills might also be dispensed with."

After playing at the Haymarket in 1781, Mrs Jewell seems to have retired from the stage. She died suddenly of an apoplectic fit at her house, No 26, Suffolk Street, on 8 September 1798 and was buried at St Martin-in-the-Fields on 16 September. Her obituary notice in the *Gentleman's Magazine* of October 1798 recalled that "she possessed a good voice, and was well acquainted with musick. She was once, and deservedly, a favourite with the publick as an acting singer; and in private life bore a very respectable character."

Mrs Jewell's husband, William, survived her by 30 years, dying in 1828. In his notice will be found information on their daughter and grandchildren.

Jewett, Randolph c. 1603–1675, organist, composer.

Randolph (or Randall) Jewett was born about 1603 either in Dublin or, less likely, Chester, and could have been the "Randle Juet" who was a chorister at Chester from 1612 to 1615. His father may have been John Jewett, precentor's vicar in 1619 at Christ Church, Dublin, or William Jewett of Dublin. Hawkins in his *General History* said that Jewett studied under Orlando Gibbons and took a B. Mus. degree at Trinity College, Dublin. Randolph's first appointment was as organist of Christ Church, Dublin, in 1631; he was also in that year made organist and vicar choral of St Patrick's Cathedral. He kept the former post until 1639 and the latter until 1642. Grove places Jewett in Chester in 1642; Pulver has him there in 1643–44. At Chester he was organist of the Cathedral, perhaps until 1646 (the records for several years are missing). In any case, he was back in Dublin as vicar choral at Christ Church and vicar choral at St Patrick's Cathedral in 1646.

By 1651, when Playford's *Musical Banquet* was published, Jewett was in London; that publication listed him as an organist living in London and a teacher of organ or virginal. In 1660 he was made almoner at St Paul's and in 1661 a minor canon and junior cardinal. He moved to Winchester in 1666 to serve as organist, lay vicar, and master of the choristers at Winchester Cathedral. Jewett died, according to an inscription at the Cathedral in Chester, on 3 July 1675 at the age of 72. He had written his will on 20 November 1674; it was proved on 17 July 1675. Jewett gave his name as Randolph in the will, and in it he directed that his son Benjamin should receive £200, his grandchild John Jewett £10, and his grandchildren Elizabeth and Mary Jewett £7 each. He left everything else to his wife, Ann, and named his son, Benjamin, and daughter, Deborah, the residuary legatees.

Jewett was the composer of a number of anthems and an evening service.

Jinghall, Mrs [fl. 1740], actress.
A Mrs Jinghall played Eurydice in *Orpheus and the Death of Eurydice* at Yeates's booth at Bartholomew Fair on 23 August 1740.

Joanna Maria. See "BARONESS, THE."

Jobson, Mr [fl. 1759–1797], puppeteer.
According to Speaight in his *History of the English Puppet Theatre*, the puppeteer Jobson seems to have made his first public appearance at Canterbury in 1759. His offering was called a *Grand Medley of Entertainments*, with "operatical moving figures" in *The Necromancer*, eight Lilliputians in a country dance, and a clockwork exhibit of six figures ringing bells. He had purchased his puppets from Lacon, who had had the figures as early as 1739 at Tunbridge Wells. Jobson was next reported at Bartholomew Fair in 1778, though he was probably exhibiting regularly over the years. When he brought his "Patagonian Puppet Show" to the fair in 1779, he claimed he was from the Covent Garden Theatre, though the bills there show no trace of him. He put on *Julius Caesar, or Punch being Emperor of Rome*, augmenting his puppet show with a hornpipe by "Little Ben," the contortions of a posture maker, four girls in a country dance, a hornpipe by Master Jobson (his son, one supposes, dancing on the puppet stage), and a display of five-foot-high waxwork figures representing a foreign court, concluding with a scene between Punch and Joan.

In 1780 at Bartholomew Fair he brought back much the same entertainment, though

this time the waxwork display concluded with Punch and the Devil in a battle. The set of puppets he used may have been restricted to Roman characters, for the shows he put on seemed regularly to have had a Roman setting. In 1790, as Speaight points out, the play was *The Rival Brothers, or the Death of Caesar*, apparently a variation on the work Jobson presented in 1779. It concluded with "a sparring match between those celebrated pugilists Mr Swatchel (alias Punch) and his wife Joaney."

The "Pie Powder Court Book" at the Guildhall shows that on 4 September 1790 Jobson and Hart paid 8s. for a license to perform a drollery, and Jobson alone paid another 8s. for a license to present his puppet show. He was at the fair again in 1793 and 1794; and in 1797, according to Morley's *Memoirs of Bartholomew Fair*, Jobson and other puppeteers were prosecuted for allowing their puppets to talk and do the business of live actors, which was against the Licensing Act.

Jobson, Master [fl. 1779], dancer.
In 1779 at Bartholomew Fair, Master Jobson danced a hornpipe as part of an entertainment presented by Jobson the puppeteer—presumably his father. The hornpipe may have been performed on the puppet stage. A hornpipe was also danced by "Little Ben," who may have been Master Jobson.

Jodgins. See HODGINS.

"Joey." See GRIMALDI, JOSEPH.

Johannot, Mr [fl. 1783–1785], box and lobby keeper.
The accounts for the King's Theatre show that a Mr Johannot served as a boxkeeper there in 1783 and as a box and lobby keeper in 1784–85. He was very likely related to the singer Richard Johannot.

Johannot, Richard d. 1815, singer, actor, manager.
In his *Memoirs* James De Castro said that Richard Johannot was engaged as a comic singer at the Royal Circus for its second season in the summer of 1783. In a bill for 9 October 1784 Johannot was cited as singing a song in *The Lover's Device* and also offering a specialty

Harvard Theatre Collection

(Richard?) JOHANNOT
engraving by Astley

song, "Four-and-Twenty Fiddlers." Sometime during the 1785 season he was in an unnamed burletta. That year also saw his first association with Astley's Amphitheatre, where he was a popular attraction every summer through 1798.

At Astley's he entertained audiences with such songs as "The Basket of Moss-Roses," "Bow-wow-wow," "Miss Jenny don't think that I care for you" (with Mrs De Castro), and numerous unnamed comic songs. He was also a Devonshire Farmer and the Commander of the Cumberland in *The Royal Naval Review at Plymouth*, Vulcan in *The Reasonable Wife*, an unnamed character in *The Generous Turk*, Clodpate in *Love from the Heart*, a Clown in *Harlequin, Emperor of the Moon*, the Mayor in *The Tythe Sheaf*, a Clown in *The Four Quarters of the World*, Jupiter in *The Good and the Bad*, Pyeman to the Camp (with a song) in *Bagshot-Heath Camp*, Saveall in *The Miser* (at Astley's

showplace in Peter Street, Dublin), and an Indian King in *The Siege of Quebec*. Johannot was cited as singing also in *Harlequin's Medley*, *My Grandmother*, and *Harlequin Invincible*.

Astley permitted Johannot to appear elsewhere during those years. An undated bill for the Royal Circus that probably belongs to the spring of 1786 had Johannot down for Sir Jasper Wilding in the burletta *Who's Who*; he was given a benefit at the Circus in 1790; and he sang between the acts at the Haymarket Theatre on 15 October 1792. Doane's *Musical Directory* of 1794 listed Johannot as a tenor who had performed not only at Astley's but also in the Handel concerts at Westminster Abbey. His address was given as York Buildings, Lambeth. Johannot appeared in Dublin during the 1795–96 season, apparently at Fishamble Street. He was there again in 1796–97 and at Crow Street in 1797–98.

Johannot enjoyed a very favorable contract with Astley. Charles Dibdin in his *Memoirs* said Astley paid Johannot seven guineas weekly or 365 guineas annually plus a benefit free of house charges and expenses each year in London, Dublin, and Liverpool. Dibdin estimated that Johannot must therefore have been making a total of £500 or £600 yearly. Astley also kept a pleasure horse for the singer's recreation and paid all of his traveling expenses. Yet after the summer of 1798 Johannot deserted Astley and went to Dublin on his own.

According to De Castro, Johannot left Astley partly in the hope of making more money and partly because he was ambitious to

make a stand in the regular drama; an elevation, no doubt, to be anxiously desired; but though an Edwin and a Wilson in a Minor Theatre, yet he possessed not the solidity of talent, the rich humour and hearty stamina of the latter in representing old men, nor the comic, eccentric manner, and incomparable rapid style of burletta singing in the former.

De Castro cited a benefit bill for Johannot at Crow Street on 26 February 1799. The singer played Justice Woodcock in *Love in a Village* and Lingo in *The Agreeable Surprise* and sang a number of songs. Tickets were available from him at No 19, Crow Street. De Castro said the benefit produced upwards of £600. Johannot failed in both of those characters at Crow Street, according to De Castro, and returned to Astley's, though at a reduced salary.

Johannot became a partner with Parker, Davis, and others in the management of a troupe of equestrian performers in 1799. The company appeared in London and in the provinces, with Johannot serving as one of the chief singers, often pairing off with Charles Dibdin in songs by Dibdin. Johannot also continued performing at Astley's, apparently through 1803. Dibdin at Sadler's Wells usually had Johannot over to sing at his benefit: ". . . I wrote Songs for his Benefits, and thus returned, and profitably to him, the Compliment. . . . [He] had originally been under the tuition of my father, had a most extraordinary voice, for strength, tone, and modulations, and was irresistibly comic on low comedy and burlesque singing. . . ."

On 26 September 1803 Johannot sang "What News?" at the Royal Circus, and on 3 October there he played the title role in *Johnny Armstrong*. On the fifteenth he sang "Paddy O'Brian's Observations on Bonaparte's intended Invasion, on the Flat-bottom Boats." He was still under contract to Astley, however, for the Royal Circus bill of 15 November said he was appearing as a singer by permission of Astley. The scanty records contain no mention of Johannot after that until 10 July 1809, when he reappeared at the Royal Circus singing Peachum in a new burletta based on *The Beggar's Opera*. The papers found him excellent in the role. He repeated it in April 1810 and was singing "Overboard he Vent" at the Circus sometime in 1812.

De Castro said that after that ". . . Johannot got on the decline in every respect; and, after experiencing as many hardships and pecuniary distresses, as before, on the contrary, he had long rolled in the lap of inconsiderate luxury, he departed this life at Bathwick, near Bath, in the month of January, 1815."

The Mrs Johannot who performed at Astley's Amphitheatre from 1785 to 1793 was probably Richard's wife. Some early sources said that a daughter of Johannot became Mrs Vining, but that woman was Jemima Marian Bew, an illegitimate daughter of John Henry Johnstone. Some sources also say that another daughter of Johannot married William Wallack, but again there was confusion with another offspring of John Henry Johnstone—Susan Johnstone, who married James William Wallack. A Mary Johannot was on the paylist

at Drury Lane Theatre from 1812 to 1816; she was probably a relative of Richard Johannot, as was, one supposes, the box and lobby keeper Johannot of the 1780s.

Hall's *Catalogue of Engraved Dramatic Portraits* in the Harvard Theatre Collection cites an engraving by H. Astley of a Tony Johannot and identifies him as an actor and the grandfather of James W. Wallack; Hall gives his death date as 1825. That engraving may be of Richard Johannot, but if it is, the Christian name, the relationship to Wallack, and the death date are surely incorrect.

Johannot, Mrs [Richard?] [*fl.* 1785–1793], *dancer, actress.*

The Mrs Johannot who performed at Astley's Amphitheatre from as early as 1785 to as late as the spring of 1793 was probably the wife of the popular singer and actor Richard Johannot. She was a member of Astley's troupe in 1785, but the first mention of a role for her came in September 1787, when she played one of the French characters in *The Siege of Quebec*. On 4 September 1789 she was a Rower in *The Royal Naval Review at Plymouth*; on 6 May 1791 she participated in a comic dance called *The Irish Fair*; and on 3 April 1793 she was in *The Generous Turk*.

"John, Little." *See* RAY, JOHN.

Johns, Mr [*fl.* 1770], *actor.*

Mr Johns played Foodle in *Tom Thumb the Great* and Heli in *The Mourning Bride* at the Haymarket Theatre on 19 December 1770.

Johns, Mr [*fl.* 1775–1777], *cheque taker, doorkeeper.*

The Drury Lane accounts show a Mr Johns to have been a pit cheque taker as of 5 October 1775. He was listed as a doorkeeper at 9s. weekly in 1776–77.

Johns, Miss [*fl.* 1785], *singer.*

Miss Johns sang with Doyle, Lowe, Mrs Baker, and others at Sadler's Wells on 15 September 1785.

Johnson. *See also* JOHNSTON and JOHNSTONE.

Johnson, Mr [*fl.* 1737–1740], swordsman.

According to Hutton's *History of Derby* (1817), Mr Johnson was one of the "heroes of the bear-garden." In 1740 at Figg's booth on the bowling green at Southwark, Egan's *Boxiana* informs us, Johnson participated in a display of swordsmanship. He was known, Egan said, for his "hanging-guard."

Johnson, Mr [*fl.* 1737?–1750], singer.

About 1740 was published *Songs and Duetts in Baucis and Philemon* as sung by Mr Johnson and Mrs Hill. Peter Prelleur's interlude was probably performed first about May 1737 at the New Wells, Lemon Street, though there is no certainty that Johnson sang in it then. The only singer named Johnson who was performing in London near 1740 was the one who sang at the Bartholomew Fair booth operated on 23 August 1743 by Yeates, Warner, and Rosomon. That Johnson was probably the man who was at Shepherd's Market, May Fair, on 11 July 1747. That performance was a benefit for Adams and Johnson, who was identified as a distiller.

At that point Johnson may have been only a semiprofessional singer. If he was the Johnson who had a music shop in Cheapside in 1746, perhaps he gave up distilling and followed a purely musical career. On 10 March of that year tickets to a concert at Hickford's Music Room in Brewer Street were available from Johnson's music shop. The same Johnson, perhaps, sang Henry de Chemin in *L'Opéra du Gueux*, a French version of *The Beggar's Opera*, at the Haymarket Theatre on 29 April 1749. With the same group on 9 February 1750, at the same playhouse, Johnson played Front d'Airain in *L'Officier en recrue*, a French translation of Farquhar's play.

Johnson, Mr [*fl.* 1742–1749], actor, dancer.

A Mr Johnson played Orasmin in *Zara* at the James Street playhouse on 7 April 1742. The following 25 August he managed to appear as Security in *The Indian Merchant* at the Phillips-Yeates Bartholomew Fair booth and also as Octavian in *Scaramouch Scapin* at the booth run by Hippisley and Chapman. On January 1743 he was again at the James Street Theatre, playing Muley Moloch in *Don Sebastian*. He took the title part in *The Royal Heroe* at Hallam's theatre at May Fair on 1 May 1744 and was a Huntsman in *The Amorous Sportsman* at Goodman's Fields Theatre on 26 December of that year. *The London Stage* lists him as a dancer because of that last assignment.

On 16 October 1746 at the New Theatre in Southwark Johnson played Sir Charles in *The Stratagem*; then on 31 October 1748 he was seen as Trueman in *The London Merchant* at James Street. The following 26 December he acted Sackbut in *A Bold Stroke for a Wife* at the New Wells, Clerkenwell, and on 23 August 1749 at Cushing's Bartholomew Fair booth Johnson played Pembroke in *King John*. There is a possibility that the appearances listed above were made not by one man but by two or even more, yet there seems to be a pattern: a performer turns up from time to time at the minor theatres, apparently jobbing in rather than becoming a company member with any troupe.

Johnson, Mr d. 1746, actor.

"Tall" Johnson, as he was called, was given particular attention by John Hill in *The Actor* (1750):

Our managers have more than once rejected persons who have offer'd themselves, not only for playing the first characters, but even the subordinate ones, merely for want of height, tho' they have not been deficient in any other particulars: and we have seen within these few years, that when Mr. *Johnson*, a person of considerable merit in tragedy, but of an enormous stature, was received by a manager [Henry Giffard] who had more good nature than the gentlemen in that station usually have; it was in vain that he attempted to bring the audience to approve him, even with the advantages of an expressive countenance, a sonorous voice, and a majestic deportment. He appear'd a giant among a nation of dwarfs; a *Gulliver* surrounded by a *Lilliputian* army: if he was engag'd in a quarrel, it was no merit in him to conquer a man whom he seem'd so vastly an over-match for; and if he made love, we had no idea but of a *Polypheme* and *Galatea*; and thought it unnatural for a little creature to venture to like him. The disproportion between this gentleman's stature and that of Mrs. *Giffard*, with whom he usually play'd, was esteem'd to be such as no audience would ever be brought to bear. . . .

Johnson made his first appearance on 27 October 1735 as Torrismond in *The Spanish Fryar* at the Goodman's Fields Theatre.

Giffard cast Johnson during the rest of the 1735–36 season as Tamerlane, Oroonoko, Henry V, King Arthur, Altamar in *The Parracide*, Dumont in *Jane Shore*, Biron in *The Fatal Marriage*, Pierre in *Venice Preserv'd*, Montezuma in *The Indian Emperor*, Bevil Junior in *The Conscious Lovers*, and Clerimont Senior in *The Tender Husband*. The Johnson who appeared at Lincoln's Inn Fields on 31 March 1736 (a night when Johnson of Goodman's Fields was free) as Obadiah in *The Committee* was surely Benjamin Johnson of Drury Lane, who frequently played that part. Our subject, though, was the Johnson who acted Zamor in *Alzira* at Lincoln's Inn Fields on 18 June. In mid-season Gray wrote to Walpole, on 3 January 1736: "they have a new man to supply Delane's place, one Johnson, with ye finest person & face in the world to all appearance; but as awkward, as a Buttonmaker; in short, if he knew how to manage his Beauties to advantage, I should not wonder, if all the Women run mad for him. . . ."

Giffard moved his troupe to the Lincoln's Inn Fields playhouse for the 1736–37 season, and there Johnson added such new roles to his repertoire as Sempronius in *Cato*, Mithridates, the King in *1 Henry IV*, Medium in *The Independent Patriot*, Sir Charles Freelove in *A Tutor for the Beaus*, Fairfax in *An Historical Play*, Gaylove in *The Maid's the Mistress*, and Claudius in *Hamlet*.

An actor named Johnson played the title role in *Cato* sometime after Barton Booth's death. Though "Tall" Johnson is not known to have attempted the part (he is only known to have played Sempronius), there seems to be no other likely candidate. Perhaps Giffard, after seeing Johnson in some leading serious roles, let him try Cato. Aaron Hill wrote a special prologue, which is the evidence of Johnson's having played the part. In part the actor was made to say,

E'er I presume, to try to night's fam'd part,
Kind to the modest, chear a doubtful heart:
No vain conceits too rash a speed create;
I bend, all conscious of a Cato's weight;
Calmly content, by measur'd steps, to rise,
I view the distant goal, with patient eyes:
Fond of the stage, where life's strong passions glow,
But shun the choaky weeds, that o'er it grow.

Unpush'd by pride, climb slow care's due degrees,
Humbly aspiring—and—but—long—to please.

Well can my mem'ry—to my blush—restore
Whose steps I tread in—WHO was here—before.
Him have you seen—A Cato, worth your praise!
Fill'd with Rome's fire, and form'd, to grace her
      BAYS!
Ill, to supply such absent splendor, sent—
Receive me—in the light—His lustre lent.
Judge me not vain, while lengths, unwish'd, I run;
See, the faint shadow—and suppose—the SUN

Johnson's predecessor in the part was, of course, Barton Booth, who had died in 1733. Though Aaron Hill penned that special prologue for the occasion and, as will be seen, wrote a concerned letter about "Tall" Johnson after the actor's death, he objected to but did not prevent the marriage of his daughter Urania to Johnson in 1739. Further information on Miss Hill may be found in Aaron Hill's entry.

When Giffard's venture collapsed, Johnson joined the Covent Garden company, making his first appearance there on 2 November 1737 as Leonato in *Much Ado about Nothing*. Johnson remained at Covent Garden through the 1745–46 season, trying out such new roles as Gaunt in *Richard II*, the King of France in *Henry V*, Bedford in *1 Henry VI*, Bajazet in *Tamerlane*, Northumberland in *2 Henry IV*, Cassander in *The Rival Queens*, the High Priest in *Mariamne*, and the Governor in *The Island Princess*. His last appearance was in *Henry V* on 11 March 1740, after which he deserted the London stage for four years.

Johnson stretched the truth when he advertised on 30 April 1744 that his appearance as Zamor (not Gamor) in *Alzira* at Drury Lane would be his first on any stage in five years. Johnson also spoke a new prologue. Drury Lane did not schedule any further performances for him, and it seems clear that he acted just for W. Giffard's benefit on that occasion. A Johnson played the title role in *The Royal Heroe* at May Fair on 1 May, but we take him to have been a different performer. A Johnson, perhaps our subject, was associated with Theophilus Cibber's troupe at the Haymarket in the fall of 1744. *The London Stage* indicates that that Johnson's occasional stage name was Hill. Johnson played Balance in *The Recruiting Officer* on 27 September; "Hill" acted Friar Lawrence in *Romeo and Juliet* on 29 September; and Johnson was Sealand in *The Conscious Lovers* on 4 October. A Mrs Hill sang at the Haymarket in October and November of 1744; that might make one question whether the actor Hill was Johnson working under a stage name for one performance or an actor actually named Hill. The Johnson who played a Huntsman in *The Amorous Sportsman* at Goodman's Fields on 26 December was, again, a different performer.

It seems certain that the Johnson who acted at Covent Garden in 1745–46 was "Tall" Johnson. On 23 September 1745 he played the Ghost in *Hamlet*; then he acted Sir John in *The Non-Juror*, Apemantus in *Timon of Athens*, Smith in *The Rehearsal*, Leonato in *Much Ado about Nothing* (which he had played in 1737 when he first appeared at Covent Garden), Bellarius in *Cymbeline*, the title role in *Volpone*, and, on 23 April 1746, his last appearance, Frontenac in *Liberty Asserted*. No one named Johnson was seen on the London stage for another two and a half years. The date of Johnson's last performance ties in with a letter from Aaron Hill to Garrick written on 30 June 1746:

Your letter said of Mr. Johnson, with a more significant propriety, than you intended the expression for, that he, but just appear'd and vanish'd. He had literally vanish'd, when you said so: and the visit, which he made you, was the last he made in life. He told his family, that to himself he had seem'd dead enough, in Hamlet's Ghost, to be the very thing he acted. Among your many just admirers, you had never any, more sincerely such, than that poor, honest, friendly, plain, good meaner. He was in the highest rapture, when he heard of your return; but (like a very mortal as he was) had form'd long prospects of delight, he was to have the shortest share in.

This melancholy accident, impress'd still deeper, by the dangerous effect it has upon his widow, whom they brought down hither, in a wildness, bordering on distraction, has for some short time, postpon'd a pleasure, I should else have press'd with great impatience.

The press reported on 12 April 1746 that "Last week died at Wandsworth, in Surrey, *Mr. Johnson*, late a comedian belonging to the Theatre Royal in Covent Garden. He married the daughter of Aaron Hill, Esq. and was a Man well respected by all that had the pleasure of knowing him." Latreille incorrectly dated that report 1742 and identified the actor as Benjamin Johnson.

Johnson, Mr [fl. 1752–1753], *property maker.*

In connection with the pantomime *Harlequin Ranger*, which played at Drury Lane Theatre beginning on 14 December 1752, Richard Cross noted in his prompter's diary that the scenes of the fountains "were design'd & made by Mr. Johnson Property maker to our House."

Johnson, Mr [fl. 1761–1762], *singer.*

On 13 November 1761 a Mr Johnson was paid 10s. 6d. at Covent Garden Theatre for singing in *The Coronation*, a spectacular afterpiece which had its first performance that night and was repeated many times during the season.

Johnson, Mr [fl. 1763–1765], *actor.*

In Foote's company at the Haymarket Theatre in the summer of 1763 a Mr Johnson acted Heeltap in *The Mayor of Garratt*, Sir Jasper in *The Citizen*, Thunder in *The Rehearsal*, Bonniface in *The Beaux' Stratagem*, Antonio in *Love Makes a Man*, and an unspecified part in Foote's presentations of *The Diversions of a Morning*. Johnson returned to the Haymarket in the summer of 1765 to perform La Fleur in *The Commissary*, Dick in *The Minor*, and a role in *The Patron*, among other parts. The Mrs Johnson who was at the Haymarket in 1763 was probably his wife.

Johnson, Mr [fl. 1766], *actor.*

A Mr Johnson was a member of Spranger Barry's Irish company that played at the King's Theatre in the summer of 1766. His roles there included Priuli in *Venice Preserv'd*, Gloucester in *King Lear*, and Oliver in *As You Like It*.

Johnson, Mr [fl. 1771], *actor.*

A Mr Johnson played Major O'Flaherty in a specially-licensed performance of *The West Indian* given at the Haymarket Theatre on 15 April 1771 by a casual company of touring players. *The Public Advertiser* carried the notice: "Benefit for Johnson. This Play will not be repeated at the Haymarket this Season, as it is a particular Act of Indulgence that it is suffered to be performed there this Evening." Possibly this actor was Samuel Johnson (fl. 1752?–1781).

Johnson, Mr *[fl. 1778],* *actor.*

A Mr Johnson acted Tom in a specially-licensed performance of *The Jealous Wife* at the Haymarket on 23 March 1778.

Johnson, Mr *[fl. 1782],* *actor.*

In the spring of 1782 at the Haymarket Theatre a Mr Johnson acted the title role in *Don Quixote in England* and Lord Stanley in *Richard III* on 4 March, Knowlife in *The Tobacconist* on 21 March, the Nephew in *The Irish Widow* on 9 April, and principal characters in *The Fashionable Wife* and *The Lawyer Nonsuited* on 6 May.

Johnson, Mr *[fl. 1783–1784],* *actor.*

At the Haymarket Theatre on 17 September 1783, a Mr Johnson, announced as from the Theatre Royal, Dublin (he was not the Irish actor J. H. Johnstone, who also made his debut in London at the beginning of that season), acted principal characters in *Cheapside* and *A New Way to Keep a Wife at Home.* Probably he was the Johnson who played a role in *The Talisman* at the Haymarket on 21 January 1784 and the "Johnston" who was named in the bills for Villars in *A Word to the Wise* on the same night. The Mrs Johnson who played Miss Montague in the latter piece probably was his wife.

Johnson, Mr *[fl. 1791–1794],* *puppet showman, exhibitor, actor.*

The "Pie Powder Court Book" at the Guildhall Library indicates that a Mr Johnson was one of the showmen who offered puppet shows and other exhibitions at Bartholomew Fair in 1791 and 1794. Perhaps he was the Johnson who acted the Clown in *The Life and Death of Harlequin* with Mrs Sturmer's company at the New Theatre in Swan Yard in September 1794, during the fair.

Johnson, Mr *[fl. 1791–1794],* *actor, singer, manager.*

In and around London between 1791 and 1794 a number of performances were given in which a Mr Johnson took parts. While we assume the same person was involved in the instances cited below, it is possible, of course, that several Johnsons were active. It is also possible that this Mr Johnson was John John-son (1759–1819), an actor-singer who later went to America with his wife Elizabeth Johnson (1771–1830), but we have no evidence to that effect.

A Mr. Johnson played the Duke in *Venice Preserv'd* and Caleb in *Taste* at the Haymarket Theatre on 24 October 1791. A Mr. Johnson acted Trudge in *Inkle and Yarico* and Flash in *Miss in Her Teens* at the Crown Inn, Islington, on 16 January 1792. The Mrs Johnson who played Narcissa in the former piece was probably his wife.

In June 1792 at Barking, Essex, nine miles from London, a Mr Johnson brought a touring company to play in the town hall, which had been converted into a theatre. "Their dresses far excel any we have ever before remembered here," reported a correspondent to the *Thespian Magazine* that month, and "Mr and Mrs Johnson are most to be mentioned: their performance has given general satisfaction, particularly the latter; who, though young on the stage, has acquitted herself much to her credit; and by a proper attention, promises fair to become a favorite actress." Mrs Johnson enjoyed for her benefit "the best house they have had here."

A Mr Johnson played Symon in the pastoral *The Gentle Shepherd* at the Haymarket Theatre on 22 October 1792.

A Mr Johnson acted Careless (with a song) in *The School for Scandal* and Gradus in *Who's the Dupe?* at the Windsor Castle Inn, King Street, Hammersmith, on 24 March 1794, for the benefit of Mr Kent and his family, sponsored by the Margravine of Anspach. The Mrs Johnson who played Candour in the mainpiece was probably his wife. They probably appeared the next night in *The Road to Ruin* and *The Poor Soldier,* but the casts are not known.

Johnson, Mr *[fl. 1799],* *boxkeeper.*

A Mr Johnson was money taker in the boxes at the Richmond Theatre, Surrey, in the summer of 1799. His name is on a list of the company for that season preserved in the Richmond Reference Library.

Johnson, Mrs *[fl. 1670–1688],* *actress, dancer.*

Mrs Johnson's first recorded part was Betty in *Sir Salomon* in April 1670 at the Lincoln's Inn Fields Theatre. She was seen as Statyra in

The Women's Conquest and as a dancer (probably the character of Theodosius) in *The Humorists* in 1670–71, and as Honour Muchland in *The Morning Ramble*, Carolina in *Epsom Wells*, Ismena in *The Reformation*, and Morena in *The Empress of Morocco* in 1672–73.

Hers was a short career that gained her much praise. In his preface to *The Humorists* in 1671 Shadwell admitted that the first performance of his play was something of a disaster, but it was "revived, after the second day, by her kindness (which I can never enough acknowledge) who, for four days together, beautified it with the most excellent Dancings that ever has been seen upon the Stage. This drew my enemies, as well as friends, till it was something better acted, understood, and liked, than at first." It has been assumed by most authorities that the dancer was Mrs Johnson. When she was Caroline in *Epsom Wells* on 2 December 1672, according to Downes, she caught the eye of an admirer. The prompter remembered that "Mrs Johnson in this Comedy, Dancing a Jigg so Charming well, Loves power in a little time after Coerc'd her to Dance more Charming, else where."

Elsewhere was in the arms of, among others, the Earl of Peterborough, who on 11 December 1677 challenged Lord Deincourt and Sir George Hewett for having "broken the windowes of one Mrs. Johnson, a lady of pleasure under his Lordship's protection. . . ." King Charles heard of the quarrel, prevented a duel, and made everyone friends. A manuscript lampoon at Harvard among some poems by Rochester and others tells how Mrs Johnson spread her favors around:

> *From Duke and from Lord pritty Johnson is fled*
> *Thus Kindly embraceing her Godfrey she said,*
> *If plenty of money my dearest had more*
> *I should not be Counted so Arrant a Whore*
> *If thou would'st maintaine me, I'de not goe astray*
> *Nor ever receive more rings from Tho: Gray.*

Sir George Etherege may have been one of Mrs Johnson's lovers, for from his post in Ratisbon he remembered her. In November 1686, when he was attracted to a young actress named Julia, newly arrived in Ratisbon, he compared her attractiveness with Mrs Johnson and Mrs Wright, his actress friends in London. In a letter written early in 1688 he told Middleton that Julia was "no less handsom and no less kind in Dutchland, than Mrs Johnson was in England."

Johnson, Mrs [*fl.* 1763], *actress.*

At the Haymarket Theatre a Mrs Johnson acted Gipsey in *The Beaux' Stratagem* on 5 September and Honoria in *Love Makes a Man* on 7 September 1763. She was probably the wife of the Mr Johnson (fl. 1763–1765) who was also with the Haymarket company that summer.

Johnson, Mrs [*fl.* 1784], *actress.*

A Mrs Johnson played Miss Montague in *A Word to the Wise* at the Haymarket Theatre on 21 January 1784. Probably she was the wife of the Mr Johnson who acted there the same night. On 8 March 1784 Mrs Johnson acted Belinda in *The Man's Bewitch'd* at that theatre.

Johnson, Mrs [*fl.* 1792–1794], *actress.* See JOHNSON, MR [*fl.* 1791–1794], *actor, singer, manager.*

Johnson, Master [*fl.* 1762], *singer.*

A Master Johnson sang in *Alexander's Feast* and *The Sacrifice*, oratorios given at Drury Lane Theatre on 3 and 5 March 1762, respectively. On 11 June 1762 he was among the singers who presented songs from *Artaxerxes* at Ranelagh Gardens.

Johnson, Bartholomew *b. 1710?, bassoonist, violoncellist, composer.*

Bartholomew Johnson was born on 3 October 1710, according to *Grove's Dictionary*. (The *Catalogue of Engraved British Portraits in the British Museum* gives his year of birth as 1700 and his year of death as 1804. Both dates are incorrect). Little is known about this musician except that he appeared as a soloist in London concerts about 1770. His hundredth birthday was observed at Freemasons' Hall, Scarborough, in 1810, when Johnson played one of his own minuets. At that time a painting of Johnson by John Jackson was presented to the Scarborough Corporation by Lord Mulgrave; an engraving of it by Henry Meyer, of Great Russell Street, London, was published on 1 October 1811 with the caption "Mr Bartholomew Johnson Aet 100."

BARTHOLOMEW JOHNSON

engraving by Meyer, after J. Jackson

Johnson, Benjamin *1665–1742, actor, singer, scene painter.*

Benjamin Johnson was born in 1665 and was, according to Chetwood's *General History*, "bred a Painter, where his Employment led him to paint, under his Master, the Scenes for the Stage. . . ." But he found that listening to the actors gave him more pleasure than painting, so, as Johnson is supposed to have said, he gave up the saint's occupation for that of a sinner—a reference to St Luke being the patron saint of painters. He apparently joined a troupe of strolling players, and then joined Christopher Rich's company at Drury Lane in 1695, just after Betterton and many of the older players had seceded from the United Company and formed their own troupe.

Johnson's first recorded role was Sir Simon Barter in *The Mock Marriage* in September 1695 at Drury Lane. The rest of his known roles during his first seasons in London indicate not only the extent of his provincial ex-

Harvard Theatre Collection

BENJAMIN JOHNSON as Ananias

from an engraving by Van Bleeck

perience but also his penchant for comedy: Gerardo in *The Rival Sisters*, Captain Driver in *Oroonoko*, Sir William Wisewood in *Love's Last Shift*, Sir Rowland Marteen in *The Younger Brother*, Sir Rustick Good-Heart in *The Lost Lover*, and (at Dorset Garden) Gripe in *The Cornish Comedy*. To the end of the century Johnson was seen in such new parts as a Player in *The Female Wits*, Coupler in *The Relapse*, Homily in *The Sham Lawyer*, Sir Dottrel Fondlove in *The World in the Moon*, Woodall in *Sauny the Scot*, Gusman Senior in *Imposture Defeated*, Dandalo in *The Fatal Discovery*, the Sieur Bondevelt in *The Campaigners*, Governor Tyrant in

The Island Princess, Lyrick in *Love and a Bottle*, Wrangle in *Love Without Interest*, Smugler in *The Constant Couple*, Sir Solomon Empty in *The Reform'd Wife*, Alphonso in *The Pilgrim*, and Alderman Chollerick in *Courtship à la Mode*. Chetwood in 1749 said that Johnson played a summer season in Ireland "about fifty years ago," but no confirming evidence has come to light.

Johnson and several other performers were charged about 1701 with acting obscene and profane plays, the works cited being *Volpone, The Humours of the Age* (which had its premiere on 1 March 1701), and *Sir Courtly Nice*. By playing a delaying game with the authorities the actors finally managed to have the case dismissed. Johnson had by the early years of the new century established himself well enough that *A Comparison Between the Two Stages* honored him with a nasty remark; Ramble and Critic are talking:

Ramb. Then there's the Noble Ben's Namesake—
Crit. Is or might be a good *Comedian*, but he has the Vice of all Actors, he's too fond of his own Merit.

The *Post Boy* of 12–14 May 1702 announced that *Theatra Vindicata*, an answer to the *Comparison*, would "speedily be publish'd" and another, *A Short Defence*, was also advertised as in press, but neither work saw print.

The prompter Downes, writing his *Roscius Anglicanus* in 1708, was high in his praise of Johnson:

He's skilful in the Art of Painting, which is a great Adjument, very Promovent to the Art of true Elocution, which is always requirable in him, that bears the Name of an Actor; he has the Happiness to gain Applause from Court and City: Witness, Morose, Corbaccio, Mr. Hothead and several others; He is a true Copy of Mr. Underhill, whom Sir William Davenant judg'd 40 Years ago in Lincolns-Inn-Fields, the truest Comedian in his Company.

Two years later in *The Life of Betterton* Gildon called (or had Betterton call) Johnson "our present Roscius." As Numphs (i.e. Wasp in *Bartholomew Fair*) Johnson acted with "such an Engagement in the Part, that I could not persuade my self, that it was acting but the Reality. . . ."

Bond's edition of *New Letters to the Tatler and Spectator* contains a piece on drama and opera signed by "Philo Patriae" and dating on or after 14 January 1710. Bickerstaff in the *Tatler* No 120 had named Doggett "the best of Comedians," but the correspondent allowed that

Ben: Johnson excells him in all Parts where Nature is to be expressed in her proper Gestures: Dogget is confind, & the same in all Parts, But Ben: is various yet just in All; and whilst he acts Corbaccio, Morose & Numpes it is Injustice to prefer any one to him, till we can see any one so masterly in three such parts as those of so different a Character.

As is evident from the references to parts in *Volpone, The Silent Woman*, and *Bartholomew Fair*, Johnson took special care to play well characters in Ben Jonson's works—because of his name, evidently, though he seems not to have been a descendant of Jonson. He also developed some other characters in the early years of the eighteenth century, many of which he kept for many years afterwards, to the delight of audiences. Among those he added to his repertoire in the first decade of the century were Fireball in *Sir Harry Wildair*, Sable in *The Funeral*, Obadiah in *The Committee*, Sir Paul Squelch in *The Northern Lass*, a Gravedigger and Polonius (but rarely) in *Hamlet*, Testimony in *Sir Courtly Nice*, Aelius in *Timon of Athens*, Hecate in *Macbeth*, Randall in *The Jovial Crew*, Foresight in *Love for Love*, Stephano in *The Tempest*, Fernando in *The Fatal Marriage*, Gomez in *The Spanish Fryar*, Belvil in *The Rover*, Savil in *The Scornful Lady*, Clodpate in *Epsom Wells*, Bluff in *The Old Bachelor*, the Carrier in *1 Henry IV*, Sir David Dunce in *The Soldier's Fortune*, a Plebeian in *Julius Caesar*, Gardiner in *Henry VIII*, Ananias in *The Alchemist*, Sir Benjamin Nickit in *The Gamester*, Raison in *Greenwich Park*, Mufti in *Don Sebastian*, and Pearmain in *The Recruiting Officer*.

That first decade of the eighteenth century was a most unstable one for the performers; not until Cibber, Wilks, and Doggett took over as managers of Drury Lane in 1710 did the situation settle down. With the opening of the new Queen's Theatre in 1705, the increasing dissatisfaction with the manager Christopher Rich at Drury Lane, and the growing popularity of Italian opera, the actors sometimes found themselves playing now at Drury Lane and now at the Queen's.

During the decade Johnson wound up in prison once, for reasons that are not clear. In

1705 he was supposed to have a benefit when Swiney's play *The Quacks* was to have its premiere, and the bill noted that Johnson was languishing in prison (for a debt?). But the performance was stopped. He seems not to have been incarcerated for long. On 11 April 1709 he signed a contract with the manager Swiney to act from the following 1 July for a period of five years at £100 annually, a benefit each April with £40 house charges, and a vacation from 10 June to 10 September each year. The irony was that no sooner had the actor signed to work with Swiney at the Queen's Theatre than the management shifted, and Johnson wound up by late November 1710 at Drury Lane under Cibber, Wilks, and Doggett.

Johnson remained at Drury Lane, playing there many of his old roles—especially those favorites with the audiences: Corbaccio, Foresight, Blunt, Obadiah, Driver, Coupler, Ananias, a Gravedigger, Morose, Sir William Wisewood, the Carrier, Hecate, Smugler, and others—until the fall of 1733, when he joined Theophilus Cibber and his rebels, and bolted Drury Lane for an experimental and ultimately successful protest against the Drury Lane management. Between 1710, when the Drury Lane management settled down, and 1733, when it was shattered, Johnson added such new roles as Jacomo in *Don John* (*The Libertine*), Sir Solomon Sadlife in *The Double Gallant*, Caliban in *The Tempest*, Squire Thomas in *The What D'Ye Call It*, Palmer in *The Comical Revenge*, Fossile in *Three Hours after Marriage*, Diego in *The Adventures of Five Hours*, and the title role in *Wat Tyler*. But after 1720 Johnson was not much interested in expanding his repertoire. He kept playing, over and over again, the parts, mostly comic, which he had established during his first ten years in London.

During those years between 1710 and 1733 little is known about Johnson other than what he played. In 1711, for example, *The Guardian* No 82 printed a supposed bill from Will Peer in connection with a revival of *The Lancashire Witches* in August: "For boarding a setting dog 2 days to follow Mr. Johnson in Epsom Wells [*sic*] . . . . . 0 0 6d." Johnson's usual part in that work was Tom Shacklehead, a country fellow. On 11 August 1711 Johnson was mentioned in passing in connection with that play in the *Spectator*, and the same journal on 5 May

1712 said of Ben's Corbaccio in *Volpone* that it "must have given all who saw him a thorough detestation of aged avarice."

"Patrick Fitz-Crambo" in 1743 published his *Tyranny Triumphant*, satirizing the contention that year between the actors and the manager Fleetwood. He recalled how Johnson had been treated under the triumvirate of Cibber, Wilks, and Doggett (and later Booth, who replaced Doggett). Fitz-Crambo called Johnson "a very worthy honest Man" who was in all his roles "a faithful Servant to Nature, and copied her close in every turn of Passion; his Action, his Attitude was so just, and so Characteristic, that no Painter would wish for a better Life to draw from. . . ." Yet he had met with cruel treatment from the Drury Lane managers, treatment of which he was too good-natured to complain. Having secured from Johnson his promise not to desert them for John Rich at the rival theatre, the managers then "compleated his ill Treatment":

One of the Triumvirate [Cibber, no doubt], when Mr. *Johnson* was ill of a Fever, had play'd, and been well receiv'd, in the Part of *Justice Shallow*, which had been cast for that Gentleman: Upon which he, envying Mr. *Johnson's* Reputation, thought fit to intrude further into his Walk, by slyly dropping several Plays in which Mr. *Johnson's* Parts were very considerable, and reviving other Plays, and ordering it so that Mr. *Johnson* should have no Part in them, so that abundance of People in praising that Actor would frequently slide into his Commendation that he was excellent in the small compass he acted, not knowing that his Compass had been much larger, and that he had excell'd in all. . . .

Davies in his *Dramatic Miscellanies* in 1784 noted that the triumvirate had about 1715 retained Johnson by giving him roles previously played by Doggett—and by raising Johnson's salary; but many of those very roles, Davies said, were in time appropriated by Cibber for himself.

There was doubtless some exaggeration in the stories about the treatment of Johnson, for the calendar of his performances shows him to have stayed in clear possession of his favorite roles and to have added few new parts associated with Doggett.

One curious piece of information concerning Johnson stems from D'Urfey's *Wit and Mirth* (1719), a collection of song lyrics. Included was the Sexton's song in *Hamlet*, "Once more to these Arms," which was stated to have been sung by Ben Johnson. Johnson is not otherwise thought of as a singer, though he may have incorporated songs into some of his roles. Despite Johnson's reluctance to try many new parts as he aged, his concentration on his favorite roles paid off in compliments. *The Comedian* in October 1732 said, "I believe if I say of *Johnson* that a truer Comedian never trod the Stage, I shall have the Assent of all who have seen him on it." And in *The Life of Gay* (1733) Curll called Johnson "the best Comedian of the present Age (in his Style of Playing) . . . "

Benjamin Johnson played Foresight in *Love for Love* for his first appearance at the Haymarket Theatre on 26 September 1733 with Theophilus Cibber's seceders. As might be expected, he did not try many new roles during the few months the rebels held forth at the Haymarket, but he did attempt some: Shallow in *2 Henry IV*, Sir Francis in *The Double Gallant*, and Dr Mummy in *The Mother-in-Law*. He kept the first and last when the troupe returned to Drury Lane in March 1734.

Johnson and some of the other Drury Lane actors at the end of the 1734–35 season, under the manager Fleetwood, considered (but evidently did not carry out) a plan to rent the theatre from Fleetwood for 15 years at £920 annually. Thus Johnson was, as one might expect, one of the signers in 1735 of a petition against the new bill before Parliament for the governing of London's playhouses. The actors' protest did not stop the passage of the Licensing Act, but then the Act did not do much harm to performers like Johnson, who was a member of a patent company. Johnson's real concern in the petition he signed was that he had just been negotiating to rent Drury Lane from Fleetwood, and Fleetwood might have taken the Drury Lane patent elsewhere.

From the spring of 1733 to his death in 1742 Benjamin Johnson remained at Drury Lane, again playing many of his old parts. The additions to his repertoire included Shallow in *The Merry Wives of Windsor*, Vellum in *The Drummer*, Fumble in *A Fond Husband*, (revived after almost 40 years), and Old Gobbo in *The Merchant of Venice*. Johnson's last appearance was in an unnamed role in *The Rehearsal* on 26 May 1742.

One report of Johnson's death, picked up by Latreille from a clipping, was incorrectly dated 12 April 1742 (*recte*: 1746): "Last week died at Wandsworth, in Surry, *Mr. Johnson* late a comedian belonging to the Theatre Royal in Covent Garden. He married the daughter of Aaron Hill Esq. and was a man well respected by all that had the pleasure of knowing him." That reference was clearly not to Benjamin Johnson but to "Tall" Johnson.

Reed's "Notitia Dramatica" in the British Library has it that Benjamin Johnson died at 77 on 3 July 1742. In the O. Smith collection at the British Library is a note that Benjamin Johnson died on 31 July at Wandsworth. Lowe's notes to Cibber's *Apology* cite Johnson's death as in August. The *Daily Advertiser* of 2 August stated that Johnson had died at Kensington Wells on 31 July 1742 at the age of 77. The last seems to be the most accurate statement. On 15 December 1742 at Drury Lane a benefit was held for Johnson's "daughter," evidently to provide her with benefit money the manager Fleetwood had owed her father. Garrick played Plume in *The Recruiting Officer*, with Peg Woffington acting Sylvia, and both Beard and Lowe sang.

Benjamin Johnson had written his will on 20 April 1742, styling himself a gentleman of the parish of St Paul, Covent Garden. He left £10 to his sister Ann Baxley and her husband and everything else to his goddaughter Margaret Callow, spinster, who proved the will on 2 August 1742 and who was, we would guess, the "daughter" mentioned in the benefit bill.

Of Johnson's personal life hardly anything has been discovered. An entry in the registers of St Paul, Covent Garden, may possibly refer to him: on 4 January 1702 Richard, the son of Benjamin and Mary Johnson was christened— but that could as easily refer to another Benjamin Johnson.

In his edition of Downes's *Roscius Anglicanus* Waldron quoted some manuscript notes by Thomas Davies: "Johnson was a very correct and chaste Comedian. He was the most exact copy of Nature I ever saw. But he wanted that warmth of Colouring which Cibber gave to his comic characters, and which Mr. Garrick has since carried still higher." In his *Dramatic Miscellanies* Davies commented most favorably on the "exhibition of comic distress" Johnson brought to the character of Morose and on Johnson's "large speaking blue eyes" that he kept on the actor to whom he spoke, and in his *Life of Garrick* Davies expressed his admiration for Johnson's handling of more serious parts. As Bishop Gardiner in *Henry VIII* "Johnson represented with critical exactness, unmixed with that buffoonery which has since been adopted by the actors of Gardiner." Hill in *The Actor* (1750) said Johnson "never appeared upon the stage, without being the greatest player on it." Such roles as Coupler and Smugler, Hill said, "ceas'd to be any thing with us, when he ceas'd to play them."

Johnson was pictured by Laguerre in his "Stage Mutiny" print in 1733; Ben is shown in the character of Testimony in *Sir Courtly Nice*, standing behind Griffin in the group picture. Van Bleeck in 1738 depicted Johnson and Griffin as Ananias and Tribulation in *The Alchemist*; Van Bleeck engraved the work in reverse in 1748.

Johnson, Charles. *See* JOHNSON, SAMUEL [fl. 1752–1781].

Johnson, Mrs [Charles, Mary?] [fl. 1748–1749], *actress, singer.*
A Mrs Johnson played Betty in *A Bold Stroke for a Wife* on 26 December and Lucy in *The London Merchant* on 29 December 1748 at the New Wells, Clerkenwell, and Moll Brazen in *The Beggar's Opera* on 2 January 1749 at Southwark. Possibly she was Mary, the widow of Charles Johnson; the widow's benefit tickets had been accepted at Covent Garden Theatre on 29 March 1748.

Johnson, E. [fl. 1794], *singer.*
E. Johnson was listed in 1794 in Doane's *Musical Directory* as a singer in the Covent Garden oratorios who lived at the Tenter Ground, Moorfields. No doubt he was related to the singer James Johnson of the same address.

Johnson, "Fiddler." *See* JOHNSON, SAMUEL 1691–1773.

Johnson, George *d. c. 1665, theatre keeper.*
The elder George Johnson was the theatre keeper at court from 26 October 1660; he was officially replaced by his son George on 10 February 1665, and it can be assumed that the elder Johnson had recently died. George Junior also took over his father's post as Yeoman of the Bows, on 13 February 1665. The theatre keeper's job, which came under the Revels Office, consisted of attending at court performances and supplying such necessaries as rushes, pans for fires, bellows, tongs, stage properties, a boat for fetching the players from the public theatres when they appeared at court performances, and a chamberpot for backstage.

The younger George Johnson probably served as Groom of the Revels Office from 1662 to before 9 September 1671, according to Boswell in *The Restoration Court Stage*. When he took over as theatre keeper after his father's death, he continued in that office until his death in 1672. A Lord Chamberlain's warrant dated 26 May 1664 put one of the Johnson's, evidently George, Junior, in possession of lodgings in the Cockpit at court which the professional actor Henry Harris, a Yeoman of the Revels Office, had occupied.

After the death of the younger George Johnson in 1672 the theatre keeper's post went to Philip Johnson, doubtless a relative, who held the job from mid-November 1672 to 24 April 1678, when he was succeeded by John Clarke.

Johnson, George *d. 1672, theatre keeper*
See JOHNSON, GEORGE *d. c. 1665.*

Johnson, Henry [fl. 1777–1788], *box bookkeeper, assistant treasurer, manager?*
Henry Johnson was a box bookkeeper at the King's Theatre between 1777–78 and 1787–88. In 1781–82 he was also an assistant to William Jewell, the theatre's treasurer. Johnson's first name is on a Larpent manuscript in the Huntington Library. Probably he was the Johnson who served as one of the acting managers (along with Badini, Carnevale, and Molini) of the King's Theatre in 1786–87.

Johnson, James [fl. 1794], *singer.*
James Johnson, who lived at the Tenter Ground, Moorfields, was listed in 1794 in Doane's *Musical Directory* as a singer and a member of the Cecilian Society. No doubt he was related to Mr E. Johnson of the same address.

Johnson, Jane. *See* CIBBER, MRS THEOPHILUS THE FIRST.

Johnson, John *1759–1819, actor, singer.*

John Johnson, born in 1759, probably was the Johnson who acted at Bath in 1783–84 and 1784–85 before he entered Tate Wilkinson's company on the York circuit in 1787. Johnson left the latter company suddenly "from some very trivial cause," as Wilkinson put it in his *Wandering Patentee*, joining Paul Redigé's company at the Wakefield and Doncaster theatres (leased, incidentally from Wilkinson). The York manager had become distressed with Johnson's conduct "relative to the moving of some scenery of mine." Wilkinson cast aspersions on his acting abilities, to which Johnson was supposed to have replied that "he should have a contemptible opinion of himself indeed, if the worst character he performed was not superior to any part" of Wilkinson's Shylock.

In the summer of 1787 Johnson acted at Colman's Haymarket Theatre, making his first appearance on 16 May as Alphonso in *The Spanish Fryar* and Congo in *Harvest Home*. By the end of the summer he had been seen as Sir Felix Friendly in *The Agreeable Surprise*, Don Pedro in *Much Ado about Nothing*, Selim in *A Mogul Tale*, Goodwill in *The Virgin Unmask'd*, Capt Slightly in *The Romp*, Juggins in *The Suicide*, Carlos in *The Widow's Vow*, Gayless in *The Country Attorney*, an Officer in *Venice Preserv'd*, Cosey in *A Beggar on Horseback*, Eustace in *Love in a Village*, Verulam in *Henry the Second*, Lorenzo in *The Merchant of Venice*, Captain Nightshade in *Seeing is Believing*, Harman in *Lionel and Clarissa*, a Planter in *Inkle and Yarico*, the Manager of the Fête in *Transformation*, Valentine in *The Intriguing Chambermaid*, Borachio in *Much Ado about Nothing*, Osmin in *The Test of Love*, Doublefree in *The Follies of a Day*, Ratcliff in *Jane Shore*, Seton in *Vimonda*, and George Bevil in *Cross Purposes*.

Johnson returned to the Haymarket each summer through 1792 (except that of 1790) to serve in modest supporting roles in comedy and musical pieces. Among the many parts he played during those seasons were Vane in *The Chapter of Accidents* and Sir Charles Freeman in *The Beaux' Stratagem* in 1788, Frank in *Half an Hour after Supper*, a principal character in *The Sword of Peace*, and the Duke of Somerset in *The Battle of Hexham* in 1789, and a Citizen in *The Surrender of Calais* in 1791. He was probably the Johnson who, by special license at the

Haymarket, acted the Duke in *Venice Preserv'd* and Caleb in *Taste* on 24 October 1791 and Symon in *The Gentle Shepherd* on 12 December 1791 and 22 October 1792.

During the winter Johnson toured the provinces. He was a singer at the Norwich theatre between January and April 1789 and in May 1790. He was there again in 1791 with his recent bride, Elizabeth, the daughter of Major Ford of Ipswich. As Miss Ford she had acted at Norwich the previous season. After playing at Norwich until May 1792, the Johnsons were at Bath in 1792–93 and 1793–94, where she was well received though over-puffed in the press. Johnson, very much in love with his wife, who was about 12 years his junior, managed to persuade Wilkinson to engage her in the summer of 1794, despite the previous bad feeling between the husband and the York manager.

The Johnsons were recruited by John Hodgkinson for the American stage in 1795. He made his American debut on 2 November 1795 at the Federal Street Theatre, Boston, as Bygrove in *Know Your Own Mind*, played by the combined Boston and New York companies. On 5 November he acted Sir Francis Wronghead in *The Provok'd Husband*, in which Mrs Johnson made her debut as Lady Townly. With Hodgkinson's American company at Boston through 20 January 1796, Johnson was seen as Drummer in *The Battle of Hexham*, Whittle in *The Irish Widow*, Rowley in *The School for Scandal*, Leech in *The School for Wives*, Osmyn in *The Sultan*, and Weazel in *The Wheel of Fortune*, among other roles.

When Hodgkinson took his contingent to New York, Johnson made his first appearance at the John Street Theatre as Sir Francis Wronghead on 10 February 1796. The *Daily Advertiser* of the twelfth thought Johnson was entitled to great praise, "though he did not, perhaps, enter fully into the *peculiar commic* [sic] *spirit* of the character; it was more happily expressed in his countenance, than in his voice and action." Among his other roles in his first New York season were the Old Man in *The Surrender of Calais*, Donald in *The Deserted Daughter*, Roque in *The Mountaineers*, Sir Jealous Traffick in *The Busy Body*, as well as many of the characters he had played at Boston. The Johnsons remained in America for three seasons, acting at New York, Boston, Hartford, and Philadelphia. His salary in 1798 was about $20 per week and that of his wife, who was a more important performer, $25.00.

Though Dunlap offered them a renewal of their articles at the Park Theatre in New York for the 1798–99 season, the Johnsons decided to return to England. Mrs Johnson made her debut at Covent Garden Theatre on 28 September 1798 as Lady Townly; during the rest of that season while earning £3 per week she acted regularly. Johnson, on the other hand, did not make his appearance at Covent Garden until 18 May 1799, as Fitzharding in *The Iron Chest* and Semblance in the first London performance of Dunlap's farce *Tell Truth and Shame the Devil*, for a benefit his wife shared with Townsend. Mrs Johnson's portion of tickets sold that night was £115 3s. 6d.

Johnson toured the provinces over the next three years, playing at Dublin, Richmond, and Sheffield in 1799 ("husband of the lady at Covent-Garden"), at Hull in 1800, and at Nottingham in 1802, among other places. In the fall of 1802 he returned with his wife to New York to act with Dunlap's company at the Park Theatre. When Dunlap went bankrupt in February 1805, a "Commonwealth of Actors," established to finish the season, selected Johnson and Joseph Tyler as joint managers. Their success resulted in their reappointment as managers for 1805–6, in which season the Johnsons' daughter Ellen Augusta Johnson, then about six years old, played in the afterpiece *The Wolf King; or, The Tale of Little Red Riding Hood*. When the directors of the Park leased the theatre to Thomas A. Cooper in the spring of 1806, the Johnsons sailed back to England, where they played the provinces for some 11 years.

In 1817 the Johnsons returned to New York, where he acted for several years at the Park Theatre until his death in that city on 25 October 1819 at the age of 60, according to his obituary in the Boston *Columbian Centinal* of 30 October 1819.

Dunlap described Johnson as having a small and light figure, well formed, with "a singular physiognomy, a nose perfectly Grecian." In his last years at the Park his powers had diminished, but he had been an important actor in the developing years of the American stage.

His wife Elizabeth had made her last appearance on the stage at the Park on 26 April 1817. She died at Whitestone, Long Island, on 16 June 1830.

The Johnsons' daughter, Ellen Augusta, born at Hull on 12 November 1800, made her debut at Drury Lane in October 1815 and began her adult association with the Park Theatre in 1817. An attractive and successful performer, in August 1825 she married Thomas Hilson, a regular member of the Park Theatre Company, who, born of "a respectable English family by the name of Hill," had adopted the professional name of Hilson. After making his debut at the Park in 1811, he enjoyed public favor as a comedian and singer. With her husband, Mrs Hilson played starring engagements in various American cities, beginning in 1831. Hilson died of a stroke at Louisville, Kentucky, on 23 July 1834, about the age of 50. Ellen Hilson died on 2 April 1837. In the Harvard Theatre Collection is an engraved drawing of a tombstone in St John's Cemetery commemorating Mrs Johnson, Mrs Hilson, and two infant children of the latter. On Mrs Hilson's death, her infant daughter Maria was adopted by Mr Simpson, manager of the Park Theatre. Maria Hilson married Alfred L. Curtis, a New York merchant, on 8 December 1853 at Calvary Church, and she died in New York in June 1869.

Johnson, Mrs John, Elizabeth, née Ford
1771–1830, actress.

Elizabeth Johnson was born in 1771, probably at Ipswich. She was the daughter of Major Ford of Ipswich and also was related to a Mr Jackaman, the town clerk. As Miss Ford she was acting by 1790 at the Theatre Royal, Norwich, where Mrs Merry knew her as a tall and awkward girl. The following year she was again performing at Norwich, but now as Mrs Johnson, having married the actor John Johnson (1759–1819), who was about 12 years her elder. She played at Bath and Bristol in 1793 and 1794. There, according to Tate Wilkinson in his *Wandering Patentee*, she was most favorably received but too lavishly puffed. Wilkinson engaged her for the York circuit in August and September of 1794 and found that she had "an excellent figure, dresses to great advantage, and has a good portion of merit," in both comedy and tragedy; "her behaviour is unexceptionable in every point, in and out of the

Tombstone of ELIZABETH JOHNSON

theatre, and indeed is such, that every person must be glad to see her in it."

In 1795 John Hodgkinson recruited Mr and Mrs Johnson for his American Company. She made her debut at the Federal Street Theatre, Boston, on 5 November 1795 as Lady Townly in *The Provok'd Husband*. At Boston through 20 January 1796 Mrs Johnson acted about 20 roles, including Lady Teazle in *The School for Scandal*, Mrs Belville in *The School for Wives*,

Widow Brady in *The Irish Widow*, Statira in *Alexander the Great*, Perdita in *Florizel and Perdita*, Bisarre in *The Inconstant*, Lydia Languish in *The Rivals*, and Louisa in *The West Indian*. When she first appeared at the John Street Theatre in New York on 10 February 1796 as Lady Townly, the critic in the *Daily Advertiser* of 12 February was excited over "Her person, elegant and graceful; her countenance pleasing, animated and peculiarly expressive of those lively emotions which she so powerfully excites; chaste and spirited in her manner; her action easy and proper; her pronunciation correct, distinct and clear." Of her performance as Julia in *The Surrender of Calais* the same critic raved that "Mrs. *Johnson* charmed our hearts! Rarely is such a form, such a face, and such a mind as all her action pourtrays found united in the same person.—Her voice is powerful, though sweet; her pronunciation just, though a little studied—this however, is a *good* fault. . . . She is strictly attentive to the *scene*. . . ." Among her other roles during her first New York season were Zoraida in *The Mountaineers*, Miss Tittup in *Bon Ton*, Emeline in *Speculation*, Juliana in *The School for Citizens*, and Beatrice in *Much Ado about Nothing*.

Playing in Baltimore, Philadelphia, and Hartford, as well as in New York and Boston, Mrs Johnson developed into an actress of substantial merit and considerable importance. She was Rosalind when *As You Like It* was performed as the inaugural production at the new Park Theatre on 29 January 1798 and acted a successful Juliet there on 9 March of that year. In his *History of the American Theatre*, Dunlap, who was her manager at the Park, wrote that Mrs Johnson was

a tall, elegant, beautiful young woman, whose taste in dress made her a model for the belles of the city, and whose manners were as fascinating off as on the stage. . . . She was almost too tall, yet the spectator did not wish her any shorter, and if any movement appeared like an approach to awkwardness, it was only to be attributed to modesty. . . . At the time we now speak of, America had not seen so perfect a fine lady in comedy.

After three seasons in America, the Johnsons determined to return to England. Announced as from the theatre in America, on 28 September 1798 Mrs Johnson made her first appearance as Lady Townly at Covent Garden The-

atre, where she had been engaged for £3 per week. (Her salary the previous season in New York had been $25.00 per week.) Afterwards she played Sylvia in *The Recruiting Officer* on 5 October 1798 and then on 11 October acted Agatha Friburg in the premiere of Mrs Inchbald's *Lovers' Vows*, a play that was performed 42 times before the end of the season. Her performances of those debut characters were commented upon at length in an informative review in the *Monthly Mirror* of October 1798:

MRS. JOHNSON—*from America*.

The part of *Lady Townley*, requires so much from the actress, that it is seldom we see a finished performance of the character. The present COUNTESS OF DERBY [Elizabeth Farren] looked, spoke, and felt it. . . . To be inferior to such a woman, can be no degradation to Mrs. Johnson; nor must we think lightly of her talents, *because* they were surpassed in *Lady Townley* by the transcendant abilities of Miss Farren.

Elegance is the charm which should preside over every scene of this character: the gay rattle of her conversation; her resolute resistance of her husband's authority; her teizing provocations; her lively raillery of *Lady Grace* and "her antediluvian notions," must be all under the control of this prevailing quality. This it is that makes it so difficult in performance; many can play it with spirit, but few with *elegance*. Mrs. Johnson's appearance and manner are highly favourable to the undertaking; but though no novice upon the stage, she is one of those ladies, who, from a native diffidence of her own powers, shrinks from the approbation that is meant to cheer her; she comes modestly and respectfully before the public, and seems more solicitous that the audience should discover her merit, than she appears forward to disclose it.

This amiable timidity prevented her from giving that sprightly effect to some of the passages which the author intended; there was a lack of the *gaieté du coeur*, the flow of spirits which never once forsakes the giddy votary of fashion, till shame, contempt, and disgrace, unite to display the horrors of her situation. The vivacity of *Lady Townley* should have no boundary, for her follies are in some measure the consequence of her youth and playful disposition, otherwise nothing could preserve her from the detestation of the audience. Mrs. Johnson was very successful in the *last scene*, which she played with great delicacy and feeling.

Her *Sylvia*, in the Recruiting Officer, is a performance of much merit; but an actress must summon up all her courage, and all her impudence to give effect to the scenes of Farquhar; his dialogue abounds in sharp reciprocations of wit, which must be delivered with force and rapidity; and his obscenity is so gross, that the performer, to do it justice, must come boldly forward upon the stage. Mrs. Johnson, we plainly see, is not equal to so formidable an encounter; for, though her first scenes were agreeably arch and animated, there wanted, in her male attire, the familiar air and frolicsome address of *Jack Wilford*. *Sylvia* must needs be supposed to be pretty well divested of her *mauvaise honte*, to attract, as a *man*, the attention of a couple of libertines like *Plume* and *Brazen*.

Mrs. Johnson is much above the middle stature, but her height, while it gives a commanding appearance to her person, is not incompatible with grace; her face is handsome, and, we think, rather femininely interesting than strongly expressive; her action is not inelegant, but it wants freedom and variety; her voice is happily suited to either department of the drama; her intonation is full and musical; she has a sort of *lisp*, that frequently reminds us of Mrs. Goodall (a lady whom we think she resembles in some other respects) but it does not materially affect her articulation; she speaks with a degree of judgment and precision which few women are able to attain: indeed, *good sense* is the characteristic of all her performances. In every point of view she is to be considered with respect.

The *Norwich Mercury* of 13 October 1798 announced that the Mrs Johnson who had recently made her successful debut at Covent Garden was the daughter of Major Ford of Ipswich and the wife of the Mr Johnson who had formerly played at Norwich.

On 15 December 1798 Mrs Johnson acted Lady Macbeth for the first time. Her other roles that season were Mrs Cleveland in *The Votary of Wealth* and an unspecified part in *Albert and Adelaide*. For her benefit on 18 May 1799, when her share of tickets totaled £115 3s. 6d., she acted Helen in *The Iron Chest* and Catherine in *Catherine and Petruchio*.

After acting a summer at Birmingham, Mrs Johnson returned to Covent Garden in 1799–1800, again for £3 per week. Her new roles that season included Mrs Metland in the premiere of Mrs Inchbald's *The Wise Man of the East* on 30 November 1799 and Miss Dorillon in *Wives as They Were, and Maids as They Are* for a benefit she shared with Emery and Mrs Thomas Dibdin on 28 May 1800, when the total receipts were £362 12s. Next season she was gone from Covent Garden.

From 1800 to 1802 Mrs Johnson was a valuable player at York and Hull, though when she acted Emily in *The Poor Gentleman* in Hull on

February 1802, the critic in the *Monthly Mirror* thought that she did not look young enough for the role, despite her playing the part "admirably."

In the fall of 1802 the Johnsons returned to New York to act at the Park Theatre under Dunlap's management. She reappeared on 17 November as Lady Bell Bloomer in *Which is the Man?*; the press reported that she performed the role "with that grace, vivacity, and easy elegance which form the character of the polished and fashionable lady," demonstrating she had "derived improvement from her transatlantic visit." Her portrayal of Lady Teazle in *The School for Scandal* on 22 November ranked "before any other" the critic in the *Evening Post* had ever seen. Her Beatrice in *Much Ado about Nothing* on 9 December was regarded by the critic in the *Morning Chronicle* as "the best we recollect to have ever seen on our stage."

Having spent four years in their second American visit, the Johnsons then made their way back across the ocean to spend 10 years of comparative obscurity in the English provinces. They were back in New York in the autumn of 1817, when Mrs Johnson acted Lady Randolph in *Douglas* on 2 December at the Park Theatre. Though her *forte* had previously been high comedy, she now was found in a different line, playing Jane Shore, Queen Elizabeth in *The Earl of Essex*, Madame Clermont in *Adrian and Orilla*, and Eugenia in *The Foundling of the Forest*, among other serious roles. She was not a success that season, though her daughter Ellen Augusta Johnson, who had been born at Hull on 12 November 1800, made her adult debut at the Park on 15 January 1817 as Amanthis in *The Child of Nature* and soon became a popular favorite. Mother and child appeared together on 25 April 1817, when Mrs Johnson's performance as Evelina in *The Castle Spectre* proved to be her last upon the stage.

Elizabeth Johnson died at Whitestone, Long Island, New York, on 16 June 1830, at the age of 59, and was buried in St John's Cemetery. Her husband John Johnson had died in New York on 25 October 1819 at the age of 60. For information on their child Ellen, who married the actor Thomas Hilson, see John Johnson's notice.

In the Harvard Theatre Collection is an engraved drawing of the tombstone which marked the graves of Mrs Johnson, Mrs Eleanor Hilson, and the infant children of the latter.

Johnson, "Maggoty." *See* JOHNSON, SAMUEL *1691–1773.*

Johnson, Philip *d. 1678?, theatre keeper, gallery keeper?*

Philip Johnson, doubtless a relative of the elder and the younger George Johnson, theatre keepers at the court of Charles II, took over the job of the younger George in 1672. Philip held the post at court until on or before 24 April 1678, when he was succeeded by John Clarke. Since court employees sometimes held outside jobs, perhaps Philip Johnson was the person cited as one of the (middle?) gallery keepers at the Drury Lane playhouse in December 1677. The document citing him was reported in *The Theatrical Inquisitor and Monthly Mirror* of July 1816—too late a source to be considered completely reliable. The gallery keeper Johnson was mentioned in the income reports for *All for Love* on 12 December 1677 and *The Rival Queens* on 26 December. The replacement of Philip Johnson as court theatre keeper in April 1678 suggests that he had recently died.

Johnson, Robert *b. c. 1645, musician.*

In *Colchester's London Marriage Licenses*, edited by Joseph Foster, is the report of a marriage at Gray's Inn Chapel on 4 December 1666 of Robert Johnson, musician, of the parish of St Giles in the Fields, bachelor, age 21, and Martha Strowd of the same parish, spinster, age 20, the daughter of Abraham Strowd.

Johnson, Robert ₍*fl.* 1794–1815₎, *violist.*

Robert Johnson of Bury St Edmunds was listed in 1794 in Doane's *Musical Directory* as a bass and tenor player in the Handelian memorial concerts at Westminster Abbey and as a member of the New Musical Fund. In 1815 he was still a subscriber to that Fund and played in that year's program for the Fund's benefit.

Johnson, Samuel *1691–1773, dancer, musician, actor, playwright.*

Samuel Johnson of Cheshire was born in 1691 and became a dancing master. From Byrom's *Private Journal and Literary Remains* we learn that Johnson gave a subscription ball in Manchester in 1722 and by 1724 was in London as a violinist. We take it, therefore, that the Mr Johnson advertised as lately arrived from Ireland who performed three violin concertos (one called "The Cuckoo") at York Buildings on 27 March 1724, was very likely Samuel. He wrote both the music and the words to *Hurlothrumbo, or the Supernatural*, which was given its premiere at the Haymarket Theatre on 29 March 1729, with Johnson

SAMUEL JOHNSON, of Cheshire, as Wildfire, playing violin, with ELIZA HAYWOOD as Lady Flame, on balcony: a scene from *The Blazing Comet*

artist unknown

playing Lord Flame, for his benefit. The odd work was remarkably successful. A wide circle of Johnson's friends lent their support, and the piece received the encouragement of the Duke of Montague (from whom the idea of the work supposedly came) and of Sir Robert Walpole. The *Biographia Dramatica* (1812) said that Johnson performed Lord Flame "sometimes in one key, sometimes in another, sometimes fiddling, sometimes dancing, and sometimes walking on high stilts." Byrom wrote an epilogue for the second performance of the work on 7 April, another benefit for Johnson, and may have helped compose the text of the play itself.

Johnson became for a while a town hero (and butt of such satirists as Fielding). He quickly wrote a new piece, a "dramatic Opera called The Cheshire Comicks or the Amours of Lord Flame," in which on 23 February 1730 he played the leading role at the Haymarket. The work did not appeal and was never published. Johnson's next effort was *The Blazing Comet: The Mad Lovers; or, The Beauties of the Poets* ("A Dramatic Every Thing"), with Johnson as Wildfire, which played at the Haymarket on 2 March 1732. Johnson apparently managed the troupe that performed his work. On 8 March he danced a hornpipe and Cheshire round, but instead of *The Blazing Comet*, which had been scheduled, *Tunbridge Walks* was performed, owing to Johnson's having a "great Cold, that renders him Incapable of executing his Part." For his benefit *The Blazing Comet* was performed twice in April, and then Johnson again revived *Hurlothrumbo*.

On 18 April 1735 at Lincoln's Inn Fields the Cheshire eccentric once more revived *Hurlothrumbo* and his part of Lord Flame, but only for a single performance. Then, on 10 January 1737 at that house, he brought out a new piece, *All Alive and Merry* ("An Opera in a Comedy"), which was never published. Again he composed the music as well as the text. According to Byrom, on the opening night of the work Johnson for some reason "was for fighting with somebody in the pit." The work was reasonably successful. On 14 May 1741 Johnson was back with *Hurlothrumbo* at the Haymarket.

On 11 April 1741 at the Haymarket another of his unpublished works, *The Fool Made Wise, or Sir John Falstaff in Masquerade*, had been performed. (Nicoll believes this was one work; *The London Stage* makes it two.) *The Dictionary of National Biography* also lists as by Johnson, *Pompey the Great*, which was never published and seems not to have been performed. *A Vision of Heaven* was published in 1738; attributed to Johnson also was *Harmony in Uproar* and a dialogue called *Court and Country*. The *New Cambridge Bibliography of English Literature* does not list Johnson.

When Johnson was not in London, he held forth in Manchester as a dancing master. From about 1745 on, however, he lived in relative retirement and isolation in Gawsworth, near Macclesfield, where he was variously known as Lord Flame, Fiddler Johnson, and Maggoty Johnson. Isaac Reed in his "Notitia Dramatica," in the British Library, recorded the death of Samuel Johnson of Cheshire on 3 May 1773:

Died at the New Hall in Gawsworth Cheshire in a very advanced age Mr Samuel Johnson commonly called Lord Flame a pesn formerly well known as an excellent Comedian a famous dancing master a masterly player on the Violin an extraordinary singer the author of a play called Hurlothrumbo and others of more eminence. He was a man of singular oddities with sharp flights of wit and a keen satirist even upon his best friends. He for above 30 years past lived in retirement at the above place having very little society with any of his neighbours kept only one maid which he called Goose Eye who lived with him 30 years even from her childhood till a few weeks before his death when she fell sick and died. He made a vault in a grove [called "Maggoty Johnson's Wood] about a quarter of a mile from Gawsworth Church and had made preparations for building a Tomb over her she in her sickness (by his persuasion) had agreed to be so buried; but two of her brothers coming to see her just before she expired frustrated his design and had her buried in Gawsworth Church. Mr. Johnson's dissapt & grief for the death of her who so long had been a faithful servt to his own desire had Christian Burial at Gawsworth Church on the 5th but was afterwards removed to the Vault which he designed for his Maid.

Johnson himself probably wrote the inscription on a stone at his tomb:

Stay, thou whom chance directs or ease persuades
To seek the quiet of these sylvan shades;
Here undisturbed and hid from vulgar eyes
A wit, musician, poet, player, lies:
A dancing-master, too, in grace he shone,
And all the arts of opera were his own.

Courtesy of Raymond Richards, Gawsworth Hall

SAMUEL JOHNSON, of Cheshire

self portrait

In comedy well skilled, he drew Lord Flame,
Acted the part, and gained himself the name;
Averse to strife, how oft he'd gravely say
These peaceful groves should shade his breathless
clay,
That when he rose again, laid here alone,
No friend and he should quarrel for a bone;
Thinking that, were some old lame gossip nigh,
She possibly might take his leg or thigh.

Johnson's ghost was said to have haunted the spot where he was buried, and, according to *Notes and Queries* on 6 January 1877, he once nearly frightened a nervous lady to death by his "polite assurance that he should consider himself bound to pay her his first visit as a ghost."

This mad, or madcap, man was shown in a print published in 1732 depicting a scene from *The Blazing Comet*. Johnson, as the mad lover Wildfire, is shown holding a violin and bow and standing on stilts, carrying on a balcony scene with Lady Flame (Eliza Haywood), a fellow lunatic. Among the portraits at Gawsworth Hall is an oil of Johnson, painted by himself.

Johnson, Samuel [fl. 1752?–1781], actor, manager.

The actor and provincial manager Samuel Johnson (not to be confused either with the great lexicographer or with the eccentric author of *Hurlothumbro*) was perhaps the S. Johnson who is listed by William Smith Clark in *The Irish Stage in the County Towns* as having acted at Belfast on 24 May 1758 and at the Smock Alley and Crow Street theatres, Dublin, in 1759–60.

In the 1760s Samuel Johnson built up a circuit of provincial theatres in Wiltshire, Hampshire, and West Sussex. His connection with those southern districts may have begun as early as 1752, for a Johnson was playing in Percy's company at Canterbury, Kent, that year. In 1763 Johnson fitted up the town hall in Winchester as a theatre and in 1764 he bought out Dymer's interest and properties in the theatrical venture at Chichester, where he converted an old malthouse. At Brighton he rebuilt a big barn, which he opened as a theatre holding about 100 people on 7 May 1764, with performances of *The Busy Body* and *The Mock Doctor*. He continued to visit Brighton until at least 1770. (In his history of the the-

atre of Brighton, H. C. Porter mistakenly gives Johnson's Christian name as Charles.)

In 1765 Johnson arranged a new theatre in Mr Bungay's Sun Inn, Fisherton Bridge, in Salisbury, which he opened on 25 January. Another new theatre, erected by subscription, was opened at Southampton on 7 July 1766. From 1767 through 1769 Johnson's companies made appearances at Portsmouth, Southampton, Salisbury, Winchester, and Newport, and on the Isle of Wight. In 1768–69 his co-manager was Collins. Samuel Johnson was probably the manager of that surname who headed a ribald company at Reading, where, according to Gilliland, the male performers were all "rogues" and the females all of unmentionable character. The anonymous author of *Candour. An Enquiry into the real merits of the Salisbury Comedians*, published on 30 November 1767, wrote of him:

Fond of Low Humour, JOHNSON *first we see,*
(How well the Humour and the Man agree)
In that, indeed his Praise can be but small,
We give enough, by giving none at all. . . .

In 1769–70 Johnson seems not to have been found with his touring company, though his wife, who had been with him in the 1760s, continued to appear in the towns in the south of England mentioned above.

He may have been the Johnson who acted Major O'Flaherty in *The West Indian* for his own benefit, by special license, at the Haymarket Theatre on 15 April 1771. Probably Samuel was the Johnson who performed in Foote's summer company at the Haymarket in 1774, playing a Scholar in *The Padlock*, La Fleur in *The Commissary*, Harry in *The Mock Doctor*, and parts in *The Bankrupt*, *The Devil upon Two Sticks*, and *The Rehearsal*.

On 23 March 1775 Johnson took the Haymarket Theatre for a benefit performance of *The Merchant of Venice* in which he acted Shylock "in the Jewish dialect" and spoke a new epilogue which he had written for the occasion. He also acted in the afterpiece *The Snuff Box*. A week prior to that event, someone had written to Johnson through the columns of the *Morning Chronicle* of 15 March 1775 to castigate him for his "bold attempt of putting a new suit of cloaths upon Shylock." The writer allowed Johnson merit as Major O'Flaherty, the Spanish Fryar, and Falstaff—roles he may have acted previously in London—but complained "what, in the name of all that is reasonable, could induce you to make so great a trial of the patience of a London audience, as to fix upon a character, where your figure cannot befriend you?" Perhaps, presumed the correspondent, "your Hibernian front and the keen air of St. George's Fields, have armed you cap-a-pee." On 22 March, the day before he essayed Shylock, Johnson replied to the same paper, admitting he was an Irishman with a brogue but thinking it "rather cruel to condemn a man before he is heard." He added that he had "ever found the London audience kind and impartial," certainly establishing he had previously been a metropolitan performer.

A license was granted to Samuel Johnson to perform at the Haymarket on 24 January 1776, but no playbill survives for that date. In the autumn of 1776, Johnson was with a company that played 12 nights at China Hall, Rotherhithe, between 23 September and 18 October 1776. Johnson's roles included Captain Savage in *The School for Wives*, Jupiter in *Midas*, the Lord Chamberlain in *Henry VIII*, Lory in *Miss Hoyden*, Sadi in *Barbarossa*, Dick in *The King and the Miller of Mansfield*, Tradelove in *A Bold Stroke for a Wife*, Hotman in *Oroonoko*, Chamberlain in *A Trip to Scotland*, Ratcliff in *Richard III*, Perdiccas in *Alexander the Great*, Woodley in *Marriage à la Mode*, Doodle in *The Life and Death of Tom Thumb the Great*, Trueman in *The London Merchant*, Selim in *The Mourning Bride*, Beaufort in *The Citizen*, Sempronius in *Cato*, Freeman in *High Life below Stairs*, and Worthy in *The Recruiting Officer*.

Probably our subject was the Johnson who over the next five or six years occasionally played in specially-licensed performances at the Haymarket. On 11 February 1777 he acted Falstaff in *King Henry IV, With the Humours of Sir John Falstaff* for a benefit he shared with West "at the Desire of the most noble Order of Bucks." Tickets could be had of Johnson at the Golden Cross, Charing Cross. On 23 March 1778 Johnson played Tom in *The Jealous Husband*, on 15 March 1779 Haughty in *The Humours of Oxford*, and on 22 January 1781 Courtly in *A Wife to be Lett* and a principal character in *The Sharper's Last Shift*.

Perhaps Samuel Johnson can be identified with Johnsons who performed in London and elsewhere over the next several decades, but we are unable to do so with any confidence. A Mr Johnson began a trial engagement at Norwich in the spring of 1769. A person of that name played at Chester in Austin and Whitlock's company in September 1775; and a Johnson was an extra at Liverpool in August 1777. At Edinburgh in 1770, when Foote's Haymarket company was playing there, a Mr Johnson was described in *A New Rosciad*:

> Next J—S—N comes—a listless thing!
> Twanger of discord's jarring string:
> Alike intun'd for joys or woes,
> Croaking he comes, and croaking goes.
> His stiff-set legs in stated track,
> Take two steps forward, two steps back:

Between 1774 and 1784 an actor named Johnson regularly played many roles, mostly in an older line, in the Edinburgh company. And the *Morning Chronicle* of 26 January 1787 reported the death on 24 January at Mildenhall of a Mr Johnson of Jerrold's, company who expired while acting Benvolio.

Samuel Johnson's wife, who acted in his provincial companies and occasionally in London, is noticed separately.

Johnson, Mrs Samuel [*fl.* 1759–1781?], actress, singer.

Mrs Samuel Johnson was acting with her husband at the Smock Alley Theatre, Dublin, by 1759–60. During the 1760s she was a member of the touring company managed by him which played at Winchester beginning in 1763, at Chichester and Brighton beginning in 1764, at Salisbury beginning in 1765, and at Southampton beginning in 1767. She also acted at Portsmouth and Newport and on the Isle of Wight, as well as at the places named above, between 1767 and 1770. At Salisbury on 30 November 1767 the author of *Candour. An Enquiry into the real merits of the Salisbury Comedians* wrote of her:

> Next, MRS JOHNSON see—if I condemn,
> May I ne'er see true modesty again.
> O! tis a Flower indeed, so seldom found,
> So very seldom on theatric Ground,
> That it deserves our utmost fostering Care,
> To cherish, to protect, and keep it there.

Perhaps Mrs Samuel Johnson was the Mrs Johnson who performed at Edinburgh in 1770. *A New Rosciad* found her movement

"Stiff and affected in her gait, / She steps by rule premediate" despite the fact that she had a form "compos'd with symmetry." The author was unimpressed with her inanimate face—"A blank insensibility"—and with her whining and expressing of terror and rage by "the stampt foot, and panting breast." She may also have been the Mrs Johnson who at Edinburgh in 1773–74 played such roles as Belinda in *The Provok'd Wife*, Calpurnia in *Julius Caesar*, Dorinda in *The Beaux' Stratagem*, Lucinda in *The Conscious Lovers*, Miranda in *The Tempest*, and Sukey Chitterton in *The Invasion of Harlequin*.

Perhaps our subject was the Mrs "Johnston" who performed Mrs Slammekin in *The Beggars Opera* on 6 September 1774 at the Haymarket Theatre, where Samuel Johnson seems to have been a member of Foote's summer company. A Mrs "Johnston" also played Diana Trapes in *The Beggar's Opera* at the Haymarket on 21 September 1775. Perhaps she acted with her husband in a company that performed at China Hall, Rotherhithe, between 23 September and 18 October 1776, but her name does not appear in the extant bills.

Probably she was the Mrs Johnson who, announced as from the Haymarket Theatre, acted Alicia in *Jane Shore* on 31 July 1779 at Norwich. A Mrs Johnson played Mrs Watchit in *The Artifice* at the Haymarket on 16 October 1781.

Johnson, Thomas [*fl.* 1758–1779?], *equestrian, proprietor.*

On 15 July 1758 Thomas Johnson, a native of Ireland, advertised in the Bristol press that, weather permitting, he would perform "Feats of Horsemanship" on Durdham Down on 17 July. He was lodging then at the Ship in March Street, Bristol. In the same year Johnson made appearances in a field adjoining the Three Hats, in Upper Street, Islington, where he became known as "the Irish Tartar." His performances included galloping round the field with three horses abreast, shifting himself from one to the other. In *The Tavern Haunter* for November 1758 a reporter described another feat: "while he was standing on the Outside Horse of the Three, with all the Reins and Whip in one Hand, he threw up his Cap several Times in the Air, and catched it again,

with the other, while the Horses were in full Speed. . . ." Johnson had acquired his "wonderful Dexterity," according to this testimony, by the practice of eight or 10 years and in 1758 appeared to be "about 25, or 26 Years of Age."

At one time Johnson's act included riding on a single horse while standing on his head, but this trick "gave pain to the spectators," so he was obliged to eliminate it. At the Three Hats on 17 July 1766 Johnson rode in the presence of the Duke of York and some 500 spectators. Johnson became the proprietor of Dobney's Bowling Green House in Penton Street sometime after the death of its owner, Ann Dobney, in March 1760. He changed the name to Johnson's Prospect and Bowling Green House and converted the bowling green to an amphitheatre. Johnson seems to have given up the place by 1769. During the 1760s he also performed equestrian feats at the Star and Garter Tavern and Gardens, Chelsea, where admission was one shilling.

Possibly he was the Mr Johnson who was a member of a troupe headed by the showman Philip Breslaw that performed "a new grand Exhibition" at the Merchant Taylors' Hall in Bristol from mid-August to mid-September 1779. Breslaw on other occasions was associated with equestrians.

At the Huntington Library is an anonymous print of "Johnson, Standing on One, Two & Three Horses in full Speed." Several similar prints, including one engraved by G. Bickham, of "Johnson the surprising Horseman," depicting him in action are in the British Museum.

Johnson, "Yorkshire" *d. 1841, actor.*

Information concerning the actor called "Yorkshire" Johnson can be found in *The History of the Theatre Royal, Dublin* (1870), where it is stated that this person had been born in London and as a young man had been apprenticed to a solicitor there. His interest in amateur theatricals, however, eventually brought him to his first professional engagement at Richmond, Surrey, and an unspecified tragic role sometime in the late 1790s. While performing at Richmond, Johnson was seen by the Irish manager Jones, who engaged him for

THOMAS JOHNSON
engraving by Bickham

the Crow Street Theatre, where he first appeared as Trudge in *Inkle and Yarico* in 1799.

Johnson soon developed a line of low-comedy characters like Zekiel Homespun in *The Heir at Law*. After playing in Dublin until 1803 he visited the Irish provinces and London. He returned to Dublin in 1805 to act at Crow Street until the opening of the Hawkins Street Theatre in 1820, playing at the latter house for another 20 years. Supposedly Johnson remained loyal to his Dublin public, though he had received an offer of £12 per week to play in America. "His private character was unexceptionable, and his manners and conversation were those of a gentleman." He was called "Yorkshire" Johnson not so much for his often performing characters from that region but for the purpose of distinguishing him from "Irish" Johnstone (John Henry) and "Scotch" Johnston (Henry Erskine).

In April 1834 while performing Isaac Mendoza in *The Duenna* he received an accidental kick from the actor of Don Carlos which led to complications and almost killed him. Evidently Johnson never fully recovered from the injury, the effects of which, it was reported, eventually caused his death. That demise, however, did not occur for another seven years. In 1840–41 his health prevented his accepting his usual engagement. On 10 December 1840 he gave his final performance as Ralph Hempseed in *X. Y. Z.*, for his farewell benefit. The following year he died, presumably in his house at No 27, Westmoreland Street, Dublin, where with his wife he had lived for many years.

Johnston. *See also* JOHNSON and JOHNSTONE.

Johnston, Mr [*fl.* 1766]. *See* BARDIN, PETER.

Johnston, Mr [*fl.* 1767], *singer.*
A Mr Johnston sang an unspecified vocal part in a performance of Milton's *Lycidas*, an afterpiece set to music by William Jackson, at Covent Garden on 4 November 1767. That person may have been John Johnston of Drury Lane, but according to the bills that actor was appearing in *A Peep behind the Curtain*, the afterpiece at his theatre that evening.

Johnston, Mr ₁*fl.* 1777₁,   *actor.*
A Mr Johnston played an unspecified role in the first London performance of Robert Hitchcock's *The Coquette* at the Haymarket Theatre on 9 October 1777.

Johnston, Mr ₁*fl.* 1786₁,   *actor.*
A Mr Johnston played minor roles in productions given by a company at the Windsor Castle Inn, King Street, Hammersmith, in the summer of 1786. His first role, a Countryman in *She Stoops to Conquer* on 5 June was followed by Roger in *The Mayor of Garratt*, servants in *The Country Girl*, *The Heiress*, and *The Belle's Stratagem*, Marcellus in *Hamlet*, Spinosa in *Venice Preserv'd*, Crusoe in *Robinson Crusoe*, Hobnail in *Peeping Tom of Coventry*, a Waiter in *The Fool*, and, for his last-known appearance there, on 5 August, David in *The Natural Son*.
The Mrs Johnston who was in the same Hammersmith company no doubt was his wife. They shared a benefit with Miss Williams on 5 August 1786.

Johnston, Mr ₁*fl.* 1798–1814₁,   *dancer, actor.*
A Mr Johnston was employed at Drury Lane Theatre as a chorus dancer for a salary of £1 per week in 1798–99 and 1799–1800. On 5 December 1798 his name was added to the bills as a dancer in *The Captive of Spilburg*, and the next night he performed as a Villager in the ballet *The Scotch Ghost*. On 19 January 1799 he danced as a Vassal in the premiere of *Feudal Times*, the younger Colman's music drama which ran for 39 performances that season. In the following season he performed a Slave in 24 performances of *Blue-Beard*. He was probably the "Johnson" who played the Second Sailor in *Hamlet* on 16 September 1800. The "Master Johnson" who appeared among the small "pantomimick characters" in *Harlequin Amulet* at Drury Lane on 23 December 1800 was probably his son.
Johnston's name continued to appear in the Drury Lane account books as a dancer through 1803–4, at least. Probably he was the "Johnson" who performed in pantomimes and ballets at Sadler's Wells in 1797, 1800, 1806, 1808, and, no doubt, other years. A "Johnson" danced at the Royal Circus in 1809 and 1810 and at the Surrey Theatre in 1814, at the latter

playing an Officer of the Persian Court in *Shamacda; or, The Desert Fiend* on 11 April. A Miss Johnston, perhaps our subject's daughter, danced at the Royal Circus regularly in 1806 and 1807.

Johnston, Mrs ₁*fl.* 1766–1767₁,   *actress.*
A Mrs Johnston was a member of Spranger Barry's Irish company that played at the King's Theatre in the summer of 1766. Her roles there included Lady Wronghead in *The Provok'd Wife*, Goneril in *King Lear*, Melissa in *The Lying Valet*, Mrs Sealand in *The Conscious Lovers*, Emilia in *Othello*, and Pulcheria in *Theodosius*. In 1767 as a member of Foote's summer company at the Haymarket Theatre she acted Sisigambis in *Alexander the Great*, Mrs Peachum in *The Beggar's Opera* and Mrs Sealand. Possibly this actress was Mrs John Johnston (d. 1785), who was a sometime company member at Drury Lane.

Johnston, Mrs ₁*fl.* 1768₁,   *actress, singer.*
A Mrs Johnston played Jenny in *The Gentle Shepherd* at the Haymarket Theatre on 19 December 1768. Performances of this pastoral piece by Allan Ramsay were usually given by actors from the north.

Johnston, Mrs ₁*fl.* 1775₁,   *actress, singer.*
A Mrs Johnston played Diana Trapes in *The Beggar's Opera* at the Haymarket Theatre on 21 September 1775. Perhaps she was Mrs Samuel Johnson.

Johnston, Mrs ₁*fl.* 1786₁,   *actress.*
A Mrs Johnston acted leading parts with a company at the Windsor Castle Inn, King Street, Hammersmith, in the summer of 1786. Her first role, Mrs Hardcastle in *She Stoops to Conquer* on 5 June, was followed by Lady Randolph in *Douglas*, Margery in *The King and the Miller of Mansfield*, Catherine in *Catherine and Petruchio*, the Queen in *Hamlet*, Mrs Cheshire in *The Agreeable Surprise*, Lady Sycamore in *The Maid of the Mill*, Mrs Sagely in *The Heiress*, the Mayoress in *Peeping Tom of Coventry*, Miss Bridget Pumpkin in *All the World's a Stage*, Iris in *A Bold Stroke for a Wife*, Lady Wronghead in *The Provok'd Husband*, Ursula in *The Padlock*, a Lady in *The Belle's Strata-*

gem, and, for her last-known appearance, on 5 August, Jacintha in *The Wrangling Lovers* and Mrs Phoebe Latimer in *The Natural Son*.

The Mr Johnston who was in the Hammersmith company no doubt was her husband. They shared a benefit with Miss Williams on 5 August 1786.

Johnston, Master [*fl. 1759*], *actor.*

A Master Johnston played Beaufort, Junior, in a performance of *Cleone* given by children at the Haymarket Theatre on 10 May 1759. Perhaps he was the son of Mr and Mrs John Johnston, performers at Drury Lane Theatre at that time.

Johnston, Alexander *d. 1775, housekeeper, box bookkeeper, proprietor, property maker? actor?*

According to "Nicholas Nipclose" (Francis Gentleman) in *The Theatres* (1772), Alexander Johnston had once been the proprietor of a puppet show in Edinburgh before he became associated with Drury Lane Theatre. That association might have begun as early as 1752–53, for on 14 December 1752 Cross wrote in his prompter's diary that the scenes of fountains in the pantomime *Harlequin Ranger* "were design'd & made by Mr. Johnson Property maker to our House." That "Johnson," however, may have been a different man though our subject's family was connected with decorations and property-making for several generations.

Johnston was, in any event, housekeeper at Drury Lane by 1761–62. Probably he was the "Johnstone" whom Garrick had ordered "to write out some of the Parts" of several pieces sent by Arthur Murphy, as Garrick reported to that author by letter on 17 September 1761. On 26 May 1762 Johnston received a benefit as housekeeper. That season he also began to serve as box bookkeeper, and the bills specified that places for the boxes could be had from him at the stage door. Either as housekeeper or box bookkeeper, sometimes as both, he was regularly listed for an annual benefit, his last coming on 20 May 1775, when he received net proceeds of £192 4s. 6d. Johnston's salary was 8s. 10d. per day, or £3 13s. per week, between 1764–65 and 1766–67.

Johnston's name appears on occasion in Garrick's correspondence. On 12 December 1774 David complained to his brother George about the pen he was using, but since Johnston was in "a damn'd humour" he dared not ask for a better one. On 16 December 1774 Garrick apologized to George Steevens for failing to keep places for him at a recent performance of *Hamlet*, absolving Johnston from blame.

Modern scholars, such as Christian Deelman in *The Great Stratford Jubilee*, have assumed that the housekeeper was "Gibby Johnson," the person who acted the role of Gibby in *The Wonder* at Drury Lane for several decades. Indeed an engraving of "Mr Jonston" in that role, by Saunders after Van der Gucht (1773), has been called a portrait of Alexander Johnston by the *Catalogue of Engraved British Portraits in the British Museum* and the Hall catalogue of portraits in the Harvard Theatre Collection. But we find no evidence to confirm that identification, and during his lifetime no mention seems to have been made of the housekeeper's acting, a circumstance which, had it occurred, most likely would have been reported. It is tempting to assume that the Johnston who regularly played the Housekeeper in *A Peep Behind the Curtain*, a popular farce by Garrick that had its premiere on 23 October 1767, was the real housekeeper. "Gibby" and the stage housekeeper, however, we believe was John Johnston (fl. 1742?–1781), who regularly performed at Drury Lane during the time the housekeeper Alexander was alive.

Alexander Johnston subscribed to the Drury Lane Fund beginning in 1766, but he never lived to claim. He died on 1 October 1775, at the beginning of Garrick's last year of management, and was buried at St Dunstan, Stepney. By his will, drawn on 2 July 1775, wherein he described himself as a "gentleman" of Russell Street in the parish of St Martin-in-the-Fields, he left his jewels, plate, books, linen, furniture, and other household effects to his wife, Mary Johnston. The rest of his unspecified estate he directed to be sold, and from the proceeds his wife was to receive £100, his son, Roger Johnston, £50, and his daughter Margaret Burrell (of Edinburgh) £50. The balance was to be invested in annuities for his wife. After Mary Johnston's death, son Roger was to receive the annual interest on £1000 for life. The will contains a very long and complex formula for passing along the trust to unnamed grandchildren. The will was proved at London by his widow on 9 October 1775.

Johnston's wife, who was a wardrobe keeper at Drury Lane, died only about a month after her husband, on 9 November 1775.

While housekeeper and box bookkeeper, Johnston also seems to have supplied decorations and properties for various pantomimes. He made the small chandeliers for the Jubilee Rotunda at Stratford in 1769. A press clipping in the British Library's Burney papers offers a poem "To the Memory of the late Mr. Johnson, Book-keeper, &c. at Drury Lane Theatre" which contains the lines: "Fam'd as thou wert for Pantomimic art, / Thou also play'dst the faithful servant's part." In *The Theatres*, Gentleman claimed that Johnston was "remarkable for Economy, obsequiousness and taste in decorations by which he has accumulated some thousands." Garrick seems to have appreciated his services. In his letter of 27 January 1765, sent from Paris, the manager asked James Love to "tell Johnston & his Wife that I have great regard for them."

Johnston's son, Roger, was a property maker at Drury Lane in the 1770s and a provincial manager. Roger's son, named Alexander after his grandfather, was an important machinist, decorator, and costume designer at Drury Lane from 1789 until his death in 1810.

Johnston, Mrs Alexander, Mary
d. 1775, wardrobe keeper.

Mary Johnston, the wife of the Drury Lane housekeeper Alexander Johnston (d. 1775), may have been the "Mrs Johnson" who shared in benefit tickets with other house servants at Drury Lane on 21 May 1761. By 1764–65 she was serving as a wardrobe keeper, earning 3s. 4d. per day, or £1 per week, a salary she was still receiving in 1766–67. In 1766 she subscribed £1 1s. to the Fund.

In his will Alexander Johnston named his wife to receive his household effects and the bulk of his estate, total worth unspecified. Johnston died on 1 October 1775 and his widow proved his will on 19 October. Several weeks later, however, on 9 November 1775, according to the *Morning Chronicle* of 11 November, Mary Johnston also died. Administration of her estate was granted to her son, Roger Johnston, a Drury Lane property maker, on 28

November 1775. She also was the mother of Margaret Burrell, of Edinburgh, who was mentioned in her husband's will.

Johnston, Alexander *d. 1810, machinist, carpenter, painter, scene designer, costume designer, dancer, actor.*

Alexander Johnston, a backstage master of many trades during the 1790s and early 1800s, was the son of Roger Johnston, a Drury Lane property maker and provincial manager, and the grandson of Alexander Johnston (d. 1775) and Mary Johnston (d. 1775), Drury Lane housekeeper and wardrobe keeper, respectively. No doubt young Alexander was the Master Johnston who played children's roles at Brighton, 1774 to 1776, during the time his father managed that theatre, and at Bristol in 1781–82.

A Master Johnston also played a Lilliputian in *Robinson Crusoe* at the Theatre Royal, Shakespeare Square, Edinburgh, on 26 January and 3 April 1782; could he have been the A. Johnston who was paid £3 3s. a month later, on 3 May 1782, for dancing at Drury Lane? Though not listed as "Master" but "Mr" A. Johnston in the account books at that time, it appears that he was still young enough for his mother to collect his salary: on 9 July 1782 "Mr. A. Johnston in full for Dancing pᵈ his Mother 5/9/–." At that time Roger Johnston, his father, was employed as a Drury Lane property maker.

During the 1780s Alexander Johnston continued to be paid by Drury Lane, presumably as a dancer. His salary in 1785–86 was £1 6s. per week. On 18 May 1787 he danced a hornpipe, and another one on 7 June. Between 1785 and 1789 a Johnston, probably Alexander, but perhaps Roger, received sums in payment for decorations and materials. From this time until far into the nineteenth century there were a number of Johnsons, Johnstons, and Johnstones working for the London theatres, off and on stage, and usually only their last names are found in bills and accounts; so it is impossible to sort them out with any certainty.

By 1788–89 we can begin to discern Alexander Johnston functioning as a machinist, earning a salary of £2 10s. per week and sharing in benefit tickets with house servants and dancers on 9 June 1789. Probably he was the "Johnson" who, according to the bill, wonderfully executed the *Figure in the Iron Cage* for the subterranean dungeon scene in *Gallic Freedom; or, Vive la Liberté* at Sadler's Wells on 31 August 1789. (Nicoll—calling it an "entertainment"— places this production at the Royal Circus on 21 August 1789.)

During the last decade of the eighteenth century Alexander Johnston grew in importance to the various London theatres as carpenter, painter, scene designer, costume designer, and machinist. He can be noted almost every season at Drury Lane, though he did not spend his time in the exclusive service of that theatre. On 7 June 1792, when the Drury Lane company was at the King's Theatre, he shared benefit receipts of £518 6s. (less house charges of £171 15s.) with the D'Egvilles, Nix, and Dale. His address then was No 15, Martlet Court, Bow Street.

At the laying of the first stone for the new Drury Lane Theatre in 1792, according to J. P. Kemble, "Mr Johnson the Machinist . . . put some coins under it." At the King's Theatre he did the decorations for Noverre's new ballet *Iphigenia in Aulide*, which opened on 23 April 1793. The "Machinery, Decorations, and Dresses" were under his direction for *Macbeth*, the inaugural production at the new Drury Lane on 21 April 1794. Other productions at Drury Lane with which he was subsequently involved included dresses, with Miss Rein, and also (often) the decorations, for *The Cherokee* on 20 December 1794, *Alexander the Great* on 12 February 1795, *Jack of Newbury* on 6 May 1795, *Venice Preserv'd* on 21 October 1795, *Harlequin Captive* on 18 January 1796, *The Iron Chest* on 12 March 1796, the Shakespeare hoax *Vortigern* on 2 April 1796, *Mahoud* on 30 April 1796, *Robinson Crusoe* on 26 December 1796, *Feudal Times* on 19 January 1799, *The Egyptian Festival* on 11 March 1800, and *De Montfort* on 29 April 1800. The *Monthly Mirror* of March 1800 commended his work in *The Egyptian Festival* because of the splendor of the production and the fact that he "attended with particular accuracy to the *costume* of the country."

Another of his triumphs was *Blue-Beard*, a popular musical drama by Colman the younger, which opened at Drury Lane on 16 January 1798 with "The Machinery, Decorations, and Dresses designed under the direction of Johnston, and executed by him, Underwood, Gay, and Miss Rein." In his *Reminiscences*, Michael

Kelly, who played Selim in that production, told of going with Sheridan and Kemble to the property room where they found Johnston, "the able and ingenious machinist, at work upon the horses, and on the point of beginning the elephant, which was to carry Blue Beard." To Sheridan's suggestion that he hire an elephant from Pidock's, in Exeter Exchange, Johnston replied, "If I cannot make a better elephant than that at Exeter 'Change, I deserve to be hanged." Kemble's great success as Pizarro on 11 December 1799 was aided to a considerable degree by Johnston's machines, decorations, and dresses. Similarly, for *Harlequin Amulet* on 22 December 1800 he was greatly credited in the press: "Mr. JOHNSTON, the celebrated Mechanist, we understand, formed the plan of the Pantomime; the whole of which does much credit, not only to his execution, but to his inventive taste." Among his effects was a "dragon of surprising terror." *Bell's Weekly Messenger*, 6 April 1807, contrasted Johnston's contribution to *The Wood Daemon; or, The Clock Has Struck* to that of Monk Lewis, the author:

For this piece the public are indebted to that ingenious mechanist, Mr. Johnston, of Drury Lane, author of several popular pieces, viz. *Cinderella, The Lady of the Rock, The Sleeping Beauty, &c., &c.* He has, unquestionably, been somewhat indebted to Mr. Monk Lewis for furnishing him with some incidents, in the nature of a story, upon which to hang his scenery; but he has suffered that Gentleman to predominate a little too much in the first and second parts of the performance, of this he received a hint during the first night's representation, and a considerable deal of the flattest fustian we ever heard (with which Mr. Lewis has interlarded the piece) has in consequence been expunged. As it is now exhibited, it forms one of the most interesting, magnificent, and ingenious spectacles we ever witnessed. The machinery is complicate and skilful beyond a parallel, and is so aptly introduced, and ingeniously worked, that it confers that kind of credit upon Mr. Johnston, which far o'ertops the ambition of the ordinary stage mechanist of the day. It raises him to something of the dignity of mechanical science and invention, and we shall scarcely think ourselves in danger of a smile, when we pronounce him to be a man, whose genius would have elevated him to very conspicuous utility and notice, had he not been condemned to waste and dissipate it in Pantomimes, Melo-Dramas, and Plays.

By the side of Mr. Johnston, Mr. Lewis appears

very small indeed. He is a perfect incumbrance upon him; a night-mare on the piece.

We will not anticipate the pleasure of our reader by entering into details; it will be sufficient to pronounce it, to be in the first rank of those spectacles, with which the town prefers to be amused in the present day.

Johnston remained at Drury Lane until his death in 1810. His salary was £5 per week in 1795–96, £6 in 1798–99, and by 1803–4 it was set, winter and summer, at £10. He also shared in large benefits; for example, on 2 June 1806, his benefit with Miss Boyce, the singer, brought £388 1s. 7d. (before charges). The Drury Lane account books at the Folger Shakespeare Library show Johnston handling large sums of money for the theatre's enterprises. He was entrusted with paying scene men and making financial arrangements for productions, as on 28 January 1799: "Mr Wright on account of Advance to Mr. Johnstone for Feudal Times £100.4s." By 1809 his activities included those of principal property manager. Johnston, who resided close to the theatre, was one of the first to discover and witness the progress of the flames that destroyed Drury Lane on 24 February 1809.

His work for other London theatres included machinery with Branscomb for *Black Beard; or The Captive Princess* at the Royal Circus in April 1798, costumes at the Haymarket in the summer of 1798, decorations and banners for *Almoran and Hamet; or, The Fair Circassian* at the Royal Circus in March 1799, properties and decorations for *Peter Wilkins* at Sadler's Wells on Easter Monday 1800, dresses and decorations for *Halloween* at the Royal Circus in 1801, and water monsters and other properties for Dibdin's aqua-dramas at Sadler's Wells in 1806–7. In August 1809 at the Royal Circus Johnston executed and supervised the grand banquet in *Macbeth*.

Alexander Johnston died in late October 1810 of a "broken heart," according to the *Examiner* (31 October). He had worked hard for Sheridan's Westminster campaign in November 1806 and loaned him money. The younger Dibdin in his *Professional and Literary Memoirs* described Johnston as "a man of the first eminence for talent; and who ruined himself as I have been given to understand, upon *good* authority, by assisting *Sheridan* to get into

Parliament in his last and unsuccessful endeavour to represent Westminster."

Johnston's wife may have been employed in the theatre during the eighteenth century, but it is impossible to identify her among so many others of the same or similar name. A Mrs A. Johnston was on the Drury Lane company list between 1804 and 1806 at £6 per week and at Brighton in the summer of 1809. (There was also a "Mrs B. Johnstone" at Drury Lane from 1803–4 through 1805–6 at £6 per week.)

Johnston was a very energetic and versatile man who served his profession well. If he did begin as a dancer, then he may also have acted or walked in his share of processions. (One Johnston appeared as the Second Sailor in *Hamlet* at Drury Lane in 1800–1801.) Early in his career he seems to have been an apprentice to Rudolph Cabanel, machinist and general supervisor of the maintenance and operation of backstage effects after Holland's reconstruction of Drury Lane in 1793–94. Johnston learned the art and craft of costuming from Mary Rein, many years the chief dress designer at Drury Lane. From his association with Gaetano Marinari and Thomas Greenwood he learned his painting and from William Underwood his carpentry.

In their *Rejected Addresses* (1812), Horace and James Smith sang Johnston's praises:

> *Amid the freaks that modern fashion sanctions,*
> *It grieves me much to see live animals*
> *Brought on the stage. Grimaldi has his rabbit,*
> *Laurent his cat, and Bradbury his pig;*
> *Fie on such tricks! Johnson, the machinist*
> *Of former Drury, imitated life*
> *Quite to the life. The elephant in Blue Beard,*
> *Stuff'd by his hand, wound round his lithe proboscis,*
> *As spruce as he who roar'd in Padmanaba.*

Johnston, Henry Erskine   1777–1845, actor, manager.

Born in Edinburgh in May 1777, Henry Erskine Johnston manifested his theatrical flair by the age of 10 in amateur dramatics, according to the *Monthly Mirror* of September 1800. The same notice states that on leaving school young Johnston was first apprenticed to a writer to the signet (notary) and then to a linen draper, whom he served for about three years. But the biographical notices of Johnston's early

HENRY E. JOHNSTON as Sir Robert Ramble
engraving by Hall, after Wageman

life are garbled. A brief obituary in the *Gentleman's Magazine* of July 1845 claimed that he was the son of a hairdresser, a detail which may or may not be true. In *Stage Reminiscences* (1866), Matthew Mackintosh reported that Johnston's real name was Somerville, that he was a cousin of Margaret Agnes Somerville, who became Mrs Alfred Bunn, and that he had first acted at York under the name of Erskine. Dibdin, however, in his *Annals of the Edinburgh Stage* rejects Mackintosh's account of Johnston as "absurdly wrong from beginning to end."

Presumably, Johnston recited Collins's "Ode on the Passions" at the Theatre Royal, Shakespeare Square, Edinburgh, for the benefit of a "friend" sometime in the early half of 1794. So impressed (the story goes) was the manager Stephen Kemble with Johnston's potential that he offered the lad, then about 17, very attractive terms; and, announced as a young gentleman, Johnston made his debut as Hamlet on

9 July 1794. There is no proof of the *Thespian Dictionary*'s assertion that he also played Harlequin that night. He repeated Hamlet with success on 11 July and then played Young Norval in *Douglas* for his benefit on the twenty-third, causing a sensation by stepping on the stage in full Highland attire—"the whole house rose and gave him a reception such as had seldom been heard within the walls of the building," reported Dibdin. The play's author, John Home, was in the audience and pronounced Johnston the "beau-ideal of his conception." That night Johnston also played the male title role in the afterpiece, *Catherine and Petruchio*. On 25 July, the next-to-last night of the season, he appeared in *Oroonoko*.

According to Dibdin, after playing that brief summer season in 1794 at Edinburgh, Johnston went to Dublin, where he acted 12 nights, seven of those as Norval; but according to the manuscript notes of the late William Smith Clark, Johnston did not make his first Irish appearance until 1795–96, when he was engaged at the Crow Street Theatre. In any event, Johnston was again at Kemble's Edinburgh theatre early in 1795, making his appearance on 16 February in *Douglas*. He also acted Don Felix in *The Wonder*, George Barnwell in *The London Merchant*, Hamlet, Jaffeir in *Venice Preserv'd*, Petruchio, Romeo, and Tancred in *Tancred and Sigismunda*. After playing at Belfast in March 1796, Johnston returned to Edinburgh on 6 April to act Zaphna in *Mahomet* and also added to his repertoire Posthumus in *Cymbeline* and Malter in *The Children in the Wood* on 16 April. On 30 May he acted Hamlet, free, for the benefit of the Charity Workhouse and on 3 June he again contributed his services for the benefit of the actors' fund. By that time he was being acclaimed the "Scottish Roscius."

Sometime in June 1796 Johnston married the young actress Nannette Parker, daughter, by his first wife, of the equestrian producer William Parker. Nannette's stepmother, Parker's second wife, was Sophia Granier, one of a large family of London dancers. Johnston's bride (not yet 15, according to the *Monthly Mirror* of October 1805, and 16, according to the *Authentic Memoirs of the Green Room*) accompanied him to Dublin, where they played at Crow Street in 1796–97.

Courtesy of the Garrick Club

HENRY E. JOHNSTON as Douglas
by Singleton

Clark places Johnston in Cork as late as 5 October 1797, so the actor must have moved with some haste to arrive several weeks later in London, where he was to begin an engagement at Covent Garden for a salary of £12 per week. There he made his debut on 23 October 1797 as Douglas. The *Morning Herald* of 24 October found that "Nature has been very bountiful" in providing Johnston "with a voice of much compass and melody" but complained that he "does not appear to have paid much attention to the cultivation of her favours," especially as his transitions were abrupt and discordant and his tones "of so strange a nature that it appears more like two distinct voices than a judicious modulation of his natural accents." The *True Briton* of 24 October observed his close copying of J. P. Kemble's performance in the role, "even to the crossing of the legs in dying." In a long review of his performance as Douglas,

the *Monthly Mirror* of October 1797 also noted his imitation of Kemble but gave him credit for taste in that regard, though the critic could not pronounce him that "*rara avis* which we understand he has been considered in the North":

His voice is unusually flexible, and its tones various; soft, sweet, melting, strong, piercing, full, capable of any depression, or any elevation. But not content with this bountiful gift, he seeks, with a perverseness which is inexcusable, to improve, but in reality to injure its value, by the most abrupt and ridiculous transitions. . . . His countenance is expressive, his figure is pretty, but boyish; it wants height and substance for an universality of character, though it sits well with the youth of Norval. His action is animated, and often graceful; the same may be said of his deportment. Here also he has his eye upon Kemble. . . .

His pathos is indeed inimitable; it flows from the pure source of feeling and cannot err.

In summing up Johnston's qualities, the *Monthly Mirror* reviewer believed that he had "finer requisites, figure excepted, than any actor on the stage"—high praise indeed for the twenty-year-old—but his intellect showed "somewhat shallow." His Scottish accent, which by 1800 he had entirely overcome, no doubt enhanced his debut role.

After repeating Douglas on 26 October 1797, Johnston's next role was Romeo on 2 November (a role he acted often that season), followed by Dorilas in *Merope* on 29 November, and Achmet in *Barbarossa* on 4 January 1798. On 28 April he played Hamlet for his benefit. Tickets could be had from him at No 31, King Street, Covent Garden; gross receipts were £230 19s. 6d. On 17 April he had played a principal character in *Curiosity*, a five-act drama translated from a play by Gustavus III, late King of Sweden. On 30 May 1798 Johnston read the part of Hortensio in *Disinterested Love* because Pope was ill.

In the summer of 1798 Johnston made his first appearance at Colman's Haymarket Theatre, as Alberto in the premiere of Holcroft's *The Inquisitor* on 23 June and subsequently was seen there as Walter in *The Children of the Wood*, Sir Edward Mortimer in *The Iron Chest*, and the Bard in *Cambro-Britons*. On 3 September 1798 he played Hamlet, and his wife, making her first appearance at the Haymarket, played Ophelia. (She had been at the Royal Circus and Sadler's Wells as Miss Parker.) Also in the Haymarket company and at Covent Garden over the next several years was the singing actor John Henry Johnstone, with whom our subject is often confused.

Returning to Covent Garden for his second season at £12 per week (and his wife at £3), Johnston acted Anhalt in the premiere of Mrs Inchbald's popular *Lovers' Vows* on 11 October 1798, Albert in the premiere of Birch's *Albert and Adelaide* on 11 December, Henry Melville in the premiere of Holman's *The Votary of Wealth* on 12 January 1799, Carrol the Irish Chieftain in *Oscar and Malvina* on 2 March, Inkle in *Inkle and Yarico* (for his wife's benefit on 5 March, when they lodged at No 47, Great Queen Street), Henry Hastings in the premiere of T. J. Dibdin's *Five Thousand a Year* on 16 March, Harry Bertram in the premiere of Dibdin's *The Birth Day* on 8 April, Daracardin in the first professional production of the Margra-

Harvard Theatre Collection

HENRY E. JOHNSTON as Hamlet

engraving by Kay

vine of Anspach's *The Princess of Georgia* on 19 April, and Count Florenzi in *False and True* on 30 April. For his benefit on 23 April 1799, when he played Sir Edward Mortimer in *The Iron Chest*, gross benefit receipts were £334 3s. 6d. Again at the Haymarket in the summer of 1799, his roles included Walwyn in *Family Distress* and Dick Dowlas in *The Heir at Law*.

In his third season at Covent Garden, 1799–1800, Johnston's salary was reduced to £10 per week, for he had not, it seems, shown the kind of improvement which writers like T. Harral in *Monody on the Death of Palmer* (1798) had expected of him. Since his first season in London he had not played high-powered capital roles. On 9 October 1799, however, he appeared as Polydore in *The Orphan* and on 14 November as Lothario in *The Fair Penitent*. On 16 January 1800 he was the original Philip in Cumberland's *Joanna* and on 8 February the original Henry in Morton's very popular comedy *Speed the Plough*. A performance of that piece scheduled for 1 April 1800 had to be postponed because of an accident suffered by Johnston. According to Thomas Dutton in *The Dramatic Censor*, Johnston, "in the full tide, flow, and torrent of his eloquence, was ambitious of adapting the *action* to the *word*. In his eagerness to show *how* he would kick *certain other persons*, he had the misfortune to kick himself!"

Other roles played by Johnston in 1799–1800 included Leontine in *The Good Natured Man*, Leeson in *The School for Wives*, Milday in *Liberal Opinions*, Guiderius in *Cymbeline*, Neville in *The Dramatist*, the title role in *Don Juan*, and Captain Douglas in *Fashionable Levities*. For a benefit with his wife on 29 April 1800 he acted Henry in *The Deserter of Naples* and Douglas; tickets were available of the Johnstons at No 24, Bedford Street, Covent Garden. Gross receipts were £380 11s. 6d. In the summer of 1800, Johnston made only one appearance at the Haymarket—on 13 June, as Dick Dowlas in *The Heir at Law*. From 17 July through 18 August he played at the Theatre Royal, Birmingham.

Johnston was one of eight performers (including Holman, J. H. Johnstone, Fawcett, Pope, Munden, Incledon, and T. Knight) who during 1799–1800 published a statement of grievances against the management of Covent Garden. In his scornful attack upon the dissenters, Dutton reported in the *Dramatic Censor* that Johnston and his wife, considering their salaries and benefit after charges, had earned £817 2s. for the theatrical year. At the insistence of the influential Fawcett, who would not remain at Covent Garden unless Johnston was reinstated, Johnston returned to that house in 1800–1801 for £10 per week. On 10 October 1800 he acted Faulkland in *The Rivals* for the first time and subsequently appeared as Harry in *Wild Oats* and the original title character in *Perouse*; the last-mentioned part he played at Manchester in March 1801. At the Haymarket in the summer of 1801 his roles were Adelbert in *Sighs*, Lealto in *False and True*, Ribbomont in *The Surrender of Calais*, Tomar in *The Corsair*, and Vivaldi in *The Italian Monk* (for the Johnstons' benefit on 11 August), and Wilford in *The Iron Chest*.

After two more seasons at Covent Garden (he was the original Caesario in *Alfonso* in 1801–2 and the original Count Romaldi in *The Tale of Mystery* in 1802–3), Johnston went over to Drury Lane, where he made his debut on 15 September 1803 as Anhalt in *Lovers' Vows* to his wife's Amelia. There he remained two seasons. Among his original roles was Count Belfior in *The Wife of Two Husbands* in 1803–4.

He returned to Covent Garden on 13 October 1805 as the original Rugantino in Monk Lewis's *The Bravo of Venice*. About that time he began to devote his time and energies to provincial activities. He had acted at Plymouth in June 1802 and at Edinburgh in July and August 1802. He was again in Edinburgh in the summer of 1805, when he lived at No 9, St James Square. In 1807 and 1808 he acted at the Crow Street Theatre, Dublin. On 4 October 1808 he wrote to Robert Dundas to apply for the position of manager of the Edinburgh theatre. In that letter (now in the Scottish National Library) Johnston reminded the patentee that he had been born in Edinburgh, had begun his career there, and in Dublin had been called upon "to take a considerable share of the management." Further, he promised to bring quality to the Edinburgh theatre equal to that of any in "the British Empire." He then affirmed his patriotic sentiments by informing Dundas that, when in London, he had been "connected with the Regiment of Loyal North Britons" and when in Edinburgh was "a member of the First Regiment of R:E:V:". The management, nevertheless, went to Henry Siddons.

Johnston's chance to manage came in 1811–12, when he leased Astley's Amphitheatre in Peter Street, Dublin, for £6000 and renamed it the Royal Hibernian Theatre. The place was altered at great expense and a patent was obtained from the Duke of Richmond. Johnston's performance there of the title role in *Timour the Tartar* received high praise in the *Irish Dramatic Censor*—"the tragedian rises triumphant from the incongruous mass of confused incident, inflated sentiment, and colloquial bombast." (That journal also charged Mrs Johnston, who by that time had gone to live with Henry Harris, the manager of Covent Garden, with adultery and abandoning her husband and infant family.)

Johnston was complimented for having brought the town many new and unexpected

Harvard Theatre Collection

HENRY E. JOHNSTON, singing "A Bundle of Truths"
engraving by Cruikshank

representations in his competition with Frederick Jones at Crow Street, but "his private
fortune," reported the journal, "all the hard
savings of a life of theatrical industry, has gone
to wreck in the contest." His speculation in
the opera company at Dublin had also weakened his resources. About that time, according
to James Morris's *Recollections of Ayr Theatricals*,
Johnston was also manager of a company at
Ayr that played in a vacated soap factory until
a new theatre was built for him in 1812, he
"being lessee and part owner." He also had
theatres at Aberdeen and Greenock.

In 1814 the theatre in Queen Street, Glasgow, was under Johnston's management, but
his Irish creditors pursued him and had him
jailed in Dundee. The young Francis Courtney
Wemyss was kind to him during his incarcer-
ation, so upon his release Johnston offered the
lad a place in the Glasgow company; but he
reneged when he heard that Wemyss did not
have the consent of his guardian uncle.

Johnston returned to Covent Garden on 10
December 1816, his "first appearance there for
twelve years," as Sir Archy Macsarcasm in *Love
à-la-Mode*. He followed with Sir Pertinax Mac-
sycophant on 27 December. On 10 June 1817
he created the role of Baltimore in *The Election*
at the English Opera House (the Lyceum). At
Drury Lane in 1817–18 he acted Pierre in
Venice Preserv'd and was the original Donald in
The Falls of Clyde and the original Rob Roy
Macgregor in Soane's adaptation from Scott;
he also served as stage manager.

His Drury Lane engagement at £8 per week
lasted through 1820–21. He took his final
benefit at that theatre on 3 July 1821, acting
Dougal in the Pocock version of *Rob Roy Macgregor* and Romaldi in *The Tale of Mystery*. From
Drury Lane he went to the Olympic Theatre,
where he acted the Solitary in *Le Solitaire; or,
The Recluse of the Alps* on 24 November 1821.
In his *Drury Lane Journal*, James Winston recorded that on 9 January 1822 "H. Johnston,

Tayleure, and Oxberry came delegated from the whole of the Olympic Theatre to say they had struck, the salaries not being paid from six to eight weeks. . . ."

Johnston assumed another management at the beginning of 1823 when he opened the Caledonian Theatre (previously the Circus) on 11 January with a production of *Gilderoy*, in which he played the title role and delivered a brief address he had composed. He gave up the Caledonian on 7 April 1823, after which he disappeared into the provinces. In October 1830 he returned to the Caledonian for four nights.

In 1838 Johnston applied for a place in Wemyss's Walnut Street Theatre in Philadelphia, a circumstance which evoked a melancholy though satisfying thought in that American manager's *Theatrical Biography*: "What strange events daily occur in this world. Who could have supposed that the Glasgow manager, who so summarily dismissed a boy of seventeen, in 1814, should in 1838, have applied to that boy for permission to act in a Philadelphia theatre, of which he had become the manager, and be refused, for want of talent, having become perfectly superannuated."

Johnston did go to America, however, and on 7 November 1837 made his debut in New York at the National Theatre, Church Street, as Sir Archy Macsarcasm in *Love à-la-Mode* and Romaldi in *The Tale of Mystery*. For his benefit on 3 January 1838 he played his original characters of Flodoardo and Rugantino. At the end of the season, on 12 June, Johnston received another benefit, as Shylock and as Walter in *The Children of the Wood*. Though admired, he was too far beyond his prime to cause much excitement in New York; and so he returned to England.

The *Sunday Times* of 23 February 1845 reported that Johnston had died on 9 February at his residence in Gillingham Street, Vauxhall Road. At the time of his death, according to the *Gentleman's Magazine* of July 1845, he was "nearly 70." Johnston was buried in the Lambeth parish church near the graves of the equestrians Robert Woolford and John Ducrow.

Having been estranged for many years, the Johnstons had been granted a divorce on 25 February 1820. (Our statement in the notice of Frances Abington in volume I of this *Dictio-*

Harvard Theatre Collection

HENRY E. JOHNSTON, in *The Exile*
by De Wilde

nary that the Jane Johnstone of Wimpole Street, who received £200 in 1815 from Mrs Abington's will, was the widow of Henry Johnston is incorrect.) Henry Erskine Johnston and Nannette Parker Johnston had at least six children by 1805. Their first, Henry William Mark Morris Johnston, born on 9 May 1798, was baptized at St Paul, Covent Garden, on 2 June 1798. A second child had been born by September 1800, when the *Monthly Mirror* reported that they had two. Their son William, born on 31 October 1800, was baptized at St Paul, Covent Garden, on 15 November 1800. In June 1802 the *Monthly Mirror* reported the birth of another son. Nannette Johnston, accounted a beautiful and fascinating woman, was still alive in 1826 but her death date is unknown to us. After his divorce, Henry seems to have remarried. Mrs Magdalen Johnston, described in the Garrick Club catalogue of portraits as his widow, presented a portrait of him as Douglas, painted by Sir William Allan, to the club in 1861.

In his best years Johnston was a versatile and popular actor whose playing of many roles offered pleasure. He was not truly excellent, in the judgment of critics like Thomas Gilliland, but he was "highly useful." Early in his career he was an extravagant sort of ladies' man, handsome and amusing. In private he performed ventriloquy, gave imitations, acted monodramas, and mimicked animals.

Portraits of Henry Erskine Johnston include:

1. By Samuel De Wilde. In *Mathews Collection Catalogue*, No 308, but not in the Garrick Club.

2. By Samuel De Wilde. In *Mathews Collection Catalogue*, No 357, but not in the Garrick Club.

3. Engraved portrait by K. Mackenzie, after R. Dighton. Published as a plate to *Thespian Dictionary*. Another impression appeared as a plate to *The Myrtle and the Vine*, published by West & Hughes, 1800.

4. By unknown engraver, after E. Smith. On a plate with a bust portrait of Mrs Johnston. The same picture of him, alone, was published as a plate to the *British Stage*, July 1820.

5. As Aegeon, with Mrs Johnston as Aemilia, in *The Comedy of Errors*. Engraving by Bromley, after Hamilton. Published by G. Kearsley, 1804.

6. As Sir Charles Easy in *The Careless Husband*. By unknown engraver. Published as a plate to *British Drama*, 1817.

7. As Donald, with S. Perley as Kenmure, in *The Falls of Clyde*. Engraving by J. Findlay, after W. M. Craig. Published by Jameson, 1820.

8. As Douglas in *Douglas*. By William Allan. In the Garrick Club (No 82). According to the catalogue, this painting was presented to the club in 1861 by his "widow, Mrs. Magdalen Johnston."

9. As Douglas. By William Owen. Location unknown. Engraving by J. Young, published 13 August 1804.

10. As Douglas, full length, holding a sword in both hands. By Henry Singleton. Exhibited at the Royal Academy in 1802. Engraving by E. Mitchell, published by J. P. Thompson, 1806. Mitchell's engraving is not, as indicated in the Harvard Theatre Collection catalogue (No 5), of the Garrick Club portrait (below) but of this painting. Another engraving by T. Wright was published as a plate to Oxberry's *New English Drama*, 1821.

11. As Douglas, half-length. By Henry Singleton. In the Garrick Club.

12. As Douglas. By unknown engraver. Published as a plate to *Hibernian Magazine*, January 1796.

13. As Douglas. By unknown engraver. (Harvard No 8)

14. In *The Exile*. Watercolor by Samuel De Wilde. In the Harvard Theatre Collection. Johnston stands in riding habit, top hat, boots, crop in right hand.

15. As Hamlet. Engraving by J. Kay. Published, 1795.

16. As Hamlet, with Nannette Johnston as Ophelia. By Robert Ker Porter. Painting exhibited at the Royal Academy in 1801. Present location unknown.

17. As Hamlet. Engraving by W. Ridley, after R. K. Porter. Published as a plate to the *Monthly Mirror*, 1800. A copy by J. Thomson was published as a plate to the *Theatrical Inquisitor*, 1817; and another copy by an unknown engraver was also issued.

18. As Hassarac in *The Forty Thieves*. Engraving by West, published 1827.

19. As Jerry Hawthorn in *Tom and Jerry*. By unknown engraver.

20. As O'Donoghue. By unknown engraver.

21. As Sir Robert Ramble in *Every One Has His Faults*. Engraving by W. Hall, after T. Wageman. Published as a plate to Oxberry's *New English Drama*, 1822.

22. As Romeo, with Mrs Pope as Juliet. Engraving by B. Reading, after A. Buck. Plate to *Bell's Shakespeare*.

23. As Rugantino in *Rugantino*. By unknown engraver.

24. In character, hussar military dress. Watercolor by Samuel De Wilde. In Harvard Theatre Collection.

25. In character, long coat, standing, paper in right hand extended. Watercolor by Samuel De Wilde. In the Harvard Theatre Collection.

26. In a satirical print entitled "A Bundle of Truths." By G. Cruikshank, published 2 September 1811. Heading verses *"Sung, with great Applause, by Mr. Henry Johnston, in Dublin, Cork, &c. &c."*

27. In a caricature, "Sprig of Shillelah and Shamrock so Green," heading songs. Published by Laurie & Whittle, 1807.

28. In a caricature, "Paddy M'Shane's Seven Ages," heading song. Published by Laurie & Whittle, 1807.

Johnston, Mrs Henry Erskine the first, Nannette, née Parker *b. 1782, actress, dancer, singer.*

Nannette Parker was born in London in 1782, the daughter of the pantomime player and equestrian producer William Parker by his first wife. Parker's second wife, Nannette's stepmother, was Sophia Granier, a member of a large family of London dancers. According to the *Monthly Mirror* of October 1805, Nan-

nette was sent at an early age to Edinburgh for her education. Her father was proprietor of the Circus at Edinburgh from 1788 to the middle of the 1790s, so it is likely that Nannette performed there. No doubt she was the Miss Parker who danced at Sadler's Wells in London in October 1793. In April 1794 at the Wells she danced in *Irish Courtship* and *Penmaenmawr* and in May in *William Tell*, pieces in which her stepmother also appeared. At the Royal Circus on 17 April 1795 Miss and Mrs Parker (the latter announced as from the Theatre Royal, Dublin) danced in *The Happy Cottagers*.

Sometime in June 1796 she married the popular northern actor, Henry Erskine Johnston, whom she had met at Edinburgh. (*Bell's Weekly Messenger* for 26 June 1796 reported that they had been married "lately.") According to Johnston's obituary in the *Sunday Times* of 23 February 1845, he used to appear nightly in a stage box at the Circus to throw bouquets to the lovely dancer. They were, it was said, the handsomest bride and groom "ever seen in England." At the time of her marriage Nannette was "not fifteen," according to the *Monthly Mirror*, and 16, according to the *Authentic Memoirs of the Green Room* (1814).

In 1797 she went with her husband to act at Dublin, where she enjoyed success as Lady Contest in *The Wedding Day* and Josephine in *Children in the Wood*. She accompanied Johnston to London in 1797–98, when he had an engagement at Covent Garden. On 2 June 1798 their first child, Henry William Mark Morris, who had been born the previous 9 May, was baptized at St Paul, Covent Garden. Evidently he was the first of six children she was to bear by October 1805.

On 3 September 1798, near the end of the summer season at the Haymarket, Mrs Johnston acted Ophelia to her husband's Hamlet. On 12 September she played Roxalana in *The Sultan*. The *Monthly Mirror* offered praise and criticism of Mrs Johnston in both roles:

This Lady is wife to the tragedian of the same name. She has fine natural requisites for the stage, and promises to become a very valuable actress. Her figure is tall and elegantly proportioned; her voice is sweet, flexible, and articulate, and there is a prepossessing softness in her features which well became the character in which she has so deservedly attracted the notice of the public. Indeed we have seldom seen a more interesting *Ophelia*. This part

Harvard Theatre Collection

NANNETTE JOHNSTON

engraving by Hopwood, after Haughton

requires neither strong tragic nor comic powers, nor very scientific singing; and yet the two finest actresses in the world, and perhaps the finest singer in the world, have all made choice of it for the display of their respective talents. It is probably the *only* character which *could* be represented by three such women as Mrs. Siddons, Mrs. Jordan, and Mrs. Billington: neither of them, in our opinion, produced the effect intended by the poet. An artless and pathetic delivery; a simplicity of action and deportment; an agreeable *ballad* voice; an easiness of transition in the "snatches of old tunes" from the grave to the gay; a gentle, not a majestic, abstraction in her madness; are what we expect from the representative of this character; and we found them all, (making the usual allowances) in Mrs. Johnston's performance of Ophelia, "the young, the beautiful, the harmless, and the pious."

Mrs. Johnston's *Roxalana* was by no means on a par with her Ophelia; but she has evidently comic capabilities which may be matured into excellence. The character was undertaken with too much precipitation;—and yet it bore a promise, that, under the auspices of the Covent-Garden manager, we hope to see realized. We cannot, we *ought* not to expect finished acting from so young a candidate. Application will surmount many difficulties, and experience and encouragement must do the rest.

She had, in fact, been engaged at Covent Garden with her husband in 1798–99, he at £12 per week, and she at £3. There she made her debut on 17 September 1798 as Ophelia, this time to Holman's Hamlet. After repeating that role on 24 September, she acted Amelia Wildenhaim in *Lovers' Vows*, Mrs Inchbald's drama which opened on 11 October 1798 and ran 42 performances before the season ended. The role had been especially written for Mrs Johnston, according to the *Monthly Mirror* of October 1805. On 12 January 1799 she created Gangica in the premiere of Holman's popular comedy *The Votary of Wealth*. That season she also played Malvina in *Oscar and Malvina*, Susan in *The Follies of a Day*, Aurelia in *Five Thousand a Year*, and Illidia in the premiere of *The Princess of Georgia* on 19 April. For her benefit on 5 March 1799, when tickets could be had of her at No 47, Great Queen Street, Lincoln's Inn Fields, she played Yarico to her husband's Inkle and took in the substantial sum of £401 15s. (less house charges).

In July 1799 the *Monthly Mirror* announced the birth of a daughter to Mrs Johnston. With a salary raised to £5, Mrs Johnston began her second season at Covent Garden on 25 September ber 1799 as Gangica. On 11 October she played Dorinda in *The Beaux' Stratagem* for the first time. On 30 November she was Ruth Starch in the premiere of Mrs Inchbald's *The Wise Man of the East*, on 8 February 1800 the original Miss Blandford in the premiere of Morton's very popular *Speed the Plough*, and on 19 February the original Theodora in *True Friends*. For her benefit shared with her husband on 29 April, when they lived at No 24, Bedford Street, Covent Garden, she acted, her first time in those characters, Jacintha in *Lovers' Quarrels* and Louisa in *The Deserter of Naples*. Gross receipts for the night were £380 11s. 6d. Several nights later, on 1 May 1800, she created the role of Virginia in Cobb's musical farce *Paul and Virginia*, and "for her vanity in attempting a *singing* character," wrote Dutton in *The Dramatic Censor*, she provoked "pity and contempt." Though she was a good actress, she displayed arrogance and presumption, Dutton said, "by coming on stage the first night with a *tambourine* in her hand, which she had not the skill to touch. She was very properly laughed out of her folly by the newspapers, and she has left the tambourine behind in succeeding representations."

Another pregnancy prevented Mrs Johnston from playing the vigorous part of Virginia on 7 October 1800, near the start of her third season, so the role went to Miss Murray, who also took on Miss Blandford in *Speed the Plough* on 21 October. A son was born on 31 October 1800 and christened William Johnston at St Paul, Covent Garden, on 15 November. Mrs Johnston was welcomed back to acting at Covent Garden on 6 December as Virginia; that season she also played Viola in *Twelfth Night* and the original Madame Perouse in *Perouse*. That summer she was engaged at the Haymarket, appearing as Josephine in *Sighs* on 22 June 1801. For her benefit there with her husband on 11 August she played Ellena in *The Italian Monk* for the first time.

At Covent Garden in 1801–2 she was the original Amelrosa in *Alfonso*. That summer of 1802 she and her husband acted at Plymouth in June, and then she made the long journey north to Edinburgh, where on 23 July she appeared as Cicely Homespun in *The Heir at Law*. Her other roles at Edinburgh included Agnes in *The Mountaineers*, Amelia in *Lovers' Vows*, Angela in *The Castle Spectre*, Cowslip in

NANNETTE JOHNSTON, fleeing Henry Harris for Drummond

by G. Cruikshank

The Agreeable Surprise, Juliet in *Romeo and Juliet*, Lydia Languish in *The Rivals*, and Yarico in *Inkle and Yarico*.

The Johnstons returned to Covent Garden in 1802–3, where she acted Clarinda in *The Suspicious Husband* and the original Caroline in *John Bull*, but a disagreement with that theatre's management caused the couple to engage at Drury Lane in the following season. They remained there for two seasons, with Mrs Johnston playing among other roles Cora in *Pizarro*, Julia in *The Rivals*, Sigismunda, and Juliet.

The Johnstons returned once again to Covent Garden in 1805–6 (after she had another child about September 1805), this time to remain for nine consecutive seasons, except for 1806–7, when she was at Bath. Among her more important roles during that period were Beatrice in *Much Ado about Nothing* in 1807–8; the original Alexina in *Exile* in 1808–9; the original Agnes in *Free Knights* in 1809–10; Desdemona in *Othello*, Marcia in *Cato*, Helena in *All's Well that End's Well*, and the original Zorilda in *Timour the Tartar* (in which she displayed the equestrian skills of her early breeding) in 1810–11; Perdita in *The Winter's Tale* and Imogen in *Cymbeline* in 1811–12; and Angelica in *Love for Love*, Sylvia in *The Recruiting Officer*, and the original Almeyda in *The Rene-*

gade in 1812–13. Her salary from 1807–8 to 1811–12 was £14 per week, and from 1812–13 to 1814–15 it was £15. She also played at Edinburgh in the summer of 1806.

During a visit to Dublin, about 1811, Mrs Johnston separated from her husband. The *Irish Dramatic Censor* of 1811–12, Johnston's supporter during his management of the Peter Street amphitheatre in that city, charged Mrs Johnston as an adulteress and a mother "who abandons the offspring she ought to cherish, and the husband whom she has sworn to love." She had gone to live with Henry Harris, manager of Covent Garden. Her relationship with Harris lasted until the beginning of 1814, when she deserted him for a London banker named Harry Drummond. A satirical print by G. Cruikshank celebrating Mrs Johnston's desertion of Harris was published on 1 March 1814. Little wonder that after the season closed she was not re-engaged at Covent Garden. A subsequent lover was Richard Curran, a Deputy Master of the Rolls.

Mrs Johnston then seems to have retired from the stage, except for an appearance for Conway's benefit at Covent Garden in 1816 and a few nights at the Haymarket. Little is known of her thereafter. On 25 February 1820 she was granted a divorce from Johnston. She was still alive when Oxberry published his

Dramatic Biography in 1826. The Miss Johnston who appeared as a singer on 23 June 1823 at the Haymarket perhaps was her daughter.

At the height of her career Mrs Johnston was a very beautiful woman, with talents in both comedy and tragedy. She was, according to the *Monthly Mirror* of October 1805, a remarkably good dancer and a pleasing if not strong singer. In her former husband's obituary the *Sunday Times* of 23 February 1845 described her as having been once "one of the most fascinating women breathing" but did not indicate whether or not she was still alive. Sometime after his divorce, Henry Erskine Johnston was married again, to a woman named Magdalen, who as his widow presented a picture of him to the Garrick Club in 1861.

Portraits of Nannette Johnston include:

1. By Samuel De Wilde. In *Mathews Collection Catalogue*, No 307, but not in the Garrick Club.

2. Engraved portrait by Alais. Published as

Harvard Theatre Collection

NANNETTE JOHNSTON as Zorilda
engraving by Dighton

a plate to the *Authentic Memoirs of the Green Room*, 1803.

3. Engraved portrait by J. Hopwood, after M. Haughton. Published as a plate to *La Belle Assemblée*, 1812.

4. Engraved portrait by Page, after W. Beechey. Published as a plate to Oxberry's *Dramatic Biography*. (Similar to engraving by Ridley.)

5. Engraved portrait by W. Ridley, after J. R. Smith. Published as a plate to the *Monthly Mirror*, 1805. A copy by an unknown engraver was also issued.

6. By unknown engraver, after E. Smith, on a plate with a bust portrait of H. E. Johnston. The same picture, of her alone, was published as a plate to the *British Stage*, 1820.

7. As Alexina in *The Exile*. Watercolor by Samuel De Wilde. In the British Museum.

8. As Alexina. Watercolor by Samuel De Wilde. In the Harvard Theatre Collection. Similar to the one in the British Museum.

9. As Aemilia, with Mr Johnston as Aegeon, in *The Comedy of Errors*. Engraving by Bromley, after Hamilton. Published by G. Kearsley, 1804.

10. As Amelia in *Lovers' Vows*. Watercolor by unknown artist. In the Harvard Theatre Collection.

11. As Lulima in *The Tyrant Saracen*. Engraving by Marks. Published by the engraver.

12. As Ophelia, with Henry E. Johnston as Hamlet. By Robert Ker Porter. Painting exhibited at the Royal Academy in 1801. Present location unknown.

13. As Rosalind in *As You Like It*. Penny plain by unknown artist. Published by W. West, 1812.

14. As Zorilda in *Timour the Tartar*. Engraving by Dighton. Published by the engraver, 1811.

15. As Zorilda. Engraving by Luigi Senzanome (De Wilde?), a satirical print entitled "Apollo in Danger," published in *The Satirist*, June 1811. Mrs Johnston rides at the head of a force of horsemen. J. P. Kemble has her horse by the tail. See *British Museum Catalogue of Political and Personal Satires*, No 11772, for background.

16. "Dress of Mrs. H. Johnston in the Venetian Outlaw." By unknown engraver. Published as a plate to the *Theatrical Recorder*, 1805.

17. In a satirical print by George Cruik-shank, entitled "Theatrical Faux Pas," published in *The Satirist*, 1 March 1814. Mrs Johnston is depicted fleeing Harris at the facade of Covent Garden to join her new lover, the banker Drummond. Over Drummond's door is the inscription *"Drummond—Pawn Broker—NB Old Pieces taken in."* Also pictured are Catherine Stephens, Mathews, Fawcett, Sally Booth, Emery, Mr and Mrs Liston, and Incledon. See *British Museum Catalogue of Political and Personal Satires*, No 12327, for background.

Johnston, John ₁*fl.* *1742?–1781*₁, *actor, singer, dancer.*

An actor named John Johnston was in the company at the Smock Alley Theatre, Dublin, in 1742. Perhaps he was the same Johnston who played Scaramouch in *Pigmalion* at the New Concert Hall, Edinburgh, on 1 March 1749 and was still in that city in 1750. The

Harvard Theatre Collection

JOHN JOHNSTON as Gibby

engraving by Saunders, after Van der Gucht

"Johnson" who was at Sadler's Wells in 1754 was perhaps that person. It seems fairly certain that the actor and pantomime player John Johnston was a regular performer in the Drury Lane company by 1751–52, though in his earlier years there his name was sometimes given as "Johnson." On 3 January 1752 his name was added to the list of performers in *Harlequin Ranger*. He may have been at Drury Lane in 1752–53, though his name did not appear in the bills. The following season, 1753–54, he again performed in *Harlequin Ranger*, was also seen in *Fortunatus*, and on 2 July 1754 played Wart in *The Humourists*.

After several more seasons in pantomimes, Johnston played his first speaking character in a play on 6 November 1756, when he performed Gibby and Garrick acted Don Felix, also for the first time, in a revival of *The Wonder*. From that point Johnston alternated between pantomime and play characters for 25 seasons at Drury Lane, never rising to very much prominence in the company or with the public. It is possible that there were actually two players named Johnston in the company over that period, one appearing in plays and the other in pantomimes, but the various surviving accounts suggest only one, and that one, we believe, was John Johnston. Some scholars, however, have indicated that the actor of Gibby was Alexander Johnston, the Drury Lane housekeeper who died in 1775. We find no evidence to support that identification. In any event, the role was regularly played by John Johnston, whose performance in it, in the opinion of the *Theatrical Review* (1772), was "so contemptible, as to raise critical indignation."

Among the characters regularly acted by John Johnston at Drury Lane were Faulconbridge in *King John*, Old Capulet in *Romeo and Juliet*, the Housekeeper in *A Peep Behind the Curtain* (or was that role played by the actual housekeeper?) a Witch in *The Witches*, Cook and Pantaloon in *Queen Mab*, as well as several female characters in pantomimes.

J. Johnston's name appeared on a Drury Lane pay sheet dated 24 January 1767 as an actor receiving a modest 5*s*. per day, or £1 10*s*. per week. (The housekeeper A. Johnston was on the same list for the higher amount of 8*s*. 10*d*. per day.) In 1775–76 he was receiving 6*s*. 8*d*. per day and in 1777–78 (according to

Winston's notation in a manuscript at the Folger Shakespeare Library) 9*s*. 2*d*. per day.

Johnston's wife, Helen, was also a performer at Drury Lane during his tenure. They may have been the Mr and Mrs Johnston who, described as sufferers from a fire, received a benefit at Drury Lane on 6 May 1769. In the 1770s the Johnstons lived at No 97, Craven Buildings, Drury Lane. The Master Johnston who played Beaufort, Jr, in a children's performance of *Cleone* at the Haymarket on 10 May 1759 may have been their son. A Master "Johnson" sang in the oratorios at Drury Lane in March 1762 and at Ranelagh Gardens in June 1762.

When the Drury Lane theatrical fund was established in 1766, Johnston subscribed £1 1*s*. and soon became the secretary. He signed his name in that capacity to the "Tesimony of Duty and Affection from the Committee of the Fund of the Theatre Royal Drury Lane to David Garrick, Esq." presented to the retired manager on 25 March 1777. The illuminated manuscript is now in the Harvard Theatre Collection.

John Johnston's death date is not known to us. He was active at Drury Lane through 1780–81. The Mrs Johnston who died in August 1785 wass37probably his wife.

An engraving by J. Saunders, after Van der Gucht, of him as Gibby in *The Wonder* was published by the engraver in 1773 and was reissued in 1774 with the address of H. Bryer. A colored drawing by S. Harding, after Van der Gucht's portrait, is in the Harvard Theatre Collection. The catalogues of the engraved portraits in the Harvard Theatre Collection and the British Museum identify the sitter as "Alexander Jonston," but the plate states simply "Mr Jonston." Consequently John Johnston the actor has often been confused with Alexander Johnston the housekeeper, to whom he may well have been related. (It is very possible, also, that the actor John Johnston was the same person as, or was related to, the music seller and copier John Johnston, fl. 1767–1778.)

Johnston, Mrs John, Helen   *d. 1785, actress, singer.*

The Mrs Johnston whose name first appeared in the London bills on 29 July 1760 as Lappet in a summer performance of *The Miser* given at Drury Lane to "Benefit a Gentleman who has written for the Stage" was, we believe, the wife of the actor John Johnston (fl. 1742?–1781). The performance that night was offered by a company constituted mainly of regular Drury Lane actors, including Johnston. Perhaps she was the Mrs Johnston who had been at the Crow Street Theatre, Dublin, in 1759–60.

The following season Mrs Johnston was in the Drury Lane company, appearing first as Lady Faulconbridge (to her husband's Faulconbridge) in *King John* on 17 December 1760, a role she played two other times before she was seen as Toilet in the first performance of Colman's *The Jealous Wife* on 12 February 1761. In addition to numerous performances that season as Toilet, Mrs Johnston acted Lucinda in *The Conscious Lovers* on 21 May, when she shared in benefit tickets, and Aranti in *King Lear* on 28 May. That summer she was in the company headed by Foote and Murphy, who had rented Drury Lane, appearing as an unspecified character in *All in the Wrong*.

Mrs Johnston's name was not in the Drury Lane bills in 1761–62, so perhaps she was the actress of that name who was at Smock Alley, Dublin, that season. She may have been the Mrs Johnston (fl. 1766–1767) who acted at the King's and the Haymarket in the summers of 1766 and 1767, respectively.

Not until six seasons later did Mrs Johnston return to the Drury Lane boards, reappearing on 16 September 1767 as Mrs Peachum in *The Beggar's Opera*. That season she played the Duchess of York in *Richard III*, Mrs Trusty in *The Provok'd Husband*, Lady Capulet in *Romeo and Juliet*, a role in *Harlequin's Invasion*, the Queen in *Cymbeline* (in which she was hissed on 10 October 1767), Dame Pliant in *The Alchemist*, Isabella in *The Conscious Lovers*, Leonora in *The Mourning Bride*, Lady Loverule in *The Devil to Pay*, Sisigambis in *The Rival Queens*, Mrs Junket in *The Absent Man*, Mrs Watchly in *Wit's Last Stake*, Kitty in *The Lyar*, and Florella in *The Orphan*.

Over another 13 seasons Mrs Johnston served Drury Lane as a supporting actress. Among the roles she filled were the Player Queen in *Hamlet*, Eliza in *The Plain Dealer*, Lucilla in *The Fair Penitent*, Lady Scrape in *The Musical Lady*, the Nurse in *Isabella*, Charmion in *All for Love*, Cleone in *The Distrest Mother*, an Attendant in *The Royal Suppliants*, Inis in

Braganza, Mrs Touchstone in *Old City Manners*, Francisca in *Measure for Measure*, Lady Clifford in *The Earl of Warwick*, and Lady Bab in *High Life below Stairs*. In 1780–81, her last season, her roles were Mrs Wisely in *The Miser*, Erixene in *The Grecian Daughter*, the Duchess of York in *Richard III*, Leonora in *The Mourning Bride*, Sisigambis in *Alexander*, Lady Bountiful in *The Strategem*, Isabella in *The Conscious Lovers*, Cephisa in *The Distrest Mother*, Lady Capulet in *Romeo and Juliet*, and the Housekeeper in *The West Indian*.

Despite her long career, there are few contemporary comments on her. The *Theatrical Review* (1772) wished that Leonora in *The Mourning Bride*, as seen on 28 September 1771, would be played "by a better Actress than Mrs. Johnston, who seems but little acquainted with any Language." Her salary from 1774–75 through 1776–77 was £1 10*s*. per week. In April 1777, when she shared a modest benefit with Mrs Bradshaw and Mrs Love, her address was No 97, Drury Lane, where she still lodged, presumably with her husband, in May 1779. On 23 April 1777, in a letter to Andrew Bowes, Garrick called Johnston and his wife "persons of great Worth & much regarded by Mr Garrick."

According to James Winston's notations in the Drury Lane Fund Book (at the Folger Shakespeare Library) Mrs Johnston subscribed £1 1*s*. in 1775 and died on 28 August 1785. Winston also provided her Christian name, Helen, but called her husband, erroneously we believe, Alexander.

Johnston, John [*fl.* 1767–1778], *music copyist, music seller, publisher, prompter?*

The John Johnston who served Drury Lane Theatre as a music copyist in the 1760s and 1770s was probably the music publisher and seller of that name who by January 1767 had a shop "at the Apollo in the Strand opposite the New Exchange Coffee Rooms." On 23 October 1767 Garrick wrote to him about the Orpheus music in *A Peep Behind the Curtain*. In March 1768 Garrick presented a bill in the amount of £4 4*s*. to the Calcutta theatre for "Mr. Johnston's bill for music." The Drury Lane treasury paid him for his music bills £19 3*s*. on 1 December 1775 and £24 2*s*. on 23 March 1776. On 21 December 1776 the Liverpool Theatre received a bill for £5 15*s*. 6*d*.

to pay "Johnson" for writing out music. Possibly he was also the Johnston who received occasional small payments as assistant prompter in March 1767. Mr "Johnson," Drury Lane underprompter, attended Mossop's funeral on 6 January 1775.

After August 1767 Johnston moved his shop to various addresses in the Strand, including "opposite Lancaster Court," "near Charing Cross," and "near Northumberland House." Between 1768 and August 1772 he settled at No 11, York Street, Covent Garden, and subsequently to "between the new Exhibition Room and Exeter Change" in the Strand until about 1776. From about 1776 to 1778 his address was No 97, Drury Lane, the same as that of the Drury Lane actress Helen Johnston, whom we take to have been the wife of the Drury Lane actor John Johnston (fl. 1742?–1781). The mutual address for the two John Johnstons may only have been a confusing coincidence, but it is possible that the two were father and son.

Johnston published several works in collaboration with Longman, Lukey, and Company. Under his own imprint appeared Dibdin's *Lionel and Clarissa* (1768), *The Padlock* (1768), *Shakespeare's Garland* (1769), *The Deserter* (1773), *The Waterman* (1774), and *The Quaker* (1775). His other publications included works by Arne, general sheet music, dances, and sonatas.

He seems to have ceased business about 1778, a date which coincides nicely with some great dissatisfaction which he had given Garrick. Evidently his business was failing, and he seems to have been the Johnston whose debts Garrick assumed on the security of his musical property. Johnston intended to reimburse Garrick by serving in the navy, to which purpose Garrick wrote in his behalf to Lord Sandwich. On 25 December 1777 Johnston wrote from Portsmouth to thank Garrick. But something went amiss, and Garrick had to pay some of Johnston's debts. In a letter to John Moody at Bristol on 16 July 1778, Garrick complained:

. . . I have done with *Johnston* for Ever—— ——I have begun to make his fortune, nor shall I tell Lord Sandwich of his Ingratitude to me, but he shall never Enter my doors again—they have deceiv'd me most egregiously & ungratefully—the Wife assur'd me, that you had accepted of an Assignment of his musical property, which was to be paid to You regularly, by the great Shop in Catharine Street—Why was I to be fool'd by such a Senseless Lye?—I am now only Sorry that such a fellow as Johnstone should draw me in to believe his protestations, & that any Person Should *know* of my folly but Y^{r}Self— —

Some of Johnston's plates and stock were acquired by Longman, Lukey and Company after his business closed.

Johnston, Roger ₍*fl. 1771–1790?*₎, *property maker, decorator, manager, actor, author.*

Roger Johnston was the son of the Drury Lane housekeeper Alexander Johnston (d. 1775) and Mary Johnston (d. 1775), a wardrobe keeper at the same house. He followed in one of his father's professional lines, as a property maker and decorator. Sybil Rosenfeld in *Theatre Notebook* (Spring 1965) suggests that Roger was functioning at Drury Lane by 1762, but we believe she has confused him with his father. Similarly, *The London Stage* indicates that Roger was a sometime actor at Drury Lane; though he did act in his own company at Brighton, we believe that Roger did not perform in London and that the Drury Lane performances credited to him in *The London Stage* were given by John Johnston, a longtime regular there. Also, the actress Mrs Helen Johnston, identified in *The London Stage* as the wife of Roger, seems actually to have been the wife of the actor John Johnston. Roger's wife acted at Brighton, but so far as we can determine not at London.

Between August and December 1771 Roger Johnston helped to fit up the theatre and paint scenery for Sir Watkin Williams-Wynn's private theatricals at Wynnstay, for which services he was paid £61 for 18 weeks of work. That year he also received £300 for work in London. On 16 March 1772 he was paid £2 15s. by Drury Lane for gilding and on 1 March 1773 his bill of £124 5s. was paid by the treasury. On 18 June 1776 he received £33 1s. 6d. for his properties bill. On 4 October 1777 Drury Lane paid him £1 1s. for three days.

In 1774 Roger Johnston took a three-year lease on a new theatre in North Street, Brighton, which the bricklayer Samuel Paine had built. Johnston and his wife also acted in the company. His final season of management

there ended on 15 October 1776. According to Hogan in *Shakespeare in the Theatre*, Johnston managed a summer company at the Mile End Assembly Room, London, in 1778.

After 1778 we lose track of Roger Johnston in theatre records, though he may have continued professionally active. Perhaps it was Roger who received sums from Drury Lane in payment for materials and decorations between 1785 and 1789, but probably that Johnston was his son Alexander. A pantomime, *The Fairy Favour; or, Harlequin Animated*, which was first produced at Drury Lane on 27 December 1790, is credited to Roger by *The London Stage*.

He was named residuary legatee, after his mother, in his father Alexander Johnston's will in 1775, first to receive £50 and then the annual interest from £1000 upon the death of his mother. She died within the year and he proved her will at London on 28 November 1775. His sister was Margaret Burrell of Edinburgh.

Roger's son, named Alexander, began to dance as a child in the provinces and then at Drury Lane but soon became a very important machinist and decorator in that theatre during the 1790s and the first decade of the nineteenth century.

Johnston, "Scotch." *See* JOHNSTON, HENRY ERSKINE.

Johnstone. *See also* JOHNSON and JOHNSTON.

Johnstone, Mr ₍*fl. 1785*₎, *actor.*

A Mr Johnstone acted a Waiter in a specially-licensed performance of *All the World's a Stage* at the Haymarket Theatre on 15 March 1785 for the benefit of Mrs Pinto.

Johnstone, Ann, later Mrs Charles Presbury ₍*fl. 1797–1807*₎, *actress.*

Mrs Ann Johnstone made her first appearance on any stage as Horatia in *The Roman Father* at Birmingham in July 1797. The *Monthly Mirror* for that July reported that "she acquitted herself well." She next performed Statira, to Holman's Alexander and Mrs Siddons's Roxana, in *The Rival Queens*.

The "Young Lady" who acted Zaphira in

Barbarossa at Covent Garden Theatre on 4 January 1798 was identified in the *Thespian Dictionary* (1805) as Mrs Johnstone. That was her only London performance before the end of the century. In 1799 she joined the Bath stage, making her first appearance on 16 November as Elvira in *Pizarro*. At Bath and at Bristol, where she acted until 1804, Mrs Johnstone became a famous tragic actress whose style was described as "Siddonian." The *Thespian Dictionary* reported her figure as "tall and elegantly proportioned, and her voice harmonious and extensive."

On 20 September 1804 she returned to London to act Elvira at Drury Lane, where she remained engaged at £6 per week through 1806–7. She should not be confused with Mrs H. Johnston, who acted comedy roles at Drury Lane during the same years.

On 2 May 1807 at St Paul, Covent Garden, Ann Johnstone, described in the registers as a widow, married Charles Presbury, a bachelor from the parish of St Martin-in-the-Fields, whereupon she gave up her engagement at Drury Lane. In the *Gentleman's Magazine* of December 1807 her husband was identified as a jeweler of New Street, Covent Garden.

Johnstone, "Irish". *See* JOHNSTONE, JOHN HENRY.

Johnstone, J. [*fl.* 1784–1794], *violinist.*
A Mr Johnstone was listed by Dr Burney as one of the first violins in the Handel Memorial Concerts at Westminster Abbey and the Pantheon in May and June 1784. Probably he was the J. Johnstone, a violinist living in Mayfair in 1794, who was noted in Doane's *Musical Directory* as a participant in the Handelian concerts at the Abbey.

Johnstone, John Henry 1749?–1828, *actor, singer.*
Accounts of the early years of John Henry Johnstone's life are full of confusion and contradiction. An obituary notice in the *Gentleman's Magazine* for February 1829 claimed that at the time of his death on 26 December 1828 Johnstone was 78, thus placing his year of birth as 1750. The *Monthly Mirror* of April 1802 gave his date of birth as 1 August 1759, and the *European Magazine* of October 1783 (the month of Johnstone's Covent Garden de-

JOHN HENRY JOHNSTONE
engraving by Bestland

but) as 1755. *The Dictionary of National Biography* states that he was born "probably" on 1 August 1749, a date also furnished by the notes of William Smith Clark. Johnstone seems to have been born at Kilkenny, the son of a quartermaster (also a riding and paymaster) in an Irish regiment of horse stationed in that city. There is no substance, it would appear, to the statement in the *Gentleman's Magazine* obituary that Johnstone was born at Tipperary into a large family sired by a farmer.

After his father died Johnstone was cared for by his mother, who, according to Oxberry, survived by dealing in second-hand clothes. About the age of 12 Johnstone was articled to Mr Jones, an eminent Dublin attorney, with whom he continued for some four or five years. He left Jones over some disagreement and, according to one source, came to London, where in a brief time he squandered all the money he had saved from his clerkship. A Dublin merchant, who had sought out Johnstone in the metropolis at the behest of the lad's mother, gave him funds to return across the Irish Sea. Johnstone soon joined the army (to avoid a bailiff in Athlone, reported Oxberry) and served for several years with a cavalry regiment at Clonmel. It is not clear whether Venus or Mars prompted the end of his military career. One story claims that "too much attention to ladies brought on ill health, which he turned to advantage by persuading the surgeon to procure his discharge." Another story, however, reports that his easily agitated nature led to a quarrel with his lieutenant which won Johnstone a court martial but that the proceedings were eventually terminated by the regiment's commanding officer, a Colonel Brown. Brown, having heard Johnstone's sweet tenor voice at military entertainments, recommended him by letter to Ryder, the manager of Smock Alley Theatre, Dublin, who engaged the inexperienced but talented young man.

Johnstone made his debut at Smock Alley on 9 November 1775 as Lionel in *Lionel and Clarissa*. Immediately after his first appearance his salary, which had been first set at two guineas per week, was doubled, and he proceeded to perform a whole range of young singing lovers. His provincial apprenticeship lasted ten years, at Crow Street in 1776–77, Fishamble Street in 1777, Crow Street from 1777–78 through 1780–81, Smock Alley in 1781–82, and at both Crow Street and Smock Alley in 1782–83. He also acted at Cork in 1777, 1779, and 1781 and in Kilkenny in 1780.

On 22 February 1778 at Dublin, he married Maria Ann Poitier, the daughter of Colonel Poitier, governor of Kilmainham Gaol. (The marriage was reported by the *Hibernian Journal* of 23 February 1778 and the *Morning Chronicle* of 4 March). As Miss Poitier, she had acted at Salisbury in 1775 and at York and Manchester in 1776. At the time of her marriage she was a member of the company at Crow Street with Johnstone. Miss Poitier had connections to a theatrical family, being the niece of the dancers Jenny Poitier (later Mrs Vernon and subsequently Mrs Thompson) and Michael Poitier (d. 1774). Among the songs published in Dublin in 1781 as sung by Mr and Mrs Johnstone were *Gentle Echo* in *The Touchstone* and *Partners of my toils and pleasures* in *The Lord of the Manor*. It was said in the *Gentleman's Magazine* of February 1829 that Mrs Johnstone, "being highly accomplished, and possessing a

profound knowledge of music, imparted to her husband the arcana of the science, and made him a finished singer."

In the summer of 1783 Johnstone journeyed to London with his wife to visit her mother. While there, upon the recommendation of Charles Macklin, the Johnstones were engaged by Thomas Harris at Covent Garden at a combined weekly salary of £12 per week (he to receive £8 and she £4), as indicated in the account books, and not the £14 reported in all the memoirs.

Johnstone made his first appearance at Covent Garden on 2 October 1783 as Lionel to an enthusiastic reception. The *Theatrical Review* reported:

This gentleman's person, voice, and action, are of the most eminent style. His person is elegant, proportionate, and handsome. His voice particularly sweet and interesting. And his action for propriety, expression, and discrimination, is superior to any we have yet seen in the character. From his performance of Lionel, we may venture to pronounce his abilities equal to the most principal parts in Comedy and Tragedy, where an excellence of person, voice, and deportment, are particularly required.

After other appearances as Lionel on 10 and 22 October 1783 and as Macheath in *The Beggar's Opera* on 14 October and Lord Aimworth in *The Maid of the Mill* on 24 October, Johnstone played his first new London role. It was Dermot in O'Keeffe's comic opera *The Poor Soldier*, which with music by Shield had its premiere at Covent Garden on 4 November 1784 and subsequently played a total of 40 times that season. The piece was so successful that subsequent operas composed by Shield had an Irish character for Johnstone, who quickly won a reputation as the stage Irishman without equal. His thick accent and unaffected stage personality made the Irish song very popular in London. On 17 April 1784 Johnstone played Edwin in the premiere of Shield's *Robin Hood* (text by Macnally) which also became a popular repertory piece. In his debut season Johnstone also appeared as Carlos in *The Duenna*, Capt Belville in *Rosina*, and the title role in *Cymon*. For his benefit on 28 April 1784, for which tickets could be had of him at No 23, Pall Mall, he performed Hawthorn in *Love in a Village* and Apollo in *Midas*. Receipts came to about £160.

Courtesy of the Garrick Club

JOHN HENRY JOHNSTONE as O'Whack
by Wellings

Sometime during his first season Johnstone became ensnared by Sarah Maria Wilson (née Adcock), an actress at Covent Garden notorious for high living made possible by the liberality of her lover, Lord Hinchinbroke. (From about 1772 to 1775 she had lived with the actor Thomas Weston, whose name she used for the stage until she became allied with the actor Richard Wilson and subsequently adopted the stage name of Mrs Wilson.) The gifts and other attentions she bestowed upon Johnstone, who seems always to have been susceptible to extra-marital affairs, turned his head and heart from his wife. Mrs Johnstone (who had made her Covent Garden debut on 17 September 1783 as Rosetta in *Love in a Village* but performed only through 22 December of that year) subsequently took lodgings at Turnham Green to absent herself from the embarrassment caused by her husband's relationship with Mrs Wilson. She died young on 15 June 1784 (not 1785 as sometimes reported) at Turnham Green. In a biographical sketch of Johnstone which appeared at the height of his career, in the *Monthly Mirror* of April 1802, the episode was glossed over by the author with the assertion that "his enemies endeavoured to propagate an invidious report . . . to throw some imputation on his character" and that on her deathbed Mrs Johnstone had declared he had been "the best of husbands to me." Johnstone's affair with Mrs Wilson was short-lived as well, for Mrs Wilson died in December 1786, "in great misery" and poverty, according to Oxberry. Johnstone then became "a very general lover" who soon "found a lady who had been settled in a handsome annuity by a friend" and lived several years with her.

Johnstone's professional career meanwhile prospered. He began his second season at Covent Garden on 17 September 1784 as Amiens in *As You Like It*. In addition to his usual roles of Dermot, Belville, Edwin, and Apollo, he performed for the first times Sir Callaghan O'Brallaghan in *Love à-la-Mode* and Lorenzo in *The Merchant of Venice* on 10 November 1784. On 16 November he played Henry in the premiere of the O'Keeffe-Shield comic opera, *Fontainebleau*. His other roles included Sir John Loverule in *The Devil to Pay*, Ferdinand in *The Duenna*, Captain Banner in *The Nunnery*, another comic opera composed by Shield, which opened on 12 April 1785, and Captain Farquhar in the first performance in London of Jephson's *The Campaign* on 12 May. On 19 March 1785, for a production in which the female and male roles were reversed, Johnstone acted Mysis in *Midas*, for Lewis's benefit.

Johnstone remained a popular performer at Covent Garden through 1802–3, playing a variety of roles, mostly of Irish characters, in comedy and many first-tenor parts in comic opera. Among the most important of the numerous characters that he offered during his 20 years at Covent Garden were Major O'Flaherty in *The West Indian*, Sir Lucius O'Trigger in *The Rivals*, Captain O'Patrick in *Love in a Camp*, Foigard in *The Beaux' Stratagem*, Inkle in *Inkle and Yarico*, Sandy in *The Highland Reel*, Count Bellegarde in *Hide and Seek*, Raymond in *The Crusade*, and McDermot in *The School for Arrogance*. On 13 April 1790 he played Lucy in a performance of *The Beggar's Opera* in which several female and male roles were exchanged; Bannister performed Polly and Mrs Wells played Macheath.

Among the principal roles Johnstone "created" was Captain O'Donnel in *The Woodman* on 26 February 1791. As second tenor in that piece he tried to imitate Incledon, the first tenor, with a trill on high C and a run up to G, but he could not make the change from falsetto to natural voice; "and apart from that," wrote Haydn in his second London notebook, "he is most unmusical. He creates a new tempo for himself, now 3/4, then 2/4, makes cuts whenever it occurs to him." Other characters he introduced at Covent Garden included the Duke of Alberossa in *The Ward of the Castle* on 24 October 1793, Dorimond in *The Travellers in Switzerland* on 22 February 1794, Captain O'Leary in *British Fortitude and Hibernian Friendship* on 29 April 1794, Michael in *Naples Bay* on 2 May 1794, Captain Pendant in *Arrived at Portsmouth* on 30 October 1794, McQuery in *The Way to Get Married* on 23 January 1796, Captain O'Neil in *Abroad and at Home* on 19 November 1796, Liffey in *Ramah Droog* on 12 November 1798, and Father Dominico in *True Friends* on 19 February 1800.

Johnstone also played regularly each summer season from 1791 to 1800 (except 1792) at the Haymarket Theatre, where he made his first appearance on 25 June 1791 as Clifford in *The Kentish Barons*. That summer there he also played Inkle, Captain Greville in *The Flitch of Bacon*, O'Carrol in the premiere of Colman's very successful *The Surrender of Calais* on 30 July 1791, and a vocal part in *The Catch Club*. Among his many roles at the Haymarket in the 1790s were Killmallock in the premiere of *The Mountaineers* on 3 August 1793, Capt Macgallaher in the premiere of *Bannian Day* on 11 June 1796, the Governor in the premiere of *The Castle of Sorrento* on 13 July 1799, and Sir Sturdy O'Tremor in the premiere of *What a Blunder!* on 14 August 1800. During the late 1780s and 1790s a number of songs were published as sung by him at Covent Garden or the Haymarket. On several occasions in the spring of 1792 he appeared with the Drury Lane company at the King's Theatre, acting O'Carrol in *The Surrender of Calais* on 29 March for young

Harvard Theatre Collection

JOHN HENRY JOHNSTONE as Dennis Brulgruddery

engraving by Thomson, after Partridge

Bannister's benefit and doing the same service on 11 April for Bensley. He played the same role at Drury Lane for a special performance on 10 December 1795.

After his career took hold in London, Johnstone, infrequently it seems, played the provinces. He returned to Smock Alley in the summer of 1785, played one night there in 1786, that year also acted at Waterford, Limerick, and Cork, and was at Crow Street, Limerick, and Cork in the summer of 1788. In the summer of 1790 he traveled on the Continent for six weeks with Michael Kelly. In July 1792 he was at Newry. Johnstone was among the London players who made up the company for the Earl of Barrymore's private theatricals at Wargrave in the winter of 1791–92. In August of 1797, Johnstone performed for four nights at Birmingham.

In 1799–1800 Johnstone and seven other performers (Holman, Pope, Incledon, Munden, Fawcett, Knight, and H. E. Johnston) were involved in a dispute with the Covent Garden proprietor over the management's reducing the amount of free orders and increasing the benefit charges. The Lord Chamberlain ruled against the actors, several of whom left that theatre; but Johnstone remained on for several more seasons, through 1802–3. In the summer of 1803 he visited Dublin, where he was acclaimed as the genuine Irishman. He returned to London that fall to take up an engagement at Drury Lane, making his first appearance on that stage (except for several benefits he had played the previous decade) on 20 September 1803 as Murtock Delany in *The Irishman in London*.

The remaining 17 years of Johnstone's career were spent at Drury Lane (and with that company at the Lyceum between 1809 and 1812). A Drury Lane casting book from about 1815, now at the Folger Shakespeare Library, lists 23 roles for Johnstone. Most of them were in the stage Irishman line, for his failing singing voice caused his gradual abandonment of musical roles. Among his old favorites on the casting list were such roles as Teague in *Honest Thieves*, Captain O'Cutter in *The Jealous Wife*, Patrick in *Sons of Erin*, McScrape in *Netley Abbey*, Dennis Brulgruddery in *John Bull*, Kenrick in *The Heir at Law*, and Tully in *The London Hermit*. He also made regular summer appearances at Edinburgh during the second decade of the nineteenth century.

On several occasions he returned to the stage of Covent Garden, particularly on 8 June 1814 as Sir Callaghan in *Love à-la-Mode* for Mathews's benefit. It was at Covent Garden, in fact, that Johnstone received his farewell benefit, as Dennis Brulgruddery in *John Bull* on 28 June 1820. He did, however, play at Liverpool that August. In his late years Johnstone's health had been failing. On 1 June 1818 he was prevented from playing in *The Review* because he had been thrown from his chaise, but he recovered. In the winter of 1820–21 he was confined for three months, and by 1 February 1821 his physician allowed him to venture out for a couple of hours each day. He made yet another appearance, for the benefit of the Irish distress districts, at Drury Lane on 18 May 1822, as Dennis Brulgruddery; in his diary James Winston noted that Johnstone was "wonderfully received"; he "lacked his wonted

spirit occasionally but shewed the great actor." The house, however, was sparse.

Johnstone lived out his retirement at his house at No 5, Tavistock Row, where he had resided from at least 1810. In April 1786 he had lodged at No 23, Pall Mall; in April 1787 at No 7, Suffolk Street, Charing Cross; in April 1788 at No 83, St Martin's Lane; in May 1789 at No 12, Norton Street, Portland Chapel; and in 1790 and 1791 at No 10, Great Russell Street. Between 1792 and his move to Tavistock Row he lived at No 19, the Piazza, Covent Garden.

His life in the theatre had rewarded Johnstone well. In the 1790s his salary at Covent Garden was £10 per week; in 1801–2 it was raised to £11. At Drury Lane he was being paid £17 per week by 1813–14; the figure was reduced to £15 in 1814–15 (his signed salary receipts for those seasons are in the Harvard Theatre Collection), at which level it remained in 1815–16 and 1816–17. Between 1786 and 1791 his benefits brought in an average of about £275, the lowest £215 on 28 April 1786 and highest £313 on 5 May 1789 (less house charges of £105 in each instance). Between 1792 and 1800 the average gross benefit increased to £391, the lowest being £333 on 29 April 1794 and the highest £489 on 25 April 1793.

Seven years after the death of his first wife Maria Ann Johnstone in 1784, Johnstone married by license Ann Bolton, a "minor," at St Paul, Covent Garden, on 23 December 1791. According to Oxberry, Johnstone had earlier eloped with her—accompanied by her sister—but, soon after, her father, a Bond Street wine merchant, became reconciled and the wedding was arranged. In the marriage register Ann was described as from the parish of St George, Hanover Square. Though Johnstone was a convivial member of such groups as the Beef Steak Club and the Anacreontic Society and maintained a dignified and gentlemanly appearance, at home he was parsimonious—his wife, it was said, frequently had to pawn parts of her wardrobe; he was characterized by Oxberry as "tyrannical at home, inconstant abroad—mean at his table, and an interloper at the table of others." Ann Johnstone died 18 years before her husband, at Tavistock Row on 19 August 1810 at the age of 39.

By his second wife Johnstone had one

Harvard Theatre Collection

JOHN HENRY JOHNSTONE as Sir Callaghan O'Brallaghan

engraving by Ward, after Shee

daughter, Susan Johnstone, who was probably born in 1793; the day that the Earl of Barrymore died, 6 March 1793, he was to have stood sponsor to Johnstone's infant daughter, reported "Pasquin" in his *Life* of that nobleman. She later acted for a while as Miss Johnstone. Her marriage to the very popular actor James William Wallack, the elder (1794–1864), in 1817 resulted in a substantial nineteenth-century theatrical dynasty in England and America before she died in 1851. Presumably Johnstone had disapproved his daughter's match to Wallack. He was the son of William Wallack and Elizabeth Granger Field. John Johnstone "Lester" Wallack (1819–1888), the son of Susan Johnstone and James William Wallack, became an important actor on the American stage.

By one of his extramarital affairs with the Edinburgh actress Lois Mary Searles, Johnstone fathered a daughter named Jemima Marian Bew. Lois Mary Searles was the daughter of a shopkeeper in the Covent Garden Piazza, where Johnstone had resided for some

years. When Johnstone abandoned her, the pregnant Miss Searles was taken in marriage by Charles Bew, also a London actor and sometime dentist. The child Jemima Marian Bew also became an actress at Drury Lane and married the actor Frederick Vining at St Paul, Covent Garden, on 2 March 1814.

John Henry Johnstone died at his house in Tavistock Row on 28 December 1828, at the age of 78 according to the register of burials at St Paul, Covent Garden, where he was interred in a vault in the eastern angle on 3 January 1829. The probate of his will in Doctor's Commons was reported in the *Gentleman's Magazine* of February 1829. His estate was valued under £12,000 in personal property (not the £40,000 or £50,000 rumored). He left some small bequests to friends and a £50 annuity to a housekeeper who had nursed him during his last years. Despite Oxberry's claim that Johnstone had behaved brutally to his natural daughter, the will provided a bequest of £500 to Mrs Vining. The bulk of his estate he left in trust to the children of his daughter Susan Wallack.

About five feet nine inches in height, possessed of a very fine head and handsome face, Johnstone retained an air of gentlemanly dignity. In 1825, at about the age of 75, he looked, it was said, no more than 50. He suffered most of his career from swollen ankles, which required him to wear boots almost constantly. His jealous rivals would "sneer at his *legs*," but as "Anthony Pasquin" wrote in *The Children of Thespis* (1788), "an *Irishman's leg* is not priz'd for its quickness, . . . For the owners ne'er use them in running away." Pasquin (really John Williams) asked:

Yet where shall we find, in these dissonant days,
An opera chief that deserves so much praise?
If he answers not every purpose of merit,
If view'd in all points, he has taste, truth, and
    spirit.

. . . .

He has one great advantage, 'mid singers most
    rare,
For in AIMWORTH *the nobleman buries the play'r;*
His person is dignified, graceful, commanding,
And his eyes shew the traits of a good understand-
    ing.

He was not much of a musician, as Haydn had noticed. He often fell out of time with the orchestra and frequently out of tune, a circumstance used to advantage in Bannister's imitations of him. His voice was good in upper ranges, discordant in the lower.

Unquestionably Johnstone was the best Teague on the stage in his day, even better than Moody according to most testimony, though Genest thought the latter superior. Johnstone's popularity was so great that Irish characters were introduced by playwrights hopeful of getting their plays accepted, even though the logic of the plots hardly supported such inclusions. Adolphus described the rage:

A play, a farce, an interlude, a pantomime, or any other piece, let the scene be laid where, and the time fixed when, the author pleased, could hardly at that stage be brought upon the stage without an Irishman. This was a severe task upon Jack Johnstone, but it was entirely his own doing: he played, he looked, he sung the character so admirably; he exhibited so much true feeling, and such spontaneous fun, that it seemed almost a fraud upon the audience, in any house where he was engaged, to exclude him from a piece in which there could be a pretence for introducing him. The cavils of criticism; its great words,—such as anachronism,—incongruity,—however ably enforced or authoritatively sounded, were lost and drowned amid the torrents of delight and thunders of applause which always greeted the unrivalled performer. Place an Irishman in Calais, in Granada, or in the Sierra de Ronde, if Johnstone were that Irishman, the criticism of the audience . . . forgot all difficulties of place and climate; and if he had made his entrance on an uninhabitable island, he would have been cordially welcome.

Two epigrammatic verses which appeared in August 1793 sum up his reputation:

"The Stage is Nature's mirror"—Right!
In further proof, the other night
Paddy exclaim'd—"O, by the Mass,
That Johnstone is my looking-glass!"

"By my faith 'tis no Bull, cries Paddy, but Fact,
When from Dub{l}in to London I roam,
Ev'ry hour I'm there, while I see Johnstone act,
By J—s—s I feel I'm at home."

Portraits of John Henry Johnstone include:
1. By Robert Dighton? Pencil sketch. In the Folger Shakespeare Library.
2. By Samuel De Wilde. In the Lady Leicester Collection.

3. By unknown artist. Nine silhouettes on paper. In the Garrick Club.
4. Engraved portrait by C. Bestland. Published by the engraver, 1791. The same engraving was published as a plate to *European Magazine*, 1793.
5. Engraved portrait by J. Condé. Published as a plate to *Thespian Magazine*, 1793.
6. Engraved portrait by Martyn. Published as a plate to the *Hibernian Magazine*.
7. Engraved portrait by W. Ridley, after Hutchinson. Published as a plate to the *Monthly Mirror*, 1802.
8. Engraved portrait by W. Ridley, after M. A. Shee.
9. Engraved portrait by W. Ridley. From a miniature. Published as a plate to Parson's *Minor Theatre*, 1794.
10. By unknown engraver. From a miniature (Harvard No 8).
11. As Apollo in *Midas*. By unknown engraver. Published by R. Butters (as a plate to an edition of the play 1789?)
12. As Sir Callaghan O'Brallaghan in *Love à-la-Mode*. By M. A. Shee. Exhibited at the Royal Academy in 1803. In the Garrick Club (No 365). Engraving by W. Ward, 1803. Copies were engraved by Maguire for the *Cyclopedian Magazine*, 1808; Kennerly (Harvard No 20); and J. Rogers for Oxberry's *New English Drama*, 1824, and Oxberry's *Dramatic Biography*, 1826.
13. As Captain Valentine, with John Edwin as Jemmy Jumps, in *The Farmer*. By unknown engraver. Published by J. Aitken, 1791.
14. As Dennis Brulgruddery in *John Bull*. Watercolor by Samuel De Wilde. In the Garrick Club (No 45d).
15. As Dennis Brulgruddery. Drawn and engraved by S. Sharpe. Published as plate to *The Universal Songster*.
16. As Dennis Brulgruddery. Engraving by Thomson, after Partridge. Published as a plate to the *Theatrical Inquisitor*, 1816.
17. As Edwin in *Robin Hood*. Watercolor by W. Loftis. In the Folger Shakespeare Library.
18. As Looney, with John Emery as John Lump, in *The Wags of Windsor* (*The Review*). Engraving by J. and H. Caulfield, after Emery.
19. As Major O'Flaherty in *The West Indian*. Engraving by P. Audinet, after De Wilde. Published as a plate to *Bell's British Theatre*, 1792. A copy engraved by S. Close was pub-

lished as a plate to *British Theatre*, 1795; another copy, by an unknown engraver, was printed for C. Cooke, 1808.

20. As Major O'Flaherty. Watercolor by Samuel De Wilde. In the Garrick Club (catalogue No 487). Not the same as above.

21. As Major O'Flaherty. Engraving by Thomson, after T. Wageman. Published as a plate to Oxberry's *New English Drama*, 1818.

22. As Murtock Delany in *The Irishman in London*. Engraving by F. Warburton, after W. Wellings. Published by Wellings, 1793.

23. As O'Dedemus. Watercolor by Samuel De Wilde. In the Harvard Theatre Collection.

24. As O'Gallagher, in Chinese costume, in *The Travellers*. By unknown engraver.

25. As O'Rourke O'Daisy, with Maria Theresa Bland as Dolly, in *Hit or Miss*. In a satirical print by Cruikshank, entitled "Huzza, for old Ireland, with Hubbaboo Whack!" published by Laurie & Whittle, 4 April 1810.

26. As O'Whack in *Notoriety*. Watercolor by W. Wellings. In the Garrick Club (No 549b).

27. As Shady O'Blarney in *Botheration*. Drawing by unknown artist. In the Widener Collection, Harvard University.

28. As Tully in *The London Hermit*. By unknown engraver, after De Wilde. Published by J. Dunford, 1816.

29. In character, arm in sling, letter in right hand. Watercolor by Samuel De Wilde, dated March 1809. In the Harvard Theatre Collection.

Johnstone, Mrs John Henry the first, Maria Ann, née Poitier *d. 1784, singer, actress.*

Maria Ann Poitier was probably born in Ireland, since she was the daughter of Colonel Poitier, governor of Kilmainham Gaol. Her theatrical relations included her uncle, Michael Poitier (d. 1774), a dancer, and her aunt Jane Poitier, an actress who first married Joseph Vernon and then became Mrs Thompson.

The earliest stage appearances of Maria Ann Poitier seem to have been made at Salisbury in 1775 and at Manchester in 1776 before she was taken by her aunt Mrs Thompson to Tate Wilkinson at York in April 1776. The York manager found that she had "an elegant person, an enchanting pipe, and was truly a charming singer." At York that spring she performed as Leonora in *The Padlock* and in the

title role of *The Maid of the Mill*, among other roles, "to excellent houses, and with unbounded applause," according to Wilkinson. That summer she played at Birmingham and later that year at Crow Street, Dublin, where she was also in 1777–78.

At Dublin on 22 February 1778 she married the Irish actor John Henry Johnstone, who was also a member of the Crow Street company. As Mrs Johnstone she continued as a Dublin performer through 1782–83, often appearing with her husband. Songs published at Dublin as sung by her included "Touchstone" and "Gentle Echo" from *The Touchstone* (*Hibernian Magazine*, February 1781), "Partners of my toils and pleasures" from *The Lord of the Manor* (*Hibernian Magazine*, June 1781), and *Rest Beautious Flowr's* (separately published, 1781?), also from *The Lord of the Manor*. It was claimed in the *Gentleman's Magazine* of February 1829 that Mrs Johnstone, "being highly accomplished, and possessing a profound knowledge of music, imparted to her husband the arcana of the science, and made him a finished singer.

After a visit to her mother, who was residing in London during the summer of 1783, Mrs Johnstone was engaged with her husband at Covent Garden for the 1783–84 season, she at a salary of £4 per week and he at £8. She made her debut there on 17 September 1783 as Rosetta in *Love in a Village*. According to the bills, this was her first appearance on that stage; Reed's "Notitia Dramatica" at the British Library states that it was "her 1^s App.^{ce} in England." So the statement in the *Town and Country Magazine* for September 1783 that she had appeared at the Haymarket a few years earlier as Miss Poitier may be erroneous; her name is in no Haymarket bills. On 19 September 1783 she made her second Covent Garden appearance, as Leonora in *The Padlock*. Subsequently she acted Mandane in *Artaxarxes* on 16 October, Norah in *The Poor Soldier* on 12 December, the title role in *Rosina* on 15 December, and Victoria in *The Castle of Andalusia* on 20 December.

After 22 December 1783, when she again played Norah, Mrs Johnstone retired from the stage. At the time, her husband was carrying on an open affair with the actress Sarah Wilson, and some reports state that Mrs Johnstone fled to Turnham Green in embarrassment and distress. According to the *Public Register* (Dublin), she died at Turnham Green on 15 June 1784 (not 1785 as sometimes reported). No issue of her marriage with Johnstone is known.

Wilkinson thought highly of her, writing in *The Wandering Patentee*: "London has an unknown loss by the death of the delightful girl; there could not have been the smallest doubt of her success, had the tyrant Death permitted her to live."

Jolli, Antonio   *c. 1700–1777, scene painter, manager?*

In his *Decorative Painting in England* Edward Croft-Murray noted that Antonio Jolli was born in Modena about 1700. He studied under Rinaldi and (Francesco?) Bibiena, and after working under Pannini in Rome he returned, in 1725, to his native city. Then he worked in Perugia and about 1735 settled in Venice, where he married. In Venice Jolli became a scene painter at the theatres of S. Cassiano, S. Samuele, and S. Giovanni Chrisostomo. He may also have painted scenery in Dresden.

About 1743 Jolli came to London. From 1744 to 1748 he painted scenery at the King's Theatre for *Rosalinda* (January 1744; designed and painted new scenes); *Annibale in Capua*, *Mitridate*, *Fetonte*, and *Bellerofonte* (1746–47; for the first and third he also designed scenery for the dances); and *Semiramide reconosciuta* (1748). Jolli signed the preface to the printed edition of *Semiramide reconosciuta* on 7 May 1748, noting that the work was "the last Opera I shall bring on this Season. . . ." That led Croft-Murray in the April and May 1941 issues of the *Burlington Magazine* to wonder if Jolli was in some way concerned in the management of the King's Theatre.

Croft-Murray argues convincingly that Jolli probably executed the panels in the painted hall at the impresario Heidegger's house at Richmond. Jolli painted two perspective pieces for the Duchess of Richmond in 1744 and two overmantel pictures in the gallery at Temple Newsam, near Leeds, for the seventh Viscount Irwin about 1745. He worked also at Fonthill House, seat of the Beckford family, and painted some views of Richmond and the Thames. His architectural and topographical paintings show the influence of Pannini and Canaletto.

About 1750 Jolli went to Madrid. He was elected a member of the Venetian Academy in

1755 and was in Naples in 1759. He returned to Venice in 1760 but settled in Naples in 1762 and was appointed to the court theatre. Antonio Jolli died in Naples on 29 April 1777.

Jolly, Mr   [*fl. 1756–1758*], *dancer, dancing master.*

Although he may have appeared earlier in the dancing chorus, the first notice of Mr Jolly at Drury Lane Theatre was on 11 May 1756, when he performed Harlequin, with Dumay as Pierrot, in a new pantomime dance. A week later on 18 May he appeared with Dumay and Cointe in a new dance, *Les Savoyards*.

In the summer of 1757 Jolly danced regularly in specialty numbers at the Haymarket Theatre, where his name sometimes appeared in the bills as Joly. There on 22 August 1757 one of his pupils, Miss Filizeau, also danced.

During the next winter season he danced at the Haymarket in *Le Carnaval de Venise* on 26 December 1757 and with Miss Dulisse on 13 March 1758.

Jolly, George   [*fl. 1630?–1673*], *actor, manager.*

George Jolly the actor-manager may have been the son of George Jolley, a barber-surgeon of the parish of St Martin, Aldersgate, who had a daughter Mary christened on 8 January 1630 at St Giles, Cripplegate. G. E. Bentley suggests in his *Jacobean and Caroline Stage* that our subject was probably the George Jolly "Player in yᵉ house of Mathew Smith Playeʳ in Whitcrostrt" whose son John was baptized at St Giles's on 9 July 1640. The boy died soon after and was buried the following 13 July, his father again being identified as "George Jolly Player." Until Bentley traced those parish register entries, it was not known that Jolly had been a pre-Commonwealth actor.

At some point Jolly went to the Continent. Hotson in *The Commonwealth and Restoration Stage* suggests that Jolly may have been a member of the Prince of Wales's troupe in Paris in November 1646. That group disbanded for lack of pay that month. In any case, existing records show us that Jolly was in Cologne at the end of April 1648; Hotson believes he went there from Paris by way of Holland, where he may have headed a troupe in February 1648.

On 26 April 1648 Jolly and his fellow players performed in the tennis court in the St Apostelnstrasse in Cologne. They were given permission to continue performing for two weeks, and that grant was extended to the end of July, after which they went to Frankfort on the Main. Jolly's company returned to Cologne in early 1649. The group styled itself English, though some members were natives, and the company performed in German. The troupe played at the August fair in Frankfort in 1651 in the Ballhaus adjoining the Gasthof zum Karchbein. But a rival company, performing plays with music and changeable scenery, proved far more popular with the audiences and caused Jolly to revamp his troupe after the Italian and French fashion—with scenes, machines, and operas. By 1653 he had modernized his group and was performing in Vienna. Cohn notes in his *Shakespeare in German* that "George Jeliphur" received 15 florins on 15 May 1653 for performing "a comedy with his colleagues before their Majesties." The following year he added actresses to his company and was prospering. He was in Frankfort again in 1654, still playing at the tennis-court playhouse, but he made enough money to propose the building of a new playhouse of his own.

Early in 1654 "Horis Jolifus," styling himself an "English and Roman Imperial Comedian" after his Vienna visit, applied to perform in Basle. He boasted that he would please Swiss audiences "with his well-practised company, not only by means of good instructive stories, but also with repeated changes of expensive costumes, and a theatre decorated in the Italian manner, with beautiful English music and skilful women. . . ." The Swiss were not impressed and refused him a permit.

During the winter of 1654–55 Jolly's players were not in Frankfort, but they returned for a long stay in 1655 and were fortunate enough to be seen in September by Charles Stuart, soon to become Charles II of England. Charles and his court were in Frankfort for the fair, incognito (at least for a while). After that, Jolly styled his troupe "The King's Servants." In September 1656 Jolly was faced with the competition of a troupe operated by two of his former actors, Schwartz and Hoffman, who rented the tennis court before Jolly had a chance to; in the spring of 1657 Jolly managed to rent the tennis court first. The rivalry continued, and in July 1657 Jolly, finding the opposing troupe at the tennis-court theatre, had to build a temporary booth theatre. The competition grew fierce, leading to brawls in taverns between rival players. Finally, on 29 September, rules were set up by the city elders governing the operation of playhouses. The rival troupes joined temporarily, but quarrels continued, a split occurred, and the city councillor banned both troupes. Schwartz and Hoffman finally left Frankfort to the Jolly company, which received permission to perform two or three times a week for a while and remained in Frankfort for the winter of 1657–58.

In the spring of 1658 Jolly once again united with the Schwartz-Hoffman company, but by July the troupe had split again. Jolly was forced out of the tennis-court theatre and reduced to eight performers; his actresses deserted him. Finally a peace was made; the companies reunited and set out for Vienna. There "Joseph Jori"—probably Jolly—called himself an "English and Heidelberg comedian" and asked permission to perform, but his plays shocked Viennese spectators, and by the spring of 1659 Jolly was performing in Nuremberg. On 29 December 1659 a child of his was christened there: "Georgius Jeliphus von Chelse in Middlsex bey London ein *Comoediant. Maria di Roy* van Utrecht in Holland." The name of the child is not known. On 31 January 1660 Jolly was expelled from Nuremberg because of a quarrel; by the following November he was in England.

On 24 December 1660 Charles II granted George Jolly a license to establish a third acting company in London—the other two, under Sir William Davenant and Thomas Killigrew respectively, were granted royal patents. Jolly rented the Cockpit in Drury Lane. By the summer of 1661 he was using the Salisbury Court theatre but, finding it unsatisfactory, he returned to the Cockpit, only to be ordered by the King to go back to Salisbury Court. He at some point evidently also used the old Red Bull Theatre. But his position in London was difficult; he held only a license, which meant that his company could live only at the pleasure of the King; he did not have a theatre he could call his own, as by 1661 both Davenant and Killigrew did, and his rivals had the rights to the most popular plays. One play which it seems certain that Joly's troupe performed, *Dr Faustus*, did not appeal to Restoration playgoers.

On 30 December 1662 Jolly was apparently happy to come to an agreement with Davenant and Killigrew: he signed over his license to them for £4 a week for the rest of his life. A bond of £2000 was posted to assure Jolly that Davenant and Killigrew would hold to the conditions of the agreement. On 1 January 1663 the Master of the Revels, Sir Henry Herbert, granted George Jolly permission to form a strolling company and play outside London and Westminster, and on 29 January the King reenforced that by calling on provincial officers to give Jolly their protection. Sybil Rosenfeld, in an article on the players at Cambridge in *Studies in English Theatre History*, said that sometime in 1662 Jolly's troupe performed *Philaster*, *The Changeling*, *The Rump*, and *Wit Without Money* at the Cardinal's Cap Inn, in St Botolph's parish.

On 15 April 1663 in the Mayor's Court Book in Norwich was entered the following:

This day George Iolly gent produced a patent from the King made to him & such psons as he shold choose for yᵉ exercising of playes opperas Maskes shoes & scenes in any place in England & wales & licence was given to him to doe yᵉ same at the Kings armes in this City.

On 3 August Jolly was allowed to continue in Norwich for five more weeks on his promise to "be benefciall to the poore," a vow which he kept. In Jolly's repertoire at Norwich, according to Dr Edward Browne's manuscript notes, were *Tu Quoque*, *Ignoramus*, *The Pinner of Wakefield*, *Muliasses*, *A Girl Worth Gold*, *'Tis Pity She's a Whore*, *The Little Thief*, *A New Way to Pay Old Debts*, and *The Faire Quarrell*.

Jolly's success at Norwich in 1663 encouraged him to return there the following year. He was back in London about March 1664, trying to get his money from Davenant and Killigrew. He discovered that they had convinced the King that Jolly had sold them his license outright and that they would use it to set up a "Nursery" for young actors. Jolly had right on his side, of course, and since Davenant and Killigrew would not pay him his due, he somehow retrieved his license and formed a London troupe. Hotson says that despite resistance from the patentees Jolly performed, apparently at the Cockpit in Drury Lane, until the plague closed all theatres in the spring of 1665.

In 1666–67, perhaps at the Cockpit, Jolly performed once again. Killigrew used his influence to have Jolly's troupe silenced in March 1667, and Jolly's license was officially revoked on 2 April. Jolly fought back, naturally, and Davenant and Killigrew finally agreed to let him serve as the patentee of the Nursery they were setting up in Hatton Garden. Jolly was paid 6s. 8d. for every day the youthful company performed, in lieu of setting up a company of his own. The Nursery operation remained in Hatton Garden until sometime in 1668. Then it moved to Gibbons's tennis court (the old Vere Street Theatre) until May 1671, when it shifted to Bun Hill, Finsbury Fields. A new Nursery in the Barbican was apparently opened in the winter of 1671–72. After the death of Sir William Davenant in 1668, Jolly served at the Nursery under Killigrew and Lady Davenant; the former continued to be at odds with Jolly, but Lady Davenant evidently treated him favorably.

The young actors at the Nursery sometimes gained experience by touring. On 22 September 1669 Jolly was given permission to perform in Norwich, and his troupe was probably made up at least partly of players from the Nursery in London. It may, indeed, have been identical with the Duke of Monmouth's players. By 8 December Norwich was trying to get rid of Jolly, and on 24 December a letter was written to Sir Joseph Williamson seeking his help in limiting the stay of visiting troupes, for "they divert the meaner sort of people from their labour in the manufactories, thereby occasioning a vain expense of time and money." By 17 January 1670 Charles II authorized the city to place whatever limits it wished on visiting companies.

Jolly remained associated with the Nursery in London until at least 1673, after which his activities have not been traced. On 12 March 1683 John Coysh was in Norwich with a troupe, presenting himself as "asignee of yᵉ Patent of Georg Jolly deceased."

"Jolly Tar, The" *b. 1748, dancer.*

A lad of seven, called "The Jolly Tar," danced a hornpipe at the Haymarket Theatre on 9, 11, and 15 September 1755.

Joly. *See* JOLLY.

Jona, Mr   *d. 1756, prompter.*

On 5 May 1756 at Covent Garden Mr Jona shared a benefit with five others. That benefit would indicate that he was employed at that playhouse, but when the *Daily Advertiser* the following 25 October reported Jona's death, he was described as a "Master of Languages and Prompter to the Opera" at the King's Theatre. On the following 8 December Jona's widow and her five children were given a benefit at Covent Garden; the bill stated that tickets were available from her in Little Warrick Street, Charing Cross. Covent Garden granted Mrs Jona and her children another benefit on 21 December 1758.

By a previous marriage Mrs Jona was the mother of the performers Miss E. Ambrose and the Miss Ambrose who later became Mrs Kelf. Thus Jona and his wife had either had three children after their marriage, or Jona had brought to the marriage three children of his own by a previous marriage.

Jonas, Mr   [*fl. 1767–1786*],   *conjurer.*

The earliest notice of Mr Jonas was December 1767, when, according to W. J. Lawrence's notes at the National Library of Ireland, Jonas was doing conjuring tricks at Napper's Great Room in George's Lane, Dublin. On 31 May 1768 "The Famous Mr. JONAS *The CONJUROR*" was holding forth at Mrs Shirley's Long Room at the Hot Wells in Bristol. He advertised on 18 June that he had just returned to Bristol from a brief excursion and was ready to "wait on any private Company, not more then Ten in Number, for One Guinea. . . ."

Wroth's *London Pleasure Gardens* places Jonas at Dobney's Bowling Green in 1769, performing feats of manual dexterity. At those performances the skeleton of a whale 60C long was shown, but Jonas may not have been responsible for that exhibition. In August 1769 the "so-much admired and unparallelled" Jonas showed his "matchless and curious deceptions" at Penny's Folly, or the Belvidere Tea Gardens in Pentonville Road; the program also featured the Learned Little Horse of Mr Zucker the proprietor and some airs on musical glasses by Mrs Zucker. Jonas was listed by the Duchess

of Northumberland in her catalogue of diversions in London in 1773.

Leathers, in *British Entertainers in France*, places Jonas, an "English Jew," in France in 1774, doing juggling and magic acts at the fairs and social gatherings. Jonas was performing at Bath in December 1776 and was at Bristol ten years later. A Bristol advertisement on 1 July 1786 said that "Mr Jonas who has been Abroad a few Years exhibits his new Deceptions and Experiments" on 3 July at Foreman's Long Room at the Hot Wells at one in the afternoon and at Taylors' Hall at eight in the evening. He planned to reveal how he did his card tricks, to help people protect themselves from sharpers.

Jonas, Mr   [*fl. 1776?–1815*],   *puppeteer, manager, actor.*

Mr Jonas appeared with Astley's London troupe from Sadler's Wells at Birmingham in December 1776 serving as a clown and acrobat. He may well have been the Jonas who was at Bartholomew Fair regularly in the 1790s and had a career as a provincial manager. The Pie Powder Court Book at the London Guildhall contains a number of citations concerning the activity of Jonas at the Fair. On 4 September 1790 he paid 8s. for a license to put on a puppet show. In 1791 he appeared as both a puppeteer and an actor; in 1792 he exhibited puppets, and in 1793 he acted. His troupe was in the George Inn Yard at the Fair in 1794 and performed *All in Good Humour* and *The Whim*. Jonas returned as a comedian in 1795. At the theatre in the market place in Hoddesdon on 23 February 1796 Jonas played Medium in *Inkle and Yarico* and Joey in *Modern Antiques* for W. Penley's benefit (Mrs Jonas also acted). In the late summer Jonas was again at Bartholomew Fair as a player. He acted there again in 1797, performed at the Fair with Penley (probably Samson Penley) in 1798, and produced a puppet show in 1799.

The *Monthly Mirror* in September 1799 reported that Jonas, from Lewes, had opened a new theatre at Eastbourne. He and Samson Penley applied in December 1803 for a license to operate a playhouse at Folkestone and by then were apparently managing several provincial theatres and had given up Bartholomew Fair. An undated note in *The Theatric Tourist* concerned the theatre at Lewes:

[Cobb] then renewed JONAS and PENLEY's lease for twenty-one years, at the annual rent of fifty pounds, including the adjoining buildings, which let for, one eight and the other ten pounds per year. The present leaseholders are in possession of some small towns in the neighborhood, of which Eastbourne is the chief. They annually "show 'em in" at Peckham Fair, and renew the days of Thespis. Bartholomew [Fair] has encountered much loss by their desertion, for these few years past. The theatre is situate at the bottom of Star Lane, in a place oftentimes called Botany Bay. Expences ten pounds, and holds seventy, at 3s. 2s. and 1s. An annual season.

By about 1814 Jonas and Penley managed theatres also at Windsor, Henley, and Peckham Rye. Possibly Jonas was the actor of that name who appeared on 7 March 1815 as Lope Tocke in *The Mountaineers* at the Ostend theatre. A Miss Jonas was also on that bill, but she seems not to have performed in the eighteenth century.

Jonathan, [Mr?] [*fl.* 1759–1761], *actor.*

A Mr Jonathan (or was Jonathan the person's Christian name?) participated in *The Fair* at Covent Garden Theatre beginning 10 December 1759 serving as (Merry?) Andrew to Yates's (mountebank) Parade. Two seasons later, beginning 13 October 1761 and continuing through 9 November, Jonathan once again played "Andrew." He was used in 23 performances and paid 5s. daily.

Joncel. *See* DUJONCEL.

Jones, Mr [*fl.* 1715–1718], *singer.*

Mr Jones sang in *The Island Princess* on 25 January 1715 at the Lincoln's Inn Fields playhouse. He was heard in *The Beau Demolished* on 9 February, and since he was named as the singer of *Now Roger and Harry* from *The Mountebank* when that song was published, it is likely that he sang in the performance of that work on 21 December 1715. On 2 January 1717 he sang Latinus in *Camilla*. The following 31 October Jones sang in *The Prophetess*, and he appeared as an entr'acte singer during the 1717–18 season at Lincoln's Inn Fields. But on 19 March 1718 he and Provo shared a benefit concert at the Tennis Court (not James Street).

Jones, Mr [*fl.* 1716–1717], *violinist.*

Mr Jones was paid £2 3s. for playing the violin in the band at the King's Theatre five nights between 8 December 1716 and 29 June 1717.

Jones, Mr [*fl.* 1717?–1732], *numberer.*

The Mr Jones who shared a benefit with the actor Diggs at Drury Lane Theatre on 30 May 1717 may have been Jones the numberer. When Jones had a benefit on 27 May 1719 his function in the company was stated. The next benefit notice for him was in May 1725, after which he was fairly regularly cited for shared benefits through at least 9 May 1732. Charles Beecher Hogan, in *Shakespeare in the Theatre*, takes Jones the numberer of the 1720s to have been the same person as Jones the box office keeper of the late 1740s, but the gap of 16 years between notices suggests to us that two different men, perhaps a father and son, are in question.

Jones, Mr [*fl.* 1721–1750], *gallery keeper, stage doorkeeper.*

The name Jones appears in the benefit bills and accounts of John Rich's company at Lincoln's Inn Fields and Covent Garden from 1721 to 1750. Though it is possible that more than one house servant named Jones worked during those many years, perhaps all the references are to the same employee. The first mention of Jones was on 6 June 1721 when he shared gross receipts of £107 19s. 6d. at a Lincoln's Inn Fields benefit. He was cited fairly regularly at benefit time through May 1729. His weekly salary during this period was £1 1s. and he was described as a gallery keeper.

For the few years following, Jones was not cited in the bills, though that does not necessarily mean that he did not continue in John Rich's employ. On 26 May 1735 at Covent Garden, Jones's benefit tickets were accepted, and the following year he split a benefit with two others. The 1735–36 accounts show his salary to have been 15s. weekly and his post that of stage doorkeeper. Jones was mentioned in benefit bills through 1737–38 but not again until May 1745. The last reference to him in the accounts was on 29 September 1749; he was cited as receiving 3s. for two days' work during the 1749–50 season. If one Mr Jones served the company all these years, his responsibilities were simplified and his salary lowered as he grew older. By 1750 he was doubtless close to retirement.

Jones, Mr [*fl.* 1723], *actor.*
A Mr Jones played Worthy in *The Recruiting Officer* on 15 April 1723 at the Haymarket Theatre.

Jones, Mr [*fl.* 1728–1731], *violinist.*
Mr Jones played violin at a concert at York Buildings on 13 March 1728 and performed at Drury Lane Theatre in a variety concert on 26 March 1729. He shared a benefit with the actor-singer Excell on 30 November 1731 at the Sun Tavern behind the Royal Exchange.

Jones, Mr [*fl.* 1729–1741], *actor, singer.*
Discriminating the Joneses who were active in the early eighteenth century is a bewildering task. One can almost make a case for there having been just one actor named Jones who was busy from the beginning of 1729 to perhaps as late as September 1756, though in a few instances he would have had to move swiftly from one playhouse to another in one evening to make engagements. It seems more likely that there were two or more Joneses who acted during that period, and we have here conjectured four.

A Jones acted Bedamar in *Venice Preserv'd* at the Haymarket on 10 January 1729; it was advertised as his first appearance on the stage. Jones acted at Reynolds's booth at Bartholomew Fair the following August, and beginning on 18 December 1729 he appeared fairly regularly at the Haymarket Theatre. On that date he was Death in *Hurlothrumbo*, the work of the eccentric Samuel Johnson of Cheshire. On 29 January 1730 he played Urlemdenny in the same piece, and on 6 February Jones was Bonniface in *The Stratagem* for one performance in the middle of the *Hurlothrumbo* run. Johnson's next play, *The Cheshire Comicks*, played on 23 February with Jones in the cast; then on 11 March Jones was Mrs Slammekin in *The Metamorphosis of The Beggar's Opera*, played Fluellin in *The Half Pay Officers* and Hob in *Flora* the following day, and on 30 March acted Dr Orator and Bookweight and spoke the prologue to *The Author's Farce*. On 6 April 1730 Jones was Scapin in *The Cheats of Scapin*; on the eighth he spoke the prologue and played Antilochus in *The Rival Father*, and on 24 April he spoke the prologue and played Lord Grizzle in *Tom Thumb*. That kept him occupied until 23 June, when he played Squeezum in *Rape Upon Rape*. He was the Duke in *Othello* on 27 June 1730 and the Bawd in *The Amorous Adventure* on 17 July (he often played skirts parts, as can be seen).

On 1 August 1730 Jones played an unnamed role in *The Rum Duke and the Queer Duke* at Tottenham Court; then at Bartholomew Fair on 22 August he was the Bawd in *Harlequin's Contrivance*. On 4 September at the fair he repeated that part and again played Lord Grizzle in *Tom Thumb*. He acted his part in *Harlequin's Contrivance* again on 9 September at Southwark Fair, and there on the fourteenth he appeared in that piece plus *Tom Thumb*, in which he played his part of Grizzle. On 18 September 1730 he began an engagement at the Haymarket (playing Foigard in *The Stratagem*) which continued through May 1732, with occasional appearances elsewhere.

At the Haymarket, after his appearance as Foigard, Jones acted Bookweight and Orator again in *The Author's Farce*, Grizzle in *Tom Thumb*, Antonio in *Love Makes a Man*, Old Mirabel in *The Inconstant*, the Bawd in *The Amorous Adventure*, Squeezum in *The Coffee-House Politician*, Lord Grizzle in *The Battle of the Poets*, Gratiano in *Othello*, Mirza in *The Generous Freemason*, Bonniface in *The Stratagem*, Dominic and Gomez in *The Spanish Fryar*, Evan ap Remnant in *The Jealous Taylor*, Sir Francis in *The Provok'd Husband*, Sir Sampson in *Love for Love*, a role in *Lupone*, Toby in *The Cobler of Preston*, Wisdom in *The Letter Writers*, William in *The Welch Opera*, Sir Thomas Delamore and a Citizen in *The Fall of Mortimer*, Scapin in *The Cheats of Scapin*, Limpo in *The Blazing Comet* (Samuel Johnson of Cheshire was back again), Reynard in *Tunbridge Walks*, Father Cadiere in *The Wanton Jesuit*, Obadiah in *A Bold Stroke for a Wife*, Jobson in *The Devil to Pay*, Kite in *The Recruiting Officer*, Polydore in *The Orphan*, Corydon in *Damon and Phillida*, and Thorowgood in *The London Merchant*. He also delivered an epilogue on an ass. The same Jones would seem to have performed all that activity, and only on 1 June 1732, when he played in *The London Merchant* at the Haymarket, was there a conflict with a performance by a Jones elsewhere: at Drury Lane on that date a Jones played the Chairman in *The Covent Garden Tragedy*. Possibly one person could have done both.

Indeed, that summer marked the beginning of an association with Drury Lane. He was seen as a Servant in *The Devil to Pay*, the Chairman in *The Covent Garden Tragedy* (noted above), a Welshman in *The Mock Doctor*, Mat in *The Beggar's Opera*, an unnamed role in *Rural Love*, and Puritan in *The Devil of a Duke*. He was at Drury Lane again during the regular winter season of 1732–33 and remained through 1734–35, playing such new parts as a Murderer in *Macbeth*, Mrs Fardingale in *The Funeral*, a Clown in *The Country Revels*, the Constable in *The Provok'd Wife*, Bounce in *Caelia*, Jaques in *Love Makes a Man*, a Chinese Guard in *Cephalus and Procris*, Dicky in *The Constant Couple*, Whisper in *The Busy Body*, Meanwell in *The Imaginary Cuckolds*, Buckram and Jerry in *Love for Love*, Toby in *The Livery Rake*, a Satyr in *Damon and Daphne*, Quaint in *Aesop*, a Collier in *The Recruiting Officer*, Sir Jealous in *The Busy Body*, Thrasillus in *Timon of Athens*, Mustacho and Sycorax in *The Tempest*, Obadiah in *The Committee*, Goodall in *The Intriguing Chambermaid*, Nym in *The Merry Wives of Windsor*, and Supple in *The Double Gallant*.

During Jones's stint at Drury Lane, which began with a possible performance by the actor at the Haymarket on a day he was on the bill at Drury Lane, there was another Jones acting in London. His activity may have begun before 1733, though until that date we have conjectured that the Jones who is the subject of this entry could have taken all the assignments. On 23 August 1732 Jones (our subject, we think) played Sir Positive Crab in a droll, *Henry VIII*, at Bartholomew Fair.

During 1732–33, while Jones was busy at Drury Lane, a second Jones appeared at the Haymarket and Covent Garden. At Bartholomew Fair on 23 August 1733 both Joneses (if not a total of three) were active, but there is no way of telling who played what. On that date the name Jones was attached to a Rival Swain in *The Gardens of Venus*, a Masquerader in *The Ridotto al'Fresco*, and Ramilie in *The Miser*. In 1733–34 our Jones played at Drury Lane and the Haymarket, the second Jones appeared at Lincoln's Inn Fields, and possibly a third acted at the James Street Theatre. It is likely that the Jones who played Dolalolla in

The Opera of Operas at the Haymarket on 28 January 1734, the Cook in *The Country House* at Drury Lane on 30 March, and Guzzle in *Don Quixote in England* at the Haymarket on 5 April was our man. A Jones (a third one, or our subject?) played Decius in *Cato* at James Street on 23 May.

The Jones who acted a full summer season at the Haymarket in 1734 was, we believe, the Jones we have been following. On 3 June he appeared as Bardolph in *The Humours of Sir John Falstaff*, after which he played Sir Francis in *The Provok'd Husband*, the first and second Buyer in *The Lottery*, Robin in *The Beggar's Opera Tragedized*, Bonniface and Foigard in *The Stratagem*, Heartwell in *The Contrivances*, a role in *The Humorous Election*, and Lockit in *The Beggar's Opera*. In view of his previous skirts parts, we take it that the Jones who appeared at York Buildings on 21 March 1735 to act Mother Punchbowl in *The Covent Garden Tragedy* and Cholerick in *Love Makes a Man* was the actor we have been following. At Lincoln's Inn Fields on 12 June he acted the Old Woman in *Rule a Wife and Have a Wife*.

As in the summer of 1734 so also in 1735 a Jones appeared regularly at the Haymarket; he played several parts he had acted in 1734 plus Alderman Muckworm in *The Honest Yorkshireman*, Barnwell, Senior, in *The London Merchant*, Teague in *The Twin Rivals*, Gerald in *The Anatomist*, Acasto in *The Orphan*, and Scrub in *The Stratagem*. Then, at Lincoln's Inn Fields, Jones acted Wasp in *Bartholomew Fair* on 25 August 1735, Charino in *Love Makes a Man* on 29 August, Grizzle in *The Tragedy of Tragedies* and Lockit in *The Beggar's Opera* on 2 September, and Ricardo in *The Carnival* on 5 September.

Jones did not return to Drury Lane full time in the fall of 1735, though he seems to have been there for two performances: Sycorax in *The Tempest* on 31 October and Jaques in *Love Makes the Man* on 19 November. During the 1735–36 season Jones apparently moved about (if we have correctly followed the same Jones during the season). After his two performances at Drury Lane he played several at the Haymarket: Kite in *The Recruiting Officer* on 13 December 1735, Duretête in *The Inconstant* on 17 December, the Mayor, Ghost of Comedy, and Physic in *Pasquin* on 5 March 1736, and the Justice in *Tumble Down Dick* on 29 April.

Then on 26 June he played Lockit in *The Beg-gar's Opera* and Sir Jasper in *The Mock Doctor*, and on 30 July he was Hunks in *The Temple Rake*. On 23 August he was in *The Cheats of Scapin* at Bartholomew Fair and on 20 September he was the Drunken Mayor in *Pasquin* at Southwark Fair. We find no roles mentioned for Jones in the late months of 1736, but he was at the Haymarket in March and April 1737 with Fielding's group playing Mynheer Maggot in *A Rehearsal of Kings*, Ground Ivy and a Politician in *The Historical Register*, and a Gentleman in *Eurydice Hiss'd*. After that, references to an actor Jones—any Jones—in London cease until the late summer of 1740.

On 23 August 1740 at Bartholomew Fair a Jones was Comedy in *Harlequin Restor'd*, and at Southwark Fair on 9 September he played the Miller in *Harlequin Doctor Faustus*. The 1740–41 season shows a number of performances here and there by one Jones or more. They could all have been played by the same person, and they appear to be, like performances noted above for the 1735–36 season, by an actor with something like the line of parts we have seen in the Drury Lane Jones, jobbing in here and there during the season. In September, October, and November 1740 Jones played Shift in three performances of *The Cheats of Scapin* at Covent Garden. On 4 December he played the Mother in *The Fortune Tellers* at Drury Lane.

At Goodman's Fields on 15 April 1741 Jones was Mercury in *Lethe*; on 4 August he was a Witch in *Harlequin Sorcerer* at Tottenham Court; and on 22 August at *Bartholomew Fair* he played Bellamy in *The Modern Pimp*. The records then show no appearances by a Jones in London until the spring of 1744, and though the Jones who acted then may have been our subject, we think it best to treat him separately.

Jones, Mr ₍*fl.* 1733–1736?₎, actor.

Though some of the roles assigned to this Mr Jones may have belonged to the Jones who was active beginning in 1729, there are dates when one man could not have encompassed the known activity in the bills. There would seem to have been at least two Joneses performing in London beginning in 1733 or perhaps earlier. The Jones who acted from 1729 in London had an engagement at Drury Lane which ran from the summer of 1732 through

the 1734–35 season, so we take it that another Jones, the subject of this entry, was the actor who was cited in winter bills at the minor playhouses and who made sporadic summer appearances.

From 20 to 26 March 1733 a Jones played a Drawer in *Love Runs All Dangers* at the Haymarket Theatre. Perhaps he was the Jones who acted at Covent Garden in July and August of that year as Menander in *Sophonisba*, Comic in *The Stage Mutineers*, and Driver in *Oroonoko*. On 26 July, a day when he was not performing at Covent Garden, he was in *The Amorous Lady* at the Haymarket. At Bartholomew Fair on 23 August both Joneses (if not both of them plus a third) performed, but there is no way of telling who played what. The bills cited a Jones playing a Rival Swain in *The Gardens of Venus*, a Masquerader in *The Ridotto al'Fresco*, and Ramilie in *The Miser*. On 4 September 1733 only one Jones was active: he played Omar in *Tamerlane* at Bartholomew Fair. Again, it is impossible to tell which Jones was the man.

On 3 May 1734 at Lincoln's Inn Fields Jones played Moneytrap in *The Confederacy*, and at the same house on 23 May he was seen as Monsieur in *The School Boy*. On 23 May a Jones (a third one?) acted Decius in *Cato* at the James Street Theatre. On 20 August Jones was again at Lincoln's Inn Fields, playing Sir Francis in *The Provok'd Husband*; at the Haymarket on 7 October he acted Jeremy in *Love for Love*. At Tottenham Court on 28 May 1735 he appeared as Gardener in *The Drummer*.

Tracing the activity of the Joneses from the fall of 1735 forward becomes even more difficult, for the Jones who had been acting at Drury Lane did not return there, yet, if we judge by some of the parts acted here and there in 1735–36, that Jones was still performing in London. The Jones we have been following may have been the one who acted Bounce in *A City Ramble* at Covent Garden on 27 March 1736, for that performance does not fall into a pattern of appearances at the Haymarket by the Jones who had just left Drury Lane.

Jones, Mr ₍*fl.* 1741₎, singer.

Mr Jones sang in *Acis and Galatea* when it was performed on 28 February 1741 at the Lincoln's Inn Fields playhouse. He was apparently a member of the chorus.

Jones, Mr ₁*fl. 1744–1750*₁,   *actor, singer.*
On May Day 1744 a Mr Jones played Fernando in *The Royal Heroe* at May Fair. That Jones may have been the one who was in London in 1741 and had acted there since 1729, but the gap of three years suggests to us that it might be best to treat the Jones of 1744 as a different performer. He was at the Haymarket on 16 May 1744 acting Sullen in *The Stratagem*, and he returned to May Fair on 7 June to play Gibbet in *The Stratagem*. At James Street the following 10 December he played Foppington in *The Careless Husband*, and on 15 April 1745 Jones was a Demon in *The Tempest* at Goodman's Fields.

After an absence of a year and a half he (or a Jones) was at Goodman's Fields on 25 November 1746 playing Obadiah in *The Committee*. His name disappeared from the bills once more, until 2 May 1748, when a Jones played Gloster in *Jane Shore* at the Haymarket. At Bartholomew Fair on 24 August of that year Jones was Menzikoif in *The Northern Heros* and the Captain in *Harlequin Captive*, and he repeated the former part at Southwark Fair in September. On 2 January 1749 at Southwark Jones played Jack in *The Beggar's Opera*. At Southwark Fair on 7 September 1750 Jones acted Jethro in *Jeptha's Last Vow*.

Jones, Mr ₁*fl. 1748–1750*₁,   *box office keeper.*
Mr Jones, identified in the bills as a box office keeper at Drury Lane, received partial benefits on 9 May 1748, 2 May 1749, and 8 May 1750.

Jones, Mr ₁*fl. 1748–1752*₁,   *violoncellist.*
A clipping in the Garrick Club reveals that the violoncellist Jones performed at a concert at Hickford's Music Room on 22 April (or May) 1748. The following 9 December at the Haymarket he participated in a benefit for Waltz, and on 28 March 1750, when *Solomon* was presented at Drury Lane for Jones's benefit, he played a concerto on the 'cello. The fact that he was given a solo benefit would suggest that he may have been in the Drury Lane band. He shared a benefit with the company dancing master (unnamed) on 29 April 1752.

Jones, Mr ₁*fl. 1755–1756*₁,   *actor.*
At Croydon on 2 October 1755 Tradelove in *A Bold Stroke for a Wife* was played by a Mr

Jones. The same actor, we would guess, was the Jones who acted Captain Bounce in *Adventures of Half an Hour* at Bartholomew Fair on 3 September 1756.

Jones, Mr ₁*fl. 1760–1763*₁,   *singer.*
Though we know of no specific performing duties for Mr Jones, he was named on the Covent Garden music list at 4*s*. 2*d*. daily on 22 September 1760, and *The London Stage* cites Jones as a singer at Covent Garden in 1762–63.

Jones, Mr ₁*fl. 1765*₁,   *actor.*
A Jones played Tom Thimble in *The Rehearsal* at the Haymarket Theatre on 30 August 1765.

Jones, Mr ₁*fl. 1765*₁,   *doorkeeper.*
In a paylist for Drury Lane dated 9 February 1765 a Mr Jones is noted as receiving 1*s*. 6*d*. daily or 9*s*. weekly as a doorkeeper.

Jones, Mr ₁*fl. 1766–1795*₁,   *actor.*
Mr Jones was in Roger Kemble's company for at least the first half of the 1766–67 season, playing at Coventry beginning 18 August 1766 and then Worcester beginning the middle of January 1767. On 12 February he acted the title role in *King Charles I* at Worcester. A Mr Jones who was described in W. J. Lawrence's notes as a specialist in Teague and Irish clowns was at the Smock Alley Theatre in Dublin during some part of the 1766–67 season, and our guess is that since the Jones who was in Kemble's troupe was not mentioned in that company's roster in the summer of 1767, he very likely went to Ireland. One role assigned to him in 1767 is MacBrogue in *The She Gallant*. Jones was at the Crow Street playhouse in Dublin in 1768–69; another Jones made his first appearance in Dublin in five years on 29 November 1770, two weeks before our Mr Jones turned up in London at the Haymarket to play Don Carlos in *The Mistake*. He appeared at the Haymarket again on 4 March 1771 as Lord Lurewell in *The King and the Miller of Mansfield* and Stanmore in *Oroonoko*. At the same house on 4 August 1772 Jones played the Taylor in *The Miser*.

Those performances may have concerned Robert Jones, but we know that on 16 May

1774 Robert was in a performance at Drury Lane the night a different Jones—the one we have been following, we believe—played an unnamed part in *The Bankrupt* at the Haymarket. The Jones of this entry seems to have set a pattern of making occasional London appearances at the Haymarket but not during its regular summer season, which fact suggests that he was a provincial player who came to London from time to time.

A Jones played Polyperchon in *Alexander the Great* at China Hall, Rotherhithe, on 7 October 1776. A year later, on 9 October 1777, a Jones was in *A True-Born Irishman* at the Haymarket. At the same house on 8 March 1779 Jones was Item in *Wit's Last Stake*, and the following 27 December there he was seen as a Constable in *The Rival Milliners*. The same Jones, we guess, appeared several times at the Crown Inn, Islington, in February, March, and April 1780, sometimes on nights when Robert Jones was busy at Covent Garden Theatre. Our Jones's roles at the Crown Inn were Lord Minikin in *Bon Ton*, Stockwell in *The West Indian*, Pantaloon in *The Death and Restoration of Harlequin*, Fribble in *Miss in Her Teens*, Richmond in *Richard III*, Benvolio in *Romeo and Juliet*, Sir George Airy in *The Busy Body*, Prattle in *The Deuce is in Him*, Trueman in *The London Merchant*, Bouilliard in *The Camp*, Aimwell in *The Beaux' Stratagem*, and Frankly in *The Suspicious Husband*.

Peripatetic Jones (unless we have assigned to one Jones work done by more than one) was at the Haymarket again on 26 March 1781 acting Porter in *Love and a Bottle*, and he returned to the Crown Inn in late March and early April to play Catesby in *Richard III* and Castalio in *The Orphan*. At the Haymarket on 21 January 1782 Jones acted Laric in *The Beaux' Duel*, and the following November there he had an unnamed role in *The Taylors*. After another absence Jones returned to the Haymarket on 21 January 1784 to take a part in *The Talisman*. He was probably the Jones who in August of that year was seen as Richmond in *Richard III*, Edmund in *King Lear*, and Hal in *1 Henry IV* at the Theatre Royal, Edinburgh. Then, on the following 16 November, he returned to the Haymarket in London to play Ghastly in *The School for Wives*. On 15 March 1785 at that house Jones acted William in *All the World's a Stage*.

On 8 January 1787 at the Haymarket Jones played Hodge in *Love in a Village*, and the following 30 March he acted Sullen in *The Beaux' Stratagem* at the Red Lion Inn, Lordship Road, Stoke Newington. A Jones was James in *The Mock Doctor* at Bartholomew Fair in 1788 and was in *The Recruiting Serjeant* at Bartholomew Fair in the late summer of 1789. In November at the White Horse, Fulham, he played Aldiborontiphoscophornio in *Chrononhotonthologos*, Medium in *Inkle and Yarico*, Taylor in *The Shipwreck*, and Sir Roger Belmont in *The Foundling*. He returned to Bartholomew Fair in 1790 to act (Fribble?) in *Miss in Her Teens*.

At the Haymarket on 22 May 1794 a Jones acted Woodley in *Three Weeks After Marriage* and Rodolpho in *Tancred and Sigismunda* and then returned the following September to play Stock in *A Bold Stroke for a Wife* and Alguazile in *The Purse*. An undated bill (grouped with bills dated September 1795) in Lysons's "Collectanea" at the Folger Shakespeare Library lists Jones as Ernesto in a performance of *The Orphan* at the Assembly Hall in Kentish Town. After that the Jones we have been following may not have performed further in London. The Jones who acted at the Haymarket and elsewhere sporadically from 1796 to 1799 was probably Robert Jones, who left Drury Lane after the 1795–96 season, performed here and there, and went to America in 1800.

Jones, Mr   [fl. 1770], *performer?*

Pinks's *Clerkenwell* has it that at the Shakespeare Head near the New Wells in 1770 a Mr Jones "exhibited a great and pleasing variety of performances, in a commodious apartment, up one pair." The nature of the performances was not stated, nor can we tell if Jones was a performer or a manager. The proprietor of the Shakespeare Head, Mr Mytton, had had a benefit at the Covent Garden Theatre on 24 April 1746, so he had theatrical connections of long standing.

Jones, Mr   *d. 1773, treasurer.*

The *London Chronicle* of 30 January–2 February 1773 reported that on 30 January Mr Jones, treasurer at Ranelagh Gardens, was leaning against a rail that gave way; Jones fell into the Thames and was drowned. Possibly Jones was related to William Jones, the architect of the Rotunda and other buildings at Ranelagh.

Jones, Mr [fl. 1783–1785], boxkeeper.

Mr Jones served the King's Theatre as a boxkeeper from 1783 to 1785, according to the Lord Chamberlain's accounts.

Jones, Mr [fl. 1783–1785], constable.

Mr Jones served the King's Theatre as constable from 1783 to 1785, according to the Lord Chamberlain's accounts.

Jones, Mrs [fl. 1728–1741], actress, singer.

Mrs Jones performed at the Haymarket Theatre in the 1728–29 season and in the spring and summer of 1730; she then returned there occasionally through the fall of 1736. It is likely that she was the Mrs Jones who appeared at Drury Lane and Goodman's Fields in 1740 and 1741. Her first notice in the bills was on 10 December 1728 at the Haymarket, when she acted Abigail in *The Lottery*. In May 1729 she was Moll Titup in *The Smugglers*, a Grace and a Nymph in *The Humours of Harlequin*, and (called, apparently in error, "Miss" Jones) Manchet in *The Beggar's Wedding*. She was in *The Beggar's Wedding* again at Reynolds's booth at Bartholomew and Southwark fairs in August and September.

From 8 April to 3 July 1730 Mrs Jones was again at the Haymarket, playing Phenicia in *The Rival Father* and Princess Huncamunca in *Tom Thumb*. She repeated her role in *Tom Thumb* at Southwark Fair in September, after which her appearances in London were occasional. She acted Madam ap Shinken in *The Welch Opera* at the Haymarket on 22 April 1731, the Queen in *The Opera of Operas* at the same house on 4 June 1733, and Davy in *The Mock Doctor* (plus an entr'acte song) there on 5 June 1734. At Goodman's Fields on 29 March 1735 she sang a song and on 23 August 1736 she was in *The Cheats of Scapin* at the Fielding-Hippisley booth at Bartholomew Fair, as was a Mr Jones. On 28 September at Lincoln's Inn Fields she appeared in *King Arthur*.

The same Mrs Jones, we believe, played Grideline in *Rosamond* at Drury Lane on 8 March 1740. She was at Goodman's Fields for the 1740–41 season, though she returned to Drury Lane in March 1741 to play in *Rosamond*

again. Her first notice at Goodman's Fields was on 31 October 1740, when she played Mrs Motherly in *The Provok'd Husband*. Then she was seen as Mrs Chat in *The Committee*, Trudge in *Love and a Bottle*, Mrs Drab and a Priestess in *The Imprisonment, Release, Adventures, and Marriage of Harlequin*, Dorcas in *The Winter's Tale*, Lady Bountiful in *The Stratagem*, Lucy in *The Beggar's Opera*, Inis in *The Wonder*, Honoria in *Love Makes a Man*, Friendly in *Flora*, the Doctor's Wife in *The Anatomist*, a character in *King Arthur*, and Thais in *Timon of Athens*. She returned to Goodman's Fields on 14 September 1741 as Lady Darling in *The Constant Couple*, but after that her name disappeared from the bills.

Jones, Mrs [fl. 1752], actress.

A Mrs Jones was listed among the actresses in the company at Richmond during the summer of 1752, but no roles are known for her.

Jones, Mrs [fl. 1770?–1792?], actress, singer.

The Mrs Jones of this entry was possibly the woman of that name who acted at Glasgow as early as 1770 and played Anne Page in *The Merry Wives of Windsor* at the Theatre Royal in Edinburgh on 9 April 1774. Mrs Jones played at Brighton in 1777. When she appeared on 10 May 1779 at the Haymarket Theatre in London as Lady Randolph in *Douglas*, she was advertised as having acted previously in Dublin. She returned to the Haymarket on 13 December 1784 to play Mrs Peachum and Diana Trapes in *The Beggar's Opera*. The *Thespian Magazine* on 2 July 1792 reported Mrs Jones in the company playing at Hoddesdon, Newcastle upon Tyne, and Shields.

Jones, Mrs [fl. 1791], house servant?

A Mrs Jones was one of many whose benefit tickets were accepted at Drury Lane Theatre on 26 May 1791. She may have been one of the house servants.

Jones, Mrs d. 1806. See GRANGER, JULIA..

Jones, Miss [fl. 1730–1743?], actress, singer, dancer.

A Miss Jones made her first appearance at the Haymarket as Charlotte in *The Half Pay Officers* on 12 March 1730. The bill implied that she had performed elsewhere previously, but there seems to be no earlier London record concerning her. At that performance she also spoke the prologue to *Flora*, and on 6 April she spoke the prologue and epilogue to *The Cheats of Scapin*. Then, from 24 April through 3 July, she played the title role in a very successful run of *Tom Thumb*. She repeated her part in that play on 4 September at Reynold's booth at Bartholomew Fair and on 14 September at Southwark Fair.

Miss Jones returned to the Haymarket in 1730–31 to play Tom Thumb again, and on 19 March 1731 at the benefit for Mr Jones (her father?) she played the part "in an entire new Habit," danced, and spoke the epilogue. On 4 May she acted another young person's part, the Page in *The Orphan*. She was then not seen on a London stage for almost a year, and when she returned she brought with her another Miss Jones, very probably her sister, who was styled Miss Jones Junior and was, we think, Jane or Jenny Jones. (Information on the girls' parentage may be found in Jane's entry.) The possibility of confusing the roles of the two girls is great, for they had similar talents—acting, singing, and dancing—and also they played similar and sometimes even the same roles.

The Miss Jones we have been following, whose first name was never cited in the bills but who was sometimes styled Miss Jones Senior, returned to the Haymarket Theatre on 16 February 1732 to play Lucia in *The Cheats of Scapin*. On 8 March she acted Belinda in *Tunbridge Walks* and danced, and in the afterpiece Miss Jones Junior played Tom Thumb in *The Tragedy of Tragedies*, coached, perhaps, by the elder Jones girl. The elder girl may have outgrown children's parts and was by 1732 near her majority. During the remainder of the 1731–32 season Miss Jones was seen as La Laguiére in *The Wanton Justice*, Betty in *A Bold Stroke for a Wife*, Rose in *The Recruiting Officer* (a part the younger Miss Jones played later), Serina in *The Orphan*, Teresa in *The Spanish Fryar*, and an unnamed character in *The Coquet's Surrender*.

She appeared at both Lincoln's Inn Fields and the Haymarket in 1732–33 on dates that are not in conflict and in parts more appropriate to her than to the younger Jones girl. On 20 November 1732 she was Cratander in *Teraminta* at Lincoln's Inn Fields; on 29 November at the Haymarket she played Maria in *The Miseries of Love*; on 7 March 1733 she played the Queen in the first of six performances of *Rosamond* at Lincoln's Inn Fields, interrupting that run on 27 March to appear as Beatrice in *The Old Debauchees* at the Haymarket. At Bartholomew Fair in August Miss Jones was a Masquerader in *Ridotto al'Fresco*.

Miss Jones joined Theophilus Cibber's Drury Lane seceders at the Haymarket in the fall of 1733, appearing as Dollalolla in *The Opera of Operas*, a Shepherdess in *The Festival*, and Aeneas in *Dido and Aeneas*. When the rebel players returned to Drury Lane in the spring of 1734 Miss Jones was seen as Pallas in *Britannia* and Ceres in *Cupid and Psyche*. (Just as soon as Cibber's players left the Haymarket another group put on *Don Quixote in England* with a Miss Jones as Miss Sneak; that would seem to have been the younger Jones girl.)

The Miss Jones who performed at the Haymarket in June, July, and August 1734 seems to have been the elder girl, judging by the roles: Nonpareil in *The Covent Garden Tragedy*, Lucy in *The Beggar's Opera Tragedized*, Lady Loverule in *The Devil to Pay*, Phoebe in *The Beggar's Wedding*, Mrs Stocks in *The Lottery*, Mrs Motherly in *The Provok'd Husband*, Mrs Sneak in *The Humorous Election*, Lucy in *The Beggar's Opera*, and, on 14 August, Mrs Wheedle in *The Miser*. Playing Mrs Wisely in the last work was a Miss Jones making her first appearance on any stage, which fact in theory rules out Jane Jones, but the bills often prevaricated in these statements. A third Miss Jones thus seems to have turned up, but as far as can be told from the confusing bills, she did not pursue her career further.

On 2 September 1734 at the playhouse in Hampstead *The Beaux' Stratagem* was performed for the benefit of the Misses Jones Jr and Sr—Jenny and our subject, we suppose. On 1 October at Lincoln's Inn Fields, *Don Quixote in England* was acted with Miss Jones playing Mrs Sneak and Miss Jones Jr acting Miss Sneak.

Our Miss Jones seems to have been the one who joined the Goodman's Fields troupe under Henry Giffard in 1734–35 and continued with that company for three seasons. Her first appearance there was on 9 September 1734, when she sang in Italian and English. During her first season there she offered entr'acte songs and was seen as Germanicus in *Britannia*, a Spirit in *The Necromancer*, Lovemore in *The Lottery*, Jupiter (*sic*) and Juno in *Jupiter and Io*, Kalib in *The Indian Emperor*, Lucy in *The Beggar's Opera*, Lady Loverule in *The Devil to Pay*, and Hunter in *The Beggar's Wedding*. She made a single appearance at York Buildings on 3 March 1735 (when she was not scheduled for anything at Goodman's Fields) to sing Polly in *The Beggar's Opera*.

In the summer of 1735 she returned to the Haymarket to play Trusty in *The Provok'd Husband*, the Maid in *The Twin Rivals*, Charlotte in *The Mock Doctor*, Serena in *The Orphan*, Mrs Coaxer in *The Beggar's Opera*, and Gypsey in *The Strategem*. To her repertoire at Goodman's Fields in 1735–36 she added Frederick (*sic*) in *The Lover His Own Rival*, a Shepherdess in *Harlequin Shipwrecked*, and Leander (*sic*) in *The Mock Doctor*. On 13 December 1735 she played Lucy in *The Recruiting Officer* at the Haymarket—a night when she had no assignment at Goodman's Fields; Miss Jones Jr acted Rose. She sang in the chorus of *King Arthur* at Goodman's Fields, or was scheduled to sing, on 17 December 1735; on that night at the Haymarket Miss Jones played Bissare in *The Inconstant* and Miss Jones Jr played Oriane, for the benefit of the elder Miss Jones. The elder girl could have managed her assignments at both playhouses, or perhaps she simply did not sing that night at Goodman's Fields. She acted Bisarre again on 19 February 1736, when she was not scheduled for anything at Goodman's Fields.

The Giffard company performed at Lincoln's Inn Fields in 1736–37, where Miss Jones appeared in several old parts and some new ones: Combrush in *The Honest Yorkshireman*, a Follower in *Harlequin Shipwrecked*, Plaitwell in *A Tutor for the Beaus*, and the title role in *Flora*. She also entertained with entr'acte songs ("Early Horn" was a favorite) and shared a benefit in May 1737 with four others. The rest of her career (unless two or more women named Jones were referred to in the bills) was erratic. The younger Miss Jones seems to have left London after 1736–37, and though the references to a Miss Jones in London are found here and there rather than consistently at one theatre, it could well be that our subject, who had never risen to a high rank in any company, simply took what employment she could find during the rest of the 1730s and the early

1740s. After Giffard's venture collapsed, Miss Jones was evidently without employment, and for a season no Miss Jones was cited in London bills.

In 1738–39 a dancer named Miss Jones was at Drury Lane, spending virtually the whole of her engagement from 30 October 1738 to the end of the year playing Mrs Marrowbone in *Robin Goodfellow*. Then the name of Miss Jones again disappeared from London bills for a year. *The London Stage* seems to be in error in listing a Miss Jones as an actress at Covent Garden in 1739–40; there appear to be no references in the bills that season to any Jones of either sex. A Miss Jones was at Drury Lane on 26 December 1739 singing in *The Tempest*, and during the remainder of the season she sang in *Macbeth* and *Don John* and played the Queen of the Gypsies in *The Fortune Tellers*, Lady Macduff in *Macbeth*, and Amphitrite in *The Tempest*. She performed at Goodman's Fields in 1740–41, playing Dorcas in *The Mock Doctor*, Sir John (*sic*) in *The Devil to Pay* (and she sang "Early Horn"), Minerva in *Harlequin Student*, and the Nurse in *Love for Love*. She also sang "The Punch's Song" with Hemskirk on 12 March 1741, a date when at the same house Mrs Jones performed.

The London Stage lists a Miss Jones in the Goodman's Fields company in 1741–42, but she was not cited in any bills, and the listing is apparently an error for Mrs Jones, who played Lady Darling in *The Constant Couple* there. Miss Jones did appear at the James Street playhouse that season, however: on 31 May 1742 she acted Semanthe in *Ulysses*. A year later at Southwark Miss Jones played Priscilla in *The Lying Valet*. Up to this point it has been possible to see at least some pattern to the career of Miss Jones, though after 1736–37 we cannot be as certain that the references to Miss Jones are to the performer of earlier seasons. After 1743 it is even more difficult to be sure, for the citations are so scattered. Since after 1743 there is a gap of five years before a Miss Jones was referred to again in London bills, it has seemed advisable here to assume that the references in 1748 and later are not to the performer we have been following.

Jones, Miss [*fl.* 1734], *actress*.
On 14 August 1734 at the Haymarket Theatre a Miss Jones made her first appearance on

any stage playing Mrs Wisely in *The Miser*. Acting Mrs Wheedle in that performance was another Miss Jones, who had been performing in London since 1730.

Jones, Miss [*fl. 1746–1757?*], *singer, actress*.

At Goodman's Fields on 22 March 1746 a Miss Jones made her first appearance on any stage singing an entr'acte song. Perhaps she was the Miss Jones who played Scullion in *The Unnatural Parents* at the Lee and Yeates booth at Bartholomew Fair on 24 August 1748. That Miss Jones repeated her role in the same work (retitled *The Fair Maid of the West*) on 7 September. On 26 July 1750 a Miss Jones, perhaps the same performer, sang between the acts, at the Haymarket. A Miss Jones acted Isabella in *The Conscious Lovers* at Richmond on 13 June 1752, and the same (?) Miss Jones played Miss Polly in *The Adventures of Half an Hour* at Bartholomew Fair on 3 September 1756. Probably it was that Miss Jones who appeared as Clara in *The Intriguing Captains* at Southwark Fair on 20 September 1756. Perhaps the same Miss Jones played Colombine in *The Restoration and Adventures of Harlequin* at Bartholomew Fair in September 1757.

Jones, Miss [*fl. 1748*], *actress*.

A Miss Jones played Miss West in *The Consequences of Industry and Idleness* at Yates's booth at Bartholomew Fair on 24 August 1748.

Jones, Miss [*fl. 1778?–1815?*], *singer, actress?*

So little is known about the Miss Jones who sang in London in 1797 that identifying her is very difficult. Perhaps she was the Miss Jones who played children's roles at Bristol from 1778 to 1784. On 23 January 1797 at the Haymarket Theatre "A Young Lady" sang in *The Battle of Eddington*; the singer was later identified as Miss Jones.

The Drury Lane accounts show that a Miss Jones was on the payroll there in 1795–96 and again, at a weekly salary of £1, in 1801. The same Miss Jones, we think, was the performer who was in *The Travelers* at Drury Lane in 1805–6, though her name was not on the company list. From 1809–10 through 1814–15 a Miss Jones was at the Lyceum Theatre at £1 5s. weekly.

Jones, Miss *d. 1803, actress*.

Miss Jones played a principal role in *The Double Amour* at the Haymarket Theatre on 25 September 1780 and was one of the Mob of Women in *The Recruiting Officer* at the Crown Inn, Islington, on 15 March 1781. She performed much more than that, for the *Gentleman's Magazine* in September 1803 gave special attention to her death. It reported that she had died in Salisbury Square, Fleet Street, and had lately been a member of the Lincolnshire company of players. "The young and promising actress," the periodical said, "was slowly recovering from an illness contracted in the exercise of her profession when she was compelled to take a journey to London; the fatigue and other consequences of which, it is presumed, put a period on her life."

Jones, C. [*fl. 1798*], *harpist*.
C. Jones played the harp at the Haymarket Theatre on 21 July 1798.

Jones, Charles [*fl. 1709?–1722*], *musician*.
The Mr Jones who was sworn a musician in ordinary in the King's Musick on 13 September 1709 was probably Charles Jones, who was cited as a royal musician in the Lord Chamberlain's accounts on 21 November 1710. He was mentioned occasionally through 19 April 1722, when he was replaced by Thomas Cuthbert.

Jones, Charles [*fl. 1731–1755?*], *actor*.
Charles Jones played Lord Puff in *The Intriguing Chambermaid* at Drury Lane on 15 January 1734 (a Mr Jones, a Drury Lane regular, played Goodall). Charles Jones would appear not to have been attached to any London troupe, though possibly some of the parts assigned to Mr Jones should be reassigned to Charles. The evidence, however, points to Charles Jones's having been a provincial actor who appeared only occasionally in London. An unidentified clipping in the O. Smith papers at the British Library, dated 8 November 1731, indicates that Charles Jones was an actor in Bath at that time and had murdered one Basil Price. He was evidently acquitted, in view of his London appearance a few years later. On 17 January 1740 a benefit was given

Charles Jones at Covent Garden; there was no indication that Jones performed, but the benefit was clearly a special one, not falling in the usual benefit period from March through May.

The London Stage lists Charles Jones as a member of the Lincoln's Inn Fields company in 1742–43, though his only known part there was Lothario in *The Fair Penitent* on 21 January 1743, and it would seem that, again, Jones simply came to town for a single appearance. The Winston manuscripts show that the unnamed gentleman who played Juba in *Cato* at Drury Lane on 27 September 1744 was Charles Jones. On 8 May 1745 at Covent Garden a benefit was held for Charles Jones, identified as the son of the late Jere Jones, who formerly kept the Selectation Tavern at Billingsgate. Rosenfeld reports that Charles Jones was a member of Simpson's troupe in 1750 (Simpson worked the Bath-Bristol circuit), so it is probable that the Mr Jones who played Stukely in *The Gamester* at the Jacob's Wells Theatre in Bristol on 31 March 1755 was Charles.

Jones, Charles ₍fl. 1759?–1764₎, *horn player, flutist.*
Charles Jones had a music shop opposite Staple Inn near Holborn Bars and in 1759 published the tunes from *The Beggar's Opera* transposed "for the Guittar." He also subscribed that year for Bezozzi's *Six Solos for the German-Flute, Hautboy, or Violin, with a Thorough Bass for the Harpsichord.* He was most probably the Charles Jones of Russell Court, Covent Garden, listed in *Mortimer's London Directory* in 1763 as a French horn player and teacher of the German flute. In 1764 that Jones from his music shop in Russell Court published *Six English Songs as sung by Mr. Lowe & Mrs. Lampe Junr. at Mary-bone Gardens. Set to music by Mr. Chas. Lampe.* Possibly Charles Jones was the son of the flutist John Jones of 1726.

Jones, Charles d. c. 1780?, *performer?*
Very little is known of Charles Jones, though his wife, Esther, née Young, had a considerable stage career. They were married about 1762, and Esther performed for many years at Covent Garden Theatre as Mrs Jones. About 1780 Jones died; on 18 May 1780 "the widow of the late Jones" had benefit tickets

out at Covent Garden. John Beard wrote to the Royal Society of Musicians about 1784 on Mrs Jones's behalf, referring to Jones as a former worthy member of "our community"— the theatrical and musical world, of which Beard was a part. Since Beard thought Mrs Jones would qualify for aid from the Royal Society of Musicians, her late husband must have been a member. We have found no mention of Charles Jones in the Minute Books of the Society, however, nor does his name appear n any theatrical records of the 1760s and 1770s. As a member of the Royal Society of Musicians he must have been a professional musician, and he may well have performed at Covent Garden.

Jones, Mrs Charles, Esther. *See* YOUNG, ESTHER.

Jones, Cyprian ₍fl. 1735₎, *musician.*
The marriage register of St Dunstan's, Stepney, carries the following entry for 8 November 1735: "Cyprian Jones of B[ethnal] G[reen] Musician Elizh. Coldcoat d[itto]. Spin[ster]."

Jones, Daniel ₍fl. 1794–1818?₎, *singer.*
Doane's *Musical Directory* of 1794 listed Daniel Jones, of No 130, St Martin's Lane, as a tenor who sang for the Cecilian Society and in the Handel performances in Westminister Abbey. A Jones sang in the chorus at Drury Lane in 1808, and perhaps our subject was the D. Jones who was on the company list of the English opera at the Lyceum Theatre in the Strand in 1817 and 1818.

Jones, Edward, supposed real name of Edward Berry. *See* BERRY, EDWARD.

Jones, Edward 1752–1824, *harpist.*
Edward Jones was born at the farmhouse, Henblas, in the parish of Llanderfel, Merionethshire, on 2 April 1752. His father, an accomplished organist, taught Edward and his brother Thomas the Welsh Harp; a third son learned to play the spinet and a fourth the violin. If Mee in *The Oldest Music Room in Europe* is correct in saying that Edward played at the Oxford Music Room about 23 October 1762 and on 22 January 1763, then young Jones's professional career began much earlier than is

usually reported. Fanny Burney in her diary spoke of a concert at the Burneys in London in May 1775 at which she met "Mr. Jones, a Welsh harper, a silly young man. . . ."

Jones's earliest public appearance in London may have been on 15 March 1776, when he played a solo on the pedal harp at the Concerto Spirituale at Covent Garden. He offered solos later that month at the same theatre in performances of Hook's *The Ascension* and Arnold's *The Prodigal Son*. The *European Magazine* in 1784 stated that Jones had performed at the King's Theatre for the benefit of the Musical Fund seven years before, in 1777, though we have not found that bill. He was, however, at Covent Garden on 3 May 1777, when his benefit tickets were accepted. On 5 July 1778 Jones was recommended for membership in the Royal Society of Musicians. He was then described as a single man. He was admitted on the following 4 October. Jones was, the *European Magazine* thought, a better music historian than a musician, and it cited his *Musical and Poetical Relicks of the Welch Bards*, which was published in 1784. Jones continued researching old Welsh airs and through his publications over the years was largely responsible for preserving 225 of them. Grove provides a list.

Jones taught music to a number of members of high society in London and in 1783 was appointed bard to the Prince of Wales, thereby gaining the title Bardd y Brenin, or the King's Bard. He also had a post in the Office of the Robes at St James's Palace and lived at the Palace for a time. Later he had lodgings at No 3, Green Street, Grosvenor Square, and then in Great Chesterfield Street, Marylebone. Doane's *Musical Directory* of 1794 gave Jones's address as Bond Street and noted that he performed for the Concert of Ancient Music.

Jones probably appeared at many public concerts, notices of which have not been found. On 6 April 1795 he was at Covent Garden, playing an accompaniment for the chorus singing some ancient British airs in the first part of *Windsor Castle*. Jones played in the Covent Garden oratorios in 1798, and he was probably the Jones who was a member of the Court of Assistants of the Royal Society of Musicians in 1802.

Jones collected a great number of rare books, some of which he sold for £300 in 1824 when he found himself in financial difficulties. On 15 March of that year he petitioned the Royal Society of Musicians for financial aid, being, he said, 72 years old, "infirm and totally unable to maintain himself by his professional pursuits." The Society granted him an allowance of £4 4s. monthly on 4 April 1824, but help came too late. Edward Jones died on 18 April and was buried in the Marylebone burying grounds. After his death the remainder of his library was auctioned off for about £800. In addition to his books on music and his collection of ancient Welsh airs Jones wrote a number of songs, lessons, marches, sonatas, and other pieces for harp or harpsichord, many of which are listed in the *Catalogue of Printed Music in the British Museum*.

Jones, Edward   *1764–1799, actor.*

Edward Jones was born in 1764 and made his only London appearances in the 1770s. Typically, he made his first effort as the Duke of York in *Richard III*; the work was performed at Covent Garden on 3 February 1772, and young Edward continued appearing in the part through 7 November 1777. His other parts as Master Jones were a Dwarf in *Orpheus and Eurydice*, beginning 13 October 1775, and the Page in *The Orphan*, on 1 November 1776. He probably had other assignments that were not noted in the bills.

He spent the ensuing years playing in the provinces, according to puffs he received later in America. Before he left England in 1794 he acted at Weymouth, Exeter, Cheltenham, and Salisbury, as did his wife, (who evidently did not act in London). Charles Stuart Powell recruited the Edward Joneses for the opening of the Federal Street Theatre in Boston in the spring of 1794. Jones played Trollie, and his wife acted Mariana in *Gustavus Vasa*, the mainpiece, and Cockletop and Nan in the afterpiece, *Modern Antiquities*. Before his appearance at the Federal Street playhouse Jones performed at the Board Alley Theatre in Boston, according to Clapp. Jones and his wife played in Portland, Maine, from 17 October to 3 November 1794 in the Assembly Room in King (later India) Street, we learn from the *New England Quarterly* in 1938. Then, on 15 December, Jones played Touchstone in *As You Like It*, at the opening of the second Federal Street Theatre season in Boston.

When Powell went bankrupt, the Joneses headed south for Charleston with Sollée. Julia Curtis, in her dissertation on the Charleston stage, cites Jones as playing Cornwall in *King Lear* on 21 January 1795 and the Earl of Worcester in *The Humours of Sir John Falstaff* on the following 6 April. In 1795–96 Jones served as manager of Sollée's troupe in Charleston and also received acclaim from audiences as an actor, especially in his low-comedy parts. As Floriville in *The Dramatist*, said the local paper, Jones was no less than "a phenomenon of this age." Jones also played during the season Solus in *Every One Has His Faults* (with his wife as Lady Eleanor Irwin), Tinsel in *The Double Disguise*, Sir Peter Teazle in *The School for Scandal* (opposite Mrs Jones as Lady Teazle), Shelty in *The Highland Reel*, Polonius in *Hamlet*, Tony Lumpkin in *She Stoops to Conquer*, the Apothecary in *Romeo and Juliet* (Mrs Jones was Juliet), James in *The Man of the Times* (with his wife as Katy), Roller in *The Robbers*, Jemmy Jumps in *The Farmer*, and the Lieutenant in *The American Heroine*.

Seilhamer states that the Joneses returned for a short engagement in Boston under John Brown Williamson in 1796–97. Edward may have been the Jones who appeared in Philadelphia in the winter of 1796, though the presence of America of another English actor, J. Jones, makes identification difficult. The Edward Joneses were in Charleston in the spring of 1797; they toured north again in the summer, playing in Boston, doing a one-night stand on 7 August in Hartford, and making their debut that month in New York at the John Street Theatre. They performed in Philadelphia and were back in Charleston by 7 November.

During the 1797–98 season Jones is known to have played Renault in *Venice Preserv'd*, Tag in *The Spoiled Child*, Mercutio in *Romeo and Juliet*, Shelty in *The Highland Reel*, and Touchstone. He continued as manager of the troupe through 1798–99. But on 21 November 1799, according to the *South Carolina Gazette*, Edward Jones died. The paper stated that "A few hours before his dissolution he took a most affecting leave of his wife and four young children who are left to mourn his loss." Jones was only 35 years of age when he died. The children were given a benefit on 8 May 1800. At the benefit Mrs Jones introduced two of her children to the stage in *Children in the Wood*. She continued serving in a managerial capacity with Williamson and Alexandre Placide for some time after her husband's death.

Jones, Edward [*fl.* 1794–1800?], singer.

Doane's *Musical Directory* of 1794 listed Edward Jones, of No 2, Snow's Fields, Southwark, as a bass who sang for the Handelian Society and in the Handel performance at Westminister Abbey and Covent Garden Theatre. Edward was probably the Jones who sang in the chorus at Covent Garden from 1797 to 1800, one of his few notices in the bills being on 16 January 1800 when he sang in *Joanna*. But there were other Joneses who sang at the end of the eighteenth century—Daniel and (J.?) Walter, who probably sang tenor, and Thomas, who was an alto.

Jones, Elizabeth *b. c. 1769, actress.*

Richard Yates's "housekeeper" made what seems to have been her only London appearance on 18 November 1793 at Covent Garden as Imogen in *Cymbeline*. It was advertised as her first appearance, and, though she was cited only as a Young Lady in the bills, the *Thespian Magazine* in December identified her as Miss Jones. She had acted previously at Birmingham, but none of her roles there are known. The day after her appearance at Covent Garden the *Public Advertiser* commented that "When next [Miss Jones] plays the part she should endeavour to hold her person erect. The crouching attitudes that she adopted in the breeches scenes, took from the captivating impression that her figure might otherwise have produced."

On 21 April 1796 Richard Yates died at his house in Stafford Row, Pimlico, at the age of 89. According to the Digges-Ward correspondence, Yates's nearest relative, Lieutenant Thomas Yates of the Navy, his brother's son, took possession of Yates's house. Miss Jones, by virtue of a will in her favor (alleged by the nephew not to be genuine), disputed the nephew's claim. Thomas Yates and his wife and Elizabeth lived in the house for a time, but, to protect her property Miss Jones brought two men, Sellers and Footner, into the house. Thomas Yates thought the men had designs on the life of his wife and himself. He sent his wife for a constable while he, to allay suspicion, walked in the garden. When he attempted to get back into the house, he found the door barred, and, while trying to get in through a back window, he was killed by a pistol shot.

An inquest was held, and Miss Jones and her two cohorts were charged with murder. On 16 September 1796 the three were tried at Old Bailey; Sellers was found guilty of manslaughter, but Footner and Miss Jones were acquitted. The killing and the trial created a great stir in London, and reports concerning the time of the shooting, the name of the victim, and Miss Jones's Christian name were often muddled in later accounts. Elizabeth was called Mary by one paper, and the victim was mistakenly identified as Richard Yates's brother, "a Lieutenant in the Army." As late as 1940 an account in *Notes and Queries* placed Richard Yates's death on 21 April 1785 and stated that the nephew was killed while forcing his entry into the house because he was not recognized by the assailant.

In any case, Elizabeth was reported in 1796, apparently correctly, to have been about 27 years old. The fifth issue of *How Do You Do* on 24 September 1796 said, "However Miss Jones may have been censured before the result of her trial, she is certainly now to be pitied. Had not she too much relied on the direction of others, a reconciliation might have taken place between all parties." In 1797 Elizabeth was officially named residuary legatee of Richard Yates's estate.

Though Elizabeth seems not to have pursued her stage career in London after her 1793 appearance, perhaps she was the Miss E. Jones who acted at the Theatre Royal, Edinburgh, in 1805–6. That actress in the spring of 1806 is known to have played Genevieve in *The Hunter of the Alps*, Philidel in *Arthur and Emmeline*, the title role in *Rosina*, and Virginia in Paul and *Virginia*.

Jones, Emanuel. *See* EMMANUEL, MR.

Jones, Francis ₁*fl.* 1701–1702₁, *musician.*
According to the Lord Chamberlain's accounts, Francis Jones was a member of the royal musical establishment in 1701 (and probably earlier) and 1702 at an annual salary of £40.

Jones, George ₁*fl.* 1793₁, *dancer.*
The Jones who danced in a crowd as one of the "Natives of the Island" in James Byrn's new ballet *The Governor* at Covent Garden on 11 March 1793 and half a dozen times through 23 April is identified in *The London Stage* as George Jones. There seems little chance that he was the equestrian and manager.

Jones, George ₁Kingston?₁ ₁*fl.* 1779–1795₁, *equestrian, manager.*
George Jones was appearing at Astley's Amphitheatre at least as early as 16 September 1779, the date of the first bill carrying a "Jones" in feats of horsemanship. His appearances were regular and frequent through at least 1782, and he was perhaps continuously an employee of Philip Astley into the late 1780s, for there is a Jones on an Amphitheatre bill of September 1787. Among the few descriptions we have of his act is one from the summer of 1782. Jones vaults "from the Ground as the Horse rises at a Leaping Bar, and flys on the Horse, as the Horse is actually passing the bar. He stands on Two Horses, and takes a flying Leap. He lays on both saddles, and takes another Leap." He also was involved in a pyramid formed on three horses, with Griffin and Miss Hotson.

After that employment, but at some time before 1794, George Jones and James Jones (apparently not related) were joint proprietors of what James Decastro in his *Memoirs* calls a "place for equestrian and stage performances . . . in Union Street, Whitechapel."

In 1794, persuaded by Charles Hughes, they took a lease on the old Royal Circus in St George's Fields for an annual rent of £210. They completely renovated the interior, dubbed it the New Royal Circus and Philharmonic Academy, and in 1795 began attracting large crowds to their spectacular bills of pantomime, tumbling, rope-walking, and equestrian daring.

The Joneses also took their company to Edinburgh in the winters and played in provincial towns coming and going. According to Decastro, the Edinburgh branch lost money, causing a reorganization which somehow resulted from George Jones's separation from the enterprise in 1798–99.

According to a notation in the James Winston Collection in the Folger Library, George Jones was around 1800 the proprietor of the Pantheon Riding School in Blackfriars Road and lived at No 4, Lambeth Road. He may have been the George Kingston Jones whose will was proved on 13 July 1809. The estate amounted to £200.

Jones, Griffith *c. 1758–c. 1789?, instrumentalist.*

Griffith Jones, according to the information supplied when he was recommended for membership in the Royal Society of Musicians on 7 March 1779, was born about 1758. He had served his musical apprenticeship under Baumgarten and in 1779 was employed at Covent Garden Theatre (in the winter season) and at the Haymarket (probably in the summer); he was single, about 21 years of age, and proficient on the violin, clarinet, organ, "etc." In 1784 he was pianist to Covent Garden Theatre, and an unidentified clipping in the Enthoven Collection dated 17 April of that year notes that Jones rote-taught Charles Bannister the songs he sang, since Bannister could not read music. The G. Jones who played tenor (viola) at the Handel Memorial Concerts at Westminster Abbey and the Pantheon in May and June 1784 was probably Griffith. He may have died in 1789; the tickets of a Griffith Jones's widow were taken at a benefit at the theatre on 18 May that year, according to the John Philip Kemble notes (not, however, noted in *The London Stage*).

We have accepted the Kemble note indicating the death of Griffith Jones, but the information concerning a Griffith Jones who had a musical career immediately following is enough like that which we have for the present subject to suggest that there may have been only one Griffith Jones, not two. The Kemble note could easily refer to another Jones—to Charles, perhaps, whose widow was in dire circumstances in 1789.

Jones, Griffith [*fl.* 1792–1814?], *violist, pianist?*

The Minute Books of the Royal Society of Musicians show that Griffith Jones played tenor (viola) at the St Paul's concert on 10 and 12 May 1792. He performed in the concerts in 1793, 1794, and 1795 as well, but his name was not listed in 1796, and on 2 July 1797 Jones explained to the Society that he had missed a Whitehall concert that summer due to illness. The *British Union-Catalogue* cites Jones as a pianist, though that could be a confusion with the earlier Griffith Jones. One G. Jones was an instrumentalist in the Covent Garden oratorios in 1798, 1799, and 1800, and a Jones, possibly a musician, was mentioned frequently in the Drury Lane accounts in the first decade of the nineteenth century at a salary, at least in 1808–9, of £1 5s. weekly. The initial G. was attached to the name once. Perhaps Griffith was the Jones who played at the Lyceum from 1811–12 through 1813–14 for £1 5s. weekly.

Jones, J. [*fl.* 1799–1805], *manager?*

A Mr Jones was granted a license to present a play at the Haymarket Theatre on 17 April 1799. *The Merchant of Venice* was performed by volunteer actors for the benefit of an infant orphan family. Tickets were available at No 17, Tufton Street, Westminster (Jones's address?). It seems likely that he was the same Jones, specified a bit more exactly as J. Jones in the Lord Chamberlain's accounts, who received another license in 1805. Unfortunately, the date and place were not specified.

Jones, [J.?] **Walter** [*fl.* 1794–1817], *bassoonist, singer?, drummer.*

Doane's *Musical Directory* of 1794 listed Walter Jones, of No 73, Holborn, as a bassoonist and a tenor (singer?) who performed with the Longacre Society, the Surrey Chapel Society, and in the oratorios at Covent Garden Theatre and Westminster Abbey. Perhaps he was the Jones who played in the band at the Richmond, Surrey, playhouse in 1799. The Haymarket Theatre accounts contain many references to a bassoonist named Jones from 1815 to 1817; his initials seem to have been J. W., and we would guess that he may have been Walter Jones. Other Joneses were cited in the Haymarket accounts, one of them an actor, so it is difficult to determine what the bassoonist's pay may have been. One note, dated 1815, has a Jones receiving £1 16s. (per week?) for playing bassoon and drums—an odd combination.

Jones, James *fl. c. 1787–1816*, manager.

Probably from about 1787 until 1794 James Jones (described by F. W. Brayley in his *Historical and Descriptive Accounts*, 1826, as one "who had been a clerk in some office under government") and George Jones the equestrian were joint proprietors of what James Decastro called in his *Memoirs* "A place for equestrian and stage performances . . . in Union Street, Whitechapel."

In 1794 the Joneses were persuaded by the equestrian Charles Hughes, whose influence with the magistrates assured him of a recurring annual performance license issued for the old Royal Circus in St George's Fields, to lease that establishment for 21 years at a rent of £200 *per annum*. They renovated the house, stage, and ring, rechristened the place the New Royal Circus and Philharmonic Academy, and raided the hippodrama-and-comedy company of Benjamin Handy at the Lyceum for performers. John Cartwright Cross, actor, author, and song writer, whose talent for devising and directing spectacular entertainments was to be one of the largest assets of the Circus until his death in 1809, came over from Covent Garden. He married Sarah Sophia,

Harvard Theatre Collection

JAMES JONES

engraving by P. Roberts

James Jones's youngest daughter, on 23 August 1798, took over part of the active management when George Jones that winter left the theatre, and was "admitted as a proprietor to the extent of one-fourth of the concern," according to Brayley. Another daughter, according to Charles Dibdin in his *Annals*, married James Grant, the Edinburgh actor.

The Joneses had opened the Edinburgh Equestrian Circus on 25 January 1790. By January 1796 it was known as "Jones's Royal Circus." The managers carried a company to Edinburgh in the winter of 1798–99, and losses incurred there were supposed by Decastro to have caused a breach in the partnership which drove George Jones from the company. Bills exist from Norwich and York showing performances of the company on their journeys between London and Edinburgh.

In March 1799 the *Monthly Mirror* declared:

The liberal manager of the Circus, in gratitude to the public, for their unbounded support, during the last three years, has entirely rebuilt the interior of his theatre, and decorated it, with all imaginable splendour, from original drawings, made by [Rudolphe] Cabanel; the stage and ceiling are raised, and the lobbies are more spacious and airy. Upon the whole, it exhibits an Arcadian simplicity, blended with Eastern grandeur: we have seen nothing in this country so truly picturesque and beautiful.

Jones has added many valuable performers to his extensive group of last year, and if crowded house, every evening, indicate public patronage, the manager has the satisfaction of witnessing a *bumper* repeated.

The Royal Circus was destroyed by fire in 1805 but was rebuilt in 1805–6.

The fire broke out between one and two o'clock in the morning of Monday the 12th of August, and burnt so furiously that in 20 minutes the whole roof fell in with a dreadful crash. The Equestrian and Circus Coffee Houses, adjoining, were destroyed, as well as the manager's dwelling-house, behind the theatre, and a neighbouring printing-office. When the engines arrived, some time elapsed before water could be procured, and in the mean time the whole of the building, with the scenery, wardrobe, properties, music, &c. became a prey to the flames. By four o'clock, nothing remained but a heap of smoking ruins. So rapid was the progress of the fire, that Mr. Jones, who was asleep in bed when the alarm was given, with difficulty escaped in his shirt, and was compelled to leave the receipts of the preceding Saturday night in his bureau behind him.

Until its conversion to a regular theatre in 1809, the bills of the circus resembled those of other arenas: filled with sound and fury, color and light, music and fireworks. There were dancing, and tight-rope walking, burlettas and farces, contortionists and sibilists. But the most constant attractions were the horses, thundering around the ring in re-enactments of battles, performing tricks, or bearing men and women riders who performed tricks on them. Among the much copied innovations of James Jones was the introduction of the pony races, which were first tried out on their majesties at Frogmore and then became a popular feature of the bill. Jones evidently was the licensee of the theatre throughout the period after 1809 when Elliston was managing, for on 25 February 1816 James Jones took a benefit and mournfully advertised "The Last Night and Final Close of this Theatre." The prognostication was false. The Circus became the Surrey after 1816 and served as a theatre through successive burnings until the 1920s.

But Jones was finished there because, he said, of the rapacity of his landlord, Temple West. The bill for 19 February 1816 carried Jones's complaint:

James Jones, begs to inform the Public in general, that in consequence of his not being able to obtain a renewal of his Lease, which expires at Lady Day next, by reason of the Ground Landlord enhancing the present Rent of 200 Guineas to £4,200 per Annum, although his Misfortunes, from the destruction of the said Theatre by fire, and the rebuilding the same on a more extensive and improved plan, at the enormous expense of £14,500, when there only remained 11 Years of the Original Lease, induced him to believe he should meet with a corresponding Liberality from such Landlord in return, upon his application for a renewal of his said Lease; but having experienced the contrary without hope of Remuneration, and not having taken a Benefit for 8 Years past, he begs leave most respectfully to announce to his Friends and the Public in general, that he has fixed on the abovementioned Night for that purpose, when he trusts he shall experience that Liberality and Patronage he has heretofore experienced, which he ever has, and will gratefully bear in his Recollection.

In 1816 John Rennie's new Waterloo Bridge, which would make it possible for audiences to travel conveniently to the Surrey Theatre, was nearing completion. Jones and a partner, James Dunn, determined to build a rival house. They put out a prospectus offering investors a return of five percent and perpetual free admission to each purchaser of a hundred-pound share. The response was slow. After John Thomas Serres, Marine Painter to the King, invested £2000, the young Princess Charlotte and her new husband, Prince Leopold of Saxe-Coburg, were induced to stand as royal patrons, and a cornerstone on which that fact was proclaimed was laid by their proxy, one Alderman Goodbehere. It was not, however, until 1818, after a wealthy merchant named Glossop had repeatedly saved the enterprise by infusions of money, that the Royal Coburg Theatre was opened. After about two years Jones relinquished control and Glossop took over the theatre's direction. It later became known as the Royal Victoria—the "Old Vic."

We do not know the name of James Jones's wife, but she is not to be confused with Martha Elizabeth Palmer, who married Dr James Jones.

A portrait of James Jones was engraved by P. Roberts.

Jones, Mrs James. *See* PALMER, MARTHA ELIZABETH.

Jones, Jane [*fl. 1732–1757?*], *actress, singer, dancer.*

W. R. Chetwood in his *General History* in 1749 said that Miss J. (Jane or Jenny) Jones was from an "antient and reputable" Welsh family and that her father "Made the Stage his refuge"—but Chetwood failed to say where. An "unforeseen misfortune" fell on Jones, whereupon he "governed a Country Company many Years, with Judgment, Honesty, and Reputation." Which of the many Joneses in theatrical annals Jenny's father may have been Chetwood did not say, but there is a possibility that he may have been Thomas Jones the dancer, who appeared in London, as did his son; the bills sometimes suggest that from time to time in London in the first half of the eighteenth century there may have been a family of performers named Jones: father, son, and two daughters, dancing being a talent in all four and acting and singing additional specialties of the girls. But identification is far from certain, and merely separating the careers of the two Jones girls in the 1730s and 1740s (if there were, in fact, only two and not more) presents problems enough.

Chetwood said that our Miss Jones was "thrust on the Stage a mere Infant, and now [1749] makes a very good Figure there. . . ." Chetwood wrote from Dublin, where Jane Jones was performing at the time. He found her a sober, discreet, and virtuous woman. Jenny may well have been performing, perhaps in her father's provincial troupe, a few years before her name appeared in London bills in 1732. At the Haymarket that year two Jones girls appeared. One, called Miss Jones Junior, played Tom Thumb in *The Tragedy of Tragedies* on 8 March; the senior Jones girl played Belinda in *Tunbridge Walks*, the mainpiece that evening, and was probably the Miss Jones who had two years before played Tom Thumb and had now graduated to somewhat more mature roles. The junior Miss Jones, then, would seem to have been Jane, a young girl playing little boys' roles. On 23 March the bill cited the Miss Jones who played the Quaker Boy in *A Bold Stroke for a Wife* as Jenny Jones; the actress who played Betty was called Miss Jones. The bills did not make such a distinction except when the two girls performed at the same theatre the same night.

Jenny acted the Page in *The Orphan* on 8 May 1732 and may then have gone to Ireland. The following fall, on 4 September at the Haymarket, Signora Violante and her troupe presented *The Beggar's Opera* "after the Irish manner" with "Miss Jenny" as Polly. Other performances in London in 1732–33 by a Miss Jones would appear to have been by the elder girl.

In 1733–34 the Miss Jones with Theophilus Cibber's rebel players at the Haymarket and then at Drury Lane would again seem to have been the elder Miss Jones. Another Miss Jones was in Dublin that season, but she does not seem to have been Jenny. On 28 June 1734, on the other hand, a Miss Jones sang at the Haymarket with Master Arne, as she did again with him at Lincoln's Inn Fields in August, and she may well have been our subject. A benefit was held on 2 September at Hampstead for both Misses Jones. Miss Jones Junior played Miss Sneak in *Don Quixote in England* on 1

October of that year at Lincoln's Inn Fields; she was so named to distinguish her from the elder Miss Jones, who played Mrs Sneak. On 3 March 1735 a Miss Jones sang Polly in *The Beggar's Opera* at York Buildings, and we would take that performance to have been by Jenny. Miss J. Jones was Myrtillo in *The Provok'd Husband* at the Haymarket on 8 August of that year; Miss Jones played Mrs Trusty.

During the 1735–36 season one Miss Jones (the elder, evidently) performed at Goodman's Fields with Giffard's troupe, as she had the previous season; the Miss Jones who was at the Haymarket that season seems clearly to have been Jenny. On 17 September she was a Lady in *Jane Shore*; then she played Rose in *The Recruiting Officer*, Oriana in *The Inconstant* (Miss Jones played Bissare), Miss Mayoress in *Pasquin*, Leander in *The Mock Doctor*, Libertine in *The Female Rake* (and she spoke the epilogue), the Tragedy Queen and Aurora's Maid in *Tumble Down Dick*, Charlot in *Guilt Its Own Punishment*, Charlotte in *The Mock Doctor*, and Sukey Ogle in *The Temple Rake*. Jenny had a solo benefit on 13 May 1736. She was probably the Miss Jones who appeared on 20 September 1736 at Southwark as the Mayor's Daughter in *Pasquin*; performing the Drunken Major was Mr Jones—perhaps a relative.

In 1736–37 Jenny seems to have been again at the Haymarket with Fielding's Great Mogul's Company of Comedians, while the elder Miss Jones played at Lincoln's Inn Fields with Giffard's troupe. But Jenny was mentioned in the Haymarket bills only for the part of a Lady in *The Historical Register* on 21 March 1737 and subsequent dates. Perhaps after that Jenny left London. "Miss" or "Mrs" Jones appeared in the bills with some frequency in the years that followed, but the fact that no bill after 1735–36 referred to a Miss J. Jones or a Miss Jones Junior suggests that distinctions were no longer needed. We know that Jenny performed in Dublin from 1746 onward, but for a period of ten years we cannot be certain of her whereabouts.

Lady Grace in *The Provok'd Husband* was played at the Smock Alley Theatre in Dublin on 17 March 1746 by Jane Jones "from England, being the first Time of her appearing in the Kingdom." She remained at Smock Alley through 1748–49 and may have been the Miss Jones who danced there in 1756–57.

Jones, John ₁*fl. 1660–1674*₁, *trumpeter.*

The Lord Chamberlain's accounts show that John Jones was appointed a trumpeter in ordinary in the King's Musick on 30 November 1660. It is probable that he was related to Peter Jones, who had served as a court trumpeter from 1625 to 1641. John received a yearly salary of £60 and served under Gervase Price, the serjeant trumpeter. He accompanied the King on a trip to Bath in the late summer of 1663 and, from 10 June 1669 to 25 August 1670, served under Lord Howard, the ambassador to Morocco. On 16 June 1674 Thomas Cressell was appointed "in the place and upon the surrender of John Jones."

Jones, John ₁*fl. c. 1717–1739*₁, *organist.*

Sometime before the death of Daniel Purcell in 1717, John Jones applied for the post of organist to the United Parishes of Allhallows, Bread Street, and St John the Evangelist. Daniel and Edward Henry Purcell and Maurice Greene were among the Jones supporters who signed a broadside, now in the British Library, commending Jones's abilities. The same John Jones, perhaps, was one of the original subscribers to the Royal Society of Musicians on 28 August 1739. Possibly he was the father of John Jones (1728–1796), who became organist of St Paul's Cathedral.

Jones, John ₁*fl. 1723–1759*₁, *trumpeter.*

The Lord Chamberlain's accounts made frequent mention of the trumpeter John Jones from 27 October 1723, when his salary of £40 annually commenced, to 1759, when he was still serving in the royal musical establishment.

Jones, John ₁*fl. 1726*₁, *flutist.*

On 30 April 1726 John Jones played a concerto on the "small Flute" at Lincoln's Inn Fields playhouse. He seems not to have performed in London again, which makes one wonder if he was the John Jones who was buried at St Paul, Covent Garden, on 30 December 1726. But the name is far too common to make a certain identification.

Jones, John ₁*fl. 1726–1729*₁, *porter.*

John Jones worked as a porter at the Lincoln's Inn Fields for 10*s.* weekly from at least as early as 1726 to 1729 and perhaps longer. He was cited several times in the company accounts.

Jones, John *1728–1796, organist, composer.*

John Jones was born in London in 1728, and on 24 November 1749, according to Grove, he became organist of the Middle Temple. The *Calendar of Middle Temple Records*, however, shows that Jones was paid £12 10*s.* on 5 October of that year for his services as organist, so he had been working there for some time before he was officially elected to succeed Vincent. The records show payments to Jones over the years of £25 annually. Since he was regularly referred to as John Jones Junior, it is possible that he was the son of the organist John Jones who was active from about 1717 to 1739.

Jones augmented his income at the Middle Temple by accepting the post of organist of the Charterhouse on 2 July 1753, succeeding Pepusch, and that of organist at St Paul's Cathedral on 25 December 1755. Two letters from Dr Burney to Thomas Twining in July and October 1783 indicate that Jones had written for publication an *Analysis of Air & Harmony*, dedicated to the directors of the Concert of Ancient Music. Burney said it was printed at Colchester. Burney called Jones a pleasant man as long as one gave his serious prejudices their head. The Burney letters are at the British Library.

In 1784 Jones served Burney as assistant director of the Handel Memorial Concerts at Westminister Abbey and the Pantheon in May and June; in 1785 he was a Governor of the Royal Society of Musicians; and on 3 June 1792 he was elected to the Committee for the Society's concert at St Paul's the following year. In addition to his service as organist in three different posts, all of which he held until his death, Jones composed a number of glees, chants, and lessons which were published between 1745 and 1796.

Jones lived at the Charterhouse for many years. The registers there note his marriage to Sarah Chaloner, spinster, at Sudbury, Derbyshire, apparently in 1753, when Jones was elected to the organist's post. Their daughter Sarah was born on 2 June 1758 and christened three days later, but she died within two weeks and was buried at Greenwich. The couple had a son John, who was born on 15 October 1759 and christened the following 27 November. A daughter Henrietta Maria was christened on 6 January 1761, and a son Thomas was born on 28 October 1762 and christened on 9 November. Mrs Jones died in 1792 and John followed her to the grave four years later, as the inscription in the Charterhouse Chapel Cloister shows:

> Here lieth the Body of
> JOHN JONES Esqr
> Organist of the Hospital
> St Paul's Cathedral
> and the Temple
> who died 17th of February 1796
> Aged 67 years.
> Also of Mrs SARAH JONES
> Wife of the above
> who died the 8th of October 1792
> Aged 62 years.
> The above John Jones
> resided in this Hospital 43 years.
> Also of HENRIETTA MARIA JONES
> Daughter of the above
> who died 22nd May 1828
> in the 68th year of her age.

John Jones was incorrectly called "William" when his burial at the Charterhouse was recorded in the registers on 22 February 1796.

Jones, John $_{[}$ *fl. 1739–1763?$_{]}$*, *violinist.*
On 28 August 1739 John Jones of the Horse Guards became one of the original subscribers to the newly-founded Royal Society of Musicians. Perhaps he was the violinist John Jones, described in *Mortimer's London Directory* in 1763 as one of His Majesty's band, who lived at Lady Vanbrugh's, Whitehall.

Jones, Julia *d. 1806. See* GRANGER, JULIA.

Jones, Patty. *See* ASTLEY, MRS PHILIP.

Jones, $_{[}$ **R.?** $_{]}$ $_{[}$ *fl. 1732–1734$_{]}$*, *dancer, violinist.*
Two Joneses, evidently a father and son, danced in London in the early 1730s, and only occasionally did the bills distinguish them carefully. The elder Jones seems to have been Tom; the younger was sometimes labeled Junior and sometimes "R." From 5 October 1732 to early February 1733 young Jones danced at

the Goodman's Fields Theatre. On 25 November 1732 the bill was specific about his work: he danced a hornpipe while playing the violin, a specialty also of the elder Jones. On 14 February "R. Jones, from Goodman's Fields," danced a hornpipe at the Haymarket Theatre. Both the junior and the senior Jones danced at the Haymarket on 16 March and subsequent dates, as on 26 May, when they appeared in a dance called the *Dutch Skipper*. They also performed at the Mills-Miller-Oates booth at Bartholomew Fair the following 23 August. R. Jones was at the Haymarket again in March 1733, dancing with T. Jones. On 4 February 1734 the junior Jones danced the role of Pluto in *Cupid and Psyche* at Drury Lane. He seems not to have pursued his dancing career beyond the 1733–34 season.

Jones, Richard $_{[}$ *fl. 1672$_{]}$*, *musician.*
A warrant in the Lord Chamberlain's accounts dated 29 February 1672 and another dated the following 2 October call for the apprehension of Richard Jones and a number of other musicians who had been performing music without a license.

Jones, Richard $_{[}$ *fl. 1674$_{]}$*, *singer.*
Richard Jones, a countertenor, was cited in the Lord Chamberlain's accounts on 14 April 1674 as one of a number of court singers who were to attend Charles II at the chapel in Windsor.

Jones, Richard *d. 1744, violinist, composer.*
Richard Jones the violinist became the leader of the Drury Lane band about 1730, succeeding Carbonelli. He was probably the Jones who composed and adapted the music for *Apollo and Daphne*, which was performed at Drury Lane in 1723. The advertisements boasted that the new music "proper Judges allow to be the best of the Kind now extant." A musician named Jones, again probably Richard, was active at Drury Lane in 1728–29, and it is highly probable that for some years before his appointment as leader of the band he was a performer in it. Michael Christian Festing was one of Jones's pupils and with Richard Charke succeeded to Jones's post.

Jones published some harpsichord lessons in 1732, a set of *Chamber Air's for a Violin and Thorough Bass* in 1736, and *Six Suites of Lessons for a Violin with a Thorough Bass* about 1741. Of his personal life virtually nothing is known. Possibly the following entry in the registers of St Paul, Covent Garden, concerns his wife: Christobell, wife of Richard Jones, was buried *in* the church on 30 March 1742. The *Daily Advertiser* on 24 January 1744 reported the death of the musician Richard Jones on 20 January.

Jones, Robert *d. 1772?, pyrotechnist.*

In March and April 1778, in her diary, Mrs Thrale commented on Captain Robert Jones, who was a pyrotechnist and had, before 1772, entertained the town with fireworks at Marylebone Gardens. Two of his effects were the Forge of Vulcan in the Cave of Mt Etna and the calling of Eurydice out of hell. Balderston in *Thraliana* notes that the Forge of Vulcan was done by the pyrotechnist Torré, not Jones. Mrs Thrale said that on 18 July 1772 Captain Jones was convicted of "Crimes against Nature" and sentenced to die. We do not know whether or not the sentence was carried out.

Jones, Robert *d. 1806, actor, singer.*

The actor Jones who married Julia Granger and died in America in 1806 was, according to an obituary in the *Columbian Centinal*, Robert Jones. It is likely that the Mr Jones who acted in London from as early as 1772 was also Robert, though discriminating among the Joneses is a nearly impossible task, and the conclusions here should be considered tentative.

On 26 December 1772 Jones was an unnamed character in *The Pigmy Revels* at Drury Lane, and he continued throughout the 1772–73 season but received only one other citation in the bills: Maw-Worm in *The Hypocrite* on 21 May 1773. He was back in 1773–74 to play in *The Pigmy Revels* again, and he was also seen as Verges in *Much Ado about Nothing*, Isaachar in *The Note of Hand*, the Bookseller in *The Committee*, and a Beggar in *The Ladies' Frolick*. At the end of the season the bills appear to present evidence that there was a second Jones performing in London: on 16 May 1774 a Jones played an unnamed part in *The Bankrupt* (mainpiece) at the Haymarket, and at Drury Lane our Jones acted Abel and the Bookseller in *The Committee* and a Beggar in *The Ladies' Frolick*.

Jones played at the Haymarket during the summer of 1774, acting an unnamed part in *The Nabob*, the Poet in *The Author*, a part in *The Devil upon Two Sticks*, the Tailor in *Catherine and Petruchio*, a part in *The Bankrupt*, Counsel in *Cross Purposes*, Paduasoy in *The Commissary*, a part in *The Rehearsal*, and Staytape in *The Patron*. He did not act at any London theatre during the 1774–75 winter season, but he returned to the Haymarket in mid-May 1775 to repeat several of his old roles plus Hellebore in *The Mock Doctor*, a part in *The Nabob*, and a part in *The Orators*.

On 13 October 1775 Jones made his initial appearance at Covent Garden playing Tom in *The Jealous Wife*. During the rest of the 1775–76 season he was seen as a Drawer in *Orpheus and Eurydice*, Dick in *The Lying Valet*, the Poet in *The Author*, the Tailor in *Catherine and Petruchio*, an unnamed character in *Prometheus*, one of the Gravediggers in *Hamlet*, the Puritan in *A Duke and No Duke*, Counsel in *Cross Purposes*, Shoemaker in *The Man of Quality*, Tom in *The Funeral*, and Tom in *The Jealous Wife*. Into his schedule at Covent Garden in May 1776 he was able to sandwich appearances at the Haymarket in *The Mock Doctor* and *The Nabob*, as the Haymarket summer season began. His summer there consisted of several of his old parts.

From 1776–77 through 1784–85 Jones played full winter seasons at Covent Garden and either vacationed or performed away from London during the summers. The account books show that he was earning £1 10s. weekly during most of that period, though in 1783–84 he was dropped to £1—which may account for his breaking away from Covent Garden after the following season. During 1776–77 and 1777–78 a Master Jones (Edward) was also in the company; one might guess he was our subject's son, though he need not necessarily have been related.

During those seasons at Covent Garden, Jones played, among other new parts and many unnamed roles, a Recruit in *The Recruiting Officer*, Peter and the Apothecary in *Romeo and Juliet*, Barnardine in *Measure for Measure*, the Anatomist in *The Royal Chace*, Taylor in *The Provok'd Wife*, Transfer in *The Minor*, Snug in *The Lady's Last Stake*, Nym in *Henry V*, the Poet in *The Twin Rivals*, an Officer in *The Comedy of Errors*, Dr Coffin in *Dr Last in His*

Chariot, Ali in *Gallic Gratitude*, Formal in *Every Man in His Humour*, Buckram in *Plymouth in an Uproar*, Alguazil in *The Wonder*, the first Carrier and Bardolph in *1 Henry IV*, Dubois in *The Shepherdess of the Alps*, Rhubarb in *The Double Gallant*, a Servant in *The Deaf Lover*, Roberto in *Love Makes a Man*, Cryer in *The Humours of an Election*, Metaphrastus in *The Mistake*, Lord Sands in *Henry VIII*, George in *The Excise Man*, Order in *A New Way to Pay Old Debts*, Remonstrance in *Seventeen Hundred and Eighty One*, an Old Beau in *The Choice of Harlequin*, a Sailor and Quid in *The Positive Man*, Justice Statute in *The What D'Ye Call It*, Ezekiel Spotless in *Retaliation*, Ghastly in *The School for Wives*, Wat Dreary in *The Beggar's Opera*, Gobbo in *The Merchant of Venice*, Counselor Plausible in *The Man of the World*, Corrigidore in *She Wou'd and She Wou'd Not*, the third Witch in *Macbeth*, Blunt in *Richard III*, Dapper in *The Citizen*, Postboy in *Fountainebleau*, the Courier in *The Follies of a Day*, Gardener in *Barataria*, and Isaacs in *The Lawyer's Panic*.

A Mr Jones was the subject of the following report in the *Public Advertiser* on 12 October 1782:

> Mr. Jones, of Covent-garden theatre, is employed to make a model of the new buildings at Somerset-house. To any body who has not seen the works of Mr. Jones, it cannot convey much idea on the subject to say that his models are done with cards, yet such is the happy effect produced by his manner of working them, that to represent any architecture not in ruins, we prefer the cards to cork. It is but justice to add of Mr. Jones, that in the discovery and pursuit of this elegant art, he spends those hours not employed on the stage.

Could that Jones have been Robert?

Jones seems not to have been making any headway at Covent Garden. His salary had been modest to begin with and had gone down instead of up with the years. He pretty regularly had his benefit tickets accepted in the spring, but he was always one of many who had tickets out. On 18 October 1785 he appeared at Drury Lane as a Countryman in *The Country Girl* to begin an engagement that lasted through the 1795–96 season—with perhaps an appearance or two elsewhere, as we shall see. But until the 1788–89 season Jones seems to have done no better than he had at

Covent Garden; indeed, he was named in the bills far less. But beginning in the fall of 1788 he was cited frequently, and though he did not graduate to major parts, he settled into a number of bit parts and secondary and tertiary characters in plays and pantomimes.

Among his named roles (he played many "Principal Characters" that were not named) were a Woodman in *Philaster*, Roberto in *The Strangers at Home*, the Second Gravedigger and a Sailor in *Hamlet*, the Tailor in *Catherine and Petruchio*, Snap in *The First Floor*, the Surgeon in *The Chances*, a Beggar in *The Pilgrim*, Gobbo in *The Merchant of Venice*, Robert in *High Life Below Stairs*, a Citizen in *Coriolanus*, Ely in *Henry V*, a Planter in *Oroonoko*, a Pedlar in *Harlequin's Frolicks*, Crowquil in *The Belle's Stratagem*, Snap in *Love for Love*, Tyrrel in *Richard III*, a Watchman in *The Fairy Favour*, Alguazile in *Don Juan*, the Doctor in *Macbeth*, Rhubarb in *The Double Gallant*, the Physician in *King Lear*, Cymon in *All the World's a Stage*, Stock in *A Bold Stroke for a Wife*, a Goatherd in *The Mountaineers*, Corrigidore in *She Wou'd and She Wou'd Not*, Scale in *The Recruiting Officer*, a Countryman in *Harlequin Captive*, a Bookseller in *The Plain Dealer*, and Abram in *Romeo and Juliet*. (Some of those parts were played in 1792 and 1793 at the King's Theatre and the Haymarket, where the Drury Lane players performed after their theatre burned.)

Either Robert or another Jones appeared elsewhere during Robert's engagement with Drury Lane. On 7 December 1785, just after Robert had begun his engagement and on a night on which he was free, a Jones, very likely Robert, played Rhubarb in *The Double Gallant* at Covent Garden—a role he had played there before and continued to act at Drury Lane. A Jones was one of the Natives of the Island in *The Governor* at Covent Garden beginning 11 March 1793 (Robert was free and may well have performed at his old theatre). Jones was granted benefit tickets to sell each spring at Drury Lane but he was always one of many.

Jones's salary at Drury Lane at the end of his engagement there in 1795–96 was £1 10*s*. He had made little progress during his more than 20 years on the London stage. Perhaps he was the Jones who made sporadic appearances in and around London in the years that followed. A Jones appeared in 1796 at the Richmond Theatre. A Jones played Dr Hellebore (Robert had played it earlier) in *The Mock Doctor* at the Haymarket on 16 September 1796, Paul Peery in *Ways and Means* there on 23 January 1797, a part in *The Battle of Eddington* there on 10 May, a part in *Forecastle Fun* at Covent Garden on 9 May 1798, and a Bricklayer in *Harlequin's Chaplet* there on 13 May 1799. Since Robert Jones certainly left Drury Lane after the 1795–96 season and did not go to America until 1800, it is very possible he was the actor in question in all those instances.

Perhaps it was during the late 1790s that Robert Jones met Julia Granger. She was performing under the name of Mrs Edward in 1797 and married Jones in 1800. Just as in England, so in America, distinguishing accurately among the Joneses is difficult. There was a J. Jones in America about the same time as Robert, and the possibility of confusing the two is easy. Apparently it was Robert Jones who was recruited by Whitlock to play at the Federal Theatre in Boston, where he made his American debut on 27 October 1800 as Bob Handy in *Speed the Plough* and William in *Rosina*. He later acted the Baron in *The Stranger*, which encouraged the *Gazette* critic to say that "Mr. Jones Possesses a very useful and pleasing versatility of talent; and in all his astonishing variety of characters, he uniformly discovers a discriminating judgment, and a chaste execution." The *Chronicle* critic, on the other hand, found Jones inattentive to his role and lacking in moderation in performance. On 16 February 1801 Jones played Alonzo in *Pizarro*, to mixed notices. Whitlock lost $4000 by the end of the season and had to disband the company.

The Whitlocks and the Joneses were at the Chestnut Street Theatre in Philadelphia in 1801–2. Durang thought Jones was "a very respectable actor in sentimental business." On 19 October Jones played Romeo, but the critics had to compare him with Cooper, unfavorably, and *The Port Folio* criticized Jones for his listless manner. Jones may not have stayed at Chestnut Street more than one season, though his wife did. They were at the Federal Street Theatre in Boston again, under Snelling Powell this time, in 1803–4, after which they journeyed to Charleston, South Carolina, where Robert Jones died in 1806. The *Columbian Centinal* on 27 August 1806 reported that Robert Jones had died on 7 August. Julia Granger Jones died the following 19 Novem-

ber, according to the same periodical, leaving four young orphans. One of the children was Julia Elizabeth Jones, born on 4 November 1800, the eldest of Jones's four children, according to Bernard's *Retrospections of the Stage*.

Since the Joneses are so difficult to distinguish, it might be helpful here to state that there was a Jones who in Ireland was considered famous as a Teague and an Irish Clown, according to the late W. S. Clark's investigations. That Jones was at Smock Alley in 1766–67 and at Crow Street in 1768–69. There seems to be nothing in the career of Robert Jones that would suggest that he was the Dublin Jones. That actor was evidently the Jones who was in Roger Kemble's troupe at Coventry in the autumn of 1766 and in Worcester in January 1767. Irish records show that Jones to have appeared at the Capel Street Theatre (first time in five years, said *Faulkner's Dublin Journal*) in November 1770. A Jones (who was evidently not the same person) made his first appearance in Ireland in 1770–71 at the Smock Alley Theatre, and that Jones Clark listed as appearing at Cork in 1770 and again in 1776 and at Youghal in 1784. Clark also found among W. J. Lawrence's papers a bill about a celebrated comedian named Jones who appeared for one night at Smock Alley in 1773–74, but one would suppose that such a one-night stand would not have been given Robert Jones, who had clearly not gained much fame.

Jones, Mrs Robert. *See* GRANGER, JULIA.

Jones, Stephen [*fl.* 1770–1794], *violinist.*

On 11 October 1770 Stephen Jones, of Sudbury, Derby, musician in ordinary to the King, appointed John Hughes of New Bond Street, Hanover Square, his lawful attorney. Similarly in 1776 Jones made James Fisher of Green Street in the parish of St George, Hanover Square, his attorney. Jones was evidently at these times being sent out of London and needed someone who could receive money owed him. It is probable that the musician in question was the Stephen Jones, violinist in the King's band and resident in Buckingham House, who was listed in Doane's *Musical Directory* in 1794.

Jones, Thomas ₁*fl. c. 1719–1742*₁, *harpist.*

The blind harpist Thomas Jones performed at Cannons about 1719 and 1720, though the records Pepusch kept of the salaries of the musicians there do not include a figure for the harpist. He played a voluntary on the "Welch" harp at Goodman's Fields on 30 June 1730. Jones was at Oxford for the Act in 1733, and he appeared in London at the Lincoln's Inn Fields Theatre on 4 May 1737 to play a Handel concerto for the Welsh harp between the mainpiece and afterpiece. In March 1738 and August 1739 he played selections from Handel and Corelli at Cuper's Gardens.

The harpist was probably the Thomas Jones who became one of the original subscribers to the Royal Society of Musicians on 28 August 1739. The *Daily Advertiser* on 5 March 1742 contained a "Notice to all Gentlemen and others, That Mr. Jones, the Harper, who play'd for seventeen Years and upwards at the Old Hercules Pillars, in Fleet Street is now remov'd to the Trumpet in Sheer-Lane, Temple Bar . . . ." Such notices are useful reminders that performers in the period covered by this dictionary were probably much busier throughout their careers than the occasional surviving notices suggest. Most advertisements are scattered and single, such as the last one we have found that seems to concern our subject: on 15 May 1742 at Drury Lane Jones played a lesson on the Welsh harp.

In the harpist Edward Jones's entry we have cited harp performances by him at the Oxford Music Room in 1762, though Edward Jones was only 10 at that time and not otherwise cited as a child prodigy; the performances may have been given by Thomas Jones.

Jones, Thomas ₁*fl. 1720?–1742?*₁, *dancer, choreographer, violinist, manager?*

There is a possibility that the Jones spoken of by the prompter W. R. Chetwood in his *General History* (1749) as a provincial performer was the dancer and violinist Thomas Jones, who was active in London perhaps as early as 1720. Chetwood was discussing Jane Jones, who was from an "antient and reputable" Welsh "family." Her father, Chetwood said, "Made the Stage his refuge" and after an "unforeseen misfortune" he "governed a Country Company many Years, with Judgment,

Honesty, and Reputation." Could he have been Thomas Jones? Chetwood was remiss in not indicating where Jones managed a provincial troupe, for that information might have made identification easier. Thomas Jones is known to have performed at Bath in the 1730s and during that decade or later may well have had a company of his own somewhere—perhaps in southern England or in Wales.

If Thomas was Jane Jones's father, then he had another daughter, older than Jane, who was active from 1730 to perhaps 1743. And, as will be seen, he had a son, R. Jones, who was an accomplished dancer.

The Jones who danced on 19 May 1720 at Drury Lane was probably Thomas Jones. So, too, probably, was the Jones who danced at the Great Booth in the Queen's Arms Tavern at Southwark on the following 3 October. At Lincoln's Inn Fields playhouse on 31 March 1722 and subsequent dates Jones danced a hornpipe, which became his specialty. He displayed his hornpipe at the Haymarket on 28 June and at the autumn fairs, identified now as Tom Jones. After the fall of 1722 Jones's name seems to have disappeared from London bills until 31 October 1730, when he danced a hornpipe at Lincoln's Inn Fields. Jones was at Lincoln's Inn Fields from January to May 1732, and a scholar of his danced at the Haymarket in March 1732. With Mrs Ogden at Lincoln's Inn Fields in March, Jones danced a *Sailor and Country Girl* of his own composing. A scholar of Jones danced *St Giles's Jog* at Drury Lane in August 1732, and either the same boy (10 years old) or another Jones pupil danced a hornpipe at Goodman's Fields in November. When our subject danced on 4 August at Tottenham Court he was identified as T. Jones from Lincoln's Inn Fields.

On 16 March 1733 at the Haymarket Jones Senior and Jones Junior danced; we take the elder Jones to have been Tom and the younger probably his son, whose initial was later given as R. The pair appeared in a *Dutch Skipper* dance four days later. On 4 June the elder Jones offered at the Haymarket a new dance of his composing, choreographed to the fifth concerto of Vivaldi, with Jones accompanying himself on the violin. Jones also appeared at Covent Garden in the spring of 1733. The *Gloucester Journal* in July of that year noted that the Bath troupe included "Mr. Jones, the eminent dancer in the footing manner, from Covent Garden, and a great performer on the violin." In August at Bartholomew Fair Jones was a Rival Swain in *The Gardens of Venus* and, with the junior Jones, offered specialty dances.

After 1733 London records of Jones cease for a number of years. Perhaps our subject was the T. Jones who was at the Aungier Street playhouse in Dublin in 1737–38. We take the Jones who danced a hornpipe while accompanying himself on the violin on 12 January 1742 at Goodman's Fields to be Tom, though no initial was mentioned in the bill to help with identification, and the younger Jones had also developed the violin-hornpipe specialty. But also dating from 1742 is a notice of a hornpipe dancer named Jones who performed at the London Spa; he was described as from Bath, and it seems likely that from 1733 onward Thomas Jones pursued his career with the Bath company, making occasional appearances elsewhere.

Jones, Thomas [fl. 1738–1759], *musician.*
Thomas Jones served in the King's Musick from 1738 (when he replaced Thomas Jackson) until 1759. His yearly salary was £40.

Jones, Thomas [fl. 1788?–1800?], *harpist, composer?*
Doane's *Musical Directory* of 1794 listed Thomas Jones, of Vine Street, Piccadilly, as a harpist who performed with the New Musical Fund. That year he was on that organization's Court of Assistants. On 22 April 1794 he played at Sadler's Wells. Perhaps he was a descendant of Thomas Jones the blind Welsh harpist of earlier in the century, and possibly he was the Thomas Jones who composed some sets of country dances in 1788 and 1789 (both listed in the *Catalogue of Printed Music in the British Museum*) and in 1800 brought out *Music purposely Composed for the Harp, etc. by T. Jones of Gaddesden.*

Jones, Thomas d. 1793, *organist.*
Musgrave's Obituary records the death of Thomas Jones on 9 October 1793 and notes that he had been the organist of St Vedast, Foster Lane, and St Michael le Querne. He died in Highgate, and it was from there the previous 23 June that he had written his will.

He asked to be buried in the Temple churchyard. To his servant Sarah Cox he left 20 guineas. He directed that his two organs and all his music books and manuscripts should be sold to the best advantage. The rest of his estate he bequeathed to his sisters, Sarah and Catherine Jones, equally. His sisters proved the will on 11 October 1793.

Jones, Thomas [fl. 1794], *singer.*
Doane's *Musical Directory* of 1794 listed Thomas Jones, of No 22, Newcastle Street, the Strand, as an alto who sang for the Handelian Society. Perhaps he also sang in the chorus at the Covent Garden playhouse from 1797 to 1800, though we take that performer to have been Edward Jones.

Jones, [W.?] [fl. c. 1765–1796], *trumpeter.*
William Rendle in *Old Southwark*, states that a Mr Jones and his pupil Master Green played trumpets at Finch's Grotto Gardens about 1765. Perhaps the same Jones was the musician who was receiving 5s. 10d. daily for playing in the band at the Covent Garden Theatre in 1767–68. Master Green, still advertised as Jones's scholar, performed at Marylebone Gardens on 21 August 1770, and he appeared at Covent Garden on 15 May 1771 and at Finch's again on 30 August. On 25 March 1774 Master Green played at the Haymarket Theatre. No accounts survive to confirm our guess that Jones was probably playing in the band at Covent Garden during these years.

Among the trumpeters who played in the Handel Memorial Concerts at Westminster Abbey and the Pantheon in May and June 1784 was W. Jones, who was probably our subject. The Drury Lane accounts from as early as 12 February 1787 cited a trumpeter named Jones. He seems to have been earning £1 weekly. The accounts mentioned him last on 3 December 1796.

Jones, Walter. *See* JONES, [J.?] WALTER.

Jones, William [fl. 1707–1708], *actor.*
William Jones, otherwise unknown, was listed in a petition by the players in 1707–8 against a proposed union of the opera and act-

ing companies. His name is in the middle of a group of prominent actors—Wilks, Pinkethman, Estcourt, Cibber, Mrs Oldfield, Mrs Knight, and others—and one would suppose that Jones, too, was an actor. The document was reported by Fitzgerald in his *New History*, so perhaps an error in transcription was made.

Jones, William Wheeler ₍*fl.* 1785–1803₎, *bassoonist, oboist.*

William Jones was a member of the Court of Assistants of the Royal Society of Musicians as of 6 March 1785. He played bassoon in the St Paul's concert in May 1792 and was listed in Doane's *Musical Directory* of 1794 as a participant in concerts by the Choral Fund and the Madrigal Society. Doane said that Jones was also an oboist and gave his address as No 6, City Road. The 1794 subscription list of the New Musical Fund included William Wheeler Jones, presumably our subject. Jones was noted as a member of the Court of Assistants of the Royal Society of Musicians in 1798 and again in 1803.

Jonno. *See* JANNO.

Jonsalino. *See* JANSOLIN.

Jonson. *See* JOHNSON, JOHNSTON, JOHNSTONE.

Jordan, Mrs ₍*fl.* 1688–1690₎, *actress.*

Mrs Jordan (or Jordain, Jorden, Jourden) played the minor part of Celia in *The Fool's Preferment* in April 1688 for the United Company at the Dorset Garden Theatre. A manuscript cast list at the Folger Shakespeare Library shows that she acted Amaryllis in an all-female production of *Pastor Fido*, probably in the spring of 1689 at Drury Lane Theatre. In 1689–90 she is known to have appeared as Antramont in *The Massacre of Paris*, Mrs Crisante in *The Widow Ranter*, Armena in *The Treacherous Brothers*, Laura in *The English Frier*, and the juvenal lead Elvira in *The Amorous Bigotte*—in late March 1690, the last record of her activity.

Jordan, Dorothy, née Bland, sometimes Miss Phillips and Miss Francis, 1761–1816, *actress, singer.*

The great comedienne who rose to fame as Mrs Jordan was baptized Dorothy, daughter of Francis and Grace Bland, at St Martin-in-the-Fields on 22 November 1761. Her father was the eldest son by a second marriage (to Elizabeth Heaton) of Nathaniel Bland, a Dublin judge and heir to Derriquin Castle and estate near Sneem, in County Kerry, Ireland. The judge's son by a former marriage, John Bland (1721–1808) had been disinherited for taking to the stage. Francis Bland did not profit by his half brother's experience and he, too, became estranged from his father after his connection with Grace Phillips became known. That his alliance with Grace was only informal seems certain, though an early account speaks of a secret ceremony before a Catholic priest in Ireland.

Grace Phillips was one of three daughters, all of whom were actresses, of a Welsh clergyman. Grace had perhaps met Francis Bland in Ireland, where she principally pursued her career and where an unreliable early account says "Captain" Bland was stationed. The record is obscure on those points, as it is on how many children sprang from the union. It is believed that there were perhaps nine, though (besides Dorothy) only three can be traced: George Bland (d. 1807), a London and provincial actor; Hester Francis Bland (who acted at Hull and York as Hester Francis); and Francis, who settled in Wales.

Nothing is known of Dorothy's childhood and education. Sometime before Dorothy was 13 years of age Francis Bland had abandoned his common-law wife and his children, for in London, at St. Botolph's Without, on 17 May 1774 he married Catherine Mahoney, an heiress of Killarney. He died in 1778. Some financial help may have come from the Bland family even after Francis and Grace parted, but it seems probable that Grace's acting was the principal source of income, certainly after Francis's death. Her wages must have been sometimes meagre and uncertain.

Grace Phillips had begun in promising fashion, as Juliet in *Romeo and Juliet* on 12 November 1756 at Dublin's Smock Alley Theatre, and during that season she had played an impressive variety of roles—21 at least, ranging from Lavinia in *The Fair Penitent* to Narcissa in *Love's Last Shift*, from Lucia in *Cato* and Desdemona in *Othello* to Lady Betty Modish in *The Careless Husband*. But, so far as can be deter-

By gracious permission of Her Majesty Queen Elizabeth II

DOROTHY JORDAN as the Comic Muse

by Hoppner

mined, she never acted in London. She apparently spent some years in the provinces, at Edinburgh, York, and smaller towns, as Miss Phillips or as Mrs Francis, but her career cannot now be followed. If her daughter Dorothy (sometimes Bland, sometimes Francis, often Phillips) inherited her theatrical talent, she may almost be said to have inherited also the emotional and financial insecurity which hung always over her life to cloud her merry disposition and dilute the satisfactions of her brilliant successes on the stage.

Dorothy made her debut at the Crow Street Theatre, Dublin, under the management of Thomas Ryder. Her initial part was Lucy in the interlude *The Virgin Unmask'd* on 3 November 1779. She played the male role of Lopez in a transvestite performance of *The Governess* on 20 May 1780. Sir Jonah Barrington wrote of her performance as Priscilla Tomboy in *The Romp*. None of her other characters are known. She was billed as Dorothea Bland throughout that and the following season. In 1781–82 she shifted to Smock Alley, where Richard Daly was manager, and there she acted under the name Dorothea Francis. Dorothy acted frequently during the season with the young John Philip Kemble. She was Adelaide in *The Count of Narbonne*, Charlotte in *The Gamester*, Selina in *Tamerlane*, Lady Anne in *Richard III*, Miss Ogle in *The Belle's Stratagem*, Louisa in *The Discovery*, Maria in *The School for Scandal*, and Catherine in *Catherine and Petruchio*. Her last Dublin appearance seems to have been on 16 May 1782, when she spoke the prologue before *The Maid of the Oaks*. Firm information about her life during those first two years of her career is fragmentary, consisting only of notes made by W. J. Lawrence from bills and from company records now lost, dim recollections (after 50 years) of P. L. Gordon in his *Personal Memoirs*, and gossip from Sir Jonah Barrington's *Personal Sketches*. Gordon remembered that Dorothy was courted by a Lieutenant Charles Doyne when she acted briefly at Waterford but that her mother made her reject his offer of marriage.

The probable reasons that Dorothy succumbed to the amorous advances of the manager Richard Daly during the months when she acted at Smock Alley have been subjected to speculative analyses by each of her successive biographers: she was unprotected and young,

her family impoverished, her mother probably actually ill; Daly was attractive, plausible, dissolute, unscrupulous; his methods of seduction were varied, and his past behavior with young actresses was notorious. Whatever the circumstances were, Dorothy became Daly's mistress, quickly found herself both pregnant and disillusioned, and fled Ireland for England owing Daly a considerable sum of money.

In July 1782 Dorothy and her mother Grace, her sister Maria, and her brother Francis applied to Tate Wilkinson, the manager of the York circuit, at Leeds. Wilkinson, who recognized Grace as having been his "first Desdemona in Dublin, in Feb. 1758," gave the bedraggled family his hospitality and Dorothy an audition, despite his skepticism—"The mamma, like other mamma's, and in particular ACTRESSES MAMMA'S, talked so fulsomely of her daughter's merits, that I was almost disgusted, and very near giving a flat denial to any negotiations." Wilkinson feared also that Dorothy, now the whole support of her family, would not warrant a salary large enough to sustain the burden. Dorothy's overconfidence only increased his trepidation; when he asked her: "But what do you play? Comedy, tragedy, farce . . . ?" She replied, "All!" But his reservations evaporated as she began to recite "lines from Calista [in *The Fair Penitent*]: (the part we had agreed on for her trial-character.) . . . At the tones of her voice . . . I felt inwardly surprised and delighted, [and] could not repress my hopes and my compliments. . . ."

Dorothy played the part on 11 July as "Miss Francis." Wilkinson first had her in the playbills as Miss Bland, but her mother made him post new ones. After the play Dorothy charmed Wilkinson and the audience with the song "Greenwood Laddie":

. . . on she came in a frock and a little mob-cap, and sung the song with such effect that I was fascinated—for managers do not always meet with jewels, but when they do, and think the sale will turn out for their own advantage, you cannot conceive, reader, how it makes our eyes sparkle.

Dorothy was signed by Wilkinson for 15 shillings per week. On 5 August, the day of her benefit, it again became necessary, pursuant to her mother's orders, to change the playbill, for by now Dorothy's pregnant condition was becoming obvious. She was no

Harvard Theatre Collection

DOROTHY JORDAN as Priscilla Tomboy
engraving by Angus, after Stothard

longer *Miss* "Frances," but, at Wilkinson's suggestion, *Mrs* Jordan. (In one of his accounts,
Wilkinson declares that he told her, "You have
crossed the water, my dear, so I'll call you
Jordan.")

Dorothy was made acquainted now, after
some successes, with the jealousy of other actresses, particularly a Mrs Smith, who, "swelled
with indignation," fomented dissatisfaction in
the other performers by claiming that Wilkinson showed unfair partiality to the newcomer. But Dorothy also encountered the
kindness of the old Dublin manager George
Cornelius Swan, who undertook to coach her:
" . . . when Mrs. Jordan [was] ill, he was
admitted to the little bed-chamber, where, by
the side of the bed, with Mrs. Bland's old red
cloke around his neck, he would sit and instruct his pupil in Hill's character of Zara."
Swan is also supposed to have paid the debt to

Daly of some £250, releasing Dorothy from
that bondage.

Dorothy experienced the usual rigors and
adventures of circuit-walking. For instance, at
Sheffield in 1782, when acting a scene with
Knight in *The Fair American*, they were almost
killed when "a roller of immense weight gave
way" and fell near them. But she also gained
there the admiration and lasting patronage of
the Duke of Norfolk. Her increasing indispositions, as her pregnancy advanced, made it
necessary to cancel performances at Hull and
she made her first acquaintance with the fickle
cruelty of audiences, who hissed her for her
supposed delinquency. In September 1782
Frances, Daly's child, was born.

Dorothy Jordan remained with Tate Wilkinson until the summer of 1785 but, according to Wilkinson, did not much improve during her final season there: " . . . she grew very
careless and inattentive; was very often really
or fictitiously ill." On 15 March 1785 she refused to sing a scheduled song at Mills's benefit
and was again disciplined by the audience. She
was soon, however, able to be as refractory as
she liked. For in the spring she obtained a trial
engagement at Drury Lane, on the recommendation of William "Gentleman" Smith. One
very fortunate accident occurred that season.
She saw Mrs J. Brown act with great success
Peggy in *The Country Girl*, kindling an ambition to play that role which afterward became
one of her best-received offerings. "It struck
Mrs. Jordan's ideas so forcibly, that she declared she would study and act that part the
following winter at Drury Lane," wrote Wilkinson.

In September 1785 Dorothy arrived in London with her mother, her small daughter
Frances, and her sister Hester. Dorothy came
into a theatre in which Mrs Sarah Siddons was
the unquestioned Melpomene. After a slow
initial start, Dorothy was destined to become
Thalia to the theatrical paragraphers. She
would remain a popular favorite for nearly 30
years. Her debut role, on 18 October 1785,
was the one she had so carefully prepared—
Peggy in *The Country Girl*, "not acted these
twelve years," and so a well-calculated novelty
to London audiences. It was repeated a dozen
times, carefully distributed at widening inter-
vals over the season.

Dorothy's other parts that first season were

Harvard Theatre Collection

DOROTHY JORDAN as Peggy

engraving by Bartolozzi, after Romney

few but successful. She appeared seldom in tragedy, but her comedy lines were various. When she first played Viola in *Twelfth Night*, on 16 November, the *Public Advertiser's* critic applauded her versatility: "The great powers of Mrs. Jordan cannot be better displayed than in the wonderful contrast of her *Country Girl* and *Viola*. In one all archness and vivacity; in the other serious, gentle, tender and sentimental." On 21 November she gave Londoners her Imogen in *Cymbeline*, which she had first performed at Leeds on 25 July 1785. Her first essay at Drury Lane of Priscilla Tomboy in the afterpiece *The Romp* (perhaps the most distinctively Jordanian part in her repertoire) gained warm approval—and a caution—from the *Public Advertiser*: "Of the low comedy of Mrs. Jordan . . . we cannot say too much in . . . praise. Let her avoid an indulgence, however, in too much buffoonery." The managers steadily raised her pay.

A notation appears in the Folger Library's manuscript Drury Lane account book for 17 December 1785 showing her beginning salary: "List Rais'd Mrs. Gordom 13s/4d pr Diem," i.e., £4 per six-day week. Her first benefit, on 28 April 1786, grossed £205 2s. 1d., a respectable showing, and before the end of the season she was making £8 per week. Periodical citations of the Folger accounts will suffice to show her financial progress: 14 March 1789, "Mrs. Jordan 2 Nights at £10:0:0 pr night." That rate obtained through 1791–92. From 1792–93 through 1794 she was paid £31 10s. for each week's acting. In 1795–96, acting sometimes four nights, sometimes five, she got £10 10s. a night. She had by now been granted a "free" benefit each season—without the large charges for use of the theatre which others were obliged to pay.

In 1796 Mrs Jordan's night earned her £658 19s. 6d. "Mrs Jordan's clear night" on 22 April 1799 amounted to £706 5s. 6d. By 1802–3 she was acting four nights a week for £57 15s. Her benefit receipts, though not as high as in 1795–96, were usually between £300 and £400, and in the 1804–5 season were £623 18s. 6d. and in 1805–6 £608 7s. In addition, she charged a substantial fee of £10 or £15 to act in benefits. In September 1807 she was dropped down to £30 for a six-day acting week but had "the privilege of writing orders—unlimited," when she engaged for the following

two years. In the provinces, where she toured nearly every summer for many years and also accepted winter engagements of one or several contiguous nights, her fees were often very high.

At Drury Lane from 1785–86 through 1808–1809 Mrs Jordan added to her repertoire the following roles: in 1785–86, Miss Peggy in *The Country Girl*, Viola in *Twelfth Night*, Rosalind in *The Jubilee*, Priscilla Tomboy in *The Romp*, Imogen in *Cymbeline*, Bellario in *Philaster*, Rosa in *The Strangers at Home*, Hippolita in *She Wou'd and She Wou'd Not* (according to the Reverend John Genest, "one of Mrs. Jordan's best characters—when I was introduced to her in 1814, and expressed the great pleasure I used to have in seeing her in Hippolita, 'Aye,' said she, 'that was one of the parts on which I used to pique myself.'"), Widow Brady in *The Irish Widow*; in 1786–87, Matilda in *Richard Coeur de Lion*, Miss Prue in

Harvard Theatre Collection

DOROTHY JORDAN as Sir Harry Wildair by unknown engraver; after William Chalmers

Love for Love, Roxolana in *The Sultan*, Rosalind in *As You Like It*; in 1787–88, Juletta in *The Pilgrim*, Sir Harry Wildair in *The Constant Couple*; in 1788–89, Corinna in *The Confederacy*, the original Beatrice in *The Pannell*, John Kemble's alteration of Bickerstaff's *'Tis Well It's No Worse*, Nell in *The Devil to Pay*, Eleanor in *The Impostors*, William in *Rosina*, Lady Bell in *Know Your Own Mind*, the first Aura in *The Farm House*, J. P. Kemble's version of Charles Johnson's *Country Lasses*; in 1789–90, the original Little Pickle in *The Spoiled Child*, sometimes ascribed to her, but probably by Isaac Bickerstaff (it was the part by which she was longest remembered), Helena in *Love in Many Masks*, the original Miss Plinlimmon in *The Welsh Heiress*, a comedy by Edward Jerningham, Lydia Languish in *The Rivals*; in 1790–91, Lettice in *The Intriguing Chambermaid*, the original Augusta Reynolds in Andrews's *Better Late than Never*.

In 1791–92, she added Fatima in *Cymon*, the original Julia Wingrove in Richardson's *The Fugitive*, Letitia Hardy in *The Belle's Stratagem*; in 1792–93, Amanthis in *The Child of Nature*, Lady Contest in *The Wedding Day*, Cowslip in *The Agreeable Surprise*, the title character in *The Old Maid*, the original Sabina Rosny in Richard Cumberland's comedy *First Love*; in 1795–96, the original Flavia in W. H. Ireland's spurious "Shakespearean" tragedy *Vortigern*, Fidelia in *The Plain Dealer*, Juliet in *Romeo and Juliet*; in 1796–97, the original Albina Mandeville in Frederick Reynolds's comedy *The Will*, Ophelia in *Hamlet*, the original Letitia Manfred in Cumberland's *The Last of the Family*, Lady Teazle in *The School for Scandal*; in 1797–98, the original Sir Edward Bloomly in *Cheap Living*, a comedy by Reynolds, the original Angela in M. G. Lewis's melodrama *The Castle Spectre*, the original Susan in Thomas Holcroft's comedy *Knave or Not*, Estifania in *Rule a Wife and Have a Wife*, Bisarre in *The Inconstant*, the original Miss Villeure in John O'Keeffe's comedy, *She's Eloped!*, Beatrice in *Much Ado about Nothing*, Susan in *The Follies of a Day*, Dorinda in *The Tempest*.

In 1798–99 Mrs Jordan added Maria in *The Citizen*, the original Cora in R. B. Sheridan's *Pizarro*, Lady Harriet in *The Funeral*, Zorayda in *The East Indian*; in 1799–1800, the original Julia in Prince Hoare's *Indiscretion*, Miss Hardcastle in *She Stoops to Conquer*; in 1800–1801,

the original Imogen in M. G. Lewis's *Adelmorn the Outlaw*, the title role in *Nina*, Lady Rackett in *Three Weeks After Marriage*, Jacinta in *Lovers' Quarrels*, Biddy Tipkin in *The Tender Husband*; in 1801–2, Miss Rackett in *Fashionable Friends*, Violante in *The Wonder*, Mrs Sullen in *The Beaux' Stratagem*, Miranda in *The Busy Body*, Widow Belmour in *The Way to Keep Him*; in 1802–3, Sophia in *The Road to Ruin*, the original Eliza in *Hear Both Sides*, a comedy by Holcroft, the original Emma in Allingham's farce *The Marriage Promise*, Flora in *The Midnight Hour*; in 1803–4, the first Widow Cheerly in *The Soldier's Daughter*, a comedy by Andrew Cherry, the original Louisa Davenant in Cumberland's *The Sailor's Daughter*, Rosetta in *The Foundling*; in 1804–5, Clara in *Matrimony*, the original Lady Lovelace in Holt's *The Land We Live In*, Belinda in *All in the Wrong*; in 1805–6, Mrs Hamilton in *The School for Friends*, Second Constantia in *The Chances*; in 1807–8, Lady Bloomfield in Kenney's *The World*, Cicely Homespun in *The Heir-at-Law*; and in 1808–9, Helen in S. J. Arnold's comedy *Man and Wife*.

Mrs Jordan's last original role was not at Drury Lane but at Covent Garden, on 20 April 1814, when she played Barbara Green in Kenney's *Debtor and Creditor*. She played at the English theatre in Brussels in September 1814 and gave a final series of 10 performances at Margate in July and August 1815. Not in London alone was she a conqueror. She became a national British institution, sallying forth summer after summer to act in the principal cities and towns of England, Scotland, and Wales. Medals were struck in her honor at Edinburgh and Glasgow.

After her first few seasons, Dorothy Jordan was in every sense a "star," almost automatically commanding the leading female roles in comedy and farce when she chose. But she was also a generous and cooperative repertory player. Some of her most memorable roles— particularly that of the schoolboy Little Pickle (which became an affectionate nickname) in the farce *The Spoiled Child*—were in dramatic trifles and would have been inconsiderable in other hands.

Dorothy was never classically beautiful. Though in her youth she had a small, neat figure and was a celebrated performer of "breeches parts," as time went on she grew corpulent. Her attractions were a voice of compelling sweetness, an infectious laugh, and a radiant stage personality.

The often-savage critic John Williams (writing as "Anthony Pasquin") in *The Children of Thespis* (1792) congratulated the Drury Lane management on acquiring her:

Behold sportive JORDAN, *that favourite fair,*
Who was sent by kind Fate to avert your despair:
With her you've successfully baited your trap;
She's in truth the best feather you have in your cap.
How you got her, to me, I must own, is a wonder!
When I think of your natural aptness to blunder.
She must have been forc'd on you, maugre your
*   sighing,*
As they give children physic in spite of their crying.
*   Be wise, if you wish she should add to your*
*   store,*
Let her put on MELPOMENE'S *buskins no more*
Tho' the Scion could play ev'ry character well,
You should keep her in those where she's own'd to
*   excel;*
For IMOGEN'S *woes, or fair* VIOLA'S *wit,*

The decrees of Propriety mark'd her unfit:
Let her polish those talents which Heaven has sent
*   her,*
And the ROMP *prove the climax to* MOODY'S
*   TORMENTOR.*
Be that her ne plus—*keep her actions in view,*
Lest she wander in labyrinths wanting a clew.
As she's mounted the summit of public applause,
Preserve her importance and husband the cause

. . . .
'Mid the wilds of blithe Nature she wanders alone,
And oft gathers flowrets to Culture unknown.

. . . .
*   In* NELL *sportive Nature's rude habits are*
*   shown,*
And the rose of vulgarity flushes full blown.
Not a ray issues forth from her keen sable eye,
But gives all the race of Refinement the lye.
The broad jolly rapture she paints with such
*   truth,*
That Surliness grins, and bares wide his foul tooth:
Yet her name's not been rais'd by illiberal arts,
She came 'fore the audience, and rush'd to their
*   hearts:*

William Hazlitt said only more eloquently what all her admirers—that is nearly all who saw her and wrote of her—seemed to seek to convey, as he wrote of

Mrs. Jordan, the child of nature, whose voice was a cordial to the heart, because it came from it, rich, full, like the luscious juice of the ripe grape; to hear whose laugh was to drink nectar; whose smile "made a sunshine," not "in the shady place," but amidst dazzling lights and in glad theatres;—who "talked far above singing," and whose singing was like the twang of Cupid's bow. Her person was large, soft, and generous like her soul. . . . It was her capacity for enjoyment, and the contrast she presented to every thing sharp, angular, and peevish, that communicated the same genial heartfelt satisfaction to the spectator. Her Nell, for instance, was right royal. . . . She was Cleopatra turned into an oyster-wench, such as she was, would have been equal to a Cleopatra; and an Antony would not have deserted her for the empire of the world.

Charles Lamb lamented:

Those who have only seen Mrs Jordan within the last ten or fifteen years, can have no adequate notion of her performance of such parts as Ophelia; Helena, in All's Well that Ends Well; and Viola. Her voice had latterly acquired a coarseness, which suited well enough with her Nells and Hoydens, but in those days it sank, with her steady, melting eye, into the heart. . . . There is no giving an

Harvard Theatre Collection

DOROTHY JORDAN

engraving by Clamp, after Chalmers

account of how she delivered the disguised story of her love for Orsino. It was no set speech, that she had foreseen, so as to weave it into an harmonious period . . . but, when she had declared her sister's history to be a "blank," and that "she never told her love," there was a pause, as if the story had ended— and then the image of the "worm in the bud" came up as a new suggestion—and the heightened image of "Patience" still followed after that, as by some growing (and not mechanical) process, thought springing up after thought, I would almost say, as they were watered by her tears.

Leigh Hunt also singled out her Ophelia for special praise:

Nothing can be more natural or pathetic than the complacent tones and busy goodnature of Mrs Jordan in the derangement of *Ophelia*; her little bewildered songs in particular, like all her songs indeed, pierce to our feelings with a most original simplicity. . . . Mrs Jordan seems to speak with all her soul; her voice, pregnant with melody, delights the ear with a peculiar and exquisite fulness and with an emphasis that appears the result of perfect conviction. . . . Her laughter is the happiest and most natural on the stage; if she is to laugh in the middle of a speech, it does not separate itself so abruptly from her words, as with most of our performers; . . . her laughter intermingles itself with her words, as fresh ideas furnish her fresh merriment; she does not so much indulge as she seems unable to help it.

Such attractions, combined with such a guileless and pliant disposition, naturally laid Dorothy open to lifelong exploitation from her lovers and her relatives. The exploitation was usually financial, often emotional as well. On 22 April 1809 she wrote to James Boaden: "From my first starting in life, at the early age of fourteen, I have always had a large family to support. My mother was a duty. But on brothers and sisters I have lavished more money than can be supposed, and more, I am sorry to say, than I can well justify to those who have a stronger and prior claim to my exertions." She worked until the last year of her life and those exertions earned enormous sums, adding up, she once estimated, to over £100,000.

Invariably, Dorothy's relationships were from their beginnings unusually complicated and grew more so as time went on. Her brief and disastrous liaison with Richard Daly has been described. It had left her with the daughter, Frances. Not long after she came to London in 1785 or 1786, she began a relationship with a young barrister, Richard Ford, son of the Court physician, Dr James Ford, a financial backer of Drury Lane Theatre. In 1787 the couple moved into a house at No 5, Gower Street, and later acquired a summer place at Richmond. Whether or not Ford promised to marry her as has been repeatedly asserted, he never did so. He shared her earnings and gave her three children—Dorothea Maria Ford, born in August 1787; a son, who died at birth, in October or November 1788; and Lucy Hester Ford, born sometime in 1789.

In 1790 Ford relinquished her to the Duke of Clarence. By a deed of settlement dated 4 November 1791 Dorothy transferred all her savings to Ford and her sister Hester for the maintenance and education of her children, promised to allow them £550 a year, began paying Hester an allowance of £50 a year, and installed her with the children in a house in Brompton. Even as she made these arrangements she was being attacked by the newspapers for "deserting" her children for a royal lover. The Duke of Clarence, near the end of November 1791, wrote a note to John Palmer asking him to use his influence with the editor of *The Morning Herald* to make him stem the slander in that paper. Richard Ford signed and published an affidavit declaring that Mrs Jordan's "conduct [towards her children] has . . . been as laudable, generous, and as like a fond mother as . . . it was possible to be. She has indeed given up for their use every sixpence she has been able to save from her theatrical profits." Neither the Duke's request nor Ford's affidavit had much effect. When illness prevented her playing at Drury Lane on 26 November 1791 the audience grew riotous. On 30 November she sent the following letter to several London newspapers:

I have submitted in silence to the unprovoked and unmanly abuse which, for some time past, has been directed against me, because it has related to subjects about which the public could not be interested; but to an attack upon my conduct in my profession, and charge of want of respect and gratitude to the public, I think it my duty to reply.

Nothing can be more cruel and unfounded than the insinuation that I absented myself from the theatre on Saturday last from any other cause than inability, from illness, to sustain my part in the entertainment. I have ever been ready and proud to exert myself to the utmost of my strength, to fulfill

The Iveagh Bequest, Kenwood

DOROTHY JORDAN as Viola

by Hoppner

my engagements with the theatre and to manifest my respect for the audience; and no person can be more grateful for the indulgence and applause with which I have been constantly honoured. I would not obtrude upon the public an allusion to anything which does not relate to my profession, in which *alone*, I may without assumption say, I am accountable to them; but thus called on, in the present instance, there can be no impropriety in my answering those who have so ungenerously attacked me, that if they could drive me from that profession they would take from me the ONLY INCOME I have, or mean to possess, the whole earnings of which, upon the past, and one-half for the future, I have already settled upon my CHILDREN. Unjustly and cruelly traduced as I have been upon this subject, I trust that this short declaration will not be deemed impertinent; and, for the rest, I appeal with confidence to the justice and generosity of the public.

Yet she was hissed when she returned to the stage on 10 December. She stepped resolutely forward and spoke:

Ladies and Gentlemen,—I should conceive myself utterly unworthy of your favour if the slightest mark of public disapprobation did not affect me very sensibly. Since I have had the honour and the happiness to please you, it has been my constant endeavour by unremitting assiduity to merit your approbation. I beg leave to assure you, upon my honour, that I have never absented myself one minute from the duties of my profession but from real indisposition. Thus having invariably acted, I do consider myself under the public protection.

She was applauded, and the furor, for the time, subsided. But throughout her association with the Duke, a period of nearly twenty years, she was from time to time subjected to ribald comment in the popular press; and many vulgar caricatures of her and Clarence, and their growing family, were published—frequently riding in some equipage on the door of which was shown a coat of arms featuring a chamberpot (a "jordan"). She learned not to respond, but she always suffered. Her feelings were salved, however, by her great popularity with the theatre-going public wherever she played.

Since the adoring James Boaden, successive generations of biographers have served as the kind of apologists whom she does not need. There is no good evidence that she did not enter her relationships with men warmly and willingly, prepared to make each *affaire* a permanent one. The observation is particularly true of the union with the Duke of Clarence which, had it been with a less exalted personage, would have amounted to a common-law marriage. There is some reason to think that, had it not been for the Royal Marriage Act, he would have made her his morganatic wife. For even though he was the most dedicated of

Harvard Theatre Collection

DOROTHY JORDAN as Hippolita

engraving by Jones, after Hoppner

rakes before he met Dorothy Jordan, he seems to have settled into a careful husband and devoted father afterward. In their twenty years together Dorothy and Prince William produced 10 children. During most of that time, she was also theatrically engaged.

At first the public saw her as a royal concubine, supported by the public purse. (An anecdote which has hung on with such surprising hardihood that one hopes it is true concerns the alleged attempt of George III to reduce by half the annuity of £1000 agreed upon by his son. Dorothy is supposed to have rejected the King's attempted retrenchment by tearing off and sending back to him the bottom part of a playbill which bore the admonition: "No money returned after rising of the curtain.") Very quickly the public attitude shifted to one directly opposite, which most biographers, led by Dorothy's friend James Boaden, eagerly adopted: Mrs Jordan was kept unwillingly at work on the stage earning vast sums to support a profligate prince. But no one has ever been able to describe authoritatively the state of the couple's finances. Even A. Aspinall, who comes closest (in *Mrs. Jordan and Her Family, Being the Unpublished Correspondence of Mrs. Jordan and the Duke of Clarence*, 1951), furnishes banking accounts which seem to contradict each other. But the accounts, and the letters, seem also to point to the judgment that Mrs Jordan when she toured sent massive amounts of money home. Most certainly a portion of it was for her own debts and insurance policies, and a great deal of it was for her children by Daly and Ford and for other members of her family. There is no doubt that for years she and her children by the Duke (while they remained in her care) received generous allowances. But it is also clear that Clarence borrowed very large sums at interest from Dorothy, and the bookkeeping on those transactions, as on the sizable cash payments she received from provincial managers, is virtually nonexistent. Both she and the Duke were extravagant. He had a very limited allowance from the royal exchequer. Debts mounted on both sides. When Dorothy died she was near bankruptcy.

The many surviving letters between "Dora" and the Duke in the possession of the Earl of Munster and of the Henry E. Huntington Library provide an appealing sketch of a warm and humorous woman, a fine professional, a shrewd bargainer, and an anxious mother and devoted consort. They show the strain she was under and the dangers and hardships she endured as she left the house at Bushy Park, which the King had given his son in 1797, to take short and profitable provincial engagements for the sake of her growing family. In 1801 she narrowly escaped injury when her carriage overturned. At the Margate Theatre on 27 August 1802 her clothing caught on fire onstage. She wrote the Duke on 31 August "I was near being burnt to death, my gown being in flames up to the waist so that I concluded my last scene in my peticoat." In 1809 she acted for a long period with a voice painfully hoarse: "I fear I caught cold in the Bristol theatre, where there is a fire but once a week." Lodging in Liverpool in that year she and her daughter Lucy were given a room divided by a thin partition from the next where a woman

"was taken in labour at one o'clock. Her bedstead was exactly close to mine, so that it was just as distressing as being in the room." She "went through (in idea) the whole business" for seven hours. Habitually rising by five-thirty, standing rehearsing all morning with painfully swollen ankles, bringing to life five characters a week, sometimes two a night, in five or six performances, she often moved about the country on the brink of exhaustion.

But these hazards and vexations were small compared to the anguish she suffered over her frequent separations from the children when they were young. Her anxieties increased when her two eldest sons by the Duke joined the fighting in Europe against Napoleon, Henry in the Royal Navy (his father's old service in which the Duke was now refused active duty) and George with the Army in the bloody and disastrous Peninsula campaign. George was wounded and taken prisoner at Talavera in 1809. But there were sustaining satisfactions to "cruising" (as she called it) in the provinces, especially the money. At Bath in the spring of 1809, for instance, despite a huge unseasonable fall of snow and then a flood when it melted, she cleared 800 guineas acting from 11 April to 2 May.

Mrs Jordan's Dublin engagement in the summer of 1809 will stand as typical for both the vexations and the triumphs. She made over £1400 by the trip (but had to leave £400 behind to pay for debts her brothers James and George had contracted). On 10 June she wrote to the Duke:

I rehearsed today and was addressed by a very *old man* who was standing at the *wing*. . . . It was the very person that brought me on the stage the first night I played. He reminded me of my running off the stage behind the scenes, and his following me, and bringing me forward by *main force*. He is not a little *proud of this*.

She was warmly entertained by Sir Jonah Barrington's family and others. Feeling ill, she sent for a physician, who turned out to be the one who had treated her measles, long ago. She played despite his advice. He gave her 60 drops of laudanum when she came off. Her audiences adored her, but she found them rude and repellent with their frequent fights in the gallery. Some other forms of adoration, though flattering, were even less acceptable. She wrote the Duke that she had been approached by a nervous emissary of the Lord Lieutenant, the Duke of Richmond, who regretted "that his *situation prevented* his doing himself the pleasure of calling on me, but that he should consider himself very much *flattered* and *extremely happy* if I would allow him to call *on me alone*, at half past 12 *that night*." She admonished the Duke of Clarence to ignore the overture, as she had done.

Jones offered her £100 a night and a second free benefit if she would extend her engagement for a week. But, tired of Irish food and customs and worn out with playing, she terminated "the most tiresome business I ever undertook," again endured a miserable crossing of St George's Channel, and, by way of Liverpool, Leicester, and Chester, came back home.

Each year seemed more arduous than the one before. Dorothy was often ill with stomach disorders and migraines but shook them off. "My throat is better, but I am quite hoarse"; she omitted scenes from the farce, therefore. "I was very unwell for a few hours, but shall start again on Monday. I should, I am sure, have made an excellent soldier. . . ." In 1811, she wrote from Worcester: "I shall have made £1007. This is certainly a large sum, but I can assure you I have worked very hard for it." From Cheltenham in 1811 she expressed her ardent wish to retire, as Mrs Siddons was about to do: "I envy her, but I cannot give it up yet, indeed I must not, however distressing it may be to me. . . ." Her expenses mounted with the growing inflation: "I pay 5 gs. per week for two *rooms*. . . ." On 1 October 1811, lamenting a wet day and a thin house at Cheltenham, she wrote:

Money, money, cruel money, since my first setting out in the world at the age of 13, at a *moderate calculation*, I have spun *fairly and honestly* out of my own brains above £100,000, and still, this cruel *pelf* robs me of even comfort and *happiness*, as I verily believe we have nothing to do with our *own fate*. I may fairly say what a strange one mine has been, and *is likely to be*.

The reflection was prescient. In her private life Dorothy Jordan's cheerful generosity and impulsive kindness were well known. Though she grumbled about her expensive relatives she never deserted them in their scrapes. She wrote to the Duke in 1807: "When I reflect on the trouble, *expence and vexation* I have suffered on the account of my brother [George] and sister [Hester] since I was 14 years old, I am more surprised than *satisfied* at *my patience*." She gave each of her daughters £10,000 for dowry. She had a fond relationship to William, the Duke's son by another woman, and grieved when he went down with the *Blenheim* in 1807. She extended her motherly concern to unhappy young George FitzErnest, the Duke of Cumberland's natural son, and even to foundlings. On 30 January 1814 she wrote her son George from Bath: "I am now going to see cloathed a poor wretched little boy that was dug out of the snow—not so big as Tuss [her son Augustus, then nine years old]. I mean to send him to London by waggon & put him into some charity school."

Mrs Jordan's dealings with managers were tough-minded and resolute. Her admirer, the easy-going Tate Wilkinson, in his whimsical way chided her in *The Wandering Patentee*: "But now, dear Mrs. Jordan, you do like the cash, and I believe and hope you take care of it; that you love to receive it I know, and so does every other manager; you *have* made us all know that." But if her needs—and her constant, driven, defensive comparison of her art with the art of Mrs Siddons—made her demand high salaries, she knew that she drew large houses. However, her generosity was available even to managers, though she in her turn felt that they "have no mercy on one." At Richmond in November 1809, after the company drew small attendance because of the lateness of the season, she declared to the Duke that she could not "think of exacting the 20 gs. per night. This would indeed be nearly as bad as Mrs. Siddons. I could not have the heart to do it; the man has six small children and is very poor. . . ." (The allusion is a report that Dorothy had heard that, earlier in the fall, Mrs Siddons—whose fee was £30—had just played to a thirty-one-pound house and expected her fee, "so that the miserable manager made £1." Dorothy received the news eagerly, like all reports which showed the Kemble family in a bad light.)

Dorothy had wit as well as courage and generosity, as her letters also show. Her trust in the Duke's faithfulness was sound enough for her to rally him on the subject. On 15

From the collection of Edward A. Langhans

"Fording the Jordan"

engraving after Gillray

December 1810, she wrote: "I like the new maid, Mrs. Reynolds, *very much*. She has two great requisites (I think) for a ladies maid; she is very attentive and *very ugly*. Perhaps the latter qualification you may not think so necessary, but that is the very reason that I *do*."

The Duke's need for money, always pressing, became acute. In 1811, in order to begin the fruitless pursuit of heiresses which made him the butt of another series of leaders and caricatures, he asked Mrs Jordan to meet him at Maidenhead to discuss terms of a separation.

On 23 December 1811 an agreement was executed which gave her £600 a year for a house and carriage, £1500 a year for the maintenance of her four daughters by the Duke, and £200 a year for each of her other three daughters. Dorothy was to forego acting. If she should return to the stage she would lose custody of the Duke's daughters and their maintenance money (and so she did when she returned to the stage in 1812).

Many even of the royal family sympathized with Mrs Jordan, and some found the behavior of the Duke reprehensible. Dorothy thought the blame lay with a ministry which would not relieve his financial situation. She moved out of the house at Bushy Park and into one in Cadogan Place. Her life plunged into fresh difficulties. A wastrel son-in-law, Thomas Alsop, married to her daughter Fanny, had to be provided a place in India and his debts at home had to be paid. Dorothy reluctantly went back to acting, and the Duke's daughters went back to their father. After a provincial tour in 1812 she secured an engagement at Covent Garden. Her debut there on 10 February 1813 was greeted with warm applause by the audience but excited a vicious attack by the *Times*, to which she replied with a dignified letter. Her retort gained her great support in the other journals. But Fanny Alsop began to take drugs, a practice which would eventually cause her death; she also acquired an illegitimate child.

Dorothy's sons George and Henry Fitz Clarence were posted to India, exiled for their part in exposing the incompetence of their Colonel (Henry had transferred to the Army). It took £3000 for outfitting to get them out to India, which Dorothy probably supplied. They left in March 1815, and she would not see them again. The Napoleonic War had regenerated and her son Frederick joined his regiment. She signed blank bonds and promissory notes for what she thought would be small amounts in favor of her trusted and favorite son-in-law, Dora's husband, Frederick March. March swindled her. In panic, and apparently at the suggestion of Sir John Barton, the agent of the Duke of Clarence, Dorothy sold the lease of her house and her furnishings and fled to France, accompanied only by a companion, Miss Sketchly, who had been her children's

governess. Living under the name "Mrs James," first at a village near Boulogne-sur-Mer, she moved to Versailles at the end of 1815, then to St Cloud, all the time waiting anxiously for some word that it was safe to return. Her only comfort was the presence for a short period of her 16-year-old son Frederick, whose regiment was in Paris. No word ever came, and despair accelerated the decline of her already failing health.

Early on the morning of 5 July 1816 Dorothy Jordan died. Eight hastily-gathered English residents of Paris attended her coffin to the cemetery at St Cloud. Her personal possessions at Paris were sold off by order of the French police. Her estate at London was administered *ex officio* by the King's solicitor. Its value was under £300.

Mrs Jordan gave birth to at least fourteen children. By Richard Daly she had Frances (Fanny), born in September 1782, who changed her name to Frances Bettesworth in 1806 and in 1808 married Thomas Alsop. Fanny was separated from her husband, took to the stage, and died (probably from an overdose of laudanum) in America in 1821.

Richard Ford fathered Dorothea Maria, born in August 1787, who married Frederick Edward March in 1809, and Lucy Hester Ford, born in 1789, who in 1810 married Samuel Hawker, later General Sir Samuel Hawker. Dorothy Bland's son by Richard Ford died at birth in October or November of 1788.

Mrs Jordan had 10 children by the Duke of Clarence. The eldest was George Augustus Frederick Fitz Clarence, born on 29 January 1794. He married May Wyndham, natural daughter of the Earl of Egremont. He had a gallant and distinguished career as a soldier in the Napoleonic campaigns and in India. In 1831 he was raised to the peerage as the Earl of Munster. He committed suicide on 20 March 1842.

Henry Edward Fitz Clarence, born on 27 March 1795, died a captain in India in September 1817. Sophia Fitz Clarence, Dorothy Jordan's first daughter by the Duke, was born in August 1796, in 1825 married the first Baron De Lisle and Dudley, and died on 10 April 1837. Mary Fitz Clarence, born on 19 December 1798, married in 1824 Charles Richard Fox, later a general, a natural son of the third Lord Holland. Mary died on 13 July 1864.

Lord Frederick Fitz Clarence was born on 9 December 1799; he became a lieutenant general. In 1821 he married Lady Augusta Boyle, daughter of George, Earl of Glasgow. He died 30 October 1854. His sister Elizabeth Fitz Clarence, born on 17 January 1801, married William George, Earl of Erroll, in 1820. She died on 16 January 1856.

Adolphus Fitz Clarence, born 18 February 1802, rose to the rank of rear admiral on active service in the navy. He died on 17 May 1856. Augusta Fitz Clarence was born on 17 November 1803. In 1827 she married the Hon John Kennedy Erskine, second son of the Marquess of Silsa, who died in 1831; in 1836 she married Lord Frederick Gordon, who assumed the name of Hallyburton. She died on 8 December 1865.

Augustus Fitz Clarence, born 1 March 1805, took orders and became rector of Mapledurham. He married Sarah Elizabeth Catherine, a daughter of Lord Henry Gordon, in 1845 and died in 1854. The last of the siblings, Amelia Fitz Clarence, was born on 21 March 1807, married Lucius, Viscount Falkland in 1830, and died on 2 July 1858.

Portraits of Dorothy Jordan include:

1. By J. T. Barber. Miniature exhibited at the Royal Academy in 1799 (No. 880). Present location unknown. Engraving by W. Ridley, published as a plate to the *Monthly Mirror*, December 1804.

2. By William Chalmers. Half-length drawing; wearing a miniature of the Duke of Clarence. Present location unknown. Engraving by R. Clamp, published as frontispiece to Carey's *Dupes of Fancy*, 1792.

3. By Richard Cosway. Miniature in the possession of the Earl of Munster.

4. By Gainsborough Dupont. (Previously attributed to Romney.) In the Garrick Club (No 370). Presented in 1887 by Mrs Fitzgerald of Sharlestane Manor, Buckinghamshire.

5. By Thomas Gainsborough. In the possession of Lord Northbrook.

6. By John Hoppner. Exhibited at the Royal Academy in 1786 (No 173) as "Mrs. Jordan in the Character of the Comic Muse, supported by Euphrosyne, who represses the advance of a Satyr." Formerly at Hampton Court, now at Buckingham Palace, in the Collection of Her Majesty, Queen Elizabeth II. Engraving by T. Park, published 1787. Another plate, with the figure of Euphrosyne omitted, by an unknown artist, was published in *La Belle Assemblée*, 1814; a half-length engraving of the same was also published, undated.

7. By John Hoppner. Oil on canvas (30 × 25), half-figure, nearly full face, looking to right; in crimson dress cut low, left arm bare to elbow. Described by McKay and Roberts in *John Hoppner, R. A.* (1914). In 1914 this portrait was in the Beef-Steak collection of Paddy Green; once it had been in Sir Henry Irving's collection in the Green Room of the Lyceum Theatre. It was illustrated in Sedelmeyer's *Six Hundred Paintings* (1900), No. 93.

8. By John Hoppner. Oil on canvas (50 × 40), three-quarter figure seated in a landscape; in low-cut white dress with short sleeves, a gold-colored glove on right hand and arm; holding in hands the strings of a satchel which rests on her lap. This picture, exhibited at the Royal Academy in 1796, was sold in the Hoppner sale in 1823 (lot 18). In 1953 it was in the hands of Messrs French & Co, New York, who sold it to a private collector. It was sold at Sotheby's on 17 July 1974 (lot 103) and is reported to be in the collection of Edward Stotesbury, Philadelphia. A photograph in color was published in *The Connoisseur*, March 1953.

9. By John Hoppner. Oil on canvas (30 × 25), half-figure to left, looking forward; in black and grayish-brown dress, cut low, and edged with white lace. Bought at the John F. Talmadge sale in New York on 20 February 1913 (lot 23) for $21,000 by Messrs Knoedler & Co; illustrated in the sales catalogue. In the collection of W. K. Bixby of St Louis in 1914.

10. By John Hoppner. Sketch at Bushey House, Middlesex (Department of the Environment).

11. By George Morland. Canvas (14 × 17), unsigned, undated. Exhibited at Burlington House, 1870, at Dowdeswell's Galleries, Bond Street, 1894. In 1907 the portrait was owned by F. Abbiss Phillips, Manor House, Stoke d'Abernon, Cobham, Surrey. Perhaps the same as No 42, below.

12. By R. K. Porter, c. 1800. As the Comic Muse. Present location unknown. Engraving by J. Godby, published by E. Orme, 1806.

13. By George Romney. Depicts her resting

her right elbow upon her knee, her hand touching chin. Called Mrs Jordan, but perhaps not. Sold by Sir W. Cuthbert Quilter at Christie's in July 1909; bought for 4800 guineas by Maurice Ruffer. Auctioned with Ruffer collection at Christie's on 29 April 1932. Present location unknown. Illustrated in *The Magazine of Art*, June 1897. A cut-down version, half-figure, was in the Ismay Collection, Dawpool, Thurstaton, Birkenhead, in 1909.

14. By George Romney. Shows Mrs Jordan's left hand resting on her right shoulder; in white muslin dress. Owned by Lady Northwick at Northwick Park in 1909.

15. By George Romney. Half-length, wearing white dress with black girdle, holding a sprig of orange blossom. Owned by Major General Mackenzie in 1909.

16. By George Romney. Seated, wearing blue sash; long tan gloves held in her left hand; marine background. Owned by Major General Mackenzie in 1909.

17. By John Russell. Playing guitar. Owned by Thomas Goff in 1965. Engraving by J. Heath, published 1802; a copy engraved by R. Page, with guitar omitted, was published by R. Souter, 1816; and another copy, with guitar omitted, was issued undated.

18. By John Russell. Owned by M. Bernstein of Paris in 1909.

19. By unknown artist. In a four-panel painting, with Anna Maria Crouch, Charles Lee Lewes, and Joseph Shepherd Munden. Once in the possession of the Earl of Munster; now in the Ashmolean Museum, Oxford.

20. By Francis Chantrey, c. 1831. Statue in marble of Mrs Jordan, with baby on her lap and a child at her knee. In the possession of the Earl of Munster. A picture of the statue is printed in Aspinall's *Mrs Jordan and Her Family*. In the Harvard Theatre Collection is an undated anonymous engraving of the statue.

21. Engraving by J. Condé. Published as a plate to *Thespian Magazine*, 1794.

22. Engraving by F. Crawley, after E. Smith. Published as a plate to *British Stage*, 1820. An undated copy by an unknown engraver was also issued.

23. Engraving by J. Heath. Published by J. Watts, 1787.

24. Engraving by K. Mackenzie, after R. Dighton. Published as a plate to *The Myrtle and the Vine*, 1800.

25. Engraving by Mackenzie. Published as a plate to the *Monthly Mirror*, 1805.

26. Engraving by R. Page. Published by Dean and Munday, 1816.

27. Engraving by A. Scratch, after Goles. Mrs Jordan as the Comic Muse. Published as a plate to *Attic Miscellany*, 1790 (Theatrical portraiture, No 7). Another impression of the same plate was issued with title "M^rs J——n as a Hoyden."

28. By unknown engraver. On a plate with another of Robert W. Elliston, marked "E. Smith, del.," published in Holcroft's *Theatrical Recorder*, 1805.

29. By unknown engraver. On a plate with another of Richard Daly, published in *Town and Country Magazine*, 1787.

30. By unknown engraver. On a plate with one of the Duke of Clarence and titled "The Juvenal Tar—The Spoil'd Child," undated.

31. By unknown engraver. Seated on the knee of the Duke of Clarence. Published as a plate to *Bon Ton Magazine*, November 1791.

32. As Belinda, with R. W. Elliston as Beverley, in *All in the Wrong*. Engraving by Alais. Published by Roach, 1808.

33. As Clara in *Matrimony*. By unknown engraver. Published as a plate to Holcroft's *Theatrical Recorder*, 1805.

34. As Cora, with babe in arms, in *Pizarro*. Painting by Samuel De Wilde. In the Mander and Mitchenson Theatre Collection, presented by Jenetta De Wilde, widow of the artist's great-grandson. Reproduced in Mander and Mitchenson's *A Picture History of the British Theatre*.

35. As Cora, standing, left arm extended; feathered coronet. Watercolor drawing by unknown artist. In the Harvard Theatre Collection.

36. As Cora, with child on ground. Engraving by Murray. Published by S. Roach. Not in Hall catalogue but in the Harvard Theatre Collection.

37. As Fidelia in *The Plain Dealer*. Engraving by P. Audinet, after J. Roberts. Published as a plate to Hawthorn's *British Drama*, 1798.

38. As Mrs Ford in *The Merry Wives of Windsor*. Watercolor by unknown artist. In the Harvard Theatre Collection.

39. As Hippolita in *She Wou'd and She Wou'd*

Not. By John Hoppner. In the possession of Sir Edward Stern in 1906. Engraving by J. Jones, published 1791.

40. As Hippolita. Engraving by J. Heath, after T. Stothard. Published by Lowndes, 1790.

41. As Hippolita. By unknown engraver.

42. As Isabella in *Isabella.* By G. Morland, unsigned and undated, but from c. 1800. In the possession of Mrs F. Abbiss Phillips in 1909. Engraving by T. S. Engleheart, on a plate with a picture of William IV, published by Cumberland; the same, without William IV, by an unknown engraver was issued as a plate to *The Casket,* 1837.

43. As Lady Bell, with R. W. Elliston as Millamour and Harriot Mellon as Lady Jane, in *Know Your Own Mind.* Engraving by C. Heath, after Singleton. Published by Longman and Co.

44. As Lady Bloomfield in *The World.* By unknown engraver. Published as a plate to Scales's edition of the play.

45. As Lucy in *The Virgin Unmask'd.* By unknown engraver. Published as a plate to an edition of the play, 1787.

46. As Lydia Languish in *The Rivals.* Engraving by Alais. Published by J. Roach, 1805.

47. As Matilda in *Richard Coeur de Lion.* According to W. J. Lawrence, in *The Connoisseur* (clipped article in the Enthoven Collection), John Hoppner painted her in this character and an engraving by H. Cook was published in 1832. Lawrence may have confused this work with the portrait by Hoppner now called Mrs Jordan as Viola in *Twelfth Night* (see below, No 77) and formerly called Mrs Jordan as Rosalind in *As You Like It.*

48. As Matilda, with John Philip Kemble as Richard, showing scene of Gothic castle and drawbridge. Engraving by Richardson. Published by A. Hogg, No 46, Paternoster Row, 28 February 1787.

49. As Nell in *The Devil to Pay,* with an actor. Sketch by unknown artist made during the performance at Cheltenham on the day Mrs Jordan heard the Duke of Clarence was to leave her. In the possession of Thomas Goff in 1965. Reproduced in B. Fothergill's *Mrs Jordan.*

50. As Nell. Engraving by J. Rogers, after Kennerley. Published as a plate to Oxberry's *Dramatic Biography,* 1825.

51. As Nell. Engraving by J. Rogers, after O. Steeden. Published as a plate to Oxberry's *New English Drama,* 1824.

52. As Nell. By unknown engraver. Published by J. Roach, 1802.

53. As Nell. By unknown engraver. Published by R. Butters as plate to an edition of the play, 1788.

54. As Miss Notable in *The Lady's Last Stake.* Engraving by Leney, after De Wilde.

55. As Peggy in *The Country Girl.* Engraving by Armstrong, after Moses. Published as a plate to *British Drama,* 1817.

56. As Peggy. Drawing by Cruikshank. Present location unknown. Engraving by Murray, published by Roach, 1799; engraving by Alais, published by Roach, 1806.

57. As Peggy. By Samuel De Wilde. In the Garrick Club. Engraving by Bromley, published as a plate to *Bell's British Library,* 1791.

58. As Peggy, with Richard Wroughton as Moody. Engraving by Fittler, after Singleton. Published by Longman and Co, 1806.

59. As Peggy. By George Romney, 1787. There are three versions of this portrait. The painting assumed to be the original was bought by the Duke of Clarence for 70 guineas on 26 November 1791. In 1830 he gave it to his daughter Lady Amelia Fitz Clarence upon her marriage to Viscount Falkland; in 1909 it was still in the Falkland collection. A second version, formerly owned by Mrs Jordan's eldest son, Colonel Fitz Clarence, first Earl of Munster, is now in the Rothschild bequest to the National Trust at Waddesdon Manor. A third version was owned by Sir Charles Tennant in 1894. According to manuscript notes by Sir Henry Russell, cited by Lawrence, Romney was capturing Mrs Jordan in an attitude she used as Priscilla Tomboy in *The Romp*; and Ogborne's engraving was published by Boydell in 1788 as such. But the print was later reissued as *The Country Girl* and the picture has been generally known by that title since. On another state of the engraving in the Harvard Theatre Collection Ogborne's name is erased and Bartolozzi's name substituted, in error we believe. Other engravings of Romney's portrait include: by W. H. Worthington, published as frontispiece to Mrs Jordan's *Life* by Boaden, 1831; by an unknown engraver, published with title "Mrs. Jordan as 'The Laughing Girl' from a picture by Cosway"; and by an un-

known engraver, published as a plate to *Dramatic Magazine*, 1830.

60. As Peggy. Engraving by Thornton. On the same plate with a portrait of Miss Brunton as Euphrasia in *The Grecian Daughter*. Published in the *New Lady's Magazine*, 1786.

61. As Peggy. Engraving by J. Wooding.

62. As Peggy. By unknown engraver. Published as a plate to *Lady's Magazine*, 1786.

63. As Peggy. By unknown engraver. (Hall catalogue, No 56.)

64. As Peggy. By unknown engraver. (Hall catalogue, No 57.)

65. As Phaedra in *Amphitryon*. Canvas by Samuel De Wilde. In the Garrick Club (No 223). Engraving by F. Audinet, published as a plate to *Bell's British Library*, 1792.

66. As Priscilla Tomboy in *The Romp*. Engraving by Carey, after Miller. Published by J. Carey, 1785.

67. As Priscilla Tomboy. Watercolor by Thomas Stothard. In the Huntington Library. Engraving by W. Angus, published by Lowndes, 1786; reverse by unknown engraver published as a plate to the *Lady's Magazine*, 1790.

68. As Priscilla Tomboy. By unknown engraver. (Hall catalogue, No 62.)

69. As Priscilla Tomboy. An unknown engraver. Published as a plate to an edition of the play, by R. Butters, 1785.

70. As Rosalind in *As You Like It*. Engraving by J. Alais, after R. Satchwell. Published as a plate to an edition of *Shakespeare*, by Roach, 1800.

71. As Rosalind. By John Hoppner. Now thought to be of her as Viola. See below, No 77.

72. As Roxalana in *The Sultan*. By unknown engraver.

73. As Sabina Rosny, with Richard Wroughton as Lord Sensitive, in *First Love*. Engraving by E. Smith, after Singleton. Published by Longman and Co, 1806.

74. As Sir Harry Wildair in *The Constant Couple*. By William Chalmers. Exhibited at the Royal Academy in 1790 (No 629). Probably the picture stippled by an unknown engraver, published by William Holland in 1788; described as very rare by Hall catalogue (No 68).

75. As Sir Harry Wildair. Watercolor by W.

Loftis, "Taken from Life . . . March 1789." In the Folger Shakespeare Library.

76. As Mrs Sullen, with John Bannister as Scrub and Dwyer as Archer, in *The Beaux' Stratagem*. Engraving by E. Smith, after C. Heath. Published by Longman and Co, 1806.

77. As Viola, dueling with Sir Andrew Aguecheek, in *Twelfth Night*. Drawing by Henry Bunbury. Represents the scene in a private production at Wynnstay. Present location unknown. Engraving by Charles Knight, published 1788.

78. As Viola. Oil on canvas by John Hoppner. In the Iveagh Bequest, Kenwood. Possibly the painting exhibited at the Royal Academy (No 81) in 1796 as "Portrait of a Lady." Sold at Christie's, from the Onley Savill Onley Collection, in 1894 for 1100 guineas, as a portrait of Mrs Jordan as Rosalind in *As You Like It*. Identified as Mrs Jordan as Viola in "The Georgian Playhouse" exhibition at the Hayward Gallery in 1975. Engraving by H. Cook, published in 1832 as a Lady in Character. (A penciled inscription on the British Museum's proof of Cook's engraving calls the picture Mrs Goodall as Frederick in *Lovers' Vows*.)

79. As Viola. By unknown engraver.

80. As the Widow Bellmour in *The Way to Keep Him*, playing on a lute. Engraving by Alais. Published by Roach, 1808.

81. As The Widow Bellmour, reading a book. Engraving by J. Chapman, after H. Moses. Published as a plate to *British Drama*, 1806.

A number of caricatures and satires of Mrs Jordan are indexed and described in *The Catalogue of Political and Personal Satires in the British Museum*. Among these are:

82. By James Gillray, entitled "La Promenade ler Famille—a Sketch from Life." It depicts Mrs Jordan walking along, reading, nonchalantly by a signpost, while the sweating Duke of Clarence pulls a go-cart full of babies and dogs.

83. By James Gillray, engraved after a drawing, entitled "The Devil to Pay—The Wife Metamorphos'd, or Neptune reposing, after Fording the Jordan." It depicts the Duke of Clarence up to his waist in a cracked chamber pot—"jordan"—looking over the edge at Dorothy, nude above the waist, reclined on a couch. Published 8 November 1791.

84. By unknown engraver, entitled "The

Spoilt Child." It depicts Dorothy standing, in breeches, nude above waist. Published as a plate to the *Man of Pleasure's Magazine*, February 1791.

85. By unknown engraver. Depicts Dorothy playing a piano and singing "Here's Songs of Love and Maids forsaken." Published by H. Humphrey, 24 October 1791.

Several portraits have mistakenly been identified as being of Mrs Jordan: Bartolozzi's engraving, after Cipriani, entitled "The Comic Muse" was issued in May 1785, before Dorothy made her debut in London; a portrait often called and exhibited as of Mrs Jordan by Lawrence is actually a portrait by Beechey of Princess Elizabeth, Landgravine of Hesse-Homburg (engraving by Cheesman); and a portrait by M. W. Peters in the J. Pierpont Morgan Collection (reproduced in *The Connoisseur Magazine*, February 1907), cannot be of Mrs Jordan, as sometimes catalogued. A mezzotint by J. R. Smith of the Peters painting was published, as "Love in Her Eye sits Playing," in May 1778, before Dorothy Francis, the future Mrs Jordan, became an actress. Peters's subject is a mature woman, not a sprightly teenager. Another portrait said to be of her is Romney's "Mirth" or "Allegro," a scene of a woman dancing, with four women playing triangles in the background; but when the picture was engraved by Dunkarton in 1771, Dorothy Jordan was a child.

Joseph, Mr [*fl.* 1746], *dancer.*
Mr Joseph danced at Sadler's Wells in April 1746, according to bills now in the British Library's Percival Collection.

Jossett, Mons [*fl.* 1749–1750], *dancer.*
Though the Covent Garden accounts cite the dancer Jossett as being paid £10 10s. for nine dates between 4 November 1749 and 24 March 1750, he was advertised as making his first appearance on the English stage on 7 February 1750, when he danced in *The Fair*. Earlier references to him may have concerned rehearsals. On 8 January 1750, a month before he made his first official appearance, the tailor, Mr Brodas, was cited in the accounts as making Jossett a dancing dress. In addition to appearing in *The Fair*, Jossett was in the *Mas-*

querade Dance in *Romeo and Juliet* on 1 March 1750 and in a *Dutch Dance* on 19 March.

Jossi. *See* JOZZI.

Joubert, T. [*fl.* 1791–1808], *dancer.*
The dancer "Juber" who on 26 May 1791 at the King's Theatre danced a pas seul and with Mlle Mozon a pas de deux was surely the dancer T. Joubert, who can be traced into the early years of the nineteenth century. The bill for the King's Theatre performance called Juber a principal dancer from France. Fuchs in his *Lexique* lists a dancer named Joubert who performed at the Hague in 1762 and, with his wife, was active into the 1780s on the Continent. Another Joubert led a troupe at Amiens in 1788, but he may not have been a dancer. In any case, there is not sufficient evidence to identify the London dancer with any other continental performer.

Joubert danced at the King's Theatre again in 1801–2 after an absence from the London stage for some years, and in 1802 he also appeared at Sadler's Wells. He was at the Wells again on 2 April 1804 and was mentioned in the Drury Lane accounts from 1805–6 through 1807–8 at £4 10s. weekly.

Joules, Mr [*fl.* 1781–1784], *actor.*
Mr Joules, surely of French extraction, played Simple in *The Merry Wives of Windsor* on 3 March 1781 at Covent Garden Theatre. He was employed there through 1783–84 but was not often mentioned in the bills. He is known to have been a Servant in *Duplicity*, a French Servant in *The Belle's Stratagem*, a French Soldier in *Henry V*, and Le Goût in *More Ways than One* (replacing Wewitzer on 18 May 1784—the last clear reference to him).

Jouron. *See* GAURON.

Jouve and **Jouvet.** *See* JOVEY.

Jovey, Mr [*fl.* 1799–1818], *double bass player.*
On 1 August 1799 the Drury Lane accounts show a payment to Mr Jovey, a member of the theatre band, of £2 0s. 10d., his arrears in pay for an unspecified period. Jovey was probably

the composer "Jouvet" who wrote the music for T. J. Dibdin's *Valentine and Orson*, performed at Covent Garden in 1804. "Jouve" was listed as a double bass player in the opera band at the King's Theatre in 1817 and 1818. There is a possibility that the musician referred to here was the French music teacher Jean Jousse (1765–1837), who resided in London after fleeing France at the Revolution, but a certain identification cannot be made.

"Jovial Pigmy, The." *See* COAN, JOHN.

Joy, Miss [*fl.* 1700], *strong woman. See* JOY, WILLIAM.

Joy, Richard [*fl.* 1699], *strong man. See* JOY, WILLIAM.

Joy, William 1675–1734, *strong man.*
William Joy (or Joyce) was born at St Lawrence, near Ramsgate, on 2 May 1675, according to the account of his life in Caulfield's *Remarkable Persons*. He showed great strength at an early age and by 1699 was exhibiting his feats in London. He excited a remarkable amount of attention, the papers giving him more space than the legitimate theatres. Tom Brown, writing facetiously to George Moult on 12 September 1699, complained about the lewdness of typical theatrical fare, which would surely kill the stage, "and the strong Kentish man will take possession of the two play-houses, as he has done of that in Dorset-Garden." Indeed, Joy exhibited his feats of strength to the London public at the rarely-used old Dorset Garden Theatre, and he showed himself as well at private parties, as on 15 November, when he performed before the King at Kensington. In December the King went to see Joy at the playhouse.

On 7 December 1699 Richard Joy (William's brother?) joined William in some feats of strength, and the London *Post* of 1–3 January 1700 carried an advertisement saying that the Kentish Strong Man's sister, a girl of 15, would be exhibited, her feat being to carry five bushels of wheat.

Most of the exhibitions of strength, however, were by William Joy himself, called sometimes "The English Sampson." Some of

Harvard Theatre Collection
WILLIAM JOY
engraving by Cook

his feats were described in the advertisements: "he drew against a horse, and lifted 20 hundred weight." He could be seen "lifting a weight of 2240*l*. Holding an extraordinary large Cart-Horse; and afterwards breaking a Rope that will bear 3500 weight." Sir Hans Sloane saw one of Joy's performances and was astounded that Joy "has nothing appears outwardly to give him such force." Caulfield noted some of Joy's other feats: seated on a stool with his legs elevated, solely by muscular power, he jumped clear of the seat; he placed a glass of wine on the sole of his foot and, without bending his head or body, raised the glass to his mouth and drank the contents. Joy also demonstrated his power in the open air. At Hampstead before an audience of hundreds he pulled up by the roots a tree a yard and a half in circumference. In 1701 he appeared at a Bartholomew Fair booth.

Tom Brown in his letter to Moult said, "I don't doubt, but that several of the Ladies who saw this Prodigy of a Man, long'd to try a *Fall* with him in private, like the Woman in Ovid, that was desirous to lie with *Hercules* . . . . " Then Brown quoted a letter to Joy from "a certain Countess that shall be nameless":

I saw you Yesterday with Satisfaction, exerting your Parts in *Dorset-Garden*, on that very *Theatre* where I have frequently beheld the *Alexanders*, the *Caesars*, the *Hercules*, the *Almanzors*, the greatest Heroes of *Greece* or *Italy*, of antient or modern Times, taking Towns, sacking Cities, overturning Empires, singly routing whole Armies, but yet performing less Wonders than you. Yet, I must tell you, it grieves me to see so noble a Talent misimploy'd, and that Strength thrown upon undeserving Houses, that cannot reward your Labour, which might much better divert the requiting Woman. Meet me therefore, thou puissant Man, in another Garden, on a better Theatre, where you may employ your Abilities with more Profit to yourself, and Satisfaction to the expecting

MELESINDA.

The Dictionary of National Biography states that after the vogue for strong men passed Joy engaged in smuggling and drowned in 1734.

An engraved portrait of William Joy at the age of 24, by P. van der Berge, was published by the artist at Amsterdam. Another portrait, also showing Joy at 24, engraved by "J. F.," was published in 1699. A copy of the latter, engraved by Cook, was published in Caulfield's *Remarkable Persons* in 1819.

Joyce. *See also* JOY.

Joyce, Mr [*fl.* 1777], *actor.*
Mr Joyce played Mause in *The Gentle Shepherd* at the Haymarket Theatre on 13 October 1777.

Joyce, Mr [*fl.* 1784], *singer.*
Mr Joyce sang bass in the Handel Memorial Concerts at Westminster Abbey and the Pantheon in May and June 1784.

Jozzi, Giuseppe [*fl.* 1746–1748], *singer, harpsichordist.*
The male soprano Giuseppe Jozzi sang in *La caduta de' giganti* at the King's Theatre on 7 January 1746, participated in a concert for the benefit of indigent musicians on 25 March, and appeared as Alexander in *Antigone* on 13 May. While in London he tried to pass off as compositions of his own eight sonatas by Al-

berti but was found out by a gentlemen just arrived from Italy with the sonatas in Alberti's hand. On 15 March 1748 at the Haymarket Theatre Jozzi played a concerto on the harpsichord for his benefit. After leaving England he became a teacher of singing at Amsterdam.

Juber. *See* JOUBERT.

"Jubilee Dicky." *See* NORRIS, HENRY 1665–1731.

"Judith and Helena." *See* "HELENA and JUDITH."

Julian, [Francis?] [*fl.* 1733–1748], *actor, singer.*
Mr Julian played the Colonel in the ballad opera *The Harlot's Progress* on 28 September 1733 at "a large commodious Room in Artichoke Yard at Mile-End during the Time of the Fair." A year later at Mile End Green he was seen as Peartree in *The Gardener's Wedding.* Then, after an absence of a number of years Julian, hailed as from the Edinburgh theatre, made his first Drury Lane appearance on 28 May 1740 as Gomez in *The Spanish Fryar.* That was the extent of his engagement at Drury Lane; in August he performed at the Hippisley-Chapman booth at Bartholomew Fair, and beginning in 1740–41 Julian was engaged at the Goodman's Fields Theatre.

His first recorded part at Goodman's Fields was Fondlewife in *The Old Bachelor* on 21 October 1740. Between then and the end of the 1741–42 season, under Henry Giffard's management, Julian was seen in such roles as Periwinkle in *A Bold Stroke for a Wife*, Learchus in *Aesop*, Vellum in *The Drummer*, Sir Francis in *The Provok'd Husband*, Smugler and the Alderman in *The Constant Couple*, Shallow in *The Merry Wives of Windsor*, Charino in *Love Makes a Man*, Foresight in *Love for Love*, Goodwill in *The Virgin Unmask'd*, Day in *The Committee*, the Carrier in 1 *Henry IV*, the Collier in *The Recruiting Officer*, Sir Solomon in *The Double Gallant*, Polonius in *Hamlet*, Squib in *Tunbridge Walks*, Sir William in *Love's Last Shift*, Coupler in *The Relapse*, one of the Witches in *Macbeth*, Cripple in *Love and a Bottle*, the Father to Colombine in *The Imprisonment, Release, Adventures, and Marriage of Harlequin*, a Shepherd in

The Winter's Tale, Foigard in *The Stratagem*, Jemmy Twitcher and Mat in *The Beggar's Opera*, Lopez in *The Wonder*, Gratiano in *Othello*, Nicias in *Timon of Athens*, Ernesto in *The Orphan*, Harry in *Pamela*, Charon in *Lethe*, Pantaloon in *Harlequin Englishman*, the Old Man in *King Lear*, and Decoy in *The Miser*. His line was very much like that of Benjamin Johnson at Drury Lane.

During that period Julian appeared at Bartholomew fair in August 1741 as Fribble in *Thomas Kouli Kan*, and before the 1742–43 season began he was at the James Street playhouse, where he may have been serving that performance as manager, on 12 October 1742, playing the title roles in *The Mock Doctor* and *The Miser* for his benefit. Then, with Giffard's troupe, he appeared at Lincoln's Inn Fields Theatre during the regular season in such new parts as Sir Francis in *The Busy Body*, Pearmain in *The Recruiting Officer*, Benedict in *The School Boy*, Muckworm in *The Honest Yorkshireman*, Forrest in *Richard III*, Butler in *The Devil to Pay*, the Steward in *All's Well that Ends Well*, and Peachum in *The Beggar's Opera*.

Julian was away from London, evidently, until the 1745–46 season, when he was in Hallam's troupe at Goodman's Field, playing, on his first appearance there on 28 October 1745, Alberto in *The Massacre of Paris*. He went on to act some of his earlier parts, as well as Poundage in *The Provok'd Husband*, the Cook in *The Lying Valet*, Subtleman in *The Twin Rivals*, one of the Mob in *The Humours of Purgatory*, a Coachman in *The Drummer*, Alphonso in *The Spanish Fryar*, Mustachio in *The Tempest*, Ratcliff in *Jane Shore*, a Maid in *Rule a Wife and Have a Wife*, a Sailor in *The Fair Quaker of Deal*, Ferret in *The Royal Merchant*, and Soto in *She Wou'd and She Wou'd Not*.

Charles Beecher Hogan suggests in *Shakespeare in the Theatre* that Julian may have been Francis Julian, who subscribed in 1746 to the *Works* of Henry Ward. After his tries at London, Julian apparently settled for provincial acting. He was at Norwich on 13 January 1748, making his first appearance there, according to Brown's list of Norwich performances.

Juliano, Master *b. c. 1788, violinist.*
Master Juliano, a child of eight, played a concerto on the violin between the acts at the King's Theatre on 10 March 1796. The advertisement noted that the boy was patronized by the Duchess of York.

Julien, Mons ₍*fl. 1786–1788*₎, *actor, dancer.*
At Astley's Amphitheatre on 4 September 1786 Mr Julien played the Umpire of Sports in a new musical spectacle called *Love from the Heart, A Trial of Skill for a Wife; or, Theodore the Heart of a Lion*. Mrs Julien played a Shepherdess in that work. On 23 August 1788, for the benefit of Monsieur and Madame Julien at the Royal Circus, Julien danced Mynheer Tunbelly in a new comic divertissement by Delpini entitled *A Dutch Teagarden* and then played the General of the Army in the divertissement *The Impressed Recruits* and the Lover in the pantomime *What You Please*. It is probable that Julien and his wife were related in some way to the Juliens active in France during the last quarter of the eighteenth century, and it is possible that Mons Julien was the father of Louis Antoine Jullien, who was a music seller and publisher, a conductor, and a composer of dance music in England in the middle of the nineteenth century.

Julien, Mme ₍*fl. 1784–1788*₎, *dancer.*
Madame Julien made what was advertised as her first appearance in London on 18 December 1784 at the King's Theatre, dancing in a divertissement. She was from the "King's Theatre" in Naples. In 1785 at the Royal Circus she was in *The Garland*, and there she danced a Shepherdess in *Love from the Heart* on 4 September 1786; Monsieur Julien, presumably her husband, also performed. On 29 May 1786 at the Circus she danced *La Provençale*. On 23 August 1788 there she and Mons Julien shared a benefit at which she and Master D'Egville danced a minuet de la cour and a gavotte, she danced a solo hornpipe, she and Mons Bedott offered a pas de deux, and she played Columbine in the pantomime *What You Please*. A Mademoiselle Julien, a dancer, appeared at the Smock Alley Theatre in 1785–86 and, unless that was an error for Mme Julien, she may have been related.

"Julietta." *See* FRASI, GIULIA.

"Jumpedo, Don" ₍*fl.* 1749₎, *dancer, acrobat.*

After the hoax pulled by the "Bottle Conjurer" William Nicholls on 16 January 1749 (he advertised that he would escape into a bottle; the audience showed up, but he did not), a rash of antics by imitators entertained London audiences. The first seems to have been at Covent Garden on 11 March: the *General Advertiser* on 13 March said that "Don *Jumpedo*, who lately was to have performed at the Little Theatre in the Haymarket, appeared on Saturday last, at the Theatre in Covent-Garden, in the Character of Harlequin in the ROYAL CHACE; in which he made his first Essay of *Jumping down his own Throat*, and was universally applauded." That announcement was repeated on 16 March and introduced into the publicity for *Apollo and Daphne* on 27 March.

Drury Lane joined the sport on 13 April with an afterpiece called *Lethe and Jumpedo*, "The whole to conclude with an extraordinary and surprising performance of the Original Seignor Capitello Jumpedo, who, after enter-

taining the audience with a *Hornpipe*, will in a manner entirely new, Jump down his own throat." On the same day, having gotten wind of what Drury Lane was up to, Covent Garden advertised that "Don Jumpedo (Tho' not the Original) will Jump DOWN his Own Throat; and (as a New Addition) afterwards Jump UP again."

The following 23 August at Phillips's booth at Bartholomew Fair the afterpiece was *The Harlot's Progress*, advertised as including "the Escape of Harlequin into a Glass Bottle," and also "the last new additional Scene of Sig Jumpedo Jumping Down his own Throat." On 30 October at Covent Garden "The Escape of Harlequin into a Quart-Bottle" was worked into *Apollo and Daphne*, and Don Jumpedo once again did his jumping down his throat and back up again. But it seems clear that the theatres had milked the routine dry, and the Jumpedo craze died. It is anyone's guess who the performers were who masqueraded behind the Jumpedo pseudonym.

= K =

K. *See* KYNASTON.

Kaempfer, Joseph [*fl.* 1776–1790?], *double bass player.*

According to the rather general account of Joseph Kaempfer in Sainsbury's dictionary, the Hungarian musician was self-taught. He went to Vienna and was received in the chapel of the Esterhazys, presided over by Haydn. Kaempfer's instrument was the double bass, which he called his "Goliath," and he developed such control over it that he could play on it difficult violin passages. In 1776, when he traveled around Germany, he had an instrument constructed that could be taken apart. He visited St Petersburg and then came to England. He resided in London for some years after 1783, was considered a fine solo performer, and was regularly engaged at concerts.

Kaiew Neika [*fl.* 1795–1796?], *performer.*

A Catawba Indian named Kaiew Neika, or White Man, was at Sadler's Wells on 18, 19, and 20 June 1795 and on later dates, with his fellow Indian Coutchee Noyai. They performed feats of archery, management of the tomahawk, and war songs and dances, and toward the end of their stay, in July, offered "an Indian Interlude of connected action called The Ambuscade," showing an attack on a hunting party. In that playlet they were assisted by 10 London performers in Indian makeup. One of the Indians was about 32, the other about 20 (the papers did not indicate which was which), and both were described as "well-looking." Perhaps the Catawba Indians who performed at Astley's Amphitheatre in April and May 1796 were the same pair.

Kamazin. *See* KARMAZIN.

Kammell, Anton *c.* 1740–*c.*1788, *violinist, violist.*

In his *History of the Violin* van der Straeten states that Anton Kammell was born in Bohemia about 1740 and was sent by Count Waldstein, Lord of Hanna, to study in Italy under the violinist Tartini. Kammell went to Prague and then came to London, where he performed and taught from about 1768. Benjamin Blake studied under Kammell for about two years, and Joseph Obermayer was also his pupil. Kammell married a wealthy woman and became a court musician. About 1790, some two years or more after Kammell is believed to have died, *The Favourite Sinfonie* by Dittersdorf was published in London; it was described as having been performed at Mr Kammell's subscription concert. Where Kammell held his concerts is not known. Kammell wrote a number of works for the violin and viola, his two instruments, and some symphonies and overtures. He was spoken of as deceased in 1788.

Kane. *See* KEAN.

Karba. *See* KARPA.

Karist. *See* KARST.

Karmazin, Mons [*fl.* 1752], *bassoonist.*

Monsieur Karmazin (or Harmozin) made his first appearance in England playing a concerto on the bassoon at Drury Lane on 16 October 1752.

Karney. *See* CARNEY.

Karpa, Godfried [*fl.* 1726], *bassoonist.*

A Lord Chamberlain's warrant dated 1 March 1726 directed that Godfried Karpa, "bason," be paid for playing in the *Te Deum* at St James's. On 11 March at the Haymarket Theatre, by royal command, a benefit concert "of several sorts of Musick" by the best hands of the "Opera" was presented for the bassoonist "Karba," who probably performed. He played on 28 April at Drury Lane Theatre for Miss Robinson's benefit.

Karst, Mr [fl. 1784], *instrumentalist. See* KARST, [JOHAN GEORGE?].

Karst, [Johan George?] [fl. 1784–1785], *instrumentalist.*

A Mr Karst was among the trombone or sackbut players at the Handel Memorial Concerts at Westminster Abbey and the Pantheon in May and June 1784. Playing second oboe was a Mr Karist (probably meant for Karst). One of these two musicians was surely Johan George Karst, who was proposed for membership in the Royal Society of Musicians on 1 May 1785 and roundly refused by a vote of 23 nays and one yea on the following 5 June.

Karver, Miss [fl. 1736–1760], *actress, singer.*

Miss Karver (or Carver) was first noticed in the playbills on 27 May 1736, when she acted Maria in *Guilt Its Own Punishment* at the Haymarket Theatre. With Fielding's Great Mogul's Company of Comedians she was Mrs Barter in *The Historical Register* at the same playhouse on 21 March 1737 and subsequent dates. Then, after an absence from London (or from the playbills, at least), Miss Karver appeared at Drury Lane as a singer in *The Tempest* on 26 December 1739 and on 13 February 1740 as the First Wife in *Don John*. She shared a benefit with others on 28 May and sang an entr'acte tune.

In 1740–41 she sang Jenny Diver in *The Beggar's Opera*, played a Gipsy in *The Fortune Tellers*, and doubtless was active in the singing chorus during the season. She again shared a benefit in the spring. Miss Karver left the London stage for several years, returning on 22 November 1748 for a solo benefit at the Haymarket. The bill identified her as the performer "who sang some years ago" at Drury Lane and "since [when?] at Mr Foote's Theatre in the Haymarket." She sang "by desire, Women and Wine." Tickets from her were available at No 2, Plough Court, Fetter Lane. She held another benefit on 14 February 1759 and was a participant in *Mrs Midnight's Concert*

and Oratory at the Haymarket on 14 February 1760.

Kater, Rose Mary, née Cooper [fl. 1794], *singer, organist.*

Doane's *Musical Directory* of 1794 listed Mrs Rose Mary Kater, late Miss Cooper, as an organist and singer who performed for the Choral Fund and the Longacre Society and lived in Black Lyon Yard, Whitechapel. There is a possibility that she was the singer who took the title role in *Polly Honeycombe* at the Haymarket Theatre on 26 August 1793, for one source identified that young woman as a Miss Cooper—but another said she was Miss Villers. We have entered the Haymarket performer as Miss Cooper.

Katharine, Mme [fl. 1754], *dancer.*

On 28 November 1754 at the Haymarket Theatre an "Aethiopian Concert" was presented, with dancing provided by a woman styled as Mme Katharine. *The London Stage* has "Mlle" Katharine dancing in the concert on the following 9 December, making her second appearance, but that surely is an error for Mme Katharine.

Katharine, Mlle. *See* KATHARINE, MME.

Katterfelto, Gustavus d. 1799, *mountebank.*

The Prussian conjurer, empiric, and mountebank Gustavus Katterfelto was operating in the Gloucester region by 1777 and in December 1780 lectured at Cox's late museum in Spring Gardens in London. Through a series of outrageous advertisements, usually headed "Wonders! Wonders! Wonders!," he gained not only much attention but a considerable following among the credulous, who were fascinated by his "proetics," "stynacraphy," and "caprimancy." A news clipping at the British Library, hand-dated 5 April 1782, was a typical puff:

This Present Evening, and Every Evening this Week, at COX'S MUSEUM, Spring-Gardens. A SON of the late Col. KATTERFELTO, of the Death-Head Hussars, belonging to the King of Prussia, is to exhibit a great variety of curious and surprising Experiments in Natural, Experimental Philosophy, and Mathematics, and such as never was seen in this Kingdom, by any other person before.

Mr. KATTERFELTO has had the honor, in his

JAMES GRAHAM and GUSTAVUS KATTERFELTO

caricature by unknown engraver

travels, to exhibit before the Empress of Russia, the Queen of Hungary, the Kings of Prussia, Sweden, Denmark, and Poland.

Mr. KATTERFELTO will, after his Philosophical Lecture, discover various arts, by which many persons lose their fortunes by Dice, Cards, Billiards, and E. O. {roulette} table.

N. B. His Philosophical Lecture will be from seven to nine o'clock, and from nine until ten he will shew and discover some of his other various arts.

During the influenza epidemic in 1782 he claimed to have a cure; he said he had discovered the secret of perpetual motion; he employed a performing black cat in some of his lectures; and he boasted of owning a "solar microscope."

He sometimes styled himself Doctor or Colonel Katterfelto and sometimes George Psalmanazar, the divine and moral Philosopher of Piccadilly, a reference to the famous "Formosan" literary impostor of that name (1679?–1763). In a typical advertisement Katterfelto stated:

The evening lecture at 8 o'clock will be continued as usual and enriched by the presence and extraordinary performance of the black cat, by which Dr Katterfelto doubts not of getting 30,000 £ in the course of the present year, especially if she should have kittens as he will not dispose of any under at least 500 guineas, as several of the 1st nobility in different parts of Europe, have already requested to have some of that most wonderful breed.

Katterfelto usually exhibited at Spring Gardens, but one advertisement, in March 1783, invited everyone to his exhibition room in Piccadilly. That month he advertised that he was going to Berlin in April, regretted by the royal family and the learned. He had been invited to have discourse with Benjamin Franklin and with the French royal family in Paris, "provided the King of Prussia can be prevailed on to dispense with his presence at Berlin." He called himself "The Prussian Newton." Perhaps he went; probably not. Rumor had it that he had ordered a £25,000 carriage, yet by the end of 1783 he was offering all his "apparatus" for sale for £2,500. The *Morning Post* on 3 June 1784 reported that the English royal family had visited Katterfelto's exhibition and had been completely satisfied by his performance, so he had either then returned to London or had never departed.

On 2 February 1787 he ran an advertisement for shows at Spring Gardens, boasting of his 16 years of traveling and noting that he planned presently to exhibit at Oxford. His advertisement in London on 22 May 1789 cried,

WONDERS of NATURE, which are beyond description, are to be seen now at No. 22, Piccadilly, late Fantoccini Rooms. This and every Day This Week from 8 to 10, from 10 to 12, from 12 to 2, and from 3 to 5 o'clock, if the sun appears at that time.

MR. KATTERFELTO will, by his new improved SOLAR MICROSCOPE, shew many thousand surprising insects, particularly those which have been advertised in all the different newspapers, and which have threatened this kingdom with a plague, if not speedily destroyed. They are of the Same kind, by

all accounts, which caused a great plague in Italy in the year 1432. They will be magnified as large as an ox, and one as rough as a bear, and a hundred persons may have a view at one time: and he will shew, in a drop of water, (the size of a pin's head) upwards of 5000 insects. —The same in Beer, Milk, Vinegar and Blood.

The *Monthly Mirror* in May 1798 reported that "Dr. Katterfelto, though killed long since by the newspapers, is, we hear, now visiting the great villages and little towns in the North, after having tired John Bull 'de bigger,' to get all he can from John Bull 'de lesser.'" *The Dictionary of National Biography* said Katterfelto was imprisoned for vagrancy in Shrewsbury but was welcomed at Whitby. He carried with him a museum of natural and other curiosities, most of which he appears to have picked up on the Yorkshire coast. One of his tricks at Whitby was to raise his daughter to the ceiling by means of a magnet that supposedly attracted the huge steel helmet she wore.

GUSTAVUS KATTERFELTO
artist unknown

Katterfelto inspired the ridicule of cartoonists and authors, as might be expected. Cowper wrote in *The Task* of "Katterfelto, with his hair on end / At his own wonders, wondering for his bread." And *Harlequin Teague* at the Haymarket in 1782 contained an imitation of Katterfelto by Wewitzer in the character of Dr Caterpillar. Peter Pindar spoke, perhaps facetiously, of the mountebank in his *Works* about 1794 as "A late celebrated philosopher and conjurer." The *Monthly Mirror* in January 1800 reported that Gustavas Katterfelto had died at Bedale, Yorkshire, on 25 November 1799. His widow married John Carter of Whitby.

In *The Shows of London* Richard Altick noted that Katterfelto was pictured in at least eight satirical prints, one of which shows him with his rival quack, Dr Graham. An unknown artist also pictured Katterfelto.

Kauntze, George H. [*fl.* 1794–1798], clarinetist, violoncellist.

The Mr Counts, whose entry appears in the fourth volume of this dictionary, we can now identify more exactly as George H. Kauntze. Doane's *Musical Directory* of 1794 called him Counts, alias Kauntz, a clarinetist and violoncellist in the band of the second regiment of the guards. He played at the Apollo Gardens and lived at No 34, Charles Street, Westminster. The *British Union-Catalogue of Early Music* identifies him as George Kauntze and conjectures, evidently incorrectly, that he was a flutist. The list of subscribers to the New Musical Fund in 1794 included a G. H. Kauntze, clearly the same person. On 15 January 1798 at the Haymarket Theatre Kauntze played in a performance of the *Messiah*.

Kaworth. *See* RAWORTH.

Kaye, Thomas 1722–1816, horn player.

Thomas Kaye (sometimes Key) was born in 1722. The earliest musical reference found for him was dated 16 December 1768: a letter of attorney from Miles Coyle to Thomas Kaye of Russell Street, Covent Garden, musician. Kaye was empowered to receive from the Lord Chamberlain's office £10 due Coyle as a former child of the Chapel Royal. By 20 August 1775 Kaye was playing in the band at Drury Lane Theatre. How long he continued there is not known; in 1783 he was in the band at the King's Theatre, playing for the operas. He was one of the French-horn players who participated in the Handel Memorial Concerts at Westminster Abbey and the Pantheon in May and June 1784. Perhaps he was the T. Kay who, with Charles Elliot, had a music shop in London from 1787 to 1791 at No 332, the Strand. Elliot also had a shop in Edinburgh from 1770 to 1793.

On 19 February 1790 Kaye played in the *Messiah* at Covent Garden, and he participated in Handel concerts there again in the three years that followed. Doane's *Musical Directory* of 1794 listed Kaye as a member of the Royal Society of Musicians and a performer at Ranelagh Gardens as well as in the oratorios. Doane gave Kaye's address as No 14, Princes Street, Westminster. In 1796 and 1797 Kaye served on the Court of Assistants of the Royal Society.

Thomas Kaye appealed to the Society for aid on 2 December 1798. He said he was then 76 years old and had no engagement except at Colman's theatre—the Haymarket—during the summers. He was granted three guineas monthly, which he dutifully relinquished the following July when the Haymarket season once again gave him employment. Similar arrangements were made in 1799 and 1800. A Mr "Kayes" was paid, along with Cornish, Taylor, Jackson (all musicians in the Covent Garden oratorios in 1800), and Dickenson for performing in *The Critic* and *A Trip to the Nore*. That notation appeared on 15 April 1800 in the Drury Lane accounts, and perhaps the two patent theatres occasionally traded instrumentalists. Covent Garden had performed *The Critic* on 30 April 1800, but the only record of a performance of *A Trip to the Nore* goes back to 27 December 1792. It probably was revived, perhaps at Drury Lane, in the spring of 1800.

Kaye appealed on 2 August 1801 for medical aid and was granted £6 6*s*. by the Royal Society of Musicians. He may have played at the Haymarket that summer, as he certainly did in 1802, when the Society supported him except for the summer season. But the aging musician was clearly unwell in 1803. On 3 April the Society was informed that for Kaye's indisposition Dr Clark prescribed sherry; it was agreed that he be allowed one dozen (bottles?) for the month of April; the bill came to £2 7*s*. 6*d*. Kaye recovered temporarily and played the summer season at the Haymarket, giving up his allowance as usual. He worked in the summers through 1806 at least, if not, as the account books seem to suggest, through 1810. The Society minutes show nothing but notations of medical aid for Kaye after 1806— 10 guineas in November 1810 and the same amount on 7 January 1816, when Kaye was 94. He died within a few weeks. His daughter requested and was granted £8 for his funeral expenses on 4 February.

Kaygill, Mr [*fl.* 1757–1782], *house servant.*

Mr Kaygill (or Cagle, Keygill) served Drury Lane as a pit doorkeeper from as early as 16 May 1757, when a benefit notice appeared in the *Public Advertiser* (*The London Stage* for that date does not cite him). He was mentioned at benefit time in most years, and a paylist dated 9 February 1765 shows that he was being paid 1s. 6d. daily or 9s. weekly for his labors. The theatre accounts on 5 October 1775 called Kaygill a pit office keeper, and under that designation in 1776–77 he was earning £1 weekly. Three times in early 1782 the accounts noted that Kaygill had made errors in his accounting, and after his last mistake, reported on 2 April 1782 for an error of 6s. made on 14 March, Kaygill's name disappeared from the company accounts and bills.

There was a machinist named Caygill or Kaygill working in Liverpool from 1786 on; perhaps he was related to the Drury Lane house servant.

Keale, Mr [*fl.* 1748–1749], *actor.*

Zanga in *The Revenge* was performed at the James Street Theatre on 30 June 1748 by "a Gentleman from the Theatre in Fort St George [in Madras, India], who never perform'd in England before." When the actor played Zanga again a year later, on 16 May 1749 at the Haymarket Theatre, he was identified as Mr Keale from Fort St George, making his second appearance in England.

Kean. *See also* KEEN *and* KEENE.

Kean, Mr [*fl.* 1771], *performer?*

A news clipping dated 1771, noted in the entry of Charles Keen, said "Mr. Kean of Sad-

ler's Wells, lately said to be dead is living. . . ." We know nothing else of Kean, and there is the possibility that he was the minor actor William Keen, who gave up his summer employment at the Haymarket Theatre after 1668 and may well have gone over to Sadler's Wells in later summers.

Kean, Mrs [*fl.* 1791–1792], *performer? house servant?*

A Mrs Kean (possibly Kear) is on the company list of Drury Lane Theatre during the season of 1791–92 at a salary of £1 5s. per week. Her duties are not known.

Kean, Edmund [*fl.* 1788–1789], *actor, monologuist.*

Edmund Kean was one of three brothers, apparently all tailors. They lived together in the 1780s at No 9 Little St Martin's Lane, where their widowed sister Mrs Price kept house for them. One brother, Aaron, remained at his trade, but Moses discovered that he had a gift for mimicry and began exploiting his talent with some success in London and elsewhere. In 1788 he was one of the rather mixed bag of performers who engaged with Jack Palmer at his famous fiasco, the Royalty. Edmund, then a clerk or draughtsman, apprenticed to the surveyor Wilmot, apparently followed his brother to that theatre after success in debating clubs at the Lyceum, Coachmaker's Hall, the Mitre, and Spring Gardens.

The playbill of 9 September 1788 featured *Sound Without Sense* "by the Author, Mr. Edmund Kean" in his first appearance on the stage. *The Gazetteer* of 9 September explains *Sound Without Sense* as "Imitations of various Public Speakers in the Debating Societies." How often Edmund appeared cannot now be determined. On 1 April 1789 Moses Kean was at Rice's Great Rooms ("Late Hickford's") engaged in his mimicry "assisted by his brother Mr. E. Kean."

Nothing more is known of the elder Edmund Kean's performing career. Present interest in him lies in the fact that he is supposed to have been the father of the great nineteenth-century actor Edmund Kean. The mother was, pretty surely, Nancy Carey, a provincial actress, daughter of the monologuist George Savile Carey.

A Mr J. Addison, writing to the *Sunday*

Times for 2 June 1833, declared that Kean "died about the age of 22 or 23, previous to which he had been disordered in his intellect. . . ." A Mr Lush, writing in the *Gentleman's Magazine* of August 1833, adds that Kean died by walking off the roof of his lodgings. But that death was given to Moses his brother by an unidentified early nineteenth-century clipping in the British Library.

Kean, Edmund   *1787–1833, actor.*

The date and place of the first theatrical appearance of the great tragedian Edmund Kean are as uncertain as his parentage, his birth date, and most other circumstances of his earliest years.

Michael Kelly, the singer, asserted in his *Reminiscences* (1826) that he had personally selected the Cupid for the lavish production of *Cymon* in which he had sung the title role on 31 December 1791. He had chosen from among a number of children. "One struck me, with a fine pair of black eyes, who seemed by his looks and little gestures to be most anxious to be chosen as the representative of the God of Love; I chose him, and little then did I imagine that my little cupid would eventually become a great actor; the then little urchin was neither more nor less than Edmund Kean." But the statement, like much else in the *Reminiscences*, is suspect. The playbill for the evening and for all the other evenings of a long run that season gave the part of Cupid to Master Gregson, a regular in the company since March 1788. A Master Kean, very likely Edmund, was listed in the Drury Lane playbill of 8 June 1796 for Robin in *The Merry Wives of Windsor*. That performance was a few days before the end of the season and the play was not repeated.

That is all the information we have on possible performances by Edmund Kean in the eighteenth century. He is, obviously, an actor of the following era. The best modern treatment of his life is Harold Newcomb Hillebrand's *Edmund Kean* (1933).

Kean, Moses   *d. 1793, actor, monologuist.*

All early accounts agree that the three brothers Kean—Aaron, Edmund, and Moses—were tailors. Aaron stuck to his trade. Edmund followed Moses onto the stage. Moses had suffered some accident which required the am-

putation of his right leg, and was thus "disqualified," in the words of Charles Lee Lewes, "for sitting cross-legged on a shop board." His success in imitating friends and notables at private gatherings determined him to take his talents to the stage.

The Young Gentleman advertised as making his "first appearance in publick" at the Haymarket on 22 March 1784 in the role of the Gentleman in the Balcony in *The Manager in Distress* was young Moses Kean. (He was named—but as "Kean" only—in the playbill of 26 August.) The March performance was a specially-licensed benefit for Mrs Margaret Cuyler in a theatre usually dark at that season. Mrs Cuyler was making use of a standard device to attract her audience—a debut, and a rather unusual one. For in the course of the evening, it was promised, the Young Gentleman would give "a much greater Variety of *Imitations* than has ever yet been offered." Clever imitations of his fellow actors and other

Harvard Theatre Collection

MOSES KEAN, imitating HENDERSON's Hamlet

artist unknown

well-known personages was to be "Mosey" Kean's specialty for the rest of his rather vagabond career.

Kean was in and out of London, traveling widely in the provinces, but most of his country engagements are either lost or confused with those of other Keans (Keens, Keenes, Kanes) who were active in England and Ireland during his years.

On 7 February 1785 he gave his imitations "at the end of the first ballet" when a company under Delpini's direction put on a performance at the Haymarket. At that theatre on 24 and 31 January and 24 February 1785 he provided his imitations for performers' benefits. On 7 May 1785 he played Dr Squib in *The Devil upon Two Sticks*, imitating Samuel Foote in the part (very faithfully, for Foote, too, had lost a leg). It was one of his two "dramatic" parts. He joined George Savile Carey at Leeds on 3 and 5 April 1786. On 17 August 1786 he gave, at the North Street Theatre, the first morning performance ever seen at Brighton. This was called his *Attic Entertainment*. He was said to be assisted in this program of readings, imitations, and music by a Mr Phillips, "reader to Dr. Samuel Johnson," and "the brothers Linley."

He played his Dr Squib again for the benefit of Harwood, the Drury Lane prompter, on 8 January 1787. He was at the Haymarket again as the Gentleman in the Balcony on 23 June and 6 July 1787. Moses alternated appearances at Bristol and Bath in January 1789—at Bristol's Theatre Royal on 5, 12, and 19 January and at the Orchard Street Theatre, Bath, on 8, 13, and 17. When Charlotte Tidswell shared a benefit with Phillimore and Barnes at Drury Lane on 4 June 1789, Moses Kean took the transvestite role of Mrs Cole in *The Minor*, the second "dramatic" role attempted during his career.

On 1 April 1789 at "Rice's Great Rooms (late Hickford's)" he gave "Senatorial, theatrical and various other imitations," assisted by his brother Mr. E[dmund] Kean. Moses was said to have just returned from a provincial tour. He was living at No 8, St Martin's Lane.

He is traceable to Brighton on 11 August 1789, where a boastful manager ("ever anxious to introduce every Species of agreeable Amusement") had

engaged the celebrated Mr. KEAN, From the THEATRES ROYAL, Drury Lane and Covent Garden, and the Hay-Market, to give his EVENING LOUNGE: Consisting of various IMITATIONS. He has been universally approved of at OXFORD, CAMBRIDGE, and many other Parts of ENGLAND, and has the Honour of being a Member of that elegant and liberal Institution the ANACREONTIC SOCIETY.

Moses was with Carey again at the Town Hall in Cambridge on 31 October 1789 and on 23 and 25 February 1790, acted his perennial Gentleman at the Haymarket again on 5 and 9 July, gave his lecture at Oxford at the Mitre Inn on 19 November, and returned (alone) to Cambridge on 11 December. On 16 September 1791, for Robert Palmer's benefit, he played the Gentleman in the Balcony, this time being joined by a Lady in the Balcony. After that date he faded from the theatrical scene. He died sometime in 1793. An unidentified and undated clipping in the British Library claims that "His death was singular. He was fond of scenery [and] remarkable views. . . ." He went to the top of his residence, "near Seven Dials," lost his hold, fell into the street, and died. But that was said by other testimony to have been the manner of death of his brother Edmund.

Moses Kean, like Aaron, has sometimes been thought to have been the father of the brilliant nineteenth-century tragedian Edmund Kean. But that distinction probably belongs to their brother Edmund, despite the close affiliation of Edmund with George Savile Carey, the father of Nancy Carey, who bore the great actor.

Moses Kean made a tolerable living imitating his colleagues, "not," says Lee Lewes, "with ignorance or malice, but by a true and picturesque manner of conveying to his admiring auditors the pleasing gesticulations and modulations in the speech and person of the actor pointed at." But like the other great mimics of his time, he himself was imitated and, like them, he was charged with mental cruelty by some critics. The author of *The Modern Stage Exemplified* (1788) gibed:

A mimick now, (a taylor's trade no more
He bears, tho' once a taylor's trade he bore)
KEAN, leaving shop-board, sheers and list behind,
Now measures manners, and cuts up mankind.

He raises laughter, like the rest of m'mes,
At ills, not vices; at defects, not crimes.

Thomas David Rees also satirized Moses playing the character Tim Thimble in the anonymous afterpiece *Thimble's Flight from the Shopboard*, which was given one performance at the Haymarket on 25 August 1789. The *Thespian Dictionary* (1805) reported that it "was disapproved of for its unjust personality."

J. T. Smith, in *Nollekens and His Times* (1829) described Moses Kean as

a stout-built man with black-bushy hair, and a wooden leg. He was always dressed in a dashing manner, in a scarlet coat, white satin waistcoat, black satin small-clothes, and a 'Scott's Liquid dye' blue silk-stocking; he had also a long-quartered shoe, with a large buckle covering his foot, a cocked hat and a ruffled shirt, and never went out without a switch or cane in his hand.

Smith added that "Mr. [John] Alefounder painted a whole-length portrait of him as large as life in the above dress, which was exhibited in the left-hand corner of the Ante-room at Somerset-House. There is also a whole-length etching of him, of a quarto size." Neither has been seen by us. An anonymous engraving of Kean in his "Imitation of Henderson's Hamlet" was published by W. Hinton in 1786. The same picture in an etching by "A. B." was also issued, undated.

"Kean of the Arena, The." *See* DUCROW, ANDREW.

Kear. *See also* KEAN.

Kear, James Thomas   *d. 1796, singer, actor.*

In the summer of 1754 James Thomas Kear, after a steady if not lustrous employment as a vocalist for 24 years, was entertaining patrons of Marylebone Gardens. He sang there again in 1757 and perhaps in the several years preceding. In a *Medley Concert* promoted by Theophilus Cibber at the Haymarket Theatre on 17 October 1757 Kear made his first appearance on the stage singing "Dorus and Cleora," a new cantata set to music by Bryan, and "Rule Britannia." Throughout that season at the Haymarket in connection with Cibber's concerts, farragoes, and plays, Kear offered such vocal

selections as "Phoebus sinketh in the West" and "School of Anacreon" on 21 October, a new song on 6 January 1758, and a song in praise of the King of Prussia on 12 January; he sang in *Acis and Galatea* on 2 February. Kear returned to sing at Marylebone Gardens in the summer of 1758, enjoying a benefit with Miss Glanville on 11 September. That year was published the song *Let ev'ry Martial Soul advance*, as sung by him.

In 1760–61 Kear was engaged as a chorus singer at Drury Lane, where he performed for the first time on 20 October 1760 in the funeral procession in *Romeo and Juliet*, a service he rendered throughout the season. On 11 May 1761 he played Damon in *The Chaplet* (for the first time) and sang Purcell's "Sing All Ye Muses" with Champness, for a benefit he shared with Fawcett and Baddeley.

Possibly Kear continued as a chorus singer at Drury Lane for the next four seasons, but his name appeared in no bills there until 1 May 1765, when he played Hymen in an adaptation of *The Tempest*. The late William Clark in his notes listed a Kear at Smock Alley Theatre, Dublin, in the 1761–62 season, but as a dancer; perhaps Kear was in Dublin then as a singer, and Clark misunderstood his function in the chorus. Announced as from Dublin, Kear performed at Norwich from 1762 to 1764, at Birmingham in the summer of 1762, and at Finch's Grotto Gardens in St George's Fields, Southwark, in 1765.

In 1766–67 Kear began an engagement at Drury Lane which lasted 11 years. His salary of £1 per week in the first season had risen only to £1 10s. by 1776–77; the size of his roles did not increase perceptibly. Throughout these years he served as a shepherd, soldier, beggar, fryar, and other obscure characters in the choruses of *Almena*, *Macbeth*, *A Peep Behind the Curtain*, *The Jubilee*, *The Witches*, *Harlequin's Invasion*, *Pigmy Revels*, *Alfred*, and numerous other pieces, and acted occasionally the Butler in *The Devil to Pay*, Joe in *The Miller of Mansfield*, Muggins in *The Cobler*, and a Coachman in *Old City Manners*. He was also heard in specialty songs, such as "The Whistling Plowman" on 13 May 1766 and "A Hunting Song" on 18 May 1770. Kear performed at Bristol in the summer of 1770.

While employed winters at Drury Lane,

Kear also sang regularly at Sadler's Wells between 1771 and 1779. On 17 June 1775 the *Morning Post* announced Kear's death, but on 21 June the *Morning Chronicle* denied the report. When he shared a benefit with Miss Dowson at Sadler's Wells on 21 September 1775 Kear's address was No 2, Stephen Street, Tottenham Court Road. He still lodged there on 6 May 1777, when he shared a benefit with Legg at Drury Lane.

A notation by J. P. Kemble on a bill at the Huntington Library that Kear "seems not to have appear'd on the Stage after the third of June 1777" is incorrect, for he was still at Drury Lane on 29 October 1777, when he played a Gardener in *The Rival Candidates*, a piece for which his name continued in the bills until 20 February 1778. On 2 March his name was omitted and did not again appear in the Drury Lane bills. He did, however, sing at Sadler's Wells in the summer of 1778 and as late as 15 April 1779.

Kear, having subscribed in 1766, claimed on the Drury Lane Theatrical Fund at Christmas 1783, and according to Kemble's notes, was supported by the Fund till he died at Norwood Green near Hounslow on 12 November 1796. His full name is in the Winston fund book at the Folger Shakespeare Library.

Keard, Thomas   [*fl. 1794*], *singer?*

Doane's *Musical Directory* of 1794 listed Thomas Keard of Wandsworth as a bass (singer?) who participated in the Handel performances at Westminster Abbey.

Kearny, Mr   [*fl. 1736*], *musician?*

At Drury Lane on 22 May 1736 the benefit tickets of Thumoth and Kearny were accepted. The performance was a benefit for Mr Winch, who played a concerto on the French horn. Thumoth was also a musician, so it is probable that Kearny was too.

Kearny, Mr   [*fl. 1768–1769*], *actor.*

The Mr Kearney who performed at the Crow Street Theatre in Dublin in 1768–69 was probably the Kearny who appeared at the Haymarket Theatre in London from late May to early September 1769. Kearny's first appearance at the Haymarket was on 24 May as Puff in *Miss in Her Teens*, after which he was seen as the Constable in *The What D'Ye Call It*, Bruin

in *The Mayor of Garratt*, Bonniface in *The Beaux' Stratagem*, Padwell in *The Vintner Trick'd*, Loader in *The Minor*, Wat Dreary and Mat o' the Mint in *The Beggar's Opera*, Guttle in *The Lying Valet*, Guildenstern in *Hamlet*, the Lieutenant of the Tower in *Richard III*, Sharper in *The Old Bachelor*, Guzzle in *Tom Thumb*, an unnamed character in *The Orators*, Metullus in *Julius Caesar*, and Gratiano in *Othello*.

Keasberry, William   *1726–1797, actor, manager.*

Very likely William Keasberry had been acting for some time in the provinces before he joined the Edinburgh theatre in 1755 at the age of about 29. His first appearance of record was as a Witch in *Macbeth* at the New Concert Hall in that city on 10 March 1755. On 31 March he acted Mat o' the Mint in *The Beggar's Opera*. His other known roles in Edinburgh included Aboan in *Oroonoko* on 29 November 1755, Gaylove in *The Honest Yorkshireman* on 6 December, Young Rakish in *The School Boy* on 3 January 1756, Sciolto in *The Fair Penitent* on 21 January, a Spouter in *The Apprentice* on 11 February, and Carlos in *The Fatal Marriage* on 24 April 1756. Also acting in the Edinburgh company with him was his wife Henrietta, the daughter of the London actress Sarah Hamilton.

In 1756–57 he began his long association with the Orchard Street Theatre in Bath. In partnership with Griffith of the Norwich theatre, Keasberry took over the management of the Bath theatre for the 1760 season. That year they also erected a temporary theatre at Winchester in order to capitalize on a nearby encampment of eight regiments. One night during their twelve-week engagement at Winchester, some olive leaves caught fire on stage during a performance of *Alexander the Great*, causing some panic in the audience and a little indignity to the actor of Clytus, who was forced to rise from his dead position on the floor and then return to it after the scare subsided.

Keasberry acted at the Jacob's Wells Theatre in Bristol in 1763. He was engaged by Love for the new Theatre Royal at Richmond in 1766 and also played there in *The Wonder* and *Midas* in 1767. With Roger Kemble's strolling players Keasberry and his wife acted at Bath from 18 September 1767 to 31 May 1768 and then returned for the summer to Richmond, where Keasberry had a benefit on 9 August 1768, when *The Beggar's Opera* was performed.

Keasberry made an excursion into London for a specially-licensed performance given for the benefit of Lee on 19 September 1768 at the Haymarket Theatre, in which he acted Volscius in *The Rehearsal* and Damon in *Damon and Phillida*. He was announced as from the Theatre Royal, Bath, where he continued to play for a number of years. In the summer of 1769 he was again at Richmond. Late in the summer of 1770 he returned to the Haymarket for Dubellamy's benefit to play Hawthorn in *Love in a Village*, Keasberry's second and evidently last performance in London, on 20 September.

Keasberry served as Palmer's manager at Bath and Bristol until 1786, in which year he and Dimond took over the proprietorship, opening the Bath theatre on 7 October. After that year Keasberry seems to have reduced his stage appearances, but in earlier years he was regarded as a good general actor. Charles Dibdin, a close friend for more than 20 years, valued his "veteran judgment" and "gentlemanly deportment." On 12 August 1774 Keasberry's death was erroneously reported by the *Morning Chronicle*, but the paper retracted the report on 22 August.

In 1795 Keasberry retired because of ill health, leaving the Bath management to Dimond. He died at Bath in November 1797, on the fifteenth according to the *Gentleman's Magazine* but on the seventeenth according to the Bristol *Journal*, at the age of 71. He was buried in Widcombe Churchyard on 20 November, to the strains of anthems sung by his theatre colleagues.

According to some reports (noted in *The Letters of David Garrick*, edited by Little and Kahrl) Keasberry had married a favorite Bath actress, Miss Carr (possibly the daughter of Oliver Carr). But it seems clear from the will of the actress Anna Giffard, dated 9 September 1776, in which Keasberry was named her executor, that he was married to Henrietta Hamilton, the daughter of Sarah Hamilton and the sister of William and Myrton Hamilton. Henrietta acted with Keasberry at Edinburgh in 1755–56 and regularly at Bath and Bristol during his management. She may have been one of the Misses Hamilton who played in

London about mid-century. According to the *Gentleman's Magazine* of June 1812, Mrs Keasberry, the relict of William Keasberry, patentee of Bath and Bristol, died at Berkeley, near Glastonbury, on 15 June 1812, after a few minutes' illness, at the age of 75.

At Bath the Keasberrys lived in a large house at the end of Philip Street. They had at least five children, four of whom were performers for a while. The eldest son, Captain William Keasberry, spent 20 years abroad in the military organization of the East India company before his death in the East Indies was reported in the Bath *Journal* in August 1797. He seems not to have acted. A second son, Master H. Keasberry, played Tom Thumb in *Tom Thumb the Great* on 9 April 1782 and then Prince Arthur in *King John* on 18 April; he continued to perform children's roles at Bath and Bristol until 1791. The youngest son, Master John Keasberry, also played children's roles at those two theatres between 1779 and 1787. He was the Lieutenant John Keasberry who was promoted in July 1800 to Captain in the East India Company, on service at Madras.

Julia Maria Keasberry, the elder daughter, danced and sang at Bath from about June 1781 through 1783–84. On 19 August 1784 at St James's, Bath, she married Nathaniel Peach of Roxborough, Gloucestershire. He was a gentleman of fortune who left her a widow with three children, one of whom was Captain Peach, sometime city treasurer of Bath and stage manager of the theatre. Another daughter, Miss H. Keasberry, played Prince Henry to her brother's Prince Arthur in *King John* on 18 April 1782. Several days later, described as not yet 14, she was praised by the *Bath Chronicle* for her performance as Adelaide in *The Count of Narbonne*.

Keating, Mr ₍*fl.* 1715₎, *performer?*

A Mr Keating, who may have been a performer, was given a solo benefit at Lincoln's Inn Fields on 31 October 1715. The bill gave no indication of his function at the theatre, if any, or of his participation in the evening's performance.

Keating, Mr ₍*fl.* 1753₎, *performer?*

At Drury Lane on 15 May 1753 benefit receipts of £170 (presumably before house charges) were shared by a Mr Keating (according to the bill; the prompter Cross wrote "Key-ton" in his diary) and three others. Keating may have been a minor performer.

Keating, Mr [*fl.* 1789], *actor.*
On 31 October 1789 at Drury Lane a young gentleman who had never appeared on any stage before took the leading role in *Oroonoko*. The Kemble notes tell of his fate: "Mr. Keating appeared first time on any stage in Oroonoko—he showed no marks of Genius, and is not to be engaged."

Keating, Mr [*fl.* 1793–1814], *pit doorkeeper.*
The accounts books for the Covent Garden Theatre show Mr Keating (or Keeting) to have been serving as a house servant at 12*s.* weekly from as early as the 1793–94 season. The books later cited his job as pit doorkeeper. In 1802–3 he was raised to 15*s.* weekly, at which scale he remained until 1813–14.

Keeble, John *1711–1786, harpsichordist, organist, composer, theorist.*
Born in 1711 in Chichester, John Keeble was brought up as a chorister in the cathedral of that city under Thomas Kelway. In 1734–35 he became a pupil of Pepusch in London. By 1736, according to Dr Burney, Keeble began to distinguish himself as a harpsichordist. In 1737 he succeeded the insane Thomas Roseingrave as organist of St George, Hanover Square, but continued to divide his salary with him until that unfortunate musician's death in 1759. Presumably Handel had recommended Keeble for the position over Matthison. Keeble was organist in the Rotunda at Ranelagh Gardens from its opening in 1742 until he was succeeded by Butler about 1772. He had many pupils for the harpsichord, including the composer John Burton (1730–1782), who became a distinguished harpsichord player and organist.

Keeble published five books of organ pieces and with Jacob Kirkman, *Forty Interludes to be played between the verses of the Psalms*. In 1784 he published *The Theory of Harmonics, or an Illustration of the Grecian Harmonica*, an ingenious and controversial work which attracted adverse reviews in the *Monthly Review* of November 1785 but favorable opinions in the *European Magazine* of the same year.

Keeble was regarded by Burney as "an excellent organist, [an] intelligent teacher, and a worthy man." He died at his house in Conduit Street on 24 December 1786 and was buried, according to his wishes in his will, in the parish church of Ramsholt, Suffolk, "in the same vault and in the same private manner as my dear Wife."

In his will, made on 27 July 1786 and proved on 16 January 1787, Keeble left numerous small bequests to friends and relatives. To his son-in-law, Captain Thomas Hamilton, husband of his daughter Sally, Keeble left all his shares in "the Mines Royal and Mineral and Battery Works Company"; upon Sally he had previously settled a trust at the time of her marriage. He left £10 each to the schools of Gray Coat Boys, Blue Coat Girls, and Red Sleeve Boys, all charity institutions in Ipswich.

The Mary Keeble, spinster, of St Martin-in-the-Fields, whose will was proved at London on 20 December 1786, may have been the musician's niece; in her will she left one guinea "to my uncle John Keeble and his wife Anne." An S. Keeble, book and music seller near the Temple Gate in 1688, may also have been related.

Keefe, Mr [*fl.* 1740–*c.* 1750], *proprietor.*
By 1740 a Mr Keefe was the proprietor of Lambeth Wells, where mineral waters and concerts had been offered since before 1697. Located in Three Coney Walk (later known as Lambeth Walk), the establishment was frequented by a boisterous and mean clientele. About 1750 the proprietorship of the Wells passed into the hands of Thomas Ireland.

Keefe, Mrs. *See* O'KEEFFE, MRS JOHN.

Keegan, Mr [*fl.* 1784], *balloonist.*
A clipping at the Garrick Club dated 27 September 1784 is a notice from the balloonist Mr Keegan from his residence at No 81, the Strand, that his balloon could not be launched from Foley Gardens as promised because of the weather. He assured the public he would take off from the gardens on 30 September.

Keelin. *See* KEILING.

Keen. *See also* KEAN and KEENE.

Keen, Mr ₍*fl. 1789–1791?*₎,   *dancer.*

Mr Keen was first carried in the Drury Lane bills as dancing a hornpipe in Act III of *The Beggar's Opera* on 8 January 1789, an exercise which he repeated each of the several times the ballad opera was given that season. He danced a highland reel with Hamoir and Miss Stageldoir on 27 May. He does not seem to have given any other solo performances, though he may have been a regular in the corps of dancers. He shared in benefit tickets with 15 others on 10 June 1789. He played some minor and unspecified character in the pantomime *Harlequin's Frolics* on 26 December 1789.

Our subject was very likely the man of that name who was dancing at the Birmingham Theatre with Miss Valois in August of 1790 and who returned there in July 1791.

Keen, Miss ₍*fl. 1785*₎,   *dancer.*

On 26 December 1785 at the Haymarket Theatre Aphra Behn's old comedy *The Amorous Prince* was revived by "Independent Ladies and Gentlemen" for the benefit of "a Performer, thirty years a Servant of the Publick." In the masquerade in the fifth act of the mainpiece a *Minuet de la Cour* was danced by a Miss Keen and a Master Corbyn, neither of whom seem to have appeared again in London. They were probably juveniles and may have been amateurs.

Keen, Charles   *d. 1771, singer.*

An unidentified newsclipping dated 1771, in the British Library, reads "Mr. Kean of Sadler's Wells, lately said to be dead is living; the person who died was Charles Keen, a prisoner in the King's Bench, who formerly sung 'The Knife Grinder' at Sadler's Wells." He was probably the Mr Keen who was on the bills as a singer at Sadler's Wells in 1765.

Keen,   Edward   ₍*fl.   1699–1735?*₎, *impresario, composer, instrumentalist?*

The *Post Boy* on 11 May 1699 carried an advertisement for "A Consort of New Vocal and Instrumental Musick, for the Benefit of Mr Edward Keene, who was the first Promoter of the Musical Entertainments in Sommerset House Garden." The concert was held at York Buildings and was the first of many benefits over the years for Keen, who was a composer of songs and, perhaps, an instrumentalist—

though the advertisements never indicated his participation in concerts he promoted. All of his known concerts were at York Buildings, with tickets available from Keen at his house in Arundel Street. Though his concerts may have continued regularly over the years, we have only one notice after 1707: on 2 April 1729 at York Buildings.

Some of Keen's songs that were published were *Jemmy told his Passion* (1700?), *Celia's bright Beautys all other's transcend* (1704?) from *The Heiress*, and *Here's Health to those Men*, otherwise called *The Northampton-shire Health* (1719 or earlier). *The 4th Book of the Compleat Flute Master*, advertised in February 1707, contained "an excellent Solo, by Mr. Edw. Keen, never before published."

Some or perhaps all of the following parish register entries may refer to Keen's family. At St Paul, Covent Garden, on 15 September 1697 was buried Edward Keen (our subject's father?); Frances Keen, "a Musician's child," was buried at St Clement Danes on 10 October 1705; Ann Keen, similarly noted as a musician's child, was buried there on 20 August 1706; and Daniel Keen, "a Musick-man's child," was buried there on 9 November 1711.

When the elder John Walsh, music publisher, made his will on 20 May 1735 he left £10 to his brother-in-law Edward Keen. The will was proved on 26 March 1736. That Edward Keen may have been our subject, but we have found no other evidence to corroborate a link between the Keen and Walsh families in the first half of the eighteenth century. A generation later the younger John Walsh made his will on 2 August 1758 and left £500 and an annuity of £50 to his cousin Mary Keene. That will was proved on 9 July 1766.

Keen, William   *1740–1775, actor, singer.*

William Keen's first London appearance was at Drury Lane Theatre on 26 December 1764 as Maigre in the afterpiece *Queen Mab*. In the remainder of that season (in which he earned 15s. per week) he essayed only Ledger in *Polly Honeycombe*, Montague in *Romeo and Juliet*, and some part unspecified in *The Rites of Hecate*. He gravitated to the Haymarket in the summer following and is recorded there as Ledger, as Paduasoy in *The Commissary*, and in some roles in *The Orators* and *The Patron*.

In the season of 1765–66 at Covent Garden

Keen added to his repertoire Elliott in *Venice Preserv'd*, Zimventi in *The Orphan of China*, Hercides in *Mahomet*, Perez in *The Mourning Bride*, Myris in *All for Love*, Derby in *Jane Shore*, Eumenes in *The Rival Queens*, the Lawyer in *Love's Last Shift*, Blunt in *The London Merchant*, and some part in *The Hermit*. He was paid £1 per week. At the Haymarket in the summer of 1766 (and at the King's Theatre on 8 August and afterward) he repeated a number of his roles and added one of the Spouters in *The Apprentice*, Paris in *Romeo and Juliet*, Gibbet in *The Beaux' Stratagem*, Cornwall's Gentleman in *King Lear*, Lord Townly's Servant in *The Provok'd Husband*, the Duke in *Othello*, Spinosa in *Venice Preserv'd*, Charles in *As You Like It*, and Attacus in *Theodosius*.

From 27 October 1766 until mid-January 1767 he sang in an entertainment put on sporadically by "Signor Placido's company" at the Haymarket. At the Haymarket in July 1767 he was the original Phillippominos in the anonymous "Tragedy for Warm Weather," *The Taylors* (repeated several times), and in August had a part in *The Countess of Salisbury*.

Keen was at the Haymarket for only one more summer, that of 1768, but he returned to Drury Lane each winter season until 1774–75. His other roles, in approximate order, were: an Officer in *Tancred and Sigismunda*, Mirvan in *Tamerlane*, Angus in *Macbeth*, Merlin in *Cymon*, Robin of Bagshot in *The Beggar's Opera*, a Knight in *The Countess of Salisbury*, Jelizer in *Zingis*, an Officer in *Douglas*, a Messenger in John Home's new tragedy *The Fatal Discovery*, Sebastian in *The Tempest*, Hortensio in *Catherine and Petruchio*, Trueman in *The Clandestine Marriage*, the Prince in *Romeo and Juliet*, a Servant in *A New Way to Pay Old Debts*, Humphrey in *The Conscious Lovers*, the Captain in *Cymbeline*, Buckram in *Love for Love*, Blister in *The Double Gallant*, Tressel in *King Richard III*, a principal character in *The Jubilee*, Scaramouch in *The Elopement*, Lucius in *Theodosius*, Aurelius in *King Arthur*, Robin in *The Author*, Lyon in *The Reprisal*, Sebastian in *The Tempest*, Blandford in *All in the Wrong*, the Player King in *Hamlet*, Carbine in *Lethe*, Sotherton in *A Trip to Scotland*, the original Bully Boy in George Downing's slight farce *The Humours of the Turf*, Sellaway in *The Gamesters*, one of the Mob in *The Alchemist*, some part in Messink's

new pantomime *The Pigmy Revels*, Bridgemore in *The Fashionable Lover*, Harpax in *Albumazar*, Lord Racket in *The Heroine of the Cave*, Traverse in *The Clandestine Marriage*, Salarino in *The Merchant of Venice*, Calippus in *The Grecian Daughter*, a part in *Harlequin's Jacket*, an Officer in *Braganza*, the Coachman in *The Committee*, and Glumdalca in *Tom Thumb*.

Keen's parts very rarely were higher than the tertiary level, and most were comic or eccentric. But he served faithfully and seems to have gained the esteem of his manager. David Garrick wrote to the comedian John Moody on 11 August 1775: "I have been much shock'd twice this Summer with the Deaths of poor [Charles] Atkins, . . . and poor Keene." Keen had died at Liverpool on 1 August, at age 35, according to the *Morning Chronicle* of 19 August.

Keene. *See also* KEAN *and* KEEN.

Keene, Mr ₍*fl.* 1736₎, *actor.*
A Mr Keene played Careless in *The Committee* on 31 March 1736 at the Lincoln's Inn Fields playhouse. The play was not repeated.

Keene, Mr ₍*fl.* 1778₎, *actor.*
A Mr Keene played Gallono in *The Covent Garden Tragedy* in a specially-licensed performance at the Haymarket on 28 December 1778.

Keene, Robert ₍*fl.* 1791–1794₎, *singer?*
Robert Keene was listed as a "bass" (singer, presumably) in Doane's *Musical Directory* (1794), living at No 14, Albion Place, Wallworth, and belonging to the Handelian Society, the Surrey Chapel Society, and the Long Acre Society. He was said to have borne a part in the "grand performances" in Westminster Abbey commemorating Handel, the most recent of which had been in 1791.

Keene, Robert ₍*fl.* 1794₎, *singer?*
Robert Keene "Junr." of Duke Street, Manchester Square, a "bass" (singer, presumably) was listed in Doane's *Musical Directory* (1794) as a member of the Surrey Chapel Society.

Keene, Theophilus 1680–1718, actor.

The biography of Theophilus Keene, supposedly written by Richard Savage and signed on 18 August 1718, implies that Keene was born in 1680. His parents, the *Life* says, were dissenters, and young Theophilus was educated at the Presbyterian Academy in Little Britain to be a dissenting teacher. But he gave up that career, along with wealthy relatives who might have helped his fortune, because he did not care to follow dissenting beliefs. He became interested in the stage, joined John Coysh's troupe of strolling players, and married a Mrs Wilmot. He then, according to the *Life*, acted in Dublin.

W. S. Clark in *The Early Irish Stage* states that the Smock Alley manager Joseph Ashbury recruited Theophilus Keene and Benjamin Husband in 1696 and gave them their first professional training. Clark has Keene remaining in Dublin until 1704, though the *Life* has Keene in London and working for Rich's company at Lincoln's Inn Fields as early as 1695. But Rich managed Drury Lane, not Lincoln's Inn Fields, and Keene was listed in no London casts until 1704–5 at the earliest. Chetwood preserved three Smock Alley Casts from 1698–99, one of which contains Keene: he played Louis in *The Comical Revenge*. He was certainly in good company: also in the cast were Booth, Estcourt, and Wilks, all destined for important London careers.

By the spring of 1705 Keene was acting in London at Drury Lane, his earliest recorded part there being Freckle in *The Quacks* on 29 March. The following July he was seen as Borosky in *The Loyal Subject*, and in 1705–6 he played Portius in *Perolla and Izadora*, Meanwell in *The Fashionable Lover*, and Balance—a role that the *Life* said was very successful—in *The Recruiting Officer*.

Owen Swiney recruited Keene and a number of other Drury Lane players for his company at the Queen's Theatre in 1706–7. There Keene played the King in *1 Henry IV* on 26 October 1706 for his first appearance, then he acted Raymond in *The Spanish Fryar*, Balance, Burleigh in *The Unhappy Favourite*, Voltore in *Volpone*, Claudius in *Hamlet*, Wheadle in *The Comical Revenge*, the Grand Vizier in *Almyna*, Lovegood in *Wit Without Money*, Casca in *Julius Caesar*, Odmar in *The Indian Emperor*, Gerrard

in *The Royal Merchant*, the Surveyor in *Henry VIII*, Cinna in *Caius Marius*, Acasto in *The Orphan*, Sir Charles Freeman in *The Stratagem*, Lycon in *Phaedra and Hippolitus*, the Mad Scholar in *The Pilgrim*, Frontenac in *Liberty Asserted*, Loveday in *The London Cuckolds*, Count Baldwin in *The Fatal Marriage*, Lord Beaufoy in *The Taming of a Shrew*, the Captain in *The Old Troop*, Maherbal in *Sophonisba*, and Justice Overdo in *Bartholomew Fair*. That was a most impressive showing and probably more indicative of Keene's abilities when he came from Ireland than was his first season at Drury Lane, where the ensconced actors already controlled many parts Keene may have had in his repertoire.

Keene returned to the Queen's in the fall of 1707, but in midseason the management of the two main theatres shifted and the players moved to Drury Lane, leaving the Queen's to the opera company. From October 1707 to New Year's Day 1708 at the Queen's, Keene played some new parts: Story in *The Committee*, Surly in *Sir Courtly Nice*, Delphia in *The Maid's Tragedy*, Sullen in *The Stratagem*, Priuli in *Venice Preserv'd*, Oswald in *The Royal Convert*, Sir Friendly Moral in *The Lady's Last Stake*, Duncan in *Macbeth*, and Oldrents in *The Jovial Crew*. At Drury Lane for the remainder of the season he added such roles as Polyperchon in *The Rival Queens*, Archilaus in *Mithridates*, Petruchio in *The Chances*, Lord Brumpton in *The Funeral*, Gonzalez in *The Mourning Bride*, Bajazet in *Tamerlane* (for his benefit on 15 April), the Governor in *Oroonoko*, Sir Edward Belfond in *The Squire of Alsatia*, Old Meriton in *Love for Money*, Apemantus in *Timon of Athens*, and the King in *Don Carlos*.

Except for a momentary stay at the Queen's in November 1710, Keene acted at Drury Lane until the end of 1714 and the opening of John Rich's new playhouse in Lincoln's Inn Fields. His roles continued to be generally of the heavy, blunt sort. Chetwood noted that Keene, "Altho' a very good Figure and Voice, his Person wanted Elegance for the soft Characters." Audiences were especially enthusiastic about Keene's Claudius in *Hamlet*, which helped earn him the description of "majestic."

Some of his new parts at Drury Lane before the end of 1714 were Sir Edward Hartford in *The Lancashire Witches*, Hannibal in *Sophonisba*,

Harvard Theatre Collection

THEOPHILUS KEENE as Cato

engraving by Hulett

Clytus in *The Rival Queens* (another role he was praised for), Montezuma in *The Indian Emperor*, Iago and Brabantio in *Othello*, Egeon and Creon in *Oedipus*, Cardinal Wolsey in *Henry VIII*, Selecus in *The Humorous Lieutenant*, Kent in *King Lear*, Serapion in *All for Love*, Ajax in *Troilus and Cressida*, Chamont in *The Orphan* (after the death of Verbruggen), Scandal in *Love for Love*, Mahomet in *Abra Mule*, Aecius in *Valentinian*, Clause in *The Royal Merchant*, the title role in *Julius Caesar*, Heartwell in *The Old Bachelor*, the King in *The Maid's Tragedy*, the Emperor in *Aureng-Zebe*, Lucius in *Cato*, and Sir Solomon in *The Cautious Coxcomb*.

The managerial troubles that plagued Drury Lane in the early eighteenth century came to a head in 1710. The inexperienced proprietor William Collier in the 1709–10 season made Aaron Hill manager of the troupe at Drury Lane. But several of the actors, including Keene, had a share in the company management and were at odds with Hill. Hill took away their power, and Keene and John Bickerstaff, the most volatile of the actors who had thus been denied, led a riot that brought about their suspension from the company by Hill on 14 June 1710, but by then the summer vacation had begun. The managerial problems were solved during the 1710–11 season, and the stable management of Drury Lane by the triumvirate of Cibber, Wilks, and Doggett began.

On 18 December 1714 the new playhouse in Lincoln's Inn Fields opened, managed by John Rich and operating under the old Duke's Company patent of Sir William Davenant. Rich had attempted to recruit a number of Drury Lane players for his new troupe, but, as the *Weekly Packet* on 18 December reported, "some of the Gentlemen who have left the Theatre in Drury-Lane for that Service, are order'd to return to their Colours, upon Pain of not exerting their Lungs anywhere. . . ." Keene, one of those lured by Rich, played Kent in *King Lear* at Drury Lane on the day Lincoln's Inn Fields opened, but by 4 January 1715 he had changed his affiliation and acted Heartwell in *The Old Bachelor* at Rich's playhouse. He remained at Lincoln's Inn Fields for the rest of his life, acting such new parts as Carlos in *The False Count*, Manly in *The Plain Dealer*, Sir John Brute in *The Provok'd Wife*, Sebastian in *The Perfidious Brother*, Brutus in *Julius Caesar*, Dorax in *Don Sebastian*, Timon of Athens, Marcian in *Theodosius*, and the Governor in *The Island Princess*. He performed through the end of the 1716–17 season.

Steele wrote to Lady Steele on 11 June 1717 that Rich was "almost broke" and that the prospects were dim for a continuation of the venture at Lincoln's Inn Fields. The manage-ment of Rich's playhouse was turned over to Keene and Christopher Bullock. Rich's patent was signed over to them at the beginning of the 1717–18 season. In the middle of that season Keene had "a very great Fit of Illness," but recovered, according to the author of the actor's *Life*. Before he could begin a second season at Lincoln's Inn Fields, Keene died, at the age of 38. Chetwood, writing years later and romanticizing, reported that "the ill Success of the Theatre, when he was a Sharer in Profit and Loss, broke his Heart." The fact was far different.

The *Weekly Journal or Saturday's Post* of 2 August 1718 reported that on 23 July Keene, riding in the country, had been thrown by his horse and had died on 25 July. The St Clement Danes burial registers note his interment on 30 July 1718, in the vault, according to the *Life*, where Mountfort, Horden, and Powell had been buried. It was, as Chetwood termed it, a "Walking Funeral." A voluntary subscription was raised by members of both theatrical houses, and Keene's body was carried from his lodgings to St Clement Danes, with actors from each playhouse as pall-bearers. Two hundred people attended his funeral, wrote Chetwood, and the actor Walker spoke a blank-verse elegy.

Many would-be wits wrote verses at Keene's death, one of them saying, according to Chetwood, that "Death was found too Sharp for Keen." Other writers were more descriptive of Keene's talent. Richard Savage set the general consensus: "Majestick roughness in his Form was seen, / And Roman Grandeur dress'd his awful Mien!" "His manly Voice the British Genius fir'd," claimed Savage. William Wilks said:

> *Where Tragedy you Acted with such Grace,*
> *Such awful Gesture, such Majestick Mien;*
> *Ev'n Hannibal appear'd himself in Keene . . .*

But "C. W." was the most human; he said he "drank many a Bottle" with Keene, and they were often "very Merry together." Whereupon he wrote a light poem calling for toasts to a departed companion. Theophilus Keene's widow was granted a benefit on 4 December 1718 at Lincoln's Inn Fields Theatre.

In Harvard Theatre Collection is an engraving by Hulett of a scene from *Cato*, published as a frontispiece to the play in 1739. An inscription in pen states, "The only portrait of Mr Kean with his hand to his chest." On the verso, in ink: "Rare / actor and sharer of Lincoln's Inn Fields / Theatre. the unsuccessful Season of / 1717–18 broke his heart." The central figure could depict Keene, but there is no way of telling whether the likeness is reliable.

Keene, Mrs Theophilus, ₁formerly Mrs Wilmot?₁ ₁*fl. c. 1696?–1748?*₁, *dresser.*

The *Life* of the actor Theophilus Keene states that he married a Mrs Wilmot, evidently before going to Ireland, where we know he went in 1696. If the couple married about that time, Theophilus would have been about 16; Mrs Wilmot sounds older. But we cannot be certain of the facts about Keene's early years, and we certainly cannot be sure that, if he did marry a Mrs Wilmot, she was the widow he left when he died on 25 July 1718.

Widow Keene received a benefit at Lincoln's Inn Fields on 4 December 1718, and regularly throughout the 1720s she was cited in benefit bills. Among the clippings in the Burney Collection at the British Library is an item dated 19 January 1720 which advertises "The Widow Keene's Masquerade Habits to be Let, at the Domino and Turk in the Hay-Market, adjoining to the Theatre; or at her House, Numb. 7, in Cook's Court little Lincoln's Inn-Fields." The advertisement clearly indicates that she had her own business, but the regular benefits at the playhouse suggest that she was also an employee there. Indeed, the Lincoln's Inn Fields accounts in 1724 show not only a bill from her on 23 November, presumably for goods from her shop, but a salary payment on 7 December of £2 6s. for six days (an extraordinarily high weekly salary for a house servant, which she evidently was, and possibly an error).

Her last shared benefit on record was on 25 May 1730. The accounts at Covent Garden in 1735–36 indicate that Mrs Keene was one of the women dressers and also supplied the theatre with feathers. As a dresser she worked 172 acting days at 20d. daily (which fact makes us suspect that the earlier salary notice was in some way in error). She was presumably the Mrs Keene who was cited regularly for payments in the Covent Garden accounts in 1746–47 and through January 1748.

Keesberry. *See* KEASBERRY.

Keeting. *See* KEATING.

Keiling, John, called "Blind Jack" ₁*fl. c. 1720*₁, *musician.*

In his *Remarkable Persons* (1819), Caulfield described John Keiling, known as "Blind Jack," a bizarre musician who was active about 1720:

John Keiling, alias Blind Jack, having the misfortune to lose his sight, thought of a strange method to insure himself a livelihood. He was constitutionally a hale, robust fellow, without any complaint, saving blindness, and having learnt to play a little on the flageolet, he conceived a notion that, by performing on that instrument in a different way to that generally practiced, he should render himself more noticed by the public, and be able to lay larger contributions on their pockets.

The manner of Blind Jack's playing the flageolet was by obtruding the mouthpiece of the instrument up one of his nostrils, and, by long custom, he could produce as much wind as most others with their lips into the pipe; but the continued contor-

Harvard Theatre Collection

JOHN KEILING

engraving by Grave

tion and gesticulation of his muscles and countenance, rendered him an object of derision and disgust, as much as that of charity and commiseration.

An anonymous engraving of Blind Jack Keiling, in oval, performing on the flageolet with his nose, was published by D. Wansell. A copy, in rectangle, engraved by R. Grave, was published in Caulfield's *Remarkable Persons*, in 1819. Another copy, by an unknown engraver, oval in rectangle, was also issued, undated.

Keiling, John Gaspar [*fl. 1688?–1696*], *musician.*

One "Keelin" attended the King at Windsor from 24 July to 20 September 1688. He was a musician and may have been one of the children of the Chapel Royal, who were required to attend during that period. On 14 January 1696 John Gaspar Keiling (the same person?) was appointed a musician without fee in the King's Musick, waiting for a salaried post to become vacant.

Keiser, Mr [*fl. 1727*], *house servant.*

An entry in the Lincoln's Inn Fields accounts dated 2 March 1727 reads "Mr Harrison by Keiser." Harrison was a hosier who dealt with the playhouse; Keiser was evidently a house servant, perhaps an office worker, who in this instance was apparently arranging for complimentary tickets for Harrison.

Keisher. *See* KISHEIR.

Keitch. *See* KYTCH.

Keith, Mr [*fl. 1723*], *actor.*

The 1724 edition of *Sir Thomas Overbury* lists a Mr Keith as Sir George Elloways. The play was given at Drury Lane on 12 June 1723.

Keith, Cornelius *1758–1800, singer, organist, violinist, guitar player.*

Cornelius Keith was the son of William and Mary Keith of Mile End Old Town. He was born on 20 June 1758 and was christened four days later at St Dunstan, Stepney. His father was (later?) organist of West Ham Church, Essex; we have no record of his having performed professionally in London. Cornelius sang tenor in the Handel Memorial Concerts

at Westminster Abbey and the Pantheon in May and June 1784, and the following 5 August at St Leonard, Shoreditch, he married Sarah Langford, spinster, of that parish. Their son Robert William Keith was born on 20 March 1787 at Stepney, according to his own letter years later to Sainsbury the biographical dictionary editor. In 1787 Cornelius Keith was the organist of St Peter, Cornhill, and of the Danish Chapel in Wellclose Square.

On 1 November 1788 Cornelius was recommended for membership in the Royal Society of Musicians. By that time he had added to his organist's posts that at the City of London Lying-in Hospital in City Road. He was also noted as proficient on the violin and guitar and the teacher of a number of music students. Keith was elected to the Society on 1 February 1789. He played violin in the St Paul's concert in May most years from 1789 through 1800. Keith apparently died between May and 7 September 1800, when his four children were granted £3 monthly for maintenance.

Sarah Keith, after a year of widowhood, married Joseph Wood at St Martin-in-the-Fields on 22 September 1801. The Royal Society of Musicians, however, continued its concern for her children. On 3 April 1803 a daughter of Cornelius Keith (named Cornelia? the Minute Books are difficult to decipher) had been placed on trial with Mr Robson, an upholsterer in Red Lion Street, Whitechapel, to learn the trade of upholstery and mantuamaking. She had been successful and was bound his apprentice. On 3 November 1811 the Society learned from Mrs Wood that her son Cornelius Keith Junior had been bound apprentice to the musical instrument maker Mr Reading, of Upper John Street, Golden Square. It seems to have been young Cornelius who, because his conduct during his apprenticeship was reported to the Society as irregular and disobedient, was refused his usual (annual?) benefaction of £10 on 7 January 1816. The elder son, Robert William, studied music under his grandfather and did not go through an apprenticeship.

Sarah Langford Keith Wood's second husband was buried at St John the Evangelist, Lambeth, on 29 June 1834, aged 56. On 10 August Mrs Wood sought aid from the Royal Society of Musicians. She wrote that she was then 66 years old and reduced to living on a

£24 annuity; Joseph Wood had died insolvent. She gave her address as No 58, York Street, York Road, Lambeth. On 7 September relief was granted her, and the record indicated that she had no children.

Keitsh. *See* KYTCH.

Kelf, Mrs. *See* AMBROSE, MISS, LATER MRS KELF.

Kellaway. *See* KELWAY.

Kelley. *See also* KELLY.

Kelley, Charles [*fl. 1739*], *musician.*
Charles Kelley was one of the original members of the Royal Society of Musicians when it was founded on 28 August 1739.

Kelley, George [*fl. 1710*], *musician.*
The Court of Burgesses of Westminster recorded in the minutes on 17 January 1710:

A petition of the Waits belonging to this City and Liberty was presented to the Court complayning of severall psons that play on Musick and receive in their Stead in the Parish of St. James's Westmr diverse Sumes of money prtending to be authorised so to do by Mr. Justice Tully and 2 other Justices of the Peace wch is much to their damage desiring relief from the Court. It is Ordered by the Cort That the consideracon of the said Peticon & prmises be putt of to the next Court day.

The following week the minutes were more specific: "John Herbert Joseph Clay and George Kelley and other Musitians living in the Parish of St. James . . . have not only this last but Christmas was twelve months taken & received severall Sumes of money." The culprits were ordered to appear before the court, but no record has been found of the outcome of the case.

Kellner, Christopher [*fl. 1794*], *oboist.*
Doane's *Musical Directory* of 1794 listed Christopher Kellner, of No 29, James Street, Westminster, as an oboist who performed for the New Musical Fund, the Concert of Ancient Music, and in the Handel concerts at Westminster Abbey. He was a member of the Court of Assistants of the New Musical Fund in 1794.

(Doane also lists a "C. Kelner," violinist and horn player in the Queen's Band at Buckingham House. Conceivably the same as the oboist, "Kelner" may also have been the son of our subject.)

Kellner, Earnest [*fl. 1794*], *horn player.*
Doane's *Musical Directory* of 1794 listed Earnest Kellner, of No 29, James Street, Westminster, as a horn player who performed for the New Musical Fund, the Concert of Ancient Music, and in the Handel concerts at Westminster Abbey. He was certainly related to Christopher Kellner of the same address and may have been the father of Ernest Augustus Kellner, who was born at Windsor in 1792 and had a musical career in the nineteenth century.

(Doane also lists an "E. Kelner" of No 12, Castle Street, Leicester Square, a bassoonist of the Queen's Band who played for the New Musical Fund. Very likely "Kelner" is either our subject or his son.)

Kellner, Ephraim [*fl. 1735?–1752*], *singer?*
A Mr Kellner (or Knellar) sang in *King Arthur* at the Goodman's Fields playhouse on 17 December 1735 as a member of Henry Giffard's company. On 20 February 1736 he was a Shepherd in *Harlequin Shipwrecked*, and when Giffard's troupe moved to Lincoln's Inn Fields in the fall of 1736, Kellner again sang in *King Arthur*. Perhaps the singer was Ephraim Kellner, who was one of the original members of the Royal Society of Musicians when it was founded on 28 August 1739. Ephraim Kellner was named in the will of Johann Christoph Pepusch, written on 9 July 1752 and proved on 21 May 1753, as co-inheritor with John Travers of all of Pepusch's moveables and books of music. The two men were also named residuary legatees.

Kellner, Johann August *1756–1835,* *instrumentalist.*
According to the recommendation for membership in the Royal Society of Musicians in 1788 of Johann August Kellner, he was born in 1756, apparently in Germany. One would guess that he may have been the son of Johann Christoph Kellner (1736–1803), the German composer who became organist of the court

church at Kassel. On 7 September 1788 Johann August was proposed for membership in the Royal Society of Musicians. He was described as married but with no children, 32 years old, a member of the Queen's band, a performer in the Ancient Music concerts in Tottenham Street, and a musician proficient on the bassoon, violoncello, trombone, and tenor (horn, one supposes, though perhaps a viola). Kellner was admitted to the Society on 4 January 1789, and every May from 1790 through 1800 and again in 1811 he played in the St Paul's concert. He usually played bassoon, but once he was listed for double bass and once for violin. In 1797 the Society minutes show that Kellner served on the Board of Governors.

Kellner's second wife was Isabella Maria Wheatly, "spinster," whom he married at St Margaret, Westminster, on 22 December 1818. Isabella on 2 October 1835 reported to the Society the death of her husband "John" August Kellner on 17 September 1835 after an illness that kept him bed-ridden and helpless for 11 months. Mrs Kellner noted that her husband's death had occurred shortly before his quarterly pension payment from the crown became due (Kellner, she said, had been an assistant in the band of George III). She found herself in embarrassed circumstances, her only support being what she earned from a day school. She asked the Society for expenses to cover her husband's funeral. The Board of Governors voted her not only £12 funeral expenses but also an allowance of £2 12s. 6d. monthly. Mrs Kellner wrote her letter from No 16, Pack Street, Windsor, and it seems probable that Kellner had died there. Mrs Kellner was twice again cited in the Society minutes, in July 1836 and July 1837, when her affidavits were admitted.

Kellom. *See* TOMLINSON, KELLOM.

Kelly, Mr [*fl.* 1732–1741], *singer, actor.*
Mr Kelly was apparently making his first public appearance when he sang Casimir in *Amelia* at the Haymarket Theatre on 13 March 1732. Almost exactly a year later, on 14 March 1733, Kelly played Plume in *The Recruiting Officer* at the same playhouse—unless that was a different Kelly. On 16 April he was Telemachus in *Ulysses* at Lincoln's Inn Fields, and at his shared benefit on 16 May he sang in Italian and English. In the fall of 1733 he performed with Theophilus Cibber's rebel Drury Lane players at the Haymarket, appearing as King Arthur in *The Opera of Operas*, a Shepherd in *The Festival*, and Mercury in *Dido and Aeneas*, From March 1734 on the performers were at Drury Lane, Cibber's argument with the management there having been settled. Kelly's first part at Drury Lane was Mars in *Love and Glory* on 21 March, after which he was a Follower of Mars in *Britannia* and perhaps Mercury in *Cupid and Psyche* (the newspapers contained conflicting casts; either Kelly or Mountier took the role).

Kelly joined Henry Giffard's company at Goodman's Fields in 1734–35, making his first appearance in the bills there on 14 February 1735 as Jupiter in *Jupiter and Io*. Before the season was over he appeared also as Rovewell in *The Contrivances*. On 2 May 1735 Kelly had a benefit at Hickford's Music Room. The following season he played Damon in *Damon and Phillida*, Rovewell, Gaylove in *The Honest Yorkshireman*, Patie in *Patie and Peggy*, Clerimont in *The Lover His Own Rival*, Paris in *Harlequin Shipwrecked*, and Jupiter in *Jupiter and Io*. On 22 April 1736 he made an appearance at Drury Lane as a principal character in *A Grand Epithalamium*—perhaps substituting for someone who was indisposed.

Giffard's group moved to Lincoln's Inn Fields theatre in 1736–37. There Kelly repeated some of his earlier parts and sang a role in *King Arthur*, Germanicus and an Attendant on Germanicus in *Britannia*, a Gamester in *The Beggar's Pantomime*, an Attendant on Polly in an alteration of *The Beggar's Opera*, a Priest in *Hymen's Triumph*, a part in *The Mad House*, and Friendly in *Flora*. In 1738–39 Kelly sang with the opera troupe at the King's Theatre. Dean in *Handel's Dramatic Oratorios and Masques* lists Kelly as a countertenor who was the High Priest in *Saul* and probably also sang in the chorus in 1739. Kelly sang in *Acis and Galatea* in 1741.

Kelly, Mons [*fl.* 1749–1750], *actor.*
With Monnet's troupe of French players was one Kelly in 1749–50 at the Haymarket Theatre. The company opened their season on 14 November, but because England was at war with France and anti-Gallic sentiment was

running high, the players found their performances frequently interrupted. The King withdrew their license in December because of the disturbances. Monnet was given a benefit the following 22 May 1750 at Drury Lane to help him recoup some of his losses, and he published an accounting that showed Kelly to have been engaged at £30 18s. Some of the members of the troupe did not receive their full salaries, but Kelly did. None of his roles were named in the bills, which is not surprising, for he was the lowest-paid member of the company.

Kelly, Mr [*fl.* 1787], *actor.*

At the end of a specially-licensed performance of *The Orphan of China* at the Haymarket Theatre on 26 March 1787, a Mr Kelly offered "a variety of *Imitations.*" He may have been any one of at least a half-dozen actors of that name who were performing in the provinces during that period.

Kelly, Mr [*fl.* 1789–1802], *equestrian, actor.*

Mr Kelly, from the Royal Circus in London, performed a Herald in a spectacular production of *Liberty Triumphant* at the Merchant Taylors' Hall, Bristol, on 26 November 1789 and several other times through 5 December. He was probably the Kelly who exhibited equestrian exercises at the Royal Circus in London in May and June 1800 and in August 1802. There on 16 August 1802 he performed Aquila in *Gonsalvo de Cordova; or, The Conquest of Granada.* That summer a Mrs Kelly, perhaps his wife, appeared in burlettas at the Royal Circus.

Kelly, Mrs [*fl.* 1743], *actress.*

Mrs Kelly played an Irish Woman in *The Glorious Queen of Hungary* on 4 August 1743 at a booth run by Daniel, Malone, and James at Tottenham Court. She repeated the role at the Turbutt-Dove booth at Bartholomew Fair on 23 August.

Kelly, Charles [*fl.* 1793–1815], *violinist, violist.*

Charles Kelly, a violinist and violist living at No 6, Barnard's Inn, Holborn, was listed in Doane's *Musical Directory* of 1794 as a member of the Academy of Ancient Music and the Amicable Society and a performer at the Oxford Meeting of 1793 and the Handelian memorial concerts in Westminster Abbey. On 27 September 1794 he became a freeman of the Worshipfull Company of Musicians. In 1815 he was listed as a subscriber to the New Musical Fund, to which he had belonged as early as 1794.

Kelly, L. [*fl.* 1791–1799], *actor.*

L. Kelly of "Malbro Place" was a member of the company at Richmond, Surrey, in the summer of 1799, according to a Winston manuscript in the Richmond Reference Library. An actor with that surname and first initial was performing at Dublin in 1791.

Kelly, Mark 1767–1833, *actor, singer.*

Born in Dublin in 1767, Mark Kelly was one of 14 children of Thomas Kelly, a wine merchant in Mary Street and Deputy Master of Ceremonies at Dublin Castle. Mark Kelly's mother, formerly a Miss McCabe from a respectable family of Westmeath, had been sent for her education to a Roman Catholic convent on Arran Quay, where she met Thomas Kelly while he was visiting a young relative. They eloped, but that impetuosity was eventually forgiven by her father, who settled a dowry of £5000 on the bride. Among Mark Kelly's brothers were Michael Kelly (1762–1826), who became very well-known as a singer and composer; Joseph Kelly (d. 1817), who acted in Ireland for several seasons in the 1790s; and Patrick Kelly, an army officer who was killed at Seringapatam in 1799. A married sister acted briefly and unsuccessfully as Mrs Trevor at Covent Garden in 1800.

Both Mark Kelly and his brother Joseph were playing in the provinces in the early 1790s. It was probably Mark who acted comic juveniles at Liverpool and Manchester in 1792, and at Bristol in 1792–93 and 1793–94, and at Chester in 1794. A notation dated 1 October 1794 on a Folger Library manuscript informs us that "A brother of Mr. [Michael] Kelly is engaged at D. L. who is likely to make a respectable Figure as an Actor, as well as in the vocal line." Mark Kelly's full name was entered on the Drury Lane salary list on 6 October 1794, when he was paid £4 4s. for 12 days. On 20 October he was put down for a nightly wage of 6*s.* 8*d*. Among his assignments that season was as one of the Satraps in *Alexander the Great*, a pantomime which opened on 12 February 1795 and ran 36 performances. The bills carried his name as "Kelly Jun" to avoid confusion with his more famous brother.

Our subject perhaps was the Kelly who performed at St Mary's Hall, Coventry, in 1796–97, at Southampton in 1801, at Newcastle in 1802, and at Bristol from 1806 through 1809.

Sometime after 1782, Kelly married the provincial actress Mary Jackson, the widow of another itinerant player. She had been born Mary Singleton on 12 August 1763, the daughter of a physician. By Jackson she had had four children, two of whom had died from scarlatina, along with their father. A third died shortly afterward from an accident. The surviving child of the marriage with Jackson was Anne (b. 1782), named after a maternal aunt Anne Ross, the wife of the London actor David Ross. (Young Anne made appearances as a child on provincial stages; then she proved a favorite on the London stage at the beginning of the nineteenth century; in 1803 she became the second wife of the actor Charles Mathews and enjoyed a stage career as Mrs. Mathews. Anne Mathews died in 1869.)

The union of Mark Kelly and Mary Jackson was made unhappy by his extravagance, which brought heavy debts. Probably he was the Kelly who was in debtor's prison at the time of his benefit at Coventry on 19 April 1790. A ne'er-do-well, who aped his brother Michael's fashionable manners and parties without possessing his resources or talents, Mark enjoyed little competence or success either socially or artistically. In 1795 he abandoned Mrs Kelly, who found herself without resources and with three children by him. The eldest, Francis Maria Kelly (1790–1882), became a very successful nineteenth-century performer; she is noticed in *The Dictionary of National Biography* and is the subject of a book by Basil Francis (1950). The middle child, Lydia Eliza Kelly (b. 1795), took to the Drury Lane stage by the middle of the first decade of the nineteenth century, but she could never remove herself from her sister's shadow. The third and youngest, Michael Crouch Kelly, evidently joined the navy.

Mark Kelly died at Canterbury on 4 April 1833. His estranged wife had died on 1 August 1827.

Kelly, Michael   *1762–1826, actor, singer, composer, musical director, manager.*

In the Harvard Theatre Collection is an engraved picture of Michael Kelly's tombstone which once stood in St Paul, Covent Garden, churchyard with a lengthy inscription, part of which read, "Born in Dublin, Augt 12th 1762." In his *Reminiscences*, published in 1826, Kelly provided neither day nor year for his birth. He was the eldest of 14 children of Thomas Kelly, a prosperous wine merchant who also served as Deputy Master of Ceremonies at Dublin Castle. Michael's mother was the former Miss McCabe, of a respectable Westmeath family. She had been placed for her education in a Roman Catholic convent on Arran Quay, where she met Thomas Kelly, who eloped with her. They were eventually forgiven by her father, who settled a dowry of £5000 on his daughter.

Harvard Theatre Collection

MICHAEL KELLY

by Condé

Michael's youth was comfortably passed in a household full of music and hospitality. No man in the city was more renowned than Thomas Kelly, claimed his son Michael, or "gave better dinners or better wine." Mr and Mrs Kelly "were both excessively fond of music, and considered to sing with taste." The father was probably the Thomas Kelly whose name was entered on treasury ledgers (destroyed by fire in 1922) in the Dublin Public Record Office as a state musician earning from £10 to £40 per year in the late 1760s. The talent for music which Michael demonstrated at an early age was fostered by his parents and cultivated by a series of teachers, beginning with Morland and then Cogan and Michael Arne for pianoforte, Passerini, Pereti, San Giorgio for singing, and Neale for violin. As a lad Michael participated in Kane O'Hara's "Fantoccini" performances at the Capel Street Theatre.

On 17 May 1777 (and not in 1779 as incorrectly remembered by Kelly), Signor Savoy having become ill, Kelly made his stage debut singing as the Count in Piccinni's *La buona figliuola* at the Fishamble Street Theatre. Tall for 15, possessed of a powerful treble voice, and well-versed in Italian, Kelly was successful beyond expectation. Under the direction of Michael Arne, Kelly sang the title-role in *Cymon* at the Crow Street Theatre for three nights, which he followed on a fourth night, 7 June 1777, with his Master Lionel in *Lionel and Clarissa* for his own benefit before a crowded house.

Heeding the advice of Rauzzini, who also had given the boy some singing lessons, Michael's father sent him to study in Italy. Departing Dublin on 1 May 1779, he arrived at Naples on 30 May to begin instruction under Finaroli, head of the Conservatorio of La Madonna de Loreto. By summer of 1780 he moved to Palermo to study voice under Aprile, who also gave him a home. Over the next four years Kelly traveled throughout Italy, giving concerts or performing at theatres in Leghorn (where he first met Stephen and Nancy Storace, 19 and 16 respectively), Pisa, Florence, Bologna, Venice, Brescia, Treviso, and Verona. He also sang in *La vera costanza* and *Zemire et Azor* at Graz in October 1782. In that year he was offered an engagement at Drury Lane by Linley, but his father disapproved, and Kelly

remained on the Continent. An account of the years in Italy occupies a substantial portion of the *Reminiscences*.

In the early summer of 1784 (not 1783 as Kelly implies) he was engaged for the Italian opera at the Vienna court theatre, making his debut probably in the old-man role of Gafferio in Paisiello's *Il re Teodoro* on 23 August. During his four years in this heady musical environment he met Haydn, worked with Gluck, and became close friends with Mozart. Among the operas he sang were *La Frascatana*, *Le gare generose*, *Alceste*, *Iphigenia in Tauride*, *Gli sposi malcontenti*, *Gli equivoci*, and *La grotta di Trofonio*. Notably, he created the roles of Basilio and Don Curzio in the premiere of Mozart's *Le nozze di Figaro* on 1 May 1786. Kelly's detailed account of that production and his remarks on the great composer's life have contributed much to Mozartiana.

In February 1787, having obtained his leave from Emperor Joseph, Kelly departed Vienna for London, accompanied by the Storaces, who had engagements waiting at the King's Theatre. Also in the traveling party were the Storaces' mother and the musician Thomas Attwood. After a visit to Mozart's father at Salzburg and some theatre-going at Paris, they arrived at London on 18 March. It was the first time that Kelly had been there.

On 20 April 1787 Kelly made his London debut at Drury Lane as Lionel in *A School for Fathers*, an alteration of *Lionel and Clarissa*. In the piece Kelly sang an Italian air by Sarti, with English words written by Richard Tickell. A duet written by French Laurence, for which Kelly composed the melody and Stephen Storace the instrumental parts, was also introduced. *A School for Fathers* was repeated on 24 April. Kelly was then seen as Young Meadows in *Love in a Village* on 11 May 1787, when he introduced the song "Love thou maddening power" and the duet "In thee each joy possessing," both composed by Gluck with words by Elizabeth Sheridan. On 19 May 1787 his name was added to the Drury Lane paylist for £1 13s. 4d. per day. At the end of May and the beginning of June he sang in the Handel memorial concerts at Westminster Abbey.

During his first months in London, Kelly had met Anna Maria Crouch (née Phillips), a beautiful young actress who played Clarissa on the night he had made his debut. Though she had married a naval officer, Rawlings Edward Crouch, in January 1785, she encouraged Kelly's attentions. He soon moved to lodgings in Rathbone Place in order to be near her home and proceeded to coach her in singing. Soon they became inseparable, offstage and on; her indolent husband seems not to have been distressed by the liaison and indeed they all lived and traveled in cozy fashion, a bizarre ménage à trois, until Crouch ran off in 1791, leaving Kelly and Mrs Crouch to live like husband and wife, which they did until her death in 1805.

When Kelly received news of his mother's death he departed London on 8 June 1787 to visit his father at Dublin, where he arrived on the twelfth. With him were the Crouches. That summer Kelly and Mrs Crouch performed 12 nights at Smock Alley to crowded houses and a reception which Kelly found "highly gratifying." The duet "In thee each joy possessing," as sung by them, was published in the October 1787 issue of *Hibernian Magazine*. After appearances at Limerick and Cork they recrossed the Irish Sea to perform during race week for Tate Wilkinson at York, beginning their engagement on 22 August as Lionel and Clarissa and then offering Macheath and Polly in *The Beggar's Opera*, Don Carlos and Clara in *The Duenna* (on the twenty-seventh when they also sang in *Cymon* what Wilkinson described as their "new-fangled whimsical duet," "O thou wert born to please me"), and Leander and Lenora in *The Padlock*. They also played for Wilkinson at Leeds and Wakefield, departing the latter place after singing Henry and Louisa in *The Deserter* on 13 September 1787, bound for London. (In *History of the Theatres of Brighton*, Porter places Michael Kelly in that company in the summer of 1787, but he mistakes him for another performer of that surname, some one of a number of itinerant Kellys.)

At Drury Lane in 1787–88 Kelly performed Young Meadows, a Bacchanal in *Comus*, Arbaces in *Artaxerxes*, the title-role in *Richard Coeur de Lion*, Henry in *The Deserter*, Lionel, Lord Aimworth, in *The Maid of the Mill*, Azor in *Selima and Azor*, Warnford in the premiere of Cobb's *Love in the East* (on 25 February 1788), and Artabanes for his own benefit in *Artaxerxes*, on 7 April, when Mrs Crouch played the male role of Arbaces and tickets could be had of Kelly at No 48, Rathbone

Place. Receipts totaled £351 5s. 6d., less house charges of £111 3s.

In the summer of 1788 Kelly and Mrs Crouch, accompanied by Mr Crouch, toured the north of England. At Drury Lane again in 1788–89 he was seen as Carlos in *The Doctor and the Apothecary*, Sir John Loverule in *The Devil to Pay*, and Macheath in *The Beggar's Opera*, among other roles. For his benefit on 17 April 1789, when he played Montano in *The Stranger at Home*, his receipts were £216 15s. 6d. (less £120 7s. 5d. in house charges) and tickets were available from him at No 7, King Street, Covent Garden. (At that time Mr and Mrs Crouch were at No 56, Titchfield Street, so evidently Kelly was not living with them. When the Crouches were legally separated in 1791 and Crouch disappeared with a sizeable allowance, Kelly and Anna Maria moved into a large house at No 4, Pall Mall. By 1794 they had gone into a larger one in Suffolk Street, Haymarket. There they stayed until the end of the 1796–97 season, when they moved to No 9, Lisle Street, Leicester Square, a house they shared until Mrs Crouch's death.)

Kelly made his first appearance at the King's Theatre on 11 June 1789, singing Almaviva in Paisiello's *Il Barbiere di Siviglia* for his friend Storace's benefit. With Mrs Crouch he passed the summer of 1789 on the Irish circuit, playing Limerick, Cork, and Waterford. After Ireland they went on to Liverpool, and in October they sang at "a grand musical festival" at Norwich.

The 1789–90 season at Drury Lane, when Kelly earned £11 per week, was marked by the premiere of Cobb's very successful comic opera *The Haunted Tower* on 24 November 1789, with Kelly as Lord William. Stephen Storace's music established him as a leading English composer. That season Kelly also acted Ferdinand in J. P. Kemble's musical alteration of *The Tempest*, Honor in *Arthur and Emmeline*, and Frederick in *No Song, No Supper*. On 3 June 1790 he again sang Count Almaviva, this time at the Haymarket, where the opera company, recently burned out of the King's, was playing.

Kelly and his mistress were with Joseph Fox when Fox opened the Duke Street Theatre at Brighton on 13 July 1790 and then Kelly and Mrs Crouch, along with her husband and the actor Jack Johnstone, spent August in Paris. It may have been his radical tendencies that

Harvard Theatre Collection

MICHAEL KELLY as Macheath

engraving by Murray, after Cruikshank

drew Kelly to Paris several times in the early 1790s, though ostensibly his purpose was "to see what I could pick up in the way of dramatic novelty for Drury Lane." Kelly also enjoyed great success at the Concerts of Ancient Music in London between 1789 and 1791, so pleasing the King and many subscribers with his rendition of Handel's "Haste thee nymph" that the song was repeated by request four times in one season.

In 1790–91, with his salary again £11 per week, Kelly created the role of the Seraskier in the premiere of the Cobb-Storace comic opera *The Siege of Belgrade*, a piece which opened on 1 January 1791, had 47 performances before the end of the season, and continued as a very popular standby in the repertory for many years. For Mrs Crouch's benefit on 3 May 1791, Kelly played Amintas in the premiere of Prince Hoare's comic-operatic afterpiece *The Cave of Trophonius* (it was not published but the manuscript is in the Larpent Collection at the

Huntington Library), again with the music principally by Storace.

Kelly went to Paris in June 1791, but returned to accompany Mrs Crouch at the Oxford Musical Festival in July (she became ill, but he performed). That summer he sang at the Chester and Newcastle Festivals, at the Concerts in the Minster and in the Assembly Rooms at York, and again in Wilkinson's company.

The autumn of 1792 found the Drury Lane company at the King's Theatre because their house had been torn down to make way for a larger edifice which would not open for another two years. At the King's, Kelly performed his usual repertoire, adding Don Altador in *The Pirate*, another comic opera by Cobb and Storace, on 21 November 1792. He also sang at Ranelagh Gardens in 1792 but spent most of the summer of 1792 at Paris, without Mrs Crouch. According to rumor, an intimacy had sprung up between her and the Prince of Wales, a charge vigorously denied by Anna Maria. In later years the Prince was a frequent guest at the brilliant routs Kelly and Mrs Crouch sponsored. The couple sang in the spring oratorios at Covent Garden in 1793.

When the opera finally resumed at the King's Theatre on 26 January 1793, Kelly found himself acting joint manager with Storace. That season he performed in *Odenato e Zenobia*, *Le nozze di Dorina*, and *I Zingari in Fiera*, in the last piece singing Perillo on 14 May, with nine costume changes. In the summer of 1793 he and Mrs Crouch toured Birmingham, Manchester, Chester, Shrewsbury, Worcester, and Liverpool. From November 1793 to the end of January 1794 they combined work with pleasure in hospitable Dublin.

The new Drury Lane Theatre opened on 12 March 1794 with a series of oratorios in which Kelly was a principal singer, along with Harrison, Storace, Mrs Crouch, and others. He sang in the chorus of Witches and Spirits which graced *Macbeth*, the first dramatic performance at that theatre on 21 April, and then on 26 April he played Frederick in *No Song, No Supper*, followed by several of his familiar parts in May. On 13 June 1794 Kemble's very successful *Lodoiska*, set to music composed and selected by Storace, opened with Kelly as Count Floreski. By the end of the month the afterpiece had enjoyed 20 performances and in the next season was seen 34 times. On 2 July 1794 he was Splicem in Sheridan and Cobb's patriotic entertainment *The Glorious First of June*. With Mrs. Crouch he spent the early summer at Edinburgh, playing Macheath, Frederick, Henry, Inkle, Lionel, Lord William, Robin, and Young Meadows; then he performed at York in late August.

By 1794, some seven years after he had made his London debut, Kelly had achieved some consequence in his profession as a principal tenor at the leading concerts and oratorios. At the King's Theatre he was established as stage manager, a position in which he was to continue for the rest of his life, though usually that earned him no extra pay except for his benefit nights. At Drury Lane his colleagues had voted him into the "School of Garrick," that congenial club of veterans which enjoyed monthly fellowship and food. He was also a member of the Academy of Ancient Music and the New Musical Fund.

At the King's Theatre in the season of 1795 Kelly was heard as Gafforio in *Il conte ridicolo*, Admeto in *Alceste*, Arsace in *Semiramide*, and Biscaglino in *L'Isola del piacere*. Thereafter he sang little there, for "Though a good musician and not a bad singer," as the Earl of Mount-Edgcumbe wrote, "Kelly had retained or regained so much of the English vulgarity of manner that he was never greatly liked at the King's Theatre." Pohl found his voice wanting in sweetness and melody and his rather effeminate features lacking in expression. His knowledge of stage business and musical direction continued to make him an important fixture. Of his contribution to Mazzinghi's *La bella Arsene* on 12 December 1795 the *Times* wrote that "The greatest treat for the ear were the choruses under the direction of Mr. Kelly; they were given with such judgment and accuracy as proves the utility of a separate direction for this department."

Though Kelly's acting was not his strong point and his voice was unremarkable, he possessed a style and technique which, combined with his stage-sense and intelligence, assured him popularity in the more vigorous tradition of English theatrical music at Drury Lane. His name is associated with some of the most popular pieces to be presented there in the last decade of the eighteenth century and the first

decade of the next. Among his roles in 1795–96 were Colonel Blandford in *The Cherokee*, Armstrong in *The Iron Chest*, and an unspecified part in *Mahoud*. The last-mentioned premiered on 30 April 1796, five weeks after its composer Storace had died on 19 March, and the music was completed by Nancy Storace and Kelly. In 1796–97 he performed Marcos in *The Prisoner*, Sir George Orbit in the premiere of Linley's *The Honey Moon* on 7 January 1797 and Count Solano in *A Friend in Need*, Hoare's new comic opera on 9 February, for which Kelly selected some old music and provided some new, the beginning really of a long series of musical settings he would concoct for Drury Lane productions. On 8 May 1797 Cumberland's *The Last of the Family* opened with songs composed by Kelly. By that year Kelly was functioning as Drury Lane's musical director.

In 1797–98 Kelly played Selim in Colman's fabulously successful musical drama *Blue-Beard*, which premiered on 16 January 1798, ran 64 performances by the season's end, and then was offered 38 times in the next season. The music was composed by Kelly, who also laced his work with selections from Paisiello. The *Times* suggested that if Kelly would "check that constant tempest of passion which tears to rags almost every sentiment he delivers, the dialogue of the piece would be much improved." That season he also wrote songs for *The Chimney Corner* (7 October 1797) and incidental music for "Monk" Lewis's *The Castle-Spectre*. Other pieces for which he composed before the end of the century included *The Outlaws* (in which he acted Anastro), *The Captive of Spilburg*, *Aurelio and Miranda*, *Feudal Times* (in which he played Edmund), and *Pizarro* in 1798–99 and *The Children*, *Of Age To-morrow*, and *De Montfort* in 1799–1800. On 16 November 1799 he played a leading (unspecified) role in the premiere of Linley's afterpiece *The Pavilion* (altered and later acted on 21 January 1800 as *The Ring*). In praising Miss De Camp's performance in his *Dramatic Censor*, Dutton, who was typically harsh on Kelly and his mistress, wrote: "Miss De Camp need never wish to have a better foil to her exquisite style of acting, than the puny efforts of Kelly and Mrs Crouch. They may be *singers*, but never should attempt to *perform*."

Kelly's tours to the provinces during the last

five years of the century included Wakefield in August 1795, Birmingham in 1796 and 1797, York in 1795 and 1798, and Brighton in 1798.

In 1801 Kelly was granted a license as acting manager of the Haymarket Theatre to perform several serious operas, and in that summer the premiere of *The Gypsy Prince* occurred on 24 July, with the overture and music composed and selected by Kelly. On 25 August Mrs Mountain sang his air from the play *Deaf and Dumb*. Between 1809 and 1811 he was also granted a license to present each June a play with concert, ballet, or other entertainments.

Anna Maria Crouch's death of "an internal mortification" on 2 October 1805 caused Kelly such great pain that he resolved to quit the stage. In 1806 he raised a monument over her grave in Brighton churchyard. She had bequeathed him for the term of his life her share of the house, No 4, Pall Mall, into which they had moved (from Lisle Street) some time after May 1801, when she had retired.

Kelly made his last appearance at Drury Lane on 17 June 1808 as Frederick in *No Song, No Supper*, the piece by his dear late friend Storace who had been so important to his early career. In August of that year with Catalani he ran an Italian opera company at Dublin, as he had also done the previous year. In 1811 he again returned as opera impresario to Dublin, where, according to his *Reminiscences*, he made his last appearance on the stage on 5 September; *Grove's Dictionary* states that his last appearance came on 1 October 1811, when he sang his song "The Bard of Erin" for his own benefit.

He continued, however, to compose for the Drury Lane company and to stage-manage at the King's through 1819–20. His last opera, *The Lady and the Devil*, came on 3 May 1820, marking the end of a prolific career which had produced compositions for at least 62 productions, a record for a British composer which Kelly claimed was exceeded only by Henry Bishop. A list of those productions is in his *Reminiscences* (repeated in *The Dictionary of National Biography* and *Grove's Dictionary*). No full scores or orchestral parts survive for any of his works, though some vocal scores were published. A list of those will be found in Roger Fiske's *English Theatre Music in the Eighteenth*

Harvard Theatre Collection

MICHAEL KELLY
by De Wilde

Century. A long list of many of Kelly's songs and airs is in the *Catalogue of Printed Music in the British Museum*.

During the first half of his career Kelly prospered financially. By 1795–96 his salary was £16 per week, a sum he still received in 1807–8. The Drury Lane account books show that payments to him and Mrs Crouch (whose salary was £14) were frequently lumped together. His benefit receipts were usually very substantial: for instance, £466 on 22 May 1797, £483 on 8 May 1799, £417 on 2 May 1803, and £569 on 20 May 1807 (all less house charges). He also was paid handsomely for his compositions, receiving 100 guineas for *The Outlaws* in October 1798, £180 for *Cinderella* in January 1804, and £50 for *The Wood Daemon* in April 1807.

From 1797 he had published and sold his compositions from his house at No 9, Lisle Street. His prosperity encouraged him to buy the lease of an old house, at No 9, Pall Mall, at the corner of Market Lane, from which to sell his music. Called the Music Saloon, that establishment was opened on 1 January 1802. From Pall Mall he also sold wine, many of his customers coming from the nearby theatres in the Haymarket. The fact that many of Kelly's compositions had been lifted from foreign sources caused Sheridan to propose that he should sign-post his shop "Michael Kelly, Composer of Wines and Importer of Music." But Kelly's preoccupations in the theatre prevented him from attending his music business, and it failed. A declaration of bankruptcy was issued in September 1811, while he was giving his last performances in Dublin. He was succeeded at No 9, Pall Mall, by the publishers Falkner and Christmas. Soon afterward he moved to a house at No 13, Great Russell Street.

The last years of Kelly's life were made painful by gout, the ravages of which prevented full engagement in his profession. Winston recorded in his papers (at the Folger Shakespeare Library) that "for more than ten years [Kelly] was unable to put a foot to the ground." During those years he passed many months at Brighton, befriended by George IV. The actor-turned-dentist, Charles Bew, wrote to Elliston from Brighton on 4 June 1822 that "Our old friend Mich! Kelly is in spite of infirmity the happiest of the happy sunning himself nightly in the beams of Royal affability—loved and respected by all."

Michael Kelly died at Margate on 9 October 1826. His body was returned to London and buried at St Paul, Covent Garden, on 17 October. The burial register described him as aged 64 and of Tavistock Row. The engraved picture of Kelly's tombstone carries the inscription:

To the / Memory of / a worthy man and distinguished / Musician, who for many years / engaged the favor of / the Public as Principal Vocalist / and Composer at the / Theatre Royal, Drury Lane, / and Acting Manager, of the Italian Opera / honoured by the great / and / courted by the gay, / his life was careless and without reproach / and he died / lamented by numerous friends / possessing but a single foe, / who together with his foibles /

lies Buried here. / MICHAEL KELLY. / was Born in Dublin, Aug: 1762, / and departed this life at Margate, / October 9th 1826.

Despite the strange and sometimes strained alliance, Kelly's life with Mrs Crouch had been a happy one. Their house became the resort of socialites and, Boaden reported, "The hospitality was of the gayest kind" and "the wit, that sparkled like the wine, flowed in just measure, and with good taste."

Michael Kelly died evidently without issue. We have found no will. Several of his numerous brothers went upon the stage. One, Mark Kelly (1767–1833), performed in London in 1794 and is noticed separately in this dictionary. He was the father of the famous nineteenth-century singing actress Francis Maria Kelly.

Another of Michael's brothers, Joseph Kelly, acted in Ireland in 1790–91. He was probably the person referred to in a press announcement of 7 December 1792 as a brother of Kelly of the Haymarket Theatre and a performer with Daly at Dublin the previous season; he had married a "Lady with 60,000£." He was no doubt the Captain Kelly who sang with Michael at Belvidere in 1810. He went abroad and was killed in a duel in 1817.

A third brother, Patrick Kelly, served a cadetship in India and died in 1799 in the battle of Seringapatam. In the *Reminiscences* Michael mentioned a half brother, unnamed, who had been educated at Douai for the Roman Catholic priesthood, so evidently Thomas Kelly, the patriarch of the family, had been previously married, or Michael's half-brother was a bastard son. A Mrs Trevor, advertised as a "sister to Mr Kelly of Drury-lane Theatre," acted for several months at Covent Garden in the second half of the 1799–1800 season. We know nothing about Micheal Kelly's other brothers or sisters.

Kelly had no extraordinary or original talents as a composer, but he was, as William Parke characterized him in his *Memoirs*, "a judicious compiler, and introduced into his operas many fine compositions of the Italian Masters." His slight airs, enriched by his knowledge of foreign languages and styles, were at least elegant. He had, according to Parke, but little knowledge of harmony; Kelly once admitted to him that he "merely wrote the melodies and

that the old Italian, Mazzanti, did the rest."
Of Kelly's contributions to *The Gypsy Prince* in
1801, that play's author, Thomas Moore,
wrote to his mother: "Poor Mick is rather an
imposer than a composer. He cannot mark the
time in writing three bars of music; his under-
strappers, however, do all that for him, and he
has the knack of pleasing the many."

Kelly's pragmatism was summarized by
Adolphus in his *Memoirs of John Bannister*:

> Kelly's pleasing and effective music [for *Blue-
> Beard*], the delight of the audience, afforded some
> ground for invidious carping; but it could not be
> depreciated by the criticisms of the envious. Men
> who delight in trumpeting forth their sagacity, by
> disclosing what never was a mystery, told us that
> the celebrated "tink-a-tink" was a Russian melody;
> Kelly never concealed or denied it. They further
> alleged that the beautiful March in the first act was
> not his; but the assertion was not more illiberal
> than unfounded: he demonstrated the fact; and his
> assertion was corroborated by Mr. Eley, the master
> of the band of the Horse Guards, to whom these
> sagacious persons had attributed the composition.
> When he introduced into "Comus" the celebrated
> duet from "La Cosa Rara," *Pace, o caro mio sposo*,—
> in the English, "O thou wert born to please me,"—
> it was published as Kelly's duet, and popularly so
> called: but he never pretended it was his; he could

not be so stupid as to imagine that he could steal,
without detection, from a popular opera, in the
height of its career, known to every musician, and
even to all the numerous shoal of dabblers in music.

Though he was "far from being a profound
harmonest," the "gift of melody to a great
degree," which Parke attributed to him, was
no doubt the key to his popular success.

Kelly's expert craft and his knowledge of
theatre techniques made it possible for him to
function under the extreme pressure often experienced at the theatres. *Pizarro* was prepared
with Sheridan's typical nonchalance, it seems,
and Kelly wrote that the piece "was advertised,
and every box in the house taken, before the
fourth act of the play was begun; nor had I one
single word of the poetry for which I was to
compose the music." At dinner one night Sheridan went so far as to offer his ideas to Kelly
by inarticulate "rumbling noises." Indeed, the
actors did not have lines for the fifth act until
they were actually performing the fourth.

Kelly possessed more power and talent as a
singer than as a composer. Commenting on
Kelly's rendition of a big aria in *The Haunted
Tower*, Boaden wrote in his *Life of Kemble*: "His
compass was extraordinary. In vigorous passages he never cheated the ear with feeble wail-
ings of falsetto, but sprung upon the ascending
fifth with a sustained energy that electrified
the audience." Dutton, however, never had a
good word for him, finding his voice disagreeable, his "croak" monotonous, and his acting
"insufferable." His manner as Macheath, according to Dutton, "evinces a total want of
feeling and conception; it is uniformly dull
and inanimate, conveying the idea of an au-
tomaton, wrought upon by unseen hands, to
counterfeit certain sounds and notions, in
which the figure is altogether uninterested."
Furthermore, to Dutton, Kelly was "the very
personification of effeminacy, and a palsied
tone of nerve." F. G. Waldron in his *Candid
and Impartial Strictures on the Performers* (1795)
also expressed the opinion that Kelly's voice
and knowledge were over-rated:

> . . . His voice is dreadfully wanting in sweetness
> and melody of tone, and may altogether be consid-
> ered deficient of almost every necessary requisite
> that constitutes a good one. With respect to his
> knowledge in vocal music we think it by no means
> equal to what the town conceives. . . . The arti-
> fices that have been practised in order to establish

Harvard Theatre Collection

MICHAEL KELLY

engraving by Turner, after Lonsdale

for the person before us a fame in the musical world, are well known to a few, and we trust by our endeavours the knowledge of it will be made more general.

Similarly, the author of *A Pin Basket to The Children of Thespis* (1796), found his voice "neither capacious nor melodious," but allowed that he owned a brogue which was "highly captivating to female ears." But "the Irish Nightingale," as Kelly was sometimes called, did possess a tenor heroic enough to fill the big roles on the musical stage until the much superior John Braham came on the scene, and when Braham went off to the Continent with Nancy Storace in the fall of 1797 for a four years' absence, Kelly's competent services were again important to Drury Lane. Kelly was, as one reviewer of his *Reminiscences* put it, "a pretty good playhouse singer, nothing more."

In 1826 Kelly's *Reminiscences* were published in two volumes and proved popular enough to

Tombstone of MICHAEL KELLY

warrant a second edition the same year. The publisher Henry Colburn, realizing that the failing Kelly could not complete the assignment, employed Theodore Hook, the son of the Vauxhall Gardens composer and musician James Hook, to ghostwrite from "rough illiterate materials" supplied by Kelly. For his cooperation Kelly received £400 and 50 copies. The *Reminiscences* contain many inaccuracies and lapses of memory. Kelly was supposedly very upset when he read some of the statements that his amanuensis had put in his mouth and was especially displeased that the "rascal Hook" had omitted things he had no right to leave out. A modern edition of the *Reminiscences* with an introduction and annotations by Roger Fiske was published in 1975.

Details concerning Kelly's composing may be found in Fiske's *English Theatre Music in the Eighteenth Century*. Kelly figures prominently in M. J. Young's *Memoirs of Mrs Crouch* (1806). Modern biographies of Kelly include *The Life of Michael Kelly* (1930) by S. M. Ellis and *The Irish Boy, a Romantic Biography* (1955), a novelistic treatment by Naomi Jacob.

Portraits of Michael Kelly include:

1. By Richard Crosse? He may have been the Kelly who, according to the ledgers of Richard Crosse, of Henrietta Street, Covent Garden, had his portrait painted by that deaf and dumb miniaturist on 12 March 1796.

2. By Theodore Hook. Pen and ink drawing. In the British Museum.

3. By Thomas Lawrence, 1787. Present location unknown. Engraving by J. Neagle. Published as a plate to the *General Magazine and Impartial Review*, 1788.

4. By James Lonsdale. Canvas in the Garrick Club. Engraving by C. Turner published by Mr Sams, 1825.

5. Engraving by J. Condé. Published as a plate to *Thespian Magazine*, 1792.

6. Engraving by H. Meyer, after A. Wivell, showing Kelly, in old age, seated at table with quill pen in hand. Published by H. Colburn as frontispiece to the first edition of the *Reminiscences*, 1826. The same picture, with the chair back deleted, was used for the second edition.

7. Engraving by W. Ridley, after M. Hutchinson. Published as a plate to the *Monthly Mirror*, 1801. Another copy of the portrait was engraved by Vendramini, Junior.

8. As Cymon in *Cymon*. Painting by De Wilde. In the Garrick Club. Engraving by W. Leney, published as plate to *Bell's British Theatre*, 1795.

9. As Cymon. By unknown engraver.

10. As Ferdinand in *The Tempest*. Watercolor by W. Loftis. In the Folger Shakespeare Library.

11. As Henry in *The Deserter*. By unknown engraver. Published as a plate to *Hibernian Magazine*, September 1787.

12. As Lionel in *Lionel and Clarissa*. Engraving by Walker, after C. R. Ryley. Published by W. Lowndes, 1788.

13. As Macheath in *The Beggar's Opera*. Engraving by Murray, after I. Cruikshank. Published by J. Roach with an edition of the play, 1799.

14. As the Mask in *The Island of St. Marguerite*. Watercolor by W. Loftis. In the Folger Shakespeare Library.

15. As Patie, with Mrs Crouch as Peggy, in *Patie and Peggy*. Engraving by Barlow. Published by J. Roach, 1789.

16. As William in *The Haunted Tower*. Watercolor by W. Loftis. In the Folger Shakespeare Library.

17. As unknown character, full-length, right hand pointing up, left hand holding plumed hat, ruff at neck. Watercolor by De Wilde. In the Harvard Theatre Collection.

18. A scene depicting the attempted assassination of George III at Drury Lane by Hatfield on 15 May 1800 presumably shows Kelly on the stage. Engraving by I. Brown, after W. M. Craig. Published by T. Ennersley, 10 February 1820.

Kelm, Mr [*fl. 1792*], *house servant?*

A Mr Kelm was listed with many other employees of Covent Garden Theatre on the 1 June 1792 benefit bill. He may have been a house servant.

Kelner. *See* KELLNER.

Kelway, Joseph. *d. 1782, organist, harpsichordist, composer.*

Joseph Kelway studied music under his brother Thomas, organist of Chichester Cathedral. Joseph and Thomas may have been the sons of either Thomas or Jasper Kelway of Windsor. About 1730 Joseph Kelway suc-

ceeded Obadiah Shuttleworth as organist of St Michael, Cornhill, a post he gave up on 1736 to succeed John Weldon as organist of St Martin-in-the-Fields. Kelway was succeeded at St Michael by William Boyce, whom he had defeated in the competition for that post in 1730.

Kelway had a number of important pupils. Charles Wesley learned harpsichord from him, as did Mrs Pendarves, and, in 1761, Queen Charlotte. In 1736 Mrs Alexander Pendarves wrote to Ann Granville, "My brother has tied me down at last to learn of Kellaway; he has paid him the entrance money, which is two guineas, and has made me a present of Handel's 'Book of Lessons.' I don't find Kellaway's method difficult at all. . . ." Ann Granville in August 1739 wrote to Lady Throckmorton: "Have you heard Mr. Kellaway upon the harpsichord? He is at Scarborough, and a most delightful player, very little inferior to Handel." Indeed, Kelway's virtuosity on the harpsichord, especially with Scarlatti's works, became a great attraction; and such musicians as Handel would go to St Martin's to hear his extemporaneous organ wizardry. Burney said Kelway's organ playing had a "masterly wildness . . . bold, rapid, and fanciful."

On 28 August 1739 Kelway became one of the founding governors of the Royal Society of Musicians. Earlier that year, in April, he had advertised *Twelve Sonata's for a Violin, with a Thorough Bass for the Harpsichord, or Bass Violin by Geminiani*, available from Kelway near Depuis's Coffee House in Conduit Street. In May 1747 he advertised some more Geminiani works, to be had of Kelway at his house at King's Row, Upper Grosvenor Street. At some point Kelway became harpsichord maker to the Queen, and so he described himself in his will, dated 14 April 1779. Kelway died in 1782, and his will was proved on 5 June 1782.

Kelway left the use of his house in King's Row, Upper Grosvenor Street, to his servant Ann Phillips for life, after which the property was to go to Kelway's grandnephew William Kelway and grandniece Ann Branch (née Ann Kelway) wife of Joseph Branch; Elizabeth Kelway, the daughter of the musician's late nephew Joseph Kelway; Ann Heather, formerly Ann Snapes, the wife of the coachmaker Robert Heather; and Elizabeth, formerly Elizabeth Snapes, wife of the musician John

National Portrait Gallery

JOSEPH KELWAY

by J. Russell

Stafford Smith. To Elizabeth Smith and Ann Heather, Kelway left all of his musical instruments and books of music. His portrait of Geminiani and his own portrait he gave to Ann Phillips. To his brother William Kelway, Joseph left £10, plus a shilling apiece to each of William's children. The relatives sold the Kelway music collection before the year was out.

Kelway published six sonatas for the harpsichord in 1764 and wrote some other small pieces. Grove reports a portrait of Kelway, probably by Batoni; a copy of it in pastel by J. Russell was acquired by the National Portrait Gallery (No 4213) in 1961.

Kemble, Charles   *1775–1854,   actor, manager, playwright.*

Charles Kemble, the eleventh child of the provincial manager Roger Kemble and his actress wife Sarah (née Ward), was born at Brecon, South Wales, on 25 November 1775. In her manuscript memoir, now at the Folger Library, his eccentric sister Ann Hatton stated that Charles's birth occurred "in the Sheep street, at the House of a Surgeon named Pow-

Harvard Theatre Collection

CHARLES KEMBLE
by De Wilde

ell." Twenty-one years earlier, Sarah, the first of Roger Kemble's 12 children, had been born in the same town, which the Kemble company visited annually. In our notice of Roger Kemble is found information on the family and its paternal and maternal ancestry. By the time Charles came along the worst of Roger's bad times as a provincial manager were over and, as Oxberry wrote in his *Dramatic Biography* (1825), the patriarch was "flourishing in comparative plenty."

Charles's elder siblings, Sarah, John, Stephen, Frances, Elizabeth, and perhaps Ann, had appeared on the stage before Charles was ten years old, so it is possible that he, too, had made a provincial appearance when a child, though no such record survives. At the age of 13 he was sent for classical study to the English college in Douai. His brother John, 18 years his elder, who had also attended Douai, paid the expenses of Charles's education. In her diary (now at the Folger Library) Jane Porter wrote about a visit Charles Kemble made to her home on 12 March 1801, during which he gave an account of his education:

He there acquired a knowledge of Pagan and Christian wisdom: But related, that from the hour of his admission, till his departure, he never read a Historian or a Poet, before the Tutors had wafered over with blank paper, any page which might tend to awaken his passions. So great was their dread of the witchery of the poets, that the room in which they were kept, was called Hell, and carefully guarded from the approach of the student. Besides this caution he never beheld a woman within the walls of the University.

After three years learning languages and reading salubrious literature, Charles suffered a serious illness which sent John across the channel to retrieve him. Through his brother's influence, in 1792 he obtained a modest situation in the Post Office in London. He moved restlessly from one position to another within that service and, inevitably, despite the dissuasions of relatives and friends, he determined for the stage.

At Sheffield in the winter of 1792–93 Charles made an appearance, on a date unknown, in his first recorded character, Orlando in *As You Like It*, but Oxberry, who provided that information, claimed that "it is well known that Mr Kemble had tried his strength in some small companies previously, though where, or when, it is now impossible to ascertain." From Sheffield he made his way to Newcastle and no doubt to some other provincial towns. Then he joined the company at the Theatre Royal in Shakespeare Square, Edinburgh, where he made his debut as Carlos in *The Revenge* on 23 January 1793. By the end of that season there he also played Bagatelle in *The Poor Soldier*, the First Player in *Apollo Turned Stroller*, Floriment in *Owen of Carron*, Paddy O'Flail in *The Volunteers*, Papillon in *The Liar*, Scruple in *Ways and Means*, and Sir Christopher Curry in *Inkle and Yarico*. He returned to Edinburgh in the early winter season of 1794 to act Captain Berry in *Half Hour after Supper*, Carlos in *The Revenge*, Laertes in *Hamlet*, Sadi in *The Mountaineers*, and Tressel in *Richard III*.

After a provincial apprenticeship of about 18 months, during which he did not prove a very successful attraction, Charles was brought to London through his brother's influence to play Malcolm in *Macbeth* on 21 April 1794, the first night that a play was performed at the new Drury Lane Theatre. The critic in the *Thespian Magazine* of June 1794 reported that Malcolm was "supported very respectably." The reviewer in the *Times* on 22 April found him "an actor of much promise—his speeches were given with good emphasis and discretion; his tones frequently reminded us of Stephen Kemble and Mrs Siddons." A press clipping in the Enthoven Collection claims that: "Mr. Charles Kemble . . . is a youth of much promise; general report would justify our saying still more,—that his conception is just, his voice and figure excellent, and his delivery and action easy." The last smacks of arrant puffery compared to Oxberry's retrospection some 30 years later which described Kemble at the time of his London debut as a "tall, awkward Youth, with what is termed a hatchet face, a figure badly porportioned, and evidently weak in his limbs; his acting was even worse than his appearance."

After several more appearances as Malcolm, Kemble acted Jaques de Bois in *As You Like It* on 25 April 1794. His brother John relinquished his usual role of Cromwell in *Henry VIII* to Charles on 1 May, causing the *Thespian*

Magazine to regret the elder Kemble's absence; "perhaps if we had never seen him in it, we should have thought Mr. *Charles* Kemble more entitled to commendation." Charles's other roles that season, in which he earned £4 per week, were Richard in *The Miller of Mansfield*, Kajah in the premiere of his brother's music drama *Lodoiska* on 9 June, Seyward in *The Hypocrite*, Lovel in *High Life below Stairs*, Papillion in *The Liar*, Belville in *The Country Girl*, and William in the premiere of Sheridan and Cobb's musical entertainment *The Glorious First of June* on 2 July. When he replaced Bannister on 28 June as Vapour in *My Grandmother*, according to an anecdote related by Oxberry, a person in the pit rose from his seat and "actually expostulated with him on the impropriety of his attempting to enact a part so far beyond his powers." (When he played the role the next season the *Times* critic punned "The Vapour of Mr. Charles Kemble put everybody into the vapours.")

In the summer of 1794 he was engaged by Colman at the Haymarket Theatre, where he first appeared on 12 July, as Papillion. Over the next two months he was seen as Ganem in *The Mountaineers*, Degagee in *The Dead Alive*, Jemmy in *Auld Robin Gray* (but even the captivating looks of beautiful Miss Leak as Jenny, lamented the *Thespian Magazine* critic in August 1794, "could not inspire him with a sufficient share of animation"), Count Fripon in *Summer Amusement*, Mons Barleduc in *Rule Britannia*, Captain Loveit in *Miss in Her Teens*, Sergeant Firelock in *Britain's Glory*, Rundy in *The Farmer*, Glanville in *The Apparition*, and Young Marlow in *How to be Happy*.

Despite his inauspicious debut season at Drury Lane, Kemble was reengaged for 1794–95 and was kept very busy in a number of inconsequential roles, which included some he had played the previous spring supplemented by Count Appiani in *Emilia Galotti*, Young Contest in *The Wedding Day* (which Oxberry claimed he had "acted with success"), Fabian in *Twelfth Night*, Lewis in *All's Well that End's Well*, Zamorin in *The Cherokee*, Orlando in *As You Like It* (his only major role, on 21 January 1795), Hephestion in *Alexander the Great*, Sigebert in *Edwy and Elgiva*, Octavio in *She Wou'd and She Wou'd Not*, Belville in *The Country Girl*, and Petruchio in *The Chances*.

Pennsylvania Academy of Fine Arts, Philadelphia

CHARLES KEMBLE as Giraldi Fazio

by Sully

In his *Candid and Impartial Strictures on the Performers* in 1795, F. G. Waldron described Charles Kemble as "A rising young actor, but with some natural defects that will ever pre- vent him from being a great one. He has more ease and sprightliness when he chooses to call them forth, than all the rest of the family put together." A year later, however, the anonymous author (not John Williams, but someone who assumed his pseudonym of Anthony Pasquin) of *The Pin Basket. To the children of Thespis* sneered:

Young Kemble will never make a player. The character he plays the best is *Vapour*—he is here to be sure inimitable, in the effect he gives it—Who can see him without having the vapours? The pride of this family who rise from a low origin. We remember, a few years since, meeting this young man with a stick over his shoulder, on which was a bundle, walking unabashed through the streets. He is now, without merit to apologize for it, as proud as any of his relations.

Yet his elder, and influential, brother John was convinced, as he told Boaden, "*He* will make an actor!" Charles, wrote Boaden, "Submitted implicitly to his brother's judgment," and we are told by William Donne in *Essays on the Drama* that John "imposed upon the young debutant a probation as strict and regular as he was in the habit of prescribing to the least gifted of his associates."

Charles was engaged at Drury Lane regularly throughout the remainder of the century, at a salary which rose gradually from £4 per week in 1795–96 to £9 in 1799–1800. He acted during that period dozens of roles, including Lawson in *The Gamester*, Carlos in Isabella (a performance admired by the *Times* critic on 21 September 1795), Prince Henry in *King John*, Laertes in *Hamlet*, Saville in *The Belle's Stratagem*, Pascentius in the ill-fated Shakespearean fraud *Vortigern*, and Paris in *Romeo and Juliet* in 1795–96; Careless in *The School for Scandel*, Axalla in *Tamerlane*, Guiderius in *Cymbeline*, Ferdinand in *The Tempest*, and the Mogul in *The Mogul Tale* in 1796–97; Lovewell in *The Clandestine Marriage*, Philotas in *The Grecian Daughter*, Theodore in *The Count of Narbonne*, Vivaldi in *The Italian Monk*, and Don Felix in *The Wonder* in 1797–98; Evander in *The Grecian Daughter*, the Earl of Richmond in *Richard III*, Percy in *The Castle Spectre*, the Duke in *The Outlaws*, Claudio in *Measure for Measure*, George Barnwell in *The London Merchant*, Norval in *Douglas*, Mr Camplay in *The Funeral*, Beauchamp in *The East Indian*, the Marquis of Vaublane in *The Castle of Montval*, and Alonzo in *Pizarro* in 1798–99; and Clifford in *Adelaide* in 1799–1800. In the spring of 1800 he became ill and could not play be-

tween 18 April and 24 May. That indisposition cost him the role of Rezenvelt in his brother John's melodrama *De Montfort*, which opened on 29 April.

During summers at the Haymarket, where he seems to have enjoyed greater success, he played, among other roles, King Edward in *The Surrender of Calais*, Radzano in *Zorinski*, Frederick in *The Jew*, Solarino in *The Merchant of Venice*, and Captain Ambush in *The Young Quaker* in 1795; La Varenne in *The Battle of Hexham*, Bassanio in *The Merchant of Venice*, Peregrine in *The London Merchant*, Captain Plume in *The Recruiting Officer*, Heartfree in *The Provok'd Wife*, Hotspur in *1 Henry IV*, and a Robber in *The Iron Chest* in 1796; the title role in *Zorinski*, Cassio in *Othello*, and Henry Morland in *The Heir at Law* in 1797; Fernando in *The Inquisitor*, Prince David in *Cambro-Britons*, and Lealto in *False and True* in 1798.

At the Haymarket on 2 July 1800 he was the original Three-Fingered Jack in the premiere of *Obi*, a pantomime by Fawcett which proved to be very successful. His performance received high praise and "Stanzas on seeing Mr. Charles Kemble in the Pantomime of Obi" by one Azuria were printed in the July *Monthly Mirror*, (The manuscript of this poem is in the Enthoven Collection; other stanzas on the small subject are in Jane Porter's small manuscript volume of poetry in the Folger Library.) Also that summer he acted on 18 July Durimel in the first performance of *The Point of Honour*, his own three-act adaptation of Mercier's *Le Deserteur*. That sentimental melodrama ran 18 performances that season, was published that year, and remained popular on the stage and in print during the first half of the nineteenth century.

At his benefit on 12 August 1800 (when tickets were available at his lodgings, No 126, Great Russell Street, Bloomsbury), Kemble performed Charles Surface in *The School for Scandal* and Three-fingered Jack in *Obi*. In the latter piece he suffered a severe accident. The usual precautions used to break his stage fall "in his leap from the precipice," according to Dutton's report in his *Dramatic Censor*, that night had been neglected and Kemble received "several violent contusions, and sprained his back in a dangerous manner." The new opera *What a Blunder!*, in which he was to play on 13 August, had to be postponed to the next night. But the injury prevented his appearing in that or any other piece for the rest of the summer.

By 1800 Kemble had made remarkable improvement as an actor. He had even overcome the liability of awkward legs—Mr Jarvis of Margate, a physician, had "attended him, and prevented an ossification of the ankle," informed Oxberry—and judgments on his acting and person became more encouraging. In a *Monody on the Death of Mr. John Palmer* (1798), T. Harral called Kemble "a promising and improving young actor," but advised that "the public would like Mr. Charles Kemble much better, if Mr. Charles Kemble liked himself somewhat less." Instead of "admiring the symmetry of his form, or the elegance of his dress, and acting entirely for himself," he should "attend to his brother performers." In the *Dramatic Censor*, Dutton observed the same defect in Kemble, which he found was widespread practice among the players, but he thought he was, nevertheless, a good actor.

As Barnwell he "appeared to particular advantage," reported the *Monthly Mirror* of December 1796, and required "only a firmer voice and a spark of his brother's fire to render him a favorite with the public." In *A Pin Basket to the Children of Thespis* (1797), John Williams wrote that, "His BARNWELL's a portrait that honors his youth; / Though not perfect 'tis something approaching to truth." Though once he had been called "a regular stick," the *Times* on 25 May 1799 could report that as Alonzo in *Pizarro* "Charles Kemble displayed so much characteristic animation in his grand scene with the tyrant as to excite the repeated plaudits of the audience." His portrayal of Cassio in *Othello*, which he first essayed on 4 September 1797, was a minor triumph of sorts; over the years many critics, such as William Robson, William Hazlitt, Leigh Hunt, and Julian Young, would hail his portrayal of the drunken lieutenant.

On 7 September 1799 Sheridan renewed Kemble's contract for four seasons, at a salary of £9 per week for the first two years, rising to £10 and £11 for the last two. On 20 November 1800 he played Faulconbridge opposite his brother's *King John* with qualified success, and that season he also acted Young Mirabel in *The Inconstant* on 9 January 1801 and appeared as

Harvard Theatre Collection

CHARLES KEMBLE as Sigismund
by De Wilde

the original Adelmorn in "Monk" Lewis's *Adelmorn the Outlaw* on 4 May 1801. He did not, however, return to the Haymarket that summer. The press announced that "Mr. Charles Kemble does not accept any theatrical engagement for the summer. He proposes, to take a continental excursion, and to reside chiefly at Vienna, for the purpose of aquiring a complete knowledge of the German language." On 30 July 1801 the papers reported that he was making a tour of Germany, accompanied by R. K. Porter, "the painter of Seringapatam."

During the next several seasons at Drury Lane Kemble's value increased, as he played Lothario in *The Fair Penitent*, Sir Brilliant Fashion in *The Way to Keep Him*, Edmund in *King Lear*, Chamont in *The Orphan*, and, for his benefit on 19 May 1803, Hamlet, a portrayal which the *Monthly Mirror* of June 1803 said "greatly increased his reputation, before deservedly high, by his chaste and animated performance." Among his roles at the Haymarket in 1802 were Frederick in *The Poor Gentleman* and Frederic in *Lovers' Vows*. He was not at the Haymarket in 1803.

Charles's articles with Drury Lane expired at the end of 1802–3. He joined Covent Garden in the autumn of 1803 at a salary of £14 per week. His brother John was also beginning an engagement there, having bought one-sixth share in that theatre. That season five members of the clan crowded the Covent Garden Green Room: John, Charles, Sarah Siddons, her husband William Siddons, and their daughter-in-law, Mrs Henry Siddons (née Harriott Murray). Charles made his first appearance there on 12 September 1803, as Henry in *Speed the Plough*. Soon he was seen as Pyrrhus in *The Distrest Mother* and Romeo.

In the summer of 1804 he journeyed to Russia. On 29 September 1804 Sarah Siddons wrote to Mrs Piozzi: "Mr Charles Kemble put himself into a Ship that was bound to St Petersburgh about three Months ago, thinking he shoud be returned by the opening of the theatre, but we hear nothing of him." The family began to fear for his ship, but he arrived safely, though a month late, to act Laertes at Covent Garden on 22 October 1804.

Charles's salary at Covent Garden remained at £14 until it was raised to £17 in 1806–7 and then to £20 in 1812–13. Important parts now came his way, including Jaffeir in *Venice Preserv'd*, Hastings in *King John*, the original Plastic in Morton's *Town and Country* on 10 February 1807, the title role in Cherry's *Peter the Great* on 8 May 1807, the Knight of Snowdoun in Morton's adaptation of *The Lady of the Lake* on 5 February 1811, and Antony in *Antony and Cleopatra* in 1811–12. He spoke the address which introduced Master Betty, the child star, on 1 December 1804. In 1806 Kemble was appointed a trustee of the actors' fund.

During that first tenure at Covent Garden, five of Charles Kemble's plays were produced. *The Wanderer; or, The Rights of Hospitality*, his adaptation of Kotzebue's *Eduard in Schottland*, opened on 12 January 1808, with Kemble as Sigismund, the leading character. The drama at first had been rejected by the Lord Chamberlain, but when Kemble changed the setting from Scotland to Sweden and the chief character from the Pretender, Charles Edward Stewart, to the son of the late King of Sweden, it was granted a license and ran 16 nights. (On 26 November 1829, the original version was played at Covent Garden as *The Royal Fugitive*, with music by Stansbury.) *The Wanderer* was published in 1808 and again in 1809.

Kemble's next stage effort was *Plot and Counterplot; or, The Portrait of Michael Cervantes*, taken from a French comedy by Michel Dieulafoy. More a translation than adaptation, *Plot and Counterplot* opened at the Haymarket on 30 June 1808 and enjoyed a long run, and was published that year. The part of Don Fernando was filled by Kemble on opening night because Putnam, who was to have played it, suddenly became ill.

Kamchatka; or, The Slave's Tribute, his adaptation from Kotzebue's *Graf Benyowsky*, was produced at Covent Garden on 16 October 1811, with Kemble as Stepanoff. His farce *The Child of Chance*, an original effort, was "stillborn," as one critic wrote, at the Haymarket on 8 July 1812 and managed two other performances. At Covent Garden on 29 May 1813, Kemble's melodrama *The Hungarian Cottage; or, The Brazen Bust* was given its first performance with him as Frederick. Despite the support of 22 pieces of music by Henry Bishop (the score is in the British Library), the play ran only four nights. None of the above three dramas was published, but they survive in manuscript in the Huntington Library. Although authorship of a farce called *A Budget of Blunders*, produced at Covent Garden on 16 February 18, has been attributed to Charles Kemble (and the play was published at Philadelphia in 1823 with his name on the title page), John Kemble's "Professional Memoranda" at the British Library and several contemporary press reports credit the play to a Mr Greffulhe.

A story was circulated in *The Festival of Wit* (1806) that Charles Kemble and the actress Maria Theresa De Camp were the joint authors of a music drama called *Deaf and Dumb*, in which they had appeared when it opened on 9 February 1801. That play was actually an adaptation by Thomas Holcroft of Bouilly's *L'abbée de l'Epée*. But, as the anecdote related, on the second night in the Green Room, young Bannister said to Miss De Camp, "You and Charles have made a good thing between you."—"Indeed," replied she, "Charles and I will never make any thing between us."

Maria Theresa De Camp's reputed Green Room retort was an ironic reflection on her somewhat odd relationship with Charles Kemble. Born in 1775 the eldest child of the musician George Louis De Camp and his wife Jeanne (née Dufour), Maria Theresa had been only 11 when she had made her debut at Drury Lane on 24 October 1786 as Julie in *Richard Coeur de Lion*. She was a pretty actress who specialized in sprightly chambermaids and singing ingenues. One night in January 1795 the usually austere John Kemble, after drinking heavily, rudely molested her in her dressing room. When he sobered, the actor-manager preferred her an abject and public apology. But the unpleasant occurrence cast a shadow over their association for some years. She and John's brother Charles Kemble appeared together in many productions at Drury Lane, and in 1800 they were betrothed. John was set firmly against the marriage, and, according to Jane Porter's "Diary," the rest of the family "soon joined John, and on pain of their everlasting displeasure, they adjudged [Charles] not to marry her." A compromise was worked out whereby John agreed to give his approval to the match if Charles still "continued in the same mind when he was thirty." On 2 July 1806, eight months after he became 30, Charles married Maria Theresa at St George, Bloomsbury, and John was there to give the bride away.

In the autumn of 1806 Mrs Kemble joined her husband at Covent Garden Theatre, where they remained through 1812–13. They also made occasional excursions into the provinces. As Hamlet and Ophelia they opened, under Trotter's management, the new theatre at Brighton on 6 June 1807 and played there that summer and the next. In 1809 they were briefly at Bath. They first appeared at the Queen Street Theatre, Glasgow, on 27 January 1812, as Hamlet and Ophelia; there they acted also Don Felix and Violante in *The Wonder*, the Duke and Juliana in *The Honeymoon*, and Captain Absolute and Julia in *The Rivals*, before they proceeded to Edinburgh.

On 13 June 1810 Charles had made his first appearance at the Haymarket in eight years, as Don Felix in *The Wonder*, with his wife as Violante. Before accepting the engagement he had pushed the manager Colman for a large salary. A letter (now in the Huntington Library) from Colman to a colleague on 21 February 1810 speaks of Charles's demands:

The terms I think are, in every point of view, enormous:—Still, as we are situated, I am for acceding to them.—Look round;—& tell me how we are to help ourselves—Among the known, & establish'd performers there is nobody left (except C. Kemble) to suit all the purposes we have in contemplation. . . .

Is it, or is it not better to strain a point (it is a *great* strain, I admit) to ascertain the assistance of one on whom we can rely, than to engage even at a *much* minor salary, a person who might (with so much weight upon his shoulders) bring us into disrepute, & into loss;—by injuring our *Stock* business, & throwing a damp upon our *novelties*?

At Covent Garden, however, Charles's career was not advancing to his satisfaction. As long as brother John continued to act there Charles would be known as "the younger Kemble." He thought of returning to Drury Lane, for he was convinced, as he wrote in a letter on 17 June 1812 (now in the Enthoven Collection), that his future depended "upon the estimation" in which he would be held for the next few years.

At the conclusion of the 1812–13 season Kemble resigned from Covent Garden and with his wife toured the three kingdoms. Early in 1814 they were playing at the Crow Street Theatre, Dublin. They were seen there in *Hamlet* that March by an anonymous playgoer who recorded in his "Journal kept in Dublin" (now in the National Library of Ireland) that neither was "found brilliant" and that while exiting from his impassioned scene with Ophelia Kemble ignominiously "bumped hard into the door & got a bloody nose." At the Theatre Royal in Shakespeare Square, Edinburgh, in April and May 18 he acted Benedick in *Much Ado about Nothing*, Charles Surface in *The School for Scandal*, Don Felix in *The Wonder*, Hamlet, Jaffeir in *Venice Preserv'd*, Richard III, Oakly in *The Jealous Wife*, Othello, Shylock, Young Mirabel in *The Inconstant*, and Young Norval in *Douglas*.

Subsequent to his provincial tour, according

CHARLES KEMBLE as Iago

by Lane

to Oxberry, Kemble journeyed to the Continent and played at Brussels, Calais, and Boulogne, among other places. He also visited Germany, it was said, to find plays he could translate for the English stage.

On 13 September 1815 Kemble returned to play Macbeth at Covent Garden, where he remained as actor 18 seasons. In the first two of those years he shared leading roles with his brother John, until John retired in June 1817. An accounting sheet in the Harvard Theatre Collection shows that for his benefit on 5 June 1817, Charles's net receipts were £197. In 1817–18 Charles acted Doricourt in *The Belle's Stratagem* (one of his finest roles, which he first played on 12 September 1817), Benedick in *Much Ado about Nothing*, Young Marlow in *She Stoops to Conquer*, the original Giraldi Fazio in *Fazio* on 5 April 1818, and the original Manfredi in *Bellamira* on 22 April. In 1818–19 he played the first Vincento in Sheil's *Evadne* and also appeared as Tamerlane, Archer in *The Beaux' Stratagem*, Sir Edward Mortimer in

Mary Stuart, Hastings in *Jane Shore*, the title role in *Ivanhoe*, and Icilius in *Virginius*. In the summer of 1819 he acted at the Haymarket.

Kemble's serious three-act play *Proof Presumptive; or, The Abbey of San Marco*, with the author as Alberto and Macready as Romani, opened at Covent Garden on 20 October 1818, but it was not popular and was not published. A manuscript copy of *Proof Presumptive* is in the Huntington Library.

In the first quarter of the century Kemble had a number of addresses in London and the suburbs. In 1809 he resided in Newman Street, Oxford Road, where on 27 November of that year his third child, Frances Ann, was born. His family then lived at Westbourne Green, afterward in a house near Paddington Church, and subsequently in a series of three residences in the Craven Hill area of Bayswater. The last of these seems to have been No 3, Craven Hill, where they were in 1821 and had as neighbors Latour the composer, Belzoni the Egyptian traveler, and Mrs Blackshaw, the sister of Beau Brummel. Kemble also kept lodgings in town to spare himself the long walk back to Paddington or Craven Hill. Between 1812 and 1815 he lodged in Covent Garden Chambers; by 1821 he was at No 35, Gerard Street, Soho; and in 1824 at No 29, Soho Square.

In November 1820 John Kemble transferred by deed of gift his entire one-sixth shareholding in Covent Garden Theatre to his brother Charles. Had circumstances been better, it would have been a handsome gift, according to some estimates worth £45,000. John's partner Thomas Harris, who had been managing the theatre while John was enjoying retirement in Switzerland, had died in October 1820, and the elder Kemble found himself faced with bickering proprietors, threatening creditors, and little prospect of profit. Charles, no doubt, considered the gift to be a great opportunity, but it proved to be ruinous. His daughter Fanny wrote in her *Records of a Girlhood*:

My father received the property . . . with cheerful courage, and not without sanguine hopes of retrieving its fortunes; instead of which, it destroyed his and those of his family; who had he and they been untrammelled by the fatal obligation of working for a hopelessly ruined concern, might have turned their labours to far better personal account.

It took Charles almost two years to wrest the management of the theatre from Henry Harris, who had inherited the principal stock from his father. Finally, after negotiation and litigation, Harris agreed to withdraw from the management and gave a lease to Kemble, John Willet, and John Forbes for a term of 10 years, commencing retroactively, 1 August 1821, for a sum of £12,000 per year. But Harris was to receive no rent until the enormous debt of the theatre was discharged. Details are found in "Harris v. Kemble," *The Vice-Chancellor's Judgment*, 12 April 1827; "Articles of Agreement between Henry Harris" and the proprietors dated 11 March 1822, a copy of which is in the Archives of the London County Council; and "Professional Memoranda of Charles Kemble," a manuscript in the British Library. A summary of these transactions and of Kemble's managerial misfortunes is offered by Jane Williamson in *Charles Kemble, Man of the Theatre* (1970).

The "Articles of Agreement" for the transfer of management were signed on 11 March 1822. When Kemble made his first appearance of the season on 19 March 1822, as Charles in *The School for Scandal*, he was warmly received by the public. The press expressed hopes for an era of "superior taste" in the new arrangement at Covent Garden, now to be managed chiefly by Kemble, a "scholar, gentleman, and perfect master of his art." Before the season ended, he offered the public highly regarded productions of *Macbeth*, *King John*, *2 Henry IV*, and *Julius Caesar*; the last opened on 22 April 1822 with Kemble as Antony, Macready as Cassius, and Young as Brutus, and was acclaimed by the *Theatrical Pocket Magazine* as "the most perfect representation that has been seen on the stage in many years."

Though beset by the usual managerial problems, Kemble's reign at Covent Garden, which had begun well, continued to prosper for several years. Testimony by his players and associates indicates that he treated them with respect, graciousness, and compassion. Edward Fitzball in his *Thirty-five Years of a Dramatic Author's Life* (1859) remembered "how agreeable and intellectual all rehearsals invariably were" under Kemble. In 1822–23, his first full season of management, Kemble continued to please in his repertoire of leading roles, and on 13 November played Cassio in support of Macready's Othello. Kemble acted the merry Friar in the new opera *Maid Marian* "with such an extraordinary abandonment and gusto," claimed William Robson in *The Old Play-Goer* (1846), that one felt transported back to Sherwood Forest.

His revival of *King John*, with historically accurate costumes by Planché, and with Charles Young in the title role and Kemble as Faulconbridge, was a great success when it opened on 24 November 1823 and is still regarded as a significant event in the development of the art of theatrical costuming. In a role somewhat uncharacteristic for him, Kemble essayed Falstaff in *1 Henry IV* on 3 May 1824; according to the *Theatrical Observer* next day, he played "better than could have been supposed." In 1824–25 he acted the original Stephen Foster in *A Woman Never Vexed* on 9 November and the original Orestes in *Orestes in Argos* on 20 April. That season was marked by the great success at Covent Garden of Weber's opera *Der Freischütz*, which ran 52 nights. Weber's *Oberon*, written at the request of Kemble, who hoped to duplicate the financial windfall brought by the earlier opera, was less successful. It was produced on 12 April 1826. But in that season Mme Vestris joined the company and proved to be a great box-office draw. On 4 May 1826 Kemble acted the original Louis Kerneguy in *Woodstock*. That fall he created the role of Francesco Foscari in Mary Mitford's *Foscari*.

In the late summer of 1827 Kemble joined other Covent Garden actors—including Miss Smithson, Abbot, and Liston—in a company brought to Paris by Laurent to present English plays at the Odéon. The company opened on 5 September, but Kemble did not act until 11 September, when his Hamlet impressed the French critics. His next character, Romeo, prompted the critic in *Le Globe* to write, "We have never perhaps seen more convincing grief on the stage." He was less successful as Othello, more phlegmatic than passionate, and his declamations displeased even the French. Fanny Kemble wrote to a friend that Kemble and his colleagues had offered "the first regularly and decently organized English theatre the French ever saw," and that her father had "obtained a most unequivocal success in Paris, the more flattering as it was rather doubtful; and the excellent Parisians have not only received him very well, but forthwith threw themselves into a headlong *furor* for Shakespeare and Charles Kemble." While it is true that the animated and somewhat passionate style of the English actors— especially Kean and Macready, who visited later in the season—greatly influenced Hugo and the French theatre, Kemble himself caused little stir actually and was found lacking when compared to Talma's brilliance. The *Courrier des Théâtres* on 28 September 1827 reported: "Mr. Charles Kemble has said farewell. We are far from recognizing in this actor the *extraordinary* talent so graciously attributed to him."

After his brief stay in Paris, Kemble returned to Covent Garden, where the 1827–28 season was marked by the engagement of Edmund Kean, who had been playing at Drury Lane. Kemble's portrayals of Richmond, Cassio, and other roles supported Kean's triumphs. Despite the throngs drawn by Kean, the fortunes of Covent Garden were in decline once more. The legacy of poor management, continuing heavy debt, complicated and wearisome litigation, escalating salaries and production costs, and some unwise managerial practices by Kemble himself, all contributed to yet another financial crisis. The annual rent of £12,000 was an enormous burden. Furthermore, F. Const, a one-eighth shareholder, was dissatisfied with the lease arrangements, concerning which he claimed he had not been consulted. He was successful in having the theatre placed under receivership commencing 19 February 1824. Kemble and Harris were in constant legal contention, it seems, for seven years, until finally on 13 October 1831 the House of Lords upheld the verdict of the Lord Chancellor (given in May 1829) which declared the lease no longer binding. But in the intervening years the troubles kept Kemble in a state of jeopardy. Fanny Kemble wrote that "The constantly darkened prospects of that unlucky theatre threw a gloom over us all."

In the summer of 1829 it seemed that the theatre would not be able to open for the ensuing season. Distress warrants for overdue taxes and rates totaling some £1700 were executed, and bailiffs took possession of the house. At the time Kemble was on summer tour in Ireland, whence his several letters (now in the Harvard Theatre Collection and the Huntington Library) indicate his determina-

tion to salvage the theatre, pointing out that the creditors could not possibly be paid unless the theatre were allowed to remain open and could have some profitable seasons. On 19 August 1829 he wrote to Bunn, the manager of the Theatre Royal, Dublin, asking to be excused from his engagement at Cork, but Bunn refused, reminding him that he was being paid a good sum for the fortnight of performances at Cork, which were scheduled for the time of the Assizes. Kemble managed to return to London in early September, and by enormous effort he worked out various projects for rescue, summarized by Williamson:

A subscription was arranged whereby "friends of the Theatre" were requested to contribute, through gifts or loans, to a six thousand pound fund-raising goal; principal creditors were asked to waive their claims for the present; Covent Garden shareholders agreed to make a complete sacrifice of profit for the ensuing season and to suspend payment of dividends for three years; various actors offered to play gratuitously for from three to ten nights; and finally, a benefit performance for Covent Garden Theatre, to take place at the King's Theatre, was announced.

The theatre opened for the season on 5 October 1829 with a production of *Romeo and Juliet* in which Kemble's acting of Mercutio, for the first time, established that role as probably his greatest, a portrayal which was called by the American actor Charles Durang "the *ne plus ultra* of high comedy." But the sensation that night was Charles's 19-year-old daughter Fanny, who in her first appearance on any stage triumphed as Juliet. Her mother came on, after having been retired for many years, to play Lady Capulet.

It is to Fanny that credit is given for keeping the theatre open and enabling it to dissolve a debt of £13,000. As a mainstay of the company for three years, she achieved a popularity which was reminiscent, at least momentarily, of the great excitement created by her famous aunt, Sarah Siddons. Kemble supported her performances, in their appearances as Pierre and Belvidera in *Venice Preserv'd*, Evander and Euphrasia in *The Grecian Daughter*, Beverley and Mrs Beverley in *The Gamester*, Shylock and Portia in *The Merchant of Venice*, the Stranger and Mrs Haller in *The Stranger*, Horatio and Calista in *The Fair Penitent*, Benedick and Beatrice in *Much Ado about Nothing*, Faulconbridge

CHARLES KEMBLE as Malcolm or Macbeth

artist unknown

and Constance in *King John*, Bertoldo and Camiola in *The Maid of Honour*, and Charles Surface and Lady Teazle in *The School for Scandal*. On 12 June 1832 they created the roles of Sir Thomas Clifford and Julia in the premiere of Sheridan Knowles's *The Hunchback*, the success of which, according to the *Times* of 13 June 1832, saved the theatre once more from bankruptcy and enabled the actors "once again, to draw their full pay." (A salary memorandum in the Harvard Theatre Collection indicates that on 3 June 1830 Kemble signed for receipt of £930, from 5 October 1829 to 3 June 1830, for 186 nights at £5 per night "leaving a balance of £120 remaining due to me.") In the summer of 1830 father and daughter had drawn great crowds when they acted at Bath, Bristol, Birmingham, Glasgow, Edinburgh, and Dublin.

When not on stage, much of Kemble's time was occupied with chaperoning his vivacious daughter to parties, balls, and other social events around town and country, and to enter-

taining visitors at their home in Great Russell Street, where they had settled in the autumn of 1830. They had lived at No 16, St James Street, Buckingham Gate since 1827. The Great Russell Street residence was close by John Kemble's former home at No 89, which gave way to the British Museum.

By the 1830–31 season the press began to notice the fact that actually Fanny was an inexperienced and uneven actress. Charles Westmacott, editor of the *Age*, attacked her in a poem which culminated a series of abuses he had heaped on the Kembles in retaliation, according to Fanny, for her father having treated the journalist coldly. On 24 October 1830 Fanny wrote to a friend about her father's exasperation and how several nights before at the theatre he "having unluckily come across Mr. Westmacott, his wrath got the better of his self-command, and he had bestowed a severe beating upon that individual." Kemble was detained by the police for a while and Westmacott threatened suit, but evidently nothing further came of the matter.

But when the more responsible press also commented on Fanny's flaws houses began to thin during 1831–32, Kemble's last year as Covent Garden manager. In October 1831 he enjoyed some success with *Henry VIII*, which he mounted with historical accuracy. He portrayed the lusty monarch "excellently well," in the judgment of the *Tatler* on 25 October, but Fanny's Katharine wanted "dignity and natural power."

That November Kemble fell seriously ill from exhaustion and "inflammation of the lungs." He almost died, but managed a recovery sufficient to allow him to resume performing on 9 January 1832, as Romeo. On 15 January he attended the opening dinner of the Garrick Club. The financial situation at Covent Garden, however, once again was critical; sparse houses required a cutback on salaries; and Kemble was weakened and very depressed. After the House of Lords had voided the lease of 1822, Kemble had agreed with Harris to manage for 1831–32; but after that season he decided not to seek a renewal.

Instead, Kemble accepted the offer of Stephen Price, manager of the Park Theatre in New York, to perform in America. After playing for a fortnight in Edinburgh and a few nights in Liverpool, Kemble and his daughter

Fanny set sail on the *Pacific* out of Liverpool on 1 August 1832. They were accompanied by Adelaide De Camp ("Aunt Dall"), spinster sister of Mrs Charles Kemble and sometime actress, who served as Fanny's devoted companion and attendant. Mrs Charles Kemble remained behind in London.

Two weeks after their landing in New York on 4 September, Kemble made his debut at the Park Theatre on 17 September 1832, as Hamlet, before a very full house on an intensely hot night. Though James Hackett thought Kemble was too old for the role, William Leggett, writing in the New York *Evening Post* of 18 September, marveled at Kemble's "exterior of five and twenty." Fanny wrote that he "looked wonderfully young and handsome." The critic in the *American* of 18 September called him "the first Hamlet we have ever had in this country." Enthusiasm was expressed for his portrayals of Romeo on 20 September, Charles Surface on 21 September, Pierre on 24 September, and Benedick, Sir Thomas Clifford, Faulconbridge, and Mirabel, which followed in quick order. The elegance of his Charles Surface was highly praised and his Pierre was acclaimed by the New York *Mirror* of 29 September 1832 as "magnificent, the best by far ever seen here." The same paper on 13 October called his characterizations "truly finished and graceful specimens of refined acting, replete with the dignity and elegance of high life, and startling the mind sometimes with bursts of tragic power, in their effect almost electric." Fanny made her debut on 18 September as Bianca and "moved, astonished, and delighted" the audience.

After playing in New York until 5 October, they made their way to Philadelphia, where they opened at the Chestnut Street Theatre on 10 October. They moved on to Baltimore and Washington in January 1833. On 18 April they opened in Boston. That season they frequently returned to New York and Philadelphia. According to Ireland's *Records of the New York Stage*, their first season in New York, 1832–33, brought more than $56,000 into the box office in 60 nights. On 19 February 1833 he acted Charles of Bourbon in Fanny's *Francis I*. In 1833–34 they performed a total of 49 times in New York. Details of their engagement in those eastern American cities (and of their excursions to Niagara Falls and elsewhere) may be found in three of Fanny Kemble's books—her *Journal*, *Records of a Girlhood*, and *Records of Later Life*—as well as in documentaries of the New York stage by Odell and Ireland and in Reese James's *Old Drury of Philadelphia*. The Kembles "made quite a sensation in the fashionable circles of society," according to Francis Wemyss; and Washington Irving recorded that they "turned the heads" of everyone. They met President Jackson in Washington and they graced the learned salons of Boston and Cambridge. The New York *Mirror* stated on 19 April 1834 that "The advent of the Kembles was an era in our dramatic history, which can be paralleled by the single instance of the arrival of George Frederick Cooke. . . . At the present day, the change produced by the Kembles in the popular style of acting must be perceptible to all."

At Christ Church, Philadelphia, on 7 June 1834, Charles Kemble gave his daughter Fanny in marriage to the wealthy lawyer and plantation heir Pierce Butler. Next day Mrs Butler and her father returned to New York for a brief farewell engagement. On 20 June 1834 they gave their last performances, in *The Stranger* and *The Day After the Wedding*, for his benefit. Fanny retired to an unhappy domesticity in Philadelphia, and Charles Kemble went home to England. "Aunt Dall" had died in Boston on 20 April 1834 of injuries suffered in a carriage upset on a trip to Niagara Falls.

Having settled at No 11, Park Place, St James, Kemble made some summer appearances at the Haymarket in 1835 and was engaged at Covent Garden in 1835–36. In March of 1836, as co-executor with Horace Twiss of the estate of his sister Elizabeth Whitlock, he proved her will, in which Charles's wife Maria Theresa was bequeathed a cottage at Addlestone.

Having decided to retire from the profession in which he had been engaged for some 44 years—since those early performances at Sheffield in 1792–93—Kemble began a last round of appearances at Covent Garden in September 1836, playing Macbeth, Hamlet, Beverley, Shylock, Charles Surface, Faulconbridge, Cassio, and Antony. His final farewell, which he had intended for the spring of that season, was precipitated by his appointment by the Lord Chamberlain on 28 October 1836 to the post of Examiner of Plays. On 23 December 1836, playing Benedick to Helen Faucit's Beatrice, Kemble took his leave of the stage. The crowd was so great that police were required to turn away the unfortunate. According to all reports it was an inspired and exquisite performance—the "*grand vin* of comedy." At the conclusion the audience, which included Princess Victoria and two distinguished actors from America, Mrs Pierce Butler and the great Edwin Forrest, rose for a 10-minute tumultuous ovation. Then Kemble delivered an affecting farewell address, which was printed in the papers next day. He was the last of Roger Kemble's children to retire from the stage, and except for eccentric Ann Julia Hatton (who died in 1838) the only one still alive in 1836.

At a dinner given by the Garrick Club at the Albion Hotel on 10 January 1837, about 100 of his professional colleagues honored Kemble with speeches, verses, and songs, including one written by J. Hamilton Reynolds and sung by Balfe, which was printed in the *Athenaeum* of 14 January 1837 (and in *Notes and Queries* of 11 November 1871) and ended with:

> *Oh! nothing can rob us of memory's gold:*
> *And tho' he quits the gorgeous, and we may grow*
>   *old,*
> *With our Shakespeare at heart, and bright forms*
>   *in our brain,*
> *We can dream up our Siddons and Kembles again.*
>   *Well! wealthy we have been; tho' fortune may*
>   *drown,*
>   *And they cannot but say that we 'have had the*
>   *crown.'*

At a private party on the stage of Covent Garden on 3 March 1840, the Duke of Beaufort presented Kemble with a large commemorative silver vase, designed by the sculptor Francis Chantrey and inscribed by 90 friends, including many leading actors.

The sinecure as Examiner of Plays held by Kemble for three years brought him £40 per year plus two guineas per license issued. The appointment was widely approved by the profession as one for which he was highly qualified, though how much personal attention Kemble gave to the licensing and censoring of plays is not clear. He suffered ill health during much of that period. And when not ill he traveled on the Continent with his younger daughter Adelaide. *The Dictionary of National*

Harvard Theatre Collection

CHARLES KEMBLE, 1840
by Lane

Biography reported that he "performed the duties by proxy." He relinquished the position to his son John Mitchell Kemble on 22 February 1840.

In response to Queen Victoria's wishes that her consort might be able to see Charles Kemble perform, he abandoned retirement to act at Covent Garden for three weeks in the spring of 1840. In his reappearance as Don Felix in *The Wonder* on 24 March, when nearly 65, he displayed the vigor and "highborn grace" which had characterized his earlier years. "Oh, when will our young men learn to be and move the love like him!" wondered *John Bull* on 29 March. He continued to amaze with Mercutio, Benedick, and Hamlet, impressing in the last on 10 April as "the master yet." He acted Mercutio on 24 and 30 March, Don Felix again on 1 April, and Charles Surface on 3 April. Hamlet was to have been performed by him as his last offering, on Tuesday, 7 April, but he played Benedick instead. Finally, he performed Hamlet on 10 April.

Obedience to his monarch, however, greatly taxed Kemble's physical powers, as Fanny had feared—"he may again relapse into feebleness, dejection, and general disorder of the system from which he appeared to be suffering before he made this last professional effort." A trip to

Italy with Adelaide had to be cut short by his rapidly deteriorating condition, and when Fanny arrived in London on a visit from America in October 1840 he was "at the point of death." Kemble made a miraculous rally, however, and soon could be moved to reside with Fanny and her husband in Clarges Street, Piccadilly, where they were also joined by Adelaide, home from a triumphant opera tour.

In 1841 and 1842 Kemble suffered bouts of severe depression. In October 1841 he traveled to Frankfort to visit Fanny but stayed only one day before returning immediately to England—"He was not at all well," wrote Fanny. That year he lost £4000 in the failure of the United States Bank of Philadelphia. By December 1841 he moved to Harley Street.

Kemble was receiving no rent from his share in Covent Garden, which yet again was in financial distress despite the artistic successes Macready and Mme Vestris enjoyed with many productions. His co-proprietors persuaded Kemble to take up the reins of the theatre in September 1842, without financial "responsibility or liability." Though the house was filled the nights Adelaide Kemble performed, and Kemble himself was, as Fanny put it, "happy as the gods" to be back in harness, the deficit continued to mount. Kemble developed a 'violent lumbago' which confined him to his bed at No 26, Upper Grosvenor Street (where the family had moved after leaving Harley Street in October and passing a short time at the Clarendon Hotel). His final managerial fling was aborted; in December the Covent Garden lease passed to Alfred Bunn.

In April 1844 Kemble gave a reading of *Cymbeline* at Buckingham Palace for Queen Victoria. It was incomprehensible to Fanny how he could "*compress* or rather *compel* the five acts into three-quarters of an hour." On 13 May 1844 he began a series of readings from Shakespeare at Willis's Rooms, which he repeated there and at Harrowgate the following year. By autumn 1845 he was living at No 44, Mortimer Street, Cavendish Square. In the late summer of 1846 he took a three-month tour of the Continent. He continued giving readings around London until his deafness forced him to give them up in 1848.

Kemble spent many days of his last years as a venerated relic at the Garrick Club. His severe deafness now necessitated the use of a hearing trumpet. "This affliction," informs one of his obituaries, "caused him at times to wear a melancholy appearance . . . but if any congenial spirit spoke to him of the 'good old times,' his eye would brighten, his voice would grow eloquent, and he would pour forth a flood of anecdote, reminiscence, and criticism most entertaining and instructive to all present."

He died on 12 November 1854, several weeks before his seventy-ninth birthday, and was buried in Kensal Green Cemetery. In his will drawn on 11 September 1851, when his address was Albany Terrace, New Road, Middlesex, he bequeathed the interest of £4000, which he had inherited from his sister-in-law Priscilla Kemble, to his son Henry (one-quarter share) and his daughters Adelaide (one-quarter) and Fanny (one-half). To Fanny he left his silver vase by Chantrey. Henry received a marble bust of his father, but which one of the four of which he is known to have been the subject was not specified in the will. Henry also inherited his father's dressing case and the "Helmet, Sword and Shield worn by my brother in Coriolanus." Small gifts were given to friends: £100 to William Loftus Lowndes, £50 to the Reverend William Harness, and £50 to Dr James Wilson. The rest of his estate went to his son and daughters, equally, with instructions that should they decide to sell his interest in Covent Garden Theatre, the shares should first be offered to the other proprietors. The will was proved at London by his executors, William Loftus Lowndes and the Reverend William Harness on 12 January 1855.

Kemble's wife Maria Theresa, who had retired in 1819, had died on 3 September 1838 at Addlestone, near Chertsey, where she frequently lived while Charles was traveling. At the time of her death, he was in Milan with his daughter Adelaide. Evidently their marriage was not made easier by Charles's reputation for womanizing in the days when he was dashing and very handsome. According to Oxberry there was gossip about him and various Covent Garden actresses, and on one occasion, about 1822, Kemble had registered at Howe's Royal Hotel in Margate with a woman he passed off as his wife. He was surprised there in bed with her by the real Mrs Kemble.

The first of Charles Kemble's five children, John Mitchell Kemble, was born in London on 11 April 1807, about a week and nine months after his parents' marriage. Educated at Trinity College, Cambridge, he became a much published philologist and historian who has received a notice in *The Dictionary of National Biography* comparable in length to that of his father. He died at Dublin on 26 March 1857 and was buried in Mount Jerome Cemetery. By his unhappy marriage in Göttingen, Germany, on 24 July 1836 to Natalie Auguste Wendt, daughter of Professor Amadeus Wendt of Göttingen, he had four children: Gertrude (1837–1882), a soprano who married the baritone Sir Charles Santley, and was the mother of the actor Michael Santley; Henry Charles (1840–1907), a colonel in the Bengal cavalry; Mildred (1841–1876), who married the Reverend Charles Edward Donne, vicar of Faversham; and a daughter, name unknown, who was born on 23 September 1842.

Philip, the second child of Charles and Maria Theresa Kemble, died in infancy. Their third child, Frances Ann (Fanny), was born in Newman Street, London, on 27 November 1809; vivacious and loquacious, she enjoyed success as an actress and socialite in Britain and America. She wrote a number of books and was the subject of several biographies, including Margaret Armstrong's *Fanny Kemble, A Passionate Victorian* (1938). Her marriage in 1834 to Pierce Butler (1810–1867) ended in divorce in September 1849. Fanny died in London on 15 January 1893 and was buried in Kensal Green Cemetery. The Butlers' children were: Sarah (1835–1908), an author who married the novelist Owen Jones Wister, and Frances Ann (1838–1910), who married the Honorable James Wentworth Leigh.

Charles Kemble's fourth child, Henry James Vincent, was born at Covent Garden Chambers in December 1812, and proved to be a handsome, pleasant, but undistinguished fellow who failed his acting audition for his father, went to Cambridge, and after drifting about had his army commission bought for him in 1832 by his sister Fanny. His affair with Mary Ann Thackeray provided Henry James with the material for *Washington Square*. By 1854 he had been hospitalized in William Stilwel's private asylum at Hillingdon, Middlesex, where his visitor William Thackeray found him hopelessly insane. Henry died there three years later on 19 August 1857. His illegitimate son

Henry (1848–1907)—"Harry the Beetle"—became an actor.

Adelaide Kemble, the fifth child of Charles Kemble, was born at Covent Garden Chambers in November 1815. According to her sister Fanny, Adelaide possessed an "unquenchable musical genius." She sang in various concerts throughout England and in 1837 began a fine opera career on the Continent. On 2 November 1841 she made her first appearance at Covent Garden, singing the title role in *Norma*; her success revived the fortunes of that theatre until she retired on 23 December 1842. On 12 July 1842 she had married Edward John Sartoris (1814–1888), M.P., at St Mary's Chapel, Renfield Street, Glasgow. Thereafter she spent much of her time in their villa at Rome. She died at Warsash House, Titchfield, Hampshire, on 6 August 1879. In his *Thirty Years of Musical Recollections*, Chorley pronounced her "the greatest, though not the best, English singer of the century." Adelaide Kemble is noticed in *The Dictionary of National Biography*. She had three children: Edward Greville (1843–1873); Mary Theodosia (1845–1925), who married Henry Evans Gordon; and Algernon Charles Frederick (1851–1892). (The marriage of Mary Sartoris and H. E. Gordon produced Margaret Gordon, who married the fifth Baron Stanley of Alderley and was the mother of the singer Adelaide Stanley and the actress Pamela Stanley; the latter married Sir David Cunynghame.)

Charles Kemble was not a great actor, though he was one of the very finest of his time. He possessed the fullest measure of Kemble beauty, picturesqueness, and "high and noble bearing." These attributes, along with an eloquent manner of speech, made him, perhaps even more than his brother John, responsible for the "Kemble school" of acting that so influenced the stage in England and America. William Macready, another very fine though not great actor, summed up Kemble as "a first-rate actor in second-rate parts." He thought Kemble's young Mirabel in *The Inconstant* "a most finished piece of acting," his Richmond spirited and chivalrous, and his Cassio "incomparable." But in such heavy roles as Hamlet, Macbeth, and Richard III, Macready found his tragic efforts to be "laborious failures." Mrs Siddons believed that Charles's Hamlet was as finely conceived as John Kemble's but not so well executed. Some of his contemporaries, like Henry Crabb Robinson and C. R. Leslie, were never fully reconciled to his acting. The latter, for example, wrote in his *Autobiography* (1816) that Kemble looked Orlando better than he played him, and he pronounced: "He is no great actor; the only character I ever liked him in was Faulconbridge."

He had an enormous number of roles of a wide range. Leigh Hunt declared that Kemble was equally superior in three classes of character:

. . . in the tender lover-like *Romeo*, in the spirited gentlemen of tragedy, such as *Laertes* and *Faulconbridge*, and as a very happy mixture of the occasional debauchee and the gentleman of feeling, as in Shakespeare's *Cassio* and *Charles Oakley* in the 'Jealous Wife.' In theatrical lovers, in that complaining softness with which the fancies of young ladies adorn their imaginary heroes, Mr. Charles Kemble is certainly the first performer on the stage.

William Donne in his *Essays on the Drama* (1858) wrote that he had never seen an actor "with more buoyancy of spirit than Charles Kemble." His Mercutio was full of fancy and overflowing with life; his portrayal of that role was, in his daughter Fanny's judgment, "*the best Mercutio, that ever trod the English stage*"—and more objective testimony suggests that Fanny may have been right. A comprehensive account of Kemble's playing of Mercutio, Hamlet, and Faulconbridge is given by Williamson.

Kemble's achievements were all the more impressive because of the fact that in the early years of his career he was looked upon as somewhat of a stick on awkward legs. But that notable Kemble discipline and genetic talent eventually brought him to the height of his profession.

He possessed few enemies and he enjoyed the highest respect and affection of his colleagues. He was, as Helen Faucit put it, "before everything pre-eminently a gentleman." Though in earlier years Charles Kemble had a roving eye, Edward Fitzball's eulogy of him is an epitaph that anyone might cherish: "As he was, before the public the prince of actors, so he was in private life, the very noblest of men."

Portraits of Charles Kemble include:

1. Attributed to Thomas Baxter. Pencil-and-red-chalk drawing, dated 1812. Sold for $90 in the auction of the property of the American Shakespeare Theatre at Sotheby, Parke, Barnet, New York City, on 15 January 1976.

2. By Henry P. Briggs. In the Dulwich College Picture Gallery, presented by George Bartley in 1854. Reproduced as frontispiece to Jane Williamson, *Charles Kemble, Man of the Theatre* (1970).

3. By Henry P. Briggs. In the Garrick Club (No 8), received in 1844 as a bequest of Edward Walpole. Half-length, standing, open shirt with collar, a white mask in each hand.

4. By Henry P. Briggs. In the Garrick Club (No 364). Provenance unknown. Head and shoulders, seated to left, black curly hair, high collar, black neckcloth and cloak, maroon coat.

5. By Henry P. Briggs. Exhibited in the National Portrait Exhibition in 1868, when it was owned by Mrs Noseda. Perhaps No 4, above.

6. By Henry P. Briggs. In J. Green's collection sold at Christie's on 22 July 1871. Perhaps No 4, above.

7. By Henry P. Briggs. Listed by the Huntington Library art file as in the O. Wister Collection, Philadelphia, this is probably the portrait mentioned in the Garrick Club catalogue as being in the possession of a descendant.

8. By Thomas Clark. In her will dated 18 May 1815 and proved on 8 July 1831 Sarah Siddons bequeathed to Maria Theresa Kemble a portrait of Charles Kemble painted by Clark. Present location unknown. Possibly it was the portrait from which Ridley did the engraving, after Clark, of Charles as Laertes; see below, No 80.

9. By Samuel De Wilde. Watercolor portrait of Kemble's head in profile, in the Harvard Theatre Collection.

10. By Samuel De Wilde. Pencil-and-red-chalk drawing, in the British Museum. Wearing feathered hat.

11. By Thomas Kearsley. A whole-length, life-size painting, in the Mathews Collection (No 360) at the Garrick Club when Kemble's notice was written for *The Dictionary of National Biography*, but evidently not now there.

12. By Thomas Lawrence. Two chalk drawings, present location unknown. Both were in

the possession of Sarah Siddons in 1830. Lithographs by R. J. Lane as pls II and IV in *Imitations of Chalk Drawings*, published by Dickinson, 1830.

13. By William Henry Nightingale. "Pencil drawing of Charles Kemble from Life," 1840, with Kemble's autograph. In the Harvard Theatre Collection.

14. By Henry Wyatt. Head and shoulders, oil painting. In the Royal Shakespeare Theatre Picture Gallery, Stratford-upon-Avon.

15. By unknown artist. Watercolor drawing presented to the Garrick Club (catalogue No 350) in 1887 by Henry Kemble. Half-length, seated on settee, his right hand on the arm; grey hair, black neckcloth and coat.

16. By unknown artist. Noted in the art file at the Huntington Library as being in Bryn Mawr, Pennsylvania; possibly in the collection of O. B. Wister of Philadelphia.

17. By unknown artist. On cardboard. Presented to the Harvard Theatre Collection in 1915 by R. G. Shaw.

18. By unknown artist, c. 1830(?). This portrait was descended through the family of Philip Rhinelander IV and has been thought to be by Thomas Sully. In 1978 in the possession of Bernard & S. Dean Levy, Inc, New York. Sitter doubtful.

19. By unknown artist. Miniature listed in Huntington Library art file as in the J. B. Robertson Collection.

20. By unknown artist. One of nine silhouettes on paper. In the Garrick Club (catalogue No 494).

21. By unknown artist. Watecolor drawing, three-quarter front. In the Harvard Theatre Collection.

22. By Timothy Butler. Marble bust exhibited at the Royal Academy, 1844. An anonymous engraving is in the Harvard Theatre Collection.

23. By Edward Davis. Bust exhibited at the Royal Academy, 1836.

24. By Lawrence MacDonald. Bust exhibited at Edinburgh, 1826.

25. By J. L. Dantan. Busts of Kemble and his two daughters were sculpted by Dantan for the Marquis of Titchfield.

26. By unknown sculptor. A plaster bust of Charles Kemble was offered in the sale of John Philip Kemble's furniture and effects at Robins on 14 and 15 December 1820.

27. Lithograph by H. Gaugain, after C. Brand. Published as a plate to Moreau's *Souvenirs du Theatre Anglais*, 1827. See also below, No 32.

28. Lithography by R. J. Lane. Published by Colnaghi & Puckle, 1840.

29. Engraving by J. Thomson. Published by Asperne as a plate to the *European Magazine*, 1822.

30. By unknown engraver, after A. H. Wall. Standing, glove in right hand, cane in left.

31. By unknown engraver. Standing at table, reading *King John*.

32. By unknown engraver, after C. Brand, 1831. A copy of the lithograph by H. Gaugain. See above, No 27.

33. By unknown engraver. Showing a portly and balding Kemble seated at table reading *Cymbeline* before Queen Victoria, Prince Albert, and 20 other members of the court at Buckingham Palace.

34. As Bassanio in *The Merchant of Venice*. Lithograph signed "M. R. [Martha Rolls] 1827." Not listed in Hall catalogue but in the Harvard Theatre Collection.

35. As Benedick in *Much Ado about Nothing*. Lithograph by R. J. Lane. Published by Colnaghi & Puckle, 1840.

36. As Benedick. Lithograph by J. H. Lynch. Printed by Graf & Soret.

37. As Cassio in *Othello*. Lithograph by R. J. Lane. Published by Colnaghi & Puckle, 1840.

38. As Charles II in *Charles the Second; or, The Merry Monarch*. Engraving by G. Adcock. Publisher by J. Gifford, 1825.

39. As Charles II in *Charles II*, with John Fawcett as Captain Copp. By George Clint, exhibited at the Royal Academy, 1825. In the Garrick Club (catalogue No 9). Engraving by T. Lupton, 1826.

40. As Charles II. By unknown engraver. Published as a penny-plain by W. West, 1826.

41. As Charles II. By unknown engraver. Published as penny-plain and twopence-colored by Hodgson, 1831.

42. As Charles Surface in *The School for Scandal*. Engraving by R. Dighton. Published by T. McLean, 1821. An anonymous lithograph copy also appeared.

43. As Cromwell, with Mrs Siddons as Queen Katharine, John Philip Kemble as Wol-

sey, Stephen Kemble as Henry, and other figures in the Trial Scene in *Henry VIII*. Painting by G. H. Harlow. The painting does not represent an actual performance, for Harlow painted many friends into it. For details on versions and engravings of this painting, see the portrait list for Stephen Kemble, No 15.

44. As Cromwell. Engraving by T. Lupton of the figure of Kemble seated at a table, with pen in hand, detail from above painting by Harlow (No 43). Published by W. Cribb, 1 February 1819. Re-impressions published 1 March 1819 and 1 July 1824. An engraving of the same picture by J. Sartain was published by R. H. Hobson, Philadelphia, and a vignette copy, bust only, by an unknown engraver was issued. Yet another copy, by an unknown engraver, with the table omitted, also appeared.

45. As Dionysius in *The Grecian Daughter*. By unknown engraver. Published as a twopence-colored.

46. As Don Felix in *The Wonder*. Engraving by R. J. Lane. Published by Colnaghi & Puckle, 1840.

47. As Don Juan in *Don Giovanni and Juan*. By unknown engraver. Published as a penny-plain by J. Bailey, 1830.

48. As Don Juan in *The Libertine*. By unknown engraver. Published as a penny-plain by W. West, 1818.

49. As Douglas in *Wallace*. By unknown engraver. Published as a penny-plain by Pitts, Printer and Wholesale Toy Warehouse.

50. As Douglas. By unknown engraver. Published as twopence-colored by J. Jameson, 1820.

51. As Duke of Aumerle, with Richard Wroughton as Bolingbroke, in *Richard II*. Engraving by A. Warren, after De Loutherbourg. Published by G. Kearsley, 1804.

52. As Falstaff in *1 Henry IV*. Seated, glass in hand. Engraving by R. J. Lane. Published by Colnaghi & Puckle, 1840. Listed in the Hall catalogue as of Stephen Kemble (No 9), but corrected to Charles in MS note in Harvard Theatre Collection. An anonymous engraving and a lithograph were also issued.

53. As Falstaff. Standing, feet apart, sword drawn. Lithograph signed "M.R. [Martha Rolls] 1827." Not listed in the Hall catalogue but in the Harvard Theatre Collection.

54. As Faulconbridge in *King John*. Engrav-

ing by R. J. Lane. Published by Colnaghi & Puckle, 1840.

55. As Faulconbridge. Engraving by T. Woolnoth, after T. Wageman. Published as a plate to Oxberry's *New English Drama*, 1819.

56. As Faulconbridge. By unknown engraver. Published as a twopence-colored by Park & Golding.

57. As Faulconbridge. By unknown engraver. Published as a penny-plain by Hodgson, 1831.

58. As Ferdinand in *The Tempest*. Standing on the shore. Engraving by Alais. Published by J. Roach, 1807.

59. As Ferdinand. Kneeling on a rock. By unknown engraver.

60. As Frank Plotwell in *The Merchant's Wedding*. By unknown engraver. Published as a penny-plain by W. West, 1828.

61. As Friar Michael in *Maid Marian*. Engraving by I. R. Cruikshank. Published as a plate to *Mirror of the Stage*, 1 April 1823.

62. As George Barnwell in *George Barnwell*. Engraving by Alais, after Cruikshank. Published by J. Roach, 1806. The same picture, engraved by G. Murray, had been published by Roach in 1799, and was said to be of John Philip Kemble, but probably the subject was Charles.

63. As Giraldi Fazio in *Fazio*. Engraving by H. R. Cook. Published as a plate to *The Drama*, 1821.

64. As Giraldi Fazio. Painting by Thomas Sully, 1833. In the Pennsylvania Academy of Fine Arts, Philadelphia.

65. As Giraldi Fazio. Engraving by G. Cruikshank. Published as a plate to the *British Stage*, March 1818.

66. As Guido, with Miss Foote as Isidora, in *Mirandola*. By unknown engraver. Published by J. Jameson, February 1821.

67. As Hamlet in *Hamlet*. Lithograph by A. De Valmont. Similar to a drawing in the Beard Collection in the Victoria and Albert Museum which is identified as J. P. Kemble as Hamlet.

68. As Hamlet. Lithograph by Ducarme. Published as a plate to *Galérie Universelle*, incorrectly titled J. P. Kemble.

69. As Hamlet, with Miss Smithson as Ophelia. In production in Paris, 1827. Lithograph by Gaugain. Reproduced in Alec Clunes, *British Theatre* (p. 106), as representing John Philip Kemble.

70. As Hamlet. Lithograph by R. J. Lane. Published by Colnaghi & Puckle, 1840. A copy by an unknown engraver was also issued.

71. As Hamlet. Engraving by J. Rogers.

72. As Henry V in *Henry V*. By unknown engraver. Published as a penny-plain by Park & Golding.

73. As Henry V. By unknown engraver. Published by J. Smart, 1821.

74. As Henry V. By unknown engraver. Published as a penny-plain by J. Thornton, 1824.

75. As Henry VIII, with Fanny Kemble as Queen Katharine and Charles Young as Wolsey, in *Henry VIII*, Covent Garden, 24 October 1831. Painting by Henry Andrews. In the Royal Shakespeare Theatre Art Gallery. Exhibited in *The Georgian Playhouse Exhibition* at the Hayward Gallery in 1975 and reproduced in the catalogue.

76. As Hotspur in *I Henry IV*. By unknown engraver. Published as a penny-plain by W. West, 1827.

77. As Iago in *Othello*. Lithograph by R. J. Lane. Published by Colnaghi & Puckle, 1840.

78. As Ivanhoe in *Ivanhoe*. By unknown engraver. Published as twopence-colored by W. West, 1820.

79. As Ivanhoe. By unknown engraver. Published as twopence-colored by Hodgson, 1822.

80. As Laertes in *Hamlet*. Engraving by W. Ridley, after Clark. Published as a plate to the *Monthly Mirror*, May 1802. See above, No 8.

81. As Leon in *Rule a Wife and Have a Wife*. Lithograph by R. J. Lane. Published by Colnaghi & Puckle, 1840.

82. As Lorenzo in *The Mistake*. Engraving by T. Chapman, after Moses. Published as a plate to *British Drama*, 1808.

83. As Macbeth in *Macbeth*. Lithograph by R. J. Lane. Published by Colnaghi & Puckle, 1840.

84. As Macbeth. Painting by Andrew Mortimer, exhibited at the Royal Academy in 1836. Presented to the Garrick Club (catalogue No 453) by Charles Kemble between 1846 and 1854.

85. As Macbeth or Malcolm? Watercolor by unknown artist. In the Garrick Club (catalogue No 608), presented in 1910 by L. L. Batten. On the brown paper backing Batten had inscribed: "This picture was given to me by Mr Soper in July 1897. It was bought by him at the sale of Mr Thomas Turner's collection of Shakespeariana at the house now St. Mary de Crypt Vicarage in Brunswick Square. In the sale catalogue which Mr. H. W. Brunton showed me it was said to be 'Charles Kemble'; and without artist's name. The sale was in 1860." Another note suggests Lawrence as the artist and the character as either Malcolm or Macbeth.

86. As Macduff in *Macbeth*. Lithograph by R. J. Lane. Published by Colnaghi & Puckle, 1840.

87. As Marc Antony in *Julius Caesar*. Lithograph by R. J. Lane. Published by Colnaghi & Puckle, 1840.

88. As Marc Antony. By unknown engraver. Published as a penny-plain by D'Ash, 1826.

89. As Mercutio in *Romeo and Juliet*. Lithograph by R. J. Lane. Published by Colnaghi & Puckle, 1840.

90. As Mirabel in *The Inconstant*. Engraving by H. Moses. Published by C. Cooke, 1806.

91. As Orestes in *Orestes in Argos*. Engraving by T. Woolnoth, after T. Wageman. Published by Cumberland, reprinted by Dolby, 1825.

92. As Orlando in *As You Like It*. Engraving by C. Warren, after De Loutherbourg. Published by Kearsley, 1804, as a plate to an edition of Shakespeare.

93. As Othello in *Othello*. Lithograph by De Valmont. Published as a plate to *Théâtre Anglais à Paris*.

94. As Othello. Lithograph by R. J. Lane. Published by Colnaghi & Puckle, 1840.

95. As Othello. Engraving by Maleuore. Published with inscription "Costume de C. Kemble, role D'Othello."

96. As Pierre in *Venice Preserv'd*. Engraving by W. T. Page, after R. Cruikshank. Published in No 267 of *Figaro in London*. A copy engraved by J. Rogers was published as a plate to *Dramatic Magazine*.

97. As Pierre. Engraving by P. Roberts. Published as a twopence-colored by O. Hodgson.

98. As Pierre. Engraving by W. Sharp, after J. Hayter. Published by Dickinson.

99. As Pierre. Watercolor by unknown artist. Sold in the Evert Jansen Wendell sale at the American Art Association, 15–20 October 1918.

100. As Pierre. By unknown engraver.

101. As Prince of Wales in *The Coronation.* Engraving by W. West. Published as a penny-plain, 1821.

102. As Richmond in *Richard III.* By unknown engraver. Published as a penny-plain by A. Park.

103. As Romeo in *Romeo and Juliet.* Engraving by "A. P."

104. As Romeo. Engraving by J. Rogers, after R. Page. Published as a plate to Oxberry's *Dramatic Biography*, 1825.

105. As Romeo. Engraving by R. Thomson, after Cowell. Published as a plate to Oxberry's *New English Drama*, 1819.

106. As Romeo. Painting by A. Wivell. In the Garrick Club (No 348). Stated in the Mathews catalogue as C. Kemble in *Hamlet.* Engraving by Thompson, 1819. Also published as a plate to Oxberry's *New English Drama*, 1821, representing Kemble as Vicentio in *Evadne.* A copy engraved by Rogers, after Wivell, was published by J. Limebird with the inscription changed to "As Romeo."

107. As Romeo. By unknown engraver. Published as a twopence-colored by O. Hodgson.

108. As Sebastian in *The Renegade.* Engraving by H. R. Cook, after De Wilde. Published as a plate to *Theatrical Inquisitor*, 1816.

109. As Shylock in *The Merchant of Venice.* Lithograph by R. J. Lane. Published by Colnaghi & Puckle, 1840.

110. As Sigismund in *The Wanderer.* Watercolor by Samuel De Wilde. In the Harvard Theatre Collection.

111. As Sigismund. By unknown engraver. Published as a plate to *Sketch of 'The Wanderer'* [1812].

112. As the Stranger in *The Stranger.* Lithograph by R. J. Lane. Published by Colnaghi & Puckle, 1840.

113. As Three-Fingered Jack with Maria Theresa Kemble (when Miss De Camp) as Rosa, in *Obi.* By unknown engraver. Published by E. Orme, 1801.

114. As Young Wilmot in *Fatal Curiosity.* Engraving by P. Audinet, after Roberts. Published as a plate to Cawthorne's *British Library*, 1796.

115. In six favorite characters. By unknown engraver. Published as twopence-colored by Hodgson, April 1832.

116. Sixteeen portraits, fifteen in character,

on one sheet. Lithograph by R. J. Lane. Published 1840. (Also in singles, published by Colnaghi & Puckle, as listed above.)

117. Six caricatures of Fanny and Charles Kemble were published by D. C. Johnston at Boston in 1835, entitled *Outlines Illustrative of the Journal of F**** A*** K*****.* "Drawn and Etched by Mr. ———." These include Kemble on stage as Hamlet before a sparse London audience which is leaving at the end of the performance: "A London Audience Getting Up In Compliment"; Kemble dining with Fanny and Aunt Dall as a vendor brings in more food; and Kemble, Fanny, and Aunt Dall strewn over the ground after their carriage accident, the injuries from which Aunt Dall eventually died.

Kemble, Mrs Charles, Maria Theresa, née De Camp *1775–1838, actress, dancer, singer, playwright.*

Maria Theresa (or Marie Thérèse) De Camp was born in Vienna on 17 January 1775. The year of her birth was given in her mother's petition to the Royal Society of Musicians and

Harvard Theatre Collection

MARIA THERESA KEMBLE

engraving by Ridley, after Barry

was provided correctly in a memoir that appeared in the *Thespian Magazine* of December 1793. That memoir was repeated virtually intact in the *Monthly Mirror* of November 1801 but with the year of her birth misprinted as 1774, the incorrect date picked up by *The Dictionary of National Biography*. She was the eldest of at least six children of the French musician George Louis De Camp and his wife Jeanne Adrienne Dufour, daughter of Jean Louis Dufour of Nancy. At the time of George Louis De Camp's marriage on 7 April 1774 he was, according to Fanny Kemble's account, a captain in the French army. It has been alleged that his real name was De Fleury and that he was descended on his father's side from French nobility. According to that story, when George Louis's father died young, his widow was forced by her proud father-in-law to abandon the name of De Fleury and to take up her maiden name again. That romantic story, told in the *Monthly Mirror* of November 1801 and embellished in the 1814 edition of the *Authentic Memoirs of the Green Room*, appears dubious.

George Louis De Camp brought his young family to London by 1777, the year in which he became a member of the Covent Garden oratorio band. Evidently his wife did not perform in England. But two of Maria Theresa's sisters, Adelaide and Sophia, and her brother Vincent, as well as her aunts Sophia and Adelaide (Mrs Louis Simonet), all were performers and are noticed separately. Information about the family is provided in the notice of George Louis De Camp.

Maria Theresa was the first of her father's children to take to the stage. At the age of eight (not six as given in several memoirs) she danced in *Les Ruses de l'Amour*, a ballet by Noverre given at the end of the opera *L'Olimpiade* at the King's Theatre on 1 May 1783—"The part of Cupid . . . by Miss De Camp, daughter to the celebrated Flute Player of that Name." Also dancing that night were her aunt and uncle, Mons and Mme Simonet, and their eight-year-old daughter Theresa. Miss De Camp again appeared as Cupid in that ballet on 8 May. The following year at the King's she was once again Cupid, but this time in D'Auberval's ballet *Le Réveil du Bonheur*, on 3 February 1784 and several times thereafter. For Mme Simonet's benefit at the King's on 11 March 1784, Miss Simonet and Miss De

Camp, both identified as pupils of Mons Simonet, danced a minuet de la cour and a gavotte. At the King's several seasons later, in the spring of 1786, she was still small enough to assume Cupid in Gardel's ballet *Le Premier Navigateur* and she also performed some specialty numbers. About that time she played the role of Zélie in a translation of the Countess de Genlis's *La Colombe* at Le Texier's theatre in Lisle Street. Thence she was engaged with Mons L'Aborie and her two young Simonet cousins to dance at the Royal Circus, where she remained only for a brief time until, as her memoirs report, she was recommended by the Prince of Wales to George Colman, manager of the Haymarket Theatre.

Her first appearance at the Haymarket was on 14 June 1786, when advertised as from the Royal Circus she danced *The Nosegay* with Master James Harvey D'Egville in the presence of the royal family. On 21 June she danced *The Polonaise* with one of the D'Egville boys and on 6 July she and Masters James Harvey and George D'Egville performed a new dance called *Jamie's Return*, which was favorably received and which inspired an engraving of the three youngsters by Sailleur, after Miller, in 1787. Her other assignments that summer included dancing in the premiere of O'Keeffe's *The Siege of Curzola* on 12 August 1786 and in *Harlequin Teague*. In the bills for the latter on 6 September her name was added as the Chair Mender (with a song in character), in which role she performed a charming turn described by Sophie v. la Roche, *Sophie in London*:

A twelve-year-old girl dressed as a poor boy who walks around with a bundle of rushes, straw and reeds to patch up old chairs, then really sits down to work on one, sang and played unusually well; indeed, was obliged to give two encores; the third time, however, announced with dignity and candour that it would not be possible, and that she feared she might be unable to take her part the next day; which would grieve her excessively, as she liked having her modest talents appreciated and applauded. Everyone clapped and praised her aloud. She is beautiful, and deserves to be the nation's darling, and will certainly become a great actress, competent to keep her voice; gesture and features in complete control, never using her talents wrongly or producing exaggerated effects.

Sometime in 1786 Maria Theresa's father had become ill, probably with tuberculosis, and he died, probably in Germany, in October 1787, at the age of 35. Her mother was reduced to living off an allowance from the Royal Society of Musicians and whatever her children could earn at the theatre. Evidently Maria Theresa's formal education had been neglected, and for some time she could speak no English; the lines she was assigned in her small roles in the earliest years of her career she mastered by imitation. Reading, writing, and arithmetic she eventually learned in her early teens from Viscountess Perceval, and music and Italian she acquired from a Miss Buchanan.

Miss De Camp made her debut at Drury Lane on 24 October 1786 as Julie in the premiere of Burgoyne's *Richard Coeur de Lion*, a melodrama which was performed 38 times before the season's end. In that production John Philip Kemble, her future brother-in-law, was a conspicuous failure as a singer in the title role. She also appeared as a Page in *The Orphan* on 7 February 1787. Over the next five seasons petite Maria Theresa was employed as a dancer and sometime actress at Drury Lane, earning £3 per week in 1789–90. Her modest assignments included regular appearances as Julie in *Richard Coeur de Lion* through 1791–92; the Prince of Wales in *Richard III*, an Italian Girl in *The Critic*, Queen Mab in *The Fairy Favour*, Jenny in *The Deserter of Naples*, and a Spirit in *The Cave of Trophonius* in 1790–91; Terpsichore in *Poor Old Drury!*, Phebe in *Cymon*, Lucinda in *The Englishman in Paris*, Madelon in *The Surrender of Calais*, and a Grace in *Dido* with the Drury Lane company at the King's Theatre in 1791–92.

Also she was regularly seen at the Haymarket each summer from 1787 through 1792 in numerous specialty dances; there she also played a Nun in the premiere of *The Surrender of Calais* on 30 July 1791 and then Madelon in that musical drama beginning in June 1792, and Sylphina in *The Enchanted Wood*, Miss Godfrey in *The Liar*, Comfit in *The Dead Alive*, Lancaster in *Henry IV*, Ismene in *The Sultan*, Emma in *Peeping Tom*, and Cecilia in *The Son in Law* in 1792. A press clipping in the Richmond Library reports that in that town on 15 October 1790 "Miss Decamp, the dancer, made her first oral essay in *Yarico* [in *Inkle and Yarico*]—making allowance for an entrée that depended more upon the head than the *heels*,

it was very creditable." In the spring of 1791 her address was No 64, Tottenham Court Road. That year she subscribed 10*s*. 6*d*. to the Drury Lane Fund (but in 1797–98, it seems, she neglected payments and allowed her subscription to lapse).

At the age of 17 she achieved her first notable success when on 15 August 1792 at the Haymarket she played Macheath in a bizarre production of *The Beggar's Opera* in which Bannister and Johnstone transformed themselves into Polly and Lucy. Young Maria Theresa was greatly applauded and encored, and the next morning, according to the *Secret History of the Green Rooms*, "crowds of her friends in carriages came to congratulate her." From that point the prospects for her career improved as her managers more and more introduced her in a "singing cast" of characters for which "An ear naturally correct—and very sedulous application to the science of music" recommended her. At the Haymarket her talents somewhat compensated for the loss of Mrs Bannister by retirement, and when Mrs Crouch was absent from the Drury Lane company at the beginning of 1792–93, Maria Theresa took over her characters with much success. At the King's with the Drury Lane company in 1792–93 her roles included Nelly and Louisa in *No Song No Supper*, a Bacchante in *Comus*, Theresa in *The Prisoner*, Marietta in the premiere of Cobb's *The Pirates* on 21 November 1792, Miss Biddy in *Miss in Her Teens*, Adelaide in *The Count of Narbonne*, and Gillian in *The Quaker*. At the Haymarket in 1793, among other roles, she performed Phoebe in *Rosina*, Miss Sukey in *Half an Hour after Supper*, Rosina in *The Spanish Barber*, and Patty in *Inkle and Yarico*.

Miss De Camp made her first appearance at the new Drury Lane Theatre on 14 May 1794, as Lady Helen in *The Children of the Wood*, and subsequently was regularly engaged there through 1799–1800, earning £4 per week in 1795–96, £5 in 1796–97, £8 in the next two seasons, and £9 in 1799–1800. She lived at No 70, Tottenham Court Road in 1793 and 1794. In June 1797 her address was No 32, Bow Street, Covent Garden. By May 1798 she had moved to No 14, Tottenham Court Road, where she lodged at least through May 1801.

Among her numerous roles at Drury Lane during that period were Charlotte in *My Grandmother*, Anne Bullen in *Henry VIII*, Statira in *Alexander the Great*, Lucy Lockit in *The Beggar's Opera*, Fringe in *The Agreeable Surprise*, and Louisa in *The Duenna* in 1794–95; Olivia in *Twelfth Night*, Columbine in *Harlequin Captive*, the original Judith in *The Iron Chest* (on 12 March 1796), Stella in *The Smugglers*, William in *Rosina*, and Widow Brady in *The Irish Widow* in 1795–96; Cherry in *The Beaux' Stratagem*, Lilla in *The Siege of Belgrade*, Fanny in *The Shipwreck*, Plautina in *A Friend in Need*, Jacintha in *The Suspicious Husband*, Flora in *She Wou'd and She Wou'd Not*, and Rose in *The Recruiting Officer* in 1796–97; Miss Sterling in *The Clandestine Marriage* and the original Irene in *Blue-Beard* (on 16 January 1798) in 1797–98; Nerissa in *The Merchant of Venice*, Catherine in *Catherine and Petruchio*, and Hippolito in *The Tempest* in 1798–99; and Eliza in *The Embarkation*, Albina in *The Will*, Lodoiska in *Lodoiska*, the original Maria in *Of Age Tomorrow*, and Miss Hoyden in *A Trip to Scarborough* in 1799–1800.

Among her roles at the Haymarket each summer were Sylvia in *The Recruiting Officer* and Floranthe in *The Mountaineers* in 1795; Lady Fanciful in *The Provok'd Wife* and Charlotte in *The Mock Doctor* in 1796; Irene in *A Mogul Tale*, Miss Neville in *She Stoops to Conquer*, Comfit in *The Dead Alive*, Rachel in *Zorinski*, Kitty in *High Life below Stairs*, Portia in *The Merchant of Venice*, Desdemona in *Othello*, and the original Caroline Dormer in Colman's *The Heir at Law* (on 15 July) in 1797; Diana in *Lionel and Clarissa*, Elinor in *Cambro-Britons*, Hero in *Much Ado about Nothing*, and Julia in *The Rivals* in 1798; Widow Belmont in *The Castle of Sorrento* in 1799; and the original Rosa in *Obi* (on 2 July) and the original Angelina in *What a Blunder* (on 14 August) in 1800.

Miss De Camp was a young woman of exceptional beauty and remarkable charm. Her daughter Fanny Kemble recalled that her "figure was beautiful, and her face very handsome and expressive." (When she appeared in the premiere of *Blue-Beard* on 16 July 1798, she was scolded by the press for wearing an immodest dress "to display the symmetry of her person.") A writer in *Blackwood's* in 1832 remembered her as "a delightful dark-eyed, dark-haired girl, whose motion was itself music ere her voice was heard." In 1795 Bellamy wrote in his *London Theatres*:

Harvard Theatre Collection

MARIA THERESA KEMBLE as Polly

engraving by Chapman, after Moses

> *To thee, DE CAMP, to thee belong*
> *The powers that charm the sportive throng;*
> *Struck with thy form, thy ease, thy grace,*
> *The mind which animates thy face. . . .*

Waldron's assessment of her in his *Candid and Impartial Strictures on the Performers*, in the same year, was more balanced:

Her person is exceedingly good; and her action in general graceful; but sometimes, in apeing the manners of the Italians in her singing, has an appearance of affectation. She will never do much more than she has already done as a vocal performer; and we think her forte in acting lies in a certain cast of sprightly parts in genteel comedy.

Her performance of Columbine in *Harlequin Captive* was thought by the reviewer in the *Monthly Mirror* of January 1796 to have been the best "we ever saw"—airy, graceful, and animated. The reviewer in the *How Do You*

Do? of 30 July 1796 commended her for her performance of Cattania in the premiere of Cumberland's *Don Pedro* at the Haymarket on 23 July, but suggested she should restrain her excessive action: "It was so redundant, that the spectator might frequently suppose . . . that he was witnessing the unnatural distortions of the Italian performers." The same journal on 5 November 1796, however, enthusiastically reported that "we never saw a better piece of acting than her *Caroline* [in *The Prize* at Drury Lane on 20 September 1796] . . . and have traced other instances of rapid improvement."

She enjoyed modest success with Portia in *The Merchant of Venice*, a portrayal which was deemed by the *Monthly Visitor* of September 1797 as "beyond what we could possibly have expected from a person of her line of acting. It was frequently above, but never below mediocrity." Dutton in *The Dramatic Censor* believed she had an "exquisite style of acting" in her line and called her Lucy in *The Beggar's Opera* "a chef-d'oeuvre" of theatrical excellence. As Caroline in *The Prize* she displayed, according to Dutton, "a versatility of talent which no other actress at the Theatre can lay claim to." At her benefit on 23 May 1800 the receipts were £431 9s. (less house charges of £217), and "The numerous and fashionable audience which crowded the Theatre" that evening, Dutton wrote, "afforded a convincing proof of the high estimation in which the talents of Miss DE CAMP . . . are deservedly held by the public."

For her previous benefit at Drury Lane on 3 May 1799 Miss De Camp had garnered an even greater sum (£447 8s., less house charges of £211) when she offered a five-act comedy of her own composition entitled *First Faults*. The author played no role in it, but chief parts were taken by Charles Kemble, Harriot Mellon, and Dorothy Jordan. It received only that one performance and was never printed, though it survives in manuscript at the Huntington Library. A plot synopsis appeared in the *Monthly Visitor* of May 1799. And the reviewer in the June *Monthly Mirror* was indulgent:

. . . We certainly do not think highly of the merits of Miss DeCamp's comedy, and if it were the production of an experienced writer, we should not hesitate to treat it with some degree of severity; but the 'First Faults' of a female must not be too narrowly scrutinized, though a little gentle reproof might, perhaps, be serviceable. As a *coup d'essai*, it is certainly creditable to her talents. There is much good sense in the dialogue, which is neatly, and sometimes elegantly, turned; the interest, towards the close, is well sustained, and there are two or three sketches of *character* that convince us she has not been unobserving of living manners. The comedy, which was very favourably received, derived great support from the acting of Mr. Bannister, Junr.

That year William Earle published a piece called *Natural Faults* and in his preface charged Miss De Camp with having pilfered his plot and people. In a letter to the *Morning Post* on 10 June 1799 she denied the accusation and countered by claiming that Earle had copied her play from recitation. Genest credited Earle's side with "the *appearance* of truth."

In the summer of 1799, at the cost of great fatigue to herself, she had made a quick trip to Brighton (during her engagement in London) to appear at Sedgwick's benefit. Her presence drew the largest crowd of the season. Since she refused to accept any money for her services, the grateful Sedgwick had a medal designed and struck which he presented to her in early January 1800. Miss De Camp wore the medal for the first time in a performance of *Lodoiska* at Drury Lane (to the delight of Sedgwick who played Khor). The inscription, according to Dutton, read:

> Woman to Man undoubtedly may prove
> Her right to friendship, unallied to love:
> And, as a token you've performed the part
> Accept this tribute of a grateful heart.

During a command performance of *Lodoiska* a month later, on 6 February 1800, Miss De Camp and Kelly suffered a fall together. A "severe contusion" rendered her unconscious. "The royal party immediately arose," reported the *Monthly Mirror*, "and left the theatre, expressing the strongest concern at the accident." A week later Miss De Camp was back at work.

For the first six seasons of the nineteenth century Miss De Camp continued at Drury Lane, adding to her repertoire such original roles as Theodore in *The Wife of Two Husbands* in 1803–4; Arinette in *Youth, Love, and Folly*

MARIA THERESA KEMBLE as Urania

engraving by Vendramini, after Jean

in 1804–5; Variella in *The Weathercock*, Ellen in *Sleeping Beauty*, Morgiana in *The Forty Thieves*, and Mrs Knightly in *Discovery* in 1805–6. Her salary in that last season was £15 per week, evidently the highest of all the women and of all but three of the men in the company. She did not reengage at the Haymarket, however, after 1800, but traveled during the summer to provincial theatres, appearing at Birmingham, Liverpool, York, Edinburgh, and Glasgow in 1801. She was again at York in 1803.

She and Charles Kemble were not joint authors, as it was sometimes reported, of the music drama *Deaf and Dumb*, in which they appeared together in 1800–1801. (That piece was an adaptation by Thomas Holcroft of a play by Bouilly.) She did write the farce *Personation; or, Fairly Taken In*, in which she also created the role of Lady Julia at Drury Lane on 29 April 1805.

Throughout her career Miss De Camp appeared in many productions with members of the Kemble family. John Philip Kemble, indeed, had been so overcome by her attractions that backstage one night in January 1795 he made a drunken assault on her. Her protesting screams quickly drew rescuers. Kemble apologized for the lurid incident in a statement to the press on 27 January 1795, declaring that her "conduct and character had in no instance authorized" his unjustifiable behavior. His private apology to Miss De Camp is contained in a manuscript (not in his hand, however) in the Harvard Theatre Collection:

As I have never been so fortunate as to find you at home, when I have Called at your house to Express my sincere regret for the disquiet I have been the occasion of to you I beg Leave to do it in this Letter; and at the same time, to Assure you, that I shall always Endeavour, by the most respectful means, to Prove my high opinion of your exemplary Conduct, in every regulation of Life.

That was the sober John Kemble with his customary graciousness. But the "high opinion" of Miss De Camp which he pledged to prove did not prevent him from standing in the way of his brother Charles's marriage to her. In 1800 Charles Kemble and Maria Theresa were betrothed. John and the rest of the family were firmly set against the match, but eventually a compromise was agreed upon whereby John promised his approval if Charles "continued in the same mind when he was thirty," an event not scheduled to occur until November 1805. Throughout much of her manuscript "Diary" at the Folger Shakespeare Library, Jane Porter recorded her feelings about the De Camp–Kemble relationship and her impressions of Maria Theresa. On 9 February 1801 she reported Maria Porter's description of the young actress:

I can see no point of her character or manners, that can unite with the softness, and dignity of Kemble's. She is lively, free, commanding, and self-assured. Exactly what she appears on the stage, only losing twenty per cent in the person, as you ap-

Courtesy of the Garrick Club

MARIA THERESA KEMBLE as Mrs Ford
by De Wilde

proach nearer. This person, tho' well shaped and of fine contour, is coarse and unfinished: it seems like the statue of an exquisite figure, which the sculptor has yet to chisel into the smooth polish of grace and beauty.

Jane Porter met "Kemble's enchantress" on 7 April 1801:

I looked at her with admiration and watched her with astonishment. I was not surprised, that her grace, vivacity, and intelligence should attract any man — but if it goes no deeper than to dazzle others, without illuminating her own mind & heart, I am amazed that she should have fired Charles Kemble. . . .

But soon Jane Porter was won over to Maria Theresa and wrote a sonnet commiserating with her for having to part with Charles when he took a voyage to the Continent in the summer of 1801.

According to Jane Porter, the lovers mu-

tually agreed to wait the five years specified. They wrote to each other and shared the same theatre, but Charles promised John he would not visit at her house, and the couple seldom found opportunity to be alone with each other. Finally, on 2 July 1806, eight months after his thirtieth birthday Charles married Maria Theresa at St George, Bloomsbury, in a ceremony witnessed by John Kemble, who had the honor of giving the bride away.

When the Kemble clan moved to Covent Garden Theatre that fall, the new Mrs Kemble joined them, making her first appearance there on 1 October 1806 as Maria in *The Citizen*. That season she was also seen as Ophelia in *Hamlet*, Dorinda in *The Tempest*, and the original Lothaire in *Adrian*. She remained with her husband at Covent Garden through 1812–13, during which period she earned a regular £15 per week and enjoyed an annual benefit. Among her original roles were Edmund in *The Blind Boy* in 1807–8, and Pertilla in *The Students of Salamanca*, Aladdin in *Aladdin*, and Mrs Templeton in *Education* in 1812–13. On 18 May 1808 she played Lady Elizabeth Freelove in her own comic interlude *The Day After the Wedding; or, A Wife's First Lesson*, for the benefit of her husband, who acted Colonel Freelove. The piece was published that year. Several weeks later, for her own benefit on 24 May 1808, she appeared in *Match-making; or, 'Tis a Wise Child that Knows its own Father*, a comedy attributed to her. It was neither repeated nor printed.

Her excursion into the provinces took her to Brighton in 1807, where on 6 June she and her husband played Ophelia and Hamlet at the opening of the new theatre under Trotter's management. A month later on 7 July she acted Jessica in *The Merchant of Venice* at the opening of the new theatre in Worthing. In 1809 they were at Bath. In January 1812 they played at Glasgow and Edinburgh, where her roles indicate that despite the fact that she had grown stout she still insisted on playing the line of characters in which she had earlier succeeded but which were by then inappropriate for her: Caroline in *The Prize*, Letitia Hardy in *The Belle's Stratagem*, Violante in *The Wonder*, Juliana in *The Honeymoon*, and Julia in *The Rivals*. She appeared at Belfast, for the first time, for a week, beginning 20 May 1812.

Mrs Kemble was not engaged in London during 1813–14 and 1814–15. She and her husband played at Crow Street, Dublin, and at Edinburgh in 1814, and perhaps afterward she accompanied him on his continental visit.

In the fall of 1815 the Kembles were back in London. Charles reengaged at Covent Garden but Maria Theresa seems to have made only a single appearance that season, as Lady Emily Gerald in her own comedy *Smiles and Tears; or, The Widow's Stratagem* on 12 December 1815. It was printed that year. She was absent from the London stage during the next two seasons, though she acted at Edinburgh. In 1818–19 she returned to Covent Garden for a final engagement. That season she was the original Madge Wildfire in Terry's *The Heart of Midlothian* on 17 April 1819. After playing Lady Julia in *Personation* for her own and her husband's benefit on 9 June 1819 she retired. Ten years later she returned to the Covent Garden stage for one final night, 5 October 1829, to play Lady Capulet on the occasion of her daughter Fanny's debut in Juliet.

Her daughter Fanny wrote that Mrs Kemble disliked London and preferred to remain in the country, where she surrounded herself with antiques. In the 1820s she lived in the family cottage at Craven Hill while her husband kept lodgings in town in order to be closer to his work at Covent Garden. She did not accompany him on his two-year visit to America from 1832 to 1834. Her last two years she passed, for the most part, in a cottage at Addlestone, near Chertsey, which she had inherited from her sister-in-law Elizabeth Whitlock in 1836. Mrs Kemble died there on 3 September 1838, at the age of 63, and was buried in Addlestone churchyard. Her husband survived her until 1854. Information on her five children is in his notice.

Genest declared Mrs Kemble "a very good actress—no person understood the business of the stage better—no person had more industry—at one time she almost lived in D. L. theatre."

Portraits of Maria Theresa Kemble, most of which date before her marriage, include:

1. By A. E. Chalon. Pen and watercolor drawing, in the National Portrait Gallery (1962).

2. By Samuel De Wilde. Black-and-red-chalk drawing, showing her holding veil over hand. In the Victoria and Albert Museum.

3. By unknown artist. Silhouette on paper. In the Garrick Club (No 494A).

4. Engraving by J. Condé. Published as a plate to *Thespian Magazine*, 1793.

5. Engraving by Mackenzie, after Dighton. Published as a plate to *The Myrtle and the Vine*, 1800, and as a plate to *Thespian Dictionary*, 1805.

6. Engraving by R. M. Paye, Jr, after E. A. Paye. Published by J. P. Thompson, 1805; another impression with title "Mrs Charles Kemble."

7. Engraving by W. Ridley, after J. Barry. Published as a plate to the *Monthly Mirror*, November 1801; reprinted by Vernor, Hood & Sharpe, 1809, with title changed to Mrs C. Kemble.

8. Engraving by J. G. Stodart. When Miss De Camp.

9. Dancing with the two Masters D'Egville in *Jamie's Return*. Engraving by Saillier, after W. Miller. Published by J. Cory, 1787. Reproduced in this dictionary, volume IV, p. 268.

10. As Aladdin in *Aladdin*. By unknown engraver, after "W. H." Published as penny-plain and twopence-colored by Hodgson, 1822.

11. As Catherine in *Catherine and Petruchio*. Engraving by Cardon, after S. De Wilde. Published as a plate to Cawthorn's *Minor British Theatre*, 1806.

12. As Catherine with J. P. Kemble as Petruchio. Engraving by J. Alais, after A. Buck. Published by J. Roach, 1802.

13. As Miss Dashaway in *The Soldier's Return*. By unknown engraver. Published as a plate to *Theatrical Recorder* (No VII), 1805.

14. As Foible in *The Way of the World*. Engraving by P. Thomson, after J. Roberts. Published as a plate to *Bell's British Theatre*, 1796.

15. As Mrs Ford in *The Merry Wives of Windsor*. Watercolor drawing by S. De Wilde, 1808. In the Garrick Club (No 518).

16. As Hypolita, with another woman as Rosara, in *She Wou'd and She Wou'd Not*. Engraving by T. Chapman, after H. Moses. Published as a plate to *British Drama*, 1817; previously printed for C. Cook, 1806.

17. As Irene in *Blue-Beard*. Engraving by

Alais, after J. Barry. Published as a plate to *Memoirs of the Green Room*, 1804.

18. As Lady Julia in *Personation*. Pen-and-ink drawing by A. E. Chalon, 1804. In the National Portrait Gallery (No 1962b).

19. As Julio in *Deaf and Dumb*. Engraving by Thomson, after S. De Wilde. Published as a plate to Oxberry's *New English Drama*, 1819.

20. As Madge Wildfire in *The Heart of Midlothian*. By unknown engraver, after "J. L. M."

21. As Patie in *The Gentle Shepherd*. Painting by S. De Wilde. In the Garrick Club (No 403).

22. As Patie. Watercolor drawing by De Wilde, similar to the Garrick Club painting. In the National Theatre.

23. As Polly in *The Beggar's Opera*. Engraving by T. Chapman, after H. Moses. Published as a plate to *British Drama*, 1817.

24. As Miss Rivers in *False Delicacy*. Colored drawing by J. Roberts, 1795. In the British Museum. Engraving by P. Audinet, after Roberts, published as a plate to *Bell's British Theatre*, 1795.

25. As Rosa in *The Caravan*. By unknown engraver. Published by A. Bengo, 1805. Reissued in 1806 in larger impression, with title "A Decamp or Exit."

26. As Rosa, with Charles Kemble as Three-fingered Jack, in *Obi*. By unknown engraver. Published by E. Orme, 1801.

27. As Rosalind in *As You Like It*. Engraving by Mackenzie.

28. As Urania. A miniature by R. Jean. On 2 February 1876 Edward Fitzgerald wrote to Fanny Kemble that his brother John wished her

to have a Miniature of your Mother which my Mother had till she died. It is full length; in a white Dress, with blue Scarf, looking and tending with extended Arms upward in a Blaze of Light. My Brother heard my Mother's History of the Picture, but could not recall it. I fancy it was before your Mother's marriage. The Figure is very beautiful, and the Face also. . . .

Fanny received the miniature in March 1876 and she carried on a correspondence with Fitzgerald about the picture for several months. She correctly identified the picture as the one of her mother as Urania, engraved by J. Vendramini, published by J. P. Thompson, 1802.

Another impression was issued with a dedication to the Hon W. R. Spencer. The present location of the original miniature by Jean is unknown to us.

Kemble, Ann Julia. *See* HATTON, MRS WILLIAM.

Kemble, Elizabeth *1761–1836*. *See* WHITLOCK, MRS CHARLES EDWARD.

Kemble, Frances, later Mrs Francis Twiss *1759–1822, actress.*

Frances Kemble was born on 28 December 1759 at Hereford, the fourth child and second daughter of the provincial actors Roger and Sarah (née Ward) Kemble. Information about her family may be found in the notice of her father, the progenitor of a very large and important theatrical dynasty. Like her brothers and sisters, Frances (or Fanny) lived as a theatre child, touring in her tender years with the company managed by her parents. A surviving playbill for a performance of *King Charles the*

Harvard Theatre Collection

FRANCES KEMBLE
by Reynolds

First at Worcester on 12 February 1767 shows the clan at work: the father and mother as General and Lady Fairfax, Master John Philip as James, Duke of York, Sarah as Princess Elizabeth, and Frances (then eight) as the Duke of Gloucester. Fanny's name is on another bill, some nine years later, for Angelica in *The Constant Couple* at Carmarthen on 20 September 1776, and no doubt there were other performances in the intervening years.

For a while Fanny was apprenticed to a milliner, but she returned to the stage. Her sister Sarah introduced her at Bath on 19 September 1780 as Jane Shore, and she also played at Bristol during the 1780–81 season. Tate Wilkinson engaged her that summer for York, where she made her debut as Lady Townly in *The Provok'd Husband* on 27 August 1781. In his *Wandering Patentee*, Wilkinson judged her an actress with "a strong understanding and a fine informed mind; but [she] was not so happy in her force on the Audience."

Fanny made her London debut at Drury Lane Theatre on 6 January 1783, as Alicia to her sister Sarah's Jane Shore. By the close of the season she had been seen another seven times in that role and as Beatrice in *Much Ado about Nothing* on 3 March 1783, Imoinda in *Oroonoko* on 17 March, and Almeria in *The Mourning Bride* on 18 March and 2 June. Another Kemble daughter, Fanny's sister Elizabeth, made her Drury Lane debut that season as Portia in *The Merchant of Venice*. The two girls remained for several seasons, Fanny usually being billed as "Miss Kemble" and Elizabeth as "Miss E. Kemble."

Fanny's critical reception during her first London season was mixed, but leaning to the unfavorable. In *The New Rosciad* (1785), J. H. Leigh claimed that as Alicia she tried to imitate the "looks of her Sister" Sarah, "but, unfortunately, in the attempt, she so *disfigured* her features, that the whole audience, as if by instinct, burst into a loud laugh." A newspaper critic, perhaps in deference to Sarah Siddons, was more tolerant and agreeable, reporting that the very large crowd who had come to see another Kemble launch a London career welcomed her with "thundering plaudits." They were rewarded, according to this critic, with a performance done well enough but far too "coldly correct" for the fiery Alicia. Compared to Sarah, Fanny revealed "not so fine a figure

as her sister, but her person is far from being other than very agreeable. Her features nearly resemble those, and her voice in some degree corresponds with that, of Mrs Siddons; though it has neither so much power, nor so much variety. In parts where there is more of a level speaking than passion, Miss Kemble, we doubt not, will prove a useful actress." In *The Children of Thespis*, Anthony Pasquin (John Williams) criticized the nepotism at the theatre and declared Fanny's performance "impudent, ignorant, gross, and absurd," complaining that "beings like *that* have Ten Guineas a week." "*The Siddons* exclaims, 'Know that Fanny's my sister; / And knowing but that, tell me *who* dare resist her?'"

Sarah's sisters returned to Drury Lane in 1783–84, when Fanny acted Alicia, Almeria, Eleanor in *The Countess of Salisbury*, Laura in *Tancred and Sigismunda*, and Statira in *Alexander the Great*. On 12 July 1784 she made her debut at Colman's Haymarket Theatre as Harriet in *The Guardian*. Her other roles were Lady Margaret in the London premiere of William Hayley's *Lord Russel*, on 18 August, and Lady Frances in the premiere of Hayley's *The Two Connoisseurs* on 2 September 1784. Boaden printed in his life of *John Philip Kemble* an exchange of letters between George Steevens, the Shakespearean, and the author Hayley concerning Miss Kemble's part in *Lord Russel*. Steevens, who, according to Boaden, "amused himself by assailing Mrs Siddons, and hoped to mortify her by magnifying the theatrical talents of her sister, to whom he paid incessant attention," petitioned from Hayley verses in praise of Fanny's performance, to be presented the next morning in order to help her overcome "her natural timidity" and "diffidence." Hayley replied that he could not accommodate because he would remain at Eartham and thus would not even see the premiere, but he suggested that as "the talents of Miss Kemble must have received infinite improvement from your critical instruction," it made better sense for Steevens to pen the lines himself.

At Drury Lane for her third season in 1784–85, Fanny played Anna to Mrs Siddons's Lady Randolph in *Douglas* on 9 October 1784, Lady Sneerwell in *The School for Scandal*, Alicia, Laura, Lavinia in *The Fair Penitent*, and Araminta in *The Confederacy*. On 23 April 1785 her benefit, shared with Elizabeth Kemble, brought her about £90. In the summer Frances joined Sarah Siddons at Edinburgh, where she appeared as Lady Bell Bloomer in *Which is the Man?*, Almeria in *The Mourning Bride*, and Perdita in *The Sheep Shearing*. The *Courant* reported that "In figure and looks" Fanny was "far from being so striking as her sister," but she did have "an agreeable countenance and a pleasing voice."

Her sister Elizabeth having married the actor Charles Edward Whitlock in June 1785, Fanny was the only "Miss Kemble" at Drury Lane in 1785–86. Among the characters she added to her repertoire that season were Lady Elizabeth Grey in *The Earl of Warwick*, the Tragic Muse in *The Jubilee*, the title role in *Zara*, for the first time on 26 December 1785 (with her brother John as Osman), Andromache in *The Distrest Mother*, Minla in *The Captives*, and Birtha in *Percy*. The account books reveal that on 6 May 1786 Miss Kemble's salary of 16*s*. 8*d*. per day was taken off the paylist. She had married the author Francis Twiss (1760–1827) by license at St Giles in the Fields on 1 May 1786, in the presence of Sarah Siddons and her husband, William. On 18 May 1786 she signed as Frances Twiss a receipt for "the Sum of Sixty Pounds in full for Benefit allowance, Salary, and all demands at Drury Lane Theatre" and retired.

Gossip had circulated in 1785 suggesting that Fanny was about to marry George Steevens. But Mrs Siddons wrote to Whalley on 15 March 1785 that "there is very little to suppose she will be soon." Sarah hoped that Fanny's "gentle spirit" would not be linked with a man of such ill temper. On 11 August 1786, Sarah could report to Whalley that Frances had married, not Steevens but Twiss, whom she called a "most respectable man, though of small fortune," adding "I thank God that she is off the stage; this is a young brother of the traveller, and is unlike him in every particular." Francis Twiss and his elder brother, Richard Twiss (1747–1821), a miscellaneous writer, were the sons of an English merchant who was resident for some time in Holland but was descended from the Twiss family of Killintierna, County Kerry. The Francis Twiss who was a proprietor and committee member of the Norwich Theatre from 1717 to 1781 may have been related, but he was not Fanny's husband.

Assisted by her husband, Mrs Twiss ran a fashionable school for girls at No 24, Camden Place, Bath, from 1807. In his correspondence George Hardinge described Mrs Twiss as well dressed though grown "big as a house." Her manner was affected, her voice measured, but she was very good-natured "and by no means deficient in materials for society or chat." In 1803 she had been left £500 in the will of her father Roger Kemble, to be received after the death of her mother (which occurred in 1807).

Frances Twiss died at Bath on 3 October 1822, several months before her sixty-third birthday. Her husband, who had published a two-volume *Complete Verbal Index to the Plays of Shakespeare* (1805), which was dedicated to John Philip Kemble, died at Cheltenham on 28 April 1827 at the age of 68.

Their eldest child, Horace Twiss (1787–1849), born at Bath on 28 February 1787, was a very successful lawyer, member of Parliament, public speaker, and prominent socialite. Among his literary efforts was *The Carib Chief*, a five-act tragedy which was performed at Drury Lane on 13 May 1819 and was published the same year. He died on 4 May 1849 and was buried in the Temple Church. Horace Twiss married his first wife, Anne Lawrence Serle (1788–1828), daughter of Colonel Serle of Montagu Place, London, at Bath on 2 August 1817. Their only child, Fanny Horatia Serle Twiss (1818–1874), married Francis Bacon (d. 1840) and then John Thadeus Delane (1817–1879), *Times* editor. After his wife's death at London on 24 March 1828, Horace Twiss married on 3 April 1830 at St George, Hanover Square, Ann Louisa Andrewenna, the widow of the merchant Charles Greenwood and daughter of the Reverend Alexander Sterky. This second marriage produced Quintin William Francis Twiss (1835–1900), who was a clerk in the treasury.

The second son of Frances and Francis Twiss, John Twiss (1798–1866), was promoted major general on 5 January 1864, served as governor of the Royal Military Academy, Woolwich, and died at London on 14 January 1866.

The Francis Twisses also had three spinster daughters who assisted with the Bath school: Frances Ann Twiss, born in 1790 and died at Hove on 24 April 1864; Amelia Twiss, born in 1791 and died at Hereford on 28 August 1852; and Elizabeth Twiss, died at Brighton on 17 February 1858. They were left some real and personal estate by their aunt Elizabeth Kemble Whitlock in 1836. A fourth daughter, born before the other three, died in infancy in January 1789.

Portraits of Frances Kemble Twiss include:

1. By John Downman. When Miss Kemble. This portrait was listed in *Mathews's Gallery* (1833). Engraving by J. Jones, 1784.

2. By Thomas Lawrence. Exhibited at the Royal Academy in 1800. Owned by A. L. Dowie in 1883. Offered at Christie's on 20 June 1930 (No 104, illustrated in the sales catalogue) and bought by Storey.

3. By John Opie, 1799. This portrait, showing the influence of Lawrence, was first owned by Amelia Opie and then was in the possession of Quintin Twiss at the end of the nineteenth century. See J. J. Rogers, *Opie and His Works*.

4. By Joshua Reynolds. When Miss Kemble. There are three versions. One was exhibited at Burlington House in 1890; it was sold at Christie's from the collection of the Rt Hon G. A. F. Cavendish-Bentinck, in July 1891 for 2640 guineas. Perhaps this was the picture bought by Bellesi at Christie's on 12 May 1950. A second version is in the collection of Mrs Wauchop, Niddrie Marischal, Craigmillar. A third is in the National Museum, Havana, Cuba. The portrait was several times engraved, each time with slightly changed features: by John Jones, 1784; another by Jones, 1786; and by S. W. Reynolds, published by H. G. & Co.

5. By unknown artist. Among the properties of Mr C. Siddons Budgen, of Winton, Wendover, Buckinghamshire, auctioned at Sotheby's on 5 April 1944 was "A Louis XVI snuff box of circular shape, with red, gold, and green striped decoration on a tortoiseshell ground, within finely chased borders, the lid insert with an oval miniature of Mrs. Twiss in low-cut white dress, full face 3⅛ in." A photograph of the miniature appears in the sales catalogue, as No 95. The snuff box was purchased by D. W. Clarke. (According to *The Dictionary of National Biography* Quintin Twiss owned some miniatures of Mr and Mrs Francis Twiss at the end of the nineteenth century.)

The *Catalogue of Engraved Dramatic Portraits in the Harvard Theatre Collection* lists Mrs Twiss as the subject of an anonymous engraving of Miss Kemble as Imogen in *Cymbeline*, but the engraving is really of Elizabeth Kemble, later Mrs Whitlock.

Kemble, Frances Crawford, later Mrs Robert Arkwright *1787–1849, actress.*

Frances Crawford Kemble was born in 1787, probably at Edinburgh and probably late in the year, for the schedule of performances given by her mother Elizabeth Kemble (née Satchell) at Edinburgh and London during the first nine months of that year seems to have gone on without interruption. Her father was Stephen George Kemble, a son of the actors Roger and Sarah Kemble and brother to several performers, including John Philip Kemble, Charles Kemble, and Sarah Siddons. Frances's younger brother Henry Stephen Kemble (1789–1836), who acted in London as a child in the 1790s and as an adult in the nineteenth century, is separately noticed in these pages.

At the age of four, announced as making her first appearance on any stage, Frances was brought onto the Haymarket boards as the Prince of Wales in *The Battle of Hexham* on 16 August 1791, and "drew forth much applause." That night her mother was taking her benefit in the role of Queen Margaret, and her father's two-act farce *The Northern Inn* was performed for the first time, as the afterpiece.

Her appearance as the Prince of Wales seems to have been her only performance on the London stage, at least in the eighteenth century. Frances's apprenticeship was served mainly in Edinburgh under her father's management and her mother's care in the winter months between 1792 and 1799. The Edinburgh bills and advertisements carry her name for the Fairy in *Selima and Azor* on 23 May and Cupid in *Cymon* on 26 May 1792, when she was about five years old. For another five years she continued in children's roles: the Duke of York in *The Royal Martyr*, Edward in *The World in a Village*, Julia in *Richard Coeur de Lion*, the Prince of Wales in *The Battle of Hexham*, and the Prince of Wales in *Richard III*. In 1797 she began to appear in adult roles, playing, over the next several years, Anna in *Douglas* (on 16 January 1797, her first time as an adult), Amanthis in *The Child of Nature*, Catherine in *Catherine and Petruchio*, Eliza in *The Jew*, Harriet in *The Jealous Wife*, Leonora in *The Padlock*,

Mrs Sterling in *The Clandestine Marriage*, and the Countess Wintersen in *The Stranger*, among other roles. No doubt when a child she also performed at Glasgow, Sunderland, Newcastle, and other towns where her father held managerial interests. Her debut as an adult at Newcastle was noted in the *Monthly Mirror* of March 1803.

At Hull on 27 June 1805 Frances married Captain Robert Arkwright (1783–1859), second son of the industrialist and inventor Sir Richard Arkwright (1732–1792). The father and another namesake son are noticed in *The Dictionary of National Biography*. Having retired from the stage, Frances Kemble Arkwright lived for many years in comfort at Sutton Scarsdale, the Arkwright family seat, near Chesterfield, Derbyshire. She died on 10 March 1849 and was buried in the private chapel there. Her husband, Robert Arkwright, died on 6 August 1859 and was also buried in the chapel. They had five children: George (1807–1856), who became M.P. for Leominster; William (1809–1857); Godfrey Harry (1814–1866); Eustace (1818–1846); and Frances Elizabeth (d. 1894), who married Sir Hew Hamilton Dalrymple, Bart.

Kemble, Henry Stephen   *1789–1836, actor, author.*

Henry Stephen Kemble was born on 15 September 1789 in a house in Villiers Street, the Strand. The story, repeated by *The Dictionary of National Biography*, that he was born immediately after his mother Elizabeth Kemble had finished acting Queen Margaret in *The Battle of Hexham* at the Haymarket, on the closing night of the summer season, appears to be untrue. Elizabeth had indeed acted the part on 14 September. But, though her name appeared in the bills for the fifteenth also, the *London Chronicle* of 16 September noted that Mrs Barresford had substituted for her in Queen Margaret; and the *Public Advertiser* of the same date reported that Miss George had taken Elizabeth's usual role, Cowslip, in the afterpiece *The Agreeable Surprise*. Nevertheless Henry Stephen Kemble's heritage was theatrical enough. His father was Stephen George Kemble, actor and son of the players Roger and Sarah Kemble, who were patriarch and matriarch of the great clan of actors which

included their children John Philip Kemble, Charles Kemble, and Sarah Siddons. And his mother was of another acting family, the Satchells.

Announced as Master Kemble, Henry at the age of four acted the Duke of York in *Richard III* on 27 January 1794 and the Duke of Gloucester in *The Royal Martyr* on 7 April 1794 at the Theatre Royal, Shakespeare Square, Edinburgh, the house managed by his father. While his mother was engaged at the Haymarket Theatre, London, in the summer of 1796, Master Kemble appeared as one of the young children in *The Children of the Wood* on 5 July. (The *Monthly Mirror* of that month identified the lad as the son of Mrs S. Kemble, but erroneously believed him to be the Kemble child who had acted the Prince of Wales in *The Battle of Hexham* in August 1791. That youngster, however, had been Frances Crawford Kemble, Henry's elder sister.) Henry also appeared in *The Children of the Wood* on 12 and 21 July 1796.

Probably young Henry made other appearances as a child with the companies managed by his father in Scottish and northern English towns, but eventually he went off to school at Winchester and then matriculated at Trinity College, Cambridge. He left the University after two years to take up the family profession. Under his father's management he appeared at Whitehaven as Frank Heartall in *The Soldier's Daughter* and acted in the north. After his father retired from management, Henry joined Maxfield, Kelly, and Collins on the Southampton and Portsmouth circuit.

On 12 July 1814 at the Haymarket he acted Octavian in *The Mountaineers* to the Agnes of his wife Mary Freize (or Freese), whom he had married on 23 January 1814 at South Shields, Durham, against the wishes of his parents. At that time he was described as a person of above middle size, with a good figure, a fine eye, but with his other features being "void of expression." The *Theatrical Inquisitor* reported that he "did not tear a passion to rags, but diluted it to the consistence of water-gruel." His wife was accounted as "pretty, lively, and vivacious" by *The Dictionary of National Biography*, but "overpowered by timidity."

As a member of the company at Bath, where he appeared for the first time on 16 November 1816 in the title role of the tragedy *Bertram*,

Harvard Theatre Collection

HENRY KEMBLE as Aslan

engraving by P. Roberts

he was regarded as a very boisterous actor. His roles there and at Bristol included Bajazet in *Tamerlane*, Gambia in *The Slave*, Daran in *The Exile*, Three-Fingered Jack in *Obi*, Octavian in *The Mountaineers*, and De Zelos in *Manuel*. In the last-named role the press reported that he met "with peals of derision, although entitled to shouts of disgust."

When his father took over the management of Drury Lane for the season of 1818–19,

Henry was engaged to play many parts beyond his abilities, making his debut on 12 September 1818 as Romeo, a role he shouted out so loudly that it was joked that he was heard at Bath. That season he also acted Julio in *A Bold Stroke for a Husband*, Harry Dornton in *The Road to Ruin*, George Barnwell in *The London Merchant*, and Biron in *Isabella* and originated Giafar in *Barmecide; or, The Fatal Offspring* and Sextus in Payne's *Brutus*, among others. On 31 December 1818 he acted Marmion in *Flodden Field*, an adaptation by himself and his father of Scott's *Marmion*.

Subsequently, Henry Kemble migrated to the minor London theatres, playing at the Surrey, Astley's, and the East London Theatre. At the Coburg in Southwark his alteration of *Flodden Field* was presented with a new title, *The Nun of St Hilda's Cave*. He proved to be a popular actor but, said one critic, with "the strongest lungs and weakest judgment." Though scion of a famous family, the advantage that could have given him was counterbalanced by his lack of talent.

By the age of 40 his hair was white and his body decrepit. He died at London on 22 January 1836 at the age of 47. We do not know when his wife died. They had at least five children, several of whom became actors and produced more actors: Blanche Kemble, actress, who married a Mr Shea, and died in 1851; Charles Kemble; Agnes Kemble (1823–1895), actress, who married the actor Thomas Clifford Cooper; Nicholas Freese Young Kemble (1825–1909); and Elizabeth Kemble, who married the actor Charles Barnett. In a letter to the editor of the *Era* on 21 July 1850, Henry Kemble's daughter Agnes denied that a Miss Adelaide Kemble, then singing on the concert stage, was her sister, and denounced her as an imposter, since the only Adelaide in the family was Agnes's aunt, Mrs Sartoris, the daughter of Charles Kemble. Agnes, however, also wrote "I have a sister, Fanny, who has occasionally sung in public." If Fanny was not a nickname for Henry's daughter Elizabeth then he had yet a sixth child.

Portraits of Henry Stephen Kemble include:

1. As Aslam the Lion. Engraving by P. Roberts. Twopence-colored published by Hodgson.

2. As the Dutch Pirate. By unknown engraver. Penny-plain.

3. As El Hyder, with Bradley as Ben Tarah, in *El Hyder*.

4. As Giafar in *Barmecide*. Engraving by J. Kennerley, after N. Freese. Published as a plate to the *Theatrical Inquisitor*, 1819.

5. As Giafar. Engraving by G. Adcock, after N. Freese. Published as a plate to Oxberry's *Dramatic Biography*, 1827.

6. As Henry VII in *The Cloth of Gold*. Engraving by W. W. Hornegold. Penny-plain published by Skelt.

7. As Korastikan. By unknown engraver. Penny-plain published by Hodgson.

8. As Marmion, with Hamblin as De Wilton, in *Flodden Field*. Engraving by J. Findlay. Twopence-colored published by Jameson, 1819.

9. As Napoleon Buonaparte. By unknown engraver. Twopence-colored published by Jameson, 1821.

10. As Richmond in *Richard III*. By unknown engraver. Twopence-colored published by Dyer.

11. As Sextus Tarquin in *Brutus*. By unknown engraver. Twopence-colored published by Hodgson, 1822.

12. As Shabico. By unknown engraver. Twopence-colored published by Park, 1837.

13. As Zamphimri, with Mrs Barrymore as Celinda, in *The Travellers*. By unknown engraver. Twopence-colored published by Jameson, 1819.

Kemble, John Philip   *1757–1823, actor, singer, manager, playwright.*

John Philip Kemble was born at Prescott in Lancashire on 1 February 1757, the first son of the provincial manager Roger Kemble. He was the second of 12 children of Roger Kemble by his wife Sarah, an actress and the daughter of John and Sarah Ward, managers of a respected company of itinerant players. John's elder sister Sarah became the famous Mrs Siddons. His brothers Stephen and Charles and his sisters Frances (Mrs Francis Twiss), Elizabeth (Mrs Charles Whitlock), and Ann Julia (Mrs William Hatton) all performed in London. His sister Jane (Mrs Henry Mason) was not on the London stage in the eighteenth century but she acted in the provinces in the 1790s. The surname Kemble, often interchangeable with Campbell, was fairly common in Herefordshire and Wiltshire, where earlier members of the family, having remained loyalists, lost lands. Perhaps the best-known ancestor was Father John Kemble (1599?–1679), who was executed for complicity in the Titus Oates plot. Information on the family background is given in the notice of Roger Kemble.

When a child, John Philip Kemble was hauled about England with his father's company, no doubt making occasional appearances in roles appropriate to his age. A surviving bill from Worcester reveals the Kemble brood at work in the yard of the King's Head Inn on 12 February 1767 in Havard's *Charles the First*, with father and mother playing General and Lady Fairfax, Sarah as Princess Elizabeth, Frances as the young Duke of Gloucester, and Master John Kemble (then age 10) as James, Duke of York. He may have played Stephano when his sister Sarah acted Ariel in *The Tempest* during that engagement at Worcester.

It was also at Worcester that John was sent to a day school for some primary education. About 10 months after playing the Duke of York at Worcester, John entered the Roman Catholic seminary at Sedgley Park, near Wolverhampton, in Staffordshire, where the account books record he arrived on 3 November 1767 with "4 suits of clothes, 12 shirts, 12 pairs of stockings, 6 pairs of shoes, 4 hats, 2 'Daily Companions,' a 'Half Manual,' knives, forks, spoons, 'Aesop's Fables,' combs, 1 brush, 8 handkerchiefs, 8 nightcaps." Roger Kemble had designed his son for the priesthood, so after five years at Sedgley Park John left on 28 July 1771 to matriculate at the English College at Douai, a favorite training ground for English Catholics taking the ecclesiastical path. At Douai he learned Greek and Latin and cultivated a penchant for matters classical. He developed fluency in French, excelled in declamations, and demonstrated a prodigious memory, one of his feats being the reciting of 1500 lines of Homer with great accuracy.

Realizing that the priesthood was not his calling and possessed, as it would seem, by a genetic prescription that was irrepressible, Kemble forsook Douai in 1775 and returned to England determined to become an actor. Despite his father's opposition, but because of his sister's support, Kemble was engaged by Crump and Chamberlain, managers of a ragtag troupe of strollers. He made his debut with

them at Wolverhampton on 8 January 1776 as the hero of Lee's *Theodosius*. His second role was Bajazet in *Tamerlane*. Much of his time with Crump and Chamberlain was passed in study and drink, activities which remained favorites in his more mature years. Anecdotes abound, but little specific survives to be reported of his apprenticeship. He left that company in the summer of 1777. During his travels about the countryside with Carleton (a stroller whose real name was John Boles Watson) he passed himself off as a Methodist preacher, and his colleague took up a "large collection." That escapade, according to a letter from Charles Kemble dated 20 February 1826 in the Harvard Theatre Collection, really took place in Yorkshire, near Tadcaster, not at Tewksbury as some early memoirs reported. Despite the slovenly appearance and habits which Oxberry related Kemble was disposed to during his youth, evidently he was dedicated to mastering his craft. He was hissed at Cheltenham, but by June 1777 he began to earn esteem in Joseph Younger's company at Liverpool, where he and Mrs Siddons had gone to perform for the summer.

On 21 June 1777 Kemble was added to the Liverpool paylist at £1 per week. He remained at Liverpool that winter, earning a weekly salary of £1 1s. between 4 October and 29 November. His characters there included Somerset in *Sir Thomas Overbury*, Coloredo in *The Heroine of the Cave*, Edwin in *Matilda*, Captain Savage in *The School for Wives*, and Roderigo in *The Pilgrim*. With Younger's company he played at Worcester, where he also spent a little time in jail for debt, and at Manchester, where he made his first appearance on 29 January 1778 playing Othello to Sarah's Desdemona and Younger's Iago. At Manchester he also acted Young Norval in *Douglas*, Glanville in *Cleone*, and Laertes to his sister's attempt at Hamlet on 19 March 1778.

At Liverpool on 27 July 1778 his tragedy *Belisarius; or Injured Innocence* was produced. Though played subsequently at Hull and York, it never was seen in London nor published. It survives, however, in manuscript at the Huntington Library. Also at Liverpool during that period he recited his poem, variously said to have been called, "The Palace of Misery" or "The Palace of Mersey." Between March and July of 1778 Kemble passed an idyllic retreat in a country lodging on Russel Moor with the Inchbalds and the Siddonses (the latter couple left the bucolic existence in April for Yorkshire), during which period he enjoyed the amiable company of Mrs Inchbald while her foolish husband was engrossed in his painting.

In a letter dated 21 June 1778 from Liverpool Kemble applied to Tate Wilkinson for an engagement in Yorkshire. To that letter, now at the Folger Shakespeare Library, he appended a catalogue of 68 roles in tragedies and 58 in comedies which he had in his repertoire, signifying that in the two brief years since his debut at Wolverhampton he had gained substantial experience. Some 29 on the list were marked with a star to indicate his favorites, including Posthumus in *Cymbeline*, Hotspur in *1 Henry IV*, King Lear, Richmond in *Richard III*, Brutus in *Julius Caesar*, Chamont in *The Orphan*, Pierre in *Venice Preserv'd*, Shylock in *The Merchant of Venice*, Ranger in *The Suspicious Husband*, Camply in *The Funeral*, Archer in *The Stratagem*, Don Felix in *The Wonder*, and Young Dudley in *The West Indian*.

Wilkinson was obliged to Mrs Siddons for the good business she had brought him the previous year. No doubt he also smelled the possibility that her brother might prove to be an advantage to him, so he engaged John. Kemble acted Captain Plume in *The Recruiting Officer* to a thin house at Wakefield on 21 October 1778. Two nights later he appeared as Beverley in *All in the Wrong*. Both roles had been on Kemble's list and the latter was marked as a favorite. Several days later the company moved to Hull, where on 30 October Kemble acted Macbeth. By 11 January 1779 he had played at Hull some 23 roles, including Archer, Laertes, Jaffeir, Falkland in *The Rivals*, Joseph Surface in *The School for Scandal*, and, on 29 December 1778, Marcus in his own *Belisarius*. Despite Wilkinson's assurance in his *Wandering Patentee* that *Belisarius* was received at Hull "with candor, credit, and applause," Kemble's play caused little stir.

Playing Orestes in *The Distrest Mother*, Kemble made his York debut on 20 January 1779. Next he was seen as Ranger on 26 January and then, through 1 May 1779, in a series of the roles he had submitted to Wilkinson. For his benefit on 27 March 1779 he revived *Belisarius* with moderate success and also played the

Master in *The Toy Shop* and Colonel Manley in *The School for Scandal Scandalized*. The latter interlude is ascribed to Kemble and was introduced at Covent Garden on 18 March 1780, before his London career began. Not published, it is now in the Larpent Collection at the Huntington Library, but Herschel Baker in *John Philip Kemble* cautions that the manuscript—once described by J. P. Collier as "entirely in Kemble's hand-writing"—offers no indication of Kemble's authorship.

That season at York, however, Kemble wrote several other plays. A farce called *The Female Officer, or Royal Volunteer*, was performed on April 1779 for Mrs Hunter's benefit. It had been licensed as early as 1 January 1778 and had been played for Kemble's benefit at Manchester on 25 March 1778. It was performed at Drury Lane on 18 February 1786 as *The Projects; or, A new way to fill an empty purse.* Licensed manuscripts for the Manchester and London productions are at the Huntington Library, and a copy is in the Harvard Theatre Collection. During his first spring at York, Kemble also offered *The Roman Actor*, a theatrical olio, altered from Massinger, and an adaptation of that author's *A New Way to Pay Old Debts*. In imitation of Thomas Sheridan he also presented "An Attic Evening Entertainment," a potpourri of passages from Sterne, Collins, Shakespeare, and the Bible.

More exciting than those early writings was the imbroglio that enveloped Kemble that spring. On 15 April 1779 he acted Teribazus in *Zenobia* to the Zenobia of a Mrs Mason (not his sister Jane). Kemble's patience was stretched by the daughter of a baronet, who, esconced in a box with a party of friends, rudely and audibly derided the actress's performance throughout, until finally, in the last act, Kemble stopped playing to announce he could not continue until "*that* lady had finished her conversation, which he perceived the going on with the tragedy only interrupted." Though the pit and galleries sided with Kemble, supporters of the lady demanded an apology, which Kemble refused, exclaiming "Pardon! ask pardon! no sirs,—*never*," and left the stage. The boxes again shouted for an apology when Kemble appeared as Douglas the next Saturday and as the Master in *The Toy Shop* the next Thursday. On the latter night Kemble stepped forward, as Boaden relates in his biography, to

The Art Institute of Chicago

JOHN PHILIP KEMBLE

By Shee

be heard before I am condemned: if when I have explained my conduct, any gentleman, or set of gentlemen, will say, in that character, that I have acted unworthily, I shall cheerfully make any repa-

ration that they may judge proper. To this there could be no *reasonable* objection, and he was heard. His fine address, his clear statement, his modesty and manliness, carried the cause, and contributed essentially to his progress in the public favour. Kemble's bravado won that day.

For his debut at Leeds on 7 May 1779 Kemble offered Hamlet and once again found himself in a squabble when Cummins, who usually played that role in Wilkinson's company, complained bitterly but soon was mollified. After two months at Leeds the company played at Pontefract for a month and then returned to York for the late summer races. Kemble's adaptation of *The Comedy of Errors*, appropriately titled *Oh! It's Impossible*, was acted at York on 26 February 1780 and was distinguished only by the fact that Kemble converted the two *Dromios* to black men. It, too, never reached print, but the manuscript is at the Huntington Library. During that period he wrote prologues for charitable benefits, gave lectures on sundry subjects, and penned Latin verses for the gravestone of Joseph Inchbald. In 1780 at York he published his *Fugitive Pieces*, a collection of 15 poetic trifles which subsequently so embarrassed him that it is said throughout his life he sought to buy up every copy he could lay his hands on in order to burn it. In April of 1780 he made a brief trip to London to debate at Mrs Cornelys's Carlisle House the question "Whether the representatives of the people ought to be answerable in a private capacity for what they may say in their official ones," and was impressive.

Kemble had labored diligently for Wilkinson, and by 1781 his reputation was established in the north. In his study of Hamlet, for example, it was said that he wrote out his role some 40 times. When he was to essay Sir Giles Overreach in *A New Way to Pay Old Debts*, a role he played for the first time on 31 July 1781 at Edinburgh, he wrote a long letter from Leeds to Mrs Inchbald to inquire how John Henderson had dressed and painted the character. Kemble had made his Edinburgh debut under Wilkinson's temporary management there as Grey in *The Chapter of Accidents* and the Master in *The Toy Shop* on 23 July 1781 and also acted there Contrast in *The Lord of the Manor*, Demetrius in *Love and Ambition*, Hamlet, Puff in *The Critic*, Oakly in *The Jealous Wife*, and Sir Giles Overreach. According to Arthur McDonald's unpublished study of his Yorkshire apprenticeship, Kemble had played for Wilkinson 102 roles in 99 plays over a

period of 345 nights by the time he terminated his engagement with his performance of Jaffeir in *Venice Preserv'd* at York on 31 August 1781.

In the autumn of 1781 Kemble engaged for £5 per week with Daly at the Smock Alley Theatre in Dublin, where on 2 November as Hamlet he made his first appearance with some success. But his portrayal of Sir George Touchwood in *The Belle's Stratagem* failed to please. According to Boaden that comic character was "totally unsuited to his powers." He recovered slightly in *Alexander the Great* and other more appropriate parts, but not until he acted Raymond in Jephson's *The Count of Narbonne* did he create any excitement in the Irish capital. The author coached his voice and hired tutors to improve his "lounging gait." The play enjoyed crowded houses for 30 nights.

For two seasons Kemble and Dorothy Francis (who became the comic darling Mrs Jordan) were the mainstays of Daly's company, supported also by Mrs Inchbald and Mrs Crawford. Kemble was also with the troupe when it played at Cork in July and October 1782. There he acted Hamlet, Jaffeir, Antony, Orestes, and Raymond, among other roles. At Limerick Kemble gallantly repulsed an attempt by some regimental officers to carry off Anna Maria Phillips, then a 19-year-old singer from Drury Lane on her first trip to Ireland. He supposedly had a "particular attachment" to her, even to the point of intended marriage, but it came to naught and she became the famous Mrs Crouch and mistress of Michael Kelly. In February 1783 Kemble acted at Kilkenny.

In Ireland there seems to have been considerable tension between Kemble and Daly, a dangerous man with a sword. John Taylor reported that they actually came to a duel because of a dispute over Kemble's salary, but he provided no details. Nevertheless, Kemble's Irish stint placed a seal on his reputation, and by the end of 1782–83, Daly was paying him £10 per week. Kemble was ready for London. As Joseph Knight summarized in *The Dictionary of National Biography*, at that point in his career

He had not reached the maturity of his powers, but on the other hand his mannerisms and affectations, though already a subject of comment, were less pronounced than they subsequently became. His appearance and general gifts, including his voice, were in his favour. He wore classical drapery with unrivalled ease and elegance, and his features were both noble and expressive.

Kemble arrived in London in mid-August 1783 and took up temporary residence in Mrs Inchbald's rooms at No 2, Leicester Court, Castle Street, Leicester Fields, while she was away. The way was prepared for his September debut by some expert publicity and by his sister's influence. Despite the disappointment the town had experienced when her brother Stephen Kemble earlier that month had made his first appearance at Covent Garden, as Othello, Mrs Siddons persuaded her friends to welcome John at Drury Lane.

On Tuesday, 30 September 1783, Kemble made his entrance upon the Drury Lane stage as Hamlet, supported by Packer as Claudius, Farren as Horatio, Baddeley as Polonius, Miss Field as Ophelia, and Mrs Hopkins as the Queen. Though he did not create the feverish interest that Garrick had caused with his debut, the event, as John Adolphus put it, was a "great" one, and the press predicted a fine future for another talented Kemble. He surprised the public and divided the critics with the originality of his particular emphases and pauses. Thomas Davies, who had been discharged by Garrick, claimed that he had never seen an audience more moved or grateful. Other critics noted espcially his electrifying transitions, an observation not often to be made later about Kemble, whose steady and unvarying style of static declamation would influence an entire school of nineteenth-century acting. John Taylor complained, however, of his "stiff, conceited, and unnatural" technique. Another critic reported "He neither walks the stage, nor turns his head, nor moves his limbs with ease." Perhaps the latter observer, hoping to see a more animated style, mistook Kemble's vaunted control for timidity.

In *The New Rosciad* (1785) the more perceptive J. H. Leigh described Kemble's restraint as he met the ghost:

Sudden he starts, each feature turn'd away,
The lips contracted, vacant is the eye;
The left hand without motion, wrist half bent,
The right hand slow moves, as if he something
                    meant;
His head and hands affected airs display,

Then opes his mouth, says nothing—walks away!
Quickly returns—stops short—quite resolute—
Exclaims "Horatio did not YOU *speak to't?"*

Kemble trailed his sword behind, rather than pointing as he followed the spectre, business well approved by the audience. His use of two miniatures rather than wall portraits in the closet scene was, however, less successful. Instead of wearing the Vandyke costume that had become traditional for Hamlet, Kemble appeared in a modern court dress, described by Boaden as "of rich black velvet, with a star on the breast, the garter and pendant ribband of an order—mourning sword and buckles, with deep ruffles." His powdered hair, in contrast to the usual short curled wig, gave greater brilliance to his eyes and flowed disheveled over his shoulders during scenes of feigned madness and agitation. Kemble's refreshing portrayal of Hamlet is detailed in Boaden's biography, in the *Theatrical Review* (1783), and in A. C. Sprague's *Shakesperian Players and Performances*. The characterization was original in details rather than outline, in tactics, as Professor Sprague points out, rather than in interpretation—"Kemble's *style* was different."

Kemble repeated Hamlet four times more before he played the title role in *Edward the Black Prince* on 20 October 1783, in which his sister Elizabeth acted Mariana. (That season three of his sisters—Sarah, Elizabeth, and Frances—were at Drury Lane, and his brother Stephen was at Covent Garden, a concentration that caused John Williams to complain they were choking the London theatres "With Kembles on Kembles.") John's portrayal of the Black Prince was received with mixed feelings by the critic in the *Morning Herald*, who found the character was

very unequally sustained by Mr. Kemble; in the impassioned scenes he was nervous and dignified; but in those less interesting, offensively emphatic, and monotonous. The character, sufficiently wretched in itself, stands in need of no additional acquatics, to drivelize it into contempt, and therefore we trust Mr. Kemble will be less lavish of his tremulous tears in future.

On 6 November 1783 he presented his third character, Richard III. (His first performance of record in that role was at Smock Alley on 26 April 1782, but it was on the list of his parts he sent Wilkinson in 1778.) Kemble's steady interpretation, in which he downplayed the character's apparent cunning because he found it vulgar, suffered much in comparison to Garrick's tremendous *tour de force*, still vivid in the memory of many spectators. A studiously fashioned and varied performance was not sufficient, for Kemble lacked what Boaden termed a "concentrated force of body and voice" that could propel him energetically through nearly four hours on the stage. Critical dissatisfaction became more widespread when he acted Sir Giles Overreach on 14 November, for he had not "the bustle, the ardour, the grasp of the man." But excitement heightened when by royal command on 6 December he appeared with Mrs Siddons, as Mr and Mrs Beverley in *The Gamester*. The *Public Advertiser* of 9 December thought his Beverley "was all we could wish"; and in the last scene with the inimitable Siddons they drew forth from the house "as many tears as ever were shed in a theatre on one evening." On 10 December he played King John to his sister's Constance, but the critics found him solemn, monotonous, artificial, and cold, an assessment with which Boaden disagreed, declaring that "The most cold-blooded, hesitating, cowardly and creeping villainy, that ever abused the gift of speech, found in Mr. Kemble the only powers competent to give it utterance." Kemble had been instructed in the role by Thomas Sheridan, thought by many to have had no competitor in that character. (A study of Kemble's King John is offered by Maarten Van Dijk in *Theatre Notebook* [1975].)

Kemble's next role in his debut season at Drury Lane was a somewhat unconvincing Shylock on 22 January 1784 (he had first acted the part at Smock Alley on 3 December 1781). He followed that with Alwin in *The Countess of Salisbury* on 13 April, with Mrs Siddons in the title role. Kemble's benefit receipts that evening were £290 15*s*. (less house charges of £106 17*s*. 7*d*.) and tickets could be had from him at No 25, Henrietta Street, Covent Garden, where he had moved when Mrs Inchbald returned to town. For his sister's benefit on 24 April Kemble acted Tancred to her Sigismunda and drew torrents of tears. One critic wrote that he knew not "who upon the Stage could have played Tancred better, nor so well," but bemoaned that though Kemble was "by far the most distinguished Actor for his Time, for

Genius," his performances were "wonderfully unequal!" He was thus compared to King William, "almost incessantly defeated, but never without Respect even in his Defeats." He was seen as Cato on 28 April, Carlos in *Love Makes a Man* on 10 May, and Jupiter in *Amphitryon* on 17 May.

In the summer of 1784 Kemble went to play for Joseph Younger and George Mattocks at Liverpool, where he had received his earliest training half a decade before. According to a memorandum of his articles at Liverpool printed in the *Theatrical Inquisitor*. Kemble was paid 10*s*. for each night of the season on which there was a play—whether he acted or not—and allotted a benefit (£35 in house charges).

Earning a salary increased to 10 guineas per week, Kemble began his second Drury Lane season on 21 September 1784, as Hamlet. Beverley, Tancred, Sir Giles, and Cato followed, and then on 22 November he created the chivalrous Arthur in the premiere of *Arthur and Emmeline*, in which Elizabeth Farren played the other title role. The two-act alteration of Dryden's *King Arthur*, by way of Garrick's adaptation, was probably made by Kemble. Purcell's music and Arne's were supplemented with compositions by Thomas Linley. On 2 December 1784 John and Sarah appeared together in the premiere of Cumberland's *The Carmelite*, in which he played Montgomeri and she Matilda. Kemble's adaptation of Massinger's *The Maid of Honour* appeared on 27 January 1785 with Kemble as Adorni and Mrs Siddons as *Camiola*. Though Kemble acted well, the frugally-mounted piece did not please. *The Maid of Honour* had only two more performances, on 29 January and 10 February; the latter, being the traditional author's night, brought receipts of £203. Not published, the text exists in a manuscript at the Huntington Library. The *London Magazine* for February 1785 reported that "This piece is considerably altered from the original; passages are expunged, and others added, in every scene; and several incidents transposed from the order in which they formerly stood." Kemble also appropriated some scenes from Beaumont and Fletcher's *The Maid's Tragedy*.

He acted a moving Othello to Mrs Siddons's Desdemona on 8 March 1785 (they had played those roles together at Manchester on 29 January 1777). Though he was grand and pathetic, he did not, Boaden thought, completely work himself into the role as he had done with Hamlet and King John—"It was, at most, only a part very finely played." *Othello* was commanded for 12 March, and subsequently John and Sarah were invited to read at Court. For his benefit on 31 March, Kemble acted Macbeth (a role usually in the possession of Smith), with Mrs Siddons in her great rendition of Lady Macbeth. The benefit cleared about £188. Kemble had made tickets available at No 2, Leicester Court, so he seems to have returned to Mrs Inchbald's lodgings. His other new Drury Lane roles that season included Maskwell in *The Double Dealer* on 4 April 1785 and Master in *The Toy Shop* on 25 April.

The summer of 1785 was spent by Kemble in Ireland, quarreling with Daly at Smock Alley and touring the county theatres. With the death of Henderson, Kemble found himself at the beginning of his third season pretty much unrivaled as the first tragedian of the London stage. The season opened on 17 September 1785 with him and Sarah in *Othello*, and John was kept busy in a line of capital roles. Within one six-day period (17–22 November) he acted Hamlet, Macduff in *Macbeth*, Posthumus in *Cymbeline*, and King John and walked as Richard III in the pageant of *The Jubilee*. On 15 October 1785 he appeared as Philotas to Sarah's Euphrasia in *The Grecian Daughter*. He acted the Duke in *Braganza* on 20 October, and his first appearance in London as Osman in *Zara* came on 26 December, with his sister Frances in the title role. On 11 February 1786 he and Sarah appeared together for the first time in London as Jaffeir and Belvidera in *Venice Preserv'd*. She was magnificent, as usual, but he, though he provided more than adequate support, was preeminently unsuited for the tumultuous and passionate Jaffeir. Later in their careers, Mrs Siddons wrote (in a letter dated 1 November 1805):

I do not like to play Belvidera to John's Jaffeir so well as I shall when Charles [Kemble] has the part. John is too cold, too formal, and does not seem to put himself into the character. His sensibilities are not so acute as they ought to be for the part of a lover. Charles, in other characters far inferior to John, will play better in Jaffeir,—I mean to my liking. . . .

For Mrs Siddons's benefit on 4 March 1786 he acted Orestes to her Hermione in *The Distrest Mother*. He created the role of Ervallin in the premiere of Delap's unsuccessful tragedy *The Captives* on 9 March; Kemble appeared on stage "in the genuine Scottish dress," but none of the other actors made a similar effort at authenticity. After being endured for three nights, *The Captives*, wrote Boaden, "like the spirit of Ossian which pervaded it, was gathered to its fathers." When he played Douglas in Percy on 25 March, the *Morning Chronicle* implored him to break his habit of running too much about the stage—"the expression of his countenance, which is well worth watching, is frequently lost to the spectator, from the difficulty in following him through all his windings and turnings." For his benefit on 6 April 1786, he played Bassanio in *The Merchant of Venice* and Petruchio in *Catherine and Petruchio*; his net receipts were about £177, and at the time he lodged at No 19, Charles Street, Covent Garden. One reviewer of the benefit performance wrote that Kemble's Bassanio received "applause and universal shout" and that his Petruchio "was among the best acting we ever saw for entertainment. It proved Kemble's comick talents beyond all dispute."

That season Kemble's farce *The Projects* (which had first been acted as *The Female Officer* on 25 March 1778 at Manchester) was brought out at Drury Lane on 18 February 1786. But it was unsuccessful and was taken off after that night. Kemble also found time that year to publish his *Macbeth Reconsidered; an Essay: Intended as an Answer to Part of the Remarks on some of the Characters of Shakespeare*. Dedicated to Edmond Malone, the 36-page pamphlet was a rebuttal to Thomas Whateley's *Remarks on Some of the Characters of Shakespeare*, published in 1785. Kemble refuted Whateley's contention that Macbeth was a coward, and, as Herschel Baker concluded, Kemble's "arguments are cogent and eloquent, and his psychological insight on the whole remarkable." The essay brought Kemble credit for graceful erudition, but criticisms that his performances on the stage were too literary persisted. In 1786 John Williams (writing as Anthony Pasquin) in *The Children of Thespis* anatomized at length his perceptions of Kemble's bad habits:

*Tho' the sense of the scene in its quickness must
   center,
Yet a pause must ensue, ere the hero will enter;
Well skill'd in the family secrets of mumming,
'Tis a trick that implies a great actor is coming;
But the time that's prescrib'd for the art being out,
Then on rushes* John, *in an outrageous rout;
With a nice painted face, and a complacent grin,
Like an excellent sign to an ill-manag'd inn;
With the lineal brow, heavy, dismal, and murky,
And shoulders compress'd like an over-truss'd tur-
   key.
   Yet he has his merits, tho' crude and confin'd,
The faint sickly rays of a half-letter'd mind.
Now excellence fascinates every sense,
Now failings appear which give judgment offense;
In* this *all the force of the Actor is seen,
In* that *glares the Pedant, and dams all the scene;
For the faults which from Nature he got in great
   store,
His pride and presumption have made ten times
   more.*

. . . .

With tragedies tortur'd the public [he] *has
   cramm'd,
Which read, were but laugh'd at; and acted, were
   damn'd;
And odes so sublime issue forth from his head,
That nine-tenths of mankind swear they cannot be
   read;
Like the vile* amphisboena *his verses assail,
For none can discover the head from the tail.* . . .

Kemble spent the summer of 1786 once more at Liverpool, receiving £162 12s. 6d. in a clear benefit on 4 September as Richard III.

In 1786–87 he added to his Drury Lane repertoire Sifroy in *Cleone*, Don Henry in the premiere of Mrs Cowley's *A School for Grey Beards* on 25 November 1786, Valentine in *Love for Love*, Lord Gayville in *The Heiress*, Raymond in *The Count of Narbonne*, Orlando in *As You Like It*, Beverley in *All in the Wrong* (for his benefit on 29 March 1787, when he netted about £188 and still lived at No 19, Charles Street), Castalio in *The Orphan*, and Lord Morden in the premiere of Holcroft's *Seduction* on 12 March 1787. On 24 October 1786 he had appeared in the premiere of Burgoyne's musical drama *Richard Coeur de Lion*, playing Richard to Mrs Crouch's Laurette and Mrs Jordan's Matilda. Despite Kemble's bad singing—in that regard he made no progress whatsoever during his career—the piece became the season's hit, running 38 performances. A more

artistic success for Kemble, however, was his appearance as Posthumus, with Sarah as Imogen, in *Cymbeline* on 29 January 1787, in which, by Boaden's testimony he was "by a thousand degrees, the best Posthumus of my time." Another fine effort by Kemble, though the vehicle was not well received by the public, was his portrayal of Mentevole in Jephson's tragedy *Julia*, which opened on 14 April 1787. The role was "truly calculated for his powers," according to Boaden, for it combined ungovernable passion with the "dark designing subtlety of the Italian."

The Drury Lane season of 1787–88 was to prove an important one for Kemble, for his professional and social positions became solidly established. It was also the season in which he married. He began in September with Hamlet and followed that with a round of his familiar characters. On 26 October 1787 *The Pilgrim*, an alteration from Beaumont and Fletcher (through Vanbrugh), was acted and then was published that year. *The Pilgrim* is usually attributed to Kemble. The Larpent copy at the Huntington Library, however, contains the notation "by Thomas King." The piece was not mentioned by Boaden but is accepted and discussed by Baker as Kemble's. With him as Pedro it lasted six performances. As Othello, on 27 October, Kemble was "judicious, but too studiously so," thought the critic in the *Public Advertiser* of 29 October, who approved his dressing the character "in the Moorish habit" but wondered if it was really necessary for Othello to be made up "as *black* as a native of Guiney?" Though correct in his address to the Senate, Kemble was "more anxious to do justice to the text of his author than the feelings of Othello"—by then a familiar complaint. His new characters included the title role in *Henry the Second*, Cleombrotus in the premiere of Mrs Cowley's *The Fate of Sparta* on 31 January 1788, Hastings in *Jane Shore* (for his benefit on 13 March, by which time he had moved to No 13, Caroline Street, Bedford Square), Manuel in the premiere of Greatheed's *The Regent* on 29 March, Belville in *The School for Wives*, Marc Antony to Mrs Siddons's Cleopatra in *All for Love*, for her benefit on 5 May, and Benedick in *Much Ado about Nothing* for Kemble's new wife's benefit, in which she acted Hero, on 30 May.

The artistic highlight of the 1787–88 season was his appearance as King Lear with Mrs Siddons as Cordelia on 21 January 1788. The text was Kemble's revision of Tate's alteration of Shakespeare's masterpiece and as such was published that year. The occasion drew £343 12s. 6d. through the doors in a clear benefit for the incomparable Sarah, and that was one of the largest sums that ever had been taken at that theatre. Boaden saw the performance and thought Kemble not far below Garrick—"as a whole, nothing ever approached the influence of Garrick in this"—but he never again was as fine as that night.

Subsequently he was too elaborately aged, and quenched with infirmity the insane fire of the injured father. The curse, as he then uttered it, harrowed up the soul; the gathering himself together, with the hands convulsively clasped, the encreasing fervour and rapidity, and the suffocation of the conclusive words, all evinced consummate skill and original invention. The countenance too was finely made up, and in grandeur approached the *most* awful impersonation of Michael Angelo.

On 8 December 1787 at St Giles in the Fields Kemble had married the Drury Lane actress Priscilla Brereton. Supposedly the marriage ceremony was repeated by a Catholic priest for John's benefit. His new wife was the 29-year-old widow of the actor William Brereton, who had drunk himself into insanity and had died in a Hoxton asylum that February, and the daughter of the Drury Lane prompter William Hopkins and his wife the actress Elizabeth Hopkins. Priscilla, or "Pop"—as she was known to friends—had ventured onto the Drury Lane stage at the age of 14 to deliver an *Address to the Town* at her parents' benefit on 19 April 1773. By 1775–76 she was acting full time at Drury Lane and specialized in soubrettes. After her marriage to Brereton at Bath in September 1777 she had acted as Mrs Brereton until his death a decade later.

Kemble's choice of Priscilla Hopkins was a surprising one, considering his earlier attachments to Mrs Crouch and Mrs Inchbald. She was pretty enough, in a peevish sort of way, but it was thought that Kemble, with his culture and taste, would marry to his advantage, probably above his station. But Kemble seems to have had his eye on Priscilla for some time. One improbable story tells of his approaching her in the Green Room to announce that, out of respect for his late friend Brereton, "I have not until this time declared my passion." Actually, if stories told by the Bannisters and others can be credited, he made his choice with characteristic deliberation, in a dispassionate manner that seems not to have inconvenienced his daily routine. It was said that Kemble decided upon her as the pawn which he needed to complete an arrangement with Lord North, who supposedly had offered him a bribe of £4000 to give up his interest in his lordship's daughter, provided the actor would marry someone else within a fortnight; when Kemble married Priscilla and claimed the money from North he was refused. That story was later branded unequivocally by Kemble as a lie. Another tale surrounds Kemble's arrival at the wedding dinner arranged by the Bannisters so late that his bride and Bannister had already departed the table for their evening's work at the theatre. Kemble worked up enough enthusiasm, at any rate, to call for Priscilla that night after her performance as Louisa Dudley in *The West Indian* and take her to his house in Caroline Street.

When Kemble returned from a summer's work at Crow Street, Dublin, at the beginning of the 1788–89 season, he learned that Thomas King, having become dismayed with the distraught manner in which Sheridan conducted Drury Lane's affairs, had resigned as the acting manager. Sheridan was engrossed with parliamentary duties, so it took him several weeks to persuade Kemble to assume the task. In a journal (now in the British Library) kept by Kemble he wrote on 23 September 1788, "This day I undertook the management of D. L. Theatre." The first play acted under his leadership was *The Jealous Wife* on 25 September, when the afterpiece was *The Lyar*. It was a shaky beginning, for originally scheduled that evening were *The Constant Couple* and *The Romp*, a bill canceled by Mrs Jordan's "Indisposition." Kemble, who was paid £500 for the season as acting manager, in a statement to the public on 10 October 1788 denied having taken over "under *humiliating circumstances*," as had been rumored, and claimed that "the power entrusted to me is perfectly satisfactory to my own feelings, and entirely adequate to the liberal encouragement of poets, of performers, and to the conduct of the whole business of the theatre."

Kemble supported his first year of management by playing more regularly than usual and by introducing himself in 18 characters he had not previously acted in London: Lord Townly in *The Provok'd Husband*, Biron in *Isabella*, Leon in *Rule a Wife and Have a Wife*, Sciolto in *The Fair Penitent*, Mirabel in *The Way of the World*, Romeo in *Romeo and Juliet*, Cromwell in *Henry VIII*, Douglas in *Douglas*, Don Felix in *The Wonder*, Zanga in *The Revenge*, Cardinal Wolsey in *Henry VIII*, Coriolanus in *Coriolanus*, Paladore in *The Law of Lombardy*, the original Norfolk in St John's *Mary Queen of Scots*, Sir Clement Flint in *The Heiress*, the Marquis in *False Appearances*, and Malvolio in *Twelfth Night*. On 24 February 1789 he was confined to bed with gout in the knee but missed only a few nights because of Holy Week and was back on the stage by 3 March as Coriolanus. On 28 November 1788 his adaptation of Bickerstaff's *'Tis Well It's No Worse* was produced as a three-act comedy called *The Pannel* and was published that day. It ran 15 nights. His comedy *The Farm House*, taken from Johnson's *The Custom of the Manor*, was first played on 1 May 1789, was published that day, and had five performances.

An important production was the revival of *Henry VIII* on 25 November 1788, with Kemble as Cromwell, Palmer as Henry, and Mrs Siddons as Queen Katharine, with new costumes, scenes, decorations, and a splendid procession. On 3 February 1788 Kemble gave up Cromwell to Robert Palmer and took on Cardinal Wolsey. Without doubt, however, the high point of the season was the production of *Coriolanus*, altered by Kemble, on 7 February 1789. It had only seven performances that season (and was published that year), but the title role came to be regarded throughout his career as one of his finest roles and was largely responsible for the identification of Kemble with "Roman" parts. He wrote in his journal on opening night that "This play was very splendidly ornamented—Mrs. Siddons was prodigiously admired {as Volumnia}, and it was said that I never acted better. The whole play was greatly applauded." With these productions of *Henry VIII* and *Coriolanus* he began

to manifest his interest in theatrical realism— or at least his enthusiasm for the picturesque classical propriety—by providing "appropriate" costumes and decorations.

During his first season of management Kemble instituted some strict discipline which included the fining of actors for professional misbehavior and the prohibiting of their friends and relatives from backstage areas. But he was plagued, as managers usually were, by altercations with actresses like Mrs Goodall, Mrs Crouch, and Mrs Jordan, and by the irritation of authors. Kemble wrote in his journal at the end of the season, "I am very sorry my Luck was to commence Manager this year— The Theatre laboured under great disadvantages from frequent Indispositions of the Performers, from the uncommon Severity of the Winter, from the Concern all People took in his Majesty's Indisposition and from their loyal joy for his Recovery. Long may he live! God everlastingly bless him, and us under him!"

During the earlier part of the 1788–89 season, in collaboration with Francis Aickin, Kemble had negotiated for the lease of the Liverpool theatre. On 1 January 1789 he wrote in his journal "This day I agreed to take the Liverpool Theatre with Mr. F. Aickin for seven years. Our rent is to be 350 Pounds per ann. We are only to use the Theatre for six months of the twelve and are to pay down twelve hundred pounds for the purchase of wardrobe, etc." On the opening night at Liverpool, Kemble delivered an address written by Miles Peter Andrews. Aickin stayed on to manage, while Kemble concentrated on his London business. Their Liverpool venture, which had good prospects, did not flourish and they lost a goodly sum. Kemble gave it up after that season.

Kemble had to face his second year of Drury Lane management without the substantial support of Mrs Siddons, who, tired of squabbles with Sheridan over the delays in paying her salary and suffering from ill health, removed herself from the stage for several seasons. He tried to compensate early in the season with a revival of *Henry V; or, The Conquest of France* on 1 October 1789. The text arranged by Kemble—or as Baker put it, "cut to tatters" by him—was published that year. Boaden was very taken with Kemble's portrayal of the leading role, thinking that not even his Coriolanus

Harvard Theatre Collection

JOHN PHILIP KEMBLE as Hamlet

engraving by Rogers, after Lawrence

Guildhall Library

JOHN PHILIP KEMBLE as Coriolanus
by Lawrence

surpassed it. "As a *coup de Theatre*, his starting up at the sound of the trumpet, in the passage where he states his attempted atonement to Richard the Second, formed one of the most spirited excitements that the stage has ever displayed."

Two other adaptations by Kemble were introduced that month: on 13 October 1789 his version of *The Tempest*, with additions from Dryden and Davenant, and on 24 October his version of Vanbrugh's *The False Friend*. Kemble did not appear in the former but he acted Don John in the latter. *The Tempest*, though mangled and trivialized, was, according to its adapter, received "with great Applause," supported as it was by the good performances of Moody, Elizabeth Farren, Kelly, and Mrs Crouch. Kemble's fourth and last literary tampering of the 1789–90 season was a five-act comedy called *Love in Many Masks* (taken from Mrs Behn's *The Rover*), which was offered on 8 March 1790 with Kemble as Willmore and was published that year.

He revived but did not act in *The Two Gentlemen of Verona* on 15 January 1790. The critics damned the play itself and Kemble wrote, "A very ineffectual Play, and I am sorry I ever took the Trouble to revive it." He added that the production had been "very ill acted," but perhaps his criticism was not intended to include his wife's portrayal of Sylvia.

Cobb's comic opera *The Haunted Tower*, in which Signora Storace made her English debut at its premiere on 24 November 1789, proved the hit of the season. By running 56 nights it assured in Kemble's second year of management an increase in business over his first—£32,750 compared to £29,644.

In addition to Henry V, Don John, and Willmore, in 1789–90 Kemble had enlarged his London repertoire with Hernandez in the premiere of Hayley's *Marcella* on 7 November 1789, Ralegh in *The Life and Death of Sir Walter Ralegh*, Sir Charles Easy in *The Careless Husband*, Doricourt in *The Belle's Stratagem*, Faulkland in *The Rivals*, and Young Marlow in *She Stoops to Conquer*, roles in which his performances did him little credit. His schedule was interrupted for a week when on 19 January 1790 he set off to retrieve his ill brother Charles from Douai. By a fortuitous coincidence they met on the road near St Omers;

Charles had recovered considerably, and on 25 January they were back in London.

By the end of his second year of management Kemble had asserted his authority to admit or forbid orders—requests by actors for free tickets for friends. Bensley and Baddeley had given him some grief over the issue, but Kemble had persisted.

The next season, 1790–91, was full of irksome quarreling with Elizabeth Farren over parts and Dorothy Jordan over money. Houses were also thinner than usual. Kemble made things no better by choosing to act Charles Surface in *The School for Scandal* on 10 November 1790. He considered the character a serious one—not a "gay, free, spirited, convivial fellow" as Taylor had tried to persuade him—so the role was played by romanesque Kemble as "merry as a funeral, and as lively as an elephant." One waggish story relates Kemble's lack of amusement in the part. It seems that in his cups one night he had insulted a gentleman on the street and when he sobered up and dutifully offered to make any honorable reparation, the abused fellow extracted a promise that Kemble would never again play Charles Surface. Kemble retained the role, nevertheless. On 17 November 1790 he was the original Saville Andrews in Reynolds's comedy *Better Late Than Never*. Kemble was ill for a fortnight in December and went to Bath for several weeks in January. On 30 January 1791 he was unanimously elected one of the four trustees for the Drury Lane Fund. He acted Osmyn in *The Mourning Bride* on 14 May. Despite the somewhat mediocre level of the season, receipts totalled £38,267 for 189 nights. For her clear benefit on 4 April 1791 Mrs Siddons, acting Mrs Beverley, brought in £412 11s., the largest gross of any night in the history of the venerable house of Garrick. Kemble while visiting York that summer struck a hard bargain with Wilkinson and acted for a week, clearing about £150.

At the conclusion of the 1790–91 season the Drury Lane Theatre, having stood since 1674, had been declared unsafe and was torn down to make way for a new theatrical facility. While awaiting the new house it was necessary for the Drury Lane company to play the 1791–92 season at the recently built King's Theatre, which upon completion had found itself without an opera patent. Kemble, earning £23 per week for acting, made his first appearance at the King's on 27 September 1791, as Charles Surface. That season he added Hotspur in *1 Henry IV*, Huniades in Hannah Brand's *Huniades* on 18 January 1792, and Oakly in *The Jealous Wife*. On 27 April 1792 he took over the role of Admiral Cleveland in *The Fugitive* from King, who had played it on opening night, 20 April; King retrieved the part at the next performance, 2 May. Perhaps the most exciting event of the season—abortive though it was—was the near-duel Kemble had with Aickin, who issued a challenge because he thought he had been insulted by Kemble during a rehearsal. They met one morning in a field near Marylebone; Kemble offered his aggressor first shot, but Aickin was so nervous that after three attempts he managed to get off one shot that missed. Whereupon the gallant Kemble fired in the air and the two stomped off the field and returned to town.

In the summer of 1792 Kemble went to help manage his brother Stephen's company at Edinburgh and also played at Glasgow and Newcastle. Among his Edinburgh roles were Coriolanus, Douglas, Henry V, Oakly, Hamlet, and Macbeth. In September he returned to manage the Drury Lane company, which played at the King's Theatre through the season, except on Tuesdays and Saturdays, from 26 January to 4 June 1793, when it was at the Haymarket Theatre. His first Haymarket appearance was as Beverley in *The Gamester* on 29 January 1793. He was the original Perithous in Murphy's *The Rival Sisters* at the King's on 18 March 1793. *The Dictionary of National Biography* and Genest assign him Horatio in *The Fair Penitent* that season, and indeed his name appeared in the Haymarket bills for that role on 23 April 1793. But the *Thespian Magazine* of June 1793 reported that Kemble had become ill, so Harley had played Horatio.

Kemble engaged for the first time with Colman's summer company at the Haymarket in 1793, making his debut on 3 August as the original Octavian in the summer patentee's extremely successful music-drama *The Mountaineers*, which enjoyed 26 performances. His performance of Octavian, according to Genest, was "very fine." Boaden termed it his "most picturesque"—"The author and the actor seem

to have asked themselves how best a series of portraits of expressive misery could be diversified and arranged; and never was an author's conception more extended and exalted, than the Octavian of Colman, was in the performance of Mr. Kemble." A long poem describing Kemble's portrayal of the varying moods appeared in the *Thespian Magazine* of August 1793. According to John Williams in *A Pin Basket to the Children of Thespis*, ill-feeling between Colman and Kemble began with negotiations for the actor's Haymarket salary.

When Mr. C. was writing his excellent play of the Mountaineers, K. chanced to be on a visit at his house, and having read part of the character of Octavian, was so delighted with it, that he entreated to play it at the little theatre. Mr. C. assured him that he could not afford him such a salary as he would demand: to which he replied, 'that he would play it for nothing, for he knew it would be the making of him.'—'Well,' was the rejoinder, 'if it will serve you I will work up the character purposely for you, and give you twelve pounds a week.' Kemble after this abused Mr. Colman, and said, he had paid him like a beggar.

Williams was no admirer of Kemble and seems to have concocted the tale, for the Haymarket paid Kemble £150 for about six weeks work that summer, about the same salary, prorated, he earned in the winter (£23 per week). His only other role that summer was Richard III on 6 August 1793 for the benefit of his sister-in-law, Mrs Stephen Kemble.

From 19 September to mid-November 1793 the Drury Lane company played at the Haymarket. Then they scattered in various directions while their new theatre was going through the final phase of preparation. Kemble spent January and February in Edinburgh working for his brother Stephen.

The new Drury Lane Theatre, with a capacity of 3611 people, was immense compared to its predecessor. The proscenium opening was 43 feet wide by 38 feet high and the stage area behind 83 feet wide, 92 feet deep, and 110 high. These dimensions obviously portended a new era of scenic investiture and splendor along with a broader and more flamboyant acting style. The theatre was opened to the public on 12 March 1794 with a concert of Handel's music performed by leading vocalists and musicians. After a series of similar

Courtesy of the Garrick Club

JOHN PHILIP KEMBLE as Coriolanus
by Harlow

concerts and oratorios, on 21 April 1794 Kemble brought his company on in the inaugural production of *Macbeth*, with elaborate sets by Capon, French, Greenwood, and others and new costumes and decorations. Kemble, who spoke a prologue written by Major General Richard Fitzpatrick, acted Macbeth, and Mrs Siddons was Lady Macbeth. Their brother Charles began his Drury Lane engagement by playing Malcolm. An epilogue written by Colman was spoken by Miss Farren. The acting version of this *Macbeth*, as altered by Kemble, was published that day. "Some alterations were made with great judgment," reported the *European Magazine* for May 1794, "particularly the omission of the visible appearance of the Ghost of Banquo, which some of the best judges of the drama had long since recommended the exclusion of. . . ." According to Boaden:

There were sundry other novelties, perhaps revivals, as to the witches and their incantations; indeed the noble firmness and compactness of the action was dreadfully broken and attenuated by the vast crowds of witches and spirits that filled the stage, and thundered in the ear a music of dire potency. The auxiliary injured the principal, and Matthew Locke became the rival of his master. Mere speech, however masterly, is weak upon the ear after the noise (call it harmony if you will) of a full orchestra, and perhaps fifty voices, with difficulty kept together in tolerable time and tune.

The *Morning Chronicle* of 22 April reported that, indeed, thunder rolled throughout the whole production and suggested that in the scene when Hecate and her companion spirit ascend on a cloud it "would better if they were not made to fly backwards." Though the new production was a great success, Kemble, suffering fatigue, was under par as Macbeth. The *Oracle* praised his dagger soliloquy, the murder, and the battle, but "all the rest was unworthy of him."

In fact he acted only occasionally before the theatre closed in early July and then went to play six nights in Edinburgh. But his afterpiece *Lodoiska*, with music arranged by Storace from several composers, had opened on 9 June 1794 and had run 20 performances that season and 34 the next. It was published in October 1794. Based on Dejaure's opera, the piece was full of Gothic nonsense in burning castles, but Kemble mounted it handsomely with scenes by Malton, Greenwood, Luppino, and Demaria and cast it with Mrs Crouch and Kelly, who earned loud applause for their exploits and voices.

Earning £17 per week, Kemble began the first full season at the new Drury Lane with a round of familiar roles. On 28 October 1794 he was the original Duke of Gustalla in Berington's alteration of *Emilia Galotti*, which closed after three nights. He acted Publius Horatius in *The Roman Father* on 15 November. His appearance as Bertram in his version of *All's Well That End's Well* on 12 December was a failure, evidently because he was so ill he should not have gone on. It was played that night only. (It had been published in 1793.) He redeemed himself, however, on 30 December 1794 with an excellent performance of the Duke in his rendering of *Measure for Measure*, which was also published that year. On 28

February 1795 he was the original Penruddock in Cumberland's *The Wheel of Fortune*, a comedy which had 18 performances by season's end. Leigh Hunt called Penruddock his "greatest performance, and I believe it to be a perfect one." It was admirable, Hunt explained, "because the very defect which hurts his general style of acting, that studious and important preciseness, which is affectation in all his other characters, contributes to the strength, to the nature of *Penruddock*." On 21 March he acted Edwy in Fanny Burney Arblay's terrible tragedy *Edwy and Elgiva*, which opened and closed that night. When Kemble tried to announce a second night the audience shouted him off the stage. For Mrs Siddons's benefit on 27 April 1795 he played Zaphna in a revival of *Mahomet the Imposter*, translated from Voltaire by James Miller.

But no on-stage performance by Kemble that season caused as much excitement as the one backstage one night in January 1795, when he made a drunken assault on the enticing actress Maria Theresa De Camp. She escaped his lust by protesting screams which drew rescuers. In his statement to the press on 27 January Kemble apologized for his brutish behavior and cleared her conduct and character. His private apology to her is contained in a manuscript (not in his hand) in the Harvard Theatre Collection. Despite the "high opinion" of her which he expressed in his apology, John stood in the way of his brother Charles's marriage to Miss De Camp for over five years.

After performing Penruddock on 9 May 1795, John and his wife left London before the end of the season, bound for Dublin, through Stratford, Coventry, and Holyhead. On 25 May 1795, as Hamlet, he made his first appearance in six years at the Crow Street Theatre, under the management of his old enemy Daly. Charles Mathews wrote that "If twenty guineas had been offered for a ticket or a place in the boxes, it could not have been purchased. In all my life I never saw people more anxious to get into a theatre." Kemble was wined and dined by Dublin society, had harsh words with C. F. Cooke, who was by comparison an unknown provincial in Daly's employ, and took £718 away for his efforts. On the way back to London John acted again for his brother Stephen at Edinburgh and also at Glasgow and Newcastle. Upon his return to London, John

appeared in *Douglas* for the benefit of Stephen's wife at the Haymarket on 29 August 1795.

The 1795–96 season at Drury Lane began badly and became worse. Cumberland's new comedy *The Dependent*, in which Kemble acted Edmund D'Alincourt, did not survive beyond its first performance on 20 October 1795. The next night Kemble's alteration of *Venice Preserv'd*, in which he acted Jaffeir and Mrs Siddons Belvidera, ran into political problems when some of the speeches about rebellion were warmly applauded by certain radical elements in the audience. The second performance on 26 October provoked a similar reaction, and by the third performance on 29 October loyalists were crying out for "God Save the King," a rendition of which Kemble managed to scrape together with a few musicians who were hanging about the theatre. Many of the audience accused the management of trying to arouse disaffection for the government. Despite the protests of the press, the play, which had been mounted with expensive new scenery and costumes, was banned after that night for seven years. When it was revived in later years, the tableau which Kemble had introduced of the conspirators being taken to their execution to the sound of muffled drums and tolling bells became a regular part of performances of that play.

On 23 November 1795 Kemble brought out his adaptation of Lee's *Alexander the Great*, complete with a battle between the Macedonians and the Persians and Alexander's triumphal entry into Babylon. The "new" scenes by Marinari and "new" costumes and decorations by Johnston and Rein were actually those used the previous season for D'Egville's spectacular ballet pantomime of the same title. Kemble's acting of Alexander somehow managed to emerge unscathed from the jam of elephants, amazons, bridges, wagons, battles, and processions. The *Monthly Mirror* for January 1796 reported that in the last scene:

the expiring tone with which [Kemble] pronounces 'Cover me'; his shivering, when wrapt round in the imperial robes; his wan and wasted countenance; the manner of his laboriously drawing his legs together, and their anguished knocking when they meet, surpass all description.

Kemble's alteration of the play was published in 1796.

On 23 January 1796 Kemble was the original Dorington in Holcroft's not very successful *The Man of Ten Thousand*. He acted Manly in his own adaptation of *The Plain Dealer*, on 27 March, but that expurgated version of Wycherley's comedy, published that year, also failed to please. He was also seen as Alonzo in the premiere of Sophia Lee's tragedy *Almeyda: Queen of Carthage* on 20 April 1796, in the title role in the premiere of Hoare's melodrama *Mahoud*, with music by Storace, on 30 April, and as Edward Clifford in the London premiere of *Julia; or, Such Things Are* for Mrs Siddons's benefit on 2 May. On the occasion of his wife's farewell benefit on 23 May, Kemble introduced another two of his alterations: *The Roman Actor*, a tragedy adapted from Massinger, in which he acted the title role; and *Celadon and Florimel*, a comedy adapted from Dryden and Cibber, in which Mrs Kemble acted Flavia, Charles Kemble acted Celadon, and Charles's future wife, Miss De Camp, acted Florimel. Neither play was published, but both survive in manuscript at the Huntington Library.

The two big events of the 1795–96 season, however, were the productions of *The Iron Chest* and *Vortigern*, and both were utter disasters. Colman's *The Iron Chest*, plagued from the first rehearsals, was given a "hasty, undigested" premiere on 12 March 1796 before a very crowded house (£471 9*s.*). Just a few hours before the curtain Kemble, who had been feuding with Colman throughout, demanded the transposition of two scenes in the second act, but the author refused. Suffering from a severe cough, Kemble hacked his way through the role of Sir Edward Mortimer. In a preface to the second edition of the play, Colman accused Kemble of deliberately sabotaging the production, calling him "a scowling, sullen, black Bull, right athwart my road;—a monster of ingratitude, of the Boeotian breed, perplexing me in my wanderings through the entangled labyrinth of Drury." At the second performance, on 19 March, Kemble was even worse, "not only dull in himself," wrote Colman, "but the cause of dullness in others." The vengeful author reported finding Kemble in his dressing room "taking *Opium Pills*; and nobody who is acquainted with that gentleman will doubt me when I assert, that they are a medicine which he has long been in the habit

of swallowing." The public revelation was mean, but the accusation was true. Kemble did take opiates to relieve the pain of his gout and asthma and also, according to a report by Scott in the *Quarterly Review* (1826), to quicken his senses for acting. Kemble remained aloof in the face of Colman's vituperation, and the preface was later suppressed, making the second edition a collector's item. In his *Pin Basket to the Children of Thespis* John Williams accused Kemble of "execrable conduct" by appearing in Colman's work only to injure it. Boaden believed that Kemble had made a serious and courageous effort to stifle his cough but that he was that night "too ill, to do more than walk through anything." The press seemed to sympathize with the actor rather than with the author. "The play failed," wrote the *Oracle* on 14 March, "and we are sorry to say did not merit to succeed." When Kemble stepped forward to apologize for his condition, the "whole audience with one voice cried out, 'No, no, Kemble—it is not your fault.'" *The Iron Chest* was subsequently revised by Colman and brought out successfully at the Haymarket on 14 August 1797 with a vigorous performance of Sir Edward Mortimer by Robert Elliston.

The storm over *Vortigern* had been gathering for some months since young William Henry Ireland and his father, the engraver Samuel Ireland, had announced their discovery of an ancient chest containing various bits and pieces of Shakespearean manuscripts as well as, wonder of wonders, two hitherto unknown full plays, *Vortigern* and *Henry II*. Sheridan won the competition over his rival patentee Harris for the privilege of producing *Vortigern*, though it seems doubtful that he believed in its authenticity. Rather, he probably sensed an extraordinary box-office event. Edmund Malone and some others tried to expose the fraud, but the production went forward in the wake of tremendous advance publicity and expectation. Mrs Siddons had the good sense to refuse to participate. Kemble was disgusted with the travesty but fulfilled his obligation to act the title role at the first and only performance on 2 April 1796 before a crush of spectators who poured £555 6*s.* 6*d.* into Sheridan's coffers. The ridiculous passages forged by Ireland soon elicited groans and laughter, and in the fifth act when Kemble quite deliberately read with derision the line, "And when this solemn mockery is o'er," the audience was convulsed into laughter for ten minutes. (Accounts of Kemble's behavior are provided by eye-witnesses in *Notes and Queries* for 6 and 20 June 1857.)

At his benefit on 18 April 1796, when he acted Coriolanus, receipts were £475 4*s*. (less house charges of £229 14*s*. 6*d*.). When the dismal season ended Kemble resigned as deputy manager, a position he had held for eight seasons, and went off to act in Ireland for the summer.

Before agreeing to return to act at Drury Lane in the fall of 1796 Kemble conducted hard negotiations with Sheridan. For a while it appeared that he would forsake London for a transatlantic excursion. The season, in fact, opened on 20 September without him. John Williams deplored the "lamenting, fulsome, and preposterous articles, with which the journals were recently pestered, upon the presumed threats of Mr. Kemble to retire from the stage. If a Foreigner had perused these absurd paragraphs, he must have imagined

Harvard Theatre Collection

JOHN PHILIP KEMBLE as King Lear
artist unknown

that the Drama superseded every other Consideration in this Country, and that Mr. Kemble was the common God of our Idolatry; that all the Community were in tears from Portland-place to Limehouse-hole; and that nothing could be well if he was ill." Finally, after settling upon articles for five years at £24 a week and £200 for his benefit, Kemble returned to Drury Lane on 29 September as Penruddock. But he would have none of the management tasks, so Sheridan appointed Richard Wroughton deputy manager. A manuscript in the British Library indicates that Sheridan actually owed Kemble some £1367 in back salary, for which, to show good faith, he gave Kemble a bond for £500 on 1 November 1796.

Kemble's new roles in 1796–97 at Drury Lane included Evander in *The Grecian Daughter*, Edward in *Edward and Eleanora*, Sextus in the premiere of Jephson's *The Conspiracy* on 15 November 1796, Young Bevil in *The Conscious Lovers*, Bajazet in *Tamerlane*, Old Wilmot in *The Fatal Curiosity*, and Varanes in *Theodosius* ("In the scene where Varanes kills himself," according to the *Monthly Visitor* of February 1797, "Kemble . . . was particularly striking. His manner of sheathing the sword in his body after he exclaimed, 'I feel the art'ry where the life-blood lies! It heaves against the point!—Now—Oh ye gods!' astonished us; and we turned, with horror from the sight"). Kemble's version of *The Merry Wives of Windsor*, published in 1797, was probably that acted 8 June 1796. *Much Ado about Nothing*, with alterations by Kemble, was played on 12 June 1797 and published in 1799.

In 1797–98 he was seen as the original Percy in "Monk" Lewis's *The Castle-Spectre*, a melodrama that enjoyed enormous success that season, and the original Stranger in *The Stranger*, Thompson's alteration from Kotzebue. He acted the original Aurelio in *Aurelio and Miranda*, Jaques in *As You Like*, the original Rivers in Lewis's *The East Indian*, the original Old Count in *The Castle of Montvale*, an original unspecified character in *Trials of the Heart*, and the original Rolla in *Pizarro*, a potboiler tragedy with music, altered by Sheridan from Kotzebue, which opened on 24 May 1799 and was acclaimed for its brilliant theatricality. *Pizarro* almost saved Sheridan's precarious financial situation. Kemble was enormously successful as Rolla; even Sheridan called his performance "Beautiful! sublime! perfection!" and Pitt declared him in that role "the noblest Actor he had ever seen." In 1799–1800 Kemble acted the original Prince Richard in Pye's *Adelaide* on 25 January 1800 and the original De Montfort in Baillie's *De Montfort* on 29 April 1800; the latter piece was, according to a notation by him on a playbill, "Adapted to the stage by J. P. Kemble."

Kemble lined his pockets with handsome receipts from summer tours to Dublin, Limerick, and Cork in 1797, Birmingham, Manchester, and Liverpool in 1798, and Brighton, Birmingham, York, and Cheltenham in 1799. One week's visit to Edinburgh in March 1799 brought him £358. At Dublin in 1800 he made £1117 in 2 weeks and on his return to London he took another £600 playing Glasgow, Berwick, and Newcastle. According to a Folger Library manuscript Kemble received in salary payments alone at Drury Lane for the 1799–1800 season a total of £1112, from 25 November to 20 May.

The expectation of a share in the patent enticed Kemble to assume the management of Drury Lane once more at the beginning of the 1800–1801 season. Sheridan desperately needed the money that Kemble possessed and could raise, and Kemble yearned to own enough of the theatre to enable him to make his own decisions. (According to the *Oracle* on 4 October 1796, when the business of the stage in *Coriolanus* "was extremely incorrect," at the time Kemble was no longer deputy manager, and some of the performers imperfect, Kemble became so disturbed that "the actor became a manager . . . and directed the scene.") On 1 February 1800 Kemble agreed to buy one-fourth share for £25,000. But when Kemble's attorney could not validate Sheridan's clear title the actor withdrew from the negotiations. Meanwhile he conducted the stage business of the theatre, for which he was to receive £500 in addition to his acting salary. Kemble was now settled in his fine house at No 89, Great Russell Street, Bloomsbury, where he had moved from No 13, Caroline Street, Bedford Square.

His version of *The Way of the World* was acted on 22 November 1800 (published 1801). His adaptations of *Hamlet*, *King John*, and *King Lear* were published in 1800. On 13 December

1800 he played the original Antonio in Godwin's failure, *Antonio*, and on 24 February 1801 he created De L'Epée in Holcroft's *Deaf and Dumb*. That season he also was the original Alfonso in *Julian and Agnes*. On 25 March 1802 he acted Leontes in *The Winter's Tale* for his first time (and his adaptation of that play was published in 1815). When his mother-in-law Mrs Hopkins died in October 1801 he did not act for a week, but claimed no salary. She named him the executor of her will. The 1801–2 season was enlivened a bit by the competition between Kemble at Drury Lane and Cooke at Covent Garden in rival productions of *Richard III*—a contest reminiscent of the Garrick-Barry duel in *Romeo and Juliet*—and generally the victory was conceded to Cooke.

At the conclusion of the 1801–2 season Kemble found he could no longer tolerate Sheridan's financial bungling and smiling promises, especially for back salaries. He resigned from Drury Lane and initiated negotiations through Mrs Inchbald to buy into Covent Garden. While he waited for Harris's decision, Kemble, leaving his wife behind, set out with Robert Heathcote in July 1802 for a grand tour. He wrote to his brother Charles of his dismay at finding his old school at Douai "in a state of ruin, poverty, and desolation, not to be described." The English and French nobility and literati in Paris threw their doors open in welcome and the press made much of his visit. He saw the best of French theatre and found it too cold, but struck a lasting friendship with Talma, who later attended Kemble's farewell from the London stage. In October 1802, in the company of Mr Ponsonby, he suffered a hard crossing of the Pyrenees, marveled at the mountains, was disappointed by Madrid—where he heard of the death of his father, the venerable Roger Kemble—and stayed for a while with Lord Holland at Valencia. Returning by way of Paris, he was back in London in March 1803.

By April 1803 Kemble concluded his deal with the Harrises, father and son, for a one-sixth share in Covent Garden, for which he was obliged for £22,000—£10,000 in cash (actually loaned to him by the Heathcotes) and £12,000 to be amortized from the anticipated profits. Kemble was to manage the operation at a salary of £200 a year and would receive

£37 16s. for acting three nights a week and £12 8s. for each extra performance. Thomas Harris retained 50 percent of the stock, his son Henry one-twelfth, and George White and Ann Martindale one-eighth each. Awaiting the opening of the next Covent Garden season, Kemble went to play at Bath's Orchard Street, making his first appearance on 12 April 1803 as Macbeth. The crush for places was great throughout his month's engagement there and at Bristol, during which he also played Hamlet, Shylock, Rolla, the Stranger, Penruddock, Orestes, Leon, and Octavian.

Covent Garden was to host a pride of Kembles in 1803–4, for John had gathered the clan. Brother Charles made his first appearance on 12 September 1803 and sister Sarah on 27 September. Sarah's son Henry Siddons and his wife Harriott (née Murray) were also brought into the company. John's Covent Garden Theatre debut occurred on 24 September 1803; the role was, suitably enough, Hamlet. Kemble met hostility from various members of the company, like Murray, some of whose roles he usurped, and W. T. Lewis, whom he replaced as manager, and especially from George Frederick Cooke, who was "much unsettled" by his rival's encroachment on his territory. To mollify Cooke Kemble gave him Richard III and played Richmond. He also acted Antonio to Cooke's Shylock, and gave him Douglas while he played Old Norval. Kemble's roles that season also included the King in 2 Henry IV and Ford in The Merry Wives of Windsor.

As manager Kemble immediately strengthened the Shakespearean repertory, as expected, spending large sums on his revivals. He was dubbed "Black Jack" by some disgruntled actors who took exception to his autocratic manner of dealing with them in his attempts to raise professional standards. The season grossed £63,182 and netted a profit of £3959, not so much when one considers that years earlier Garrick and Lacy regularly made higher profits on lower grosses. The theatre lost an enormous potential revenue through the granting of orders for free seats; on 25 June 1804 the appalled Kemble wrote in his notebook that £17,182 had been the "Amount of orders this Season!!!" So evidently he did not exercise as much authority over that situation as he had done at Drury Lane. According to Baker, how-

ever, Kemble did well personally, drawing £2000 from the treasury and sharing £1260 from a private box with Harris; he also received £315 in lieu of a benefit.

In 1804–5 Kemble brought on lavish productions of Pizarro and Hamlet and acted originally Villars in Reynolds's The Blind Bargain, Sir Oswin Mortland in Mrs Inchbald's To Marry or Not to Marry, and Barford in Colman's Who Wants a Guinea?; he also acted Octavian in The Mountaineers and Eustace de St Pierre in The Surrender of Calais. During that season occurred the extraordinary hysteria surrounding the debut and subsequent performances of Master Betty, whom Kemble welcomed to his theatre for strictly commercial exploitation. John and Sarah refused to appear on stage with the 13-year-old boy, who commanded enormous sums each night and whose acting as Douglas, Achmet in Barbarossa, Rolla, and Hamlet was cheered as superior to anyone's, even Kemble's. When the craze subsided and a certain degree of sanity returned to idolatrous audiences, Kemble admitted that he had never thought much of the boy's talent. To his fellow-members at the Beefsteak Club he confided his opinion that the mass hysteria over the Infant Roscius "was a recollection that should call shame to the cheek of modern London." Kemble's sufferance of the appearance of seven-year-old Miss Mudie in The Country Girl next season can only be explained as box-office prostitution. That poor child failed and was hooted from the stage in the middle of her performance.

Beyond the promotion of Miss Mudie's abortive appearance, in 1805–6 Kemble busied himself with a display of familiar roles, and in performances with his sister he reestablished some of the credit the theatre had lost. Holcroft praised him highly "for the correct and classical manner in which many pieces, tragedies especially, have been performed under his management." Kemble acted Gloster in Jane Shore, Pierre in Venice Preserv'd, and the title role in Reynolds's new play The Delinquent. His performance as Wolsey in his revival of Henry VIII earned him great praise. Kemble probably had a hand in writing or revising parts of The Romantic Lover; or, Lost and Found, a comedy attributed to Allingham that played at Covent Garden on 6 January 1806.

Over the next two seasons Covent Garden sailed on a fairly even keel. There were no extraordinary events or achievements but at least there were some competent though ostentatious productions. Kemble revived *The Tempest* on 8 December 1806, playing Prospero and altering the play into what one critic thought to be a piece "As tasteless as indecent . . . and totally subversive of the simplicity of Shakespeare's drama." He created laughter and controversy by persisting in pronouncing the word "aches" ("Fill all thy bones with aches") as two syllables, with the "ch" soft, in the Elizabethan manner. On 10 February 1807 he was Reuben Glenroy in Morton's *Town and Country*, his last original role. In 1807–8 he acted Iago to Cooke's Othello and was damned. He failed as Lear, and his production of *The Two Gentlemen of Verona*, in which he acted Valentine, was boring. The season ended, appropriately and forebodingly, with Kemble playing Macbeth with a "distressing lameness" in his knee.

Kemble was now drinking more and suffering regular spells of incapacitating gout. Friends and audiences were beginning to notice that at the age of 51 his virility and endurance were waning. Moreover, audiences and critics were preparing to turn away from the dignified intellectualism of Kemble's art to embrace the undisciplined passion of Kean's. And the noble Roman was about to suffer the two greatest calamities of his career.

On 20 September 1808 Covent Garden Theatre was consumed by a fire that killed 22 persons, injured many more, and destroyed valuable scenes, costumes, production books, and the vast music library, including many manuscript scores of Handel and Arne. The financial loss was well over £100,000, only £44,500 of which was covered by insurance. Kemble, already heavily in debt because of his recent investment in the patent, was nearly ruined. But friends rallied 'round, and a bond issue of £50,000 was subscribed to by the King, the Duke of York, and the public. The Duke of Northumberland made a gift of £10,000. A cornerstone for a new theatre designed by Smirke was laid on the same site by the Duke of York on 31 December 1808, just three months after the conflagration. The company meanwhile acted from 26 September to 3 December 1808 at the King's Theatre and was housed for the remainder of the season at the Haymarket.

At the conclusion of the makeshift season Kemble joined Mrs Jordan for a tour of Ireland, making his first appearance in five years at the Crow Street Theatre in Dublin on 15 May 1809. For his benefit on 12 June he acted Alexander in *The Rival Queens*. It was reported that he made £1400 during his two months in Ireland.

The new Covent Garden Theatre was a huge cavern, badly designed for sight and sound. Boaden described the halls, stairways, lobbies, and salons as "really wretched, when compared to the contrivances of Wyatt at Drury-Lane," but he judged the stage itself "certainly the most perfect with which I am acquainted." The building had been erected at a "hand-gallop, without check, without control, without superintendence," while Kemble was in Ireland. Just one year after the terrible fire it was ready. Kemble did take charge of the events leading up to the gala opening, which occurred on 18 September 1809 and was prelude to the most miserable three months of his life.

About a week before the opening the management announced the "absolute necessity" of raising prices from 6s. to 7s. in the boxes and from 3s. 6d. to 4s. in the pit. Additionally they reduced the number of available gallery seats by building 26 private boxes, a provision which for many of the public portended the intrusion of what Holcroft called "unhappy or improper persons"—that is, prostitutes. The situation was made worse by the engagement, at a fee of £75 per night, of the celebrated Italian soprano, Mme Catalani. When the theatre was inaugurated on 18 September 1809 with a lavish production of *Macbeth* it was jammed by a very ill-tempered public that soon became a frightening mob. Upon his appearance to read Horace Twiss's prologue ("positively the worst poetry in the English language"), Kemble was greeted by catcalls and whistles which rendered him inaudible. The cries of "Old Prices!" swelled up, and for the rest of the night not a word spoken by Kemble, Mrs Siddons, or anyone else could be heard. Kemble numbly persisted while the audience stood on the benches, their backs to the stage. The battle was drawn when at two in

Harvard Theatre Collection

JOHN PHILIP KEMBLE
engraving after Lawrence

the morning Kemble called constables to persuade the ugly rioters to leave. The hooting
continued through *The Beggar's Opera* on the
second night (When a riot threatens "always
act an Opera" wrote Kemble in his journal for
1791, "for Musick drowns the Noise of the
Opposition"), and through Cooke's attempt at
Richard III on the third night.

A blue-ribbon committee, consisting of Sir
Charles Price, Bart, M.P.; Sir Thomas Plumer,
the Solicitor General; John Sylvester, Recorder
of the City of London; John Whitmore, Governor of the Bank of England; and John Julius
Angerstein, after a careful investigation of the
theatre's books for the previous six years reported in favor of the management, stating
that the rate of profit had averaged 6⅜ percent, or £8345 6s. 2d. on a capital of about
£130,900. Total receipts for the six seasons
preceding 1809–10 were £365,983 17s. 1d.,

an average of £60,997 6s. 2d. per season, but
the annual disbursement was £52,652, or
£263 per night. In all, the proprietors cleared
about £37 per night, a very modest amount
considering the investment and work. It was
the committee's judgment that at the proposed
increased prices the annual profit would
amount only to 3½ percent because of insurance costs and other factors of amortization,
and if the old prices were retained the proprietors would suffer an annual loss of ¾ percent
upon their capital.

The rioters were not impressed with the
figures. Despite humiliating appeals from the
stage by Kemble and other attempts to dis-
suade the rioters, including legal means, the
disturbances continued for 67 nights. Poor
Kemble became the central focus of abuse. The
Earl of Carlisle wrote to Edward Jerningham
that he had gone twice to Covent Garden, once
to see the riot and another time to hear the
play. He had no trouble hearing and seeing the
riot, but of course he did not hear the play.
"The tumult was disgraceful to the country,"
wrote Carlisle, "but Kemble produced the vio-
lence by the absurdity and arrogance of [his]
behaviour." Kemble was accused of fueling the
fire by sending prize fighters (some of whom
were described as athletic Jews) into the house
to attempt to quell the disturbance. A number
of medals were struck at the time and worn by
the rioters as proud badges. One of these
showed John Bull on an ass which bore Kemble's face, another pictured Kemble's head
wearing a fool's cap, and a third depicted Kemble's head with an ass's ears, representing avarice and folly and bearing the ugly inscription
"This is the Jew which Shakespeare drew."

The press for the most part sided with the
public and their champion, a barrister named
Henry Clifford. He had charged that he had
been grievously set upon by the boxkeeper
Brandon, and in a jury trial before Justice
Mansfield, Clifford was awarded token dam-
ages of £5.

Some interpreted the riots as a rebellion by
consumers against unfair merchandizing practices. Others, like William Corbett, saw them
as a clear violation of the rights of property
and deplored the "attempt to compel people to
sell entertainment at the price pointed out by
the purchaser." A body of polemic literature

was spawned, including the following hand-bill:

Britons be firm!—your private RIGHTS *maintain,*
In spite of KEMBLE, *and his Venal Train;*
Disdain submission to a Tyrant's Will,
Nor JEWS! *nor* ORDERS! *o'er [e'er] this House*
    shall fill;
No Crim. Con. Boxes SHALL *our sight disgust,*
Remember, KEMBLE, *that what must be, must!!*

The Old Price Riots finally ended on 14 December 1809 when Kemble joined the leaders of his opposition in a banquet at the Crown and Anchor tavern, with Clifford as toastmaster. Kemble was appropriately apologetic and a compromise was reached, which included the immediate dismissal of Brandon. The street ballad called "Uproar at Covent Garden Theatre," printed and sold by J. Pitts, sums up Kemble's unhappy state:

O DEAR! *what can the matter be?*
Dear, dear! what can the matter be?
O dear! what can the matter be?
King Johnny is all in a rage;

He laugh'd in his sleeve, call'd John Bull a fool
    sir,
He thought he was sure the fiat he could rule sir,
But alas, he has found he will not be a tool sir,
To any proud King of the Stage.
    O dear, &c.

He built a large house, they say, only for pride sir,
He thinks to gull us by the out-side sir,
But he'll find his mistake or else he is blind sir,
For Johnny don't mean to be Hoax'd.
    O dear, &c.

He engag'd Madam Catil they say, for her croak-
    ing
But that would not do, which was cursed provok-
    ing,
For Johnny Bull swore he'd have no such token,
Which made the great Johnny to cry.
    O dear, &c.

When the prices he rose he thought he was certain,
Not minding or caring, who he was hurting,
But his threats will turn out, all my eye Betty
    Martin,
The great John he's left in the dumps.
    O dear, &c.

Indeed the great John was "left in the dumps." Proud Kemble endured as Covent

Garden manager through 1811–12, but he could not overcome his bitterness or disillusionment. The double-pronged disaster of the fire and the riots had drained away his spirit and ambition, it seems, and turned him old in the prime of life.

Kemble struggled through the shambles of the first year in the new Covent Garden Theatre and then sought the summer stillness at Wroxton Abbey, Lord Guilford's seat. In 1810–11 his spirits no doubt were rejuvenated a bit by the enthusiastic reception the fickle public gave to his performances of Macbeth, Wolsey, Octavian, and Hamlet. He declined an offer of $5000 and expenses to play 80 nights in America. That summer he performed several weeks in Edinburgh. He acted his last new character, Brutus in *Julius Caesar*, on 29 February 1812, and was superb; it was a production, according to C. M. Young, that was "the greatest intellectual recreation." He acted Macbeth at Mrs Siddons's farewell performance on 29 June 1812 and wept on the occasion. At the end of the season, without much pomp or circumstance, Kemble himself decided to resign from managing and acting at Covent Garden. He also hoped to sell his share in the patent but at a price of £25,000 there were no takers. (In the Harvard Theatre Collection is a note, dated 9 March 1812, for £24,000, signed by John Philip Kemble to George White, one of his partners.)

He acted at Liverpool, Edinburgh, and Dublin in the summer of 1812, played triumphantly at Bath and Bristol during the season, and returned to Edinburgh in February 1813. In the autumn he traveled with his wife and sister to Paris, where he was received with deference as his country's "grand tragique." He was in London again briefly in November to see Young act Antony in a version of *Antony and Cleopatra* that had been prepared by Kemble and was published that year. (Item 1677 in the auctioneer's catalogue of Kemble's library is: "Anthony [sic] and Cleopatra, 2 copies, corrected for the Stage by Mr. Kemble, and also two copies in MS.") Early in December 1813 he was once again in Dublin, acting Wolsey at Crow Street on the fourth. There he also played Zanga, Lear, Brutus, Shylock, Coriolanus, Macbeth, and Rolla, taking his benefit in the last to a "tumultuous" overflowing house on 20 December. The *Monthly Museum*

Nelson Gallery–Atkins Museum, Gift of Mrs Edwin W. Shields, Kansas City, Missouri

JOHN PHILIP KEMBLE as Rolla

by Lawrence

thought that he lacked vitality as Macbeth and that his Lear revealed nothing "beyond that we have formerly seen." The critic did not like "his falling on both knees," as Shylock, "in the public state to thank God for the ruin of Antonio."

After an absence of two years Kemble returned to the Covent Garden stage, as Coriolanus, on 15 January 1814, and his first entry was stupendous—"the whole pit rose simultaneously to welcome him," wrote Boaden, "and while he bent in grateful acknowledgment to the people before him, a circlet of *laurel* fell from the boxes at his feet." In 21 performances he made £1102 10*s*. A ledger sheet in the Harvard Theatre Collection, signed by Kemble on 19 February 1814, acknowledges receipt of £840 for the first 16 nights of playing. All agreed that Kemble was at the height of his powers. But on the twenty-sixth of that month Edmund Kean acted Shylock at Drury Lane. The gratification and security that Kemble had felt earlier that month faded as the London public turned to worship a new idol. All now was Kean's. "The old man's sun was setting," as Herschel Baker put it, "and he realized it, but to the last he held his place: the first gentleman of the stage was not one to scurry away in terror before every young pretender." Though many critics, like Hunt, deserted him in ecstasy over Kean, Hazlitt, who was no great proponent of Kemble, at least remembered that he was a magnificent actor: "Mr Kemble stood on his own ground, and stood high on it."

During his last two seasons on the stage Kemble was really preparing for his retirement. In 1815 he published *A Select British Theatre*, a collection in eight volumes of his alterations for the stage. In 1817 he published a revision of his essay on *Macbeth, and King Richard the Third*. During 1814–15 he announced four times his intention to act Falstaff in *1 Henry IV* on 22 May, but illness prevented his doing so, and he never did act the role. Mathews reported that Kemble had rehearsed the part twice and "had a very good conception of it, but did not possess physical powers to execute it." He performed in Edinburgh in March of 1815 and 1816.

When Kemble became quite ill in May 1816 false news of his death circulated about town. When he acted Macbeth on 8 June 1816

the *Times* described him as "the ruin of a magnificent temple, in which the divinity still resides." In the summer of 1816 he gave a somewhat pathetic farewell performance of Othello at Dublin, to a half-filled house; according to Macready, who was there, Kemble "walked through the play" and the audience's reception was as frigid as the recitation—not one round of applause as the curtain fell in silence. He had worked up some energy, however, by the time he played Coriolanus in Liverpool, where he was well-received as usual. He then relaxed at Haddo House, Lord Aberdeen's estate in Scotland.

Kemble's final season on the stage commenced with a round of the established repertoire. In January 1817 he played at Bristol, and in March he traveled to Edinburgh for his last appearances there, acting Penruddock, Wolsey, Coriolanus, Richard III, Hamlet, and, for his final performance on 29 March, Macbeth. On the last night he sobbed through a speech of appreciation which Sir Walter Scott had helped him write:

> As the worn war-horse at the trumpet's sound
> Erects his mane, and neighs and paws the
>   ground—
> Disdains the ease his generous lord assigns,
> And longs to rush on the embattled lines,
> So I, your plaudits ringing on my ear,
> Can scarce sustain to think our parting near;
> To think my scenic hour for ever past,
> And that those valued plaudits are my last.
> But years steal on—and higher duties crave
> Some space between the theatre and grave;
> That, like the Roman in the capitol,
> I may adjust my mantle, 'ere I fall.
> . . . .
> But my last part is play'd, my knell is rung,
> When e'en your praise falls fault'ring from my
>   tongue;
> And all that you can hear, or I can tell,
> Is—friends and patrons, hail, and fare ye well!

At a banquet attended by Edinburgh's elite, he was presented with a gold snuffbox (purchased from London for about 80 guineas).

Returning southward he played at Newcastle and arrived in London early in May. That month and the next he offered a final roll call of the best roles of his career, which had begun at least 50 years before in his father's strolling company. Thirty-four of those years had been spent on the London stage.

Kemble's last efforts, sorry to say, were distinguished only by the nature of the occasion. Hazlitt thought his Posthumus on 30 May "feeble and unimpassioned." As King John on 14 June he was "hollow and artificial," and ill, to boot. His Stranger on 21 June, however, remained superb. It was a good time to retire, the painter Lawrence regretfully wrote—"His personal powers are much weakened, & his formal, measured stiffness more expressed than when He was younger."

All the boxes had been let two weeks in advance for the final night of 23 June 1817. Even the pit was jammed with persons of rank and distinction, including the great Talma, come from Paris to witness the passing of an era. When Kemble came on as Coriolanus the house arose for a five-minute ovation. And Kemble, it was reported, played "with an abandonment of self-care, with a boundless energy, a loose of strength, as though he felt that he needed to husband his powers no longer." The curtain fell on the prostrate Roman to cheers and shouts of "No farewell!" After a few moments of respite in his dressing room Kemble came forth to deliver an affecting address, in which he said, in part:

Ladies and Gentlemen, I entreat you to believe, that, whatever abilities I have possessed,—either as an actor, in the performance of the characters allotted to me,—or as a manager, in endeavouring at a union of propriety and splendour in the representation of our best plays, and particularly of those of the divine Shakespeare;—I entreat you to believe that all my labours, all my studies, whatever they have been, have been made delightful to me, by the approbation with which you have been pleased constantly to reward them.

It was the kind of speech that Garrick could and did make openheartedly and without inner reservation. Kemble, like Garrick on a similar night, was deeply moved and almost overcome by tears, yet he spoke his final words, according to Boaden, "with hurry, and eagerness to be relieved." Garrick's night had been a national event. Kemble's, though somewhat less momentous, was full of honest sentiment and respect for the last of the Romans. In Hazlitt's account of the event in his *General View of the English Stage*—he was a critic who claimed never to be able to find the heart in Kemble—a melancholy aura pervades:

. . . There is something in these partings with old public favourites exceedingly affecting. They teach us the shortness of human life, and the vanity of human pleasures. . . . It is nearly twenty years since we first saw Mr. Kemble in the same character; yet how short the interval seems. The impression seems as distinct as if it were of Yesterday. . . . We forget numberless things that have happened to ourselves, one generation of follies after another; but not the first time of our seeing Mr. Kemble, nor shall we easily forget the last. *Coriolanus*, the character in which he took his leave of the stage, was one of the first in which we remember to have seen him; and it was one in which we were not sorry to part with him, for we wished to see him appear like himself to the last. Nor was he wanting on this occasion: he played the part as well as he ever did—with as much freshness and vigor. There was no abatement of spirit and energy—none of grace and dignity: his look, his action, his expression of the character, were the same as they ever were: they could not be finer.

Hazlitt's name is not to be found among the list of 336 persons who subscribed two guineas each for their tickets to Kemble's farewell dinner at the Freemasons' Tavern on 27 June 1817. The record of the events of that night were preserved in *An Authentic Narrative of Mr. Kemble's Retirement from the Stage; Including Farewell Address, Criticisms, Poems, &c. Selected from various Periodical Publications; with an Account of the Dinner given at the Freemasons' Tavern, 27 June 1817; an Alphabetical List of the Company Present; Speeches of Lord Holland, Mr. Kemble: Mr. Campbell's Ode, &c. &c. To which is prefixed, an Essay, Biographical and Critical*, published on 5 August 1817. During the festivities, which lasted until after midnight, 21 toasts were drunk, a group of "Vocal Gentlemen" rendered nine songs and anthems, Young spoke Campbell's "Pride of the British Stage," and a band played selections from Handel. Ten speeches and replies were made. A silver medal worn by the committee had been especially struck by Warwick for the occasion; it showed Kemble's profile on one side and contained the legend "Thou Last of all the Romans Fare Thee Well" on the other. A silver vase by Flaxman, bearing a long inscription by John Poole, was intended for presentation but was not finished in time. The present location of the vase is not known.

Through careful arrangement of his personal and professional financial affairs, Kemble's years in retirement were comfortable. With his wife he traveled in Scotland and then in France, stopping at Paris for some months and settling at Toulouse for over a year. Southern France brought him tranquillity and improving health; but eventually he found it too expensive, so in the spring of 1820 he moved up to Lausanne. The death of his partner Thomas Harris brought him back to London in November 1820 to settle his involvement in Covent Garden. His house on Great Russell Street having been sold he visited with his brother Charles's family on Gerard Street. His niece, young Fanny Kemble, remembered him then as remotely dignified, white-haired, and good-natured. In order once and for all to free himself of litigation he gave Charles his entire one-sixth holding in Covent Garden. The gift was calculated to be worth about £45,000, but it was an investment hardly likely to yield a profit. John sold his library and furniture, made his will, and returned by year's end to Switzerland. His last years at Lausanne were spent gardening, reading (supposedly he read his Bible daily), and talking to local friends. His sister Sarah visited, as did other English travelers on occasion. Mrs Kemble wrote home of their contentment in their beautiful situation overlooking Lake Geneva and the mountains.

In the autumn of 1822 Kemble journeyed to Italy, for the first time. He admired Venice, but Rome, of course, was the object of his greatest curiosity and admiration. When the annual malaria began, he made the hard trip back to Lausanne, where he arrived exhausted. It appeared that his health had rallied during the winter, but he suffered a stroke on Monday, 24 February 1823. He died two days later, on Wednesday morning, 26 February 1823. He was buried on 1 March in a black marble vault in the foreign cemetery on a hillside outside Lausanne. The service was conducted by Mr. Cheesebrough, resident Protestant clergyman to the English colony, all of whom attended. In a letter to London just after Kemble's death, Cheesebrough described the late actor as a member of his "little flock," so it appears that Kemble had turned from Roman Catholicism. Boaden rationalized, "He avoided the indecency of disclaiming the *mode* of religion followed by his father; and looked only to its *vital* character. If the most enlarged charity towards

ALL men be *foolishness* to the Catholic, I then, from his repeated declarations, pronounce Mr. Kemble to have been a Protestant."

Rules of the cemetery at Lausanne prevented his widow from raising a monument to him. A statue of Kemble as Cato, executed by Hincliffe after a design by Flaxman, was placed in the north transept of Westminster Abbey, though prejudicial objections to immortalizing "a mere player" were raised in the press in August 1824. In 1865, with the permission of his niece Fanny Kemble, the statue, a poor piece of sculpture, was removed from the Abbey. Two cenotaphs to the memory of Kemble and Mrs Siddons have been placed in St Andrew's Chapel, in the Abbey. A street in Covent Garden, formerly Princes Street, was given his name.

Kemble had made his will on 22 November 1820 during his last visit to London. In it he described himself as late of Great Russell Street and at present residing in Argyle Street. The full value of his estate is unknown, but it was substantial. Kemble left his wife Priscilla an annuity of £1000 from leases he had out to George Lambton of Durham. She received all his household goods and effects and the interest from £17,000. She could dispose of £4000 of that amount at her pleasure but the remaining £13,000 was marked for Charles Kemble, as residual legatee. His sisters Ann Hatton and Jane Mason received annuities of £60 and £20, respectively. The former complained bitterly in her letters about John's callously cutting them off without providing the comfort he easily could have assured them. Kemble directed that the remainder of his estate be converted to cash for purchasing more annuities for Priscilla. The will was proved at London by Priscilla and Charles Kemble on 26 April 1823.

Priscilla Kemble survived her husband by 22 years, dying at Leamington in 1845 at the age of 87. Kemble had no children, but he was related through his family and his wife's to a vast network of theatrical families which extended into the twentieth century and included the surnames Ward, Banks, Siddons, Hopkins, Sharp, Menage, Murray, Frieze, Barnett, Whitlock, Satchell, Bland, Betterton, Glover, and De Camp.

Most of Kemble's worldly goods had been disposed of before his death. The house at No

89, Great Russell Street, was occupied after Kemble left London by Alexander Murray, his solicitor, and eventually was absorbed in the British Museum. In 1818 Kemble had sold his theatrical costumes to the Covent Garden proprietors for £300; in the Harvard Theatre Collection is his autographed receipt of £15 annual interest that year for the wardrobe debt. His furniture and effects were auctioned by Messrs Robins of the Great Piazza in Covent Garden on 14 and 15 December 1820. The 111 lots listed in the sales catalogue included fine furniture, mirrors, a billiard table, numerous wines, and services of Nankin and English china.

Kemble had also amassed a valuable and extensive library. In 1798 Thomas J. Mathias wrote in *The Grove*: "Mr. Kemble, having no children, has now adopted the off-spring of ancient authors. . . . His fondness for obsolete books has obtained him, among the book-auction *cognoscenti*, the name of *Black-Letter Jack*. In pursuit of his propensity . . . [he] will outbid 'titled heads, and even Nicol [the king's bookseller] himself." On 24 January 1814 the actor "Gentleman" Smith wrote to his banker-friend Coutts that Kemble "persuades the ignorant that he is classical novel & learned, & would convince his followers that Garrick was ignorant & unletter'd." Smith's remark was ungenerous in light of Kemble's fine classical education and evident intellectual capabilities. Kemble's purpose, which he began to pursue soon after his London debut, was to buy every early play he could get his hands on. He also was an assiduous collector of "everything collateral to his art" and thus he gathered the ephemera of theatrical history. His general library, moreover, was a remarkable collection, really much more than "the library of a highly cultivated and learned English gentleman" characterized by Baker. As Joseph Donohue points out in *Dramatic Character in the English Romantic Age*, the intellectual endowments Kemble gained from his library were brought to bear with full effect on his characters and productions. He studied the details of dress, architecture, and manners in "the antiquities of his own and other countries," wrote Boaden, for to be "critically exact was the great ambition of his life."

Kemble's collection of old plays, especially the priceless Elizabethan quartos, did rival and then exceed Garrick's. And his collection of theatrical documents, especially playbills was extraordinary. A letter now in the Folger Shakespeare Library contains Kemble's reply on 19 October 1798 to a request from the editors of the *Monthly Mirror*:

. . . As the Collection of Play-bills, which they mention so flatteringly, consists of above a hundred Quarto volumes, to read them all would be putting them to Trouble and Expence unnecessarily. Perhaps the Proprietors would do Mr. Kemble the Pleasure of saying to what Year their Enquiries refer, or whereabouts, and then that Volume should be immediately sent. . . . Or if they prefer commissioning any Gentleman to call and search the Play Bills, Mr. Kemble will be very happy to see him.

Like Garrick's, Kemble's library informed the leading scholars of his day—William Gifford, for example, used it to prepare his edition of Jonson—and, like Garrick's, it has served scholars as an invaluable resource since.

Upon retirement Kemble sold 4000 plays and 40 volumes of playbills to William Spencer Cavendish, sixth Duke of Devonshire, for £2000. The Devonshire Collection, considerably expanded to more than 7500 plays and 111 volumes of playbills, was bought at Sotheby's in 1914 by Henry Huntington and now constitutes the nucleus of the marvelous theatrical resources in the Huntington Library. The remainder of Kemble's library, portraits, and prints was auctioned by Evans at No 93, Pall Mall, in a 10-day sale that began on 26 January 1821. An annotated sales catalogue in the Harvard Theatre Collection reveals that 1677 separate titles, 181 prints and drawings, and many manuscripts and notebooks brought a total of £2575. Kemble's First Folio of Shakespeare, according to Ryan's *Table Talk*, was purchased for £112 7s. by Boswell. After Kemble's death his widow had his Lausanne library shipped to London; she wrote to her solicitor Murray from Cheltenham on 19 August 1823:

Many thanks for your information with regard to the arrival of the Books—but I had not the least idea being sent to Hambourgh that they would have cost so much in coming over—as to a Catalogue—the state of mind we were all in at the time they were packed, made it forgotten—and George [Kemble's man-servant] says there is none—I think if you think it not an improper request that Mr

Courtesy of the Garrick Club

SARAH SIDDONS as Lady Macbeth and JOHN PHILIP KEMBLE as Macbeth
by Beach

Payne the Bookseller of Pall Mall who had the care of all Mr Kembles Library before it was disposed of would if I wrote to ask give them Warehouse Room 'till I knew when I shall eventually fix myself. . . . I shall do all you desire with regard to the deeds—the purchase of my Carriage and various expenses will make this a heavy ½ year to me however I must regulate myself accordingly—I am in spirits and health just as I was and I am very sorry I have taken my House till May, as I am not at all better for the waters indeed with an afflicted mind what medecine can be of much use.

In addition to the collection of Kemble materials at the Huntington Library, important caches of his letters, notebooks, annotated journals, and other manuscripts are in the British Library, the Harvard Theatre Collection, and the Folger Shakespeare Library. His many promptbooks at the Folger Library have recently been published in a facsimile collection edited by Charles Shattuck. Also at the Folger are 33 bound quartos of Kemble's most important parts; the characters' speeches and cue lines are written out in his own hand.

Handsome, elegant, and intelligent, Kemble cut a formidable figure in society. His charm and dignity made him seem to the manor born, and by position and talent he was able to cultivate the cultivated almost to the extent that Garrick had. In certain respects, Kemble actually consorted higher, having been among the earliest confederates of the Prince Regent, later George IV. He enjoyed the company of Lord Barrymore, Lord Derby, the Duke of Norfolk, and John Ballantyne. He visited for long periods with Francis North, fourth Earl of Guilford, at Wroxton Abbey, where they often sat into the middle of the morning drinking themselves into a stupor. He was a frequent guest at Bentley Prior, Lord Abercorn's country estate, described as "the resort of the most distinguished part of the fashionable world." Haddo House, the Earl of Haddo's estate at Aberdeen, often gave comfort to Kemble after his drinking bouts and trials of management and provided a retreat where he could work up new roles.

Kemble's relationship with Thomas Lawrence improved over the years, and that painter's enormous romantic portraits of the actor remain the most impressive and familiar. The sculptor John Flaxman and Sir Joshua Reynolds were his companions, as were the artists Francis Bourgeois and Noel Joel Desenfrans, all of whom did portraits of him. Bourgeois and Desenfrans left him money in their wills.

Walter Scott was a good friend and a warm correspondent. Kemble dined often with Edmund Malone and visited the Piozzis at Streatham. Sheridan, of course, was his working associate, but they also socialized frequently. Often when Kemble appeared at the Sheridans' for dinner, the incorrigibly unreliable Sherry would fail to come home. A decorous loyalist, Kemble closed the theatre for royal misfortunes: on 24 January 1793 because of the death of the French king and on 11 March 1802 because of the funeral of the Duke of Bedford. In the former instance, according to Michael Kelly, Sheridan was incensed, it being "an invariable maxim with him that neither politics nor religion should be taken notice of in his playhouse."

The private Kemble could be aloof and intimidating. His imperious manner caused both friends and enemies to call him "Black Jack." But Walter Scott crowned him "King John," and the *Thespiad* (1809), in deference to his intellectual bent and classical disposition, called him the "Euclid of the Stage." His vanity sometimes became ridiculous. It was said by Samuel Rogers that while residing at Lausanne Kemble resented the homage paid to Mont Blanc. His gallantry involved him in several scrapes, and his acceptance into the Sublime Society of Beefsteaks belies his reputation for piety and signifies his clubbability. He and his brother Charles were privileged frequenters of the Wrekin, a "coffee house" in Broad Court which served only wine to its select visitors. Though Cooke and Kean earned far greater notoriety for their drinking, which with each was a sickness, it is clear that Black Jack often heard the chimes at midnight. Boaden wrote apologetically that drink made Kemble "utterly and mischievously ungovernable," and indeed it often did. When sober Kemble could sit for hours with company and speak little. He would resent boisterous or off-color conversation. But when drunk, he was himself oafishly unpleasant—witness the attack upon Miss De Camp—and abandoning his habitual dignified modesty he would praise his own talents extravagantly. Anecdotes relate how immoderate drinking would start him from his seat to swear that he was a member of Parliament and to begin a declamation, as though he were addressing that body.

Nevertheless, his colleagues seem to have had the highest esteem for Kemble's talents and leadership. For many years he was a trustee of the actors' fund. Occasionally his sometime haughty manner put off his colleagues. Mrs Jordan wrote to the Duke of Clarence on 6 June 1809 from Dublin that Kemble, then performing there with his sister, was "very much *disliked* in *private*." But then Dorothy

Jordan was an old enemy who enjoyed tweaking Kemble; she informed her Duke in the same letter that "Kemble is in a rage at my being here so long before the conclusion of his engagement. Mrs. K. says it was on purpose to injure her husband." During that two-month engagement in Dublin, however, Mrs Jordan did not make as much money as she expected while Kemble's Irish flocks brought him 1400 guineas.

Despite his drinking, most of the time Kemble behaved in an exemplary professional manner. On occasion, however, that prodigious memory which made it possible for him to ingest large roles in single gulps would fail him onstage. Possibly in those instances his mind was befogged by drink or, as with all actors at some times in their careers, he drew a blank because of temporary lack of concentration. Boaden reported that when Kemble acted Lear on 6 March 1792 the bustle of the audience at the box doors "caught his ear, and routed all his meditated effects; and he found it absolutely impossible to do that at night which he had thrown out during the rehearsal in the morning." Another spectator recalled (in *Notes and Queries*, 22 September 1866) seeing Kemble go blank in the last act of *Richard III* whilst giving instructions for the battle to Catesby. "The performer's bearing became somewhat disconcerted; every moment it grew worse." His furtive attempts to get help from the prompter failed. The tension was broken when Kemble stamped his foot on the stage and confessed, "I cannot recollect it." But no sooner done, than he recalled the lost line— "See that my staves be sound, and not too heavy"—and was rewarded by a good-natured round of applause. "Kemble bowed his thanks, and the performance proceeded without further interruption to its close." As one of his biographers put it, Kemble was a stylist both on and off the stage.

His correspondence with close friends and relatives reveals Kemble as a man of sensibility and sensitivity. He cared well for his mother and father in their golden years, he cultivated career opportunities for his brothers Charles and Stephen, and he had an affectionate relationship with his sister Sarah.

Kemble has been branded as champion of a chisled, cultivated classicism, the idol of a religion shattered by Kean. Leigh Hunt anatomized Kemble in 1807 as "a genius more compulsive of respect than attractive of delight."

He does not present one the idea of a man who grasps with the force of genius, but of one who overcomes by the toil of attention. He never rises and sinks in the enthusiasm of the moment; his ascension, though grand, is careful, and when he sinks it is with preparation and dignity. There are actors who may occasionally please more, but not one who is paid a more universal or profound attention.

Kemble occupied a position in the evolution of acting history which was at once a blessing and a curse. He lacked the quixotic spirit and the extraordinary emotional range that had made Garrick's acting so mercurial and affecting; he did not possess in any great measure the fiery passion that in Kean's acting consumed all before it. But he surpassed any one of his contemporaries. In his own right he must be accounted one of the great actors of the English stage.

"We feel more respect for John Kemble in a plain coat, than for the *Lord Chancellor* on the woolsack," wrote Hazlitt. It is a truism that Kemble belonged to—even created—the grand school. Essentially his acting was characterized as stately (some said academic and frigid), lacking in fire if not in force. Brander Matthews likened his acting to "the splendor of a towering iceberg; it was awful in its effect and overpowering." His full measure of Kemble beauty—"he had the finest head, perhaps, that has ever been seen," wrote Boaden—and his high intelligence made him unrivaled in characters of classic simplicity. William Charles Macready saw him act Cato at Covent Garden on 25 October 1816, shortly before retirement, and left an account which has memorialized his majesty:

. . . As he sat majestically in his curule chair, imagination could not supply a grander or more noble presence. In face and form he realised the most perfect ideal that ever enriched the sculptor's or the painter's fancy, and his deportment was in accord with all of outward dignity and grace that history attributes to the *patres conscripti* [the Roman Senate]. . . . The tragedy, five acts of declamatory, unimpassioned verse, the monotony of which, correct as his emphasis and reading was, Kemble's husky voice and laboured articulation did not tend to dissipate or enliven, was a tax upon the patience of the hearers. The frequently-recurring sentiments on patriotism and liberty, awakening no response were listened to with respectful, almost drowsy attention. But, like an eruptive volcano from some level expanse, there was one burst that electrified the house. When Portius entered with an exclamation,—

"Misfortune on misfortune! grief on grief! My brother Marcius,"—

Kemble with a start of unwonted animation rushed across the stage to him, huddling questions one upon the other with extraordinary volubility of utterance—

"Ha! what has he done?—
Has he forsook his post? Has he given way?
Did he look tamely on and let them pass?"

Then listening with intense eagerness to the relation of Portius,—how

"Long at the head of his few faithful friends
He stood the shock of a whole host of foes,
Till, obstinately brave, and bent on death
Oppress'd with multitudes, he greatly fell"—

as he caught the last word he gasped out convulsively, as if suddenly relieved from an agony of doubt, 'I am satisfied!' and the theatre rang with applause most heartedly and deservedly bestowed. This was his great effect—indeed his single effect; and great and refreshing as it was, it was not enough so to compensate for a whole evening of merely sensible cold declamation. I watched him intently throughout—not a look or a tone was lost by me; his attitudes were stately and picturesque but evidently prepared; even the care he took in the disposition of his mantle was distinctly observable. If meant to present a picture of Stoicism, the success might be considered unequivocal, but unbroken except by the grand effect above described; though it might satisfy the classic antiquary, the want of variety and relief rendered it uninteresting, and often indeed tedious.

Kemble's grandest character probably was *Coriolanus*. Galt asserted that "Had he only acted in that character he would have been deemed the very greatest male actor ever seen." In a letter from London on 19 June 1817, the actor John Howard Payne wrote:

I can never forget Kemble's *Coriolanus*; his *entrée* was the most brilliant I ever witnessed. His person derived a majesty from a scarlet robe which he managed with inimitable dignity. The Roman energy of his deportment, the seraphic grace of his gesture, and the movements of his perfect self-possession displayed the great mind, daring to command, and disdaining to solicit admiration. His

form derived an additional elevation of perhaps two inches from his sandals.

Scott, who admired Kemble in all his Roman roles, was most impressed with his "command of muscle and limb" when cut down by the three Volscian assassins: "There was no precaution, no support; he dropped as dead and as flat on the stage as if the swords had really met within his body." Kemble disdained "all that rolling, gasping and groaning" which which heroes usually died on the stage.

Hazlitt complained that Kemble played Hamlet "like a man in armour," but he was writing of the later years of Kemble's career when the character had crystallized. As Bertram Joseph points out, Kemble's later Hamlet was "the result of his conception of the part, not of his inability to act otherwise." Indeed he did play Hotspur with "speed and enthusiasm" and his energy in that role spawned a caricature of him with "robes acting like a windmill." His earlier interpretation of Hamlet, in fact, was marked by "pantomimic powers" and sudden transitions. When Horatio and Marcellus tried to hold him back from the Ghost, Kemble responded with "every vein tense and swollen," and in other places he impressed with what Brandes called an "outbreak of wildest fire." Reviewing his performance of the role on 19 September 1797 the *Morning Chronicle* reported: "The agitation of Hamlet in the course of the Play which he prepares to try the King, and his violent transports on gaining the certainty of his uncle's villainy by the effect of the piece were strongly characterized." In *A Short Criticism on the performance of Hamlet by Mr. Kemble* published in 1789 he was criticized for moving his arms about too much in the scene with the Ghost.

A certain melancholy in his face suited Kemble for Hamlet and if he had owned a "sweeter and fuller" voice he might have equalled, even excelled Garrick in the part. Kemble's Hamlet was inevitably compared to Garrick's and Henderson's. Arthur Colby Sprague in *Shakespearian Players and Performances*, in a chapter devoted to Kemble's Hamlet, reminds us that Kemble was the only English actor of distinction who was not called "natural" by his contemporaries, yet they regarded him as preeminent as Hamlet. Lamb found it difficult to "disembarrass the idea of

Courtesy of the National Gallery of Ireland

JOHN PHILIP KEMBLE as Raymond
by Sadler

Hamlet from the person and voice of Mr. Kemble." Boaden's description of his debut in the role at Drury Lane on 30 September 1783 points out Kemble's originality, insofar as he had no great actor to copy:

His style was formed by his own taste or judgment, or rather grew out of the peculiar properties of his person and his intellectual habits. He was of a solemn and deliberate temperament—his walk was always slow, and his expression of countenance contemplative—his utterance rather tardy for the most part, but always finely articulate, and in common parlance seemed to proceed rather from organization than voice. . . .

Kemble, according to James Winston, was 20 minutes longer in his performance of Hamlet than any of his contemporaries.

In roles like Richard III and Sir Giles Overreach, of course, he bowed to Kean and Cooke, perhaps because he associated tragedy with dignity rather than with the attributes of fire and cruel facetiousness. Incapable of the "dreadful energy" of Garrick as Richard III and inclined to see the character as "refined in manners," Kemble acted it, according to Boaden, with "greater *subtlety* than had usually been displayed." That subtlety deepened into a "triumphant expression of dignified scorn" in such successful portrayals as Edward the Black Prince, Varanes, and Pierre. He had not been commanding as Jaffeir in *Venice Preserv'd*, but his Pierre, the role he first acted in that play on 7 November 1805, was, in Hazlitt's words, a character not "of blunt energy, but of deep art," and "one of the happiest and most spirited of all Mr. Kemble's performances." It was an interpretation more sarcastic than fierce, wrote Hazlitt, "and even the fierceness is more calculated to wound others than to shake or disturb himself. He is a master-mind that plays with the foibles and passions of others and wields their energies to his dangerous purposes with conscious careless indifference." The character of Pierre was in accord with Kemble's own nature, and when he indulged in morbid rancorous raillery, his tone was "in unison with the actor's reluctant contemptuous personifications of gaiety."

Supposedly Kemble's inability to play a lover prevented him from shining in Othello and Romeo. In the former he was more philosophical than impetuous and in the latter,

Boaden explains, "the thoughtful strength of his features was at variance with juvenile passion." Lear eluded him essentially because although he was deeply affecting in places he could not soar, as had Garrick, into those sublime upper regions where unspeakable human anguish dwelt.

Though Kemble was clearly best in vehicles which evoked the beauty and grandeur of the antique, it is interesting to observe that the new characters in which he proved successful, like Penruddock, Rolla, Octavian, and the Stranger, were romantic and melodramatic. Moreover, Joseph Donohue has demonstrated in his detailed reconstruction of Kemble's portrayal of Macbeth and Mrs Siddon's of Lady Macbeth (*Theatre Notebook*, 22) the extent to which romantic ideas about tragic experience pervaded their performances of that play.

Kemble was not always at his best in comedy. Yet he was superb as Petruchio and as Valentine in *Love for Love* (in which he was in Lamb's opinion "faultless"). When he acted Don Felix opposite Elizabeth Farren as Viola in *The Wonder* one anonymous reviewer thought them inimitable: "The passions of love and jealousy are pourtrayed in their strongest colouring; and we, who well remember *Garrick*, think the acting of Kemble very little inferiour to him." No man, wrote Lamb, could better

deliver brilliant dialogue, the dialogue of Congreve or Wycherley, because none understood it half so well as John Kemble. . . . The relaxing levities of tragedy have not been touched by any since him; the playful court-bred spirit in which he condescended to the players in Hamlet, the sportive relief which he threw into the darker shades of Richard, disappeared with him.

Boaden observed that Kemble subscribed to Sir Joshua Reynolds's belief that the expression of violent passion "is not always the most excellent in proportion as it is the most natural," because displays of feelings in extremity cause a departure from "the deliberate and stately step, the studied grace of action, which seems to enlarge the dimensions of the actor, and alone fill the stage." Kemble's studied demeanor also can be explained, in part, by the constitutional asthma he suffered. In person he was "decidely heroic," wrote Scott, but he had to reserve his energy and wind for certain pas-

Princeton University Library

"Theatrical Leap Frog"

by Rowlandson

sages—those bursts of passion "to which he gave such sublime effect." He really lacked the endurance for Macbeth or Lear. By necessarily pacing himself he brought down upon his head accusations of being too refined, too studied, too frigid. Such restraint certainly annoyed Leigh Hunt.

Some observers, like John Taylor in *The Stage*, understood and appreciated Kemble's achievement despite the handicap:

Oft when the hurricanes of passions rise,
For correspondent tones he vainly tries,
To aid the storm no towering note combines,
And the spent breath th' unequal task declines:
Yet, spite of Nature, he compels us still
To own the potent triumph of his skill;
While the dread pauses, deepen'd accents roll,
Whose awful energy arrests the soul.

Kemble's diction was precise and his pronunciation punctilious. He possessed some affectations, such as deliberately broadening the letter *e*—beard was bird, cheerful was churful, fierce was furse—but despite these aberrations he was acknowledged the supreme master of elocution.

As a manager and producer Kemble preferred to offer a classical, tragic repertory, though financial exigencies and audience taste often dictated otherwise. Boaden wrote that Kemble "saw the elder dramatists, alone afforded him sufficient scope, and he was too excellent a critic not to feel the palpable deficiency of the writers for the modern stage." He read from 75 to 100 new plays each season but produced few of them and then usually only at Sheridan's insistence.

Kemble inherited Garrick's mantle as the high-priest of Shakespeare, and for some 30 years the public saw and heard their Shakespeare through Kemble's conceptions, interpretations, and alterations. One contemporary exclaimed that "no man has studied Shakespeare more critically—none more happily conceives him." Less impressed critics like Hazlitt, Shaw, Lounsbury, and others found his alterations barbarous and debasing.

By his series of Shakespearean revivals, however, Kemble earned for himself the title of first great "producer" of Shakespeare on the English stage (though some might believe that it more appropriately belongs to Garrick or even to the dramatist himself). In respect to scenery and costumes and other elements of stage production Kemble's claim would seem secure. His antiquarian interests stimulated what Donohue calls "innovations in atmospheric scene design," in the hands of Capon and Malton, in which were reflected the same concern for aesthetic unity "fundamental to the landscape gardening and Gothic architecture of the day." These efforts for stylistic unity, of course, also reflected his own concerns as an actor. The impetus Kemble gave in the direction of the illusion of reality was, in the view of most historians, his most influential legacy. Though his preference may have been for classical simplicity—as authentic as possible—from the earliest years of his management he showed a willingness to introduce eye-catching stage effects. His promptbooks reveal his skill in handling large crowds in spectacular processions and tableaux. Indeed, the larger theatres that later came under his direction necessitated a heavy concentration on the visual elements, as witnessed in his lavish production of *Macbeth* with which the new Drury Lane Theatre was inaugurated on 21 April 1794. (That production, with its 22 scenes and opulent costumes, is detailed by Donohue in *Theatre Notebook*, 21.)

Some 58 plays are attributed by Nicoll to Kemble. Most of these were alterations or arrangements of the works of earlier dramatists, including 29 plays of Shakespeare. Most were published, often in several editions, and the others are found, as noted above, in the Larpent Collection at the Huntington Library.

In addition to Nicoll's, other lists of his works are provided in *Biographia Dramatica* (1812), the *Cambridge Bibliography of English Literature*, and Carl Stratman's *Bibliography of English Printed Tragedy 1565–1900* (1966).

Many of Kemble's alterations were published as *A Select British Theatre; being a collection of the most popular stock pieces of the London Theatres (including all the acting Plays of Shakespeare), formerly adapted to the stage by Mr. Kemble*, 8 volumes (1816). Discussions of the alterations are found in H. Child, *The Shakespearian Productions of John Philip Kemble* (1935) and in Joseph Donohue's important *Dramatic Character in the English Romantic Age* (1970). The latter also offers an excellent treatment of Kemble's acting style, as does Bertram Joseph in *The Tragic Actor* (1959). The *Covent Garden*

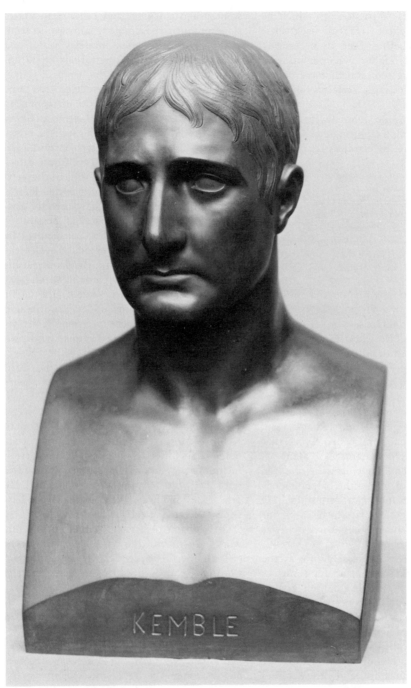

National Portrait Gallery

JOHN PHILIP KEMBLE

by Gibson

Journal (1810) by Stockdale gives a full account of the O. P. Riots, and a long list of works published about that event is provided in Arnot and Robinson's revision of Lowe's *Bibliographical Account of English Theatrical Literature*. Kemble's early poetic efforts were published at York in 1780 as *Fugitive Pieces*. His essay on *Macbeth and Richard the Third* was published in 1817 (the essay on *Macbeth* having appeared separately in 1786). A quarto volume entitled *Kembliana: being a Collection of the Jeu d'Esprits &c. that have appeared respecting King John* was issued in 1804.

Numerous specialty studies of particular aspects of Kemble's acting and producing have been published over recent years, especially in *Theatre Notebook*. Chief biographies include the anonymous *Life of John Philip Kemble, Esquire* (1809); John Ambrose Williams, *Memoirs of John Philip Kemble, Esq* (1817); James Boaden, *Memoirs of the Life of John Philip Kemble, Esq* (1825); Percy Fitzgerald, *The Kembles* (1871); and Herschel Baker, *John Philip Kemble: the Actor in His Theatre* (1942).

John Kemble was the subject of more original portraits and engravings than any other actor in this dictionary, except David Garrick and Sarah Siddons. No claim for completeness is made for the list that follows. The portraits are not described in detail. More information about a picture may often be found in the catalogue of the gallery owning it or in studies of the artist.

The iconography is organized as follows:

I. Original paintings and drawings of Kemble in private character, known now to exist or to have existed, listed alphabetically by *artist*. Engraved versions are sub-listed alphabetically by engraver.

II. Engraved portraits in private character for which no original paintings or drawings are known or identified, although an artist may have provided a design, listed alphabetically by *engraver*.

III. Original and engraved portraits in stage roles listed alphabetically by name of the *character* portrayed. Within the character listing, the items are given alphabetically by artist or engraver. Engraved versions of original portraits are sub-listed.

IV. Portraits in other media: sculptures, medallions, porcelains. Other Kemble artifacts.

For more convenient reference, we have placed in parentheses the numbers of the descriptions, when applicable, of engravings listed in the *Catalogue of Engraved Dramatic Portraits in the Harvard Theatre Collection*.

I. ORIGINAL PAINTINGS AND DRAWINGS IN PRIVATE CHARACTER.

1. By Beaumont. Present location unknown. Thomas Holcroft wrote on 31 July 1798 that "The head of Kemble painted by him [Beaumont] for Desenfans [a French art dealer] is a fine likeness, and a good picture."

2. By William Beechey. Oil on canvas. Exhibited at the Royal Academy, 1799. In the Dulwich College Gallery. Another version in the Garrick Club.

a. Engraving by Hopwood, published by Symonds, 1808. (1)

b. Engraving by Roberts, published as plates to the *Thespian Dictionary*, 1802 and 1805. (2)

c. By unknown engraver. (3)

d. Engraving by Mackenzie, in reverse. Published by Hurst, 1804. (4)

3. By J. Chinnery. Bust, full face, in fur-edged gown. Present location unknown.

a. Engraving by Edwin. Published as a plate to the *Mirror of Taste*. (9)

b. Engraving by Health. Published by Heath, and Daring & Thompson, 1799. (7)

c. Engraving by Holl. Published as a plate to the *Lady's Magazine*, 1817. (8)

d. By unknown engraver. Lithograph published with caption "Mr. Kemble from a picture by Lawrence." (10)

4. By George Clint. Present location unknown to us. A photograph is in the Harvard Theatre Collection.

5. By Richard Crosse, the deaf and dumb miniaturist of Henrietta Street, Covent Garden. Kemble sat for this artist on 6 November 1776 and 26 May 1780. Present location unknown.

6. By George Dance, 1795. Pencil drawing. Sold at Christie's on 1 July 1898, the property of the Reverend George Dance, "deceased," grandson of the artist. Present location unknown. Engraving by William Daniell, published 1810. (6)

7. By Samuel De Wilde. Head studies of John Kemble, Edmund Kean, Mary Wells, and Sarah Siddons, in pen and black ink, red chalk, pencil, and watercolor, on a single

sheet, 1802. In the Yale Center for British Art.

8. Attributed to Robert Dighton. Watercolor drawing. In the Garrick Club.

9. By John Emery. Supposedly the comedian Emery, while waiting in the wings at Sunderland, sketched a likeness of Kemble which later brought a very high figure. Present location unknown.

10. By John Gibson. Pencil drawing, quarter-length, profile to left. In the British Museum.

11. By John Gibson. Three studies in pencil, probably done in preparation for one of Gibson's busts of Kemble. In the British Museum.

12. By G. H. Harlow. At Rossie Priory.

13. By Horace Hone. Enamel, 1809. In the Garrick Club.

14. Attributed to Thomas Lawrence, probably the portrait exhibited at the Royal Academy, 1804. Seated, book resting on his crossed legs; right hand on arm of chair; left hand under chin, elbow resting on table. This portrait was sold in the Viscount Bedford sale at Christie's on 13 July, 1895, bought by Blakeslee for £273. In 1905 it belonged to Jacob Secker, art dealer of Brooklyn, from whom Francis Bartlett acquired it. In 1909 Bartlett gave it to the Boston Museum of Fine Arts, where it now resides. A copy, after Lawrence, is at Haddo House, Aberdeen.

a. Engraving by W. Say. Published by the engraver, 1814. (12)

b. By unknown engraver. Published by Johnson, Wilson, & Co, New York. (13)

15. Attributed to Thomas Lawrence, probably exhibited at the Royal Academy, 1797. Looking up, left; dark dress, high white stock. Owned by C. K. B. Wister of Philadelphia, by descent from Fanny Kemble.

16. By Thomas Lawrence. According to the *Gentleman's Magazine* of July 1845, at her death Mrs Kemble left a Lawrence portrait of her husband to the Earl of Aberdeen. A portrait described as "after Lawrence," now owned by the Earl of Haddo, at Haddo House, Aberdeen, is a copy of Lawrence's painting of Kemble that was exhibited in 1804; see above, No 14.

17. By Thomas Lawrence, Oil sketch. In the Garrick Club.

18. Possibly by Lawrence, about 1815. In dark green coat, white stock. Owned by Rowland Stephenson of Scaleby Castle, 1825; sold by John Gibbons at Christie's, 29 November 1912, bought by Freeman. A copy is in the Royal Shakespeare Theatre Gallery, Stratford-upon-Avon.

a. Engraving by C. Turner. Published as a plate to Boaden's *Life of Kemble*, 1825.

19. By Thomas Lawrence. "Satan Summoning up his Legions," exhibited in 1797 at the Royal Academy, where it still hangs. The nude figure of Satan was posed for by the pugilist John Jackson, but the face is that of J. P. Kemble.

20. By Thomas Lawrence. Pencil sketch. In the Garrick Club.

a. Engraving by Cheesman. Published as a plate to *An Authentic Narrative of Mr. Kemble's Retirement from the Stage*, 1817. Proof in the Harvard Theatre Collection (15) with addition below title, "The last Likeness ever taken."

b. Engraving by Holl. (16)

c. Lithograph by Marlet, in reverse. Title in English and French. (17)

21. By John Opie. In red cloak, with flowing hair. Once the property of Mrs Gordon of Plymouth, from whom it was bought in 1883 by James C. Inglis, who still owned the picture in 1911. Present location unknown.

22. By Martin Archer Shee. Exhibited at the Royal Academy, 1800. In the Art Institute of Chicago, the gift of Mr and Mrs William Owen Goodman. A copy done in January 1825 by John Stephano Coydell of South Carolina was bought by a Mr Lawler for $40 at the Evert Jansen Wendell sale at the American Art Association, 15–20 October 1918.

a. Engraving by W. Sharp. Published, 1803. (18)

b. Engraving by W. Sharp, smaller than above. (19)

c. Engraving by Annan & Swan. Published as a plate to Doran's *Annals of the English Stage*. (20)

d. By unknown engraver. Published as frontispiece to Fitzgerald's *Lives of the Kembles*. (21

23. By Gilbert Stuart. In the National Portrait Gallery, presented by J. T. Delane.

a. Engraving by Ridley, after "Stewart," from a portrait in the possession of Mr Twiss.

Published as a plate to the *Monthly Mirror*, 1797. (23)

b. Engraving by Pinkerton. In the British Museum.

c. By unknown engraver. Published as a plate to Smeeton's *The Unique*, 1824.

24. By Amelia Twiss. Oil on ivory. In the Westminster Public Library.

25. By unknown artist. Listed as No 313 in the *Mathews Collection Catalogue*, but not at the Garrick Club.

26. By unknown artist. In the Garrick Club, painting presented in 1918 by Lieutenant Colonel Hugh Warrender and Sir Victor Warrender.

27. By unknown artist. Panel, seated, right arm resting on back of chair and thumb resting on lower lip. In the Victoria and Albert Museum.

28. By unknown artist. Oil painting. Kemble in blued steel and gilded corslet, right hand on heart. In the Royal Shakespeare Theatre Gallery, Stratford-upon-Avon.

II. ENGRAVED PORTRAITS IN PRIVATE CHARACTER FOR WHICH NO ORIGINAL PAINTINGS OR DRAWINGS ARE KNOWN OR IDENTIFIABLE.

29. Engraving by T. Cook. Published as a plate to the *Universal Magazine*, 1783. (5)

30. Engraving by J. C. Easling, after M. A. Shee. Published by the engraver, 4 May 1807. (22)

31. Engraving by W. N. Gardiner, after S. Harding. Published as a plate to the *European Magazine*, 1797. (11)

32. Engraving by J. Godbey, after R. K. Porter. Standing, full face, cup in left hand; with title, "Tragedy." Published by E. Orme, 1806.

33. Engraving by "M. & W." Bust, with facsimile of Kemble's note of acceptance to his farewell dinner. (36)

34. Engraving by Neeles. (24)

35. Engraving by R. Page. "From an original picture." Seated, hands joined. (25)

36. Engraving by R. Page. In armor, cloak with ermine trimming over right shoulder. Published as a plate to the *British Ladies' Magazine*, 1817. (37)

37. Engraving by E. Portbury. Medallion head. Reproduction of medal worn by the committee at Kemble's retirement dinner. Published as a plate to *An Authentic Narrative of Mr. Kemble's Retirement from the Stage*, 1817.

38. Engraving by W. Read. Published as a plate to *Dramatic Table Talk*, 1825. (27)

39. Engraving by Silvester. Ticket to Kemble's farewell dinner, with head, right profile. Published as a plate to *An Authentic Narrative of Mr. Kemble's Retirement from the Stage*, 1817. (28)

40. Engraving by "S. W." Bust profile on a sarcophagus, Tragic Muse standing at right. (29)

41. By unknown engraver. Published as a plate to the *Hibernian Magazine*, January 1783. (31)

42. By unknown engraver. Published by B. Crosby, 1795. (32)

43. By unknown engraver. Published by J. Robins & Co, 1823. (33)

44. By unknown engraver. Seated, legs crossed, holding a book on knees. (30) Though identified in Harvard Theatre Collection as of John Philip Kemble, we find that attribution doubtful.

45. Satirical print: "Apollo in Danger." An assault on Apollo is made by Tartar horsemen, headed by a woman (Mrs Henry Johnston, the actress). Kemble has her charger by the tail. Satire on the production of *Timour the Tartar* at Covent Garden on 29 April 1811. Engraving by "Luigi Senzanome" [De Wilde?]. Published in *The Satirist*, June 1811. *Catalogue of Political and Personal Satires in the British Museum*, No 11,772.

46. Satirical print: "The Centaur-ian Manager." Kemble as a centaur serves as a mount for Mrs Siddons. A satire on equestrian performances at Covent Garden. Engraving by "The Caricaturist General." Published in *The Satirist*, 1 October 1811. *Catalogue of Political and Personal Satires in the British Museum*, No 11,773.

47. Satirical print: "Melpomene in the Dumps, or Child's Play Defended by Theatrical Monarchs." Kemble attempts to placate Mrs Siddons, who had refused to appear on stage with Master Betty, the child prodigy. Engraving by Rowlandson. Published by Ackermann, December 1804.

48. Satirical print: "Theatrical Leap Frog." Young boy (Master Betty) jumps on Kemble's

back. Engraving by Rowlandson. Published by Ackermann, November 1804.

49. Satirical print: "Theatrical Mendicants relieved." The Duke of Northumberland gives Kemble £10,000 for rebuilding Covent Garden. Engraving by Gilray. Published by Humphrey.

The "Old Price Riots" spawned a number of satirical prints featuring John Philip Kemble. These included (with number in British Museum *Catalogue of Political and Personal Satires*):

50. "The *Set-Too* between *Old Price* and Spangle Jack the Shewman." Engraving by Williams. Published by Walker, October 1809. (No 11,420)

51. "Kings Place & Chandos Street in an Uproar." Engraving by I. and G. Cruikshank. Published by Fores, 20 October 1809. (No. 11,421)

52. "Is this a Rattle which I see before me?" Engraving by I. Cruikshank. Published by Fores, 30 October 1809. (No 11,422)

53. "A Parody on Macbeth's Soliloquy at Covent Garden Theatre." Engraving by Williams. Published by Walker, October 1809. (No 11,423)

54. "Imitation Bank-Note." Published by Fores, 1 November 1809. (No 11,424)

55. "Killing No Murder. As Performing at the Grand National Theatre." Engraving by I. & G. Cruikshank. Published by Tegg, November 1809. (No 11,425)

56. "The Strol^{rs} Pro^{ss}—p^{te} ^{3d}." Engraving by Cruikshank. Published by Tegg, November 1809. (No 11,427)

57. "The Strollers Progress Pl^{te} 5th." Engraving by Cruikshank. Published by Tegg, 9 November 1809. (No 11,428)

58. "The O P Spectacles." Engraving by I. & G. Cruikshank. Published by Tegg, 17 November 1809. (No 11,428)

59. "Counsellor O. P.—Defender of our Theatric Liberties." Engraving by Gilray. Published by Humphrey, 5 December 1809. (No 11,430)

60. "Imitation Bank-Note." Sold by Luffman, 5 December 1809 (No 11,431). A reissue, with year removed and 1818 inserted in pen, and imprint altered to "Sold by S. W. Fores 50 Picadilly." (No 11,431a)

61. "The Boxes." Engraving by Rowlandson. Published by Rowlandson, 12 December 1809. (No 11,433)

III. ORIGINAL AND ENGRAVED PORTRAITS IN STAGE CHARACTERS.

62. As Alexander in *Alexander the Great*. By unknown engraver. Published as penny-plain by West, 1818; as twopence-colored by De Burson, 1827. (39)

63. As Alexander. By unknown engraver. Published as penny-plain by West, 1828. (38)

64. As Alonzo in *Pizarro*. Engraving by Dighton. Published by the engraver, 1799. (40)

65. As Arthur, with Elizabeth Farren as Emmeline, in *Arthur and Emmeline*. Drawing by Thomas Stothard. In the Henry E. Huntington Library.

a. Engraving by Heath. Published by Lowndes, 1786.

66. Possibly as Arthur, with three other actors. Painting by Francis Wheatley. In the City Museum and Art Gallery, Birmingham. This painting usually has been regarded as a scene from *The Tempest*, but Phillipe Downes suggests that it may represent a scene from Kemble's *Arthur and Emmeline*. If so, then the other actors are William Brereton as Oswald, Francis Aickin as Merlin, and Elizabeth Farren as Emmeline. For further information see Elizabeth Farren's list of illustrations, in this dictionary, V, 174, No 26.

67. As Bajazet in *Tamerlane*. Painting by De Wilde. In the Garrick Club.

a. Engraving by Audinet. Published as a plate to *Bell's British Library*, 1792 (41) and as a plate to *British Drama*, 1808. (42)

68. As Barnwell in *George Barnwell*. Engraving by Murray, after Cruikshank. Published by J. Roach, 1799. This portrait was also engraved by Alais and labeled C. Kemble; probably it is of Charles, not John. (43)

69. As Beverley, with Mrs Siddons as Mrs Beverley, in *The Gamester*. Engraving by Alais. Published by Roach, 180?. (46)

70. As Beverley, with Mrs Siddons as Mrs Beverley. Engraving by T. Cook, after W. Miller. Published by T. Davies, 1783. In the British Museum.

71. As Beverley, with Mrs Siddons as Mrs Beverley, and two others. Engraving by Heath, after Stothard. Published as a plate to *New English Theatre*, 1783. (45)

72. As Beverley. By unknown engraver. (44)

73. As Cardinal Wolsey in *Henry VIII*. Engraving by J. Archer. (48)

74. As Cardinal Wolsey. Engraving by De Latre, after De Loutherbourg. Published by Kearsley, 1803. (47)

75. As Cardinal Wolsey in the Trial Scene in *Henry VIII*. By G. H. Harlow. The painting does not represent an actual performance, though the central figure is Sarah Siddons as Queen Katharine, and Stephen Kemble appears as Henry VIII and Charles Kemble as Cromwell. Harlow also painted many friends into the picture. For details on versions and engravings see our portrait list for Stephen Kemble, in this dictionary, No 15.

76. As Cato in *Cato*. By Samuel De Wilde. Watercolor drawing in the Harvard Theatre Collection.

77. As Cato. Engraving by Gauci, from the bust by J. Gibson. Published by N. Chater & Co, 1823. (51)

78. As Cato. Engraving by J. J. Lane, after J. Boaden. Published by J. Dickinson, 1826. (49)

79. As Cato. By Thomas Lawrence. Seated in large chair, hands holding scroll on lap, left foot on stool. Commissioned by the Earl of Blessington, then bought by John Burton Philips, Heath House, Tean. A replica by Lawrence, painted for Charles Mathews, is in the Garrick Club. A copy, sold several times in New York, was purchased at Parke-Bernet, 21–22 September 1945; buyer unknown.

a. Engraving by W. Greatbach. Published as a plate to *The Amulet*, 1833, and printed as a photogravure by Gebbie & Co, 1888. (53.54)

b. Engraving by S. W. Reynolds. Published by Colnaghi, 1841. (52)

c. Engraving by W. Ward.

80. As Cato. Engraving by Murray, after Cruikshank. (50)

81. As Cato. Drawing by T. Wageman, 1804? In the Beard Collection, Victoria and Albert Museum. Similar to the engraving by Rogers, after Wageman, published as a plate to *The Drama*, 1822. (55)

82. As Cato. Painting by Westall. Listed in the *Mathews Collection Catalogue*, but not in the Garrick Club. Probably this is the picture engraved by Audinet, after Westall, published as a plate to *Bell's British Library*, 1791. (57)

83. As Cato. Engraving by Woolnoth, after Wageman. Published as a plate to Oxberry's *New English Drama*, 1823. (56)

84. As Cato. By unknown engraver. Published as twopence-colored by Hodgson & Co. (58)

85. As Coriolanus in *Coriolanus*. Engraving by Alais. Published by Roach, 1806. (63)

86. As Coriolanus. Attributed to Thomas Baxter, 1806. Pen-and-ink watercolor. Sold for $90 as lot 98 in the auction of the property of the American Shakespeare Theatre, at Sotheby Parke Bernet, New York, 15 January 1976.

87. As Coriolanus. Oil by Peter Francis Bourgeois, exhibited at the Royal Academy, 1797. In Sir John Soane's Museum.

88. As Coriolanus. Engraving by I. R. Cruikshank. Published as twopence-colored by West, 1817. (60)

89. As Coriolanus. On a plate with Talma. Heads only, in clouds. Engraving by H. Dawe, after Lawrence and Gerard. Published by Dawe, 1832, (62)

90. As Coriolanus. Miniature ivory by T. Hargreaves, copy after Lawrence. In the Garrick Club.

91. As Coriolanus. Painting by G. H. Harlow. In the Garrick Club.

92. As Coriolanus. By G. H. Harlow. In the Folger Shakespeare Library; bought from Michelmore, 1928.

93. As Coriolanus. Engraving by R. J. Lane, after J. Boaden. Published by Dickinson, 1826. (59)

94. As Coriolanus. By Thomas Lawrence. Large picture (113 × 70½) exhibited at the Royal Academy, 1798. Originally puchased from Lawrence by Sir Richard Worsley. Now in the London Guildhall Art Gallery, presented by the Earl of Yarborough, 1906. A small copy, after Lawrence, is in the Victoria and Albert Museum. A copy by Washington Allston is in the Players Club, New York, the gift of Mrs W. H. Osborn, 1895. See also below, No 95.

a. Engraving by R. M. Meadows, 1805.

b. Engraving by W. O. Burgess. Published by Holloway, 1839. (61)

95. As Coriolanus. By Thomas Lawrence. A sketch for the larger finished picture, above No 94, was bought by Harrison in the Lawrence sale at Christie's, 15 May 1830 (lot 20). Garlick (*Catalogue of Paintings* of Lawrence) suggests that this sketch, presumably in oils, was the version "from the late President's col-

lection" sold in the W. H. Trent sale by Foster, 12 June 1832 (lot 139).

96. As Coriolanus. Watercolor by William Loftis, about 1792. In the Folger Shakespeare Library.

97. As Coriolanus. Engraving by H. Melvill. Published as a plate to Kemble's memoirs by J. A. Williams. (64)

98. As Coriolanus. By unknown engraver. (65)

99. As Dionysius in *The Grecian Daughter*. Engraving by Cruikshank. Published as penny-plain and twopence-colored by West, 1817. (66)

100. As the Duke of Norfolk in *Mary Queen of Scots*. Watercolor drawing by William Loftis, about 1792. In the Folger Shakespeare Library.

101. As Hamlet in *Hamlet*. Engraving by W. Barnard. (83)

102. As Hamlet. Caricature by G. Cruikshank. Titled "A startling effect." Published as a plate to Dickens's *Memoirs of Grimaldi*. (85)

103. As Hamlet. Lithograph by R. J. Lane, after J. Boaden. Published by Dickinson. (67)

104. As Hamlet, standing in graveyard, skull in left hand. By Thomas Lawrence. Large painting (120 × 78) exhibited at the Royal Academy, 1801. Bought by George IV in 1824 for 500 guineas. Presented in 1836 by William IV to the Tate Gallery. A smaller version was owned by the Earl of Northbrook in 1910; another (half-length) is owned by the heirs of W. H. Lee Ewart, Mont-au Prêtre, Jersey. A less-than-life-sized version, once in the Lord Leverhulme Collection, was bought by Henry Folger from Anderson Galleries, New York, in February 1926 for $1320; sold by the Folger Shakespeare Library to the American Shakespeare Theatre, Stratford, Connecticut, in February 1962. A repetition, an heirloom, is owned by C. K. B. Wister, Philadelphia, a descendant of Fanny Kemble. A copy, after Lawrence, bought from Michaelmore in 1928, is in the Folger Shakespeare Library. Another copy, after Lawrence, is reported to be in the Players Club, New York.

At least 14 engravers reproduced the picture:

a. Engraving by G. Adcock. Published as a plate to Jerden's *National Portrait Gallery*, 1833. Reprinted, 1834; another impression, 1844. (70)

b. Engraving by Beyer. (71)

c. Engraving by Bromley, 1834.

d. Engraving by J. C. Buttre. Published as a plate to an edition of the play, 1855. (72)

e. Engraving by H. Dawe. Published by James Bulcock. (68)

f. Engraving by J. Egan. Published by Hodgson & Graves, 1838. (69)

g. Engraving by C. Marr. Published by Virtue as a plate to *Cabinet Gallery* (73)

h. Engraving to S. W. Reynolds. Published by Boydell & Co, 1805. (74)

i. Engraving by J. Rogers. Published by J. Robins. Also reprinted. (75, 76)

j. Engraving by Sartain.

k. By unknown engraver. Published by Bulcock, 1834. (77)

l. By unknown engraver. Published as a plate to Tallis's *Dramatic Magazine*. (79)

m. By unknown engraver. (80)

n. By unknown engraver; lithograph. (81)

105. As Hamlet. By Thomas Lawrence. Pencil sketch for the painting. In the National Portrait Gallery, bequeathed by R. H. Bath, 1933.

106. As Hamlet. Painting, studio of Thomas Lawrence. In the Garrick Club. Oil sketch for the larger canvas in Tate Gallery.

107. As Hamlet, seeing the Ghost. Black chalk drawing by Thomas Lawrence, about 1800. In the Ashmolean Museum, Oxford.

108. As Hamlet. Watercolor and ink drawing, after Lawrence. Sold for $50 (lot 126) in the property of the American Shakespeare Theatre at Sotheby Parke Bernet, New York, on 15 January 1976.

109. As Hamlet. Drawing by unknown artist. In the Beard Collection, Victoria and Albert Museum. Full-length, left hand upraised, right hand holding sword, tip on ground. Identified as John; but possibly this shows Charles, because of similarity to lithograph of the latter in the role by De Valmont.

110. As Hamlet, standing, right hand upraised, extended to left, with book dropping from it. By unknown engraver (84). In "Kemble's Hamlet Costume," *Theatre Survey* (May 1972), Raymond Rentzell makes a case for this print being an illustration of the conversion made by Kemble to "modern dress' for his London debut and away from the traditional Van Dyke costume as Boaden reported.

111. As Henry V in *Henry V*. Watercolor

drawing by William Loftis. In the Folger Shakespeare Library.

112. As Henry V. Caricature by A. Scratch. Published as a plate to *Attic Miscellany*, 1789, with caption. "How to tear a Speech to tatters." Reprinted, as "Engraved for the Carlton House Magazine," with new title, "The Theatrical Ranter." (87)

113. As Henry V. By unknown engraver. (86)

114. As Hotspur in *1 Henry IV*. Engraving by J. Bailey. Published by the engraver as twopence-colored, 1828. (90)

115. As Hotspur and Glendower in *1 Henry IV*. Oil by Henry Fuseli. In the City Art Gallery, Birmingham. Supposedly Kemble sat for both characters for this scene, painted about 1784, but no documentary evidence has been found for this attribution. The painting is reproduced in F. Anatol, *Fuseli Studies*, 1956.

116. As Hotspur. Engraving by C. Picart, after J. Boaden. Published as a plate to the *Theatrical Inquisitor*, 1820. (88) A variant lithography by R. J. Lane was published by Dickinson. (89)

117. As Hotspur. By unknown engraver. Published as penny-plain by Fairburn. (91)

118. As King Charles in *King Charles I*. Engraving by Audinet, after De Wilde. Published as a plate to *Bell's British Library*, 1793. (93)

119. As King John in *King John*. Engraving by Cruikshank. Published as twopence-colored by West, 1817. (95)

120. As King John. Engraving by R. J. Lane, after J. Boaden. Published by Dickinson. (94)

121. As King John, with Robert Bensley as Hubert, 1793. Watercolor drawing by William Loftis. In the Folger Shakespeare Library.

122. As King John, with three other figures. By unknown artist. Oil painting in the Folger Shakespeare Library. Possibly representing a cast from 1793, including Aickin as King Philip, Phillimore as Austria, and Mrs Siddons as Constance.

123. As Jaffeir, with Mrs Siddons as Belvidera, in *Venice Preserv'd*. Engraving by J. Alais, after A. Buck. Published by J. Roach, 1802.

124. As King Lear, 1788. Watercolor drawing by William Loftis. In the Folger Shakespeare Library.

125. As King Lear, with Mrs Siddons as

Cordelia. Engraving by Reading, after Buck. Published by Roach, 1801. (96)

126. As King Lear. Watercolor drawing by unknown artist. In the Harvard Theatre Collection.

127. As King Lear. By unknown engraver. (97)

128. As Macbeth, with Mrs Siddons as Lady Macbeth. Painting by Thomas Beach, exhibited at the Royal Academy, 1786. Said to have been painted for Lord Le Despencer. Sold with his effects from Mereworth Castle. Also sold (lot 138) at Christie's on 9 May 1865 and at Puttick & Simpson's (lot 159) on 13 July 1921. Presented in 1940 by F. J. Nettlefold to the Garrick Club, where it now hangs.

129. As Macbeth. Lithography by R. J. Lane, after J. Boaden. Published by Dickinson. (98)

130. As Macbeth, 1792. Watercolor drawing by William Loftis. In the Folger Shakespeare Library.

131. As Macbeth, May 1794. Watercolor drawing by William Loftis. In the Folger Shakespeare Library.

132. As Macbeth. By Gilbert Stuart. The *Morning Chronicle* in February 1786 reported that Stuart "has made a head of Kemble for Macbeth, marvelously exact." Present location unknown.

133. As Macbeth. By unknown engraver. Published as twopence-colored by Dryer. (99)

134. As Macbeth. By unknown engraver. Published as penny-plain and twopence-colored by Hodgson & Co, 1823. (100)

135. As Macbeth. By unknown engraver. Standing, facing and looking to right. Figure and dress are nearly identical with a portrait of Garrick in the role by C. White, after Parkinson. (101)

136. As Macbeth. By unknown engraver. (102)

137. As Mentevole in *Julia*. Engraving by S. Harding. Published as a plate to the *Hibernian Magazine*, September 1788; reissued by Richardson, 1798. (103) An engraving in reverse, by an unknown engraver, was also issued. (104)

138. As Montgomeri in *The Carmelite*. By C. R. Ryley. The last scene of the fifth act as performed at Drury Lane on 2 December 1784; others in the painting include Aickin as De Courci, Smith as St Valori, Packer as Gyfford,

and Mrs Siddons as Matilda. "The Original Picture, from which no engraving has been made," sold as lot 1025 in the sale of the James Winston Collection at Puttick & Simpson's, 15 December 1849; bought by Makepeace for £7 7s. 6d. Present location unknown.

139. As Octavian in *The Mountaineers.* Engraving by Warburton, after Wellings. Published by Wellings, 1793. (105)

140. As Oedipus in *Oedipus.* Watercolor drawing by Samuel De Wilde. In the Harvard Theatre Collection.

a. Engraving by Thornthwaite. Published as a plate to *Bell's British Library,* 1791.

141. As Orestes in *The Distrest Mother.* Engraving by Chapman, after Moses. Published as a plate to *British Drama,* 1807. (107)

142. As Orestes. Painting by Gilbert Stuart. Mentioned in Boaden's *Life of Kemble* (1825) as being in the possession of the Reverend C. Este. Present location unknown.

143. As Penruddock in *The Wheel of Fortune.* Painting by Samuel De Wilde. In the Garrick Club. Similar to De Wilde's watercolor, below.

a. Engraving by Hopwood. Published as a plate to *The Cabinet,* 1808. (110)

b. Engraving by Scriven. Published by Bell & De Camp, 1809. Reprinted as a plate to the *Theatrical Inquisitor,* 1814. (109)

144. As Penruddock. Watercolor drawing by Samuel De Wilde. In the Garrick Club. Similar to De Wilde's oil painting, above.

145. As Penruddock. Pencil drawing by T. Wageman. In the Beard Collection, Victoria and Albert Museum.

a. Engraving by Wright. Published by Simpkin & Marshall, 1820. (111)

146. As Petruchio, with Mrs Charles Kemble (when Miss De Camp) as Catherine, in *Catherine and Petruchio.* Engraving by Alais, after Buck. Published by Roach, 1802. (112)

147. As Petruchio, with Mme Vestris as Catherine, and others. Painting by George Clint. Purchased by Henry C. Folger for $250 from E. Parsons, 1 September 1927. Sold by the Folger Shakespeare Library to the American Shakespeare Festival Theatre, Stratford, Connecticut, in February 1962. Sold for $650 in the auction of the property of the American Shakespeare Theatre at Sotheby Parke Bernet, New York, 15 January 1976; reproduced in the sales catalogue.

148. As Philaster in *Philaster.* By unknown engraver. (113)

149. As the Prince in *Edward the Black Prince.* Engraving by Audinet, after Hamilton. Published as a plate to *Bell's British Library,* 1791. (114)

150. As Walter Ralegh in *The Life and Death of Sir Walter Ralegh,* 1789. Watercolor by William Loftis. In the Folger Shakespeare Library.

151. As Raymond in *The Count of Narbonne.* Chalk drawing by William Sadler. In the Irish National Portrait Gallery.

a. Engraving by unknown artist. Printed for William Allen, Dublin.

152. As Richard, with Dorothy Jordan as Matilda, in *Richard Coeur de Lion.* By unknown engraver. Published by Alexander Hogg, 28 February 1787.

153. In the collection of Raymond Mander and Joe Mitchenson. As Richard III in *Richard III.* By William Hamilton. A canvas after Hamilton is in the Victoria and Albert Museum.

a. Engraving by F. Bartolozzi. Published by Darling & Thompson, 1794. (115)

b. Engraving by F. Bartolozzi. Published by Darling & Thompson, 1814. (116)

154. As Richard III. Pencil drawing by H. Harding. In the Garrick Club.

155. As Richard III. Watercolor by William Loftis, about 1792. In the Folger Shakespeare Library.

156. As Richard III. By Gilbert Stuart, 1786. Present location unknown.

a. Engraving by Houston. Published by Freeman & Co, Philadelphia, 1796, with artist's name spelled "Stewart." (117)

b. Engraving by Keating. Published by Boydell, 1788. (118)

c. Engraving by Meyer. Published as a plate to *The Cabinet,* 1808. (119)

d. Engraving by Rogers. Published as plate to Oxberry's *Dramatic Biography,* 1825, as by Harlow and "As Hamlet." (120)

e. Engraving by Thornthwaite and Browne. Published as a plate to *Bell's British Theatre,* 1786. (121) Painter's name spelled "Stewart."

157. As Richard III. By Thomas Sully, a copy of the painting by Stuart. According to a notation in the art file of the Huntington Library this portrait is in the National Gallery, Washington, but the Gallery's art information service records no portrait of Kemble by Sully.

158. As Richard III. Watercolor drawing by unknown artist. Sold for $3.00 to "GDS" in the Evert Jansen Wendell sale, American Art Association, New York, 15–20 October 1918.

159. As Rolla in *Pizarro*. Engraving by Alais. Published by Roach, 1807, and as a plate to the *Thespian Perceptor*, 1810. (132)

160. As Rolla. Oil painting on glass in three levels, attributed to De Loutherbourg. This scene from *Pizarro* shows Rolla, who "bears a remarkable likeness to Kemble," Pizarro, three soldiers, a palm tree, and a bridge over a waterfall. In the possession of Anthony Oliver and John Saunders, who reproduce and discuss the painting in *Theatre Notebook* (Autumn 1965). Raymond Mander and Joseph Mitchenson in *Theatre Notebook* (Summer 1966) reproduce and discuss an oil painting similar to the glass painting. The canvas, "belonging to a gentleman in Australia," bears the initials T. N. and the signature J. Simpson (perhaps John Simpson, who was a copyist in Lawrence's studio). Mander and Mitchell believe that the glass picture and the oil "derive from a 'lost' original of some integrity, perhaps by De Loutherbourg?" The scene shown in both renditions is the one illustrated in J. Fittler's engraving, after a drawing by E. Pugh, of a command performance of *Pizarro* at Covent Garden in 1804.

161. As Rolla. Drawn and engraved by R. Dighton. Published June 179[9]. In the Harvard Theatre Collection but not in the Hall catalogue.

162. As Rolla. Engraving by B. J. Holl, after Wageman. Published as a plate to Oxberry's *New English Drama*, 1824. (131)

163. As Rolla. By Thomas Lawrence, exhibited at the Royal Academy, 1800. Large painting ($11' \times 7'$); holding a child in left hand and staring at dagger held in right hand. The muscular figure was supposedly posed for by the pugilist John Jackson. The model for the child held aloft reputedly was the infant Charles Sheridan, son of R. B. Sheridan by his second wife, Esther Jane Ogle. Lawrence painted this scene over his picture of "Prospero Raising the Storm," which had been exhibited in 1793. Purchased from Lawrence by Sir Robert Peel. Bought by Robson at Peel sale, Robinson & Fisher, 10 May 1900; sold at Blakeslee sale in New York, 23 April 1915, to E. W. Shields, whose wife presented it to the Kansas

City Art Institute; on loan since 1947 to the William Rockhill Nelson Gallery of Art, Kansas City. In 1964 smaller versions were with Sir George Armytage at Kirklees Park, near Brighouse; A. E. Tail at Sunbury-on-Thames; and the Ruskin Gallery, Stratford-upon-Avon. Another smaller version, not signed but said to be by Lawrence, was bought by Lawler for $65 in the Evert Jansen Wendell sale, American Art Association, New York, 15–20 October 1918.

a. Engraving by H. Daw. (123)

b. Engraving by A. L. Dick. (124)

c. Engraving by Normand. (125)

d. Engraving by J. P. Quilley. Published by McCormick, 1832. (126)

e. Engraving by S. W. Reynolds. Published by Boydell, 1803. (127)

f. By unknown engraver. Published by Bulcock, 1834; another impression was issued with the publisher's name changed to J. & F. Harwood. (128)

g. By unknown engraver. Published by Holmes & Charles. (129)

h. By unknown engraver. With quotation, "Who moves one Step to follow me, dies on the spot." (130)

164. As Rolla, with Barrymore as Pizarro. Engraving by Rogers, after Harlow. Published as a plate to Oxberry's *Dramatic Biography*, 1825. (122)

165. As Rolla. Engraving by T. Milton, after A. Buck. (137)

166. As Rolla. By unknown engraver. (133)

167. As Rolla. By unknown engraver. Published by Harrison, Cluse & Co, 1800. (134)

168. As Rolla. By unknown engraver. Published as twopence-colored by J. Bailey, 1829. (135)

169. As Rolla. By unknown engraver. Published as penny-plain by R. Forse, 1826. (136)

170. As Romeo in *Romeo and Juliet*. By unknown artist. Listed in the art file at the Huntington Library as in the D. Minlore Collection.

171. As Shylock in *The Merchant of Venice*. By unknown engraver. Published by Walker, 1809. (138)

172. As Shylock, with Mrs Siddons as Portia. By unknown artist ($19 \times 25\frac{1}{4}$). In the possession of John Boyt, Boston, Massachusetts, in 1968. A photograph is in the Harvard Theatre Collection.

173. As the Stranger in *The Stranger*. Engraving by J. Collyer, after G. Hounsom. Published by Hounsom, 1799. (139)

174. As the Stranger. Lithography by R. J. Lane, after J. Boaden. Published by Dickinson. (140)

175. As the Stranger. Painting by William Owen. Graves Art Gallery, Sheffield.

176. As the Stranger. Oil sketch by Thomas Lawrence. In the Museum of Art, Rhode Island School of Design.

177. As the Stranger. By unknown engraver. (141)

178. As Tancred, with Mrs Siddons as Sigismunda, in *Tancred and Sigismunda*. Engraving by C. Watson, after C. Sherreff. Published by Sherreff, 1785. (142)

179. As Tancred. By unknown engraver. (143)

180. As Timon in *Timon of Athens*. Colored drawing by J. H. Ramberg, 1785. In the British Museum.

181. As Timon. Engraving by W. Sharp, after J. H. Ramberg. Published as a plate to *Bell's British Library*, 1785. (144)

182. As Vincentio in *Measure for Measure*. By unknown artist. Painting in the Victoria and Albert Museum.

IV. SCULPTURES, MEDALLIONS, PORCELAINS. OTHER KEMBLE ARTIFACTS.

183. Bust head. By George Bullock. Exhibited at the Egyptian Hall, 1812.

184. Bust. By John Flaxman. Plaster, 15″ high. In Sir John Soane's Museum.

185. Statuette as Cato. By John Flaxman, about 1826. Plaster, 13″ high. First sketch for a marble statue for Westminster Abbey. In Sir John Soane's Museum. See below, No 187.

186. Bust, shoulders bare. By John Gibson, 1814. Bronze 13½″ high. In the National Portrait Gallery.

187. Bust. By John Gibson, about 1816. Plaster (18″ high) version of the bronze in the National Portrait Gallery. In Sir John Soane's Museum.

188. Statue. By J. E. Hinchliffe, after a design by Flaxman. For Westminster Abbey, 1826. Unfinished.

189. Bust. By C. M. Westmacott. Exhibited at the Royal Academy, 1822.

190. Bust, plaster. By unknown sculptor. In the Kemble sale at Robins, 14 and 15 December 1820. Perhaps this is one of those listed above.

191. On plaque, in low relief, "Kemble inspired by the genius of Shakespeare." Modeled by E. A. Baily, after a design by John Flaxman, 1826. Sketch model of a relief for a silver vase presented at Kemble's retirement. In Sir John Soane's Museum.

192. On plaque, in low relief, "Kemble crowned by Melpomene." Modeled by E. A. Baily, after a design by Flaxman, 1817. In Sir John Soane's Museum.

193. Portrait on Wedgwood. Attributed to John Flaxman, about 1784. Example in the Wedgwood Museum, Barlaston.

194. Effigy in wax. As Hamlet, based on Lawrence's portrait. In Madame Tussaud's Gallery by 1835.

195. Effigy in wax. As Coriolanus, "taken from life" in 1800. In Madam Tussaud's Gallery, probably by 1802.

196. Effigy in wax. Exhibited at Clark's Wax-Works, No 17, Fleet Street, in the late eighteenth century. See notice of Mr Clark, d. 1812, in this dictionary, III, 296.

197. Porcelain statuettes of Kemble as Hamlet (Staffordshire), Richard III (Staffordshire and Derby), and Romeo, with Miss Smithson as Juliet (Staffordshire) are to be found in various museums and in the hands of private collectors. For information see George Savage, *Eighteenth-Century English Porcelain* (1952); P. D. Gordon Pugh, *Staffordshire Porcelain Figures* (1971); and articles in *Theatre Notebook*, 11 and 29. Among the leading authorities on theatrical porcelain are Raymond Mander and Joseph Mitchenson, who have catalogued several hundred pieces, about 150 in their own collection.

198. A copper token, one inch in diameter, was struck to exploit the "Old Price Riots." On one side is a caricature portrait of Kemble. See *A Catalogue of the Montague Guest Collection of Badges, Tokens, and Passes*, published by the British Museum, 1930.

199. Ewer, with Kemble as Hamlet, after Lawrence. Bloor Derby. By John Haslem?, about 1830. In the Mander and Mitchenson Collection.

200. The sword, shield, and helmet used by J. P. Kemble as Coriolanus were left by Charles Kemble to his son Henry. The helmet is now in the Garrick Club, the shield is in the

hands of a private collector in America, and the location of the sword is unknown. Other artifacts pertaining to J. P. Kemble are in the Garrick Club, the Mander and Mitchenson Collection, the Folger Shakespeare Library, and the Royal Shakespeare Theatre, Stratford-upon-Avon.

Kemble, Mrs John Philip, Priscilla, née Hopkins, formerly Mrs William Brereton *1758–1854, actress, dancer.*

Priscilla Hopkins was born in London on 17 December 1758, the younger daughter of the actor William Hopkins, who later served as the Drury Lane prompter for 20 years, and his wife Elizabeth, née Barton, who later acted at Drury Lane for 35 years. At the time of Priscilla's birth, however, her parents were young provincial performers. Announced as appearing on the stage for the first time, Priscilla delivered an *Address to the Town* at the conclusion of *As You Like It* at Drury Lane on 19 April 1773, at her parents' benefit. "Miss P. Hopkins" was next noted in the Drury Lane bills on 25 September 1775, when she played the Page in *The Gamesters*. On 3 March 1774 the treasurer paid her 5s. for one night, probably the earlier September appearance.

Not until 1775–76, Garrick's last season as actor-manager, did Priscilla become a full-time actress at Drury Lane, at the age of 17. Announced as "a Young Lady," she acted Celia in *The School for Lovers* on 24 October 1775, and her father entered in his diary "Miss P. Hopkins made her first appearance in Celia—great applause." (In his notation on a manuscript now at the Folger Library, Winston errs in identifying Priscilla also as the Miss Hopkins who acted Celia in *As You Like It* in April 1773; that actress was her elder sister Elizabeth, later Mrs Michael Sharp.) On 9 November 1775 Priscilla played Mildred in the premiere of *Old City Manners*, Mrs Lennox's adaptation of *Eastward Hoe!*. After several repetitions of that role, she acted Lady Elizabeth Gray in *The Earl of Warwick* on 14 November, then Fanny in *The Clandestine Marriage* on 20 November ("very well and great applause" wrote her father in the prompter's diary), and Maria in *The Maid of the Oaks* on 28 November ("well received").

Before the end of the season she was also seen as Louisa Medway in *The Discovery*, Har-riet in *The Jealous Wife*, the original Harriet in Mrs Cowley's *The Runaway* on 15 February 1776, the original Eliza in Colman's *The Spleen* on 7 March, Miss Leeson in *The School for Wives*, Harriet in *The School for Rakes*, Miss Fuz in *A Peep behind the Curtain*, and Prince Edward in *Richard III* (on the last nights, 27 May, 3 and 5 June 1776, on which Garrick played the role). That season she subscribed 10s. 6d. to the Drury Lane Theatrical Fund.

Earning £2 per week (the same sum as her sister), Priscilla Hopkins continued at Drury Lane in 1776–77, adding to her repertoire Clarissa in *The Hotel*, Silvia in *The Old Bachelor*, Arabella in *The Committee*, and Maria in *The School for Scandal* (at the first performance on 8 May 1777). On 7 April she performed Foible in *The Way of the World* and Miss Kitty Sprightly in *All the World's a Stage* for a benefit shared with Elizabeth. Tickets could be had of the Misses Hopkins at No 7, Little Russell Street, the address of their parents, and receipts amounted to £237 11s. 6d. (less house charges of £65 2s. 6d.).

In the summer of 1777 Priscilla went to play soubrettes at Bristol and Bath. By that time, when she was 19, she was involved with the Drury Lane actor William Brereton, who was then about 26. The pretty and piquante Priscilla married him at Bath on 24 September 1777, under circumstances which were perhaps awkward. In a letter to Garrick on 10 August 1777 written from Bristol, Hannah More evidently referred to the young Priscilla: "The girl is returned, and they expect the man will marry her: I wish he may, for the sake of the poor father and mother. She must be a silly, romantic girl: once I find she has eloped in her feathered head and full dress, after playing Miss Tittup." Though she had become Brereton's wife by the time she returned to Drury Lane for the 1777–78 season, she continued to act as Miss P. Hopkins. Her new roles that year included Mademoiselle in *The Provok'd Wife* and Maria in *Twelfth Night*.

After acting with her husband at the Crow Street Theatre, Dublin, in the summer of 1778, she returned to Drury Lane, where, on 8 October 1778 her name appeared in the bills as Mrs Brereton for the role of Louisa Dudley in *The West Indian*, in which Brereton acted Charles Dudley. Under her married name she worked at Drury Lane for another eight years.

Harvard Theatre Collection

PRISCILLA KEMBLE

engraving by Lane, after Lawrence

In 1782 her sister Elizabeth joined her hus-band Michael Sharp at Norwich, leaving Priscilla some of her Drury Lane roles.

Mrs Brereton's repertoire now included, among others, Bridget in *Every Man in His Humour*, Maria in *George Barnwell*, the Lady in *Comus*, Mrs Ford in *The Merry Wives of Windsor*, Dorinda in *The Strategem*, Mrs Strickland in *The Suspicious Husband*, Perdita in *The Winter's Tale*, Lady Franklin in *Variety*, Lady Anne in *Richard III*, and Charlotte in *The Gamester.* Her original roles were Harriet in M. P. Andrews's *The Reparation* on 14 February 1784, Elizabeth in Mrs Cowley's *Who's the Dupe?* on 10 April 1779, and Donna Viola in Mrs Cowley's *The School for Greybeards* on 25 November 1786. In May 1779 the Breretons lodged at No 11, Tavistock Street and in May 1786 at No 10, Charles Street, Covent Garden.

No doubt she was a good wife, but about five years after their marriage Brereton began to exhibit signs of the mental illness which finally incapacitated him. His distress, it was thought, had been brought on by an unrequited infatuation for Sarah Siddons (who eventually was to be Priscilla's sister-in-law). A disapproving public hissed Mrs Siddons when she came on the stage of Drury Lane on 5 October 1784 as Mrs Beverley in *The Gamester* because of an ill-founded rumor that she had refused to play for Brereton's benefit in Dublin. The performance was interrupted for 40 minutes during which Mrs Brereton, who was playing Charlotte, "was near enough to sneak off the stage," reported the *Town and Country Magazine* in October 1784, "and leave her to stand the insults of a malicious party tho' [Mrs Brereton] knew the whole disturbance was on her account and that her husband had at least been obliged to contradict the reports that concern'd him."

Brereton's excessive drinking only intensified his problem. On the Portsmouth stage one night in the summer of 1785 as Lovel in *The Clandestine Marriage* he obliged Mrs Brereton, as Fanny, to dance a minuet which was not part of the production. It was said that he tried several times to kill himself, and when he attempted to kill her he was restrained at a Hoxton asylum, where he died on 17 February 1787 at the age of 36. That year Williams wrote of Mrs Brereton in *The Children of Thespis*: "Her face is impress'd with the seal of despair; / The mate of her bosom, poor nymph, she has lost. . . ."

She continued to act at Drury Lane as Mrs Brereton through 8 December 1787, when she played Louisa Dudley in *The West Indian.* On that day, however, she married John Philip Kemble at St Giles in the Fields in the presence of her mother and his father. The register records Priscilla as from the parish of St Mary le Strand. In his biography *John Philip Kemble* (1942), Herschel Baker, who erroneously places the marriage at St Martin's and in 1788, claims the ceremony later was "repeated by a Catholic priest for the benefit of the groom."

Kemble's choice of "Pop" Hopkins—as she was commonly known—was made with characteristic deliberation and he seems not to have allowed the marriage to interrupt his calm routine. It was rumored that Kemble had accepted a bribe of £4000 from Lord North to abandon an attachment to his lordship's young daughter, with a further stipulation that he undertake a substitute marriage within a fortnight; Kemble decided on Mrs Brereton as the pawn, but when he claimed his money, Lord North refused to pay. In later years, Kemble emphatically branded the story as a lie. Another bit of gossip was that on the afternoon of his marriage he arrived so late at the wedding meal arranged by the Bannisters that the new Mrs Kemble and Bannister had already departed the table to report to their evening's acting assignments. Kemble did manage to rouse himself sufficiently to call for his bride after the performance and escort her to her new home in Caroline Street, Bedford Square.

When Priscilla acted Lady Anne in *Richard III* and the Lady in *Comus* two nights later on 10 December 1787, she was billed as Mrs Kemble. The next night she acted Olympia in *Julia*, when Kemble played Mentevole and Mrs Siddons played the title role. On 14 December she played Margaret, the daughter to Kemble's Sir Giles Overreach in *A New Way to Pay Old Debts.* Her marriage to Kemble seems not to have forwarded her career greatly, and she continued in her usual supporting service to the Drury Lane company for nine seasons more, earning in her last season on the stage, 1795–96, £6 per week. Among her roles during that period were the original Aurora in *The Pannel* on 28 November 1788 and Flora in *The Farm House* on 1 May 1789, both afterpieces

Harvard Theatre Collection

PRISCILLA KEMBLE as Peggy

engraving by Collyer, after Dodd

Harvard Theatre Collection

JOHN PALMER as Bajazet and PRISCILLA KEMBLE as Selima

engraving by Walker, after Barralet

written by Kemble. On 8 March 1790 she acted the original Valeria in Kemble's comedy *Love in Many Masks*. While the company was playing at the King's Theatre she created Miss Manly in the premiere of Richardson's *The Fugitive* on 20 April 1792.

In the *Secret History of the Green Rooms*, Mrs Kemble was described as somewhat below middle size, of a pretty and agreeable figure with a countenance "like her mother's, which is rather peevish." In his *Candid and Impartial Strictures on the Performers* (1795), Waldron judged her "A lady of no great advantage to the drama, in whatever light we consider her; her person tolerable; her action and deportment stiff and formal; her face thought by some pretty, but has always to us the appearance of her having been just tasting *a lemon*. We can only impute her situation in the the-

atre to the interest of which she was of course in possession." She succeeded in sentimental ladies in comedy, but was weaker in tragedy.

Genest was not impressed with her talent but thought her best in parts like Maria in *The School for Scandal*. She took her leave of the stage on 23 May 1796, playing Flavia in *Celedon and Florimel*, a new comedy by Kemble altered from Dryden and Cibber's *The Comical Lovers*. At the conclusion of that piece she spoke a farewell address of four lines written for her by Bertie Greatheed; "so great was her agitation," reported the *European Magazine* of June 1796, "that she was nearly incapable of delivering them."

Thereafter Mrs Kemble stepped back into the domestic shadow, serving as dutiful wife to a man whose fame, eye for women, and attachment to the bottle could not have made him easy to live with. She accompanied him on his various travels after his retirement from the stage and the sale of their grand house at No 89, Great Russell Street, which eventually was absorbed by the British Museum. They lived at Toulouse from 1818 to 1820 and then at Lausanne, where he spent the last years and where he died on 26 February 1823. She returned to England, settling at Leamington in ample financial and social comfort, performing many charitable deeds. Kemble had left her a minimum of £1000 per year and all his household goods and effects and other properties, including his library and prints, the sale of which brought her large sums.

She was the essence of propriety, a bit too stuffy for her spirited niece Fanny Kemble Butler, who often visited her. Mrs Kemble retained her well-stored memory and lively conversation to the end of her 87 years. A letter from her to an unknown recipient, dated 11 December 1843 and now in the Enthoven Collection, reveals that her advancing age had required her to give up "society indoors and out," but she still possessed all her faculties, "and especially my sight I do not use Spectacles to work or read which in the very secluded life I am oblig'd to lead is a great blessing as I can amuse myself." She died at Leamington on 13 May 1845 and was buried in the private chapel of the Greatheed family in St Mary's Church, Guy's Cliffe, near Warwick.

Priscilla had no children by John Kemble; therefore the largest share of her property went to her brother-in-law Charles Kemble and his children, according to her obituary in the *Gentleman's Magazine* of July 1845.

Portraits of Priscilla Kemble include the following, all of which, except No 1, were engraved when she was Miss Hopkins.

1. By Thomas Lawrence. Pencil-and-chalk drawing. In the possession of Mrs Siddons in 1830. Present location unknown.

2. Engraving by R. J. Lane, after Lawrence, published by J. Dickinson, 1830.

3. As Aura in *Country Lasses*. Engraving by Pollard, after J. Roberts. Published as a plate to *Bell's British Theatre*, 1778.

4. As Lavinia in *Titus Andronicus*. By unknown engraver, after J. Roberts. Published as a plate to *Bell's British Theatre*, 1776.

5. As Miss Notable in *The Lady's Last Stake*. Engraving by Thornthwaite, after J. Roberts. Published as a plate to *Bell's British Theatre*, 1778.

6. As Peggy in *The Country Girl*. Engraving by J. Collyer, after D. Dodd. Published as a plate to *New English Theatre*, 1777.

7. As Selima in *Selima and Azor*. By unknown engraver. Published as a plate to *Theatrical Magazine*, 1778.

8. As Selima, with John Palmer as Bajazet, in *Tamerlane*. Engraving by Walker, after J. Barralet. Published as a plate to *New English Theatre*, 1776.

Kemble, Roger *1722–1802, actor, manager.*

Roger Kemble was born in Hereford on 1 March 1722. He was a descendant of a Catholic family which took its name, it is said, from the Wiltshire village of Kemble. The name, however, was a common one and often was interchangeable with Campbell. His father, also Roger Kemble, settled at Hereford about the turn of the century and made his living as a barber. The elder Roger Kemble once described himself as "fatherless." Nothing is known of his wife, our subject's mother.

Several members of the family, remaining royalists, had been dispossessed of their lands. Several others were priests. One of the latter, Father John Kemble (1599?–1679), was executed for complicity in the Titus Oates plot. That martyr's nephew, Captain Richard Kemble, fought for the King in the battle of Worcester; it was from the Captain that the Hereford line issued. The family also had associations in Gloucestershire.

Several pieces of property were owned by the elder Roger Kemble. In the Hereford City Library are two Kemble documents: a bill dated 2 May 1741, from Roger Kemble, barber, to Mme Mornington, with a receipt signed by his son Roger, and the lease of a house in Capuch Lane, in the possession of Roger Kemble, barber, to Richard Bethel. The elder Roger at one time resided at Lydbrook, Gloucestershire, in a house opposite the Anchor Inn. And there used to be two Kemble tombstones, one dated 1712, in the Lydbrook churchyard at Welsh Bignor. According to Nicholls in *Personalities of the Forest of Dean*,

ROGER KEMBLE

by Humphrey

"the house was out of the family for a time, but came back in 1757, when his niece bequeathed the property to 'Roger Kemble, of Hereford' [our subject], who left it to his son, John, who sold it."

Young Roger Kemble was trained as a barber, but at the age of 30, in 1752, having decided to become an actor, he engaged with Smith's company at Canterbury, according to the story told by Charles Lee Lewes in his

Memoirs. There he made "a very tender connexion" with the actress Fanny Furnival: "In return for his tender affection she flattered him with the promise of making an actor of him." After an intensive training period, Kemble made his debut as Serjeant Kite in *The Recruiting Officer*, but he failed. Smith would not keep Kemble, so he and Fanny applied to John Ward at Birmingham. Roger was employed by Ward, but there was no room in the company for Fanny. She joined Quelch's Coventry troupe, soon rejected Roger, and took another lover. Though Lewes wrote that Roger referred to Fanny as his wife, it is doubtful that they had ever married. At Canterbury, however, she had been billed as Mrs Kemble, or, more frequently as Mrs Campbell.

At Cirencester on 6 June 1753, Roger Kemble married Sarah Ward, his manager's 17-year-old daughter. She had been born at Clonmel, Ireland, on 2 September 1735. It was to the Ward side of the family that Roger and Sarah Kemble's numerous and illustrious offspring were to owe their aristocratic bearing, their Roman features, and their theatrical genius. Ward, an Irishman, had a superior reputation in the provinces. He became a Methodist and applied stern discipline to his children and company. His wife Sarah, also a performer, was the daughter of Mr and Mrs Stephen Butcher, provincial players. In her letters at the Folger Shakespeare Library, Ann Kemble Hatton, one of the children of Roger Kemble, provides information about the Wards and the early relationship of her parents. John and Sarah Ward had numerous children but only three survived—William and Stephen, who had little theatrical talent, and Sarah, who acted in her father's company. "She inherited the strong mind and genius of her father," wrote Mrs Hatton; "she had his dark intelligent eyes, his handsome haughty countenance with the tall and masculine figure of her mother."

As headstrong as she was beautiful, Sarah had married Kemble against her parents' hopes and wishes. She had turned away the suits of a wealthy Quaker and a young nobleman; the latter, according to Mrs Hatton, "died for the love of Sarah Ward." Her encouragement of Kemble's attentions led John Ward to compel her "under the terror of parental malediction to swear she never would marry an actor." After the marriage Ward consoled himself, as Mrs Hatton put it, with the thought that "My daughter Swore she would never marry an *Actor*, and by G-d Sir, she has religiously kept her word."

The newlyweds returned to Ward's "sullen forgiveness" and their places in the company. Roger Kemble did not form his own company soon after his marriage, as *The Dictionary of National Biography* suggests, but remained with his father-in-law for about eight years. During that period, when the company was touring Wales in 1755, their first child, Sarah Kemble (the future Mrs Siddons) was born on 5 July at the Shoulder of Mutton Inn in Brecon. Sarah was baptized at St Mary's in Brecon on 14 July, when her father's name was incorrectly entered into the register as "George Kemble a Commedian." Sarah was baptized a Protestant, the persuasion of her mother, as were all the subsequent Kemble daughters. The sons were raised in their father's church. Mrs Hatton mistakenly claimed that her sister had been born "at Denbigh (not Brecon) in the year 1753." She was also wrong about the year of birth of the Kemble's next child, John Philip; he was born at Prescot, Lancashire, on 1 February 1757, and not in 1755. A third child, Stephen George, was born at Kington, Herefordshire, on 3 April 1758. Their fourth child Frances was born at Hereford on 28 December 1759; she married Francis Twiss in 1786.

About 1761 the Kembles seem to have left Ward's company to strike out on their own. At Warrington, Lancashire, their fifth child, Elizabeth, was born on 2 April; she married the actor Charles Edward Whitlock in 1785. The Kembles remained on their own until 1763, when a sixth child, Mary, was born at Stratford-upon-Avon on 3 January 1763. She died in infancy. The Kembles returned to Ward's company that year, and when Ward retired to Leominster in the spring of 1766, Kemble took over the management, on 24 May.

For the next 15 years Roger Kemble led his company throughout England's western counties, playing in inns, barns, and ill-equipped playhouses. His troupe was steadily swelled by the births of his children. In addition to the six cited above, another six came along during the first 11 years of his management: Ann

Victoria Art Gallery, Bath

ROGER KEMBLE
by Beach

Julia, born on 29 April 1764 at Worcester, married C. Curtis, an actor in 1783 and then Wiliam Hatton in 1792; Catherine, born on 4 July 1765 at Hereford, died in infancy; Lucy, born on 28 July 1767 at Worcester, died in infancy; Charles, born on 25 November 1775 at Brecon; Jane, born on 30 September 1777 at Warwick, became the wife of the actor Henry Mason in 1801.

Though supposedly Roger Kemble wished

for none of his children to go upon the stage, each surviving one did, and all, except Frances, married performers. Their parents succeeded, for the most part, in their efforts to provide each with a good education, despite the constant travel and the distractions theatrical life presented to the children. Roger was a handsome, dignified, and apparently easygoing person, and Sarah, in her father's tradition, was the disciplinarian who kept the company and the children in line. A well-known playbill of a performance of *Charles the First* at Worcester on 12 February 1767 records five Kembles in the cast: Roger as Colonel Fairfax; Mrs Kemble as Lucy Fairfax; Sarah as Princess Elizabeth; Frances as the Duke of Gloucester; and John as the Duke of York.

Roger Kemble's professional journal, now in the Harvard Theatre Collection, records in his own hand the company's movements and repertory from mid-August 1766 through 4 June 1768. They were at Coventry for about five months, taking between £15 and £20 per night; then they gave 65 performances at Worcester from 15 January 1767 until 13 July, when they began a three-week stint at Droitwich and Bromgrove. They opened on 26 September at Bath, where they gave 94 performances before their closing night, 4 June 1768. Kemble took his players to Worcester regularly from 1767 through 1778. They visited Kington and Leominster until 1778, between 1775 and 1778 they played regular six-month engagements at Hereford, and they made calls at Monmouth, Brecon, and Carmarthen in the 1770s. Among the company's last performances under Kemble's management were those at Gloucester and Stroud in July 1780.

In 1781 Kemble retired, having disposed of his stock and "good will" to J. B. Watson. Kemble's troupe, according to one-time member Thomas Holcroft, had been "more respectable than many other companies of strolling players; but it was not in so flourishing a condition as to place the manager beyond the reach of the immediate smiles or frowns of fortune." His productions were orderly and of a high standard compared to other bands of strollers, and he enjoyed a good name.

Roger and Sarah sought "a quiet asylum in London for the remainder of their lives," basking in the enjoyment (and, one would think, the security) that the careers of their illustrious children, especially Sarah and John, brought to them. Yet Genest relates spending the winter of 1786–87 in London and hearing one evening from Mr Bonney of Percy Street

that he had been at some Banker's in the course of the day, and had heard the Banker observe, that he had a sum of money deposited in his hands for charitable purposes, and that Roger Kemble had applied to him for a part of it—his answer was, that he could not consider the father of Mrs. Siddons, who was making so much money, as a fit object of charity.

At the age of 66, Roger Kemble made his only known professional appearance in London. On 26 August 1788 he came out of his retirement to act at the Haymarket Theatre for the benefit of his daughter-in-law, Elizabeth, the wife of Stephen Kemble. His role was the Miller in *The Miller of Mansfield*. An address written by John Taylor and spoken by Elizabeth Kemble to introduce the patriarch was printed in *European Magazine* in September 1788. A critic in the *Morning Post* of 28 August wrote kindly that Kemble's performance "was replete with so much spirit and humour, and displayed so correct an idea of character, that the public have reason to lament so good an actor should be in such advanced life." The *Public Advertiser* reported on 27 August that "Here and there we could perceive the liberty of the country performer, by saying more than was set down by the author." The *European Magazine* was gracious: "considering, the motive, this performance is entitled to escape criticism, and therefore we shall be silent about it." Another critic's observations, preserved in a press clipping in the Folger Shakespeare Library, were, it seems, more frank:

His performance was in itself of no value. He has lost his teeth and his articulation; so that it is impossible to conjecture, from what he is, of what he may have been.—There was no great shew of the barn about him. . . . He would only perhaps have acted better not to appear at all; but the motive, we own, is more than a justification.

He spent the last years of his life with his wife in a cottage in Kentish Town, making frequent trips to town for various social events, especially dinners given by their son John. In 1792 he was granted the coat of arms of a gentleman. James Boaden, in his life of *John*

Victoria Art Gallery, Bath

Sarah Kemble

by Lawrence

Philip Kemble, described meeting the elder Kembles "in their decline of life":

. . . I can safely say that I never was more struck than by the sight of his venerable parents. His father had the same style of head as his own, except that the features were more delicately finished, and somewhat less energetic. But his countenance excited reverence beyond any that I have seen; to which the silver curls of his hair contributed, and the sweet composed and placid character of his deportment.

He was sitting in his son's library, and from a peculiar costume that he had adopted from liability to take cold, (a partial silk covering for the head,) he looked to me rather like a dignitary of the church two centuries back. . . .

His mother had been a distinguished beauty in

her youth, and had once been tempted by a coronet. What remained of her was of the highest order. She had a very uncommon vivacity and point in her conversation. . . . Her utterance was, like that of Mrs. Siddons, deliberate, careful in enunciation; and her diction had a nervous and exact propriety, such as we have all admired in her son.

Roger Kemble died at his house in Great Russell Street on 6 December 1802, at the age of 80. At the time, Sarah Siddons was out on tour and John Philip Kemble was in Madrid, whence he wrote to his brother Charles on 1 January 1803: "Nothing could be better judged than you interring my poor father without the least affectation of any parade; and I agree with you entirely that his remains should be protected by a simple stone" on which his age should be inscribed. The place

Harvard Theatre Collection

JOHN HENDERSON, SARAH SIDDONS, and ROGER KEMBLE, rehearsing in the Green Room

by Rowlandson

of burial was not mentioned, but probably it was at St Marylebone, where his wife was buried five years later.

In his will drawn on 14 January 1802, Kemble described himself as "of the City of Hereford but now of Saint Giles's in the ffields." To his wife Sarah he left his stocks, his household goods, his money out on mortgages, and his five renter's shares in Drury Lane Theatre. After her death the property was to be disposed as follows: his renter's shares to daughters Sarah Siddons and Elizabeth Whitlock and sons John, Stephen, and Charles; to daughter Frances Twiss £500; to daughter Jane Mason £400; to daughter Ann Hatton £20 a year, to be paid by John who should not do so "without a receipt from under the said Ann Hattons own hand." John and Charles were named co-executors with their mother. The will was proved on 6 April 1803.

Sarah Kemble had never appeared on the London stage, though between her confinements she had been a leading actress in her husband's company. She died in London on 24 April 1807, at the age of 71, and was buried at St Marylebone on 29 April.

Their sons John Philip, Stephen George, and Charles and their daughter Frances (later Mrs Francis Twiss) are noticed on these pages. Their daughters Sarah Siddons, Ann Julia Hatton, and Elizabeth Whitlock are noticed under their married names.

Roger Kemble's daughter Jane did not perform in London in the eighteenth century. She acted at Newcastle in 1796 and Edinburgh in 1797 and 1799. On 20 July 1801 she married the actor Henry Mason in Durham, Ireland. He made his debut at the Haymarket in 1814, and he died in Boston, Massachusetts, on 1 April 1851. Jane Mason's death at Edinburgh on 6 January 1833 was reported in the *Scotsman* of 12 January 1833; but according to a letter by her sister Ann Hatton's amanuensis, dated 17 August 1834 (and now in the Folger Library), Mrs Mason died on 10 January 1834. The Masons had at least five sons, three of whom became actors in America: Charles Kemble Mason, who was born in Peterborough, Northamptonshire, on 7 November 1805 and died in Brooklyn, New York, on 11 July 1875; John Kemble Mason, who was born in Edinburgh about 1806 and died in New Orleans in February 1873. Their daughter

Jane Mason, who was born in Edinburgh about 1810, married the actor Henry Hillyard in 1839, and died in Brooklyn on 13 March 1885.

Roger Kemble had at least two brothers and a sister. Thomas Kemble, a grocer of Cannon Street, London, married a Miss Cooper, "a beauty of Swindon," on 23 March 1737. She died on 21 August 1774. Thomas Kemble died on 21 March 1795 in Tokenhouse Yard, Coleman Street. Administration of his estate was granted to Roger Kemble, brother and next of kin, on 13 April 1795. Another brother, Richard Kemble, who was blind, died in a fire at Hereford in 1799, at the age of 86. The death of their sister, Elinor Kemble, spinster (who received the interest on £837 10s. in Thomas's will), was announced in the *Hereford Journal* in May 1804.

Portraits of Roger Kemble include:

1. By Thomas Beach. Exhibited at the Royal Academy in 1787. Now in the Victoria Art Gallery, Bath. Engravings by W. Ridley as plates to the *General Magazine and Impartial Review* in 1791 and the *Monthly Mirror* in 1808; a woodcut by an anonymous engraver, after Beach, was also issued.

2. By Ozias Humphrey. Watercolor on ivory, in the gallery of the Royal Shakespeare Theatre, Stratford-on-Avon.

3. By Thomas Lawrence. In 1942 this picture hung in the Deanery at Hereford. It had been taken there by a daughter of Fanny Kemble Butler when she married the Dean, James Wentworth Leigh. Lawrence's portrait of Roger's wife Sarah is in the Victoria Art Gallery, Bath.

4. By Thomas Rowlandson. Watercolor caricature showing Roger Kemble rehearsing in the Green Room with Sarah Siddons and John Henderson. In the National Trust, Ellen Terry Museum, Smallhythe; a copy in the Victoria and Albert Museum.

5. By Michael Sharp. Present location unknown. On 1 January 1803 John Philip Kemble, in Madrid, wrote to his brother Charles, "You see Michael Sharpe, sometimes, I suppose. Pray desire him to take care of my father's picture for me—it is like him, though not quite what I could wish—at least, I used to think so."

6. By unknown artist. India ink and wash, in the British Museum.

Kemble, Mrs Roger the first?, Elizabeth, "Fanny." *See* FURNIVAL, MRS THOMAS.

Kemble, Sarah *1755–1831.* *See* SIDDONS, MRS WILLIAM, SARAH.

Kemble, Stephen George *1758–1822, actor, manager, author.*

The second son and third child of the actors Roger and Sarah (née Ward) Kemble was born at Kington, Herefordshire, on 3 April 1758 and baptized as Stephen Kemble there on 21 April. When or why he later adopted the middle name George is not known. Reportedly his mother acted Anne Boleyn in *Henry VIII* on the night of his birth. Even if his arrival in the world had not been quite so dramatic as the myth relates (for similar stories are told about the peculiar births of others of Mrs Roger Kemble's children), there can be no doubt that Stephen was a child of the theatre. Though it is said that Roger Kemble wished for none of his children to become actors, they could hardly have avoided the profession as they hopped from one country theatre to another with their parents. Stephen's birth occurred during the regular annual visit of the Ward-Kemble company to the barn theatre at Kington. Probably he was sent on when still a youngster to act a fairy or cupid from time to time.

Though his elder brother John Philip and his younger brother Charles both were sent for schooling to the monastery in Douai, Stephen was apprenticed at the age of 14 to a Mr Gibbs, a chemist or surgeon at Coventry. But he soon went the way of the Kembles and joined a traveling company of actors. In the early 1770s he was at Painswick with Mark Moore's troupe. Kemble joined Wilkinson's company when it was at Doncaster where he acted the Earl of Essex in October 1781. Though severely ill he acted the title role in *St Ignatius* at York on 29 December 1781. He remained with Wilkinson at York and Leeds in 1781–82, and then in the summer of 1782 he made his Irish debut as Pyrrhus in *The Distrest Mother* at Cork on 2 August. Among the other roles he acted at Cork was Wellborn in *A New Way to Pay Old Debts* on 10 October. He was en-

STEPHEN KEMBLE

engraving by Heath, after Smith

gaged in 1782–83 at the Capel Street Theatre in Dublin, where one of his roles was Shylock.

Stephen George Kemble was employed by the Covent Garden management for the 1783–84 season at £3 per week, no doubt in hopes of capitalizing on the growing family reputation, since John Philip Kemble and Sarah Siddons were members of the rival company at Drury Lane that season. On 24 September 1783, announced as from the Theatre Royal in Dublin, Stephen Kemble made his Covent Garden debut as Othello to the Desdemona of Elizabeth Satchell, a young actress who would very soon become his wife. (*The Dictionary of National Biography* errs in giving 1784 as the year of his debut and in stating that they were already married.)

Critical comment in the *London Magazine* of

October 1783 predicted Stephen's star would never belong in the shining constellation formed by his brothers John and Charles and his sister Sarah: "he has not, and we speak charitably, any pretentions to a first or second rank in the theatre. We are sorry for this, as he seemed to labour earnestly, but in vain." In his *Life of Mrs Siddons*, Thomas Campbell described the claque assembled by the family for Stephen's London debut:

The Siddons and the Kembles were seated over the stage-box . . . to see their brother Stephen Kemble's first appearance. Nature whose effusions have in public secured to the former an universal admiration, operated very powerfully and so frequently on this occasion. The tears of sensibility stole down her cheek, and with a sister's sympathy, spoke all the brother felt.

But the Covent Garden management seems not to have been so moved. Kemble repeated Othello on 29 September 1783 and then was named in the bills for only a few more roles. His portrayal of Sealand in *The Conscious Lovers* on 8 October impressed the writer of the *Theatrical Review* (1783):

Mr. S. Kemble is indisputably an actor of feeling and judgment. He performed the part of Sealand with force, propriety, and interest. The part seemed more suitable to his nature and style of acting than Othello. His countenance is manly, agreeable, and expressive; and his voice particularly adapted to give energy to such paternal feelings, as Sealand is described to have. His greatest deficiency is—a taste of manner, and elegance of person.

Kemble acted Bajazet in *Tamerlane* on 4 and 5 November, Othello again on 27 December, Richmond in *Richard III* on 29 December, Pembroke in *King John* on 16 January 1784, and Colredo in *The Heroine of the Cave* on 22 March. He spoke prologues to *The Shipwreck* on 10 February and *Bribery on Both Sides* on 4 May, and on 17 May he delivered Collins's *Ode on the Passions* in a musical entertainment called *A Jubilee in Commemoration of Handel and Shakespeare*. A theatre pay sheet for 1783–84 (now in the Harvard Theatre Collection) indicates that he received a total of £95 for 190 nights, so he must have come on often in less significant roles not mentioned in the bills.

Kemble was not reengaged at Covent Garden for the next season. He migrated to the provinces again for several years, playing at Exeter, Chester, York, Leeds, Newcastle, Edinburgh, and Glasgow. He was accompanied by his wife, the former Miss Satchell, whom he had married at St George, Bloomsbury, on 20 November 1783. An actress of some consequence, forced by her marriage to leave a promising London career (except for summers at the Haymarket), Mrs Kemble was more favored for her talents in these provincial towns than was Stephen. They made their debuts at Edinburgh on 23 February 1786 (not 1785 as given in *The Dictionary of National Biography*) as Othello and Desdemona. Among his other roles there that season were King John, Chamont in *The Orphan*, Don Carlos in *The Revenge*, Hotspur in *1 Henry IV*, King Lear, Old Norval in *Douglas*, Shylock, and Sir John Flowerdale in *Lionel and Clarissa*. In late spring they rejoined Wilkinson at York, but Mrs Kemble's illness prevented their playing *Othello* before the season ended.

After working a busy repertory at Edinburgh again in the first half of 1787, the Kembles returned to London to keep a summer engagement at Colman's Haymarket. Stephen made his appearance there on 16 May 1787 as Dominick in *The Spanish Fryar*. Two nights later he acted Claudius for his wife's debut as Ophelia. He then was seen as Leonato in *Much Ado about Nothing*, Sir Wilful Wayward in *The Country Attorney*, Old Meanwell in *Tit for Tat*, the Abbot in *Henry the Second*, the title role in *Sir John Cockle at Court*, and Rothsay in *Vimonda*. Over the next four years, though still relegated to the provinces during the winters, he returned each summer to the Haymarket, where his roles included Sir Christopher Curry in *Inkle and Yarico*, Bonniface in *The Beaux' Stratagem*, Sir William Wealthy in *A Quarter of an Hour before Dinner*, David Northcote in *The Sword of Peace*, and the King in *The Miller of Mansfield* in 1788; Freeport in *The English Merchant*, Mr Sturdy in *Half an Hour after Supper*, Baron de Fortsheim in *The Swop*, Lord Glenmore in *The Chapter of Accidents*, Oran in *The Friends*, and Father Bernardo in *A Wife Well Managed* in 1789; Tradewell Classick in *The Married Man* and Sir Ambrose Crab in *Modern Breakfast* in 1790; and Roundfee in *Ways and Means*, Mr Manly in *Next Door Neighbours*, and Barton in *The Battle of Hexham* in 1791. On 16 August 1791 Kemble's two-act farce *The Northern Inn; or, The Days of Good Queen Bess* (altered from Heywood's *The Fair Maid of the West*) was performed at the Haymarket for the benefit of his wife. She did not appear in the piece but acted that night Queen Margaret in *The Battle of Hexham*; the cast included their four-year-old daughter Frances Crawford Kemble as the Prince of Wales. Never published, *The Northern Inn* survives in manuscript at the Huntington Library.

In February 1790 Kemble turned up as manager of a small company of actors, numbering about 16, which played almost every night at Coventry through 5 June. This venture may not have been his first at management but it precedes the claims made by scholars for Newcastle upon Tyne in March 1791 and Edinburgh in 1792.

At Coventry, Kemble reserved many of the capital roles like Lear, Othello, Hamlet, and Sealand for himself. His wife played leading roles and also sang and danced. On their benefit night, 26 April 1790, she favored the audience with Polly in *The Beggar's Opera* and he recited the popular epilogue "Belles Have at Ye All" and introduced "Hobby Horses," another recitation which included treatises on the various professions and trades, among them being "Kemble's Hobby." All concluded with the patriotic spectacle *Gallic Freedom; or, Vive la Liberté*, the main feature of which was the storming and demolishing of the Bastille. At the bottom of that evening's playbill Kemble offered "a few Observations on the Business" of the stage, comprising points of his managerial philosophy and practice, including his resolution to forbid his players to solicit in person for their benefit nights. Furthermore, "conscious that the Person, who conducts the THEATRE is *alone Responsible* for any Pieces acted at the Benefits," he pledged that "none shall be produced but such as are fit for Representation."

On 7 March 1791 Kemble assumed management of the recently-built Theatre Royal in Newcastle at an annual rent of £300. He paid £1000 to the previous manager, his brother-in-law Charles Edward Whitlock (husband of Elizabeth Kemble Whitlock), for the properties, scenery, and costumes. The deal included interest in theatres of the northern circuit in Chester, Lancaster, and Sheffield. (Details of his Newcastle management, which lasted for 15 years, are provided by S. E. Robinson in *The Eighteenth-Century English Stage*, edited by Richards and Thomson, 1971).

When John Jackson put his Edinburgh and Glasgow theatres up for leasing on 2 November 1791, Kemble obtained them and became embroiled in a confusing and tumultuous battle which was fought in the press and at the bench. The story is told through a series of publications issued on both sides: John Jackson's *A Statement of Facts, Explanatory of the Dispute Between John Jackson and Stephen Kemble, Relative to the Theatre Royal of Edinburgh* (1792, and reprinted with slight variations in Jackson's *History of the Scottish Stage*, 1793); *Answers for Robert Playfair . . . to Petition of Stephen Kemble* (1793); *A Comparative View of the Rights and Merits of Mrs. Harriet Pye Esten, &c. and of Mr Stephen Kemble* (1793); *Petition of Stephen Kemble, Manager of the New Theatre of Edinburgh, against Lord Swinton's Interlocutor* (7 February 1793); and several other publications, including Charles Lee Lewes's *Memoirs* (1805).

Though points of view differ, the facts seem essentially the same. Jackson persuaded Kemble to take the lease at a rent of £1350 for one year, believing that before the end of that period he could settle his debts, whereupon, as he had promised, he would keep Kemble as a partner. Jackson claimed that he preferred to give the lease to Harriet Esten but that her delays complicated that possibility. Lewes, on the other hand, claimed that Jackson persuaded Kemble in order to prevent Mrs Esten from obtaining the lease, fearing it would never revert to him. Kemble won the lease, and when Jackson presented his security for one-half the rent, Kemble found it insufficient and refused to allow Jackson back into the management. When Jackson accused Kemble of sharp practices Kemble refused him admission to the building. On 9 August 1792 the arbitrator Henry Erskine, Dean of the Faculty of Advocates, ruled that Kemble was required to give Jackson half the profits so long as he leased the theatre from his creditors; but while only half proprietor, Kemble was to be sole manager at a salary to be set by the Dean. Meanwhile, on 19 January 1792, Kemble had opened the season with *The Beggar's Opera* with his wife as Polly and had appeared himself in a number of roles during the year. John Kemble and Sarah Siddons came up to bolster the cause with *Venice Preserv'd.*

Harvard Theatre Collection

STEPHEN KEMBLE as Hamlet

by Dighton

But Jackson had been busy applying pressure and a little subterfuge. In July 1792 Jackson persuaded his trustee Robert Playfair to lease the Edinburgh theatre to Mrs Esten for the ensuing season at a rent of £1000, substantially lower than Kemble had paid. A scramble began for the patent at that point, with solicitations on all sides to the Duke of Hamilton and Henry Dundas, to whom it originally had been issued. Dundas asked the Lord Advocate, the Dean, and the Lord Provost to decide. They nominated Kemble, but Hamilton meanwhile had already authorized Mrs Esten to use the patent, and she had the lease. So she opened the Theatre Royal while Kemble managed to obtain permission from Jones to fit up the Circus as a theatre, which he opened on 12 January 1793. His establishment was shut down on 6 February as unauthorized. The mess was resolved by the following January 1794, when Mrs Esten gave up the lease of the Theatre Royal to Kemble, who agreed to pay Jackson's creditors £1000 and Mrs Esten £200 each year for its use.

While the disposition of the Edinburgh lease was being resolved Kemble had kept busy with his Newcastle circuit. There in January 1793 he had played Jaques, his wife Rosalind, and young Henry Siddons (son of Sarah) Orlando in *As You Like It*. By September 1792 he had also added Sheffield to his holdings. There that fall he had a dispute with the younger John Edwin over salary that resulted in letters *To the Public* published by both in Newcastle in June 1793. Kemble opened theatres at Berwick Upon Tweed on 11 August 1794 and in Alnwick in 1796, the latter under the patronage of the Duke and Duchess of Northumberland. A newly erected theatre was opened by him at Aberdeen early in September 1795 with a "good Poetical Address written by himself," which was published in the *True Briton* of 9 September. In 1799 he acquired from Cawdell the Durham circuit, which included Scarborough, Sunderland, Stockton, and North and South Shields.

With the problem of the lease and patent settled at Edinburgh, Kemble opened the Theatre Royal, Shakespeare Square, on 18 January 1794 with *Hamlet*, with his wife as Ophelia, John Kemble as Hamlet, and Charles Kemble as Laertes. For another six years Stephen managed the Edinburgh house with success and spirit. In the earlier part of his management he did not often appear on the stage; but in the latter years, when the quality of his company deteriorated, he was seen more frequently. In addition to his usual standby roles cited above, he also played at Edinburgh, among others, Bellarius in *Cymbeline*, Dumont in *Jane Shore*, Horatio in *The Fair Penitent*, Mr Harmony in *Every One has His Fault*, Mr Strickland in *The Suspicious Husband*, Sir Anthony

Absolute in *The Rivals*, Sir John Falstaff in *The Merry Wives of Windsor*, Sir William Meadows in *Love in a Village*, and the title role in *Zorinski*.

During the 1790s Kemble began to gain weight. Eventually he grew to weigh over 18 stone (over 252 pounds), though he was only five feet nine inches tall. The critic Timothy Plain (pseudonym of Moncrieff Threepland) published regular reviews of the Edinburgh theatre in the *Scots Chronicle* from 1797 to 1800 (collected and published in 1800 as *Letters respecting the performances at the Theatre Royal, Edinburgh*) in which Kemble was often dealt with severely but sometimes was given due credit for his acting. In a certain line, thought Timothy Plain, he "may be agreeable." For example, despite his ponderous, unwieldy figure, even with his imperfections, he was the best Horatio in *Hamlet* the critic had seen "these several years," for he sustained "both the sedateness and spirit of the character with propriety." The critic was sorry, however, to have seen Kemble as Richard III: "though I think him energetic in sentimental declamation, and in the blunt, honest, manly cast of parts, I cannot be of opinion that he is a proper representative of the 'lean, shrunk, withered' Richard." After several such comments Timothy Plain shrugged "with regard to his *figure* I pass it over" and determined to confine himself to Kemble's acting. As Macbeth, Kemble was unvaried in feature, deportment, and action, keeping his voice "raised above his natural pitch. . . . He *fought* through the part as if the whole merit consisted in turbulence, noise, and declamation;—it was painful to see his over-exertions." He was "an absolute stranger" to the character of Sir Anthony Absolute, "too fierce" as Bajazet, "mechanical and laborious" as Old Norval, and quite unqualified in Shylock because he either growled or screamed. When John Kemble went to play Richard III at Edinburgh in August 1800 (as he had done for his brother from time to time), Stephen acted King Henry well enough, but his "fair round belly" prevented the audience from believing that he and ill-fortune were familiar—and when he fell, "the ears of the audience were rent in twain!—the house shook!"

Near the end of his Edinburgh management, the quality of the company declined to a deplorable state and he relied on bringing in

London stars for brief and costly engagements. In 1795 his sister Mrs Siddons played for him; she earned £800 for herself but brought £1600 into his treasury. Timothy Plain complained that, with some notable exceptions, Kemble had given Edinburgh audiences "the *dross* of all theatres, merely because the Manager now and then treats us with a peep of his Sister . . . and his brother John." In Crito's *Letter to the Manager of the Edinburgh Theatre* (1800), Kemble was similarly attacked for bringing on the "refuse, the scum, the rubbish of those wretched strolling parties, who in village barns earn a miserable subsistence from ignorance and stupidity." The case seems overstated (and his management at Newcastle seems to have been received with general respect), but audiences did decline sufficiently for Kemble to give up the Edinburgh and Glasgow houses in 1800.

That summer he had opened with John Kemble as an attraction in a company otherwise called by Timothy Plain an "insult." At the conclusion of *Pizarro* on 30 July 1800, Stephen Kemble came forward to deliver his farewell address. After thanking the public for their support, he stated "though his followers might be more successful, they could not be more ambitious or anxious to please—he might almost take it upon him to assert he *had* given satisfaction." As James Dibdin continued the account in his *Annals of the Edinburgh Stage*:

At this point he was interrupted with considerable murmurs and some hissing; but he continued—"I once thought to have left Edinburgh without a single enemy behind me"—the hissing then increased, but he proceeded. "It is, however, not wonderful that I am disappointed, for even our great Redeemer had his enemies; and after his great example (at this phrase he clapped his hands on his great fat paunch) I will be meek and submissive"! The row that ensued upon this was tremendous, and after again essaying to speak, Kemble had to retire in terror of being pelted!

Thus Kemble gave over his Edinburgh management to John Jackson and Francis Aickin.

In 1806 he relinquished management of the Newcastle circuit to Macready, but though his fortunes had been in decline there his departure was accomplished with a bit more grace. On 21 June 1806 the *Newcastle Chronicle* wrote:

"Mr. Kemble, tho' on the eve of resigning management, appears still indefatiguable to please the public, as if determined we should be obliged to confess that 'the weary sun would make a golden set'." His last benefit at Newcastle, on 1 November 1806, brought him £106.

In the autumn of 1802 Kemble returned to the Drury Lane stage for a few nights, now so corpulent he could play Falstaff without padding. The *Monthly Mirror* of October 1802 thought that the fat knight was the only character in which he could have presented himself before the audience with any probability of success. Kemble wrote a humorous address for the occasion which was delivered by the younger Bannister and poked fun at himself:

But all good honest flesh and blood, and bone
And weighing, more or less, some thirty stone.
Upon the Northern Coast by Chance we caught
*   him,*
And hither, in a broad wheel'd waggon, brought
*   him,*
For in a chaise the varlet n'er could enter,
And no mail-coach on such a fare would venture.

The description of his playing of Falstaff provided by the *Monthly Mirror* critic suggests that Kemble rested more upon his physical attributes than his acting talents:

In the satirical passages he was exceedingly happy, and his vain-glorious boast in the last act 'there's Percy for you,' was as admirable in the delivery as it was new and just in the conception. The soliloquy on *honour* was also given with due force. The principal deficiency was that of *humour*, a quality which Mr. Kemble does not appear to possess in any extraordinary degree; at least his expression of it is dry, and rather forced, and wants that natural richness which is so necessary to give the requisite effect to several of the scenes in which *Falstaff* is engaged. Mr. Kemble sometimes seemed to be merely *reciting the text, in the habit of Falstaff*, instead of entering into the true jovial spirit of the character. His action was likewise too nimble, and his manner and appearance altogether too youthful for one who is called by the prince 'reverend vice, grey iniquity, father ruffian, vanity in years, white-bearded Satan,' &c.

But, upon the whole, the performance was truly respectable, and while it has proved a source of reputation and profit to the actor, Mr. Sheridan, who invited him to London, has the most solid reasons for congratulating himself on the event of the engagement.

He received £52 10s. for three nights in October 1802 and similar payments in December. On 15 December he was paid £347 10s. 6d. from a special benefit. (In the will of his father Roger Kemble, proved on 6 April 1803, Stephen was left, together with Sarah, Elizabeth Whitlock, John, and Charles, two renters' share of Drury Lane, with the interest, to be divided equally among them upon the death of their mother.)

In November 1802 he also attracted large audiences at Bath. There and at Bristol he appeared in 1803–4 as well. He made his debut as Falstaff in 1 Henry IV at Manchester in June 1804: "The discovery of Falstaff on a Couch, in his first scene, as if awakening," in the opinion of the Townsman (No XXI), "was an excellent idea of Mr Kembles; for his question . . . 'what time of day is it' had a much better effect than the common method of walking." He followed with Falstaff in The Merry Wives of Windsor, in which his acting was "infinitely superior to that in the other play."

Kemble returned to London in 1806 to play Falstaff in 2 Henry IV and then Falstaff in The Merry Wives of Windsor at Covent Garden on 17 and 24 September, respectively. In the autumn of 1813–14 he was back at Drury Lane (paid £105 on 16 October 1813). The actor William Smith had written to Thomas Coutts on 10 October 1813: "the Great Kemble, if not much mended since I saw him is like the Devonshire Ox, to be valued only for his weight."

Kemble managed at Whitehaven and Paislie about 1814 and acted at Crow Street, Dublin, in 1814–15. He was again acting at Drury Lane in 1816–17 and then became that theatre's temporary stage manager for 1818–19, during which period his son Henry Stephen Kemble was brought on in a series of capital roles for which he was unsuited. Flodden Field, a romantic drama based on Scott's Marmion, written by Stephen and his son, was first presented on 3 December 1818 (printed 1819). The following season Elliston became manager and Kemble stayed on to act. But the great attraction at Drury Lane in 1819–20 was Edmund Kean. Because of Kean's astonishing success as King Lear, the bills announced that

"Mr. S. Kemble . . . has consented to close his Engagement by performing in Afterpieces." The Miller in The King and the Miller of Mansfield on 26 April 1820 was Kemble's last performance in London.

Stephen George Kemble's death came on 5 June 1822 at the Grove, near Durham, and he was buried in Durham Cathedral in the Chapel of the Nine Altars. His wife, who survived him by 19 years, was buried by his side on 25 January 1841. One of their children, George, had died soon after his birth at Edinburgh on 21 April 1786. Their children Frances Crawford Kemble (1787–1849), an actress who married Robert Arkwright, and Henry Stephen Kemble (1789–1836), an actor, are noticed separately in these pages, as is Mrs Stephen Kemble. Stephen's children and grandchildren formed a large network of per-

Courtesy of the Garrick Club

STEPHEN KEMBLE as Falstaff
by De Wilde

formers in the nineteenth century. By his wife, Stephen was related to the Satchell family of performers, and by the marriages of his sisters-in-law he was connected to the Blands and Wilsons.

In his earlier years Kemble had been a competent actor. His best role, after Falstaff, was Sir Christopher Curry in *Inkle and Yarico*, a piece in which his wife's Yarico was highly regarded. He had the Kemble physiognomy, though not the hauteur. But, as most critics took pains to state, he was not qualified to shine in the same hemisphere with his sister Sarah's resplendent lustre, and despite Stephen's substance of form, it was his brother John who was the "Great Kemble."

In addition to *The Northern Inn* and *Flodden Field*, Stephen Kemble wrote *Odes, Lyrical Ballads, and Poems*, published at Edinburgh with a portrait in 1809. He also wrote a number of miscellaneous addresses delivered from the stage by himself and others. One such was "A Comic-Satiric Address, In the Character of Touchstone, Riding On an Ass," which Oxberry had success in speaking and which he published in his *Actor's Budget* (1820). Kemble also gave country recitations of various biblical chapters to tide him over from time to time. He was a member of an Edinburgh convivial society called the Knights Companions of the Cape and also presided sometimes over meetings of the Sunderland Shakespeare Club. Parodies emanating from the "Durham Wags" upon Kemble's poetry and social affectations were published in the fourth volume of Hogg's *Poetical Works*.

Portraits of Stephen George Kemble include:

1. By S. De Wilde. Red chalk and India ink and watercolor wash. Dated May 1817. In the British Museum.

2. By John Downman. In the list of portraits in the artist's sketch books from Butleigh Court. "Stephen Kemble, the Actor, 1812. An excellent Sir John Falstaff without stuffing." Present location unknown.

3. Engraving by S. Freeman, after T. Kearsley. Published as a plate to the *Monthly Mirror*, 1807; a vignette copy by an unknown engraver was also issued.

4. Engraving by J. Heath, after J. R. Smith. Published by S. Kemble, Newcastle, 1808.

5. By unknown engraver. Published as a plate to the *British Stage*, 1820. The same picture was also issued on a plate with one of Miss Smith.

6. As Falstaff in *1 Henry IV*. Watercolor by W. Loftis, "Taken from Life." In the Folger Shakespeare Library.

7. As Falstaff in *1 Henry IV*, standing beside prostrate figure of Hotspur. Engraving by C. Warren, after De Wilde. Published by G. Kearsley, 1804.

8. As Falstaff in *The Merry Wives of Windsor*. Watercolor by S. De Wilde, dated 1805. In the Garrick Club (catalogue No 56).

9. As Falstaff in *The Merry Wives of Windsor*. Watercolor by S. De Wilde. In the Harvard Theatre Collection. Kemble stands in a slightly different posture and is not as heavy as in No 7, above.

10. As Falstaff in *The Merry Wives of Windsor*, handing letters to a boy. Engraving by Meyrion, after Singleton. Published as a plate to Oxberry's *Dramatic Biography*, 1825.

11. As Falstaff in *The Merry Wives of Windsor*. Engraving by J. Rogers, after G. Harlowe. Published as a plate to Oxberry's *Dramatic Biography*, 1825.

12. As Falstaff (in *The Merry Wives of Windsor*?). Miniature oil on wood panel, by unknown artist. Owned by John Boyt, Boston, Massachusetts.

13. As Falstaff in *The Merry Wives of Windsor*. Drawing by unknown artist, dated 2 November 1802. In the Beard Collection, Victoria and Albert Museum, where it is identified as of John Philip Kemble; but the date coincides with the return of Stephen to play the role at Drury Lane.

14. As Hamlet. Drawn and engraved by R. Dighton. Caricature with title: "Hamlet in Scotland. A Large manager in a Great Character." Published 1794.

15. As Henry VIII in George Henry Harlow's painting of "The Court for the Trial of Queen Katharine" in *Henry VIII*. Though Stephen Kemble and his brothers John Philip and Charles and sister Sarah Siddons form the central focus of the picture, the scene does not represent an actual performance, for Harlow painted many of his friends into it. The large canvas (63 × 86), exhibited at the Royal Academy in 1817, was originally owned by a music teacher named Welsh; eventually it

came into the possession of James Morrison at Basildon Park, where it still remains by descent. In 1819 an engraving by G. Clint was published by W. Cribb, with a key to the persons pictured; another engraving was published in 1829. Smaller copies of the painting after Harlow are in the Garrick Club (No 180) and the Royal Shakespeare Theatre Picture Gallery (No 59). Another copy, after Harlow, was bought by Henry C. Folger in 1928; in 1962 it was sold by the Folger Shakespeare Library to the American Shakespeare Theatre Association, Stratford, Connecticut. As an item in the American Shakespeare Theatre Association's sale at Sotheby, Parke, Bernet in New York on 15 January 1976, that copy (Lot 114) sold for $150. Probably that was the version sold at Sotheby's, London, on 6 July 1977 (Lot 88) and again on 26 July 1978 (Lot 65) and reported now to be in a private English collection. Harlow's original painting from Basildon Park was shown in an exhibition of "Shakespeare's Heroines in the Nineteenth Century" at the Buxton Museum and Art Gallery in the summer of 1980. For additional information on the painting, see the exhibition catalogue written by Geoffrey Ashton.

16. Caricature titled: "Kemble and the Butcher." By unknown engraver. Depicts Kemble standing with stick in hand, and a butcher holding a leg of mutton.

17. Caricature titled: "Vide Criticism in the World, May 19, 1787," with three lines describing Kemble. By unknown engraver.

The engraving by R. J. Lane, after T. Lane, which is listed in the Harvard Theatre Collection catalogue (No 9) as being of Stephen Kemble as Falstaff is actually of his brother Charles Kemble.

Kemble, Mrs Stephen George, Elizabeth, née Satchell *1762?–1841, actress, singer.*

Elizabeth Satchell was born in 1762 or early January 1763 in London, the daughter of John Satchell of Great Pulteney Street, Golden Square, who was later (about 1792) musical instrument maker to the Prince of Wales. He probably was the J. Satchell who in 1782 had an instrument shop in Bedford Court, Covent Garden. In 1794 a firm of instrument makers, Satchell and Forschle, operated at No 21, Mark Lane. The Elizabeth "Setchel" from St Pancras who was buried at St Paul, Covent

Harvard Theatre Collection

ELIZABETH KEMBLE
engraving by Goldar

Garden, on 5 July 1830, aged 85, may have been her mother. Our Elizabeth had at least three sisters, who also went on the stage: Susanna Satchell, born in 1758, married the actor Robert Benson, acted in London and the provinces, and died in 1811; Catherine Mary Satchell married the lawyer John Lewis Duill in 1780, acted at Covent Garden in 1786, married the poet John Taylor in 1788, and died in 1789; and a sister, Christian name unknown, married the actor James Bland and played in the provinces but not in London. The Sarah Satchell who married John Farr at St George, Hanover Square, on 6 February 1780 was probably also a sister.

It was claimed in *The Secret History of the Green Room* that Elizabeth Satchell studied voice in secret with "Mr Baker, a Musician connected with Covent Garden Theatre," because her parents disapproved her attraction to the musical stage. But that is an unlikely story, inasmuch as three other sisters took up stage careers. Elizabeth's teacher was Thomas Baker, the elder (fl. 1745–1785?), singer at Covent Garden for over 30 years; he was paid £50 on 23 October 1782 by that theatre "in consideration of his giving up Miss Elizabeth Satchell's Article."

By that time, however, she already had two years of professional experience, having made her debut at Covent Garden as Polly in *The Beggar's Opera* on 21 September 1780, when the bills announced her as "A Young Lady" making her first appearance on any stage. Next day the *Morning Post* reported that despite her stage fright, caused by "delicate sensibility," her acting had succeeded—"Her person is exquisitely pleasing"—and her songs had been received with applause. "If Miss Satchell would put herself under the direction of a master eminent in the science of music, and well acquainted with stage effect, we plainly perceive she would shortly become a valuable jewel in the theatrical cabinet," wrote the critic; so perhaps at that time she was not yet Baker's apprentice. She repeated Polly on 22 September and 25 October before acting Ophelia in *Hamlet* on 26 October, announced as the young lady who had played Polly. On 25 November 1780 her name was printed for the first time in the bills as a principal character in the premiere of Charles Dibdin's comic opera *The Islanders*; in the published song book she was assigned to the role of Flametta. By the season's end she also had performed Patty in *The Maid of the Mill*, Sidney Grubb in *Second Thoughts Are Best*, Miss Bellmont in *Seventeen Hundred and Eighty One*, Cecilia in *The Son-in-Law*, and Constantia in the premiere of Charles Macklin's comedy *The Man of the World* on 10 May 1781.

She began her second season at Covent Garden on 17 September 1781 as Margaret in *A New Way to Pay Old Debts* and then came on as Juliet on 24 September. On 17 November she acted Adelaide in the first performance of *The Count of Narbonne*, Jephson's tragedy which owed its scenes and dresses to the direction of Horace Walpole, who wrote to the play's author the morning after the premiere that the "poor child Miss Satchell was very inferior to what she appeared at the rehearsals. . . . Her voice has no strength, nor is she yet at all mistress of the stage." Walpole thus had

"begged Miss Younge to try what she can do with her by Monday." Evidently Miss Younge's efforts were not in vain, for according to *The Secret History of the Green Room* Adelaide became Miss Satchell's most successful character, establishing her reputation solidly with the public. That season she also appeared in several other parts of some importance: Cynthia in *The Double Dealer*, Cynthia in *The Wife's Relief*, Agnes in *The Walloons*, Celia in *As You Like It*, and Cecilia in *The Chapter of Accidents*.

In 1782–83, her third season, in which she earned £3 per week, she added to her repertoire Julia in *Which is the Man?*, Miss Richley in *The Discovery*, Erato in *Philodamus*, Lady Touchwood in *The Belle's Stratagem*, Marianne in the premiere of Cumberland's *The Mysterious Husband* on 28 January 1783, a Turkish Captive in *The Knight of Malta*, Leonora in *The Maid of the Oaks*, Zanga in *The Revenge*, Lassie in *The Royal Chace*, and Perdita in *The Winter's Tale*. Probably she was the Miss Satchell who acted Statira in *Alexander the Great* on 24 May 1783, but that actress may have been her sister Susanna Satchell, who had made her debut at Covent Garden on 17 May 1783 as Floretta in *The Quaker*. That summer Elizabeth performed at Liverpool; in September 1783 a poem by "Merseius" praising her portrayal of Perdita there appeared in the London *Morning Chronicle*.

The season of 1783–84 began ambitiously for Miss Satchell. With her salary raised to £4 per week, by the end of October she had played Juliet, Margaret, Ophelia, and Perdita, roles already in her possession, and came forward for the first time as Desdemona in *Othello*, Lady Anne in *Richard III*, Cordelia in *King Lear*, Selima in *Tamerlane*, and Indiana in *The Conscious Lovers*. The *Theatrical Review* was pleased to notice the improvement of this "rising actress" and found that as Indiana on 8 October 1783 "her plaintiveness of tone, her extreme tenderness of feeling, her judicious emphasis, and her pleasing aspect, won upon our hearts as much as they satisfied our minds." She did, however, punctuate her speech too often with pauses.

On 20 November 1783 at St George, Bloomsbury, she married Stephen George Kemble, then a member of the Covent Garden company earning £1 less per week than his bride. He was one of Roger and Sarah Kem-

ELIZABETH KEMBLE as Imoinda

engraving by Leney, after De Wilde

ble's clan, which included his brother John and his sisters Sarah, Elizabeth, and Fanny, all then performing in London. On 24 November, four days after her marriage, billed as Mrs Kemble, Elizabeth acted Miss Dormer in *The Mysterious Husband*. Several weeks later, on 6 December, she created the role of Arabella in the premiere of Mrs Cowley's *More Ways than One*. To her repertoire that season she also added Charlotte in *The Two Gentlemen of Verona*, Drusilla in *The Prophetess*, and Lady Charlotte in *The Funeral*. At her benefit on 18 May 1784, when tickets could be had of her at No 22, Great Queen Street, Lincoln's Inn Fields, she acted Arabella in *More Ways than One* and Daphne in *Midas*; net receipts were a modest £37 13*s*.

When her husband was discharged from Covent Garden at the close of the 1783–84 season, Mrs Kemble migrated with him to Exeter, Chester, Leeds, Newcastle, York, Glasgow, and Edinburgh. In those towns she char-

acteristically received more favor than her spouse. In his *Children of Thespis*, John Williams chided:

> "Ah! where is the nymph . . .
>
> . . . .
> Who gave rural STELLA the heart-wounding
>   moan?
> Who made simple YARICO's terrors her own?
> That nymph . . .
> Is now making a circuit thro' half-peopled towns,
> And led by harsh Fate 'fore illiterate clowns
>
> . . . .
> For, abhorring the arts of an EMPEROR's lust,
> With the grace to be poor, and the wish to be just,
> She is sentenc'd to Want, by a TYRANT's com-
>   mand,
> And lives an example that's shewn round the land.

Playing Othello and Desdemona, the Kembles made their debuts at Edinburgh on 32 January 1786; some of her subsequent roles there were Dorinda in *The Tempest*, Gillian in *The Quaker*, Lady Teazle in *The School for Scandal*, Louisa in *The Deserter*, Nannette in *Fontainebleau*, Narcissa in *The Rival Candidates*, Norah in *The Poor Soldier*, Ophelia, Pastora in *The Perjured Clown*, Patty in *The Maid of the Mill*, and the title role in *Rosina*. She appeared at York in *More Ways than One* on 26 May 1786 but became so ill she could not play Desdemona next night. At Leeds a short time later she offered Letitia Hardy in *The Belle's Stratagem*.

After playing numerous roles at Edinburgh again in the early months of 1787, the Kembles were engaged by Colman for the Haymarket, where he appeared on 16 May 1787 as Dominick in *The Spanish Fryar* and she made her debut on 18 May as Ophelia (with Kemble as Claudius). The critic in the *European Magazine* welcomed her return to London and praised her performance for its "affecting simplicity and real excellence" but noted that she wanted spirit and vigor in the stronger and more declamatory parts. After playing Cowslip in *The Agreeable Surprise*, the title role in *Polly Honeycomb*, Dinah Primrose in *The Young Quaker*, and Nancy Buttercup in *A Beggar on Horseback*, she was the first Yarico in Colman's *Inkle and Yarico* on 4 August 1787 and then acted the title role in the premiere of McDonald's *Vimonda* on 5 September.

Though Mrs Kemble for many years was

obliged to spend the winter months of her career assisting her husband's managements in the north, she enjoyed regular summer engagements at the Haymarket through 1796, offering a very large repertoire and creating many original roles in plays by Colman, O'Keeffe, and others. Among them were Julia in *The Surrender of Calais* on 30 July 1791, Una in *The Enchanted Wood* on 25 August 1792, and Zorayda in *The Mountaineers* on 3 August 1793. (Our subject Elizabeth Kemble should not be confused with another Elizabeth Kemble, Stephen Kemble's sister, who married the actor Charles Edward Whitlock in 1785, or with another Mrs Kemble, born Priscilla Hopkins, who married John Philip Kemble and acted as Mrs Kemble at Drury Lane during some of the years Mrs Stephen Kemble was at the Haymarket.)

Addresses given for her at her benefits included No 26, Villiers Street, York Buildings, in August 1789; next door to the Old Slaughter's Coffee House, St Martin's Lane, in August

By permission of the Trustees of the British Museum

ELIZABETH KEMBLE as Cowslip
by Shee

1791; Adams's Masquerade Warehouse, Haymarket, in 1792; No 24, corner of Panton Street, Haymarket, in 1793 and 1794; No 9, Haymarket, in 1795; and No 11, Haymarket, in 1796. Her benefit on 16 August 1791, when she acted Queen Margaret in *The Battle of Hexham*, was marked by the appearance of her four-year-old daughter Frances who "drew forth much applause" as the Prince of Wales. Her benefit on 29 August 1795 was supported by special appearances of her brother-in-law John Philip Kemble as Douglas and her sister-in-law Sarah Siddons as Lady Randolph.

The *Thespian Magazine* in 1792 (p. 94) offered a tribute to Mrs Kemble's talent and character:

Mrs. S. Kemble is deservedly respected not only as the chief ornament of the Haymarket Theatre, but as a lady who for her elegance of manners, sensibility of mind, and morality of conduct, has obtained and preserves both the affection and esteem of her acquaintance (which report mentions to be extensive and valuable) and the illimitable applause of the public—the submissive duties of a wife and the affectionate attentions of a mother, are both equally conspicuous in her domestic character—In short, she is the pride of *Social* life, and an honour to the *trionic* profession. The nervous and elevated language of young Colman in his delineation of the martial consort of the VI. Harry, she delivers with energy and judgment——the nice distinctions of look and expression in the *heroine* of the episode introduced in the "Surrender of Calais" are *alone* characterized in Mrs. K's performance; and in the wild incoherence of Ophelia, and the plaintive sorrow of Mrs. Euston, she alike makes certain progress to the heart.

The exquisite sensations of disinterested love which her soul is admirably formed to experience, she transfers to the breasts of the audience; and the gentle complaint of injured attachment delivered in tones of the most superlative and enchanting melody, summons the resistless tear of compassion into the eyes of the most rugged and insensible—and while sympathy and feeling shall hold a place in the human heart, her representation of Yarrico [*sic*] will be attended with delight, and remembered with the most unbounded admiration.

The *Gazetteer* on 29 August 1791 praised the "modest, tender Mrs Kemble" for her "*bye-play*," the quality of "always *enacting*, whether in speech or not," which was a faculty she possessed "perhaps, more than any person upon the stage, more even than Mrs Siddons."

She co-managed with her husband at Coventry from February to June 1790 and she acted at Newcastle, Sunderland, Windsor, Sheffield, and Glasgow—all places where her husband managed at times in the 1790s. In the autumns of 1795 and 1796 she acted at Liverpool for Aickin. Her main activity, however, was at Edinburgh between 1792 and 1800, where Stephen Kemble held the Theatre Royal in 1792, the New Theatre (the former Circus) in 1793, and the Theatre Royal again from 1794 until his Edinburgh farewell in July 1800.

The years at Edinburgh brought the Kembles considerable litigation and public abuse. During that period Mrs Kemble acted at least 150 roles of a most varied nature, ranging throughout the eighteenth-century repertory. A small selection includes Angela in *The Castle Spectre*, Belvidera in *Venice Preserv'd*, Catherine in *Catherine and Petruchio*, Cora in *Pizarro*, Cordelia, Donna Violante in *The Wonder*, Fanny in *The Clandestine Marriage*, Isabella, Jane Shore, Julia Melville in *The Rivals*, Juliet, Lady Teazle, Madge in *Love in a Village*, Miss Hardcastle in *She Stoops to Conquer*, Miss Tittup in *Bon Ton*, Polly in *The Beggar's Opera*, Portia in *The Merchant of Venice*, Roxalana in *The Sultan*, a Singing Witch in *Macbeth*, Stella in *Robin Hood*, Venus in *Poor Vulcan*, and, of course, Yarico.

Announced as making her "first, and only" appearance on that stage, Mrs Kemble acted Ophelia in *Hamlet* and Cowslip in *The Agreeable Surprise* at Drury Lane on 20 October 1800. A contemporary hand on an annotated bill in the British Library informs us that she was "Admirable, tho' I have seen her more happy in the past." That night John Philip Kemble played Hamlet and Charles Kemble played Laertes.

Nineteen years after the death of her husband in 1822, Elizabeth Kemble died, on 20 January 1841 at the Grove, near Durham, at the age of 78, and on 25 January was buried by his side in the Chapel of the Nine Altars, Durham Cathedral. Their daughter Frances Crawford Kemble (1787–1849), who made her debut at the age of four at the Haymarket in 1791, acted at Edinburgh and Newcastle and in 1805 married Robert Arkwright. Their son Henry Stephen Kemble (1789–1836), who also appeared as a child at the Haymarket

in 1796 and married the actress Mary Freeze in 1814, performed in London during the first several decades of the nineteenth century. Both children are noticed separately in this dictionary. Stephen and Elizabeth Kemble's firstborn, named George Kemble, died in infancy soon after his birth at Edinburgh on 21 April 1786.

Most assessments of Elizabeth Kemble's talents attest to a varied excellence and an ability to play the range from "engaging innocence" to "deep-toned pathos." In the *Memoirs of John Bannister*, Adolphus praised her "generous affection" as Sophia in *The Road to Ruin* and the "heart-rending distress" of Desdemona. Though Timothy Plain, the Edinburgh critic, thought that roles like Lady Teazle and Letitia Hardy were out of her line, roles like Cora in *Pizarro* nicely suited her gentility, sweetness, and earnestness—Cora "was a picture of feeling, conjugal affection, and parental tenderness." Boaden, in his *Life of Mrs Siddons*, was effusive: "The stage never in my time exhibited so pure, so interesting a character as Miss Satchell. . . . No one ever like her presented the charm of unsuspecting fondness or that rustic simplicity which, removed immeasurably from vulgarity, betrays nothing of the world's refinement." Mrs Kemble, however, often exhibited displays of temper and in one instance gave Henry Erskine Johnstone a deep bite on his shoulder.

A critic in *Blackwood's Magazine* in 1832 praised her clear voice and thought that she was "a delicious Juliet, and an altogether incomparable Yarico" as well as an excellent Catherine in *Catherine and Petruchio*. As Polly Peachum she was praised warmly by the *Courant* of 19 January 1792 for her "natural and impressive style" of acting, for the "elegance of her figure, and the genuine simplicity of her demeanour." Timothy Plain suggested that she wanted spirit in the role, playing too simply and singing too solemnly.

Waldron noted in his *Candid and Impartial Strictures on the Performers* (1795) that her person was "engaging," her face "beautifully simple," and her manners "pleasing and unaffected." Her drawling tone, however, did not suit her, in his judgment, for speaking blank verse. Others suggested she was not a particularly good singer, though she displayed much feeling.

Portraits of Elizabeth Kemble include:

1. Engraving by J. Goldar. Published as a plate to the *General Magazine and Impartial Review*, 1790.

2. As Cowslip in *The Agreeable Surprise*. Painting by M. A. Shee. Present location unknown. Photographs of the painting appeared in a sales catalogue of the *Blakeslee Galleries Collection*, New York, 1915, and in Spielmann's *British Portrait Painting*, 1910.

3. As Imoinda in *Oroonoko*. Painting by S. De Wilde. In the Garrick Club (No 219). Engraving by W. Leney, published as a plate to *Bell's British Theatre*, 1791. The same picture with a different background was engraved by "A. H. W."

4. As Juliet in *Romeo and Juliet*. Engraving by C. Sherwin, after J. H. Ramberg. Published as a plate to *Bell's British Theatre*, 1785.

5. As Yarico, with John Palmer as Inkle, in *Inkle and Yarico*. Engraving by Barlow, after Cruikshank. Published by J. Roach as a plate to an edition of the play, 1790.

6. As Yarico. Pen and pencil drawing by Roberts. Location unknown. A notation in a manuscript at the Folger Shakespeare Library, dated "Aug. 12 [1795?]," reads *Roberts, who successfully manages the Pen as well as the Pencil, is proceeding very fast with a promising Likeness of Mrs. Kemble* in Yarico."

Kemm, Samuel [*fl.* 1794–1797?], *organist, singer?*

Doane's *Musical Directory* of 1794 listed Samuel Kemm, of Holiday Yard, Creed Lane, as an organist and alto (singer, presumably) who participated in the oratorio performances at Westminster Abbey and Drury Lane Theatre. In the Drury Lane accounts are three notes concerning one "Kern"—possibly a transcription error for Kemm. He was paid 3*s.* on 13 June 1794, 5*s.* on 3 December 1796, and 5*s.* on 17 December 1797.

Kemp, Mr [*fl.* 1723], *actor.*

Mr Kemp played Sir Charles in *The Stratagem* on 14 March 1723 at the Haymarket Theatre. On the following 15 April he was seen as Balance in *The Recruiting Officer*, and on 22 April he acted Martin in *The Anatomist*.

Kemp, Mr [*fl.* 1744], *actor.*

A Mr Kemp played List in *The Miser* at the Haymarket Theatre on 10 May 1744. It is highly unlikely that he was the jeweler William Kemp, who in 1743 took over Parlous Pond and turned it into Peerless Pool, a pleasure garden devoted to sportsmen.

Kemp, Mr [*fl.* 1759–1760], *lampman.*

The account books at Covent Garden Theatre cited Mr Kemp the lampman several times in 1759–60. On 15 December 1759 he was paid £40 for 25 nights at £1 12*s.* per night. On 8 January 1760 he received £20 16*s.* "for Lamps" for 13 nights. His last mention in the books was on 28 May 1760, when he was paid £11 4*s.* for seven nights.

Kempton, Matthew [*fl.* 1663–1681], *scenekeeper, actor.*

Matthew Kempton was first cited in the Lord Chamberlain's accounts on 6 June 1663, when he was described as a scenekeeper for the King's Company at the Bridges Street playhouse. From time to time over the following 18 years Kempton was mentioned in the accounts. On 20 July 1663 Alice Cooper was allowed to take Kempton to court; William Collins sued Matthew on 26 October 1667 and Arthur Babington went against him for a debt on 5 July 1671. The last mention of Kempton in the Lord Chamberlain's accounts was on 29 June 1681, when he was again listed as a King's Company scenekeeper—by then at Drury Lane.

Kempton evidently took on small parts in plays on occasion—at least we have one piece of evidence to suggest it: he played a Messenger in the burlesque *Empress of Morocco* in the summer of 1673 (not, according to Robert Hume, December of that year). The troupe was at the time temporarily housed at the Lincoln's Inn Fields playhouse. Sometime that season he acted a Servant in *The Maides Tragedy*.

Kempton, Mrs [Matthew?] [*fl.* 1677], *house servant.*

A Mrs Kempton, possibly the wife of the King's Company scenekeeper Matthew Kempton, was named in a document reported in the July 1816 *Theatrical Inquisitor and Monthly*

Mirror, a source to be approached cautiously. The document purported to be accountings of two performances at Drury Lane in December 1677. In the account for *The Rival Queens* on 26 December, at the end of the list of boxkeepers, pitkeepers, and gallery keepers, is "Mrs. Kempton. . . . . 5[*s.*]" Her position is not clear, for the various parts of the house appear to be otherwise accounted for. She may have been a doorkeeper or cheque taker.

Kena. *See* KEENA.

Kenaston. *See* KYNASTON.

Kendal, Mrs. *See* TWEEDALE, MISS.

Kendall, John [*fl.* 1772], *musician.*
John Kendall, of No 38, Old Change, became a freeman in the Worshipfull Company of Musicians on 20 October 1772.

Kendrick. *See also* KENRICK.

Kendrick, Joseph *b. 1755, singer?, sculptor.*
According to Rupert Gunnis's *Dictionary*, Joseph Kendrick was born on 4 June 1755 and attended the Royal Academy Schools in 1771. In addition to his career as a sculptor, Kendrick was active in London musical circles up to 1805. Doane's *Musical Directory* of 1794 gave his address as No 3, Upper Marylebone Street, near Howland Street, and described him as an alto (singer, presumably) who participated in performances by the Concert of Ancient Music, the Portland Chapel Society, and the New Musical Fund, and in the oratorios at Drury Lane and Westminster Abbey. He had performed at the Oxford Meeting, Doane said, in 1793. Kendrick was a member of the Court of Assistants of the New Musical Fund in 1794, 1805, and 1815. He was evidently not the singer Kenrick, who sang popular songs at Covent Garden Theatre and the Haymarket from 1786 to the early years of the nineteenth century.

Emma Kendrick (1788–1871) the miniaturist and Josephus John Pinnix Kendrick (1791–1832) the sculptor were Joseph Kendrick's children. After 1805 the elder Ken-

drick apparently moved from London to Portsea. Much of his signed work dating from 1774 to 1811 was done in the provinces.

Kene. *See* KEAN, KEEN, KEENE.

Keneston, Keninston, Keniston. *See* KYNASTON.

Kenna, Mr [*fl.* 1771–1794], *actor.*
Mr Kenna and his wife were acting at the Smock Alley Theatre, Dublin, in 1771. In the same year they were at Manchester. Kenna acted Glenalvon in *Douglas* at the Mill Gate Theatre, Belfast, on 6 September 1773; he returned to that city with his wife in August 1774, when his son Master John Kenna also performed. *The London Stage* places Kenna in a list of players who acted occasionally at the Haymarket Theatre during the winter of 1777–78, but we do not find his name in any of the bills; possibly some of the roles attributed to Mr Kenny belonged to him. In the *Memoirs of Harriot Mellon* by Mrs Baron-Wilson, it is stated that Kenna had been a manager of a provincial company before serving in some temporary capacity at one of the London theatres in 1777, and that having finished his engagement in one of the pantomimes he left London to travel with his wife the route of the strolling player. Kenna was acting in Worcestershire in 1778.

In the middle of the 1780s Kenna took his family to America. In addition to his wife, the group included his daughter Miss Kenna, his son John Kenna, and John's wife. According to Dunlap, Mr and Mrs Kenna made their debuts at the John Street Theatre, New York, in May 1786 as Lissardo and Isabella in *The Wonder*. On 12 December John Kenna and his wife played in *The School for Scandal*. The elder Kenna opened a theatre at Newbern, North Carolina, in June 1788 and with the same company opened another theatre in July at Wilmington. The family all acted at Philadelphia in 1791 and 1792. In 1793–94 they were at Charleston, South Carolina, where Kenna is known to have played Old McGilpin in *The Highland Reel* on 11 February 1793 and Tipple in *The Flitch of Bacon* and Faddle in *The Foundling* on 29 September 1794, the last notices of him.

His wife may have been the Mrs Kenna who played Lucy in *The Beggar's Opera* on 26 December 1794 and Regan in *King Lear* on 21 January 1795 at Charleston, but more likely that actress was John Kenna's wife. John Kenna acted many roles at Charleston between 1793 and 1795, and he and his wife were probably the Kennas who played at Providence in 1795. The dates and places of the deaths of the elder Mr and Mrs Kenna are unknown to us. Their son John died at Norfolk late in 1795 or early in 1796.

Kennedy, Mr [*fl. 1737–1760*], *actor, manager.*

The Mr Kennedy who was acting at Smock Alley Theatre, Dublin, in the spring of 1737 and shared a benefit there on 25 May was not Lawrence Kennedy, as W. S. Clark incorrectly indicates in *The Irish Stage in the County Towns*. Lawrence Kennedy, who was born about 1729, would have been too young to have been this person, but he may well have been our subject's son.

Mr Kennedy remained a member of the Smock Alley company through 1741–42. On 14 May 1741 he received a benefit there. He was, we believe, the Kennedy who made his debut at Goodman's Fields Theatre on 14 February 1745 as Stephano in *The Tempest*, in which his wife also made her debut as Ariel. He played Stephano again for five more nights, but on 20 February replaced Goodfellow as Ferdinand, a role he acted throughout the remainder of the season. On 7 March 1745 he acted Ramilie in *The Miser* and he may also have appeared in other productions for which no casts are known.

He and his wife were again in Hallam's company at Goodman's Fields in 1745–46. On 11 November 1745 he played Trueman in *The Twin Rivals*, and he was then seen as Gibbet in *The Stratagem*, Charles in *The Busy Body*, Sir Joseph in *The Old Bachelor*, Tinsel in *The Drummer*, Lorenzo in *The Spanish Fryar*, Laertes in *Hamlet*, the title role in *Oroonoko*, Young Laroon in *The Debauchees*, Trueman in *George Barnwell*, the Duke in *Rule a Wife and Have a Wife*, Hubert in *The Royal Merchant*, Polydore in *The Orphan*, Philip in *She Wou'd and She Wou'd Not*, Sir Charles in *The Fair Quaker of Deal*, Loveworth in *Tunbridge Walks*, Lord Hardy in *The Funeral*, Tattle in *Love for Love*,

and Lord Foppington in *The Relapse*. On 4 March 1764, when he shared a benefit with Miss Smith, Kennedy acted Macheath in *The Beggar's Opera*; tickets could be had of him at No 2, Lambeth Street.

At the beginning of the summer of 1746, Kennedy was with the Covent Garden company for a brief time, playing Ratcliff in *Richard III* on 16 June and Donalbain in *Macbeth* on 27 June. Then he and his wife joined Macklin's company to play at Canterbury. In the autumn he returned to Covent Garden at a salary of 10s. per week and was seen as Bernardo in *Hamlet* and Westmoreland in *1 Henry IV*. Before the end of that season, however, he and his wife (who still had been acting at Goodman's Fields) joined Simpson's company at Bath. When they were at Bristol's Jacob's Wells Theatre on 31 October 1747 he acted Pandolpho and his wife Flavia in *Albumazar*.

Within a few months Kennedy returned to Covent Garden, acting Bernardo in *Hamlet* there on 9 December 1747, Blunt in *Richard III* on 28 December, Nym in *The Merry Wives of Windsor* on 12 January 1748, and the First Merchant in *The Royal Merchant* on 27 January, but by February 1748 he departed once more. He and Mrs Kennedy were back at Bath on 4 April 1748, when they shared a benefit.

In 1749 Kennedy became manager of a small playhouse in Exeter. He also continued to perform with Simpson's company at Bath during the early 1750s. In the *Theatric Tourist*, James Winston identified him also as the manager of theatres at Plymouth and Portsmouth during these years. In 1758 at Portsmouth his troupe was dubbed "the Brandy Company" because of the intemperance of its members. Wilkinson recalled in his *Memoirs* seeing Kennedy at Portsmouth in 1758, at which time he was "an elderly man." About 1758 Kennedy sold the Exeter house to "Harlequin" Pitt, and after the 1760 season he gave up the Portsmouth venture to Arthur.

The Miss Kennedy who performed at Bath from 1750 to 1753, went to London in the season of 1753–54, and was at Dublin from the fall of 1754 through the fall of 1759 was probably his daughter.

Kennedy, Mr [*fl. 1778–1779*], *actor.*

A Mr Kennedy, announced as making his first appearance on any stage, played an unspecified role in *The Macaroni Adventurer* performed by novices at the Haymarket Theatre on 28 December 1778. In the afterpiece, *The Covent Garden Tragedy*, he acted Lovegirlo. Probably he was the Mr Kennedy who played Sancho in *The Wrangling Lovers* and delivered the prologue to *The Humours of Oxford* at the Haymarket on 15 March 1779.

Kennedy, Mrs ₍fl. 1745–1755₎, *actress, singer.*

Mrs Kennedy, the wife of the actor and provincial manager Mr Kennedy (fl. 1737–1760), probably acted with her husband in the provinces prior to her debut at Goodman's Fields Theatre on 14 February 1745 as Ariel in *The Tempest*, "with the songs proper to the character." That night Mr Kennedy made his London debut as Stephano. Mrs Kennedy repeated Ariel several times throughout the season. On 7 March she played Harriet in *The Miser*; and she probably appeared in other productions for which no casts are known.

In 1745–46, her second season at Goodman's Fields, Mrs Kennedy appeared as Dorinda in *The Stratagem*, Rosara in *She Wou'd and She Wou'd Not*, Lucy in *Tunbridge Walks*, Betty in *A Woman Is a Riddle*, Mlle D'Epingle in *The Funeral*, and Jiltup in *The Fair Quaker of Deal*. She and her husband joined Macklin's company at Canterbury in the summer of 1746. She returned to Goodman's Fields in the autumn, though her husband was then engaged at Covent Garden. She acted Myrtillo in *The Provok'd Husband*, Isabella in *The Stage Coach*, and Teresa in *The Spanish Fryar*, among other roles. Before the end of the season, however, she left Goodman's Fields to join Simpson's company at Bath, where she and her husband had a benefit on 2 March 1747. At the Jacob's Wells Theatre, Bristol, on 31 October 1747 she acted Flavia in *Albumazar*.

Mrs Kennedy remained with Simpson's Bath company at least through 1754–55. No doubt she acted also in the theatres managed in the 1750s by her husband at Exeter, Plymouth, and Portsmouth. As discussed in her husband's notice, she may have been the mother of the actor Lawrence Kennedy and the actress Miss Kennedy, who played at Bath between 1750 and 1753 and at Dublin from 1754–55 through 1758–59.

Kennedy, Mrs ₍fl. 1782₎, *actress.*

At the Haymarket Theatre on 21 April 1782, a Mrs Kennedy delivered a monologue with the substantial title of *Phelimoguffinocarilocarneymacframe's Description of a Man of War and a Sea Fight, with Explanations.*

Kennedy, Mrs ₍fl. 1792₎, *singer.*

At the Haymarket Theatre on 26 November 1792, a Mrs Kennedy sang "Poor Jack," in character, at the conclusion of *The Mourning Bride.*

Kennedy, Miss ₍fl. 1750–1759₎, *actress.*

The Miss Kennedy of this notice was very likely the daughter of the provincial and London actor and sometime country manager Kennedy (fl. 1737–1760) and his wife (fl. 1745–1755), an actress, both noticed above. She was probably also sister of the well-known actor and manager Lawrence Kennedy (c. 1729–1786).

Miss Kennedy first comes to our attention in a notice in the *Bristol Weekly Intelligencer* for 11 August 1750 announcing a benefit performance which she would share with Mrs Bishop at Jacob's Wells Theatre, Bristol, on 14 August. She returned to Bristol the following summer, but she had meanwhile joined the company at the Orchard Street Theatre, Bath, in the season of 1750–51. There she acted also in the winter seasons of 1751–52, 1752–53, and 1753–54, according to Arnold Hare's *The Orchard Street Calendar 1750–1805.* Hare gives no roles, but B. S. Penley in *The Bath Stage* reports that on 29 February 1753 she played Charlotte in *The Gamester.* And we get a further indication of her line from some doggerel praise in *The Bath Comedians* (1753; probably by John Lee):

> *I swear by th' Roses and the Lillies*
> *In her Cheeks, she's a good* Phyllis;
> *And farther I'll be bold to tell her,*
> *She pleases me in* Biddy Bellair;
> *And in the* School-Boy *my Pen itches*
> *To praise her when she's dress'd in Breeches.*

At Bath she continued to share benefits with Mrs Bishop. The elder Kennedys cited above were also in the Bath company during those four seasons.

Our erroneous assertion (in volume 5, pages 374–376) that the actress-novelist Elizabeth

Griffith had acted at Covent Garden as "Miss Kennedy" led us to assign Miss Kennedy's London parts to Mrs Griffith. We restore them now, thanks to the vigilance of Professor Betty Rizzo who is preparing a study of Elizabeth Griffith and her works and has sent us corrective information.

After playing leading roles at Bath in the fall of 1753 (the last bill in which she was carried at Orchard Street Theatre was the one for 29 October) Miss Kennedy sought a London engagement. On 10 December 1753 the Covent Garden playbill for *The Suspicious Husband* gave the cast as it had stood on 14 September, except for Clarinda, who was now played by "A Gentlewoman from Bath (who never appeared here before)." She was "Miss Kennedy from Bath" the prompter Cross jotted in his diary. She had success enough in her single performance of that part to be cast in the secondary role of Pamela in MacNamara Morgan's bombastic new tragedy *Philoclea*, which was critically derided but which ran nine nights on and after 22 January 1754.

Miss Kennedy's opportunities at Covent Garden were diminished by the crowding out of legitimate drama by Rich's latest brainstorm, the burlettas of the Giordani family, which also occupied the theatre from time to time that season. She was allowed to play Ophelia in *Hamlet* for her benefit, shared with Bencraft, on 19 April 1754 and then she retreated to Dublin's Smock Alley Theatre, where she remained in the winter from 1754–55 through 1757–58. She went over to the Crow Street Theatre in 1758–59. After that, she was heard from no more.

Kennedy, Lawrence *c. 1729–1786, actor, manager.*

According to his obituary notices in July 1786, Lawrence Kennedy had died at the age of 56 and had been on the stage nearly 50 years. If this information is accurate, he was born about 1729 or 1730 in Dublin and was acting by about 1736, at the age of six or seven. He was probably the son of Mr Kennedy who was acting at Smock Alley, Dublin, by 1737, at Goodman's Fields and Covent Garden in the 1740s and at Bath between 1746 and 1756, and also managed theatres at Exeter, Portsmouth, and Plymouth in the 1750s. Lawrence Kennedy's mother was probably the

Mrs Kennedy who also played in London in the mid-1740s and later at Bath.

Though he may have appeared in some provincial theatres with his parents earlier, the first definite notice of Lawrence Kennedy's career was as a member of the Smock Alley company in 1748–49, when his roles included Careless in *The Committee* on 17 October 1748, Witling in *The Refusal* on 7 December, Lodovico in *Othello* on 31 January 1749, and the Governor in *Oroonoko* on 29 May. In his *General History of the Stage*, published in 1749, Chetwood testified that Kennedy, a Dublin native, had a "good Figure, agreeable Voice, and genteel easy Carriage," attributes that rendered him "a pleasing Actor." It is apparent from Chetwood that Kennedy was still a young man in 1749 and had never played anywhere but Dublin.

Sometime in 1749, after the middle of May, Kennedy married the young Smock Alley actress Elizabeth Orfeur, who was the daughter of performers, Mr and Mrs Orfeur, and the younger sister of the Irish actress Mrs Thomas Farrell. The Kennedys were at Smock Alley in 1749–59 and also at the Aungier Street Theatre in 1750; then they went to play at Edinburgh in 1750–51. His first appearance at the New Concert Hall in that city was probably as Lothario in *The Fair Penitent* on 23 November 1750, followed by the Ghost in *Hamlet* on 28 November and Captain Plume in *The Recruiting Officer* two nights later. At Edinburgh Kennedy's roles were of sufficient number and consequence to suggest a promising future: Iago in *Othello*, Jaffeir in *Venice Preserv'd*, Buckingham in *Richard III*, Dumont in *Jane Shore*, the Bastard in *King John*, Polydore in *The Orphan*, and Myrtle in *The Conscious Lovers*, as well as, among other less important roles, Bassanio in *The Merchant of Venice*, Friendly in *Flora*, Lovemore in *The Lottery*, Sir John Loverule in *The Devil to Pay*, and Benvolio in *Romeo and Juliet*.

The Kennedys returned to Smock Alley in 1751–52, where they played four seasons through 1754–55. Then, leaving his wife behind in the late autumn of 1754, Kennedy went again to Edinburgh to play under John Lee's management for a season; his roles included Captain O'Blunder in *The Brave Irishman*, Roderigo in *Othello*, Captain Brazen in *The Recruiting Officer*, Dick in *The City Wives'*

Confederacy, Old Clincher in *The Constant Couple*, and Sir George Airy in *The Busy Body*. Upon his return to Dublin in the autumn of 1755, he experienced unexpected difficulties in retrieving his position at Smock Alley. As Lee Lewis told the story:

Conjugal love and paternal affection, with almost a certainty of a very good engagement, powerfully stimulated him to return home to his wife and family. He arrived in Dublin in 1755, after about a year's absence. Mrs. Kennedy was re-engaged at her former salary [£4 per week], but without being able to obtain any provision for her husband. She expostulated with the managers on the cruelty of separating man and wife, and did not fail to remind them, that in Mr. Sheridan's management, her husband had, for the last three years, three pounds a week, and for which he had done a great deal of business. They would not give any such salary; but, to oblige her, they offered to allow him thirty shillings a week, which, they said, was as much as they could possibly afford him. . . .

When the warm-tempered Kennedy was told by his wife of the circumstances, he approached Sowdon, one of the managers, with a pistol in each hand and demanded satisfaction for the insult. Sowdon, however, blamed Victor, whereupon Kennedy sought out the co-manager and brought the two face to face, preventing either from accusing the other. Deciding on discretion rather than valor, the managers immediately signed Kennedy. His intrepidity brought Kennedy the nickname of "Bold Lary," as well as a salary of £3 per week for the 1755–56 season at Smock Alley, where he and his wife continued to be engaged through 1759–60.

After some 12 years in the provinces, "Bold Lary" and his wife obtained engagements with Garrick at Drury Lane Theatre. Mrs Kennedy made her debut as Mrs Marwood in *The Way of the World* on 10 October 1760, but not until 29 December was Kennedy seen for the first time in London, as Blunt in *The Committee*. Though his wife appeared frequently that season in capital roles, Kennedy's name was found in the bills only for Capulet in *Romeo and Juliet* and the Lord Chamberlain in *Henry VIII*. Perhaps he performed some unspecified minor parts. The following season, 1761–62, he was seen more often, playing the Lord Chamberlain, Tressel in *Richard III*, Axalla in *Tamerlane*, Harlow in *The Old Maid*, Alonzo in *Rule a Wife*

and Have a Wife, Laertes in *Hamlet*, Philario in *Cymbeline*, Douglas in *1 Henry IV*, Paris in *Romeo and Juliet*, Don Duart in *Love Makes a Man*, and Dick in *The Confederacy*. For his benefit with Mrs Kennedy on 26 April 1762 he acted Aimwell in *The Stratagem*.

Failing to obtain renewed articles after their second London season, the Kennedys found themselves back in the provinces. They played at Cork in the autumn of 1762 and then joined the company at Edinburgh, where Digges and Mrs Bellamy were then the main attractions on and off stage. Mrs Kennedy was much admired in Edinburgh, but Kennedy made his main impact in a quarrel with Beat, one of the managers. "*Beat* threatened to broughton him," reported the *Theatrical Review* of May 1763, and "*Kennedy*, who does not want courage, chose rather to fight like a gentleman.— He collar'd *Beat*, insisted upon putting on his sword, and going out with him. *Beat* went out, it is true, but not to fight. He very valiantly swore the peace against *Lary*." That year Kennedy also acted at Norwich.

In the summer of 1763 Kennedy returned to London to act for Foote at the Haymarket Theatre, where he made his debut on 9 May as Counsellor Quirk in Foote's *Lectures on English Oratory*. He also played a part in *The Diversions of the Morning*, Johnson in *The Rehearsal*, Archer in *The Beaux' Stratagem*, and Clodio in *Love Makes a Man*. On 20 June 1763 he acted an unspecified role in the premiere of Foote's very successful comedy, *The Mayor of Garratt*; on 7 September he delivered the monologue *Bucks Have at ye All*.

For another ten years Lawrence Kennedy worked the provinces. His roles at Edinburgh in 1767–68 reflected his middle age: Capulet, the Duke of York in *Richard III*, Lord Randolph in *Douglas*, Mr Peachum in *The Beggar's Opera*, Oberon in *The Oracle*, and Sir Callaghan O'Brallaghan in *Love à-la-Mode*. He was a member of a company that gave 12 performances in the new theatre at Stratford in March 1771.

In 1772 Kennedy became co-manager with Booth of the New Barton Street Theatre in Gloucester. Their company also acted in the Coopers' Hall next to the Bristol Theatre in King Street from November 1772 to April 1773. Then in the summer of 1773 Kennedy and Booth succeeded Love as managers of the

Richmond Theatre for a year. On 4 April 1774 Kennedy took a benefit at the Haymarket Theatre in which he acted Peachum and the King in *The King and the Miller of Mansfield*. He announced that he had intended that performance before the benefits at the patent houses had begun but had been detained at Bristol.

After the Haymarket benefit Kennedy and his wife stayed in London to visit with Joseph Younger in King Street, Covent Garden. With them was a young female friend. At 2:00 A.M. on the morning of 4 May 1774 the young woman fell asleep while reading in bed, without putting out the candle. In the terrible fire that ensued Mrs Kennedy and her friend were burned to death and Kennedy and Younger managed to escape. In the attempt to save his wife, Kennedy had been so severely burned in the face that his future career was done considerable injury. On 6 May Garrick's treasurer at Drury Lane made a present of £21 to Kennedy and Younger; several weeks later on 25 May 1774, Drury Lane also provided Kennedy with a benefit that brought him a profit of £44 14*s*. 6*d*.

Within a few weeks after the fire, Kennedy's son Thomas, who had been acting at Bristol and Dublin, played an unspecified role in *The Bankrupt* at the Haymarket on 16 May. He was, no doubt, the Kennedy who continued to perform at the Haymarket that summer. On 17 September 1774 a license was issued to one of the Kennedys for a benefit performance shared with Fearon at the Haymarket. Lawrence seems not to have acted that night, but his son played a role in *The Fair Orphan* and Sam Simple in *The Rival Fools*.

After his recovery, Kennedy went with his son to act at Dublin. He was at Birmingham in the summer and autumn of 1775 and the summer of 1776, then played at Bristol in the summers of 1777 and 1778 and in 1778–79. He probably was the Kennedy who performed at Cork in October 1779. Thereafter he seems to have ceased acting, a circumstance probably necessitated by the paralytic stroke which his obituary reported he had suffered. His distressed circumstances, it was said, were relieved by the generosity of his friend, the actor John Henderson, who provided a weekly stipend. When Henderson died in November 1785, Kennedy's situation became desperate, and on 22 June 1786, according to the *Hiber-*

nian Journal of 28 June 1786, he killed himself with a razor, in his sixty-sixth year.

Kennedy, Mrs Lawrence, Elizabeth, née Orfeur *c. 1730?–1774, actress.*

Elizabeth Orfeur was the daughter of the Mr and Mrs Orfeur who acted in London, Richmond, and York in the 1720s. If we judge by the roles Elizabeth played when she went upon the stage at Dublin in the late 1740s, she had been born about 1730. She was the younger sister by some 20 years, according to George Anne Bellamy, of the Miss Orfeur who married the Irish actor Thomas Farrell. Probably it was the elder Miss Orfeur who was acting at Smock Alley Theatre, Dublin, in 1740–41. Elizabeth, however, was performing at Smock Alley by 24 January 1747, when she signed her name to an affidavit to *Faulkner's Daily Journal* concerning a dispute at that theatre, though her first role there known to us was as Miss Biddy in *Miss in Her Teens* on 25 January 1748. In the spring of 1749 she acted Tagg in the same play on 3 May, Lucy in *The Recruiting Officer* on 5 May, and Wheedle in *The Miser* on 8 May (and she may have played the last-mentioned role earlier that season).

Sometime in 1749, after the middle of May, Elizabeth Orfeur married the young Irish actor Lawrence Kennedy. On 19 March 1750, advertised as Mrs Kennedy, she acted Flora in *She Wou'd and She Wou'd Not* and on 5 April she acted Honoria in *Love Makes a Man*. Between her marriage and her reappearance on the Smock Alley stage she had probably given birth to her son Thomas, who would be introduced as a child actor at Smock Alley in 1755–56.

In the autumn of 1750 the Kennedys went to play at Edinburgh. At the New Concert Hall she appeared as Rose in *The Recruiting Officer* and Biddy on 30 November. Her other known roles there were Phillis in *The Conscious Lovers* on 5 December, the First Countryman in *Merlin* on 7 December, Serina in *The Orphan* on 19 December, Mrs Slammekin in *The Beggar's Opera* on 28 December, the Second Spirit in *Comus* on 14 January 1751, and Tattleaid in *The Funeral* on 28 January. In 1751–52 the Kennedys returned to Smock Alley, where they were engaged regularly through 1759–60 (except for 1754–55 when Lawrence Kennedy left his family to play again at Edinburgh). During most of that decade Mrs Kennedy was articled at £4 per week. She also acted at Cork in the late summers of 1757 and 1758.

In the summer of 1760 Mr and Mrs Kennedy were engaged by Garrick for the next season at Drury Lane. Sometime in August Garrick, in a letter to Arthur Murphy about the casting of *The Way to Keep Him*, wrote that "Mignionet is now so good a character that I think Mrs. Kennedy should play it." (But when that comedy was revived at Drury Lane on 10 January 1761 Mrs Bradshaw acted Mignionet.) Mrs Kennedy made her Drury Lane debut on 10 October 1760 as Mrs Marwood in *The Way of the World*. Her second role was Lady Graveairs in *The Careless Husband* on 14 October. Several days earlier Garrick had written to Joseph Austin, "Mrs Kennedy must be spoke to for *Lady Graveairs*, this night, & a very good Second Appearance it will be—it is in her cast of Parts." On 17 October she played Jacintha in *The Suspicious Husband* and on the twenty-second appeared as Lady Wronghead in *The Provok'd Husband*. Her other roles that season included Mrs Honeycombe in *Polly Honeycombe*, the Countess of Nottingham in *The Earl of Essex*, the Nurse in *Romeo and Juliet*, Lady Randolph in *Douglas*, Elvira in *The Spanish Fryar*, Clarinda in *The Double Gallant*, and Ruth in *The Committee*. In the following season, 1761–62, she played Mrs Marwood, Mrs Honeycombe, Emelia in *Othello*, Miss Harlow in *The Old Maid*, and the Countess of Nottingham.

After two seasons at Drury Lane, the Kennedys left London. They returned to Smock Alley for a while, played at Cork in the summer of 1762, and then went again to Edinburgh for the 1762–63 season, where Mrs Kennedy, according to the *Theatrical Review* of May 1763, was much admired. Among her roles were Lady Wronghead, Miss Harlow, Marwood, Lettice in *The Intriguing Chambermaid*, Lady Brute in *The Provok'd Wife*, Sylvia in *The Recruiting Officer*, Zara in *The Mourning Bride*, Alicia in *Jane Shore*, Kitty in *High Life Below Stairs* and Portia in *The Merchant of Venice*. "Mrs. Kennedy had merit in some parts," according to George Anne Bellamy in her *Apology*, "and as she had been in several travelling companies, she was studied in every character. Though she was far from handsome, she was a good figure."

In 1764 Mrs Kennedy again engaged at Edinburgh with her husband and son, but a skin eruption on her face limited her performances to only four that season. One night Mrs Kennedy had been announced for Zara in *The Mourning Bride*, but she was taken ill, so her sister Mrs Farrell undertook the role at the last minute. The audience expressed disapproval of Mrs Farrell's performance throughout. When it came time for her death scene, Mrs Farrell "rose from between the mutes" and told the audience of her concern that she could not satisfy in the role, explaining that she had taken it on "merely to serve the person whose benefit it was." Thereupon, she returned to her prone position and covered her face with a veil, causing the house to dissolve into laughter from which, according to George Anne Bellamy, "it was impossible to compose them for the rest of the evening."

After playing in the Irish towns in 1763 and 1764, Mrs Kennedy joined Foote's summer company at the Haymarket in 1765, appearing as Miss Harlow, Mrs Honeycomb, Patch in *The Busy Body*, and Mrs Mechlin in *The Commissary*. She then toured for several years with her husband, playing at Edinburgh in 1767 and 1768 and at Stratford in March 1771. No doubt she acted at Gloucester in 1772 where her husband managed the theatre in Barton Street for a season. Between November 1772 and April 1773 she performed at the Coopers' Hall, Bristol, and then in 1773–74 at the Richmond Theatre under the management of her husband and Booth.

In May 1774 the Kennedys were visiting Joseph Younger in King Street, Covent Garden. At 2:00 A.M. on 4 May a young friend who had accompanied them to London fell asleep while reading in bed, failing to extinguish the candle. The conflagration killed Mrs Kennedy and the friend. Younger and Kennedy, though the latter was severely burned in the face from the vain attempt to rescue his wife, managed to escape. According to James Winston in his *Theatric Tourist*, Elizabeth Kennedy was buried in the north side of the Richmond churchyard, but her name is not found in the burial register.

Elizabeth Kennedy often has been confused with her elder sister, Mrs Thomas Farrell, who also acted at Dublin early in her career as Miss Orfeur. In his *History of the Theatres of London and Dublin* (1761), Benjamin Victor gave Mrs Farrell's first initial as *E*, and modern historians, such as Clark and Sheldon, have called her Elizabeth. But the fact that her younger sister was named Elizabeth is verified in the register of her marriage, in a letter to the press, and in the baptismal record of her grandchild at St Michael le Belfry, York: on 14 March 1790, was baptized Sophia "8th child of Thomas Kennedy, son of Lawrence and Elizabeth, daughter of —— Orfeur, and Agnes daughter of Thomas and Mary Holmes." It is possible, of course, that Mrs Farrell's Christian name also was Elizabeth, or Esther, or some other beginning with *E*, as Victor stated. She was married to Thomas Farrell by 1757. Together they played at Dublin, Belfast, and Edinburgh, until her death at Belfast in December 1773. Their two daughters acted at Edinburgh, Dublin, and Belfast between 1768 and 1779.

Kennedy, Mrs Morgan Hugh, Margaret, née Doyle, earlier Mrs Farrell   *d. 1793, actress, singer.*

According to Parke's *Musical Memoirs*, the singer and actress Mrs Margaret Kennedy was a native of Ireland and when a young woman served in a pub near St Giles, London, where she sang to guests; she was heard by some Covent Garden performers, who recommended her to Dr Arne. Impressed by her talents, Arne took her under his instruction. Actually Margaret's maiden name was Doyle and she was no doubt born in Ireland. A notation on a playbill in the British Library for 23 November 1778 identified her as the sister of John Doyle, a well-known Irish singer in London between 1778 and 1794; the singer James Doyle, who performed in the Covent Garden oratorios in 1794, was probably also her brother, or otherwise related. It is likely that Margaret Doyle was older than her brother John. She was married to a Mr Farrell by the time Arne became her teacher. Probably she was the Mrs "Farrel" who with Miss Brown (later Hester Jackson?) sang *One Kind Kiss before we part*, a song that was published in 1770 and probably had been heard at Sadler's Wells.

In *The London Stage* entry for 5 November 1773, Margaret is mistaken for Polly Kennedy (d. 1781), alias Mrs Bevon, a courtesan whom John Baker saw in the audience at Covent Gar-

Harvard Theatre Collection

CHARLES FREDERICK REINHOLD as Artabanes and MARGARET KENNEDY as Artaxerxes

artist unknown

den Theatre that night and described in his *Diary*. Our subject, who did not become Mrs Kennedy until 1779, could not have been the object of Baker's attention.

Margaret Farrell was introduced to the London stage in a performance of Arne's *The Sot*, a two-act comic entertainment (altered by Arne from Fielding) that was presented by his pupils at the Haymarket Theatre on 16 February 1775. The bills listed all the characters to be played by unnamed young ladies and gentlemen for that performance and the next on 9 March, but for the third night, on 1 May 1775, Mrs Farrell's name was found for Fairlove. In this piece she introduced Arne's famous "A-Hunting we will go." About a year later she played an unspecified part in Arne's operetta *Phoebe at Court* at the Haymarket on

22 February 1776. Her next notice was on 16 March 1776 at Covent Garden, when she made her first appearance as a Bacchante and Euphrosyne in *Comus*.

In 1776–77 Mrs Farrell was engaged at Covent Garden at £5 per week. On 6 December 1776 she performed a principal vocal character in the premiere of *Caractacus*, a dramatic poem by William Mason set to music by Arne, which had many performances that season. Though she possessed a large, clumsy figure, she won favor by her intelligence, fine enunciation, and the deep compass of her voice. When she played Ariel, her next character, on 27 December, the *Morning Post* noted that she was at least a head taller and several inches wider than Hull, who acted Prospero. Such a physique allowed her to appear with frequent success in male roles, as in the title role of *Artaxerxes* on 25 January 1777. That season she also offered occasional songs and performed a principal vocal part in the oratorio *The Prodigal Son*. A press clipping in the British Library, dating from about that time, reported that she was "married, and a mother," but probably she was not living with her husband.

In the summer of 1777 Mrs Farrell appeared at Ranelagh Gardens, singing on occasion James Hook's "Yellow Hair'd Laddie," a song she rendered in subsequent years at Vauxhall Gardens along with many others by the same composer. Returning to Covent Garden in 1777–78 at a salary of £6 per week, Mrs Farrell caused some protest on 17 October 1777 when she appeared for the first time as Captain Macheath in *The Beggar's Opera* (adding to her songs Arne's "A-Hunting we will go"), but she gained favor in the role. As Euphrosyne in *Comus* on 30 October she sang "Sweet Echo," with Leoni, and then offered that song and other specialty numbers throughout the season. On 18 November 1777 she acted the male role of Bellford in the premiere of Hull's comic opera *Love Finds a Way*, with music by Arne. The songs *How dear I love her* and *Oh Love thou Delight* were published that year as sung by her in that piece. For her benefit at Covent Garden on 1 May 1778, when she appeared as Macheath and Euphrosyne, she received net proceeds of £161 3s. 6d., and tickets could be had of her in Bow Street, Covent Garden. She also performed in the oratorio *Acis and Galatea* at Drury Lane on 6 March 1778, when it was

announced that as there were very few songs in the oratorio "that can be adapted for Mrs Farrell's voice, she will sing a *cantata The rosy morn with crimson dye* between the Acts." A similar announcement appeared when she sang again at Drury Lane in *Alexander's Feast* on 18 March. When *Acis and Galatea* was repeated on 27 March, she sang Handel's "Verdi Rale" between the acts.

The 1778–79 season in London was called by J. P. Kemble "the Coalition Season, the Actors of both Theatres playing at either house indiscriminately." Mrs Farrell began her season at Drury Lane on 17 September in her roles in *Comus*, in which she also sang "Sweet Echo" with Leoni. Next night she played the male role of Colin in *Rose and Colin* at Covent Garden, then returned to Drury Lane for several more performances of *Comus* before settling in at her regular house for a while. At Covent Garden she acted Lubin in *Annette and Lubin*, Patience in *Henry VIII*, Macheath, and Cicely in *The Lady of the Manor*. On 4 January 1779 she played Feridon in the premiere of Dibdin's *The Touchstone*, a popular afterpiece that was

Harvard Theatre Collection

MARGARET KENNEDY as Macheath

artist unknown

performed 42 times before the end of the season.

At St Paul, Covent Garden, on 24 January 1779 Mrs Farrell, described as "a Widow," married Morgan Hugh Kennedy, a London physician. When she appeared as Feridon at Covent Garden on 26 January her name was given in the bills as Mrs Kennedy. The next night she sang a song in Act III of *The Comedy of Errors*. Her roles the rest of the season included Young Meadows in *Love in a Village*, Telemachus in *Calypso*, Ester in *The Chelsea Pensioner*, Ariel, and a vocal part as one of the British Virgins in *Elfrida*. She signed a pay sheet, now in the Harvard Theatre Collection, as "Marg^t Kennedy," for a total salary of £296 13*s*. 4*d*. in full for the 1778–79 season.

After acting at Birmingham in the summer of 1779, when her brother John Doyle also performed, Mrs Kennedy returned to Covent Garden for the next ten seasons, playing numerous musical roles, male and female. Among her most successful parts were Carlos in *The Duenna* and Ceres in *The Mirror* in 1779–80. She made her first appearance as Lucy in *The Beggar's Opera* on 16 October 1781 and as Fanny in *The Maid of the Mill* on 25 September 1782. The roles she created in new pieces included Orra in Dibdin's comic opera *The Islanders* on 25 November 1780, a Midshipman in Messink's pantomime *The Choice of Harlequin* on 26 December 1781, Don Alphonso in *The Castle of Andalusia* on 2 November 1782, William in *Rosina* on 31 December 1782, Patrick in *The Poor Soldier* on 4 November 1783, Stella in *Robin Hood* on 17 April 1784 (but later her role became Allan-a-Dale), Mrs Casey in *Fontainebleau* on 16 November 1784, Oediddee in *Omai* on 20 December 1785, Saib in *Love and War* on 12 March 1787, Peggy in *Marian* on 22 May 1788. At Covent Garden her salary was £11 per week in 1785–86, £11 10*s* in the next season, and £12 in 1787–88 and 1788–89. During most of the 1780s Mrs Kennedy lived in a house at No 36, Great Queen Street, Lincoln's Inn Fields. In benefit receipts she received (all less house charges of £105) £320 9*s*. 6*d*. on 27 April 1784, £257 2*s*. on 2 April 1786, and £312 6*s*. on 3 May 1787.

Mrs Kennedy also sang in oratorios at the Haymarket in February 1785, the Handel Memorial Concerts at Westminster Abbey in 1784, 1786, and 1791, and the Frogmore fête in 1791. Between 1777 and 1787 she sang in the summer at Ranelagh and Vauxhall, and many songs by Arne, Hook, and Shield were published as rendered by her at the pleasure gardens as well as in Covent Garden productions. In the summer of 1786, when she was advertised as "the celebrated Mrs Kennedy," she appeared at Edinburgh in her favorite roles, including Macheath, Alphonso, Carlos, Euphrosyne, and William.

She made her last appearance on the stage at Covent Garden on 2 April 1789 as William in *Rosina*. According to *The Secret History of the Green Room* (1790), she resigned because of a quarrel with the manager Harris, and as she "generally officiated in male characters in the vocal line," she was replaced in the next season by Duffey. Parke described her as having "one of the finest counter-tenor voices ever heard," with "a rich tone and perfect intonation." Her "powerful correct melody," reported the *Secret History*, made one entirely forget her "coarse robustness." Toward the end of her career she tended to drink too much. In *The Children of Thespis* (1788), John Williams praised "the force of her song," but indicated that her attraction as a performer of male roles was temporary.

Mrs Kennedy died at Bayswater House on 23 January 1793 and was buried at St Anne, Soho. Her husband, Dr Kennedy, died in Charlotte Street, Fitzroy Square, on 13 May 1805. He had been physician to the Lying-in Hospital in Bayswater and previously for several years an apothecary in Great Queen Street. Miss Reynolds, a singer, who made her first appearance as Arbaces in *Artaxerxes* at Covent Garden on 3 May 1787, was Mrs Kennedy's niece.

When Mrs Farrell, Mrs Kennedy was depicted by an anonymous engraver as Artaxerxes, with Charles Reinhold as Artabanes. An anonymous engraving of her as Macheath was published by J. Bew in 1778 as a plate to the *Vocal Magazine*.

Kennedy, Thomas *c. 1750?–1808, actor.*

Thomas Kennedy was born, probably about 1750, about a year after his parents married in Dublin. His father, Lawrence Kennedy, was probably the son of provincial actors who played for a brief period in London in the

1740s; his mother, Elizabeth Orfeur, was also the child of provincial actors and the younger sister of the actress Mrs Thomas Farrell.

By about the age of five or six, Thomas was performing as Master Kennedy with his parents at Smock Alley, Dublin, in 1755–56. Though he was in the Smock Alley company each year through 1759–60, only a few of his assignments are known: Tom Thumb on 1 April 1757, the prologue to *The Author* on 3 April 1758 ("being the first and only Time of his Appearing this Season") for his parents' benefit, and the monologue *Bucks, Have at ye All* in the spring of 1759, again for the Kennedys' benefit. In August and September 1758 he also played at Cork.

Accompanying his parents to Drury Lane in the autumn of 1760, Master Kennedy made his first appearance there in an unspecified role in *The Rehearsal* on 3 October, prior to his mother's debut on 10 October and his father's on 29 December. He appeared again in *The Rehearsal* on 12 December and was named in the bills on 17 December for Prince Arthur in *King John*, a role he played several other times that season; he also performed Elfina in *Edgar and Emmeline* on 31 January 1761 and a number of times thereafter. In the next season, 1761–62, he was seen again as Elfina and as a Fairy in *Queen Mab* and a Page in *Love Makes a Man*. On 28 December 1761 he played an unspecified role in a revival of *The Genii*, an entertainment that was repeated some 40 times that season.

Over the next decade young Kennedy was acting with his parents at various provincial theatres. He played at Cork occasionally from 1762 to 1764 and at Edinburgh between 1763 and 1768, when some of his roles were Daniel in *The Conscious Lovers* on 10 March 1763, a Page in *The Orphan* on 2 November 1765, Ariel in *The Tempest* on 10 April 1766, and Ranger's Servant in *The Suspicious Husband* on 13 April 1768. In March 1771, he was ten nights at the new theatre in Stratford. Between November 1772 and April 1773 he performed at the Coopers' Hall, Bristol, advertised as T. Kennedy, in order to distinguish him from his father, who managed the company. He also played with that company at Richmond in 1773, when his father became co-manager there with Booth for a season.

Soon after his mother was killed by fire in

Younger's lodgings in King Street, Covent Garden, on 4 May 1774, Kennedy appeared at Foote's Haymarket Theatre, advertised as Kennedy, Junior, from Dublin. He acted an unlisted part in *The Bankrupt* on 16 May 1774, and then played during the summer such roles as Chapeau in *Cross Purposes*, Sam Simple in *The Rival Fools* (for his benefit on 17 September), Dick in *The Apprentice*, and parts in *The Nabob*, *The Trip to Portsmouth*, and *The Duellist*.

With Younger's company, Kennedy acted at Birmingham in the summers of 1775 and 1776. After appearing at Bristol in 1777, he joined Wilkinson's company on the York circuit, acting fops and harlequins. While at Doncaster, he abandoned Mrs Taplin ("who had depended on the false vows of the seducing Kennedy," according to Wilkinson in his *Wandering Patentee*) to take up with a young actress, Agnes Holmes, whom he soon married. Agnes was reported by Wilkinson to have declared "she would rather starve with Kennedy than live with a Prince," but Wilkinson, writing in 1795, added somewhat insinuatingly, "How far she sticks to that declaration and opinion at present, I know not, nor is it my business or wish to inquire or be informed about." Kennedy played at Dublin in 1776–77, York in 1778, Bristol and Edinburgh in 1778–79, and Cork in September 1779.

In 1784–85 he and his wife were engaged at Covent Garden, where he made his first appearance on 4 October 1784 as a Witch in *Macbeth*. That season he also acted Lake in *The Positive Man*, Poins in *1 Henry IV*, Pistol in *2 Henry IV*, Jockey in *Fontainebleau*, Quildrive in *The Citizen*, Henry in *The Maid of the Oaks*, a role in *The Critic*, a Brother in *Comus*, a Tailor in *Barataria*, Charino in *Love Makes a Man*, Counselor Bantas in *The Lawyer's Panic*, Simple in *The Merry Wives of Windsor*, Lord Sands in *Henry VIII*, and Juggle in *The Israelites*.

After playing at Richmond in the summer of 1785, Kennedy returned to Covent Garden at £2 10s. per week for two more seasons in which he acted a similar line of farce and low comedy roles, including, among others, Dupely in *The Maid of the Oaks*, Biondello in *Catherine and Petruchio*, Brush in *The Lady's Last Stake*, Simon Pure in *A Bold Stroke for a Wife*, Verges in *Much Ado about Nothing*, the French Valet in *The Belle's Stratagem*, and Jack Meggot in *The Suspicious Husband*. For his benefit with his wife on 26 May 1786 Kennedy was obliged to announce that "Many Tickets of Mr Kennedy's having been stolen, he gives public Notice that no Tickets sold at the Doors or Avenues of the Theatre will have Admission this Evening." Tickets, however, were available from him at No 44, Great Queen Street, in Lincoln's Inn Fields. That night the receipts were £108 4s. 6d., leaving Kennedy with little profit after he paid £105 in house charges. The Kennedys were again at Richmond in the summer of 1786. On 23 May 1787, his last Covent Garden benefit, when he acted Jack Meggot, the receipts were £222 14s., but he had to share the money and the house charges with King. Kennedy's address then was No 49, Great Queen Street. His salary that season had been raised to £3 per week.

Kennedy passed the remainder of his career in the provinces, at York and Edinburgh from 1778 to 1791, at Manchester in 1790, at Richmond in 1791, and at Dublin from 1791 to 1797, serving as Daly's deputy manager at Crow Street from 1791 to 1793. He was probably the Kennedy who played at Edinburgh in the spring of 1801, his last-known role there being Crabtree in *The School for Scandal* on 20 April. He then, it seems, went into some business at Dublin and thrived. According to Wewitzer, Thomas Kennedy died in January 1808.

Agnes Kennedy survived her husband by 24 years, dying at Lambeth in 1832. She had been the daughter of Thomas and Mary Holmes, who was a wardrobe keeper and mantua maker at Sadler's Wells. Agnes's sister married a Mr Bates who kept a hotel at Holyhead; their daughter Mary Bates, an actress, married the playwright and performer Charles Isaac Mungo Dibdin in 1797.

Thomas and Agnes Kennedy had at least nine children. Perhaps she was the Mrs Kennedy who according to the *Morning Chronicle* of 27 March 1778 had given birth to a daughter in lodgings in Bow Street the previous day. A daughter named Maria was buried at St Michael le Belfry, York, on 3 May 1789. The registers of that church record the baptism on 14 March 1790 of Sophia, "8th child of Thomas Kennedy, son of Laurence and Elizabeth, daughter of —— Orfeur, And Agnes, daughter of Thomas and Mary Holmes." The

Miss Kennedy who acted at Crow Street in July 1796 was one of their children. The *Hibernian Journal* of 22 April 1793 reported the birth of another daughter at Dublin on 17 April. That child, at least the ninth, was probably Miss Agnes Kennedy, who began to act at Sadler's Wells, managed by her uncle Charles I. M. Dibdin, in 1813–14. She married Simon, a French dancer at the Opera House, and as Mme Simon was performing at the Surrey Theatre in the 1830s.

Kennedy, Mrs Thomas, Agnes, née Holmes *c. 1759–1832, actress.*

Agnes Holmes was born about 1759, the daughter of Thomas and Mary Holmes. Her mother was a wardrobe keeper and mantua maker at Sadler's Wells in the 1780s and 1790s. Agnes's sister married a Mr Bates who kept a hotel at Holyhead; their daughter, Mary Bates, married the playwright and performer Charles Isaac Mungo Dibdin in 1797.

Having been recommended by Mrs Hull to

Harvard Theatre Collection

AGNES KENNEDY

artist unknown

Tate Wilkinson, Agnes Holmes made her stage debut at York on 13 March 1777 as Miss Aubrey, with the epilogue, in *The Fashionable Lover*. She displayed "great nearness and much promise," according to Wilkinson in his *Wandering Patentee*, where he described her as "about 18" at her first trial. For her benefit at York on 29 April, when she acted in *A Woman Is a Riddle*, with Henry and Sarah Siddons, she was an "entire stranger," but she made "rapid improvement" under Wilkinson's management. While acting on the circuit at Doncaster that year she caught the eye of another company member, young Thomas Kennedy, who gave up his interest in Mrs Taplin to marry Agnes. According to Wilkinson, Miss Holmes had declared "she would rather starve with Kennedy than live with a Prince."

Announced as Mrs Kennedy from York, she made her debut in Foote's summer company at the Haymarket as Amelia in *The English Merchant* on 16 July 1779. Next day the *Morning Chronicle* offered praise but wondered at her choice of role: "This young actress has performed for a season at York, & we are told has a considerable share of merit in the lively cast in comedy; we are therefore not a little amazed at seeing her announced to appear in so grave a character as that which she played last night." She had, however, delivered the lines with "great good sense, proper energy, & judicious emphasis." The *Gazetteer* of 19 July found her figure and manner "extremely well suited to the part." On 17 July she acted Lucy in *A Widow and No Widow*, a role she repeated eight times that season. She also acted Miss Tittup in *Bon Ton* on 20 July and Amelia again on 14 August.

After six years in the provinces with her husband, some of which were no doubt occupied by bearing and caring for some of the nine children she eventually had, Mrs Kennedy returned to London in 1784–85 to take up an engagement at Covent Garden, where her husband was also employed. Announced as from the Newcastle stage, she appeared at Covent Garden on 16 November 1784 as Maria in *The Citizen* and Miss Bull in *Fontainebleau*. Also in the latter piece, playing Mrs Casey, was Margaret Kennedy (the former Mrs Farrell), with whom Agnes Kennedy has often been confused. Agnes played Mrs Brittle in *Barnaby Brittle* on 20 November, and Emelia in *Retaliation* on 25 November. The next night, when Miss Younge was suddenly taken ill, Mrs Kennedy played Juliet at very short notice. Her other roles that season were Maria in *George Barnwell* on 27 December, Ismene in *Phaedra and Hypolitus* on 3 March 1785, Angelica in *The Constant Couple* on 29 March, Miss Naivette Winkle in *The Israelites* on 1 April, Constance in *The Fashionable Levities* on 2 April, Isabella in *Women Pleas'd* on 11 April, and Angelina in *Love Makes a Man* on 6 May.

In her second season at Covent Garden, when she was paid £2 10s. per week, Mrs Kennedy added to her repertoire Miss Hardcastle in *She Stoops to Conquer*, Mrs Strickland in *The Suspicious Husband*, Nancy in *Three Weeks after Marriage*, Birtha in *Percy*, Valeria in *The Roman Father*, the title role in *Jane Shore* (taken on at the last minute for the ill Mrs Wells on 20 December 1785), Miranda in *The Busy Body*, Maria in *George Barnwell*, Luciana in *The Comedy of Errors*, Lady Harriet in *The Funeral*, Leonora in *The Mistake*, Angelica in *Love for Love*, Constantia in *The Man of the World*, and Serina in *The Orphan*. In September 1786 she played Mrs Euston in *I'll Tell You What* at Richmond.

In her third and final Covent Garden season, 1786–87, her salary was raised to £3 per week and she acted, among other roles, Lavinia in *The Fair Penitent*, Lady Jane in *Know Your Own Mind*, Flora in *The Wonder*, Jacintha in *The Suspicious Husband*, Miss Walsingham in *The School for Wives*, and Viola in *Twelfth Night*.

Mrs Kennedy then rejoined Wilkinson's company, playing at Hull in 1787 and at York from 1780 to 1790. The *Theatrical Register* of 1788 commented on her very elegant and expensive stage dresses and noted that as Wowski in *Inkle and Yarico* she surprised with her musical talents, though she was visibly frightened when singing her song. At Manchester on 28 April 1790 she was announced as making her first appearance there in eight years, as Letitia Hardy in *The Belle's Stratagem*. She and her husband played frequently at Manchester into June, and lived at No 17, Piccadilly. In the first half of 1791 they played at Edinburgh and then they joined the Crow Street Theatre in Dublin, where Mrs Kennedy was still acting in 1797–98. After performing at Edinburgh again in the spring of 1801, Mrs Kennedy acted at Liverpool, where it was reported that she "rather caricatured" the role of Mrs Bedford in *The Poor Gentleman*. In November of 1801 her benefit at Liverpool brought £105.

After her husband's death in 1808, Mrs Kennedy remained professionally active, playing three seasons at Covent Garden from 1815–16 through 1817–18 and then in 1818 joining the Sadler's Wells company, which was managed by the younger Charles Dibdin, her niece's husband. She then retired from the stage in 1819, but Dibdin persuaded her to return once more to act in his musical farce *The Bear*, which opened at the Surrey Theatre on 12 September 1825. In his *Memoirs* Dibdin acknowledged his debt to Mrs Kennedy, "a dignified Lady of the *vieille cour*."

Agnes Kennedy, according to O. Smith's papers at the British Library died at Lambeth in May 1832. Smith would seem to have erred in claiming that she died at age 93, for that unlikelihood would place her birth in 1739; Wilkinson, as we have noted above, described her as about 18 when she made her debut in 1777. Moreover, Mrs Kennedy was still bearing children as late as 1793. Smith also called her "an actress of great merit, and a distinguished member of the Garrick school," a somewhat generous and exaggerated compliment.

Information on her children will be found in the notice of Thomas Kennedy. A pencil drawing of Agnes Kennedy by J. Roberts is in the Harvard Theatre Collection, where also is found an engraved portrait by an unknown artist.

Kenneston or Kenniston. *See* KYNASTON.

Kenny, Mr [*fl.* 1713–1726], *bassoonist.*

On 23 February 1713 at Stationers' Hall a benefit concert was held for Messrs Kenny and Wells. They shared another benefit there almost exactly a year later, and one on 2 May 1715. At the same hall on 10 May 1717 Kenny had a solo benefit, and he had another on 12 March 1718 at the Tennis Court. On 19 March 1724 at the Lincoln's Inn Fields Theatre Kenny was identified as a bassoonist and performed with Eversman accompanying on the harpsichord. They gave a repeat performance a month later. A benefit for Kenny that was

noted in the Burney Collection at the British Library but did not get into *The London Stage* was held "At Mr. Symond's Great Room at the King's Head in Enfield" on 15 August 1726. Music "by the best Masters from the Opera" was to be offered, and a ball was to take place following the concert. The clipping hinted that Kenny had had a similar benefit the previous year, and the phrasing of the advertisement suggests that he may have played in the opera band at the King's Theatre.

Kenny, Mr *d. 1784, actor, singer.*

At the new theatre at the White Hart in Launceston, Cornwall, Mr Kenny (or Kenney) played Sir Walter Blunt in *Henry IV* and an unspecified role in the burletta *Midas* on 5 May 1772. On 3 June he had a vocal part in *The Jubilee*. Kenny acted at China Hall, Rotherhithe from 25 September to 18 October 1776, playing the Duke of Suffolk in *Henry VIII*, Simon Pure in *A Bold Stroke for a Wife*, Daniel in *Oroonoko*, Gaylove in *The Honest Yorkshireman*, Perez in *The Mourning Bride*, John in *The Election*, Tom in *High Life below Stairs*, and Thomas Appletree in *The Recruiting Officer*.

It seems most probable that the Mr Kenny who began appearing at the Haymarket Theatre in February 1777 was the same performer. On 11 February he acted Northumberland in *Henry IV*; then he reappeared in the summer to play Fingerfee in *The Devil upon Two Sticks*, Laguerre in *Polly*, a Servant in *Rule a Wife and Have a Wife*, Snout in *The Fairy Tale*, Peto in *1 Henry IV*, Tyrrell in *Richard III*, Eustace in *Love in a Village*, a Mutineer in *Cato*, Bardolph in *The Merry Wives of Windsor*, and Bernardo in *Hamlet*.

He was back at the Haymarket from January through mid-September 1778. He played such parts as Alphonso in *The Spanish Fryar*, Russet in *The Jealous Wife*, Ratcliff in *Richard III*, Sackbut in *A Bold Stroke for a Wife*, Carbuncle in *The Country Lasses*, Mr Harlowe in *The Old Maid*, a Servant in *The Female Chevalier*, a Passenger in *Man and Wife*, a Shoemaker in *Tony Lumpkin in Town*, a Soldier in *Bonduca*, Lint in *The Mayor of Garratt*, Dr Broadbrim in *The Devil upon Two Sticks*, and the second Watchman in *The Provok'd Wife*.

In 1778–79 and 1779–80 Kenny performed at Drury Lane during the regular season, usually in small or unnamed parts, yet he was seen as Ariel in *The Tempest* both seasons. W. S. Clark in *The Irish Stage in the County Towns* placed Kenny at Cork on 19 October 1778. His schedule in London at Drury Lane (at least the appearance of his name in the bills) shows a gap between 24 September and 2 November of that year, and Kenny may well have gone over to Ireland for a brief engagement. At Drury Lane in 1778–79 Kenny was earning a monthly salary of £2 6*s* 8*d*. His chores there both seasons included singing in the chorus, notably in *Macbeth*. In the summers of 1779 and 1780, as in previous years, he played at the Haymarket, adding to his list of parts such characters as John in *The Jealous Wife*, Capucius in *Henry VIII*, Hounslow in *The Stratagem*, Nancy in *Fire and Water*, Regulus in *Bonduca*, and Mervin in *The Maid of the Mill*. He also took on numerous unnamed roles and played servants, officers, and other bit parts.

Kenny was at the Haymarket again in the summers through 1783, adding, among other parts, Black in *The Dead Alive*, John in *The Patron*, Molly Brazen in *The Beggar's Opera*, Carpenter in *A Preludio*, Cudden in *The Agreeable Surprise*, Twilight in *The Candidate*, the Prompter and an Attendant in *The Life and Death of Common Sense*, a Fighting Quaker in *Harlequin Teague*, Easy in *The Quaker*, Anvil in *Gretna Green*, and his usual bit parts. During those years his winters cannot always be fully accounted for. In 1781–82, for example, he played Sir Philip Moneylove in *The Artifice* on 16 October 1781—a month after the Haymarket summer season was over; the rest of his winter is a blank, so far as London is concerned. In 1782–83 he was at Drury Lane but perhaps only from December 1782 to the end of the season. Typically, he had a number of unnamed parts plus a Watchman in *The Apprentice*, a Servant in *The School for Vanity*, Fribourg in *The Triumph of Mirth*, and a Beggar in *The Ladies' Frolick*.

Kenny played at Drury Lane in 1783–84, his final season. He was William in *All the World's a Stage*, a Waiter in *The Gamester*, Robert in *The Deaf Lover*, and a Jailer in *A Duke and No Duke*, along with a few of his earlier parts and a smattering of unnamed assignments. His final appearance on any stage may have been on 24 May 1784 in *All the World's a Stage*. Reed in his "Notitia Dramatica" stated that Kenny died in the summer of 1784.

Kenny, Mrs $_{[}$*fl.* 1776$_{]}$, *actress.*
Mrs Kenny played Decius in *Cato* at China Hall, Rotherhithe, on 16 October 1776. Also at that playhouse in the fall of 1776 was Master Kenny, probably her son. Her husband was very likely the Mr Kenny who acted at the Haymarket and Drury Lane in the 1770s and 1780s.

Kenny, Master $_{[}$*fl.* 1776–1778$_{]}$, *actor.*
Master Kennedy spoke the prologue to *Barbarossa* at China Hall, Rotherhithe, on 27 September 1776 and played the Duke of York in *Richard III* at the Haymarket Theatre on 24 March 1778.

Kenrick. *See also* KENDRICK.

Kenrick, Mr $_{[}$*fl.* 1783$_{]}$, *actor.*
At the Haymarket Theatre in 1783 a Mr Kenrick acted a principal role in *A New Way to Keep a Wife at Home* on 17 September and played a Lieutenant in *Richard III* on 15 December. On both nights he also delivered a monologue, *The Farmer's Blunder.*

Kenrick, Mr $_{[}$*fl.* 1786–1802$_{]}$, *singer.*
A Mr Kendrick was a chorus singer at Covent Garden Theatre between 1786–87, when he earned £1 1*s*. per week, and 1800–1801. Among the parts for which his name appeared in the bills were a Bacchanal in *Comus* in 1786–87, a Shepherd in *Orpheus and Eurydice* in 1791–92, an Irish Peasant in *Bantry Bay* in 1796–97, an Indian in *Ramah Droog* and a Peasant in *The Old Cloathsman* in 1798–99, and an Infernal Spirit in *The Volcano* in 1799–1800.

During the summers Kenrick also sang in the chorus at the Haymarket regularly between 1791 and 1802, performing in *The Battle of Hexham* and *The Mountaineers* in 1794, *Zorinski* in 1795, *The Italian Monk* and *Cambro-Britons* in 1798, *The Castle of Sorrento* and *Tars at Torbay* in 1799, and *Obi* and *What a Blunder* in 1800.

Kent, Mr $_{[}$*fl.* 1780–1810?$_{]}$, *actor.*
The provincial actor Mr Kent performed at Dover in April 1780, at which time he introduced his daughter Mary Anne, age four, to the stage. Announced as from the Theatre Royal, Norwich, Kent acted Moneses in *Tam-*

erlane at the Haymarket Theatre on 6 March 1786, a specially-licensed performance given for the benefit of Griffiths, a former Drury Lane actor.

No doubt that person was the Kent who acted at Brighton in the summer of 1787. In March 1794 Kent brought his family to London to play for his benefit at the Windsor Castle Inn, King Street, Hammersmith. On the twenty-fourth he presented *The School for Scandal* in which he acted Sir Peter Teazle and one of his daughters, probably Miss Mary Anne Kent, evidently the eldest, acted Maria. In the afterpiece *Who's the Dupe?* he played Old Doiley and his daughter performed Charlotte. She also gave a recitation of Garrick's *Picture of a Modern Fine Lady* at the end of the mainpiece. Another daughter, Miss C. Kent, age five offered an *Address to the Ladies*. The evening concluded with an *Address of Thanks*, "written by a Lady purposely for Mr Kent & Family, spoken by Kent." The "Lady" may have been the Margravine of Anspach, who evidently was Kent's sponsor for the event. He had anxiously advertised:

Benefit for Kent and Family. By Desire of Her Serene Highness, the Margravine of Anspach. Kent's most respectful Compliments waits on the Ladies and Gentlemen of Hammersmith, and its Vicinity, informs them that Mr Newman has kindly granted the Assembly Room for one or two Evenings; to accomodate Her Highness the Margravine and principal Inhabitants: Kent has spar'd neither trouble or expence to render it conveniant [*sic*] as possible, the Room itself being very respectable & the Entrance unexceptionable. He earnestly solicits the company of his Friends in general, assuring them that every endeavor will be exerted for their Entertainment; the Interest of every Lady & Gentleman will be ever most gratefully remember'd, as very highly contributing to Kent's extricating himself from a Situation obvious to all acquainted with the Expence he has been at, and the ill Success he has met with. To begin exactly at 6:30. Admittance 2*s*. Tickets to be had at the Winsor Castle, of Kent, and Miss Connard in Union Court, and of Miss Kent, at Mrs Bevias.

On the following night Kent offered *The Road to Ruin* and *The Poor Soldier*, for which no casts were listed. Perhaps there were subsequent performances as well.

Kent brought his family—now larger—

back to London to play at the White Lyon in Wych Street on 19 June 1795 for the "Benefit of a Family in Distress"—presumably his own. In the mainpiece, *The Child of Nature*, he acted Alberto and W. Kent, probably his eldest son, was Count Valentio; Miss Mary Anne Kent played Amanthis. In *The Oracle*, the afterpiece, Mary Anne was the Fairy Queen, Master Kent Oberon, and Miss Sophia Kent, a third daughter, Cynthia. Miss C. Kent, now six, gave her *Address to the Ladies*, Mary Anne delivered her *Picture of a Modern Fine Lady*, the girls also sang, and Kent concluded with an *Address of Thanks*.

Returning to the provinces, Kent circulated through Barnstable, Taunton, Poole, and Guernsey in 1799, no doubt with his performing brood. He may have been the Kent who acted at Edinburgh in 1809–10, but the youthful nature of the roles performed that season suggest that actor was either W. Kent or the grown-up Master Kent: Belcour in *The West Indian*, Captain Absolute in *The Rivals*, Doricourt in *The Belle's Stratagem*, and Paul in *Paul and Virginia*, among others.

Kent, Mr ₍*fl.* 1799–1804₎, *doorkeeper.*
A Mr Kent was a gallery doorkeeper at Drury Lane Theatre from 1799–1800 through at least 1803–4. In 1803–4 his salary was 9*s.* per week.

Kent, Master ₍*fl.* 1795₎, *actor. See* KENT, MR ₍*fl.* 1780–1810?₎.

Kent, Miss C. *b. 1789, actress. See* KENT, MR ₍*fl.* 1780–1810?₎.

Kent, James *1700–1776, organist, composer.*
According to Grove, James Kent was born in Winchester on 13 March 1700, the son of a glazier. He served as a chorister under Vaughan Richardson at Winchester Cathedral from 1711 to 1714 and then joined the Chapel Royal under Croft. In 1717 he was appointed organist at Finedone, Northamptonshire, a post he kept until 1731, when he was made organist of Trinity College, Cambridge, He remained there until 13 January 1737, when he became organist of the Cathedral and Col-

By permission of the Warden and Fellows of Winchester College

JAMES KENT
by "M. H."

lege of Winchester. At some point he married Elizabeth Freeman, the daughter of the singer John Freeman (c. 1666–1736). Kent resigned his posts at Winchester in 1774 and died in that city on 6 May 1776. He published during his later years some anthems, and others were published posthumously. A portrait of Kent by "M. H." is at Winchester College.

Kent, Mary Anne *b. 1776, actress, singer.*
On 22 April 1780 the *Kentish Gazette* announced that four-year-old Miss Mary Anne Kent was to perform at Dover with her father, the provincial actor Mr Kent (fl. 1780–1810?). She was no doubt the Miss Kent who later played under Butler's management at Gainsborough, Lincolnshire, in December 1792. On 24 March 1794 she joined her father and her younger sister Miss C. Kent for a benefit at the Windsor Castle Inn, King

Street, Hammersmith, where Mary Anne acted Maria in *The School for Scandal* and Charlotte in *Who's the Dupe?* and delivered Garrick's *Picture of a Modern Fine Lady* at the end of the mainpiece. She probably performed the next night in *The Road to Ruin* and *The Poor Soldier*, but no casts for that evening are known.

On 19 June 1795 Mary Anne again accompanied her family for their benefit at the White Lyon in Wych Street. She acted Amanthis in *The Child of Nature* and the Fairy Queen in *The Oracle*; also she offered her *Picture of a Modern Fine Lady* and sang. In addition to her father, her brothers W. Kent and Master Kent and her sister Miss C. Kent and Sophia also performed.

Sometime in late 1795 or early 1796 Sheridan wrote to an unidentified associate who was going to Margate to observe Miss Kent, then acting in that place and desirous of an engagement at Drury Lane. Sheridan's scout evidently recommended her, for on 20 April 1796 the Drury Lane treasurer paid Mary Anne £3 10*s*. for "3 weeks before on list." Her name appeared in no Drury Lane bills that season, so her services there remain obscure. When she played at Tunbridge Wells in August 1797, however, she was announced as from Drury Lane. On 13 January 1798 the *Norwich Mercury* announced her debut there. She seems to have retired from the stage after appearing in her benefit at Norwich on 10 April 1800, supported in the performance of *As You Like It* by her sister Sophia.

In 1804, John Howe, Baron of Chedworth, who was particularly fond of the Norwich theatre, left in his will generous bequests to a number of Norwich players, including £600 to Mary Anne Kent, "late of the Theatre Royal, Norwich, and now of Barnes in Surrey, Spinster."

Kent, Sophia [*fl. 1795–1800*], *actress.*
Miss Sophia Kent acted Cynthia in *The Oracle* on 19 June 1795 at the White Lyon, Wych Street, for the benefit of her family. Also performing that night were her father, Mr Kent (fl. 1780–1810?), her brothers Mr. W. and Master Kent, and her sisters Miss Mary Anne and Miss C. Kent. Sophia acted at Norwich in 1800, appearing in a performance of *As You Like It* on 10 April for the benefit of her sister Mary Anne.

Kent, Thomas [fl. 1669–1678], pit-keeper, scenekeeper?

Perhaps there were two Kents active at the same time in the King's Company in the 1670s, for it seems odd to find one person described now as a pitkeeper and now as a scenekeeper; one would think that the two posts would not have been handled by one person, though it would not have been impossible. There was a Thomas Kent in the King's Company, and perhaps he did hold both positions. *The London Stage* lists him as a pitkeeper in 1669–70, and two warrants in the Lord Chamberlain's accounts in January 1670 cite Kent as a scenekeeper.

A document reported by *The Theatrical Inquisitor and Monthly Mirror* in July 1816 (not too reliable a source) shows the income at the King's Theatre on 12 and 26 December 1677 for performances of *All for Love* and *The Rival Queens*. "Mr. Kent's pit" is cited in both accounts, and it would appear that he was one of two pitkeepers. His colleague Mr Britain supposedly could have taken care of the pit once the performance started if Kent was required backstage—and he would not have been until the first scene shift.

Mrs Cecily Smith was allowed by the Lord Chamberlain to go to law against Thomas Kent and Robert Shatterell of the King's players on 4 June 1678, probably for a debt. The Thomas Kent who was active in the United Company in the 1690s and the first decade of the eighteenth century may well have been our subject's son. The fact that he was called "Young Kent" suggests that he had to be distinguished from an elder Kent in the troupe, though we have no record of the elder Kent's employment in the theatre after 1678.

Kent, Thomas [fl. 1690–1708], actor.

The Kent active in the last decade of the seventeenth century was often called "Tommey" or "Young Kent," at least through 1694, presumably to distinguish him from an elder Kent in the troupe. His father may have been the King's Company house servant of the 1670s, also named Thomas Kent, and, if the elder Kent was no longer employed at the theatre, his son may have been well enough known by playgoers (he was a pitkeeper) that cast lists needed to make a distinction or call special attention to the son of one of the theatre's own families.

The earliest role for young Thomas Kent would appear to have been the Servant to Ilford in *Sir Anthony Love* in November 1690 (according to Robert Hume; probably not as early as September, as *The London Stage* reports). "Tommey" played Prince Edward in *Richard III* sometime during the 1690–91 season, according to a manuscript cast in the Hickmott copy of the 1634 edition of the play. Only two other roles are known for Kent before the United Company divided in 1695: Rogery in *The Traytor* and Toby in *The Canterbury Guests*.

Kent remained with Christopher Rich at Drury Lane after the split, playing, before the end of the century, Diego in *The Rival Sisters*, Brittone in *The Younger Brother*, the Prince of Syana in *The Island Princess* (*The London Stage* is in error in listing that part for Mrs Kent), Lurcher in *Love without Interest*, and Ratcliff in *Richard III*. It is worth noting that from 1698 forward Thomas was called Mr Kent. That fact suggests that about that time he may have reached his majority. The scanty records of early eighteenth century casts tell us of only a handful of other parts Kent essayed: a Neapolitan Lord in *The Unhappy Pentitent*, Donato in *The Patriot*, Belloon in *Love the Leveller*, a Clerk in *The Northern Lass*, Shab in *Farewell Folly*, a Merchant and Snap in *The Royal Merchant*, Scruple and Appletree in *The Recruiting Officer*, and Ralph in *Wit without Money*. Because of the management difficulties Drury Lane had late in the first decade of the new century, the players could sometimes be found there and sometimes at the Queen's Theatre. In 1706–7 Kent performed at the Queen's, and the last record we have of him is a performance of Snap in *The Royal Merchant* on 14 February 1707. Four days earlier he had been replaced in the role of Appletree in *The Recruiting Officer* by Fairbank, and the indication is that Kent left the company before the season was concluded—or at least was not able to perform. In the winter of 1707–8, when the Lord Chamberlain restricted operas to the Queen's Theatre and ordered the players to return to Drury Lane, the performers signed a petition. Thomas Kent was on the list, but he is not known to have been active on stage that season. His wife Mary, on the other hand, performed for another ten years.

Kent, Mrs Thomas, Mary ₁*fl. 1692–1718*₁, *actress.*

Mary Kent, the wife of the Drury Lane actor Thomas, was first noticed in the bills on 8 November 1692, when she appeared at Drury Lane as Rosamund's Woman in *Henry II*. The rest of her roles before the breakup of the United Company in 1695 were Florence in *The Maid's Last Prayer*, the Nurse in *Love Triumphant*, Dona Rodriguez in *2 Don Quixote*, and Mrs Breeder in *The Canterbury Guests*. With her husband she continued performing at Drury Lane under the management of Christopher Rich to the end of the century, playing Bianca in *Agnes de Castro*, Megra in *Philaster*, Flareit in *Love's Last Shift*, Lady Young-Love in *The Lost Lover*, Betty Useful in *The Female Wits*, Young Fashion in *The Relapse* (that was not a misprint; she played it occasionally in later years), Hortentia in both parts of *Aesop*, Lettice in *Woman's Wit*, Friskit in *A Plot and No Plot*, Merope in *Phaeton*, Gusset in *The Campaigners*, Eugenia in *Love without Interest*, and Lucy in *Courtship à la Mode*.

Her parts at Drury Lane from about October 1700 to March 1710 included Placentia in *The Perjured Husband*, Delia in *The Bath*, Tattleaid in *The Funeral*, Lamorce in *The Inconstant*, Isabella in *The False Friend*, Honoria in *The Patriot*, Vainlove in *The Tender Husband*, Mrs Goodfellow in *Tunbridge Walks*, Mrs Trainwell in *The Northern Lass*, Lady Wouldbe in *Volpone*, Eugenia in *The London Cuckolds*, Roselia in *The Sea Voyage*, Laula in *The Empress of Morocco*, Goneril in *King Lear*, Young Fashion again in *The Relapse*, Nottingham in *The Unhappy Favorite*, Mrs Day in *The Committee*, and Phaedra in *Amphitryon*. During that period Mrs Kent appeared regularly except for 1705–6 and 1706–7, during which time her husband seems to have continued performing. The cause of her temporary retirement from the London stage is not known.

During the summer and early fall of 1710 William Pinkethman operated a theatre in Greenwich, using players from both London playhouses, including Mrs Kent, to whom he assigned a number of significant parts: Isabella in *The Fatal Marriage*, Aquilina in *Venice Preserv'd*, Leonora in *Sir Courtly Nice*, Roxana in *The Rival Queens*, Hippolyto in *The Tempest*, Belinda in *The Fair Quaker*, Mrs Woodly in *Epsom Wells*, Elaria in *The Emperor of the Moon*, Lady Wealthy in *The Gamester*, Isabella in *The Busy Body*, Camillo in *The Mistake*, the Queen of the Amazons in *The Sea Voyage*, Angelica in *The Rover*, Araminta in *The Confederacy*, Aminta in *The Maid of the Mill*, Nourmahal in *Aureng-Zebe*, and Haily in *Tamerlane*. Perhaps that taste of playing much more important roles than she had been allowed at Drury Lane discouraged Mrs Kent from pursuing her stage career there any further.

For a few years Mrs Kent contented herself with another kind of theatrical activity. The puppeteer Powell from Bath visited London regularly, George Speaight says in his *English Puppet Theatre*, from 1710 to 1714, and each year he granted Mrs Kent a benefit, she being one of his two assistants (Betty Smith was the other; she received only one benefit during that period, so her post was inferior to Mrs Kent's). The performances were initially at Punch's Theatre in St Martin's Lane, and some of London's future performers—the younger Boman, Henry Norris, Jr, Miss Younger, Miss Porter, William Mills—received some of their training there.

After her work with puppets Mrs Kent returned to the stage. The new Lincoln's Inn Fields playhouse, under the management of John Rich, opened in December 1714, and for it Rich had to recruit a full complement of players and house servants. He lured a number of actors from Drury Lane, and from Punch's Theatre he picked up Mrs Kent. She was first seen at the new playhouse on 4 January 1715 as Laetitia in *The Old Bachelor*. During the rest of the season she played Nottingham in *The Unhappy Favorite*, a Barmaid in *The Fair Quaker*, Charlotte Weldon in *Oroonoko*, and Lady Youthful in *The Doating Lovers*. She was granted a solo benefit on 12 May, but it brought in gross receipts of only £72 1s. 6d.

Mary Kent remained with the Lincoln's Inn Fields company through the beginning of the 1718–19 season, playing such new parts as Rodriguez in *2 Don Quixote*, Madam Bertrand in *The Lucky Prodigal*, Lady Cardivant in *The Northern Heiress*, Lady Pride in *The Amorous Widow*, Lady Fantast in *Bury Fair*, Johayma in *Don Sebastian*, Mrs Prim in *A Bold Stroke for a Wife*, Decoy in *The Artful Husband*, Oriana's Mother in *The Traytor*, and Mrs Furnish in *The Fair Example*. Her part in *The Traytor*, which she first played on 11 October 1718, was omitted on 27 October. By then she may have left the company.

Kent, W. [*fl. 1795–1810?*], *actor. See* **KENT, MR** [*fl. 1780–1810?*].

Kent, William *1685–1748, painter, sculptor, architect, landscape gardener, scene painter.*

Born at Bridlington, Yorkshire, in 1685 and apprenticed to a Hull coachman at 14, William Kent enjoyed a successful career primarily as a painter, architect, and sculptor. Details of his substantial nontheatrical work will be found in lengthy notices in *The Dictionary of National Biography* and in Howard Colvin's *Biographical Dictionary of British Architects 1600–1840* (1978).

Kent painted scenery for *The Feast of Hymen*, an opera by Porpora, which was produced at the King's Theatre on 4 May 1736 in celebration of the wedding of the Prince of Wales. Peter Scheemakers executed Kent's design for the statue of Shakespeare which was placed in Poets' Corner of Westminster Abbey in 1741.

GUILIELMUS KENT
Magnæ Britanniæ Regis Pictor et Architectus

By permission of the Trustees of the British Museum

WILLIAM KENT

engraving by Ravenet, after Aikman

At Goodman's Fields on 3 March 1741 in a production of *Harlequin Student; or, The Fall of Pantomime*, one of John Devoto's scenes revealed "the *Monument* of Shakespeare, *exactly represented, as lately erected in* Westminster Abbey."

Other theatrically-related works by Kent included a monument to Congreve at Stowe; publication of two folio volumes of *The Designs of Inigo Jones* in 1727, in collaboration with the Earl of Burlington; and paintings at Hampton Court depicting the interview of Henry V and Princess Katharine and their marriage. Hogarth, who was his enemy, proclaimed that neither England nor Italy ever produced a more contemptible dauber than Kent—a verdict on his painting which time has not much softened. Horace Walpole was also critical of Kent's painting but regarded him highly in other branches of art.

Kent became principal painter to the crown in 1739 and also was master carpenter, architect, and keeper of pictures, with a total income of about £600 per year. His architecture included the Royal Mews, the Horse Guards and Treasury buildings in Whitehall, Devonshire House in Piccadilly, Kensington Palace, Burlington House, the Law Courts at Westminster, and a choir screen in Gloucester Cathedral, among many other commissions.

Kent died at Burlington House on 12 April 1748 and was buried in Lord Burlington's vault at Chiswick. According to Walpole, "His fortune, which with pictures and books amounted to about 10,000£, he divided between his relations and an actress, with whom he had long lived in particular friendship." The actress was Elizabeth Butler, who made her first appearance at Drury Lane in March 1726 and continued to act there for some 22 years. In his will, made on 13 October 1743 and proved on 15 April 1748, Kent left £600 to "Elizabeth Butler of the parish of St Paul, Covent Garden"; she did not live to enjoy the legacy, dying on 16 September 1748. Her son George and daughter Elizabeth, whom William Kent had probably sired, each received £300. Kent also made numerous bequests of pictures and small sums to his friends, patrons, and relatives, but the bulk of his estate he left to his nephew William Pearson and nieces Esther and Mary Pearson, children of his sister Esther Pearson.

A number of portraits of William Kent are known or recorded, though not all the attributions are definite. More details about the portraits listed below will be found in Margaret Jourdain, *The Works of William Kent* (1948) and John Kerslake *Early Georgian Portraits in the National Portrait Gallery* (1978).

1. By W. Aikman. At one time with Lord Castlemain at Wanstead, but present location unknown. Engravings were done by S. F. Ravenet; by A. Bannerman for an edition of Walpole's *Anecdotes*, 1762; and by J. W. Cook for another edition, 1862.

2. By Lady Burlington, "painted like Kneller." At Hardwick in 1865. Present location unknown.

3. By Lady Burlington. In crayon. Noted by Vertue at Lady Burlington's great room at Piccadilly, about 1748.

4. By Michael Dahl, 1725. Noted by Vertue. Present location unknown.

5. By Bartholomew Dandridge. *Perhaps* William Kent. In the National Portrait Gallery (No 1557).

6. By Bartholomew Dandridge. Present location unknown. At No 31, Old Burlington Street in 1910 when reproduced in the *Connoisseur*.

7. By Gawen Hamilton. In a painting of a group entitled "An Artists' Club in 1735." In the National Portrait Gallery. Reproduced in this dictionary with the notice of Joseph Goupy.

8. By William Hogarth. In Hogarth's plate "Masquerades and Operas, Burlington Gate" (1724), the statue of Kent surmounts the gate of Burlington House.

9. By William Hogarth. In Hogarth's plate "The Man of Taste" (1732), the statue of Kent is found in the same place as in Hogarth's "Masquerades and Operas, Burlington Gate."

10. By William Kent. Self-portrait. Engraving by S. F. Ravenet, 1743.

11. By William Kent. Self-portrait. Owned by the Reverend R. V. Harcourt in 1867, when it was exhibited at South Kensington.

12. By William Kent. Self-portrait, small profile drawing. At Chatsworth, with the Chiswick Miscellanies.

13. By William Kent. Self-portrait, with palette; in the decorations of the King's Stairs, Kensington Palace.

14. By William Kent. Self-portrait, probably; in the allegorical "Mercury and the Arts," in the Red Velvet Room at Chiswick House.

15. By Benedetto Luti, 1718. In the Devonshire Collection, Chatsworth.

16. By George Vertue. Miniature, 1743. In the National Portrait Gallery (No 4684).

17. By Viviani. Kent shown with the Duke of Grafton in Rome. At Euston Hall.

18. By unknown artist. In a sketch in oils of a group entitled "A Society of Artists that Existed about the Year 1730." At Oxford University. An engraving by R. Cooper was published by W. B. Tiffin, 1829.

19. By unknown artist. Sitter possibly William Kent. Oil in possession of Judge Lock at Bridlington, Yorkshire, 1919.

20. Two profile heads by unknown artist. Called "Chiswick Miscellanies." At Chatsworth. Possibly these two drawings are items 2 and 3 above, by Lady Burlington.

Kentzen. *See* KUNTZEN.

Kenyon, Mr [*fl. 1753*], *exhibitor.*
A Mr Kenyon, advertised in the Bristol papers on 24 February 1753 as from London, exhibited at the Naked Boy, next to the Guildhall in Broad Street, a machine for cutting silhouettes and a mechanical organ.

Kerman, Mlle Frederick [*fl. 1740–1742*], *rope dancer.*
Mademoiselle Frederick (*sic*) Kerman, the daughter of the ladder dancer Hendrick Kerman and his wife, was advertised in a Sadler's Wells bill of 13 April 1740 as providing audiences with a variety of rope dances. Arundel in his *Story of Sadler's Wells* assumed the bill was either in error or that a female impersonator was the performer, but Mlle Kerman seems to have been a young girl who had a masculine name. She and her father were at Sadler's Wells again in the summer of 1742; bills on 19 June and 3 July noted her rope-dancing performances.

Kerman, Hendrick [*fl. 1740–1746*], *ladder dancer, rope dancer, actor, acrobat.*
Hendrick Kerman, often cited in advertisements only as Hendrick, appeared in Paris with the London dancer Ferguson in a *fête anglais* in 1740, and the pair played minor parts

with the Grande Troupe Etrangère for some years. Ferguson did not return to England until 1747, but Kerman came over in the spring of 1741, perhaps just for a short engagement. He joined Sadler's Wells for a revival of a dance called *The Pigmalion*; Kerman was called Mr Hendrick, the famous ladder dancer from Russia—where he may have performed, though he seems to have been of Dutch origin.

He was at Sadler's Wells again in the summer of 1742. Bills for 19 June and 3 July advertised a variety program involving a mixture of local and foreign performers, with Kerman participating in a tumbling act and several ladder dances. Back again in 1744, Kerman performed in August at the New Wells, Clerkenwell, according to Pinks's *Clerkenwell*. He danced on a rope with a wheelbarrow before him, "out of which are displayed several curious fireworks," said the *Daily Advertiser*. Hendrick Kerman returned to Sadler's Wells in 1746 with his ladder dance.

On occasion Kerman's wife performed with him, as did Mlle "Frederick" Kerman, who was evidently their daughter.

Kerman, Mme Hendrick [*fl.* 1744], rope dancer, acrobat.

At the New Wells, Clerkenwell, in August 1744, according to the *Daily Advertiser*, 600 people watched Mme Kerman dance on the stiff rope, then on stilts. She jumped over a "garter" ten feet high at one point, apparently on her stilts. She was the wife of the ladder dancer Hendrick Kerman.

Kern. *See* KEMM.

Kérodack, Kérodat. *See* TÉRODAT.

Kerridge, Mr, stage name of Mr Haymes [*fl.* 1785–1795], singer, actor, dancer.

The performer who used Kerridge as his stage name was a Mr Haymes—probably not Thomas Haynes but possibly G. K. Haymes. The evidence, which derives from *The Mirror of Taste* in February 1811, when Kerridge was reported to have acted at Exeter about 1785 with William Warren, is not detailed enough to permit certain identification. From 27 June to 27 July 1785 Kerridge performed at Hammersmith, appearing first as Lord Randolph in

Douglas and then as Eustace in *Love in a Village*, Belmour in *Jane Shore*, a Frenchman in *The Death and Revival of Harlequin*, Tug in *The Waterman*, Lord Aimworth in *The Maid of the Mill*, Colonel Tivy in *Bon Ton*, Serjeant Flower in *The Clandestine Marriage*, Pedro in *The Spanish Fryar*, Pan in *Midas*, a Frenchman in *Mother Shipton*, Captain Constant in *The Ghost*, Scaramouch in *Harlequin Skeleton*, Captain Fitzroy in *The Poor Soldier*, Doublefee in *The Follies of a Day*, Slango in *The Honest Yorkshireman*, Pierrot and a Fryar in *Robinson Crusoe*, and Rossano in *The Fair Penitent*. In addition to the singing and dancing required of him within the pantomimes, Kerridge on 8 July performed the title part in an entr'acte dance entitled *The Wapping Landlady*.

A Mr Kerridge, probably our subject, served as an interpreter for a group of Italian rope dancers at the Theatre Royal, Norwich, in 1787. Kerridge was a minor singer in Bristol in 1794–95 and in late April 1795 was in the afterpiece *The Banditti* at the Theatre Royal in Bath (a troupe essentially the same as that performing in Bristol).

Kerton. *See* KIRTON.

Ketch, William [*fl.* 1720–1721], oboist.

A Lord Chamberlain's warrant dated 7 March 1721 shows that a William Ketch played oboe in a *Te Deum* performance at St James's on 13 November 1720. "Keitch" performed again at St James's on 9 July 1721. It seems likely that he was related to Jean Christian Kytch.

Kew, Nathaniel [*fl.* 1672–1682], actor.

Nathaniel Kew (or Cue, Kewe, Q) played Boyster in *The Wise Women of Hogsdon*, probably in the summer of 1672 with John Coysh's touring company, some of whom were players from the "Nursery" for young actors in London. With the King's Company in London Kew acted Lightning in the epilogue to *The Empress of Morocco* (Duffett's burlesque, not Settle's original work) at the Lincoln's Inn Fields playhouse in the summer of 1673 (suggests Robert Hume, as opposed to *The London Stage* dating of December of that year). In the burlesque proper Kew played Muley Hamet. In 1673–74 he acted a Servant in *The Maides*

Revenge. Sometime between about 1673 and 1675 he was one of the guards in *Brennoralt*, according to manuscript notes in a Bodleian copy of the play.

Kew's name did not appear in discovered records again until in mid-June 1677, when he acted the servant Jack Drayner in *Wits Led by the Nose* at Drury Lane. In *The Rambling Justice* in late February 1678 at the same playhouse Kew acted Spywell, and possibly he was on tour with Coysh's troupe, called the Duke of Monmouth's Company, in Edinburgh in the spring of 1679. The Lord Chamberlain's accounts on 8 April 1682 show that Kew was still a member of the King's troupe, but he may not have continued performing after the union of the two Restoration patent companies.

It seems very likely that the Nathaniell Kewe of St Olave, Hart Street, who left a nuncupative will on 22 December 1676 was the father of the actor. His will made his son Nathaniel Kewe his sole heir and executor. The younger Nathaniel Kewe proved the will on 14 December 1676.

Keyes. *See* KEYS.

Keygill. *See* KAYGILL.

Keynlas, Mr [*fl.* 1784], *actor.*
Mr Keynlas played Captain Constant in *The Man's Bewitch'd* on 8 March 1784 at the Haymarket Theatre.

Keys, Mr [*fl.* 1791–1813], *box office keeper.*
A Mr Keys was box office keeper at Covent Garden Theatre by 1791. He shared in benefit tickets with other house personnel there on 2 June 1791, and he was at that theatre in 1791–92. He was probably the same Mr Keys who in the first decade of the next century was a house servant at Drury Lane Theatre; the account books list him as a ticket taker in 1806, as servant from 1806–7 through 1811–12, and as boxkeeper at 18*s.* per week in 1812–13.

Keys, Miss. *See* MILLS, MRS HENRY.

Keys, Sarah Jane. *See* LEE, MRS HENRY.

Keys, Simon [*fl.* 1787–1799?], *actor, dancer.*
The parents of Simon Keys were perhaps the Mr and Mrs Keys who were members of Austin's touring company from Dublin that visited Wrexham, Wales, in the summer of 1766; in the town hall there on 4 July Keys acted Poundage and Mrs Keys acted Trusty in *The Provok'd Husband*. The company remained at Wrexham till 19 September, then played at Denbigh in October, and was at Ostwestry by 10 November 1766. It is possible, but unlikely, that Mr Keys was an equestrian of that name who was a member of Astley's company that performed on Durdham Down, Bristol, in October 1772.

Most of Simon Keys's obscure career was passed in the provinces. He was at Smock Alley, Dublin, in 1787–88 (making his first appearance in that country according to the *Hibernian Journal* of 28 December 1787). No doubt he was the actor-dancer who was a minor performer in the various pantomimes and reviews at Drury Lane Theatre (and at the King's Theatre and the Haymarket when occupied by the Drury Lane company) between 1791–92 and 1796–97, appearing for the first time it seems on 5 November 1791 in *Don Juan*. He also danced in *The Pirates* in 1792–93, *Lodoiska* and *The Cherokee* in 1794–95, and *Harlequin Captive* and *The Iron Chest* in 1795–96. On 3 December 1796 his name was on the Drury Lane pay list for £1 5*s.* per week.

After his London tenure, Keys returned to the provinces, playing at Norwich for a while, at Brighton in 1798, and with a company circuiting Barnstaple, Taunton, Poole, and Guernsey in 1799. Soon after, he left the stage to live at Ringwood, Hampshire, according to *The Secret History of the Green Room*.

Key's first name was provided by O'Keefe in his *Reminiscences*. George Parker in his *Society and Manners* reported that to his abilities as a performer, Keys

annexed the more valuable one of being a good man. . . . He was possessed of those general qualifications which render a man peculiarly useful in the Country. He was a pleasing Tragedian, as well as a very good Comedian; and to these he added likewise the adroitness, agility, and dexterity, which are required in a Harlequin. With this Gentleman and his Wife many of my hours were passed very chearfully.

Key's wife no doubt acted with him regularly in the provinces. She was, according to William Clark, at Kilkenny in 1793. Though she did not perform in London in the eighteenth century, she was a member of the Haymarket company in 1804. In September 1804 the *Monthly Mirror* called her a "well-known actress at Weymouth." The *Gentleman's Magazine* for November 1811 recorded the death of Mrs Keys, a member of Mrs Baker's company, at Tunbridge Wells on 31 October 1811; but the age of that deceased actress was given as 33, so Mrs Keys may not have been Simon Keys's first wife nor the mother of his two actress daughters. One of those daughters, Sarah Jane Keys, married the actor Henry Lee and died young in 1797; the other, Christian name unknown, married the actor Henry Mills and died in 1804. Evidently Simon Keys was also the father of a son, an obscure musician.

Keysberry. *See* KEASBERRY.

Keyse, Thomas *1722–1800, proprietor, painter.*

Born in 1722, Thomas Keyse was a self-educated artist who exhibited paintings of still-life flowers and fruits at the Free Society of Artists from 1761 to 1764. One of the founders of the Society of Artists, about 1765 he was instrumental in erecting a large building for the members; this building, however, soon was sold to one Langham who leased it for various entertainments and exhibitions until in 1809 it was converted to the Lyceum Theatre. Keyse also exhibited paintings occasionally at the Royal Academy and in 1768 received an award from the Society of Artists for his development of a new method of setting crayon drawings.

About 1765 Keyse bought the Waterman's Arms, a tavern in Bermondsey, along with some three acres of adjoining ground, and opened a tea-garden. A chalybeate spring was discovered on the grounds about 1770, whereupon the establishment was named Bermondsey Spa Gardens. It was said that the ambiance was enhanced by the cheery landlord's special preparation of cherry brandy.

In 1784, having obtained a license for musical entertainments from the Surrey magistrates, Keyse spent about £4000 on improvements intended to make his Spa Gardens a

By permission of the Trustees of the British Museum

THOMAS KEYSE

by Drummond

humble imitation of Vauxhall. He kept the establishment open on week-nights and on Sundays during the summer. Admission was usually one shilling (on some special occasions a half-crown or three shillings) which entitled the bearer of an admission token to six-pence worth of refreshments. During Keyse's tenure as proprietor, entertainments consisted of instrumental and vocal recitals, burlettas, interludes, and duets, and an occasional display of fireworks. Keyse designed the apparatus for the set-piece of a representation of the Siege of Gibraltar, probably first introduced about 1786, with fireworks, bombs, and transparencies. An important attraction was a permanent exhibition of his own paintings and drawings housed in his "Gallery of Paintings," next door to the tavern, where for an admission fee of sixpence Keyse showed his very large reproductions of such local scenes as a butcher's shop and a greengrocer's stall. In his *Book for a Rainy Day*, J. T. Smith told of a visit to the gallery in 1795 and a humorous conversation with the artist-proprietor, whom he described "a little, thick-set man, with a round face, arch look, and closely-curled wig." By that time, the popularity of the gardens was waning and the quality of the entertainment quite diminished. The spa bore the disadvantage of a lonely situation, which evidently could not be overcome despite Keyse's advertisements that "the road is lighted and watched by patroles every night, at the sole expense of the proprietor."

Keyse died at his house on the grounds of Bermondsey Spa Gardens on 8 February 1800 at the age of 79. His pictures were sold at auction. His successors could not make the gardens pay. The place was closed about 1805 and the site on Spa Road was subsequently built upon.

A *Description of some of the Paintings in the Prepetual Exhibition at Bermondsey Spa* was published about 1785. The paintings have disappeared, but the one of the butcher shop was exhibited in a Leicester Square gallery in 1818, when a writer in the *Literary Gazette* on 25 July was very impressed by its realistic details— "Nothing that ever was painted surpasses this extraordinary performance in regard to the exact representation of *still life*, as we trust *dead meat* may very properly be called." The pigment was "wonderful pure and natural." Keyse's whites remained bright, as he explained to Sir Joshua Reynolds, because the canvases were constantly exposed to fresh air.

A water-color drawing of Keyse by S. Drummond was engraved by J. Chapman and published in *The Monthly Visitor* for December 1797. Perhaps the portrait was that owned by J. H. Burn, along with a pen-and-ink sketch of the spa. At the Burn sale at Puttick's about 1880 these were bought by a Mr Gardner; subsequently they were owned by Arthur W. Waters.

Illustrations

Operas, Promptbooks, and Parts

Frontispiece to *Ariadne, or The Marriage of Bacchus*, libretto by Pierre Perrin and music by Louis Grabu, produced at Drury Lane Theatre on 30 March 1674

BEGGAR'S OPERA, Act III.

When my hero in Court appears, &c.

From the Original Picture, in the Collection of his Grace the Duke of Leeds

The Beggar's Opera, by John Gay and John Christopher Pepusch, Act III; produced at Lincoln's Inn Fields Theatre, 29 January 1728. Engraving by William Blake, 1790, after Hogarth

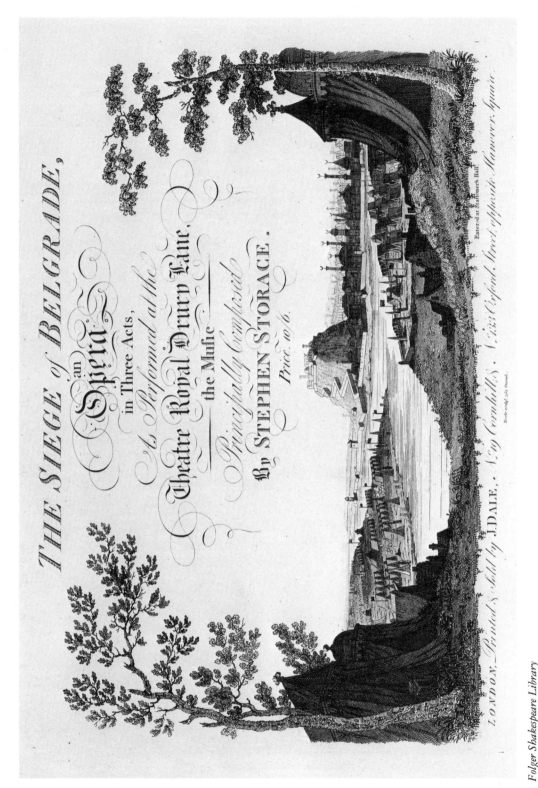

Folger Shakespeare Library
Title page, *The Siege of Belgrade*, by James Cobb and Stephen Storace, n.d.; produced at Drury
Lane Theatre, 1 January 1791

Schoenbodie del.

R. Hewlett sculp.

THE KING'S THEATRE, *HAYMARKET*.

This Theatre, destroyed by Fire 17th June 1789 rebuilt by Michael Novosielski Esqʳ in 1790-1
Was opened by the Drury Lane Company, while their Theatre was rebuilding, in March the same year.
The present Elevation after a design by John Nash Esqʳ was completed in 1819.

London Published 27th September 1820 by Robert Wilkinson, Nᵒ 58 Cornhill, 1820.

The King's Theatre opera house. Engraving by Robert Wilkinson, 27 September 1820

Mo. They are gone, I'l see his complexion;
Who's this?

Fa. Our own Son *Piperollo?*

Pi. Pray Father give me your bleſſing, ah---
Mother do not ſtone me to death with that
Money bag, I am your Son.

Mo. My Son? I know thee not.

Pi. A liar, you know Mother, is worſe than a
Theef; do not deſtroy the hopes of your Family,
Alas, I was drawn in, and made a theef
In my own defence, they ſwore to cut my throat
Elſe, do you think I had ſo little grace --

Mo. Did they ſo? I'l try what I can do.
                         She draws her knife.

Pi. Oh my quibibles! ſweet Mother, remember
You were a woman in your days, that knew
What's what, and the true difference of things.
I am a man yet, your forgiveneſſe may
Make me a true man. Libbing and hanging
Are no helps to poſterity, I am your own
Sweet fleſh and bloud--- Oh.

Mo. Kick him out of doors.

Pi. I thank you, this Correction may do me good;
Gently, ah gently; ſhall I not ask you bleſſing,
A twelve-month hence?

Both Never.

Pi. I wo'not.
My Mother has a deadly lift with her leg.

Fa. Boh, you tadpole.   *Exeunt.*

Pi. I ſhall do no good o'this trade.
Now to my wits, this is no world to ſtarve in.
                                        Exit

Enter Lucio, Giovanni, Stephanio, with white Staves.

Lu. This is very fine; do not theſe Staves become us?
But will my Lady be thus mad, and give

                                        The

The Lord *Contarini* Audience in ſuch State?
She takes upon her like a very Princeſs.   (here

Gio. But is't not ſtrange, her Uncle ſhould thus humor

Ste. He gave her the firſt hint; which ſhe purſues
To his vexation.

Luc. But will my Lord ſtoop to this mockery?

Gio. He is prepar'd by her Uncle; 'twil be ſport,
If ſhe but carry it with pride enough.

Gio. Let her alone.

St. And if my Lord wants confidence

Gio. I think her impudence will make him bluſh,
And put him out; I have ſeen a Counterfeit
With ſuch a Majeſty compoſe himſelf,
He thought himſelf a Prince, could frown as ſcornfully,
And give his hand out to great Lords to kiſs,
With as much grace, as all the Royall bloud
Had muſterd in his veins.

Lu. Some Monarch
Of Innes a Court in *England* ſure; but when
His reign expires, and Chriſtmas in the grave
Cold as the Turkies coffind up in cruſt,
That walk like Ghoſts, and glide to ſeverall Tables,
When Inſtruments are hoarſe with ſitting up,
When the gay triumph ceaſes, and the treaſure
Divided, all the Offices laid up,
And the new cloathes in Lavender, what then?

Gio. Why then the man that kiſt his highneſs hand
O'r night, may juſtle him for the wall next morning,
And have it too; if he come off with all
His wits, the Play is paid for, and he thanks
For travelling.

        *Enter Contarini, Antonio, Vergerio,
                they whiſper.*

My Ladies Uncle, and the Lord *Contarini.*

Ver. My Lord *Contarini* expects when he
May have the happineſs to preſent his ſervice

                                        To

Ready for horrid Musick. 77
mr. Osborn ready

Mat: Of what Order?

Julia: Like other Bodies-aggregate; of none, nor ever
reducible under any.

Mat: At least your Superiors' name:.

Jul: I never own'd any.

Mat: Tell me I pray; —And fizbeo: — ~~Is there Absoluta potentia~~
~~Afmade; sive Cujusvis aly; Ex a vitium Corporis, as Say~~
~~the learned~~ — What made ye first possesse her:

Jul: Look on her, and answer your self: She's young & handsome.

Mat: So was your wife, Sirrah: —And yet —[She falls into a fitt.]
This will work presently —[aside]—How long have ye been there:

Julia: Much about the tyme, you crackt a Comandment with your
Taylors Wife — [Mat starts.] —Are ye Concern'd Gentleman! Ha, hah!

Mat: Bring me the Flagellum Dæmonum, —Ile taw ye.

Julia: Or rather give your self the first discipline; —And Ile help
to lay it on, — Ha, ha, hah.

Mat: Once more I say, turne out, — Or by the phoberon, phoberotaton,
Ton de Apomeisomenos, And Heautontemorumenos, —~~Sing wee~~
~~Rhodos Colippan, Palamis Chias, Argæ, Athene~~; —Ile — —

Jul: What: —My new Conjurer; What: — Hoh, hoh!

Mat: Ile lead ye about the Countrye, like a Beare by the Nose; make
ye turne spitts, like A Dog in a Wheel: And if that won't doe't
have ye chain'd, like a flea in a Box, —And therefore dispatch;
And let me know what signe you'l give of your departure.

Jul: Thunder, thunder, thunder, — As thus Rascal: [she flyes on him.]

Mat: Ile have ye bound over for bloodshed & Battery.

Julia: I fear no Justice under heaven.

Mat: Ile bring ye into the Spirituall Court; And have ye
Excomunicated.

Julia: I am no member of your Church: Or if I were, I have no
mony to pay fees.

Mat: Ile have ye burnt in Effigie; —~~with Brimstone Galbanum~~
~~Aristolochia Hypericum, and Rew~~; in a more terrible Capp,
and painted Coate, than the Inquisition, yet ever thought of —
And if all this faile; Ile send ye back to your wife.

Julia

Folger Shakespeare Library
Promptbook for John Wilson's *Belphegor*, produced at the Smock Alley Theatre, Dublin, 1677–
78 or 1682–83

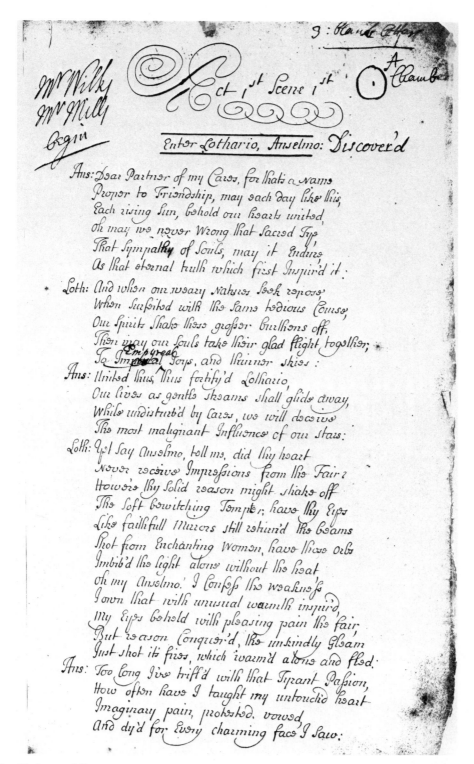

Mr Wilks
Mr Mills
begin

Act 1st Scene 1st

Enter Lothario, Anselmo: Discover'd

Ans: Dear Partner of my Cares, for that's a Name
Proper to Friendship, may each day like this,
Each rising Sun, behold our hearts united,
Oh may we never Wrong that Sacred Tye
That Sympathy of Souls, may it endure
As that eternal truth which first Inspir'd it:

Loth: And when our weary Natures seek repose,
When Surfeited with the Same tedious Course,
Our Spirits Shake these grosser burthens off,
Then may our Souls take their glad flight together;
To Empyreal Joys, and thinner Skies:

Ans: United thus, thus fortify'd Lothario
Our lives as gentle streams shall glide away,
While undisturb'd by Cares, we will deceive
The most malignant Influence of our stars:

Loth: Yet say Anselmo, tell me, did thy heart
Never receive Impressions from the Fair?
Howe're thy Solid reason might shake off
The Soft bewitching Temper; have thy Eyes
Like faithfull Mirrors still return'd the beams
Shot from Enchanting Women, have these orbs
Imbib'd the light alone without the heat
Oh my Anselmo' I Confess the weakness
I own that with unusual warmth inspir'd,
My Eyes behold with pleasing pain the fair,
But reason Conquer'd, the unkindly Gleam
Just shot its fires, which warm'd alone and fled:

Ans: Too long I've trifl'd with that Tyrant Passion,
How often have I taught my untouch'd heart
Imaginary pain, protested, vowed,
And dy'd for Every charming face I Saw:

Folger Shakespeare Library
Promptbook for Charles Johnson's *The Force of Friendship*, produced at the Queen's Theatre, 20
April 1710

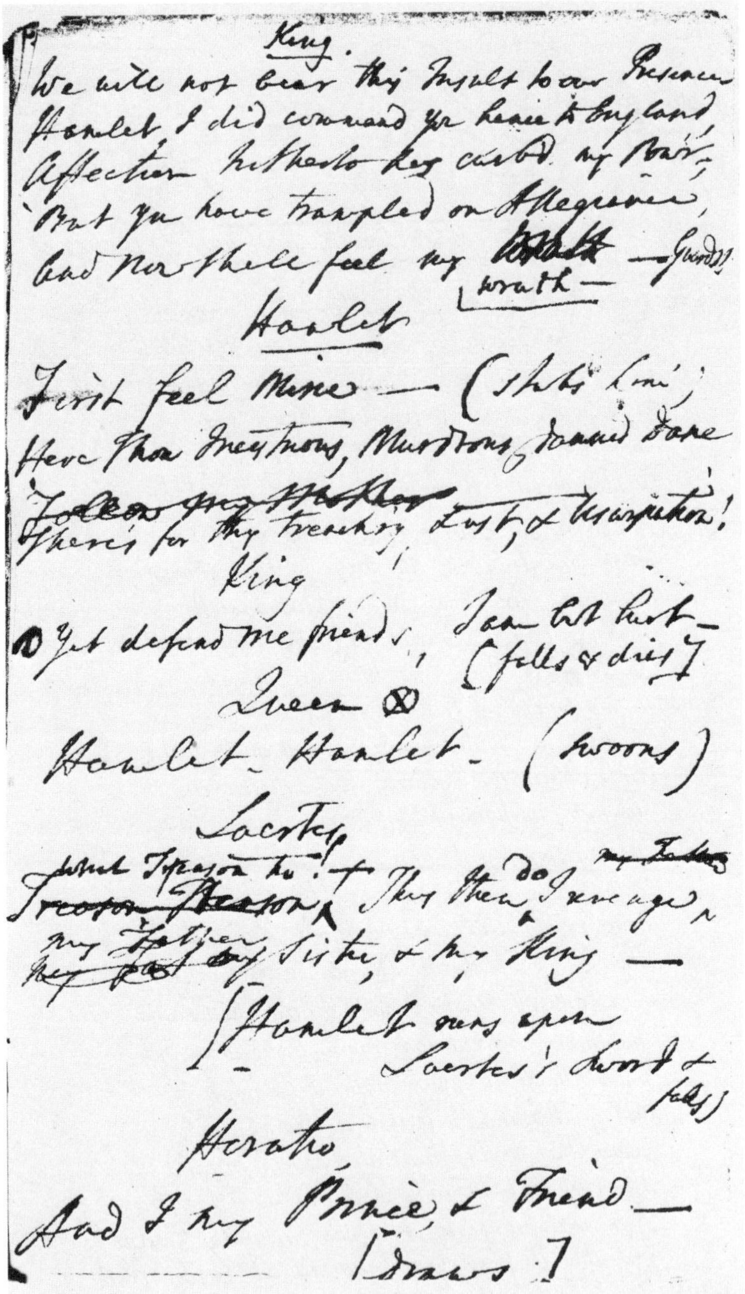

King
We will not bear this Insult to our Presence
Hamlet, I did command you hence to England,
Affection hitherto has curb'd my Pow'r,
But you have trampled on Allegiance,
And now shall feel my ~~wrath~~ wrath — Guards!!
Hamlet
First feel Mine — (stabs him)
Here thou incestuous, Murd'rous, damned Dane
~~Follow my Mother~~
There's for thy treachery, Lust, & Usurpation!
King
O yet defend me friends, I am but hurt —
[falls & dies]
Queen ⊗
Hamlet — Hamlet — (swoons)
Laertes
~~Treason Treason~~ What Treason too! — Then do I revenge ~~my Father~~
my Father ~~my Father~~ my Sister, & my King —
[Hamlet runs upon Laertes's Sword & falls]
Horatio
And I my Prince, & Friend —
[draws]

Folger Shakespeare Library
David Garrick's preparation book for Shakespeare's *Hamlet* produced at Drury Lane Theatre, 10 February 1773

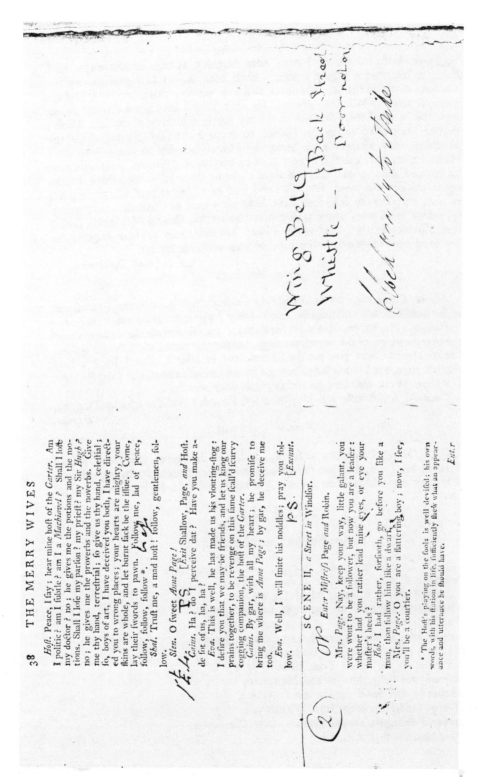

George Colman's promptbook for Shakespeare's *The Merry Wives of Windsor*, produced at the Haymarket Theatre, 24 August 1781

(41)

Quick. Hah, hah ha ha. I have been laughing at my self above this half hour, to see what a Figure I am; I have been Agent in a great many Intreagues in my life time, but never had any yet like this; this is a Masterpiece, a piece of Wit like *Hains*; for here have I insinuated my self so far into this grave Fool, Sr. *Charles*, by my subtle discovery of the late Affair; that he has trusted me in this Habit, to prepare the Old Quaker about the Writings, and afterwards to bring the Heiress her self to him——to him! Ha ha ha ha, there's the Jest now; and to receive as a Reward fifty Guinea's; ha ha ha! Alas poor shallow Knight! little does he think what's hatching in this Brain of mine: for, what will I do now? but instead of carrying her to him, keep her my self, and make her Marry me, or Compound swingeingly, which is all one; there's Wit now! ha, ha, ha; there's Mischief! Gad I love Mischief dearly: And when I have had her three or four Nights, let her hang me afterwards if she can, or any one else for me.

[Call Quickwitt.

Enter Marmalett.

Marm. Come Sir, are ye ready? the Doctor's just gone home,——bless me, to see how Clothes will disguise one! Why? you look like a meer *Ananias.*
Cunning. Ha, ha, ha, don't I? Methinks I am filled with the out-goings of the over-flowings, of the Bowel-yernings, and for the humh, and hah! *[in a Cant.* Let me alone. Come give me the Letter, and be assur'd, tho' I Jok'd a litte the last time, yet I'le not fail to bring a better Business about, e're long for thee.
Marm. Well, well Sir; go and dispatch your own first.
Cunning. An Heiress, and fifty thousand Pounds! Gad I'm a lucky Dog, ha, ha, ha.
[Exeunt.

—— *Reenter* Quickwitt.

Quick. Here's a rare Rogue for ye, had not I discovered the Plott, he had betrayed his Trust, and got the Heiress for himself; but as things go, will miss of his aim damnably: Now for my Quaking Faculty I must make one amongst 'em.
[Exit.

SCENE 2.

Enter Fulvia *and* Christopher.

Fulv. Oh Love! How many strange, and different ways
Dost thou disturb the Quiet of our Minds?
If amongst all the Race of Male Deceivers,
With Curious search we chance to find out one,
That we can fancy Honest; some cross Doubt
Straight fills us, with a fear he may prove Haggard,
And then, Alas! we split against a Rock.
That ruins us for ever: I dreamt last Night,
Frederick was False, Sordid and Mercenary:
And that he only lov'd me for my Fortune;
I give no credit to sleeps Idle Whimseys:
But yet it strangely troubles me——now *Christopher.*
VVhat Noise is that within?   G

Christ.

A trace of prompt copy ("Call Quickwitt") from Thomas D'Urfey's *The Richmond Heiress*, 1693

11.

& that must be by an artificiall spott
upon your chak in resemblance of a mole
by which sir you shall pass for Antoninus.
———————— what then Trico?
that you shall understand.
ith' interim, Jle comend you to an Artist
shall do your work without the least suspition
———————— all things.
then all things shall go well; now let us hence
and prosecute our plott with confidence

Ex: { Anton:
        Trico.

Actus Tertius. Scen: 1.
Ent Trico.
J'aue taught my schollar to understand his lesson
his mole is fix'd so artificially
'twould challenge Nature in exactness
———————— mad-caps.

(Ent Dulman)

what haue we here?
———————— gelding.
Dulman, o my conscience
Cupes, Cupes, away away, here's Dulman.
———————— honest man.
who calls me? would you speak with me my friend?
———————— know him pray.
Block! what kind of face?
———————— Portugale
he has a crooked neck, has he not?
———————— they say.
an hundred to one but its my Master.
———————— may be so.
do you know the first letter of his name?
———————— J do.
does it begin with a B?
———————— A B — no
G?
———————— G — no.
R?
———————— R — no.
T?
———————— J T. T.
Torcol?
———————— his seruant?

Trico's part in Ferdinando Parkhurst's translation of Ruggle's *Ignoramus*, played by Matthew
Medbourne at court, 1 November 1662

hasty Passion, — it is the Transport of a Love
sincere. — O, Violante! Violante! —
    Ruin'd past Redemption.
No, no, no, my Love; I can leap from the Closet
Window. <u>× O.P.</u> — The O.P. Door is clapped to, and
    bolted withinside.
Confusion! — Somebody bolts the Door withinside. —
O, Violante! — hast thou again sacrific'd to my
Rival? <u>× P.S. ∝ draws his Sword.</u>)
    Father find you here. — Distraction! —
Indeed but I shall; — unless you command
this Door to be open'd, and that Way conceal
me from his Sight. (<u>Struggling to get to the Door.</u>)
    Convince me by your Obedience.
That's not the Matter in Debate. — I will know
who is in this Closet, let the Consequence be
what it will. — (<u>Still struggling with Violan.</u>)
Nay, nay, you strive in vain: — I will go in. —
    You sha'n't go in.
I will go in.
    Why, who are you, Sir? <u>En. Pedro — P.S.D.</u>
What shall I say now?   <u>Violante × C.</u>
    Would be asham'd to own.

Folger Shakespeare Library

Don Felix's part in Susannah Centlivre's *The Wonder*, played by John Philip Kemble at Drury
Lane Theatre, 1 January 1789. The part was written out, with stage directions, by Kemble